Lecture Notes in Computer Sc

Commenced Publication in 1973
Founding and Former Series Editors:
Gerhard Goos, Juris Hartmanis, and Jan van Leeuv

Werner Grass   Bernhard Sick
Klaus Waldschmidt (Eds.)

Architecture of Computing Systems – ARCS 2006

19th International Conference
Frankfurt/Main, Germany, March 13-16, 2006
Proceedings

 Springer

Volume Editors

Werner Grass
Bernhard Sick
University of Passau
Innstr. 33, 94032 Passau, Germany
E-mail: {grass, sick}@fmi.uni-passau.de

Klaus Waldschmidt
University of Frankfurt/Main
Robert-Mayer-Str. 11-15, 60325 Frankfurt, Germany
E-mail: waldsch@ti.informatik.uni-frankfurt.de

Library of Congress Control Number: 2006921397

CR Subject Classification (1998): C.2, C.5.3, D.4, D.2.11, H.3.5, H.4, H.5.2

LNCS Sublibrary: SL 1 – Theoretical Computer Science and General Issues

ISSN   0302-9743
ISBN-10   3-540-32765-7 Springer Berlin Heidelberg New York
ISBN-13   978-3-540-32765-3 Springer Berlin Heidelberg New York

Springer is a part of Springer Science+Business Media

springer.com

© Springer-Verlag Berlin Heidelberg 2006
Printed in Germany

Typesetting: Camera-ready by author, data conversion by Scientific Publishing Services, Chennai, India
Printed on acid-free paper   SPIN: 11682127   06/3142   5 4 3 2 1 0

Preface

Technological progress is one of the driving forces behind the dramatic development of computer system architectures over the past three decades. Even though it is quite clear that this development cannot only be measured by the maximum number of components on a chip, Moore's Law may be and is often taken as a simple measure for the non-braked growth of computational power over the years. The more components are realizable on a chip, the more innovative and unconventional ideas can be realized by system architects. As a result, research in computer system architectures is more exciting than ever before.

This book covers the trends that shape the field of computer system architectures. The fundamenatal trade-off in the design of computing systems is between flexibility, performance, power consumption, and chip area. The full exploitation of future silicon capacity requires new architecture approaches and new design paradigms such as multiple computers on a single chip, reconfigurable processor arrays, extensible processor architectures, and embedded memory technologies. For a successful use in practical applications, it is not enough to solve the hardware problems but also to develop platforms that provide software infrastructure and support effective programming.

A quantum jump in complexity is achieved by embedded computing systems with an unprecedented level of connectivity linking together a growing number of physical devices through networks. Embedded systems will become more and more pervasive as the component technologies become smaller, faster, and cheaper. Their complexity arises not only from the large number of components but also from a lack of determinism and a continual evolution of these systems. The research effort needed to design systems so that they can be developed, deployed, maintained, configured, managed, and trusted will be a key issue for many years. Pervasive computing is therefore much more than an Internet access by mobile devices. The papers presented in this book set out the broadness of the research area established by pervasive computing approaches: input devices for wearable systems, mobile collaborative applications, measurement data acquisition, location awareness, QoS awareness, and context awareness.

One possibility to cope with the growing complexity of computing systems is to make them organic or autonomous, that is, to make them self-learning, self-organizing, self-configuring, self-optimizing, self-healing, self-protecting, and proactive.

In this context, completely new problems arise that should be addressed by an interdisciplinary effort. Natural organic and self-organizing systems have been studied in other scientific discplines such as philosophy and biology, and their results should now be considered by architects of organic computing systems. Some of the key questions are:

1. Do organic systems feature properties that cannot be derived from the properties of its components? Is this emergent behavior desirable in any case or not?
2. Can we really expect to completely control systems with an emergent behavior?
3. Which mathematical formalisms can help in constructing and analyzing this type of system?
4. How is user privacy maintainable?
5. What is the role of trust?

These questions were discussed during the conference stimulated by two keynote and three invited speeches. Two of the speakers have taken the opportunity to present their ideas in this book.

Organic computing is a research area initiated by the special interest group ARCS of the German computer societies (GI and ITG) that are responsible for the organization of the ARCS conference series. Future ARCS conferences will therefore continue to give a platform to revolutionary ideas for a new generation of organic computing systems.

The great interest of the research community in the research field of this conference is expressed in a large number of submitted papers. Altogether, we received 174 papers, 32 of them were accepted and are presented in this book. We were especially pleased by the wide range of countries represented at the conference. We thank all the members of the Program Committee, who did a great job. Many additional reviewers supported us in selecting the best papers. We thank all reviewers for their elaborated reviews which greatly helped the authors to further improve their papers. Readers will appreciate this effort yielding a book with high quality.

The organization of this conference was done at two different locations. Organizational tasks were performed at the University of Frankfurt a.M., while the work on the program was done at the University of Passau. We thank all staff members for their excellent work making this conference a success. Special thanks for their excellent work go to: Markus Damm, Diana Firnges, Jan Haase, Johannes Herr, Wilhelm Heupke, Joachim Höhne, Alexander Hofmann, Andreas Hofmann, Eva Kapfer, Anita Plattner, Franz Rautmann, Rüdiger Schroll.

March 2006   Werner Grass
                                                        Bernhard Sick
                                                  Klaus Waldschmidt

Organization

ARCS 2006 was jointly organized by GI (German Informatics Society) and ITG (Information Technology Society).

Executive Committee

General Chair: Klaus Waldschmidt (University of Frankfurt, Germany)

Program Chair: Werner Grass (University of Passau, Germany)

Workshop and Tutorial Chair: Wolfgang Karl (University of Karlsruhe, Germany)

Program Committee

Nader Bagherzadeh	University of California, Irvine, USA
Jürgen Becker	University of Karlsruhe, Germany
Michael Beigl	University of Karlsruhe, Germany
Riccardo Bettati	Texas A&M University, College Station, USA
Uwe Brinkschulte	University of Karlsruhe, Germany
Hermann De Meer	University of Passau, Germany
Francois Dolivo	IBM, Zurich Research Laboratory, Switzerland
Stefan Dulman	Ambient Systems, Enschede, The Netherlands
Marc Duranton	Philips Research, Eindhoven, The Netherlands
Alois Ferscha	University of Linz, Austria
Marisol Garcia-Valls	University Carlos III, Madrid, Spain
Jean-Luc Gaudiot	University of California, Irvine, USA
Werner Grass	University of Passau, Germany
Paul Havinga	University of Twente, The Netherlands
Oliver Heckmann	Technical University of Darmstadt, Germany
Wolfgang Karl	University of Karlsruhe, Germany
Rudolf Kober	Siemens AG, Munich, Germany
Spyros Lalis	University of Thessaly, Greece
Paul Lukowicz	University for Health Sciences, Medical Informatics and Technology, Austria
Erik Maehle	University of Lübeck, Germany
Tom Martin	Virginia Tech, Blacksburg, USA
Christian Müller-Schloer	University of Hanover, Germany
Timothy M. Pinkston	University of Southern California, Los Angeles, USA
Ichiro Satoh	National Institute of Informatics, Tokyo, Japan
Hartmut Schmeck	University of Karlsruhe, Germany
Martin Schulz	Lawrence Livermore National Laboratory, Livermore, USA
Karsten Schwan	Georgia Institute of Technology, Atlanta, USA

Bernhard Sick	University of Passau, Germany
Peter Steenkiste	Carnegie Mellon University, Pittsburgh, USA
Roy Sterritt	University of Ulster at Jordanstown, UK
Jürgen Teich	University of Erlangen-Nuremberg, Germany
Yoshito Tobe	Tokyo Denki University, Japan
Kishor Trivedi	Duke University, Durham, USA
Rich Uhlig	Intel Microprocessor Research Lab, USA
Theo Ungerer	University of Augsburg, Germany
Klaus Waldschmidt	University of Frankfurt, Germany
Ralph Welge	University of Lüneburg, Germany
Sami Yehia	ARM Research, Cambridge, UK

Additional Referees

C. Albrecht	C. Hochberger	F. Picioroaga
F. Bagci	C. Hoertnagl	A. Pietzowski
J. H. Bahn	A. Hofmann	T. Pionteck
P. Basanta-Val	T. Hofmeijer	G. Rey
M. Berger	R. Holzer	F. Rochner
G. Brancovici	C. Holzmann	S. Roos
J. Brehm	I. Iliadis	Y. Sazeides
I. Buhan	C. Ilioudis	A. Schill
C. Cachin	G. Karjoth	T. Schöler
J. Camenisch	S. Karlsson	W. Schröder-Preikschat
Z. Chamski	T. Kirste	P. Scotton
S. Cho	D. Koblitz	T. Smaoui
V. Desmet	R. Koch	P. Sobe
O. Durmaz Incel	W. P. Kowalk	P. Soulard
S. Eilers	M. Litza	M. Stolze
I. Estevez-Ayres	T. Loukopoulos	D. Tavangarian
L. Evers	N. Luttenberger	P. Trancoso
F. Fuchs	G. Mahmoudi	J. Trescher
R. Gemesi	M. Marin-Perianu	W. Trumler
M. Gönne	R. Marin-Perianu	V. Turau
M. Graf	N. Meratnia	E. Van Herreweghen
A. Größlinger	M. Mnif	S. Voigt
K.-E. Grosspietsch	F. Mösch	S. Wang
C. Gruber	M. Mühlhäuser	E. Zehendner
A. Hatanaka	K. Muthukrishnan	A. Zell
A. Hazem El-Mahdy	F. Neeser	Y. Zhu
E. A. Heinz	E. Özer	
J. Henkel	H. Pals	

We also thank all additional referees whose names are unknown to the Executive Committee.

Table of Contents

Invited and Keynote Papers

Life-Inspired Systems and Their Quality-Driven Design
Lech Jóźwiak 1

The Robustness of Resource Allocations in Parallel and Distributed
Computing Systems
*Vladimir Shestak, Howard Jay Siegel, Anthony A. Maciejewski,
Shoukat Ali* 17

Pervasive Computing

FingerMouse – A Button Size Visual Hand Tracking and Segmentation
Device
Patrick de la Hamette, Gerhard Tröster 31

An Ad-Hoc Wireless Network Architecture for Face-to-Face Mobile
Collaborative Applications
Gustavo Zurita, Miguel Nussbaum 42

Background Data Acquisition and Carrying: The BlueDACS Project
Thomas Wieland, Martin Fenne, Benjamin Stöcker 56

Prototypical Implementation of Location-Aware Services Based on
Super-Distributed RFID Tags
Jürgen Bohn 69

Combined Resource and Context Model for QoS-Aware Mobile
Middleware
Sten Lundesgaard Amundsen, Frank Eliassen 84

Distributed Modular Toolbox for Multi-modal Context Recognition
David Bannach, Kai Kunze, Paul Lukowicz, Oliver Amft 99

Memory Systems

Dynamic Dictionary-Based Data Compression for Level-1 Caches
*Georgios Keramidas, Konstantinos Aisopos,
Stefanos Kaxiras* 114

A Case for Dual-Mapping One-Way Caches
Arul Sandeep Gade, Yul Chu 130

Cache Write-Back Schemes for Embedded Destructive-Read DRAM
Haakon Dybdahl, Marius Grannæs, Lasse Natvig 145

A Processor Architecture with Effective Memory System for Sort-Last
Parallel Rendering
Woo-Chan Park, Duk-Ki Yoon, Kil-Whan Lee, Il-San Kim,
Kyung-Su Kim, Won-Jong Lee, Tack-Don Han, Sung-Bong Yang 160

Architectures

Controller Synthesis for Mapping Partitioned Programs on Array
Architectures
Hritam Dutta, Frank Hannig, Jürgen Teich 176

M^2E: A Multiple-Input, Multiple-Output Function Extension for
RISC-Based Extensible Processors
Xiaoyong Chen, Douglas L. Maskell 191

An Operating System Infrastructure for Fault-Tolerant Reconfigurable
Networks
Dirk Koch, Thilo Streichert, Steffen Dittrich, Christian Strengert,
Christian D. Haubelt, Jürgen Teich 202

Architectural Tradeoffs in Wearable Systems
Nagendra Bhargava Bharatula, Urs Anliker, Paul Lukowicz,
Gerhard Tröster 217

Multiprocessing

Do Trace Cache, Value Prediction and Prefetching Improve SMT
Throughput?
Chen-Yong Cher, Il Park, T.N. VijayKumar 232

Scalable and Partitionable Asynchronous Arbiter for Micro-threaded
Chip Multiprocessors
Nabil Hasasneh, Ian Bell, Chris Jesshope 252

GigaNetIC – A Scalable Embedded On-Chip Multiprocessor
Architecture for Network Applications
Jörg-Christian Niemann, Christoph Puttmann, Mario Porrmann,
Ulrich Rückert 268

Energy Efficient Design

Efficient System-on-Chip Energy Management with a Segmented
Bloom Filter
  Mrinmoy Ghosh, Emre Özer, Stuart Biles, Hsien-Hsin S. Lee 283

Estimating Energy Consumption for an MPSoC Architectural
Exploration
  *Rabie Ben Atitallah, Smail Niar, Alain Greiner, Samy Meftali,
  Jean Luc Dekeyser* 298

An Energy Consumption Model for an Embedded Java Virtual Machine
  Sébastien Lafond, Johan Lilius 311

Power Awareness

PASCOM: Power Model for Supercomputers
  *Arrvindh Shriraman, Nagarajan Venkateswaran,
  Niranjan Soundararajan* 326

Power-Aware Collective Tree Exploration
  Miroslaw Dynia, Miroslaw Korzeniowski, Christian Schindelhauer 341

Biologically-Inspired Optimization of Circuit Performance and Leakage:
A Comparative Study
  Ralf Salomon, Frank Sill 352

Network Protocols

A Synchronous Multicast Application for Asymmetric Intra-campus
Networks: Definition, Analysis and Evaluation
  *Pilar Manzanares-Lopez, Juan Carlos Sanchez-Aarnoutse,
  Josemaria Malgosa-Sanahuja, Joan Garcia-Haro* 367

A Real-Time MAC Protocol for Wireless Sensor Networks: Virtual
TDMA for Sensors (VTS)
  *Esteban Egea-López, Javier Vales-Alonso,
  Alejandro S. Martínez-Sala, Joan García-Haro,
  Pablo Pavón-Mariño, M. Victoria Bueno-Delgado* 382

An Effective Video Streaming Method for Video on Demand Services
in Vertical Handoff
  Jae-Won Kim, Hye-Soo Kim, Jae-Woong Yun, Sung-Jea Ko 397

Security

A High-Throughput System Architecture for Deep Packet Filtering in
Network Intrusion Prevention
Dae Y. Kim, Sunil Kim, Lynn Choi, Hyogon Kim 407

A Hierarchical Key Management Approach for Secure Multicast
Jian Wang, Miodrag J. Mihaljevic, Lein Harn, Hideki Imai 422

A Cache Design for a Security Architecture for Microprocessors (SAM)
Jörg Platte, Edwin Naroska, Kai Grundmann 435

Distributed Networks

Constraint-Based Deployment of Distributed Components in a Dynamic
Network
Didier Hoareau, Yves Mahéo 450

Comparative Analysis of Ad-Hoc Networks Oriented to Collaborative
Activities
Sebastián Echeverría, Raúl Santelices, Miguel Nussbaum 465

Fault Tolerant Time Synchronization for Wireless Sensor Networks
Soyoung Hwang, Yunju Baek 480

Author Index 495

Life-Inspired Systems
and Their Quality-Driven Design

Lech Jóźwiak

Eindhoven University of Technology,
Den Dolech 2, 5600 MB Eindhoven, The Netherlands
L.Jozwiak@tue.nl
http://www.ics.ele.tue.nl/~ljozwiak/

Abstract. The recent spectacular progress in modern microelectronics
that enabled implementation of a complete complex system on a single
chip created new important opportunities, but also new serious difficulties. This paper briefly analyses the situation, trends and problems
in the field of the modern microelectronic-based systems. However, the
main aim of the paper is to discuss the paradigms of life-inspired systems
and quality-driven design that seem to be adequate to overcome the difficulties, and consider their application to the architecture synthesis for
complex real-time embedded systems.

1 Introduction

The recent spectacular progress in modern microelectronics and information
technology enabled implementation of a complete complex information processing system on a single chip (SoC), global networking and mobile wire-less
communication, and facilitated a fast progress in these areas. New important opportunities have been created. The traditional applications can be served much
better and numerous new sorts of systems became technologically feasible and
economically justified, especially for applications that require miniaturization,
high performance, low power dissipation, and wire-less or distant communication. Various measurement or control systems that can be put on or embedded in
(mobile, poorly accessible or distant) objects, installations, machines or devices,
or even implanted in human or animal body can serve as an example. A big
stimulus has been created towards development of various kinds of application-
specific embedded systems.

On the other hand however, the spectacular advances in microelectronics and
information technology introduced *unusual complexity* :

- *Silicon Complexity*, in the sense of huge numbers, density, diversity, and small
  dimensions of devices and interconnections, huge length of interconnections,
  new materials and mixed technologies, and
- *System Complexity*, in the sense of a huge number of possible system states,
  number and diversity of subsystems, and extremely complex interactions and
  interrelations among the subsystems.

W. Grass et al. (Eds.): ARCS 2006, LNCS 3894, pp. 1–16, 2006.

Due to the *Silicon Complexity*, and especially: extremely high device densities, small physical dimensions, power supply reduction, and very high operating frequencies, many previously ignorable phenomena have now a great impact on the system correctness and other quality aspects. This results in *many new difficult to solve hardware issues*, such as:

- power and energy crisis, increased leakage power, and fluctuations in the on-chip power density distribution,
- on-chip communication problems, including delay variation due to substrate coupling and cross-coupling,
- decreased reliability, due to numerous reasons (noise, interference, signal integrity problems, increased defect density, manufacturing process variability, gate insulator tunneling, joule heating, electromigration, single event upsets and transients etc.),
- decreased design predictability (due to the above mentioned and some extra reasons),
- manufacturability problems and decreased yield,
- high manufacturing NRE and production costs, etc.

The *System Complexity* also results in *serious system and design challenges*, such as:

- design, quality assurance and validation of the highly complex and heterogeneous systems with exponentially growing number of states,
- ensuring of the systems' responsiveness, reliability and safety in the light of changing, noisy and unreliable environment and interior,
- reducing the design productivity gap, time-to market, and design NRE costs.

More details and explanations can be found in [1][3][6].

The *application-specific embedded systems are especially difficult to develop and validate*. In addition to the above listed issues, they must appropriately react in real-time to the signals from their surroundings and to be fine-tuned to particular applications through satisfying application specific constraints and objectives related to such attributes as functional behavior, reaction speed and throughput, power dissipation, geometrical dimensions, price etc. Moreover, many of them are used in safety critical applications that impose extremely high quality requirements (e.g. measurement or control systems built in various machines, robots, assembly lines, planes, cars, telecommunication equipment, military systems, safety systems, medical instruments or human body). One more main source of difficulties is related to the fact that *embedded systems play an extremely remarkable role in today's life and are used more and more commonly in virtually all fields of human activity, in all sorts of technical, social and biological systems, in more and more important and demanding applications.* They are even implanted in our bodies. Our life is to a higher and higher degree dependent on their adequate operation. Therefore, the individual and society expectations regarding their quality grow rapidly. In consequence, their responsiveness, robustness and dependability are becoming more and more critical.

Unfortunately, due to the rapidly growing silicon and system complexity, both the hardware and software of the future chips tends inherently to be less reliable and more sensitive to noise and interferences with the environment. However, we certainly cannot tolerate that the future systems will be less reliable.

Consequently, the *development of the future systems should aim at the total multi-objective quality maximization of the systemic solution, with a special focus on the robustness, responsiveness, dependability, safety, security, adaptability, and validation aspects.* However, these important aspects are not new and were already taken into some consideration in the past. What is thus new or different now?

The *new or different character of the current situation includes* the following:

- due to the huge and rapidly growing complexity, more and more demanding applications and growing danger of attacks and manipulations, it will be *more and more difficult to guarantee the system quality,* and particularly, responsiveness, dependability, robustness, safety, security and validation;
- due to the common usage of systems in various kinds of social, technical and biological systems, the whole life on the Earth more and more depends on them; in consequence, their *quality, and specifically responsiveness, dependability, safety and security are becoming more and more critical; also applications considered previously as non-critical are becoming more and more critical,* because we more and more rely on them.

Consequently, *high responsiveness, dependability, robustness, safety and security must now become much more common* than in the past when they were seriously considered in relation to only some very special critical systems (i.e. mission or life-critical systems for space, flight, military and similar applications). Due to the common application, reasonably *low-cost solutions must be used.* This means that these features cannot anymore be added on the top of the designed or implemented system, when using simple, but expensive means. *These features must be accounted for from the very beginning of the system specification and design process, implemented using sophisticated effective and efficient solutions, considered in parallel with all other important system aspects to possibly share the implementation costs and account for the consequences of their implementation.* This will allow for an adequate tradeoff exploitation and multi-objective optimization and result in more coherent, compact, comprehensive, reliable, robust and lower-cost solutions.

Moreover, due to the embedded and/or mobile character of the new applications, growing application complexity, power and energy crisis, increased leakage power, and fluctuations in the on-chip power density distribution, power and energy issues are more and more serious.

Summing up, the transition:

- from the *multi-chip systems* to *systems-on-a-single-chip,*
- from the *general-purpose stand-alone computers* to *application-specific embedded systems,*

- from the *separated systems* to *networked systems*,
- from the *wire-based communication* to *wireless communication*,
- from the *static systems* to *mobile and dynamic systems*

is not a gradual change, but a real **paradigm shift**:

- it *opens new opportunities*,
- but it also creates **new very serious difficulties**

that cannot be adequately resolved without an adequate system and design methodology adaptation.

The **adequate system and design paradigms** to solve the problems seem to be the paradigms of:

- *life-inspired systems*, and
- *quality-driven design*.

Predicting the current situation, several years ago I proposed the methodology of the quality-driven design of the microelectronic-based systems [2][3][5], and subsequently, supplemented it with the paradigm of the life-inspired systems [6]. In recent years, together with our collaborators we successfully applied the quality-driven design methodology and the paradigm of the life-inspired systems to the semi-automatic system architecture exploration and synthesis for the generic platform-based heterogeneous real-time embedded SoCs [3][7][8], and to the multi-objective optimal circuit synthesis [4][5].

The main aim of this paper is to discuss the paradigms of the life-inspired systems and quality-driven design, and their application to the system architecture exploration, when focusing on the important issues of parallel heterogeneous architectures, generic and re-configurable system solutions, and automatic system architecture synthesis, and using as an example our recently developed system-level design exploration method [3][7][8].

2   Quality-Driven Design

What **system design** is about is a **definition of the required quality**, in the sense of a satisfactory answer to the following two questions:

- What (new or modified) quality is required? and
- How can it be achieved?

Actually, *what is quality?*
A lot of various definitions can be found in literature, but none of these definitions is precise enough to enable the systematic consideration, measurement and comparison of quality that are necessary for quality-driven design [2][3].

Therefore, I proposed the following new definition:

Quality *of a purposive systemic solution is its* **total effectiveness and efficiency** *in solving the original real-life problem. Effectiveness is the degree to* which a solution attains its goals. *Efficiency* is the degree to which a solution uses resources in order to realize its aims. *Effectiveness and efficiency of a systemic solution together decide its grade of excellence* - their aggregation expresses quality. In turn, effectiveness and efficiency can be expressed in terms of measurable parameters, and in this way *quality can be measured.*

In particular, quality can be modeled in the form of *multi-objective decision models*, being partial and abstract (reduced to the relevant and/or feasible concerns and precision levels) models of the required quality, expressed in the decision-theoretical terms. The multi-objective decision models together with the methods and tools for the estimation of the design parameters of these models related to the relevant design aspects and performances (e.g. timing, power-dissipation, costs) enable application of the *multi-objective decision methods* for construction, improvement and selection of the most promising solutions [2][3][8].

The **main concepts of the quality-driven design** can be briefly summarized as follows:

- designing of *top-quality systems is the aim of a design process*;
- *quality is modelled and measured* to enable invention and selection of the most promising design alternatives and quality analysis and comarison and in consequence quality improvement;
- *quality models are considered to be heuristics for setting and controlling the course of design*, and as such, they are also a subject to design and change;
- *the design process is evolutionary* and it basically consists of:
  - constructing the tentative quality models,
  - using them for constructing, selecting and improving the tentative solutions,
  - analysing and estimating them directly and through analysis of the resulting solutions,
  - improving them, and using again, etc.
- *in the design process, a balance is sought for* between the multiplicity of the system life-cycle aspects considered in parallel and amount of iteration, design reuse and innovation, art and science in the design, designer's involvement and automation; *criterium for this balance is total effectiveness and efficiency* of a design process.

The quality-driven design paradigm considers system design to be an *evolutionary quality engineering process* in which the concepts of predicting, testing, learning and adapting are very important. This process starts with an *abstract, imprecise, incomplete and possible contradictory initial quality model* (initial requirements), and tries to transform the initial model into a *concrete, precise, complete, coherent, directly implementable, and optimized to quality final model.* The *quality-driven design space exploration* basically consists of the alternating phases of the *exploration of the space of the abstract models of the required quality*, and *exploration of the space of solutions* obtained with the selected quality models. With the total quality-driven design approach, all the important design aspects can be explicitly accounted for, given necessary attention, modeled, analyzed, and traded off against or combined with another aspects just from the beginning of the design process, to result in more coherent, compact, comprehensive, reliable, robust and lower-cost systems. In the quality-driven system design, the *design reuse, plays an extremely important role*, especially in the form of the generic system solutions and architectures, as for instance the generic (re-)configurable system platforms and architecture templates. Design reuse simultaneously enhances the system quality due to the "maturity" of the reused designs, as well as, the development and/or fabrication efficiency due to elimination of some costly and time consuming development and/or fabrication phases.

3   Life-Inspired Systems

The paradigm of the **life-inspired systems** originates from the observation that:

- *the operation domains, roles and complexity of the microelectronics-based systems*

more and more resemble

- *the operation domains, roles and complexity of (parts of) the (intelligent) life organisms or organized populations of such organisms.*

Based on this parallel, I formulated the hypothesis that: *the future microelectronics based systems should have characteristics that resemble the characteristics of (parts of) the (intelligent) life organisms or their organized populations. Consequently, the basic concepts, principles, functional and structural organization etc. of the microelectronics-based systems should resemble these of the (intelligent) life organisms or their populations.* "Resemble" does not of course mean to be identical. We have to account for the differences, as for instance, in the nature of the life and technological systems, their materials, implementation technologies, etc. Since the whole life on the Earth more and more depends on the microelectronics-based systems, and they more and more often are embedded in the life-organisms or play important roles in their populations, the systems must be life-inspired also for this reason.

Similarly to a real brain, a *life-inspired system* should not limit itself to the traditional basic functions of an information technology system of collecting, transmitting, storing, processing, and presenting information in relation to some external systems. In addition to these functions, it *should solve complex problems, take and implement difficult decisions, learn, discover new ideas, etc., also in relation to itself.*

To achieve these diverse aims effectively and efficiently in relation to complex and demanding applications and in the light of changing, noisy and unreliable environment and own interior, a *life-inspired system has to be a largely autonomous, self-contained, robust, self-organizing, self-adapting, self-regulating dynamic evolutionary system.* Like a real organism or brain, it should be *highly decentralized* and composed of *largely autonomous, diverse, having own particular aims and optimized for these aims sub-systems* (organs or centers). However, *the sub-systems should be adequately (hierarchically) organized, interconnected with an appropriate network of efficient communication channels, properly coordinated and adequately collaborating with each other to synergistically achieve the global system aims.*

Analogously to the life organisms, the *life-inspired systems should have adequate **self**-protection, **self**-testing, **self**-diagnosis, **self**-repair, fault-tolerance and other **self-organization, adaptation and regulation mechanisms**.*

To avoid the memory and communication bottlenecks, processing time and energy inefficiency etc.:

- *information, intelligence and computational resources* of the life-inspired system *should be properly distributed* over all its sub-systems,
- *effective application-specific operators* should be used,
- *parallel processing should be extensively applied* for tasks involving parallelism, and
- *effective communication* should be provided between the sub-systems.

This requires:

- *local distributed memories* for the sub-systems,
- (more) global *multi-port memories* for sharing data and communication between the sub-systems,
- *memory-centric processing* for massive data - the computations must come to the data and not the data to the computations (re-configurable computing),
- *simple effective communication mechanisms without unnecessary overheads,*
- *(massively) parallel processing sub-systems* involving *application-specific in hardware implemented operators,*
- *re-configurable hardware* to implement the application-specific (parallel) processing and memory-centric processing effectively and efficiently.

4 Importance of the Generic and Re-configurable System Solutions

In the life inspired-systems, ***re-configuration will play a very important role and serve numerous purposes***, including the following:

- computation speedup, as well as, power and energy savings in comparison to software solutions with the traditional CPU-centric instruction-stream-based computers, due to the distributed parallel processing and effective implementation of the application/program-specific operations and (massively parallel) computation patterns directly in the re-configurable hardware,
- product differentiation and changes in relation to applications (e.g. to cover large application domain, differentiate within a product family, react to changing standards, enhance, update or improve the product after fabrication, etc.),

- adaptability to changing operation conditions due to changes in the system's surrounding or interior, including: self-organization, self-regulation, self-protection etc. (e.g. adaptive control, filtering, interfacing, etc., but also fault-tolerance, self-testing, self-diagnosis and self-repair),
- design reuse and computational resource sharing;
- development and fabrication effort re-use that results in the reduction of the design productivity gap, shortening of the time-to market, and reduction of the design and fabrication NRE costs.

Actually, what is *re-configurable system?*
Many various definitions of re-configurable system can be found in literature. Unfortunately, all definitions that I was able to find are not general and not precise enough to enable any serious discussion. Therefore, I proposed the following definition: *re-configurable system is a system whose sub-systems and/or sub-system configurations can be changed or modified after fabrication to (better) serve a certain purpose.* Observe that this definition is independent of the system implementation aspects, and covers both the hardware and software re-configuration.

To efficiently develop the complex microelectronics-based systems, an adequate mixture of the design reuse at the system and/or sub-system levels with the automatic synthesis from the system and/or sub-system levels is needed. Generic system solutions and architectures, not necessary related to re-configurable systems, and particularly the **generic system platforms and architecture templates**, in parallel to serving similar aims as re-configuration, enable such adequate mixture of design reuse and innovation. In particular, they enable efficient *automatic system architecture synthesis, process scheduling and mapping.* If the problem (application) at a hand belongs to a certain well-defined abstraction class containing problems (applications) with similar requirements, a general form of a solution can be developed for the whole class and reused. The general form constrains the solution search space to such a degree that the construction of particular solution instances fine-tuned to particular applications can be performed by well-defined mapping, search and decision processes, based on evaluation of the solution's quality model. The mapping, search and decision processes can be automated to increase the designer's productivity and the overall quality of the design process. This sort of reuse is very important for the complex SoCs. For a certain application field, an appropriate generic architecture template can be developed and the nature of the core system's modules and interfaces between the modules and with the external world can be defined. Some families of (configurable) core system modules and interfaces suitable for different sub-fields of the application field can be developed. For a particular application, the generic architecture template and some selected core system's modules and interfaces are reused and adequately instantiated to appropriately serve the application, but also some new problem-specific modules and interfaces may be added. Observe, that the concept of *generic system solution* is strictly parallel to *genotype in the life organisms*:

- the generic solution is adequately instantiated to better serve a particular application,
- the genotype is mutated to better fit to particular conditions.

Also the *system re-configuration* is strictly parallel to the *adaptation in life organisms*.

5 System-Level Design

For complex systems such as SoCs, the system-level design forms a bottleneck and its costs are becoming dominant in the total costs of a microelectronics-based system. In addition to the difficulties with development of the modern embedded systems that were considered in the previous sections, we can expect that in the future the *more and more complex systems will be more and more on a single chip*. Observe moreover, that *SoCs and other modern embedded systems are application-specific and at the "system level"*, in the sense that they represent an important or decisive part of the actual complete product or system. Consequently, they are closer to application than to implementation technology, and they are appreciated, estimated and evaluated by the product-level attributes related to a particular application. The components of SoCs and other embedded systems tend also to be more and more at the system level and application-specific, but additionally, more often virtual (IP), flexible (customisable, re-configurable, programmable), and mixed (hardware/software, digital/analog).

For SoCs and other complex embedded systems, the *system-level design is a critical issue*. At the system level:

- the most important global design problems and tradeoffs must be decided: the main decisions are taken on the general form and nature of the future system, but also on the system's design, production, usage and disposal processes,
- the design problems are typically less structured and more complex than at the lower design levels, where we deal with only some partial problems and the design freedom is limited by the previous design decisions,
- more factors influence the design decisions than at the lower design levels, and their interrelations and tradeoffs are more complex.

Since the utility functions corresponding to various system attributes and interrelationships between various design characteristics are strongly non-linear, a huge increase of value for one characteristic is often possible without sacrificing too much of another one. Therefore, *appropriate design exploration, trade-off exploitation and decision analysis at the system-level can result in a very large improvement of the total system's quality*. Thus, besides the behavioural and structural modelling and analysis, extensively used also at the lower design levels, the **system-level design methods and tools should adequately support the parametric and the trade-off modelling and analysis, as well as,** *enable construction of various multi-objective decision models and usage of multi-objective decision methods.* The system-level design should be much more focused on the construction and validation of the design models and use of the design models and estimates for the design-space exploration by "what if" analysis. Thus, at least partially, a different kind of design support is needed here than that offered by the traditional design automation tools developed for the lower design levels. Due to the high importance, complexity and difficulty of the system-level design tasks, the *effective and efficient system-level design automation is crucial for enabling the adequate system-level design.* As explained above, in the system-level design and its automation the generic system solutions and their reuse play a crucial role - in particular, the generic system platforms and architecture templates that represent the generic system infrastructure. This infrastructure is appropriately instantiated and used by the application processes to realize the required system behaviour when satisfying certain objectives and constraints. Some of the *main design tasks the system-level EDA-tools should serve* are the following:

- application-specific generic system architecture template creation and instantiation,
- system component (IP) creation and instantiation,
- architecture template based system architecture exploration and (semi-) automatic synthesis, including automatic computation process scheduling and mapping on the selected system platform instance, when using multi-objective modeling, decision making and trade-off exploitation,
- design analysis, parameter estimation and evaluation,
- automatic hardware and software synthesis from the system-level specification,
- automatic system assembly according to the selected system architecture from the re-used IP components and the newly synthesized components,
- system design validation and system testing (including design for test and validation).

6   System Architecture Synthesis

Together with our collaborators, we applied the quality-driven design methodology, the paradigm of the life-inspired systems, and many other concepts discussed above to the semi-automatic system architecture exploration and synthesis for complex heterogeneous real-time embedded systems.

The system architecture design phase is located on the embedded system design trajectory, between the system requirement specification and hardware/software design and implementation (see Fig. 1). The *core activities of the system architecture design* for the embedded heterogeneous real-time hardware/software systems involve:

- *generic architecture design and modeling* (once for an application/system class)
- *generic architecture template instantiation* (for each particular application/system),

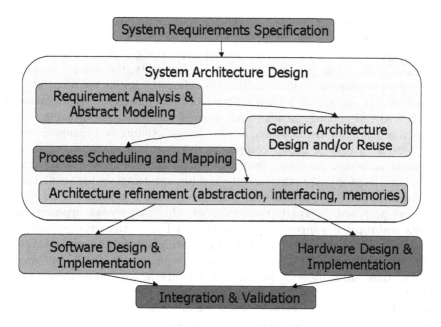

Fig. 1. System architecture design

- *abstract requirement modeling* (for each particular application/system),
- *process scheduling and mapping on the generic architecture template instance* (for each particular application/system).

To perform the system architecture exploration and synthesis effectively and efficiently, a generic architecture platform corresponding to a given application class and its main modules (processors, memories and communication) have to be developed in advance, based on the analysis of the application class and using the prior knowledge and experience related to applications/systems from this class or analogous classes. Also, a generic architecture template, has to be developed, being an abstract system-level model of the architecture platform and its modules, adequate for the architecture exploration and synthesis issue. Moreover, the original system requirements have to be analysed and an abstract system-level model of the behavioural and parametric requirements being adequate for the architecture design issue has to be constructed. The actual system architecture exploration starts with this abstract model comprising a network of collaborating computation processes and a set of parametric constraints and objectives. This network of processes have to be appropriately scheduled and distributed over the structure of modules of an adequate instance of the generic architecture template, to define the actual system architecture - i.e. the selection and interrelationships of the platform modules, assignment of the computational processes to the platform modules and their schedule - that satisfies the specific (structural, physical, etc.) constraints and optimizes the objectives of the parametric requirements in the context of specific trade-off preferences between the objectives.

Since the abstract requirement modelling, generic architecture instantiation, and process scheduling and mapping have to be performed for each particular application/system anew, and an adequate design space exploration of complex systems requires re-iterations and refinements, these three processes should be automated to a high degree. Providing the initial requirements are in any formal language, their abstract model can be automatically constructed through a sort of parsing, analysis and abstract translation. Comparing to the architecture template instantiation, the process scheduling and mapping seems to be a decision task of higher complexity, because it involves a complicated network of numerous processes that have to be appropriately scheduled and assigned on the proposed multiprocessor architecture template instance. Therefore, the automatic support for this task is of primary importance. In consequence, we proposed the *system architecture design process organization and its automatic support* as represented in Fig. 2. Both the requirement model and generic architecture template are developed before the actual system architecture exploration starts, although they both are not sacred and inviolable, but they are subject to re-design during the architecture exploration if necessary.

To start the actual architecture exploration and synthesis, based on the initial requirement analysis the designer makes a proposal of the generic architecture platform instance and its resource allocation that are expected to be adequate to

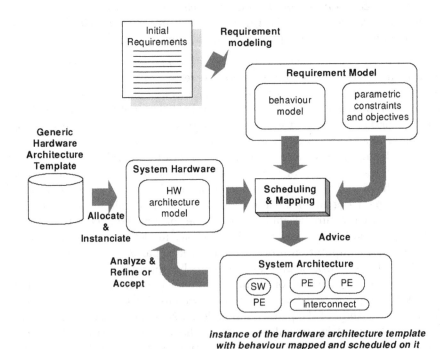

Fig. 2. Organization and automation of the system architecture design

realize the required system behaviour and satisfy the parametric requirements. His decision is implemented through instantiation of the corresponding IP models of the generic architecture template and of its modules that is supported with adequate design automation means. Using the requirement model and the IP models of the architecture template instance and of its modules, the scheduling and mapping are performed of the network of collaborating computation processes defined by the behavioural requirements on the proposed architecture template instance. Its result is a decomposition of the required network of the system's computational processes into a network of sub-systems that realizes the required processes. Each of the sub-systems corresponds to a module of the generic system architecture template instance with a sub-set of the computation processes scheduled and mapped on it. Each of the sub-systems executes a part of the required computations and all the sub-systems collaborating together realize the total required system's behaviour. This network of sub-systems represents the system architecture, i.e. the generic architecture template instance with the computational processes scheduled and mapped on this instance. The result of scheduling and mapping has not only to realize the required system's behaviour, but as well to satisfy specific constraints and optimize certain objectives in the context of some specific trade-off preferences between the objectives. The constructed system architecture is subsequently examined and analysed to check to what degree this all is satisfied. In the architecture design process that we proposed, the scheduling, mapping and architecture analysis processes are fully automated. We developed a *method and corresponding prototype EDA tool for the automatic system architecture construction and selection* through scheduling and mapping of the abstract behavioral model on the platform instance selected, when using an adequate decision model and parametric estimates. We also developed a parameter estimation method and tool for the relevant system architecture parameters, by using information from the abstract behavioral model, mapping configuration, schedule, and characteristics of the hardware resources. From our automatic EDA-tool, the designer receives feedback composed of the constructed architecture model and important characteristics of the constructed architecture showing to what degree the design objectives and constraints are satisfied by this architecture. Using this feedback, the designer can decide:

- to finish the architecture exploration end synthesis phase (if he is satisfied with its result) or to stop it (if it turns out to be impossible to realize the required system given the available resources),
- to make a new proposal of the generic architecture template instance and its resource allocation that are expected to be more adequate to realize the required system behaviour and satisfy the parametric requirements than the previously proposed (if he is not satisfied with the degree to which the design objectives and constraints are satisfied),
- to modify the generic architecture platform, some of its modules or design requirements (if it turns out that it is impossible to realize the required system with the currently used generic architecture).

In the last two cases, after making a modified platform instance and/or requirement proposal, the next iteration of the scheduling, mapping and architecture analysis is started.

The generic architecture template that served as an example in our research involved:

- instruction set processors cores,
- application-specific (reconfigurable) hardware co-processors and accelerators,
- distributed local memories placed directly in/by corresponding processing moduls,
- main memory sub-system, and
- communication sub-system (interconnections and interfaces).

The generic architecture template and the designs of some processors, memories, buses and interfaces contained in the design system library are reused and instantiated during the co-design process, but some new hardware co-processors, interfaces etc. can be synthesized and re-configurable subsystems can be re-configured especially for a specific application. The computational processes mapped to:

- instruction set processors are considered to be software modules, and
- application specific hardware co-processors and accelerators - hardware modules.

Software of the software modules is then automatically generated, compiled and executed on the instruction set processors. For the hardware modules an appropriate hardware implementing their behavior is synthesized.

The overall design aim: **find a high-quality system architecture** is expressed by a number of sub-objectives (e.g. minimize the resource usage, maximize the processing modules utilization, minimize the inter-module communication), constraints (e.g. the maximum latency and the maximum module utilization) and trade-off information. The sub-objectives and constraints are expressed as functions of some basic parameters possible to estimate based on the processors', memories' and communication models and the execution characteristics from the static behavioral analysis [7][8]. The sub-objectives are formulated as utility functions [2][3][8]. The decision model of the system partitioning issue thus constructed enables usage of the multiple-objective decision methods and tools for the invention and selection of the high-quality system architectures [2][3][8].

For complex designs, the estimation of the basic architecture parameters directly from the original behavioural specification is very difficult. Therefore, a much more abstract and simpler transition system model should be extracted for this particular design issue from the original behaviour model. To efficiently deal with design complexity, an **abstraction** is used that consists of:

- *data hiding*,
- *process abstraction and encapsulation* (the internal transformation behavior is modeled as an atomic action),

- *grouping of "zero-time" internal events into compound transitions,* and
- considering the *compound transitions with interleaved events to be equivalent.*

In this way, based on the original system behavior model, an **abstract transition system model** is constructed that is expressed in our case as an elementary net system model [8]. For this transition system model, the state reachability analysis is performed to determine the traces implementing a particular system function for the typical system use cases, and based on those traces, the precedence and conflict relations between the transformations (see Fig. 3). This information is used together with the processor models and hardware estimators to estimate the resource usage (e.g. hardware resource usage, execution time). The resource usage estimates are then used as values of some basic parameters in the formulas expressing the constraints and objectives in the decision model of the system architecture synthesis issue, and this way guide the architecture synthesis process. Using the concepts above discussed, we developed a **behavioral analysis method and tool** for an efficient automatic construction of the abstract behavioral models from the SA/RT models and use cases specified by the designer or user (see Fig. 3). We also developed a corresponding **parameter estimation method and tool** for the relevant system architecture parameters, by using information from the abstract behavioral model, mapping configuration, schedule, and characteristics of the hardware resources.

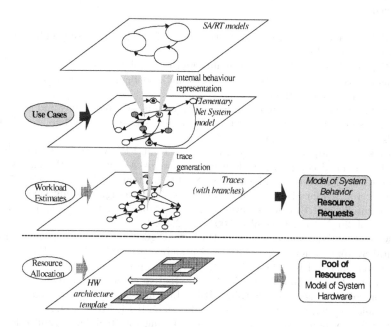

Fig. 3. Scheduling, mapping and architecture estimation using the abstract behavior and architecture models

7 Conclusion

Using the prototype EDA-tools that we developed for various issues of the system architecture design and applying them to two medium-size real-world design problems (the H263 video encoder and radio modem of a 3rd generation mobile phone), we performed a series of experiments with the proposed system architecture design method and EDA tools [8]. The experimental research confirms the adequacy of the proposed system architecture exploration and synthesis approach, and of the paradigms of the life-inspired systems and quality-driven design constituting the base of this approach. Their application should result in higher quality of systems, due to the usage of systemic solutions more adequate in the context of the emerging and future technologies and new demanding applications, and due to a more coherent, systematic, highly-automated, effective and efficient design process.

Acknowledgements

The author is indebted to his former PhD student S. A. Ong for implementing the architecture synthesis tools and performing experiments, and to K. Tiensyrja and other collaborants from VTT-Electronics, Oulu, for their kind and very effective collaboration related to the architecture synthesis tools.

References

1. Jóźwiak, L.: The 2003 International Technology Roadmap for Semiconductors, SIA, San Jose, CA, USA
2. Jóźwiak, L.: Modern concepts of quality and their relationship to design reuse and model libraries. in Current Issues in Electronic Modeling, Chapter 8, Issue 5 Kluwer Academic Publishers, 1995.
3. Jóźwiak, L.: Quality-driven design in the System-on-a-Chip era: why and how? Journal of Systems Architecture, April 2001 Elsevier Science, Amsterdam, The Netherlands, 2001, Vol 47/3-4, 201–224
4. Jóźwiak, L., Chojnacki, A.: Effective and efficient FPGA synthesis through general functional decomposition. Journal of Systems Architecture, Elsevier Science, Amsterdam, The Netherlands, Vol. 49, No 4-6, September 2003, pp. 247–265.
5. Jóźwiak, L.: Advanced AI search techniques in modern digital circuit synthesis. Artificial Intelligence Review, Kluwer Academic Publishers, Dordrecht, The Netherlands, Vol. 20, No 3-4, December 2003, pp. 269–318
6. Jóźwiak, L.: Life-inspired systems. Proc. DSD'2004 - Euromicro Symposium on Digital System Design, August 31st - September 3rd, 2004, Rennes, France, IEEE Computer Society Press, Los Alamitos, CA, USA, pp. 36–43
7. Ong, S.A., Jóźwiak, L., Tiensyrja, K.: Interactive co-design for real-time embedded control systems. Proc. ISIE-97 - IEEE International Symposium on Industrial Electronics, Guinaraes, Portugal, July 7-11, 1997, IEEE Press, 1997.
8. Ong, S.A.: System-Level Design Decision-Making for Real-Time Embedded Systems. Ph.D. Dissertation, Faculty of Electrical Engineering, Eindhoven University of Technology, The Netherlands, 2004, pp. 1–221.

The Robustness of Resource Allocations in Parallel and Distributed Computing Systems

Vladimir Shestak[1], Howard Jay Siegel[1,2],
Anthony A. Maciejewski[1], and Shoukat Ali[3]

[1] Department of Electrical & Computer Engineering
[2] Department of Computer Science,
Colorado State University, Fort Collins, CO 80523-1373, USA
{Shestak, HJ, AAM}@colostate.edu
[3] Department of Electrical & Computer Engineering,
University of Missouri-Rolla, Rolla, MO 65409-0040, USA
shoukat@umr.edu

Abstract. This corresponds to the material in the invited keynote presentation by H. J. Siegel, summarizing the research in [2, 23].

Resource allocation decisions in heterogeneous parallel and distributed computer systems and associated performance prediction are often based on estimated values of application and system parameters, whose actual values are uncertain and may be differ from the estimates. We have designed a model for deriving the degree of robustness of a resource allocation—the maximum amount of collective uncertainty in parameters within which a user-specified level of system performance can be guaranteed. The model will be presented, and we will demonstrate its ability to select the most robust resource allocation from among those that otherwise perform similarly (based on the primary performance criterion). We will show how the model can be used in off-line allocation heuristics to maximize the robustness of makespan against inaccuracies in estimates of application execution times in a cluster.

1 Introduction

This is an overview of the material to be discussed in the invited keynote presentation by H. J. Siegel; it summarizes our research in [2, 23].

This research focuses on the robustness of a resource allocation in parallel and distributed computing systems. What does robustness mean? Some dictionary definitions of robustness are: (a) strong and healthy, as in "a robust person" or "a robust mind," (b) sturdy or strongly formed, as in "a robust plastic," (c) suited to or requiring strength as in "a robust exercise" or "robust work," (d) firm in purpose or outlook as in "robust faith," (e) full-bodied as in "robust coffee," and (f) rough or rude as in "stories laden with robust humor." In the context of resource allocation in parallel and distributed computing systems, how is the concept of robustness defined?

The allocation of resources to computational applications in heterogeneous parallel and distributed computer systems should maximize some system performance measure. Allocation decisions and associated performance prediction are often based

W. Grass et al. (Eds.): ARCS 2006, LNCS 3894, pp. 17–30, 2006.
© Springer-Verlag Berlin Heidelberg 2006

on estimated values of application parameters, whose actual values may differ; for example, the estimates may represent only average values, or the models used to generate the estimates may have limited accuracy. Furthermore, parallel and distributed systems may operate in an environment where certain system performance features degrade due to unpredictable circumstances, such as sudden machine failures, higher than expected system load, or inaccuracies in the estimation of system parameters (e.g., [1, 3, 4, 5, 8, 11, 13, 14, 16, 17, 22]). Thus, an important research problem is the development of resource management strategies that can guarantee a particular system performance given bounds on such uncertainties. A resource allocation is defined to be *robust with respect to specified system performance features against perturbations (uncertainties) in specified system parameters* if degradation in these features is constrained when limited perturbations occur. An important question then arises: given a resource allocation, what extent of departure from the assumed circumstances will cause a performance feature to be unacceptably degraded? That is, how robust is the system?

Any claim of robustness for a given system must answer these three questions: (a) what behavior of the system makes it robust? (b) what uncertainties is the system robust against? (c) quantitatively, exactly how robust is the system? To address these questions, we have designed a model for deriving the degree of robustness of a resource allocation—the maximum amount of collective uncertainty in system parameters within which a user-specified level of system performance can be guaranteed. The model will be presented and we will demonstrate its ability to select the most robust resource allocation from among those that otherwise perform similarly (based on the primary performance criterion). The model's use in static (off-line) allocation heuristics also will be demonstrated. In particular, we will show how to maximize the robustness of makespan against inaccuracies in estimates of application execution times in a heterogeneous cluster. In general, this work is applicable to different types of computing and communication environments, including parallel, distributed, cluster, grid, Internet, embedded, and wireless.

Section 2 describes the FePIA procedure for deriving a robustness metric for an arbitrary system. Derivation of this metric for a given allocation of independent applications in a heterogeneous distributed system is presented in Section 3, with an experiment that highlights the usefulness of the robustness metric. Section 4 discusses heuristics developed to generate static resource allocations of independent applications in distributed systems such that the robustness of the produced resource allocations is maximized. Section 5 extends the work presented in Section 4 for distributed systems where the dollar cost for processors is a constraint. Some future work is described briefly in Section 6.

2 Generalized Robustness Metric

This section presents a general procedure, called *FePIA,* for deriving a general robustness metric for any desired computing environment [2]. The name for the above procedure stands for identifying the performance *fe*atures, the *p*erturbation parameters, the *i*mpact of perturbation parameters on performance features, and the *a*nalysis to determine the robustness. A specific example illustrating the application of the FePIA procedure to a sample system is given in the next section. Each step of the FePIA procedure is now described, summarized from [2].

1) Describe quantitatively the requirement that makes the system robust (question (a) in Section 1). Based on this *robustness requirement*, determine the QoS performance features that should be limited in variation to ensure that the robustness requirement is met. Identify the acceptable variation for these feature values as a result of uncertainties in system parameters. Consider an example where (a) the QoS performance feature is *makespan* (the total time it takes to complete the execution of a set of applications) for a given resource allocation, (b) the acceptable variation is up to a 20% increase of the makespan that was predicted for the given resource allocation using estimated execution times of applications on the machines they are assigned, and (c) the uncertainties in system parameters are inaccuracies in the estimates of these execution times.

2) Identify the uncertainties to be considered whose values may impact the QoS performance features selected in step 1 (question (b) in Section 1). These are called the *perturbation parameters*, and the performance features are required to be robust with respect to these perturbation parameters. For the makespan example above, the resource allocation (and its associated predicted makespan) was based on the estimated application execution times. It is desired that the makespan be robust (stay within 120% of its estimated value) with respect to uncertainties in these estimated execution times.

3) Identify the impact of the perturbation parameters in step 2 on the system performance features in step 1. For the makespan example, the sum of the *actual* execution times for all of the applications assigned to a given machine is the time when that machine completes its applications. Note that 1(b) states that the actual time each machine finishes its applications must be within the acceptable variation.

4) The last step is to determine the smallest collective variation in the values of perturbation parameters identified in step 2 that will cause any of the performance features identified in step 1 to violate its acceptable variation. Step 4 is done for a given, specific resource allocation. This will be the *degree of robustness* of the given resource allocation (question (c) in Section 1). For the makespan example, this will be some quantification of the total amount of inaccuracy in the execution times estimates allowable before the actual makespan exceeds 120% of its estimated value.

3 Robustness Metric Example

3.1 Derivation of Robustness

In this section summarized from [2], the robustness metric is derived for a system that assigns a set of independent applications to a distributed set of machines. In this system, it is required that the makespan be robust against errors in application execution time estimates. Specifically, the actual makespan under the perturbed execution times must be no more than a certain factor (> 1) times the predicted makespan calculated using the estimated execution times.

A brief description of the system model is now given. The applications are assumed to be independent, i.e., no communications between the applications are needed. The set $\underline{A}$ of applications is to be assigned to the set $\underline{\Omega}$ of machines so as to minimize the makespan. Each machine executes a single application at a time (i.e., no multi-tasking). Let C_{ij} be the *estimated time to compute* (*ETC*) for application a_i on machine m_j. It is assumed that C_{ij} values are known *a priori* for all i, j. This assumption is commonly made (e.g., [15]). Approaches for doing this estimation are discussed in [10]. In addition, let F_j be the time at which m_j finishes executing all of the applications assigned to it.

It is assumed that unknown inaccuracies in the ETC values are expected (e.g., a task's actual exact execution time may be data dependent). Hence, it is required that the mapping, denoted by μ, and based on the ETC values, be robust against them. More specifically, it is required that, for a given resource allocation, its actual makespan value $\underline{M}$ (calculated using the actual application computation times (not the ETC values)) may be no more than $\underline{\tau}$ (> 1) times its *predicted value*, denoted by M^{pred} . The predicted value of the makespan is the value calculated assuming the estimated ETC values. Following step 1 of the FePIA procedure in Section 2, the system performance features that should be limited in variation to ensure the makespan robustness are the finish times of the machines. That is, $\{F_j \leq \tau M^{pred}$ for $1 \leq j \leq |\Omega|\}$.

According to step 2 of the FePIA procedure, the perturbation parameter needs to be defined. Let C_i^{est} be the ETC value for application a_i on the machine where it is assigned. Let $\underline{C_i}$ be the actual computation time value. Let $\underline{C}$ be the vector of the C_i values, and $\underline{C}^{est}$ be the vector of the C_i^{est} values. The vector C is the perturbation parameter for this analysis.

In accordance with step 3 of the FePIA procedure, F_j has to be expressed as a function of C. To that end,

$$F_j(C) = \sum_{i:\, a_i \text{ is assigned to } m_j} C_i. \tag{1}$$

Following step 4 of the FePIA procedure, the set of boundary relationships corresponding to the set of performance features is given by $\{F_j(C) = \tau M^{pred}$ for $1 \leq j \leq |\Omega|\}$.

The *robustness radius*, denoted by $r_\mu(F_j, C)$, for machine j provides the largest Euclidian distance, i.e., l_2-norm, at which variable C can change in any direction from the assumed point C^{est} without the finish time $F_j(C)$ exceeding the tolerable variation:

$$r_\mu(F_j, C) = \min_{C:\, F_j(C) = \tau M^{pred}} \left\| C - C^{est} \right\|_2. \tag{2}$$

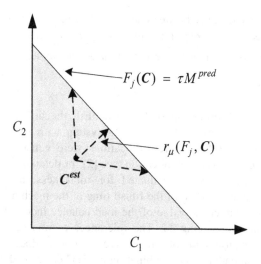

Fig. 1. Some possible directions of increase of the perturbation parameter C. The set of boundary points is given by $F_j(C^{est}) = \tau M^{pred}$. The robustness radius $r_\mu(F_j, C)$ corresponds to the smallest increase that can reach the boundary. The shaded region represents the area of robust operation.

That is, if the Euclidean distance between any vector of the actual execution times and the vector of the estimated execution times is no larger than $r_\mu(F_j, C)$, then the finish time of machine m_j will be at most τ times the estimated makespan value.

For example, assume only applications a_1 and a_2 have been assigned to machine j (depicted in Fig. 1), and C has two components C_1 and C_2 that correspond to execution times of a_1 and a_2 on machine j, respectively. The term $F_j(C^{est})$ is a finish time for machine j computed based on the ETC values of applications a_1 and a_2. The boundary line is determined by $F_j(C) = \tau M^{pred}$. Note that the right hand side in Equation 2 can be interpreted as the perpendicular distance from the point C^{est} to the hyperplane described by the equation $F_j(C) = \tau M^{pred}$. Using the point-to-plane distance formula [21], Equation 2 reduces to

$$r_\mu(F_j, C) = \frac{\tau M^{pred} - F_j(C^{est})}{\sqrt{\text{number of applications assigned to } m_j}}. \tag{3}$$

The *robustness metric*, denoted by ρ_μ, is given as

$$\rho_\mu = \min_{1 \le j \le |\Omega|} \{r_\mu(F_j, C)\}. \tag{4}$$

That is, if the Euclidean distance between any vector of the actual execution times and the vector of the estimated execution times is no larger than ρ_μ, then the actual makespan will be at most τ times the predicted makespan value.

3.2   Utility of Robustness

The experiments in this subsection seek to establish the utility of the robustness metric. The experiments were performed for a system with five machines and 20 applications. A total of 1000 resource allocations were generated by assigning a randomly chosen machine to each application (see [2] for details).

The resource allocations were evaluated for robustness, makespan, and *load balance index* (defined as the ratio of the finish time of the machine that finishes first to the makespan). The larger the value of the load balance index, the more balanced the load (the largest value being 1). The tolerance, τ, was set to 120%. In this context, a robustness metric value of x for a given resource allocation means that the resource allocation can endure any combination of ETC errors without the makespan increasing beyond 1.2 times its estimated value as long as the Euclidean distance of the errors is no larger than x seconds.

Fig. 2(a) shows the "normalized robustness" of a resource allocation against its makespan. The *normalized robustness* equals the robustness metric value divided by the predicted makespan. A graph for the normalized robustness against the load balance index is shown in Fig. 2(b).

There are large differences in the robustness of some resource allocations that have very similar values of makespan. Thus, when selecting a resource allocation with low makespan, the robustness calculation allows one to select an allocation that also provides high robustness. Fig. 2(b) shows that load balancing does not provide an accurate measure of robustness. These observations highlight the fact that the information given by the robustness metric could not be obtained from the makespan and load balance performance measures.

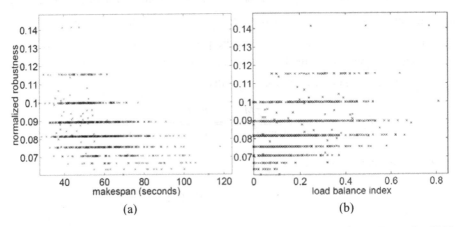

Fig. 2. Normalized robustness against (*a*) makespan and (*b*) load balance index for 1000 randomly generated resource allocations

4 Robust Resource Allocation Under a Makespan Constraint

4.1 Problem Statement

This section summarizes a part of the research described in [23]. An important research problem is how to determine a *mapping (resource allocation)* so as to maximize the robustness of desired system features against perturbations in system parameters. The general problem of optimally mapping applications to machines has been shown to be NP-complete [7, 9, 12]. Thus, the development of heuristic techniques to find near-optimal solutions for the mapping problem is an active area of research (e.g., [6, 18, 19, 20]). *Static* mapping is performed when the applications are mapped in an off-line planning phase such as in a production environment. Static mapping techniques take a set of applications, a set of machines, and generate a mapping. These heuristics determine a mapping off-line, and must use estimated values of application computation times.

As described in the previous section, the allocation of independent applications in parallel systems is considered robust if the actual makespan under the perturbed conditions does not exceed the required time constraint. The goal of this study was to find a static mapping of all applications to machines so that the robustness of the mapping is maximized; i.e., to maximize the collective allowable error in execution time estimation for the applications that can occur without the actual makespan exceeding the constraint. Mathematically, this problem can be stated as finding a mapping of $|A|$ applications to $|\Omega|$ machines such that the actual makespan is within the *absolute time constraint* $\underline{\alpha}$ while maximizing ρ_μ, given by (4). Equation (3) is restated in this study as

$$r_\mu(F_j, C) = \frac{\alpha - F_j(C^{est})}{\sqrt{\text{number of applications asiigned to } m_j}}. \tag{5}$$

A distributed system with eight machines and 1024 independent applications was simulated in this study. Two different cases of ETC heterogeneities were used in this research, the high application and high machine heterogeneity (*high-high*) case and the low application and low machine heterogeneity (*low-low*) case (see [23] for details about the simulation setup). The value of the time constraint α of 5000 seconds was chosen so that it presents a feasible mapping problem for the heuristics to solve. A total of 100 trials (50 trails for each of the cases) were performed, where each trial corresponded to a different ETC of C_{ij} values matrix. The wall clock time for each of the heuristics to determine a mapping was arbitrarily required to be less than or equal to 60 minutes to establish a basis for comparison.

Six static mapping schemes were developed in this study: Max-Max, Greedy Iterative Maximization (GIM), Sum Iterative Maximization (SIM), Genitor, Memetic Algorithm (MA), and Hereboy Evolutionary Algorithm (Hereboy). Two are described here.

4.2 Max-Max

The Max-Max heuristic is based on the Min-Min (greedy) concept in [12]. In step 2 of the Max-Max heuristic, to find the *fitness* function for assigning a given application i to a given machine j, the robustness radius of machine j given by equation (5) is evaluated based on the applications already assigned to machine j and the possible assignment of application i to machine j.

The Max-Max heuristic can be summarized by the following procedure:

1)   An application list is generated that includes all the unmapped applications.
2)   For each application in the application list, the machine that gives the application its maximum fitness value (first "Max") is determined (ignoring other unmapped applications).
3)   Among all the application/machine pairs found in the above step, the pair that gives the maximum fitness value (second "Max") is chosen.
4)   The application found in step 3 is then removed from the application list and is mapped to its paired machine.
5)   Repeat steps 2 to 4 until all the applications are mapped.

4.3 Genitor

This heuristic is a general optimization technique that is a variation of the genetic algorithm approach. It manipulates a set of possible solutions. The framework used here is based on the Genitor approach used in [24]. In our study, each *chromosome* represents a possible complete mapping of applications to machines. Specifically, the chromosome is a vector of length $|A|$. The ith element of the vector is the number of the machine to which application i is assigned. A fixed population of 200 chromosomes is used. The population includes one chromosome (seed) that is the Max-Max solution based on robustness (described above) and the rest of the chromosomes are generated by randomly assigning applications to machines. The entire population is sorted (ranked) based on their robustness metric values given by (4). Chromosomes that do not meet the makespan constraint are allowed to be included in the population. The ranking is constructed so that all chromosomes that meet the constraint are listed first, ordered by their robustness metric value (highest first). The chromosomes that do not meet the makespan constraint are then listed, again ordered by their robustness metric value (which will be negative).

Next, a special linear bias function [24] is used to select two chromosomes to act as parents. These two parents perform a crossover operation, and two new offspring are generated. For the pair of the selected parent chromosomes a random cut-off point is generated that divides the chromosomes into top and bottom parts. For the parts of both chromosomes from that point to the end of each chromosome, crossover exchanges machine assignments between corresponding applications producing two new offspring. The offspring are then inserted in the population in ranked order, and the two lowest ranked chromosomes are dropped.

After each crossover, the linear bias function is applied again to select a chromosome for mutation. A mutation operator generates a single offspring by perturbing the original chromosome. A random application is chosen from the chromosome and the mutation operator randomly reassigns it to a new machine. The resultant offspring is considered for inclusion in the population in the same fashion as for an offspring generated by crossover.

This completes one iteration of the Genitor. The heuristic stops after 250,000 total iterations.

4.4 Experimental Results

The simulation results are shown in Fig. 3. All the heuristics run for 50 different high-high and 50 different low-low scenarios, and the average values and 95% confidence intervals are plotted. The Genitor performed among the best, comparable to GIM, SIM, and MA (i.e., overlapping confidence intervals). A discussion of all the results is in [23].

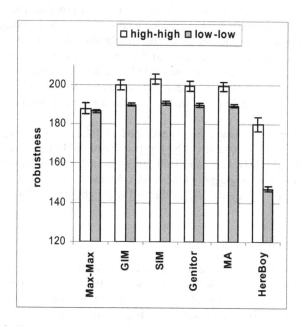

Fig. 3. Simulation results for robustness for a given fixed set of machines

5 Mapping Under Makespan and Dollar Cost Constraints

5.1 Problem Statement

This section summarizes another part of [23], which extends the idea in Section 4. The research environment here differs from Section 4 with the addition of a *cost constraint* for the machines and choosing a subset of all the available machines to be used. Thus, problem addressed here is how to select (purchase) a fixed set of machines, within a given dollar cost constraint to comprise a cluster system. It is assumed that this fixed system will be used in a production environment to regularly execute the set A of applications with known estimated computational character-stics. The machines to be purchased for the set are to be selected from five different classes of machines, where each class consists of homogeneous machines. The machines of different classes differ in dollar costs depending upon their application execution speed. The dollar cost of machines within a class is the same. Machines in class i are assumed to be faster than machines of class $i+1$ for all applications, for $1 \leq i \leq 4$. Correspondingly, class i machines cost more that class $i+1$ machines.

In this study, one must: (1) select a subset of machines so that the cost constraint for the machines is satisfied, and (2) find a static mapping of all applications to the subset. Sub-problems 1 and 2 must be done in a way so that the robustness of the mapping is maximized. For sub-problem 2, the machine assignment heuristics described in the previous section are used as components of the heuristics developed in this research.

A method used to generate 100 high application and low machine heterogeneity (*high-low*) ETC matrices for 1024 independent applications was identical to that used in the previous work (see the details of the simulation setup in [23]). Experiments with simple greedy heuristics were used to decide the value of the cost constraint to be 34,800 dollars and the time constraint α to be 12,000 seconds. Choosing different values for any of the above parameters will not affect the general approach of the heuristics used in this research. The wall clock time for the mapper itself was set as in Section 4.

Six static mapping schemes were developed in this research: Negative Impact Greedy Iterative Maximization (NI-GIM), Parition/Merge Greedy Iterative Maximization (P/M-GIM), Cost and Robustness Sum Iterative Maximization (CR-SIM), Selection Genitor (S-Genitor), Max-Max Memetic Algorithm (MMMA), and Max-Max Hereboy Evolutionary Algorithm (MM-Hereboy). The S-Genitor heuristic is described next.

5.2 Selection Genitor

The S-Genitor heuristic developed in this work consists of two phases. For phase 1, a chromosome is a vector of length five, where the ith element is the number of machines used in i^{th} class. The phase 1 of S-Genitor operates on a fixed population of 100 chromosomes. The entire population is generated randomly such that the cost constraint is met. To evaluate each chromosome, a mapping was produced using the Max-Max heuristic based on robustness (described in Subsection 4.2). The entire population is sorted in descending order based on the robustness metric.

In the crossover step, for the pair of the parent chromosomes selected by applying the linear bias function, a random cut-off point is generated that divides the chromosomes into top and bottom parts. A new chromosome is formed using the top of one and bottom of another. An offspring is inserted in the population after evaluation only if the cost constraint is satisfied (the worst chromosomes of the population are discarded to maintain a population of only 100).

After each crossover, the linear bias function is applied again to select a chromosome for mutation. A mutation operator generates a single offspring by perturbing the original chromosome. Two random classes are chosen for the chromosome and the mutation operator increments the number of machines of the first chosen class by one and decrements the number of machines of the other by one. If the chromosome violates the cost constraint it is discarded. Otherwise, the resultant offspring is considered for inclusion in the population in the same fashion as for an offspring generated by crossover.

This completes one iteration of phase 1 of S-Genitor. The heuristic stops when the criterion of 500 total iterations is met. The best machine combination found from phase 1 is used in phase 2, which derives a mapping using this combination of machines to maximize robustness based on the Genitor implementation described in Section 4 (a total of 100,000 iterations is used here to stop phase 2 of S-Genitor).

5.3   Experimental Results

The simulation results are shown in Fig. 4. All the heuristics run for 100 different scenarios and the average values and 95% confidence intervals are plotted. The S-Genitor is among and the best heuristics, comparable in performance with the P/M-GIM heuristic. Both of these heuristics, on average, had all of the available machines from Class 4 and Class 5. A discussion of all the results is in [23].

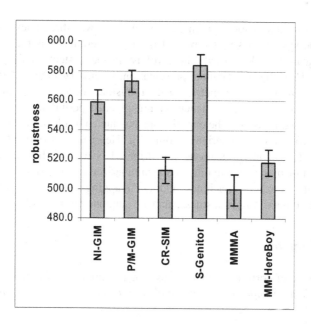

Fig. 4. Simulation results for robustness. Machine sets were determined heuristically.

6   Future Work

There are many directions in which the robustness research presented in the paper can be extended. Examples include the following.

1) Deriving the boundary surfaces for different problem domains.
2) Incorporating multiple types of perturbation parameters (e.g., uncertainties in input sensor loads and uncertainties in estimated execution times). Challenges here are how to define the collective impact to find each robust radius and how to state the combined bound on multiple perturbation parameters to maintain the promised performance.
3) Incorporating probabilistic information about uncertainties. In this case, a perturbation parameter can be represented as a vector of random variables. Then, one might have probabilistic information about random variables in the vector (e.g., probability density functions) or probabilistic information describing the relationship between different random variables in the vector or between different vectors (e.g., a set of correlation coefficients).
4) Determining when to use Euclidean distance versus other distance measures when calculating the collective impact of changes in the perturbation parameter elements.

7 Summary

Any claim of robustness for a given system must answer three questions: (a) what behavior of the system makes it robust? (b) what uncertainties is the system robust against? (c) quantitatively, exactly how robust is the system? This paper, which corresponds to H. J. Siegel's keynote presentation, summarizes the material from two papers related to robustness. A metric for the robustness of a resource allocation with respect to desired system performance features against perturbations in system and environmental conditions, and the experiments conducted to illustrate the utility of the robustness metric, are summarized from [2]. Heuristics developed to generate mappings of independent applications in distributed systems such that the robustness of the produced mappings is maximized are summarized from [23]. Finally, heuristics for (1) selecting a set of machines and (2) mapping applications to the set of machines, both to maximize robustness, also are summarized from [23].

Acknowledgment

An earlier version of portions of this manuscript appeared as an invited keynote paper in *8th International Symposium on Parallel Architectures, Algorithms, and Networks (I-SPAN 2005)*.

References

1. S. Ali, J.K. Kim, Y. Yu, S. B. Gundala, S. Gertphol, H. J. Siegel, A. A. Maciejewski, and V. Prasanna, "Utilization-based techniques for statically mapping heterogeneous applications onto the HiPer-D heterogeneous computing system," *Parallel and Distributed Computing Practices*, Vol. 5, No. 4, Dec. 2002.

2. S. Ali, A. A. Maciejewski, H. J. Siegel, and J.-K. Kim, "Measuring the robustness of a resource allocation," *IEEE Transactions on Parallel Systems*, Vol. 15, No. 7, July 2004, pp. 630–641.

3. S. Ali, A. A. Maciejewski, H. J. Siegel, and J.-K. Kim, "Robust resource allocation for distributed computing systems," *2004 International Conference on Parallel Processing (ICPP'04)*, Aug. 2004, pp. 178–185.

4. P. M. Berry, "Uncertainty in scheduling: probability, problem reduction, abstractions and the user," *IEE Computing and Control Division Colloquium Advanced Software Technologies for Scheduling*, Digest No. 1993/163, Apr. 1993.

5. L. Boloni and D. C. Marinescu, "Robust scheduling of metaprograms," *Journal of Scheduling*, Vol. 5, No. 5, Sept. 2002, pp. 395–412,

6. T. D. Braun, H. J. Siegel, N. Beck, L. L. Boloni, M. Maheswaran, A. I. Reuther, J. P. Robertson, M. D. Theys, B. Yao, D. Hensgen, and R. F. Freund, "A comparison of eleven static heuristics for mapping a class of independent applications onto heterogeneous distributed computing systems," *Journal of Parallel and Distributed Computing*, Vol. 61, No. 6, June 2001, pp. 810–837.

7. E. G. Coffman, Jr. ed., *Computer and Job-Shop Scheduling Theory*, John Wiley & Sons, New York, NY, 1976.

8. R. L. Daniels and J. E. Carrillo, "β-Robust scheduling for single-machine systems with uncertain processing times," *IIE Transactions*, Vol. 29, No. 11, Nov. 1997, pp. 977–985.

9. D. Fernandez-Baca, "Allocating modules to processors in a distributed system," *IEEE Transactions on Software Engineering*, Vol. SE-15, No. 11, Nov. 1989, pp. 1427–1436.

10. A. Ghafoor and J. Yang, "A distributed heterogeneous supercomputing management system," *IEEE Computer*, Vol. 26, No. 6, June 1993, pp. 78–86.

11. S. D. Gribble, "Robustness in complex systems," *8th Workshop on Hot Topics in Operating Systems (HotOS-VIII)*, May 2001, pp. 21–26.

12. O. H. Ibarra and C. E. Kim, "Heuristic algorithms for scheduling independent applications on non-identical processors," *Journal of ACM*, Vol. 24, No. 2, Apr. 1977, pp. 280–289.

13. M. Jensen, "Improving robustness and flexibility of tardiness and total flowtime job shops using robustness measures," *Journal of Applied Soft Computing*, Vol. 1, No. 1, June 2001, pp. 35–52.

14. E. Jen, "Stable or robust? What is the difference?" *Complexity*, Vol. 8, No. 3, June 2003.

15. M. Kafil and I. Ahmad, "Optimal task assignment in heterogeneous distributed computing systems," *IEEE Concurrency*, Vol. 6, No. 3, July. 1998, pp. 42–51.

16. V. J. Leon, S. D. Wu, and R. H. Storer, "Robustness measures and robust scheduling for job shops," *IEE Tranactions*, Vol. 26, No. 5, Sept. 1994, pp. 32–43.

17. M. Sevaux and K. Sorensen, "Genetic algorithm for robust schedules," *8th International Workshop on Project Management and Scheduling (PMS 2002)*, Apr. 2002, pp. 330–333.

18. V. Shestak, E. K. P. Chong, A. A. Maciejewski, H. J. Siegel, L. Benmohamed, I. J. Wang, and R. Daley, "Resource allocation for periodic applications in a shipboard environment," *14th Heterogeneous Computing Workshop (HCW 2005)* in proceedings of 19th International Parallel and Distributed Processing Symposium (IPDPS 2005), Apr. 2005, pp. 122–127.

19. S. Shivle, P. Sugavanam, H. J. Siegel, A. A. Maciejewski, T. Banka, K. Chindam, S. Dussinger, A. Kutruff, P. Penumarthy, P. Pichumani, P. Satyasekaran, D. Sendek, J. Sousa, J. Sridharan, and J. Velazco, "Mapping of subtasks with multiple versions on an *ad hoc* grid environment," *Parallel Computing,* Special Issue on Heterogeneous Computing, Vol. 31, No. 7, July 2005, pp. 671–690.

20. S. Shivle, H. J. Siegel, A. A. Maciejewski, P. Sugavanam,T. Banka, R. Castain, K. Chindam, S. Dussinger, P. Pichumani, P. Satyasekaran, W. Saylor, D. Sendek, J. Sousa, J. Sridharan, and J. Velazco, "Static allocation of resources to communicating subtasks in a heterogeneous *ad hoc* grid environment," *Journal of Parallel and Distributed Computing,* accepted, to appear.

21. G. F. Simmons, *Calculus with Analytic Geometry, Second Edition,* McGraw-Hill, New York, NY, 1995.

22. Y. N. Sotskov, V. S. Tanaev, and F. Werner, "Stability radius of an optimal schedule: A survey and recent developments," *Industrial Applications of Combinatorial Optimization,* Vol. 16, 1998, pp. 72–108.

23. P. Sugavanam, H. J. Siegel, A. A. Maciejewski, M. Oltikar, A. Mehta, R. Pichel, A. Horiuchi, V. Shestak, M. Al-Otaibi, Y. Krishnamurthy, S. Ali, J. Zhang, M. Aydin, P. Lee, K. Guru, M. Raskey, and A. Pippin, "Robust static allocation of resources for independent tasks under makespan and dollar cost constraints," *Journal of Parallel and Distributed Computing,* accepted, to appear in 2006.

24. D. Whitley, "The GENITOR algorithm and selective pressure: Why rank based allocation of reproductive trials is best," *3rd International Conference on Genetic Algorithms,* June 1989, pp. 116–121.

FingerMouse – A Button Size Visual Hand Tracking and Segmentation Device

Patrick de la Hamette and Gerhard Tröster

Wearable Computing Lab, ETH Zürich, Switzerland
{pdelaham, troester}@ife.ee.ethz.ch
http://www.wearable.ethz.ch

Abstract. In this paper, we present a button-sized (43mm×18mm) visual input system for wearable computers, the FingerMouse. It is a fully integrated camera and vision processing system, with a specifically designed ASIC computing images at 20GOp/s consuming 78mW. Worn on the body, it captures the user's hand and processes in real-time its coordinates as well as a 1-bit image of the hand segmented from the background. This paper describes the architecture of the FingerMouse and compares it to other implementations.

1 Introduction

As a new generation of computers, wearable computers are worn on the user's body or are even integrated in his textiles. This allows for new application scenarios: the computer becomes a digital assistant helping the user perform certain tasks. The system shall not obstruct the user in any way, his hands should be free. Ideally the digital assistant provides useful information (e.g. via a head-up display, or sound) without requiring explicit user interaction. In many situations though, user input to the system will be necessary. Obviously the classic input devices like a keyboard or a mouse do not fit into the wearable computing scenario. A new class of human-computer interaction (HCI) devices is required.

This paper describes such a new wearable device, the FingerMouse. It captures the user's hand when moving in front of the device's cameras, enabling him to interact with the wearable computer using his bare hands.

The FingerMouse uses it's own processing power to run vision algorithms, to acquire:

1. Hand movement: The hand position (absolute coordinates) in the captured images is computed.

   This allows the user to control an X-Y pointer, similar as a PC-mouse does. For more simple interactions, hand movements (up, down, etc.) are also useful, since they don't require visual feedback, as a pointer does.
2. Hand shape: The hand shape is acquired as a 1-bit bitmap through background segmentation.

   The FingerMouse transmits this image to a computer, acting as a segmenting-camera. A possible application is the recognition of hand signs by higher-level algorithms running on the wearable computer ([1]).

W. Grass et al. (Eds.): ARCS 2006, LNCS 3894, pp. 31–41, 2006.
© Springer-Verlag Berlin Heidelberg 2006

Fig. 1. Application scenario: FingerMouse worn on the body

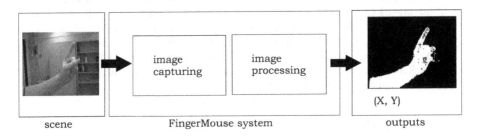

Fig. 2. FingerMouse: real-time scene capturing with hand tracking and segmentation

The following features characterize the FingerMouse:

1. Full integration
   The system includes all the parts used for image capturing, image processing and power regulation off a battery voltage. It computes the results mentioned above autonomously and transmits them to a (wearable) computer.
2. Real-time operation
   As a HCI device, the computation has to be done online. The FingerMouse operates in real-time, processing several frames per second.
3. Low latency
   When using the system with visual feedback (e.g. X-Y pointer on a screen), the user and the machine become a closed-loop system. The smaller the tracking latency (or lag) is, the higher the usability. HCI research suggests that values under 50ms are acceptable and that latency is more important to usability than the measurement accuracy. ([2] [3]) .
4. No calibration
   The device immediately works after power-up. This allows it to be turned on shortly only when user-interaction is needed.
5. High computation performance
   The FingerMouse processes images at 320x480 resolution and 15fps, achieving an image throughput of 5 Mpixels/s. We developed a specific ASIC for the image computation, which computes at 20 Goperations/sec.
6. Small size
   The current implementation is sized 43mm x 18mm.

7. Low power
The current implementation consumes less than 200mW at full operating speed (ASIC: 78mW). This value has to be seen in conjunction with the possibility to switch the system on and off very quickly.

2   Image Processing

To achieve the hand recognition, we evaluated several methods:

Table 1. Comparison between hand recognition algorithms

Method	Description	Problems
Background subtraction	Two subsequently captured images are subtracted. Moving objects can be retrieved.	If the device is worn on the body, the whole scene is always in motion. The method is not applicable.
Color segmentation	The image is segmented by using a skin color tone reference. If a pixel is similar to the reference, it's classified to the hand. [4]	Needs calibration to calculate the color reference. Changing lighting requires new calibration.
Active lighting	The foreground is illuminated by a light source of a specific spectrum. The image is captured through a spectral filter. Close objects should show a higher brightness.[5]	Lighting requires a lot of power. Outdoors, the sunlight outperforms lighting over most of the spectrum. [6]
Contour tracking	A geometrical contour of the hand is tracked over time. In new images the tracker adjust the contour to follow the hand. [7] [8] [9]	Needs calibration to initially put the contour on the hand. If the tracking is lost, new calibration is required.
Stereo vision image substraction	The image from two parallel cameras is subtracted. Since the background coincides, it disappears. [10]	The foreground is badly retrieved as an overlay of two subtracted hands. Medium distanced objects produce a lot of noise.
Stereo vision depth mapping	Using two cameras, the depth of a scene can be computed. The hand is classified by its proximity to the cameras. [11] [12]	High computational effort

We use stereo vision depth mapping in our FingerMouse system, because of its good segmentation, outdoor ability and the absence of calibration. The problem of the high computation amount is addressed by a FingerMouse ASIC, specifically developed for the task.

As seen in fig. 3, two parallel cameras, offset by b (baseline), synchronously capture an image of the scene. For each pixel, a depth Z can be computed, by comparing the two images. Objects in the two stereo image are horizontally

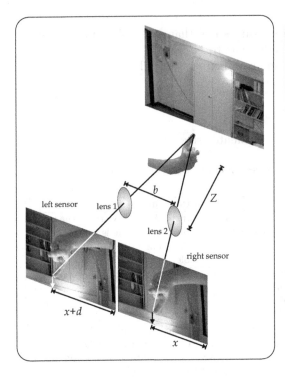 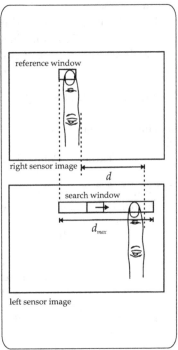

Fig. 3. *Left:* scene capture through stereo vision *right:* stereo matching

translated by the so called disparity d $[pixels]$. The disparity d of an object is inversely proportional to its distance Z from the cameras:

$$d = b \cdot f \cdot \frac{1}{Z} \cdot \frac{x_r}{x_s} \ [pixels].\tag{1}$$

(f = focal length of the lenses; x_s = image sensor width (light sensitive area); x_r = horizontal image resolution $[pixels]$).

The disparity is calculated for each pixel and then classified into foreground (high disparity) or background (small disparity). To compute a disparity, a reference window, a block (3×5 pixels) around the pixel, is compared to blocks in the other stereo image, along a horizontal search window, of width d_{max}, the highest disparity to be expected (c.f. fig.3:right). The block with the highest correlation to the reference block appears at the given disparity. The hand must not be closer than Z_{max}, the distance corresponding to d_{max}.

The correlation between blocks is calculated with 2 different functions operating on the pixel intensity (brightness): the SAD (sum of absolute differences) and the census function. The census function maps a 3×3 block to 8 bits, each bit indicating wether a border pixel is brighter than the center pixel. A 5×3 block is mapped to 3×8 bits, the combination of the results from the three

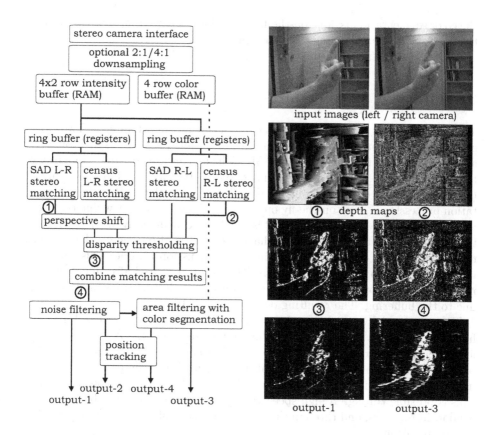

Fig. 4. Vision processing flow in the ASIC, sample images

3×3 blocks inside the 5×3 block. Blocks are compared by the hamming distance of their census function. The census and SAD matching both produce noise, but have different properties. By combining their results, noise can be reduced.

The block matching search is done both from the left to the right (L-R matching) image and vice versa (R-L). The results are different, because of occlusions occurring from the different perspectives of the two cameras [13]. The occlusions are overcome by combining the results from L-R and R-L matching.

The algorithm is shown in fig. 4. It includes the processing flow inside the ASIC and some sample images at different processing stages.

The segmented image resulting from the combination of the 4 stereo-matching operations is median filtered, to reduce noise. The resulting picture is output-1. The hand coordinates, output-2, are derived from a center-of-gravity computation.

At a second stage, the output-1 image is enhanced (fill-up) using color segmentation. The color tone (hue) reference is derived from the output-1 image (which shows parts of the hand and noise). Pixels that have a similar color and are close to foreground pixels in output-1 are classified as foreground in the output-3 image. The corresponding hand coordinates are called output-4. Since the color segmentation is done on-the-fly, the color reference is always taken from the previous image. The use of color is optional.

Similar systems are described in [14] [15] [16] [17] [18].

3   Hardware Architecture

The architecture of the system and its components are shown in fig 5. Two cameras are arranged in parallel, with a baseline of 25mm. They work synchronously and are clocked by the FingerMouse-ASIC. The images are not stored in a frame buffer, eliminating the need for an image-RAM. Instead, a window of only 4 (stereo-)lines from each stereo image is buffered inside the ASIC. The segmentation processing is done on-the-fly on the first 3 lines, while a new line is stored in the buffer. The segmented output is available concurrently with the image transmission from the cameras. The hand-tracking is also done on the fly, and the result is ready directly after the image transmission is done. This way, the result computation has practically zero latency (if measured after image transmission). The output image is delayed by only 1 single row transmission time, due to the buffering. The resulting delay is around 100 μs.

The cameras deliver pictures of 320x480 resolution at a frame rate of 15fps. To handle this amount of data and do online stereo matching, the ASIC has to perform over 20 GOperations/sec. (This value is based only the on stereo matching part, and only counting operations [subtract, accumulate, compare, fetch value] inside the loops, without any overhead. The complete figure is much higher.) This is possible through a high speed ring buffer, which stores the block search window in registers, and through the use of parallel combinatorial structures for the computation.

A small microcontroller (TI MSP430) controls the cameras, configures the ASIC and transports the tracking results via a RS232 interface. The segmented images are directly output by the ASIC, over a parallel interface.

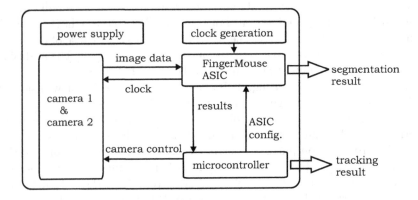

Fig. 5. System architecture

Table 2. FingerMouse ASIC Specifications

Supply voltage	2.5V / 3.3V (core / I/O)
Chip size	$2227\mu m \times 2227\mu m$ (excluding sealring and bonding areas)
Chip technology	umcL250, 250 nm
Pin count	28 input; 22 output; 20 power; 14 empty
On-chip RAM	4Kbytes (3.432 KBytes used)
Camera clock output	1/8 ASIC clock
Camera input format	B/W 8 bit/pixel or YUV 4:2:2 16 bit/pixel
Image size format	width: max. 1360 (internal: max 340, after factor 1,2 or 4 downsampling) height: max. 1020
Image data rate	5 Mpixel/s (2.5 Mstereo-pixels/s) @80 MHz
Power dissipation at full processing rate	78mW @80MHz and 96mW @100MHz clock speed
Interfaces	configuration, tracking results: RS232 segmented image output: 16-bit parallel interface @312.5KHz

4 Achievements and System Comparison

The architecture is implemented on a 4-layer PCB. The FingerMouse ASIC die is directly bonded onto the PCB, without a package. Two image sensors (Omnivision OV7649, low voltage color CMOS VGA imager) in chip-scale package were used, together with small board-lenses. The system further includes an MSP430F1611 in a standard package (backside), and interfaces for communication. A battery voltage of 2.7V-5.5V is regulated to the different voltages needed onboard, using a single micro-power-management integrated circuit (MAX8620Y).

Table 3 gives an overview of the components' power consumptions. Fig. 6 (left) shows the PCB with the optics, no electronics mounted.

Table 3. FingerMouse system power budget

Component:	Power:
FingerMouse ASIC	78 mW
Cameras	2× 30 mW
MSP430	5 mW
Clock generator	23 mW
Total internal dissipation:	166 mW
Power regulation effiency:	89%
Total input power from battery:	187 mW

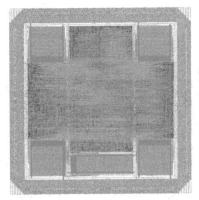

Fig. 6. *Left*: FingerMouse prototype PCB (next to 2 Euro "button") *right*: ASIC layout

4.1 Algorithm Processing Efficiency on the Different FingerMouse Implementations/Architectures

To give a notion of the system's performance, we provide an overview over 3 other prototypes that have been implemented at our lab. They all use stereo vision to segment and track the hand, but the underlying processing architecture is different.

1. The first prototype system was built in 2001/2002. It uses a DSP and a very rudimentary algorithm: for the background/foreground segmentation, two corresponding stereo-vision pixels were compared (image subtraction) and classified via a threshold. In a second step, the resulting segmentation is filtered with morphological operations. This results in a "dirty" segmentation of the background and the overlay of the hands (translated in the stereo images) which was nevertheless usable for tracking. Image processing is done after complete image transmission, resulting in some latency (13.5ms). [10]
2. The second prototype was developed in 2003/2004. It uses the same algorithm as the first prototype, with some further refinements. It uses an FPGA for the computation, which allowed zero latency and a much higher data rate than the first prototype, thanks to parallel processing and concurrent image transmission.
3. Implementation of the new algorithm on a desktop PC with additional optimizations. It uses two USB cameras and does not use the color segmentation processing step.

Even though the DSP/FPGA based FingerMouse prototypes run a much more rudimentary algorithm requiring less calculations per pixel, the efficiency comparison shows that the architecture based on our ASIC clearly outperforms the other architectures.

Table 4. Comparison between the different systems

	DSP based FingerMouse	FPGA based FingerMouse	Desktop PC based implementation	ASIC based FingerMouse
Processing architecture	DSP (TI TMS320VC33)	FPGA (Xlinix Spartan II)	PC (Intel Pentium 4)	FingerMouse-ASIC
Internal image res.	128×128 @15frames/s	640×480 @15frames/s	640×480 @1frames/s	320×480 @15frames/s
Clock	75 MHz	20 MHz	2.8 GHz	80 MHz
Power (only processing)	130 mW	1000 mW	>50 W	78 mW
PCB size	4672mm^2 73mm×64mm	3381mm^2 69mm×49mm	-	774mm^2 43mm×18mm
Thickness PCB+optics	35mm	45mm	-	8mm
Segmentation quality	low	low	high	high
Output latency	13.5ms	<1ms	1000ms	<1ms
Image data rate	0.5 Mpixels/s	10 Mpixels/s	0.6 Mpixels/s	5 Mpixels/s
Efficiency (E / Pixel)	0.26 μJ	0.1 μJ	>83 μJ	0.016 μJ

5 Conclusion

We developed a fully integrated real-time vision capturing and processing system that achieves a high performance although working under strict constraints. Due to its architecture, the small size and low power consumption, it qualifies for use within a wearable system.

Outlook. The size of such a system could certainly be further reduced, when resorting to more complex construction techniques, like multi-chip modules. On the other hand, the size reduction is limited by the need of an offset between the two stereo cameras. Reducing this offset would influence the vision processing, reducing the depth measuring resolution.

A further reduction in power consumption is still possible. Switching from $250\mu m$ to sub $100\mu m$ CMOS technology allows for a decrease of the ASIC's power dissipation by a factor of 5 without degradation of the computing performance. The trend in CMOS camera development also shows dropping power consumption while sensor performance is increasing.

The current size indicates that autonomous vision processing devices could already be used in wearable systems, and could even be integrated into mobile phones or PDA's, e.g. for user interaction or possibly to eliminate the background in video phone communication (reducing the amount of image data to be transferred and preserving the privacy of other people in the background).

Acknowledgments

We would like to thank Andreas Burg and Marc Wegmüller for their assistance in the ASIC design process. Most of the hardware implementations of the new prototype were done within student projects. Therefor, we thank the students Roman Gmünder, Julian Heeb, Thomas Koch and Sven Kuonen for their hard work. We also thank Martin Lanz, for his assistance with the die-bonding.

References

1. Starner, T., Weaver, J., Pentland, A.: A wearable computer based american sign language recognizer. Digest of Papers.,First International Symposium on Wearable Computers (1997)
2. Crowley, J.L., Coutaz, J., Bérard, F.: Perceptual user interfaces: things that see. Commun. ACM **43**(3) (2000) 54–ff.
3. Card, S.K., Newell, A., Moran, T.P.: The Psychology of Human-Computer Interaction. Lawrence Erlbaum Associates, Inc., Mahwah, NJ, USA (1983)
4. Habili, N., Lim, C.C., Moini, A.: Segmentation of the face and hands in sign language video sequences using color and motion cues. Circuits and Systems for Video Technology, IEEE Transactions on (2004)
5. Gandy, M., Starner, T., Auxier, J., Ashbrook, D.: The gesture pendant: A self-illuminating, wearable, infrared computer vision system for home automation control and medical monitoring. In: ISWC '00: Proceedings of the 4th IEEE International Symposium on Wearable Computers, Washington, DC, USA, IEEE Computer Society (2000) 87
6. de la Hamette, P., von Waldkirch, M., Tröster, G.: Laser triangulation as a means of robust visual input for wearable computers. In: ISWC '04: Proceedings of the 4th IEEE International Symposium on Wearable Computers, Doctoral Colloquium, Washington, DC, USA, IEEE Computer Society (2004) 18–20
7. Blake, A., Isard, M.: Active Contours. 1st edn. Springer, ISBN: 3-540-76217-5 (1998)
8. Grewal, M.S., Andrews, A.S.: Kalman Filtering: Theory and Practice. Prentice Hall (1993)
9. Blake, A., Curwen, R., Andrew, Z.: A framework for spatio-temporal control in the tracking of visual contours. International Journal of Computer Vision (1993)
10. de la Hamette, P., Lukowicz, P., Tröster, G., Svoboda, T.: Fingermouse: A wearable hand tracking system. Adjunct Proceedings of the 4th International Conference on Ubiquitous Computing (2002)
11. Hartley, R.I., Zisserman, A.: Multiple View Geometry in Computer Vision. Second edn. Cambridge University Press, ISBN: 0521540518 (2004)
12. Faugeras, O.: Three-dimensional computer vision: a geometric viewpoint. Third edn. Cambridge: MIT Press, ISBN: 0-262-06158-9 (1999)
13. Egnal, G., Wildes, R.P.: Detecting binocular half-occlusions: empirical comparisons of five approaches. IEEE Transactions on Pattern Analysis and Machine Intelligence (2002)
14. Porter, R.B., Bergmann, N.W.: A generic implementation framework for fpga based stereo matching. IEEE TENCON (1997)

15. Woodfill, J., Herzen, B.V.: Real-time stereo vision on the parts reconfigurable computer. The 5th Annual IEEE Symposium on FPGAs for Custom Computing Machines (1997)
16. Corke, P., Dunn, P.: Frame-rate stereopsis using non-parametric transforms and programmable logic. IEEE International Conference on Robotics and Automation (1999)
17. Kanade, T., Yoshida, A., Oda, K., Kano, H., Tanaka, M.: A stereo machine for video-rate dense depth mapping and its new applications. IEEE Computer Society Conference on Computer Vision and Pattern Recognition (1996)
18. Konolige, K.: Small vision systems: Hardware and implementation. Eighth International Symposium on Robotics (1997)

An Ad-Hoc Wireless Network Architecture for Face-to-Face Mobile Collaborative Applications

Gustavo Zurita[1] and Miguel Nussbaum[2]

[1] Universidad de Chile, Departamento de Sistemas de Información y Auditoria,
Escuela de Economía y Negocios, Diagonal Paraguay 257, Santiago 9227, Chile
gnzurita@facea.uchile.cl
[2] Pontificia Universidad Católica de Chile, Departamento de Ciencia de la Computación,
Escuela de Ingeniería, Casilla 306, Vicuña Mackena 4860, Santiago 22, Chile
mn@ing.puc.cl

Abstract. An architecture for building an ad-hoc wireless network is presented in which various face-to-face, peer-to-peer collaborative applications function simultaneously and the interconnections between group members are highly dynamic and self-organizing. To illustrate how the architecture implements communication, examples of client-server and point-to-point communication are given. An interconnection architecture of a Mobile Computer Supported Collaborative Learning (MCSCL) environment is analyzed in detail. Its communication protocols are showed with sequence diagrams. The paper concludes with an evaluation of the architecture's performance.

1 Introduction

An ad-hoc network [8] is a transitory or permanent association of nodes or mobile devices that do not depend on any fixed support infrastructure to establish intercommunication among them [1]. Connection and disconnection is controlled by the distance among nodes and the face-to-face requirements of the implemented peer-to-peer (p2p) application, which may be educational [3], commercial [7], [11] or collaborative [13].

According to [6], a mobile p2p system inherits many of the features of ad-hoc networks. Specifically, it will be (a) self-organizing: as a side effect of the movement of devices within a limited physical space, the topology of a mobile p2p system constantly adjusts itself, discovering new communication links and managing various ad-hoc sub-networks as required by the application; (b) fully decentralized: each peer is equally important and no central node exists; and (c) highly dynamic: communication endpoints can move and change frequently and independently of one another.

The mobile nodes in these systems can function in any location and change their configuration and/or membership in various sub-networks within a single network to adapt to the face-to-face social interactions that users engage in and that the network must support. The disadvantages of wireless data transmission systems are that they have relatively less bandwidth, more latency, less connectivity stability, and less predictable availability [2]. Additional constraints are a) decentralized control, to have synchronization even when a node fails, b) fault tolerant, when a node fails the other have to be operational, and c) dynamic reconfiguration, sub-networks are formed on demand.

W. Grass et al. (Eds.): ARCS 2006, LNCS 3894, pp. 42–55, 2006.
© Springer-Verlag Berlin Heidelberg 2006

This study presents an architecture for building an ad-hoc wireless network in which various face-to-face, peer-to-peer collaborative applications function simultaneously and the interconnections between group members are highly dynamic and self-organizing.

2 MCSCL Communication Support (MCSCL-CS)

A face-to-face Mobile CSCL (or MCSCL) environment enables several small groups (3 to 5 members) to work collaboratively while moving around freely with handhelds [12], [13]. This capability facilitates flexibility in social interactions and easy management of group composition.

When an MCSCL environment is used in a setting such as a school classroom, the ad-hoc network must not only interconnect all of the collaborative workgroups, but must also simultaneously maintain various sub-networks for each of the 3-to-5-member groups, which function in different collaborative activities that at any given moment are at varying stages of completion.

The proposed ad-hoc network architecture is intended for use with any MCSCL-type p2p application, and enables the interchange of group members in real time. The scenario described here is an environment in which each student in the classroom has a handheld which is used as a support tool for performing collaborative activities together with fellow group members. As well, this environment allows dynamic reconfiguration of the groups.

2.1 Specification of the Proposed Architecture

The specifications of the proposed architecture are:

- Mobility. The application must function anywhere.
- Ad-hoc Network. The network does not depend on any infrastructure beyond that formed by the handhelds themselves. Within a single ad-hoc network, various other sub-networks may be created as required for establishing interconnections between members of the collaborative groups.
- Social and Technological Network. Users can communicate not only over the technological (ad-hoc) network, but also through the "social" network, that is, face-to-face communication between peer groups.
- Configurable. Applications may need to configure different types of interconnection between nodes. In other words, they may need to establish various ad-hoc sub-networks simultaneously as well as configure a variety of intercommunication topologies between nodes, such as client-server, point-to-point, one-to-many or many-to-one.
- Dynamic reconfiguration. The environment must permit reconfiguration of sub-networks in real time.
- Extensible. This feature is necessary to enable the addition of applications not contemplated when the architecture was originally designed.

- Efficient. The architecture's level of performance must be sufficient for the application, meaning that communication times will be undetectable by the user.
- Manageable. Within the same ad-hoc network, one of the handhelds (the teacher's) must be able to reconfigure and manage in real time.

2.2 General Architecture

MCSCL Communication Support (hereafter MCSCL-CS) is derived from DACIA [10] and includes certain aspects of its group communication design. Thus, collaborative groups are defined as closed groups because they develop activities independently of those of the other groups and so do not need to be aware of the latter's external messages. Communication has been modeled as a hierarchical group, which does not limit the different forms of communication a particular activity may be required to establish so that group members can carry out the roles that activity defines. As for membership control, this is handled inside the group. The management of the collaborative groups has therefore only one point of access, making possible the Dynamic Reconfiguration of Groups (DRG). Maintaining consistency of the messages exchanged by different groups hosts is accomplished through a consistent ordering, given a hierarchical structure that facilitates message management, thus rendering global ordering unnecessary. Finally, as regards the scalability of the system, it must be ensured that the system works independently of the number of groups created and the number of group members. Since the scalability of distributed systems can be negatively affected by design decisions that tend to centralize them, MCSCL-CS was conceived for use in classrooms, whose numbers of system users are known and finite, thereby reducing the adverse impact of the groups' hierarchical structure.

MCSCL-CS is made up of a variable number of components referred to as Comp-CS that provide the necessary functionality for performing an MCSCL activity, which requires diverse structures and models of intercommunication (Fig. 1). Each Comp-CS combines the *Display* of the user interface and the logic of the collaborative activity (*Application's logic*). In Fig. 1, each system application is composed of *n* Comp-CS's, one for each node used by a specific peer.

Communication among Comp-CS's is carried out at two levels. Among components residing in the same host it is executed using an adaptation of the design pattern Events Notifier [5]. Thus, a component is subscribed to the events that other components publish, connecting and disconnecting the components of the p2p system. Communication among components, which is necessary for the collaborative performance of the activity, occurs via the exchange of messages through ports. The components can dynamically request a number of variable ports in real time. All the ports activated in a host are administered by an *Operator* that resides in each client application. Each application's Comp-CS has *n* associated ports to communicate with *n* remote components (Fig. 1).

Communication among hosts within the collaborative group and the connections between pairs of components that reside in different hosts is administered by a *Coordinator* (which may reside in any handheld). In similar fashion to the telephone system, the *Coordinator* is responsible for the wireless connections among the members of a given group of users (sub-network). That is, the *Operator* of a given node asks the *Coordinator* to establish a connection with another node *Operator* (Fig. 1).

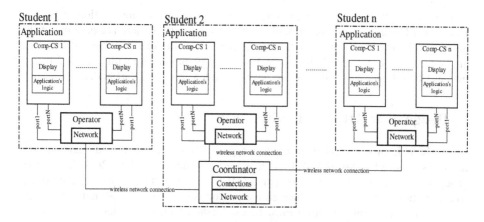

Fig. 1. Generic architecture of a system based on MCSCL-CS

2.3   Architecture Examples: Client-Server and Point-to-Point Communication

The architecture described above is general enough to be able to implement any type of communication. In what follows, two basic types of communication are presented: client-server and point-to-point.

Scenario A of Fig. 2 is an example of client-server communication with three clients, one of them acting as the server and each having its own application logic. The server application has as many ports (named PStudent 1, PStudent 2 and PStudent 3) as there are clients in the group (including its own client), and provides communication service to the other clients. To communicate with the server (PortStudent 3) the clients only need one port. If, for example, Student 1 wants to communicate through its Comp-CS Client with Student 2, the requirement is sent through PortStudent 3 ports that have been established by the Server Comp-CS (resident in Student 3).

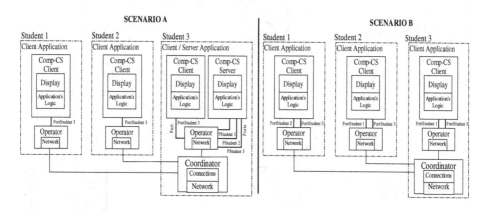

Fig. 2. Architectures for client-server (A) and point-to-point communication (B)

In scenario B of Fig. 2, an example of point-to-point communication is shown. Here, each Comp-CS component will need as many ports as there are partners in the group (excluding itself) in order to communicate with the others, which in this case are two. So, for example, when student 1 wants to communicate with student 2 (using his/her Client Comp-CS) s/he does so through student 2's port (PortStudent 2).

3 Design of an MCSCL Environment

In an MCSCL environment there are two types of actors, teachers and students. The teacher's handheld (MCSCL-Tch) configures and manages the p2p collaborative group activities. The students' handhelds (MCSCL-Stu) run the collaborative educative activities, communicating through the ad-hoc network [12], [13] and [14]. Interconnections and communication must be established with the students' applications so that they can form collaborative groups, start the activity and, when necessary, modify the group configurations.

The specific requirements of the MCSCL-Tch application are: a) management and selection of students' handhelds during the MCSCL activity; b) management and configuration of the groups that develop the activity; and c) management and configuration of the specific MCSCL activity. The requirements for the MCSCL-Stu application are: a) student handhelds assignment information; b) student group assignment information; and c) Rules and roles for the MCSCL activity.

3.1 Architecture of the System

Fig. 3 shows an MCSCL-Tch teacher's application and three groups with a total of nine MCSCL-Stu student's applications, the latter represented by solid-line circles each with an *Operator* component. The *Operator* of the MCSCL-Tch application

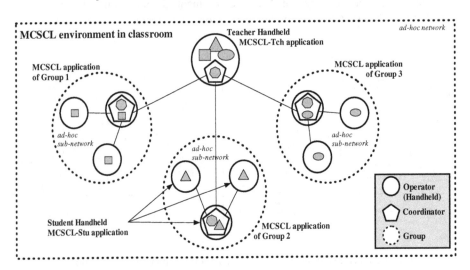

Fig. 3. Characteristics of an MCSCL environment

creates the three classroom groups containing the students, and through the group *Coordinator* (see hexagon inside pentagon) invites the *Operators* of each MCSCL-Stu application to form a part of the specific groups. Once the students are identified, the MCSCL-Tch application configures and manages three components from the nine MCSCL-Stu applications (in the ad-hoc network), that contain a *Coordinator* (the handhelds with a pentagon) which in turn configure and manage two other MCSCL-Stu applications, to form three ad-hoc sub-networks: Group 1, identified by a square; Group 2, by a triangle; and Group 3, by an ellipse.

The lines without arrowheads joining all the circles (handhelds) constitute the ad-hoc network's interconnections. Each of the dotted circles corresponds to an ad-hoc sub-network, whereas the dotted square represents the ad-hoc network. In each sub-network the same or some other application may be executed. The MCSCL-Tch application and one of the MCSCL-Stu applications in each group has a *Coordinator* component that is responsible for establishing communication between MCSCL-Tch and each group formed in order to coordinate activity development in the latter.

3.2 MCSCL-Tch Application

Fig. 4 shows the MCSCL-Tch application. The *Connection Manager* component establishes the links with the classroom group *Coordinator* and with each *Coordinator* of the students' collaborative groups (in one of the group's handhelds). When the application is executed, each component is created and performed, as are the application *Operator* and the group *Coordinator* in the classroom. Finally, the *Operator* is subscribed to this group, as explained in section 2.2

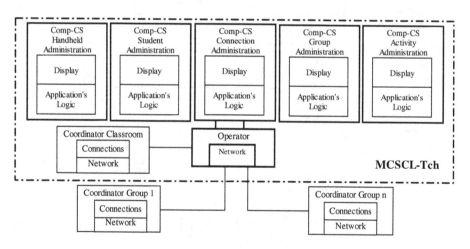

Fig. 4. Scheme of the MCSCL-Tch application architecture

3.3 Group Formation

The system's networking is exclusively p2p. This means that all users will have the same program running on their handhelds and there is no central service. The program recognizes the presence of other participants and establishes a secure communication with them in order to transfer data for synchronizing the applications. This is done via multicasting, peer discovery and synchronization via point-to-point data communication. Group formation is a basic function of the p2p MCSCL application. It is composed of three clearly distinguished stages:

- The *Operator* of the MCSCL-Tch sends connection invitations to the *Coordinator* so that connections are established with the *Operators* of the MCSCL-Stu applications residing in the students' handhelds.
- The *Operator* of the MCSCL-Tch application requests its *Coordinator* to create a new *Coordinator* among the MCSCL-Stu student application *Operators* that were previously connected.
- A group must be formed with the *Coordinator* just created. This *Coordinator* receives the connections from the *Operators* of the MCSCL-Stu application of each student that belongs to the group. The messages indicating that those *Operators* are to connect again to the new *Coordinator* are sent to the *Operator* of the MCSCL-Tch application through the teacher *Coordinator*.

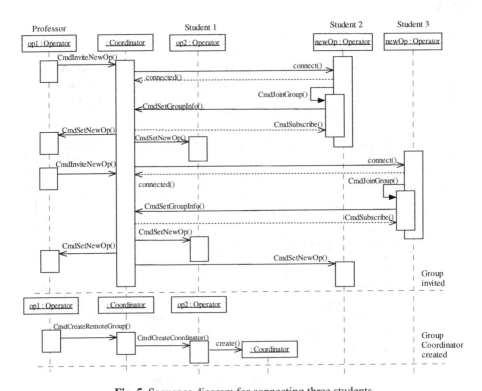

Fig. 5. Sequence diagram for connecting three students

Fig. 5 is a sequence diagram illustrating how the teacher connects three students and asks each one to create a group *Coordinator*. The *op1:Operator* of the MCSCL-Tch application sends a *CmdInviteNewOp()* command connection invitation to its *Coordinator* to establish a connection with a new *Operator* of the MCSCL-Stu student application (*NewOp:Operator*). As can be seen in Fig. 5, *op2:Operator* (of Student 1) is already connected to the teacher's *Coordinator*, and two new *Operators* corresponding to students 2 and 3 are in the process of being connected. Once all the students' *Operators* have been connected (Fig. 5, the teacher's *op1:Operator* asks its *Coordinator* by means of a *CmdCreateRemoteGroup()* command to create a *Coordinator* among of the three *Operators* that were connected. The decision as to who will be the *Operator* that creates the new *Coordinator* is made by the MCSCL-Tch application; in Fig. 5, *op2:Operator* of Student 1 is chosen. The teacher's *Coordinator* asks *op2:Operator* through the *CmdCreateCoordinator()* command. Each group formed has a group *Coordinator*, and the MCSCL-Stu applications of each student who has joined a group have an *Operator* connected to that group *Coordinator* and to the *Coordinator* defined by the teacher.

Fig. 6 is the sequence diagram showing how the teacher's *Operator* and *Coordinator* and the students' *Coordinator* and *Operators* form a three-member collaborative group. The *Operators* created in Fig. 6 are now called *op3:Operator* and *op4:Operator*, corresponding to students 2 and 3. The communication is established through the teacher's *Coordinator* and the group *Coordinator* of the three connected students.

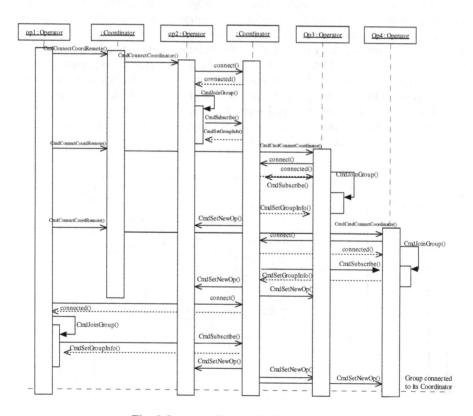

Fig. 6. Sequence diagram for forming a group

To form a group of students, the teacher must send the applications to each member of the group. For example, in order to add student 1 to the group, the teacher's *Operator* asks its *Coordinator* for that application through a *CmdConnectCoordRemote()* command. The teacher's *Coordinator* then asks student 1's *op2:Operator* by means of a *CmdConnectCoordinator()* command to include Student 1 in the collaborative work. The Student 1 *Operator* asks the group *Coordinator* (in this case, contained within itself) for a connection, and the *Coordinator* then joins *CmdJoinGroup()* and subscribes *CmdSubscribe()* Student 1 to the group.

In the scenario illustrated in Figs. 5 and 6, the teacher connects and forms a group of three members only. The procedures followed to connect more students and create new collaborative work groups are similar.

3.4 Starting and Sending Messages

Once the group is formed, a protocol based on the logic of the collaborative activity must be established for communicating among the group members. The sequence diagram in Fig. 7 shows the establishment of communication under a client-server protocol. This protocol, as requested of the collaborative group *Coordinator* by the teacher's *Operator*, must start (*CmdStartComp()*) and update (*CmdUpdate-CompInfo()*) with the *ClientMCSCL* information component of the MCSCL application for each member of the group, including the teacher's *Operator*. A new *ServerMCSCL* component of the MCSCL-Stu application must then be created. This way, neither the *ClientMCSCL* component nor the *ServerMCSCL* component knows that they reside in the same place, which allows any MCSCL-Stu application to start that component. Finally, the group *Coordinator* requests and creates communication ports among all the *ClientMCSCL* and *ServerMCSCL* components.

Once communication between the ports is established, each member of the collaborative group is ready to send and/or receive information.

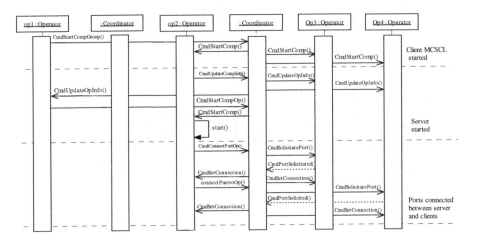

Fig. 7. Sequence diagram for communication between ports under server protocol

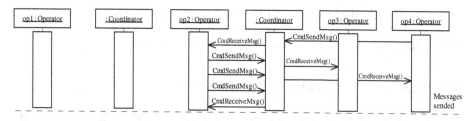

Fig. 8. Sequence diagram for the delivery of messages among the members of a collaborative group

The sequence diagram in Fig. 8 is an example of how the Student *op4:Operator* sends a message (*CmdSendMsg()* command) to the *op2:Operator*, who then forwards the same message (or a different one) to the other two students *op3:Operator* and *op4:Operator*. Note that the request to send a message is delivered to the group *Coordinator*, who redirects it to the *Operator* that needs the information (*CmdReceiveMsg()* command). The MCSCL-CS architecture is such that this procedure is independent of the logic and requirements of the MCSCL collaborative activity.

Any other communication protocol that an MCSCL activity might require can be designed based on the described functionality of MCSCL-CS, which demonstrates its flexibility, extensibility and adaptability.

3.5 Dynamic Group Reconfiguration (DRG)

For a DRG to be carried out, there must be at least one group to be reconfigured. Fig. 9 shows the sequence diagram for dismantling (disarming) the group formed in Fig. 6. The student group *Coordinator* is eliminated by the *delete()* command. After this operation, the students remain connected to the group defined by the teacher (Fig. 5).

To execute a DRG, the teacher chooses the new members of the collaborative groups who are to work on a given activity through the MCSCL-Tch application. Once all the members of the groups have been selected, the teacher's *Operator* (*op1:Operator* in the case of Fig. 5) must create the new *Coordinators* for each collaborative group again. In the case shown in Fig. 5 the *Coordinators* should be started again since the students are already connected to the teacher's *Coordinator*, the only remaining task then being to create a new group *Coordinator* and connect the students' *Operators* to it. Recall that Fig. 5 shows the case of one teacher and only three students; if there were more students connected, the DRG would choose other components of the MCSCL-CS as group *Coordinators* in the students' handhelds.

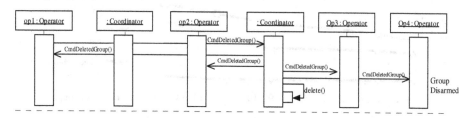

Fig. 9. Sequence diagram to dismantle a three-student group already formed

Finally, the MCSCL groups must be formed with their respective *Coordinators*. An example of this may be seen by referring back to Fig. 6, which shows the sequence diagram for creating a three-student collaborative group.

4   MCSCL-CS Performance Evaluation

The architecture proposed here has been employed with the MCSCL applications discussed in [12], [13] and [14], and implemented on the eMbedded Visual Basic (eVB) Runtime for Windows Mobile-based Pocket PC 2002 platform. The applications are executed over a wireless p2p Wi-Fi network and TCP/IP on Compaq iPAQ handhelds. For the permanent storage of configurations and results of the groups, Microsoft SQL Server CE 2.0 was used. TCP Sockets from the WinSock 3.0 eVB library provided the necessary elements to create, eliminate, connect and manage the socket connections established among the handhelds [4]. Since the eVB development environment is only a subgroup of Visual Basic, it cannot support dynamic object creation, i.e., at runtime. To solve this problem for the applications developed here, the socket-time creation was simulated based on a defined number of static objects created in implementation time. In this way, the objects needed at runtime were handled as an array of objects.

To measure the architecture's performance, the teacher's handheld (MCSCL-Tch application) interconnection delay before formation of the defined groups (MCSCL-Stu applications) was timed. MCSCL-Tch will form an ad-hoc network with MCSCL-Stu, which in turn will form ad-hoc sub-networks for each group. The group formation evaluation was conducted on a teacher's handheld for 1, 2, 9, 12 and 15 groups, each group consisting of 3 handhelds, thus forming ad-hoc networks of up to 45 students (the typical Chilean classroom size). For each of the five different quantities of groups, time performance was evaluated for delivery of 3 different information package sizes: 128 bytes, 256 bytes 512 bytes (MCSCL applications transfer small volumes of information).

As shown in Fig. 10 the time taken for all the groups to form their ad-hoc sub-networks depends on how many groups there are. According to the protocol, this time should be independent of their number, but the more groups there are the more acknowledgements must be sent to their handhelds, all of whom share the same bandwidth. Furthermore, time is needed to form the groups' ad-hoc network (controlled by MCSCL-Tch) once they have all created their ad-hoc sub-networks.

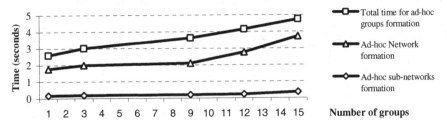

Fig. 10. Formation time of ad-hoc network and sub-networks

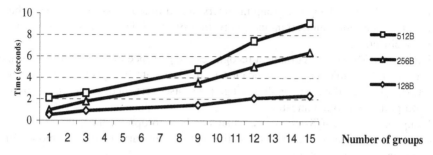

Fig. 11. Time taken for sending packages of various sizes (512B, 256B, 128B) to different number of groups (1, 3, 9, 12 and 15)

The chronometers measured only the time the teacher's handheld took to form the groups plus the time taken to send the information through the communication ports to all members of the group. In both cases, the MCSCL-Tch application receives acknowledgments of group formation (ad-hoc sub-networks) and of sent information for each group.

Fig. 11, shows the time taken for sending packages of various sizes to different numbers of groups. Sending time increases as the number of groups to which information is sent thought the ports increases. This occurs because each sub-network replicates the information, thereby overloading the wireless interconnection. In Fig. 10 the results obtained with the different numbers of groups reveals how group formation times increase linearly as the quantity of groups to be formed increases. The chronometers measured only the time the teacher's handheld took to form the groups and the ad-hoc network. This does not mean that all the collaborative groups wait for that number of seconds before continuing with their activity; rather, the number refers to the time the MCSCL-Tch application takes to execute the last phase of the protocol for the last group serviced. For example, with 15 collaborative groups, at worst each one will have to wait an average of 9.102/15 seconds to receive 512 bytes of text information before being able to return to its activity. The total number of 9.102 is explained by the fact that MCSCL-Tch must wait until the last group acknowledgement of information received has arrived and the information has been replicated to the group's ad-hoc sub-network. Once the ad-hoc network and the ad-hoc sub-networks of each of the groups have been formed, the sending and/or receiving of information does not result in heavy loads on the environment because the communication ports between group members, and the ports between them and the teacher's handheld, have already been created.

5   Final Remarks

When an MCSCL environment is used in a setting such as a school classroom, the ad-hoc network must not only interconnect all of the collaborative workgroups, but must also maintain various sub-networks, which function in different collaborative activities at various stages of completion at any given moment. The proposed ad-hoc network architecture is intended to be used with any MCSCL-type p2p application, and enables the interchange of group members in real time necessary to achieve high levels of student communication and motivation [9], [13], [14], necessary to achieve learning objectives.

Initially the MCSCL environment recognizes the presence of other participants and establishes a fault tolerant communication to transfer data for synchronizing the applications. This is done via multicasting, peer discovery and synchronization via point-to-point data communication.

Using the MCSCL-CS architecture that has been proposed here, the number of ad-hoc network nodes in a p2p collaborative system can vary up to 45 or more without causing network instability.

With MCSCL-CS, a teacher's handheld can (a) manage all other ad-hoc sub-networks, (b) configure the formation of new network nodes without having to reboot, (c) simultaneously maintain sub-networks working with different collaborative applications, (d) maintain sub-networks with 3, 5 or more nodes per collaborative work group, and (e) reboot and reconnect a collaborative work group when a group node crashes.

Once initiated by the teacher's handheld, each ad-hoc sub-network can function independently while always maintaining an open interconnection with the teacher in case rebooting or a change in the membership of a work group is necessary.

Acknowledgements

This work was supported by FONDECYT #1050601.

References

1. Bartram, L., Blackstock, M.: Designing Portable Collaborative Networks. Colligo Networks, ACM Queue 1(3) (2003) 41-49
2. Buszko, D., Lee, D., Helal, A.: Decentralized ad-hoc groupware API and framework for mobile collaboration. GROUP 2001 (2001) 5-14
3. Danesh, A., Inkpen, K.M., Lau, F., Shu, K., Booth, K.S.: Geney[TM]: Designing a Collaborative Activity for the Palm[TM] Handheld Computer. Proceedings of the Conference on Human Factors in Computing Systems (CHI 2001) Seattle, USA (2001) 388-395
4. Grattan, N.: Pocket PC Handheld with Microsoft embedded Visual Basic. NJ: Prentice Hall PTR (2001)
5. Gupta, S., Hartkopf, J.M., Ramaswamy, S.: Event Notifier, a Pattern for Event Notification, Java Report, SIGS Publications 3(7) (1998) 19-36
6. Kortuem. G.: Proem: A Peer-to-Peer Computing Platform for Mobile Ad-hoc Networks. In Advanced Topic Workshop—Middleware for Mobile Computing, Heidelberg, Germany, Nov. 2001. Banavar, G. Editor. Retrieved on December 2005 from http://www.cs. rizona.edu/mmc/10%20Kortuem.pdf
7. Malloy, A., Varshney, U., Snow, A.: Supporting mobile commerce applications using dependable wireless networks. Mobile Networks and Applications archive 7(3) (2002) 225 - 234

8. Murphy, A.L., Roman, G.C, Varghese, G.: An Exercise in Formal Reasoning about Mobile Communications. Proceedings of the Ninth International Workshop on Software Specifications and Design, IEEE Computer Society Technical Council on Software Engineering, IEEE Computer Society Ise-Shima Japan (1998) 25-33

9. Pintrich, P.R., Schunk, D.H.: Motivation in education: Theory, research, and applications, Prentice Hall Merrill, Englewood Cliffs NJ (1996)

10. Radu, L.: Providing Flexibility in Distributed Applications Using a Mobile Component Framework. Ph.D. dissertation, University of Michigan, Electrical Engineering and Computer Science, Sep. 2000. Retrieved on December 2005 from http://www.eecs. mich.edu/~aprakash/papers/radu/dissertation_radu.pdf

11. Tarasewich, P.: Designing mobile commerce applications. Communications of the ACM. SPECIAL ISSUE: Mobile commerce opportunities and challenges, 46(12) (2003) 57 - 60

12. Zurita, G., Nussbaum, M.: A Constructivist Collaborative Learning Environment supported by Wireless interconnected handhelds. Journal of Computer Assisted Learning, 20(4) (2004) 235-243

13. Zurita, G., Nussbaum, M.: Computer Supported Collaborative Learning using Handheld Computers. Computer & Education, 42 (2004) 289-314

14. Zurita, G., Nussbaum, M. Sharples: Encouraging face-to-face collaborative learning through the use of handheld computers in the classroom. Human Computer Interaction with Mobile Devices and Services. Springer, Verlag Lecture Notes in Computer Science 2795 (2003) 193-208.

Background Data Acquisition and Carrying: The BlueDACS Project

Thomas Wieland, Martin Fenne, and Benjamin Stöcker

Department of Electrical Engineering and Computer Science,
University of Applied Sciences Coburg,
96450 Coburg, Germany
{wielandt, fenne, stoeckeb}@fh-coburg.de

Abstract. As an alternative to ad hoc wireless sensor networks, we propose to utilize the mobile devices that are carried by people who walk along the site on which the sensors are deployed. Each sensor establishes a wireless connection to a mobile station and transmits its current measurements. On encounters two mobile stations can exchange their data for increasing redundancy and likeliness of delivery. When a mobile station approaches the sensor network server, it unloads all data which is saved there in a data base, processed, and published in local or global networks. In this paper, we describe our realization of this approach, the communication mechanisms that have been developed for it, as well as its potential usage. This approach is mainly characterized by the smooth integration of an additional data service in existing work processes utilizing only commercial off-the-shelf components.

1 Introduction

Wireless sensors are usually deployed in a significant number so that they set up an ad hoc network [1, 2]. The measurements of the sensors are transmitted over this network from one sensor to another until an interface station is reached. These stations are typically connected also to a LAN or have other means of processing the received information. Although the promise of sensor networks lies in the simplicity and multitude of sensors, the electronic components available today turn out to be rather expensive – especially when purchased in small quantities. In addition, there are numerous scenarios where a few number of actual sensors is sufficient; more would only be required for data transmission.

So if the sensors are singularly deployed in a distance that they cannot reach each other, different ways of data transport have to be found. This might cause a large delay in the overall communication route. But on the other hand the capacity of the network as well as its robustness can increase [3]. One way can be utilizing electronic devices that are in some way brought close to the sensors.

The set-up of a wireless sensor network infrastructure requires more than merely the sensor nodes. In a small network with limited spatial expansion all measurements are collected and processed directly by a server. When the number of nodes grows or when they are deployed in disjoint areas, regional relay stations must be used. These mobile stations act as concentrators (collectors) for an area of sensors and forward all

W. Grass et al. (Eds.): ARCS 2006, LNCS 3894, pp. 56–68, 2006.

data gathered in this area to the sensor network server (SNS). This architecture has proven to be useful for instance in environmental research [4].

The basic idea in this paper is to install isolated sensors that have wireless network connectivity, but are unable to reach any other sensor. The collectors are mobile devices carried by people who come into sufficient proximity. When two of these mobile devices come in the transmission range of each other, they can mutually exchange the data they have currently stored. As soon as a device is close enough to an SNS, it delivers its data and removes it from its RAM.

In the following sections, we are going to describe the setup of our prototype. The system that has been developed is called 'BlueDACS' as an acronym for 'Bluetooth-based Data Acquisition and Carrying System'. It uses its own protocol on the application layer for a light-weight binary data transmission. Various solutions to several technical problems that had to be found are also explained. We describe our experiences with the overall system and describe some application scenarios. Finally we give a perspective for future work.

2 System Components

The entire system comprises three subsystems: the sensors nodes, the mobile phones as collectors, and the server domain. The phones are the data carrying units, communication with the other subsystems and with each other. The server domain consists of the server itself and optional relay stations, allowing a more frequent data delivery with shorter paths to go. The overall communication relationships are shown in Figure 1.

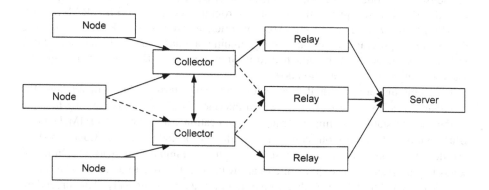

Fig. 1. Communication paths of the BlueDACS system. The nodes forward their data to the carrier which may exchange it among one another and eventually send to a receiver station.

2.1 Radio Communication

In sensor networks where several nodes are to coexist, a spread-spectrum approach on the radio communication layer can reduce interferences. A widely used incarnation of this technology is the Bluetooth protocol (IEEE 802.15). Originally designed as a cable replacement for home and office peripheral devices, it can be found today in a vast number of environments at steadily decreasing costs. This is one reason why Bluetooth has already been used for sensor networks [5-7].

However there are a few general problems with the usage of Bluetooth for sensor networks:

- Of the Bluetooth protocol stack, a sensor should at least use the network layer, maybe the LLC layer too. Depending on the type of nodes and their usage, this might impose a considerable overhead.
- The entire Bluetooth protocol is considered to be rather complex and thus power-intensive.
- The proposed scatternet functionality that would be valuable for sensor networks is currently not included in commercial products.
- Bluetooth-based nodes have to establish a connection before exchanging data. In this connection, one node acts as master and the other as slave. So a rigid role concept is necessary.

There is, however, an outstanding advantage: Bluetooth is included in numerous consumer devices on the market. So for realizing a showcase that is supposed to work with such components, Bluetooth is today the only choice for the radio communication.

Some of the aspects mentioned above may, however, even turn out as benefits: The standardized network layer, e.g., allows the developer to rely on a consistent communication channel with media access control and error detection.

2.2 Sensor Nodes

As sensor components we use ATmega128 RISC devices from Atmel [8]. They provide 128 kB self-programming flash program memory, 4 kB SRAM, 4 kB EEPROM, and 8 Channel 10-bit A/D-converter, as well as two RS232 ports. The device can be programmed in the C programming language and consumes acceptably little energy. Sensors can be attached to it directly at the A/D-converters or digitally via a separate sensor aggregation board.

For communicating with the collector units an external Bluetooth adapter, the Stollmann BlueRS, connected to the serial interface, is used [9]. For sending the data to the mobile station, a simple serial communication using the RFCOMM layer of Bluetooth is sufficient. In our configuration, the sensor node acts as a Bluetooth slave and does therefore not emit inquiry scans for other communication partners. In fact it sends inquiry packets once in a while to allow the mobile node to detect it. The sensor node is designed to deliver its data to the mobile stations exclusively. This procedure can still be optimized and leaves room for further work: Due to security reasons the sensors should not send any inquiry packets at all, at least in some scenarios. In this case, the mobile stations have exact location information about the sensors and may detect them with AGPS. This would also allow the mobile station to reduce the frequency of their inquiry scans.

The nodes use their local buffers for their own measurements. If there is an overflow, the oldest data set is skipped, acting like a normal ring buffer.

For the scenarios that are anticipated for this network configuration, a permanent power supply (long-lasting battery, dynamo, solar cell, or power outlet) can be assumed.

2.3 Mobile Phones as Data Collectors

The collectors are mobile phones that are carried by people walking across the site. From the view of the sensor network, their walking routes may be random. The deployment of a node should be planned in a way that there is a real chance that at least once a day at least one person comes in the reach of this node. It is obvious that this requirement is essential, making data gathering in less frequently visited areas unfeasible. It should, however, be realistic for many interesting applications.

As soon as such a mobile station comes in reach of a sensor node, a Bluetooth connection can be established. A handshake mechanism, a simple form of authorization, guarantees that only qualified devices get access to the data and accidentally approaching Bluetooth devices of other persons are not affected.

The mobile phones act as Bluetooth masters when communicating with the sensor nodes and the server or its relay stations. One may also take the role of a slave when talking to another mobile node. In order to fulfill their master role, the devices send out regularly an inquiry scan for detecting other devices in reach. The frequency of the scans depends on the actual usage scenario. Commonly, one scan every two or three minutes is a good trade-off between power consumption for the scan and reachability of other nodes. With this feature enabled, the power reserve of a mobile phone lasts between 4 and 8 hours.

We used Nokia 6600 and Siemens S65 phones as off-the-shelf components. Both have Bluetooth capabilities and can be programmed in Java utilizing the Mobile Information Device Profile (MIDP), version 2.0. The drawback is that currently on most devices such Java applications cannot run in background and have to be activated manually. Thus after a phone call, the bearer has to start the BlueDACS program again. Some phones with the Symbian operating system (like the Nokia 6600) are able to put the virtual machine in background during other activities; but the VM is suspended during this time. At least the application is resumed automatically and need not be restarted. This type of problem will more and more disappear as the operating systems of the mobile devices get more powerful. Alternatively, PDAs or pocket computers may be used; they have typically a larger power reservoir and allow background applications. We also made some tests with HP IPAQ PocketPCs.

The usage of standard, wide-spread consumer devices represents the special advantage in this approach. Relaxing the need for sensors to communicate with one another makes the entire system more flexible and less expensive. Although sensor nodes are thought to be deployed as rather tiny electronic components in large numbers, the current costs for such nodes – either off-the-shelf or self-configured – are still considerable, especially when purchased in small quantities. On the other hand, the solution proposed here gives the existing devices an additional task and leverages previous investments with an added value.

2.4 Relay Stations and Sensor Network Servers

As there is only one sensor network server for all sensor nodes of a specific group or even for all the sensors in the system, the chance that a mobile station comes in reach of Bluetooth transmission range of this server is rather low. (It may be installed in a place every worker must pass, like the factory gate, but this leads to other drawbacks and is not practicable for any application.) So it is helpful to install some additional relay servers that act as local points of delivery for the data. The relay servers are connected to the sensor network server (SNS) by LAN or over the Internet. They are therefore similar to the notion of "infostations" introduced in [10].

The SNS is realized as a usual PC with Bluetooth connectivity. It stores the data in an XML data base and allows access through various interfaces depending on the actual application, the data privacy, and the technical infrastructure, e.g. web-based reports, XML web services, and specialized applications making use of the data. Such applications may generate daily profiles from the measurements, graphical summaries, analyses of threshold exceedances with a hierarchical alarming system, etc. There are, of course, even much more sophisticated applications possible (see below).

From the communication perspective a relay station shows the same behavior as a sensor node in the BlueDACS system. It acts as a Bluetooth slave and sends out inquiry signals periodically to allow mobile nodes to find it.

3 The Communication Process

The description of the overall communication process can be divided into three different aspects: The format for storing the data, the procedures performed for transmitting, and the protocol used in this transmission.

3.1 Data Format

A uniform binary format that is used in all subsystems simplifies the handling of the acquired data and avoids reformatting. A BlueDACS data packet consists of the following elements:

- The number of data sets in the packet (n, 2 bytes)
- The length of each data set (m, 1 byte)
- A device identification number specifying the node that has acquired the data (DID, 2 bytes)
- A data acquisition number enumerating all packets generated by this node (DAN, 1 byte)
- The actual data sets, usually containing one or more measurement values and a time stamp, with length m and quantity n as indicated by the numbers above
- An error check array of m values, the result of an XOR operation among the data sets

The width of the DAN of 1 byte is clearly a restriction. It means that the node can generate a maximum of 256 packets until it has to overwrite its memory. It is, however, no real handicap for the practical usage. As each packet may consist of 65536 data sets at the most, a single node can still create more data than a carrier might be able to retrieve. And after all, the memory of the node is fairly limited such that these constraints are fully acceptable.

As we have designed here communication packets for the application layer, we do not have to include a very strong error-checking, but should be able to rely on what is already done on the network layer. So a simple XOR-generated code will certainly be sufficient.

3.2 Transmission Procedures

As soon as a mobile station comes in reach of a sensor node, a Bluetooth connection can be established. The sensor node transmits its most recent measurements via the existing connection to the mobile station. The data exchange protocol uses acknowledgements to ensure the success of the transmission. The mobile station checks the XOR field of the message and sends an ACK if everything is all right. Only after receiving this ACK, the node may delete the transmitted data sets from its buffer.

Like the sensor nodes, also the mobile stations keep all data that has not been transmitted as long as there is sufficient memory. The data is stored in the flash memory of the devices; thus it is still available when the phone has been switched off or has run out of energy.

If two mobile stations come close to each other (e.g., when their bearers walk by each other), they can forward mutually all measurements they currently store. They establish a Bluetooth connection, verify their authorization, and send the respective data sets. The communication is again safeguarded by XORs and ACKs to ensure that only uncorrupted data is stored. Data sets that are already stored on the respective device are discarded.

The data exchange of two mobile stations does not mean the forwarding of the complete data packets. Thus the data sets are not removed from each other's buffer after the transmission. This procedure just increases the redundancy of the entire system and the chance that any mobile station delivers the data to the SNS in the end.

As soon as a collector comes close to a relay station or the SNS, both sides establish a Bluetooth connection. The relay server just forwards all datagrams. If the transmission, again using XOR and ACKs, is successful, the mobile station removes the data sets from its buffer. The protocol is similar to the one described above for the communication between sensor node and mobile station. The SNS saves the measurements in a data base, provided that there has been no record with the same DID/DAN combination in the last 24 hours.

As pointed out in [11] and [12], there are numerous variants of this procedure. E.g., the transmission between two mobile stations may only be performed with certain likelihood, the stations may record which packets they have passed on, and they may even keep information about the IDs of those packets that – as far as the station knows – have already been successfully delivered to the SNS. For our prototype, the procedures described above seemed sufficient. Nevertheless it is clear that it strongly depends on the actual application which kind of strategy is used here.

3.3 Communication Protocol

A BlueDACS communication session is done in rounds. At the beginning of each round both partners negotiate who will be sender and who will be receiver. For this purpose, both partners send one byte (in the structure shown below) and the partner with the higher value – interpreted as an integer –becomes sender. Now a data packet is transmitted. Afterwards a new negotiation is performed, which includes an acknowledge flag for confirming the correct reception of the last packet. If the comparison of the bytes indicates that no further communication is necessary, the connection is closed. In the case that the ACK fails, the packet in question is re-sent.

The structure of the negotiation byte is as follows:

WS	RA	RA	RA	RA	RA	WR	ACK

The individual bits have the following meaning:

- WS: "wants to send". This bit is set if the sender has data to transmit.
- RA: random. A random number is used to clarify the precedence of transmissions. The partner with the higher number is to send first. A sensor node sets all bits except the last one to 0, making sure that he has the primary right to send. A relay station sets all bits to 0, as it does not have anything to send at all. The mobile stations always set the first bit to 0 and the last bit to 1, while selecting a random combination for the other ones.
- WR: "wants to receive". This bit is set if the sender is ready to receive data. Sensor nodes, e.g., set it to 0.
- ACK: acknowledge. This bit is set if the last transmission was successful (not used in the handshake procedure).

This arrangement of the flags allows interpreting the byte as a number. The communication partner with the higher number gets the right to send first. A communication is only established if one partner is willing to send (WS = 1) and the other is willing to receive (WR = 1). If this is not the case, no data exchange is necessary and the connection is closed.

If this handshaking procedure should result in equal random bits, the negotiation is repeated. This case can only happen between two mobile phones.

The big advantage of this protocol is its simplicity. It is easy to implement on any platform, meets all communication requirements, and uses the resources very efficiently. The header is rather small, i.e. reduced to the absolutely necessary issues. This is especially important for applications of the proposed type, which imply low data rates. A small header assures that the data size /packet size ratio and thus the effective bandwidth is high.

Moreover the sensor nodes are small embedded systems without much processing power. For this platform a protocol should be preferred that allows a succinct implementation. This fact also leads to a reduced error probability – which is a considerable benefit for embedded devices that might be produced and deployed in numbers. Updates of the firmware could become difficult and expensive.

4 Results and Experiences

The system has been realized as described above and tested on a prototype level. A number of experiences during development and testing could be gained.

The on-board memory of the sensor boards and the mobile stations were fairly sufficient. The code of the applications has a footprint of less than 5 kB which leaves enough memory for data storage, even on the Atmel boards.

A more serious limitation was that the Atmel boards we used do not have onboard clocks. So the tagging of the packets can only be performed with a counter. In extreme cases this might cause overflow confusions. To allow an accurate and unique identification of the packets, an additional time-stamp would be desirable. In the present hardware configuration, this could, however, only be achieved by external clock components.

The energy consumption of the Bluetooth adapter at the nodes may reach, according to the manufacturer, up to 45 mA with a BT connection, but no traffic, and 70 mA with data traffic at 115 kBit/s. As we assume a reliable power supply for the nodes, these values (which are considerably lower than the ones reported in [7] for another BT-based node) are acceptable for the anticipated usage scenarios. If the application requires a low power consumption, the BT module may be switched off after one successful delivery for some time until enough measurements are gathered again that need to be forwarded.

The programming interfaces both of the BT adapter and the mobile phones do not allow the manipulation of the radio communication on a low level. So it was not possible to test the influence of time slot aggregations and variations of encoding redundancy. For small payload packets, however, this influence is normally negligible.

The limitations of the Bluetooth protocol with respect to multiple communication partners turned out to be rather uncritical for the transmission between a node and a mobile station is, since there are hardly any other devices around that could interfere the connection. The same holds partially for the communication between mobile stations, provided they do not meet in very crowded areas. The contact between the mobile station and the SNS (or relay stations) may be more difficult. But as our experience from the test bed shows, the establishment of a connection succeeds in most cases, even if sometimes a little delay has to be accepted.

An unexpected result of the laboratory showcase experiments was that the inquiry scan, which is executed regularly by the mobile stations, takes a relatively long time, up to 30 seconds. The performance can be improved if the addresses of known devices are stored on each mobile station and only connections to these are tried periodically. This procedure assumes that the information about the devices in the system is configured at deployment time. This step makes the deployment more complex, but improves the overall performance significantly. In a repetition of the experiment with stored addresses the entire communication sequence took only a few seconds.

The mobile stations have the most complex task in the BlueDACS systems since they have to act as servers waiting for incoming connections as well as clients trying to connect to other stations. The communication is done via sockets on exactly this basis. So making data exchange during random encounters possible requires a sophisticated multithreading, switching between an open server socket and opening a client socket. The Java implementation on the mobile phones used in the prototype fulfilled this task without major problems.

The system tends to be rather reliable. The crucial aspect is the probability of the encounter of the communication partners. Theoretical calculations show that even if the probability of a mobile station meeting a node is less than 1% for a system with five carriers, all data of the node can eventually be delivered and no overflow occurs. In experiments in the university all sensor nodes could forward their measurements completely, thus fulfilling the task of the entire system satisfactorily. The behavior of all subsystems were as required; it was even possible that the sensor nodes generated data packets event-driven, i.e. only when the measured value changed. Long-term experiences can reasonably only be gained in the context of a real application. So the set-up of a real-world test bed and the evaluations of the respective results are still part of ongoing and future work (see below).

All in all, the prototype showed that the approach proposed above can actually be realized with off-the-shelf standard components, especially with standard consumer devices. The rather intensive energy consumption on the mobile phones and the long delays during BT inquiry scans and sometimes also during connection establishment give room for further research in optimization strategies. An extension in progress is, e.g., to make the server maintain a list of all communication partners in a BlueDACS environment and their BT data. This list is distributed as configuration information by the relay stations to the mobile phones which forward it to one another if necessary. So all devices know about the valid communication partners and can confine themselves to making BT connections with these only.

5 Usage Scenarios

The BlueDACS system is not thought for the classical sensor network scenarios, as these generally rely on a real-time wide-range data distribution [1, 2]. Yet there are various fields of usage where the longer time that the data might take to travel from the sensor to the server is acceptable. Some of these fields are discussed in the following.

5.1 Home Care of Elderly People

The Western industrial societies are more and more aging. An increasing number of persons need individual care, but they also want to stay in their familiar environment as long as possible. The care of these persons is often done by specially trained nurses and other assistants who visit their clients regularly, giving them the care they actually need.

The caregivers usually carry a mobile phone with them. More and more of this group also have PocketPCs for accounting the services they give. On the other hand the clients can have electronic devices measuring some physiological quantity, e.g. blood sugar or cardiograms. These devices can act as the sensor nodes described above, recording the recent measurements and transmitting it wirelessly. The mobile station in the pocket of the nurse visiting the client establishes a Bluetooth connection with the devices at the respective home and stores the data it receives.

At the end of the day the nurse returns to the central office of her organization where the corresponding relay station with BT connection is located. Her mobile device transmits the data it has gathered throughout the day to the server. There the health conditions of the clients can be analyzed based on the knowledge about their maladies and medications. If some discrepancies are detected, an alarm is issued, e.g. recommending the client to see a doctor.

The advantage of BlueDACS in this scenario is that it exactly fits in the processes that are currently run. Without much additional effort, a considerable improvement of the home care could be achieved. The challenge in this scenario is to fine-tune the sleep and wake-up sequence of the Bluetooth module in the client's device to certify that the data is actually delivered to the caregiver, without wasting two much energy by sending all day long.

5.2 Environmental Measurements

The quality of weather forecasts and the evaluation of water level changes at creeks and rivers crucially depend on measurements of the environment. The more measurements of temperature, wind speed, and air pressure are available, the more accurate a forecast can be. The same holds true for the prediction of floods, allowing detailed warnings and countermeasures. But the measurement places are often out of reach of public data networks. In the more dense populated areas of Europe, the data is frequently transmitted via cellular networks which causes air-time costs. In other areas often a visit of the measurement stations by staff persons is necessary. They denote the current values on pencil and paper, entering them later in their computers by hand.

This tedious task could be automated and made more reliant by a system like BlueDACS. The measurement stations act as the sensor nodes, receiving their energy from solar panels, possibly storing hourly measurements for one or two days. The data gathering task could be completed by people that pass the station anyway, offering a small fee for their service. If this is unfeasible, either more ore less regular visits are still necessary, but can be done faster and more efficiently. In any case, a Bluetooth connection with a mobile device is used to transmit the measurements. When the person comes home or to his/her office, a PC there could act as a relay station, taking up the data from the mobile phone and forwarding it to the nation-wide weather office (or other authorities) for further processing.

The data is usually not very sensible; thus no special security measures have to be taken. All in all, BlueDACS can automate the tasks and complement other data gathering technologies. In this scenario, the trade-off between the probability to reach a carrier and the energy consumption is also an issue. But as these outdoor devices will usually be powered by solar cells, a higher consumption of the radio unit is acceptable.

5.3 Monitoring of Operation Times of Heavy Machine

On construction sites of roads, bridges, and other complex buildings heavy and very specialized machines are used, e.g. steamrollers or tar-sealing machines. Often they are required just for one step in the entire work process, but are designed to fulfill this task very efficiently. For construction companies the purchase of such machines is often uneconomically; so they obtain them under leasing or renting contracts. More and more renting of such machines is done on a per-work-hour basis. The renting company has only to pay for the time the machine is actually in action. But for a correct and instant accounting the information about the operation times has to reach the machine owner in a reasonable time frame.

This problem could be solved with a system like BlueDACS. The machines would have built-in (and hopefully manipulation-resistant) clocks for recording the operation times. At least the foreman on the construction site carries a mobile phone which receives the operation data from the machines via a Bluetooth connection. If he meets other people involved in the construction, like architects or engineers, his device may exchange the data with their mobiles. As soon as one of them comes back into his office, the data can be transmitted to a relay station that is deployed there. This will then send the information about the operation times to the machine owner so that the billing can be processed in a precise and timely manner.

Again, BlueDACS does not require an abrupt change, but integrates well in the current processes. It is not essential how long the data actually takes from the machine to the owner. This electronic way will be in any case certainly much faster than written notices. But security is an important issue here that has not been discussed so far. The construction machine should encrypt the data, e.g. with a public key, leaving only the address of the owner permanently readable. At the server decryption can be done with the respective private key. So privacy and accuracy are protected on the way.

6   Related Works

A similar approach has already been described in related works. The basic idea of the protocol to bridge disconnected parts of ad hoc networks by mobile nodes is known as the epidemic routing protocol [13]. Much of the work in this field followed this idea, but mostly in a naïve, straightforward way. The approach of Chen and Murphy [14], the so-called Disconnected Transitive Communication paradigm, is certainly similar to ours, but describes more a general framework than a practical realisation. Musolesi et al. [15] concentrate on the routing algorithms and how to make them context-aware, demonstrating their results only by simulations. On the other hand, Lindgren et al. [16] emphasise the probabilistic aspect in their routing mechanisms, trying to connect entire clouds of nodes. They rely on the transitivity of the model and calculate the probability of delivery based on this assumption. In our approach, transitivity is also supported; the system does, however, not rely on it indispensably. In fact, it depends on the actual usage scenario whether the data exchange between the mobile stations is essential or not.

One of the first examples of the application of routing in partially disconnected ad hoc networks involving wireless sensor nodes is the ZebraNet project [17]. It employed sensors attached to animals for studies of wildlife behavior using flooding-like routing protocols. The idea of animals carrying data was also seized in DataMules [18] where, rather similar to our approach, mules are thought to visit sensor nodes and forward their measurements. The probability of delivery depended crucially on the visiting frequency of the mules. Small and Haas [11, 12] who proposed to attach the sensor nodes to whales focused primarily on theoretical comparisons between several data dissemination strategies.

Our results, however, differ in a several aspects. First of all, we have realized a working prototype that proves the feasibility of this concept; only a few of the approaches cited above did that. Second, this prototype does not rely on special hardware, individually adapted to this specific problem. As shown above, we used standard mobile phones as collectors, connecting via IEEE 802.15 (Bluetooth) protocol. And third, we separated the roles of sensors and collectors such that the sensors do not communicate with one another and the collectors do not have sensing capabilities, respectively. But most of all our system is designed to be non-intrusive. As illustrated by the usage scenarios, BlueDACS can integrated smoothly in the processes that are carried out anyway. The usage of BlueDACS does not require any additional efforts, especially not from the people carrying the mobile stations. It just introduces a significant additional value to a process that is already there.

7 Conclusion

Our experiments show that Bluetooth can be used for transmitting data acquired by sensors and other measurement devices. The approach of data gathering and carrying by more or less encountering mobile devices does certainly not replace the sensor network concept, for the delivery times are magnitudes larges than with direct wireless connection. As outline in the scenarios, however, there may be a couple of situations where the drawback of the long over-all transmission time is acceptable. Particularly when the data transmission integrates smoothly in existing processes, it can be a complimentary method worth evaluating.

The prototype described above has proven the feasibility of this concept. For utilizing standard consumer devices, Bluetooth is currently the technology of choice for the radio communication. But as we have outline, there are certain disadvantages with this protocol that raise the need for looking for alternatives. A possible candidate can be ZigBee (IEEE 802.15.4); this protocol was designed for energy-efficient transmission of small data streams. It is thus perfectly suitable for the applications described here. Maybe with the wider dissemination in the industrial area it may also find its way into mobile devices.

The BlueDACS protocol proposed here seems to be fairly sufficient for the anticipated use cases. The only missing issue is security. This could be added by taking an encrypted data set as payload for a packet. But the integration of security in the overall system has clearly to be the subject of further research.

Acknowledgements

The team that realized the prototype comprised the authors as well as Tobias Beer, Wladimir Beylin, Christoph Neumann, and Markus Wachter. So thanks go to all participants for their contributions.

This work was in parts supported by Siemens Corporate Technology, Munich, whom we are also grateful.

References

1. Akyildiz, I.; Su, W. et al.: A Survey on Sensor Networks. IEEE Comm., vol. 40 (2002) 102-114
2. Zhao, F.; Guibas, L.: Wireless Sensor Networks: An Information Processing Approach. Morgan Kaufmann Publishers, St. Louis, MO (2004)
3. Grossglauser, M., Tse, D.N.: Mobility Increases the Capacity of Ad Hoc Wireless Networks. IEEE/ACM Transactions on Networking, vol. 10/4 (2002) 477–486
4. Martinez, K.; Hart, J.; Ong, R.: Environmental Sensor Networks. IEEE Computer, vol. 37/8 (2004) 50-56
5. Milanovic, N.; Radovanovic, A. et al.: Bluetooth Ad hoc Sensor Network. In: Proc. IX. Telecommunications Forum TELFOR, Belgrad, Serbia (2001)
6. Leopold, M., Dydensborg, M.B., Bonnet. P.: Bluetooth and Sensor Networks: A Reality Check. In: Proc. 1st ACM Conf. Embedded Networked Sensor Systems (SenSys 2003). ACM Press, New York (2003)
7. Beutel, J., Kasten, O. Mattern, F. et al.: Prototyping Wireless Sensor Networks with BTnodes. In: 1st European Workshop on Wireless Sensor Networks (EWSN 2004), Springer LNCS, vol. 2920, Berlin (2004) 323-338
8. www.atmel.com
9. www.stollmann.de
10. Goodman, D.J., Borras, J., Mandayam, N.B., Yates, R.D.: INFOSTATIONS: A New System for Data and Messaging Services. In: Proc. IEEE VTC '97 (1997) 969-973
11. Small, T., Haas, Z.: The Shared Wireless Infostation Model - A New Ad Hoc Networking Paradigm (or Where there is a Whale, there is a Way), Proc. 4th ACM MobiHoc, Annapolis, MD (2003) 233-244
12. Small, T., Haas, Z., Purgue, A., Fristup, K.: A Sensor Network for Biological Data Acquisition, Chapter 11 in: Ilyas, M. (ed.): Handbook of Sensor Networks, CRC Press, (2004)
13. Vahdat, A., Becker, D.: Epidemic Routing for Partially-Connected Ad Hoc Networks. Duke University Technical Report CS-2000-06 (2000)
14. Chen, X., Murphy, A.L.: Enabling disconnected transitive communication in mobile ad hoc networks. In: Proc. of Workshop on Principles of Mobile Computing, collocated with PODC'01, Newport, RI (2001) 21-27
15. Musolesi, M., Hailes, S., Mascolo, C.: Adaptive Routing for Intermittently Connected Mobile Ad Hoc Networks. In: Pro. 6th IEEE Intern. Symp. World of Wireless Mobile and Multimedia Networks (WoWMoM'05), Messina, Italy (2005) 183–189
16. A. Lindgren, A. Doria, and O. Schelen. Probabilistic routing in intermittently connected networks. SIGMOBILE Mobile Computing and Communications Review, vol. 7/3 (2003) 19-20
17. Juang, P., Oki, H., Wang, Y. et al.: Energy-Efficient Computing for Wildlife Tracking: Design Tradeoffs and Early Experiences with ZebraNet. In: Proc. of 10th intern. conf. on Architectural support for programming languages and operating systems, San Jose, CA (2002) 96-107
18. Shah, R., Roy, S., Jain, S., Brunette, W.: Data MULEs: Modeling and Analysis of a Three-tier Architecture for Sparse Sensor Networks. In: Elsevier Ad Hoc Networks J., vol. 1/2-3 (2003) 215-233

Prototypical Implementation of Location-Aware Services Based on Super-Distributed RFID Tags

Jürgen Bohn

Institute for Pervasive Computing,
ETH Zurich, Switzerland
bohn@inf.ethz.ch

Abstract. We provide evidence of the feasibility and effectiveness of a middle-ware architecture for mobile devices which employs dense distributions of small computerized entities for providing fault-tolerant location-aware services. We do so by describing exemplary implementations based on radio frequency identification (RFID) as an enabling technology. Firstly, we present prototypical implementations of the hardware abstraction layer and of selected core middleware services. The latter enable a mobile device to store and retrieve data and position information in physical places in a fault-tolerant manner, and to identify places based on a location abstraction which is robust against failure of individual tags. Secondly, we investigate the feasibility of some higher-level services and applications by developing and evaluating prototypical systems for tracing and tracking, self-positioning, and collaborative map-making.

1 Introduction

Different from conventional means of RFID tag deployment and utilization, massively-redundant tag distributions provide novel RFID-based services and applications to mobile user devices [1]. By deploying cheap passive RFID tags (i.e., tags without a built-in power supply) in large quantities and in a highly redundant fashion over large areas or object surfaces, one obtains a so-called *super-distributed RFID tag infrastructure* (SDRI). Based on such an SDRI, [1] identifies a number of technical challenges and describes potential benefits and first prototypical results. The practical relevance of this concept is reflected in the recent appearance of industrial products that make use of such redundant RFID tag distributions, such as the "first carpet containing integrated RFID technology" presented by Vorwerk in cooperation with Infineon Technologies [2].

As a generalization of the SDRI concept, we propose *super-distribution* of small computerized (and therefore "smart") entities as a general design principle for the development of reliable and highly available location-dependent services for mobile devices. For that, we developed a layered *service middleware architecture* [3] that exploits two fundamental characteristics of the resulting infrastructure for achieving fault-tolerance and serviceability: the high degree of redundancy with regard to smart entities (abundance aspect), and the support for localized interaction between mobile devices and their immediate physical environment (locality aspect).

While [3] focuses on theoretical middleware aspects, in this paper we describe a number of concrete prototypical implementations based on super-distributed smart

W. Grass et al. (Eds.): ARCS 2006, LNCS 3894, pp. 69–83, 2006.

entities, using RFID as an enabling technology. In doing so, our major aim is to provide first-hand evidence of the practicability and effectiveness of the suggested approach by demonstrating the capabilities and performance of exemplary middleware service implementations, rather than presenting specific state-of-the-art solutions for the particular application domains we cover in the process.

In the following, we define a *smart entity* (SE) as a physical artifact that is enhanced by embedded computing technology in such a way that it has a globally unique identifier, a built-in memory with data read/write capabilities, and support for close-range wireless ad-hoc communication. Likewise, we refer to *super-distribution of smart entities* as the process of deploying and distributing SEs in a dense, highly redundant fashion. The resulting substrate is called a *super-distributed smart-entity infrastructure*.

2   Middleware for Super-Distributed Smart Entity Infrastructures

2.1   Middleware Architecture

Our service middleware for super-distributed SE infrastructures described in [3] is based on a five-layered architecture (Fig. 1): The distributed physical smart entities in their entirety constitute the physical infrastructure on the lowest level (*Hardware Layer* or Layer 0). The access to this layer is controlled by the *Hardware Abstraction Layer* on the next higher level (Layer 1). It is represented by an *Entity Read/Write* (ERW) service, which defines a generic and unifying interface to the underlying physical SE infrastructure. The *Core Service Layer* (Layer 2) consists of fundamental abstractions and generic services that operate with individual SEs by means of the ERW service. The *Higher-Level Service Layer* (Layer 3) is represented by a collection of specialized services and service templates. These services do not directly operate on individual SEs of the underlying physical infrastructure but rely on the core services instead. Finally,

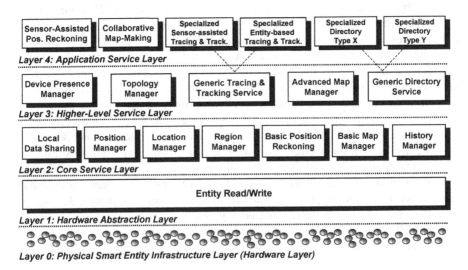

Fig. 1. Overview of the service middleware for super-distributed smart entities

in the *Application Service Layer* (Layer 4), we find application-specific services and specialized instantiations of service templates.

2.2 Middleware Employment

From the user's perspective, interaction with the SE infrastructure is performed by means of a *mobile user device* (MUD), which features a wireless communication interface for communicating in an ad-hoc fashion with SEs in its immediate vicinity. On each MUD, an independent instance of the service middleware is installed, executing the individual middleware services as separate processes. Services can be turned on or off and configured separately. A MUD can be carried by a user or may be part of other devices, such as being integrated into a vehicle or into a blind man's stick, for example.

The execution of the service middleware on the MUDs themselves (rather than providing the services as part of a fixed background infrastructure) empowers the devices to interact with the super-distributed smart-entity infrastructure in an autonomous fashion. In particular, by maintaining information in SEs at the physical places where it is required, middleware services on a MUD can remain operational even in the case of physical damage in other areas of the infrastructure, and in the absence of network connectivity or the unavailability of remote services.

2.3 Prototypical Reference Implementations

For our prototypical implementation, we selected a number of exemplary middleware services based on both a bottom up and top down approach: On the one hand, we implemented services of the lower layers that provide general basic functionality, which includes the Hardware Layer, the Hardware Abstraction Layer, and three essential services of the Core Services Layer: Local Data Sharing, Location Manager, and Position Manager. On the other hand, based on these services, we investigated the feasibility and practicability of some higher-level services by developing and evaluating prototypical systems for tracing and tracking, self-positioning, and collaborative map-making.

In our implementations, the SEs were represented by passive RFID tags. As a result, the Hardware Layer in our prototype implementation constituted a super-distributed RFID tag infrastructure (SDRI) as described in [1]. We therefore use the terms "RFID tag" or simply "tag" synonymously with "smart entity" in the remainder of the article. The MUD executing the service middleware software was represented by a notebook computer, to which a mobile RFID reader and antenna were attached to enable a localized interaction with the SDRI.

3 Implementation of Basic SDRI Middleware Services

3.1 Hardware Layer: Super-Distributed RFID Tag Infrastructure Prototype

The RFID hardware we used for the SDRI consisted of ISO 15693 compliant smart labels (transponders) that operated at a frequency of 13.56 MHz. As transponders, we employed Philips I·CODE tags (Type 1) [4], with a dimension of 7.5 cm×4.5 cm×0.1 cm. The I·CODE RFID tags feature 64 byte of physical memory, which is organized into 16 slots á 4 byte (of which 11 slots are rewritable). This allowed us to store the data of

Table 1. Properties of plastic foil templates used for building a prototypical SDRI

Dimension of plastic foil templates	123 cm × 128 cm
Mean distance between two adjacent RFID tags	17.5 cm
Standard deviation of tag distribution	2.1 cm
Number of tags per plastic foil template	61 tags/foil
Average area covered by a single RFID tag	258 cm^2
Average RFID tag density per square meter	39 tags/m^2

several middleware services (e.g., Position Manager and Tracing and Tracking Service) directly on the physical memory of individual tags during our experiments.

For building the SDRI, we attached the transponders onto four identical plastic foils using the same pseudo-random distribution pattern. This yielded four RFID-tagged templates with equal characteristics as shown in Table 1.

3.2   Hardware Abstraction Layer: Entity Read/Write (ERW) Service

For the realization of the Entity Read/Write service on the Hardware Abstraction Layer, we used the RFIDStack [5], which offers a manufacturer-independent API to applications and incorporates drivers for various types of RFID hardware. Based on the RFID-Stack, the ERW service provides the interface for writing data to and reading data from the underlying RFID tags of the SDRI, masking the complexity and hardware-specific characteristics of the underlying RFID hardware from the higher service layers. The writing of data can either be performed physically, writing to the physical tag memory, or virtually, storing the data in the so-called virtual tag memory. The latter is managed by a service instance of the RFIDStack residing in the Internet, which can be accessed by means of XML messages sent via a TCP connection [5]. The virtual tag memory not only mirrors the physical memory of a tag, but also provides an extended storage space. Our ERW implementation only allows a MUD to access the virtual memory of a tag if that entity is physically present within communication range.

The ERW service also implements the data management for the physical and virtual tag memory. It emulates a simple file system for the physical tag memory, where Service Data Units represent files and the Smart Entity Directory represents the root directory. A Service Data Unit constitutes a service-specific data unit that encapsulates the information that a service requires to be stored on a single tag for a well-defined purpose. To detect incomplete or inconsistent data units on tags caused by interrupted, incomplete write operations, CRC error checking is performed.

In particular, the ERW service provides the following basic methods for accessing the physical memory of individual tags: `listTags`, `listTagDirectory`, `writeTagFile`, `readTagFile`, `deleteTagFile`. Parameters include tag ID, file type, file data, and flags that indicate the use of the virtual memory and declare if a file should be stored persistently or can be overwritten at a later point in time (persistence flag).

3.3   Core Service Layer: Local Data Sharing (LDS) Service

The LDS service provides MUDs with an API for sharing data in physical places of the SDRI with other devices. In doing so, the LDS service exploits the high tag density in the SDRI for fault-tolerant data storage by replicating Service Data Units across multiple tags in antenna range at the current location. Data can be shared in situ by using method `shareData`, which is parameterized with the service-specific data type and the persistence flag. Previously shared data can be retrieved by means of the `getData` method.

The API of the LDS service allows the user to set the replication degree, which can be defined as an absolute number and which is targeted on a best effort basis, or as a relative percentage value. These values apply to the initial replication and the later replication maintenance procedure. The actual replication management is hidden from the service clients. For accessing the tags of the SDRI, the LDS service is based on the API of the ERW service. Further the LDS service allows to set a tolerance threshold for the number of failed tag identify/read/write attempts of the underlying ERW service. For example, if data is to be read from or written to eight different tags, failed read/write attempts for two of the tags are tolerated given a tolerance threshold of 25%. This enables the service to deal with known imperfections of RFID systems (e.g., tags in range may not be detected, or read/write operations may abort [6]). When Service Data Units are retrieved from local tags, the LDS service transparently filters duplicates.

3.4   Core Service Layer: Location Manager (LM) Service

The LM provides an API to define and resolve abstract locations: a *Location* has a unique identifier and is defined by the set of (stationary) SEs that are detected in a well-defined range of the MUD executing the service [3]. The *Location* identifiers are directly stored on the defining SEs themselves.

The main contribution of the LM is the `getLocation` method, which determines an abstract *Location* L as the set of RFID tags $tagIDSet_l$ detected at the respective physical place l in the SDRI: $L := tagIDSet_l := \{tagID_t : inRange(t, l, r)\}$, where $tagID_t$ is the unique identifier of tag t, and $inRange(t, l, r)$ a Boolean predicate that equals `true` iff tag t is within distance r of the field of the RFID antenna at place l and `false` otherwise. In our prototype system, the range r of the RFID system was defined by the characteristics of the used RFID hardware. Ideally, the range of the RFID reader/antenna should be customizable to enable the integration of different RFID systems with variable characteristics.

If the `getLocation` method is called to determine the *Location* of the current place, then the LM searches for predefined *Location* identifiers on all tags in range r. The *Location* whose identifier is stored on the majority of the detected tags is returned as the current *Location*. In case no predefined *Location* is available, or if the number of tags containing the dominant *Location* identifier is below a well-defined percentage value T, then the LM automatically defines a new *Location* and stores the corresponding *Location* identifier on the affected tags. This ensures that adjacent *Locations* only overlap in up to $(100 - T)\%$ of the tags, which in return enables a robust and selective *Location* detection in situations where individual tags fail to respond temporarily.

3.5   Core Service Layer: Position Manager Service

The main contributions of the Position Manager service are the methods `getPosition` and `setPosition`. The `setPosition` method enables a MUD to locally store its current position p^M obtained from a third party positioning service on the nearby tags. In doing so, for each tag, the new position p^t_{new} is calculated as the weighted mean of the MUD's position p^M and the old position p^t_{old} of the tag, using the number of previous write operations w as a weight: $p^t_{new} := (p^M + w \cdot p^t_{old}) : (w + 1)$. Vice versa, upon calling getPosition, the Position Manager first scans all tags in antenna range and extracts their individual position coordinates if available. Then it calculates an estimate for the current position as the mean over all obtained individual tag positions.

4   SDRI Tracking and Positioning Prototype

The SDRI Tracking and Positioning prototype provides two main services: laying and following of data traces, and self-positioning.

4.1   Prototype Description

We have developed a fully functional SDRI Tracking and Positioning prototype, which consists of two major hardware components. Firstly, a trolley with the RFID equipment (RFID reader and antenna) and the MUD (in our case represented by a notebook computer running the SDRI Tracking and Positioning application). Secondly, four RFID-tagged templates forming a prototypical SDRI (Fig. 2).

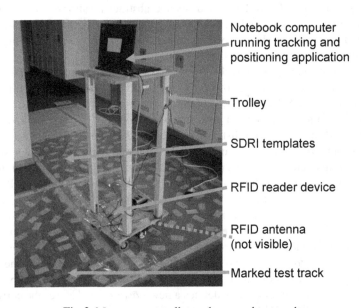

Notebook computer running tracking and positioning application

Trolley

SDRI templates

RFID reader device

RFID antenna (not visible)

Marked test track

Fig. 2. Measurement trolley and prepared test track

The RFID hardware consisted of an ISO 15693 compliant mid range RFID reader, and an external mid range RFID antenna[1]. The RFID reader supported collision resolution, which enabled it to simultaneously identify multiple transponders within antenna

---

[1] Manufacturer: Feig Electronic, model: OBID *i-scan* HF ISC.MR100 and OBID *i-mid* ISC.ANT340/240.

range. The RFID antenna was attached underneath the center of the bottom pane of the trolley, at 10 cm above the floor space. At this distance, the approximately square operating area of the RFID antenna was about 50 cm×50 cm. For constructing the prototypical SDRI, the four RFID-tagged templates described in Sect. 3.1 were arranged in an L-shape around a corner of a corridor in our office building (Fig. 2). On the templates, we manually marked a test track for our experiments with a total length of 526 cm.

4.2 SDRI Tracing and Tracking Service

The SDRI Tracing and Tracking Service features a tracing mode, which enables the MUD to leave a digital data trace in the SDRI, and a tracking mode, which allows a MUD to follow a previously laid data trace. Each mode itself is divided into a basic and advanced version, which we describe in the following.

Tracing mode. A *basic trace* is represented by a sequence of trace data objects stored on tags of the SDRI. Each *trace data object* (TDO) consists of an anonymous trace identifier (trace ID), which is generated by random, and a timestamp. A trace ID only has to be unique in the local area where it is applied, but not on a global scale. Further, all TDOs are flagged as non-persistent, and over time, the SDRI Tracing and Tracking Service overwrites the oldest TDOs on a tag with newer traces if memory space is short.

In our prototypical implementation, we replaced the timestamp in the TDO with a trace counter serving as logical clock to obtain a more compact, memory-space-saving representation. This was feasible since it is usually only necessary to locally distinguish the age of detected TDOs belonging to the same trace, which we achieve by applying a sliding-window approach. In addition, we adapted the TDO overwrite strategy to selecting a random TDO for replacement, as the use of logical clocks no longer allows to identify the oldest TDO on a tag. Memory-wise, we used 1 byte for the trace ID and one for the trace counter (with a window size of 12) per basic TDO, which fit into a single slot of our physical RFID tag memory.

If tracing is active, new TDOs are stored in a redundant fashion on the RFID tags at the current position of the MUD (by using the Local Data Sharing service) at a well-defined update rate (specified in milliseconds). For preventing repetitive trace updates at the same physical location, which would lead to a discontinuity of the trace counter values, the IDs of the locally detected tags are cached. A new TDO is only written to the SDRI if at least K percent of the local tag IDs have changed. Concretely, we used a trace update rate of 500 ms and set the update tolerance to $K = 50\%$.

The *advanced tracing mode* uses position information (e.g., obtained from the Position Manager or from a third-party positioning service) to create an *augmented trace*: the individual trace data objects are augmented with the current information about direction (orientation), change of direction, and speed of the MUD.

Tracking mode. The tracking mode of the SDRI Tracing and Tracking Service enables a MUD, the *follower*, to follow a trace by detecting the corresponding TDOs in the tags of the SDRI. We call the MUD that previously laid the trace the *forerunner*. Initially, the forerunner has to reveal its randomly chosen trace ID of the trace to the devices that are to become its followers, and to inform them about potential starting points for picking up the trace (which are not necessarily equal to the starting point of the trace).

Once a follower has detected or rediscovered the trace (i.e., tags in the SDRI which contain a TDO with the forerunner's trace ID), the follower repeatedly searches for tags with more recent trace information and moves into this direction. More precisely, the follower continuously seeks TDOs of the wanted trace ID with either a more recent timestamp, or with a higher trace counter value (based on the counter window calculated using modular arithmetic). In our system, the detected trace counter values for a specified trace are displayed in a graphical user interface window (GUI). If an RFID tag map of the prototypical SDRI is available, the GUI visualizes the tags of the trace that have been detected so far, and highlights the most recent trace information. In case of an augmented trace, the GUI also displays the augmented information, such as the current direction and change of direction (as numerical values and visually by means of an arrow symbol).

4.3 SDRI Positioning Service

The SDRI Positioning Service enables the MUD to store position information to or to retrieve it from individual RFID tags of an SDRI, either using the physical on-tag memory or a remote virtual tag database.

Calibration mode. For the calibration of the SDRI with position information, the SDRI Positioning Service supports two modes of operation: Firstly, the *exact* calibration mode allows the user to calculate the individual tag positions of all RFID tags of an SDRI template at once, based on two manually entered reference positions per template. The determined exact tag positions are then stored on the physical tags and/or in the virtual tag database. The physical tag calibration procedure is supported by a tool that shows the progress and status of the calibration with the help of a graphical display.

Secondly, the *incremental* calibration of the SDRI uses the position information of a third-party positioning service to update the position coordinates on the individual tags by calculating a new weighted mean as described in Sect. 3.5. This procedure can be performed in a collaborative fashion by independent MUDs. In the process, the accuracy of individual tag position coordinates usually increases with the number of positions that are stored on the respective tags: as the actual positions of the MUDs performing the calibration are typically scattered around individual tags, the errors of the single position values that are averaged tend to cancel each other out.

Positioning mode. The implemented *position calculation* or *positioning* procedure of the SDRI Positioning Service uses the positioning procedure of the Position Manager: First the tag position coordinates stored on the single RFID tags within antenna range are retrieved. Then the arithmetical mean of the obtained single tag position coordinates is calculated and used as the estimated position (x, y, z) of the MUD.

4.4 Experimental Results

We performed our experiments by pushing the trolley at a constant speed along the marked test track (Fig. 2). We further calibrated the tags of the SDRI with local positioning coordinates using the exact calibration tool.

Efficiency of virtual and physical tag memory access. For our positioning measurements, we used both the virtual and physical tag memory.

For accessing the virtual tag memory, which was maintained in a database on the MUD itself, it was sufficient for the ERW service to retrieve the IDs of all RFID tags within antenna range with a single command call (`identify`). The duration of the `identify` command was independent from the number of tags within range, and took approximately 200 ms on average (using 16 time-slots for multi-tag-detection as part of the anti-collision protocol of the reader). This enabled a maximum rate of up to 5 Hz for multi-tag detection and subsequent position calculation.

The efficiency of the physical tag memory was more than one order of magnitude lower, since our particular RFID hardware required sequential scans for reading out a data slot: one `identify` command followed by a separate `read` command for each detected tag. In our implementation, we needed two physical memory slots to store positioning coordinates on a tag. Therefore, for attempting to read the two data slots from four RFID tags detected during an inquiry, the duration of the scan varied from approximately 2 seconds (8 successful reads), if no errors occurred, to up to 5 seconds (8 failed reads) in the worst case if all eight sequential read operations failed. These numbers are based on timing measurements for successful and failed attempts for reading a single data slot, which for our RFID hardware were approx. 250 ms and 600 ms respectively. However, if we used a more advanced RFID system that supported the direct and parallel reading of a data slot from multiple tags in range without a prior `identify` operation, the duration of the physical tag memory access would be reduced to the order of magnitude of the duration of the virtual tag memory access.

Accuracy of the positioning procedure. Due to the comparably slow physical tag memory access of our RFID hardware, we used the virtual tag memory for our experiments. We performed three test runs at a speed of 50 cm/s, using exact manual

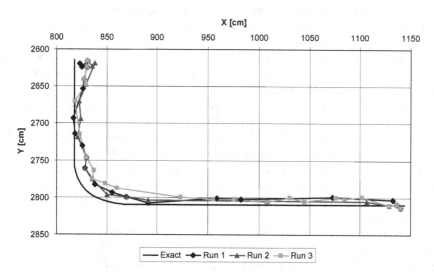

Fig. 3. Three positioning experiments of the SDRI Positioning Service performed at 50 cm/s

measurements of the test track as reference (Fig. 3). The resulting mean absolute positioning error was approx. 15 cm. Given our specific configuration, the maximum tolerable speed of the trolley is 2.5 m/s, which is determined by the tag inquiry time of approx. 200 ms (required by the ERW service for determining the tag IDs for accessing the virtual tag memory) and the length of the antenna field in moving direction of 50 cm.

5   Collaborative SDRI Mapping Prototype

The prototypical Collaborative SDRI Mapping system has two main tasks: The *localization* and *mapping* of RFID tags in an SDRI by means of autonomous vehicles, and the *merging* of overlapping partial RFID tag mappings, which were constructed independently from each other by these vehicles as part of a collaborative effort.

We do not aspire to contend with state-of-the-art solutions for the general collaborative map-making problem, which has been in the focus of research in the domain of mobile robots for decades (cf. to the work by Burgard, Fox, et al. [7, 8], for instance). Our primary goal is to demonstrate the feasibility and practicability of using a super-distributed RFID tag infrastructure for the realization of collaborative activities, which is not considered by traditional map-making systems. In contrast to our approach, RFID tags for positioning have so far only been used in the function of dedicated artificial *landmarks* on walls or floor spaces, providing auxiliary support to dedicated positioning and navigation systems [9, 10, 11].

5.1   Prototype Description

The Collaborative SDRI Mapping prototype consists of the following components: a model vehicle, a prototypical SDRI, an on-board vehicle control application (for evasive driving and dead reckoning), an off-board RFID tag mapping application, and a stand-alone collaborative map-merging application for fusing partial map observations obtained during independent test runs.

The *model vehicle* was constructed using Lego Mindstorms [12] technology. It is self-propelled, featuring two actuated parallel wheels in the back (each equipped with a rotation sensor and an electrically powered motor) and one castor wheel in the front for stabilization. A bumper sensor connected to a front bumper is used for collision detection. An on-board LEGO Mindstorms RCX controller hosts the software for controlling the motors of the vehicle, and for monitoring the rotation and bumper sensors. In addition, the model vehicle is equipped with an on-board RFID reader (Fig. 4), and an RFID antenna[2] mounted at the bottom at 1 cm distance from the floor space (Fig. 5). Due to the size of the model vehicle, the vehicle control application was executed on a separate notebook computer, which was connected to the RCX controller and the RFID reader by cable.

For obtaining a *prototypical SDRI test area*, we evenly distributed 32 mu-chip inlets across a wooden panel of the size of 50 cm×50 cm (Fig. 4). This corresponds to a tag density of 128 tags/m^2. Each mu-chip tag features a unique 128-bit ID stored in its

---

[2] Manufacturer: Hitachi Kokusai Electric Inc., model: MRE200 No. 1010 and PA1-2450AS.

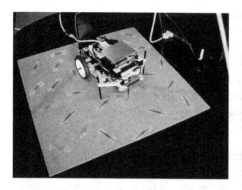
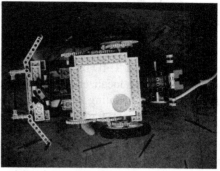
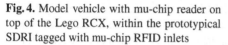

Fig. 4. Model vehicle with mu-chip reader on top of the Lego RCX, within the prototypical SDRI tagged with mu-chip RFID inlets

Fig. 5. Bottom view of the model vehicle prototype showing the wheel configuration, front bumper, and the mu-chip antenna

read-only memory (ROM). The test area of was rounded off with a solid wooden barrier to mark off its boundaries.

The *on-board vehicle control application* is executed on the RCX controller and performs the following actions: It triggers an evasion manoeuvre whenever the bumper sensor connected to the front bumpers reports an obstacle. It also continuously monitors the two rotation sensors and calculates the current position by means of a basic dead reckoning algorithm. The *RFID tag mapping application* is executed off-board on the notebook computer. It is connected to the RFID reader and continuously maps detected RFID tags, using the latest dead reckoning position information obtained from the RCX controller of the model vehicle as reference.

Overlapping partial map observations, which were created during independent map making runs, are merged with a single, gradually growing comprehensive map of the area by the *collaborative map-merging application*. The map merging algorithm uses an affine coordinate transformation between two arbitrary maps with different local (or global) coordinate systems. The transformation is unambiguously defined by a translation vector and a rotation angle given two or more overlapping tags (i.e., tags that are contained in both maps). The affine transformation is calculated numerically using a least squares metric for minimizing the overall transformation error.

5.2 Experimental Results

Experimental Method and Validation. Four map-making test runs were carried out in our test area of 2500 cm^2. Starting from a random position (which served as the origin of the local coordinate system for the measurement), the model vehicle drove along a straight trajectory within the SDRI at a constant speed of 3.6 cm/s. Whenever the bumpers hit the encircling barriers, the vehicle stopped and performed an approx. 90-degrees turn on the spot, and resumed its straight movement. While driving, the off-board application recorded the tag IDs together with the corresponding local position coordinates of the tags detected by the RFID reader on the vehicle. The position coordinates were obtained from the dead reckoning program running on the vehicle's RCX controller. Each test run lasted approx. 90 seconds, during which the vehicle performed

6 turns (each of which took approx. 6 seconds). Thus, on average, the vehicle covered a distance of approx. 200 cm per test run.

To validate our experimental results, we have manually measured the exact local position coordinates of all RFID tags in the test area as a reference. To assess the quality of an experimental RFID tag map, we calculated the overall minimum, maximum, and mean absolute tag localization error. For an individual tag, the localization error was determined by calculating the Euclidean distance between its estimated position and its corresponding exact reference position.

Dead reckoning error. The driving distance of the model vehicle was approx. 0.33 cm per rotation sensor increment. The average absolute error of the dead reckoning algorithm for an approx. 90° turn of the vehicle on the spot was about 4%, and its lateral drift approx. ± 7 cm per meter during straight driving. When considering several consecutive turns, the occurring negative and positive errors partly annihilate each other, leading to a lower effective error. In our case, the overall error of six consecutive turns was reduced to approx. 1.4 %, which corresponds to an accumulated drift of only about 2 cm per meter of straight driving.

Tag localization error. The specific RFID antenna we used detected tags inside an area of approximately 6 by 9 cm around its center point, at approx. 1 cm distance from the floor space. Since each mu-chip of our SDRI test area covered an area of approx. 78 cm^2, only one tag was within antenna range at a time. Therefore, whenever the model vehicle took its current reckoned position as a position estimate for a detected RFID tag, the error caused by the uncertainty about the exact tag position within the antenna tag reception area, which we call *tag localization error*, added to the dead reckoning error.

In our prototype system, the tag localization error equaled the distance between the center of the tag reception area of the antenna and the center point of the mu-chip inlet. Concretely, assuming that the center point of the vehicle is also the center point of the RFID antenna tag reception area, the mean tag localization error amounted to approx. 2.7 cm. In the worst case, if a detected tag was situated in one of the corners of the tag reception area, the resulting maximum tag localization error was approx. 5.4 cm.

Tag mapping error. During the mapping, the deviation e_{TP} of experimentally measured tag position coordinates from the true coordinates, which we call *tag mapping error*, is determined by two factors: the error e_{DR} of the dead reckoning system (which is proportional to the distance traveled since the initial starting position was set), and the tag localization error e_{TL}, which depends on the properties of the RFID hardware and RFID tag distribution: $e_{TP} = e_{DR} + e_{TL}$.

Evaluation of mapping procedure. As a result of the four map-making test runs, four partial maps were created. In the process, on average 11 tags were detected per test run, and 21 different tags were detected altogether. Each two created maps overlapped in two or more tags. The resulting tag mapping errors for the tags of each partial map in comparison to the tags of the exact reference map are shown in Table 2. The average tag mapping error over four experiments was 4.1 cm, with little variation (standard deviation $\sigma = 1.4$ cm). The overall maximum tag mapping error remained below 8 cm.

Table 2. Tag mapping errors of four experimentally constructed partial maps

Partial map	No. of tags	Min. error	Max. error	Mean error	Std. dev. of mean error
1	10	2.5 cm	6.7 cm	4.3 cm	1.3 cm
2	9	1.0 cm	5.2 cm	3.2 cm	1.3 cm
3	11	1.9 cm	7.3 cm	4.3 cm	1.8 cm
4	14	2.0 cm	7.9 cm	4.4 cm	1.3 cm
Average:	11	1.9 cm	6.8 cm	4.1 cm	1.4 cm

Table 3. Tag mapping errors of pairwise merged partial maps

Maps joined	No. of Tags	Min. error	Max. error	Mean error	Std. dev. of mean error
1+2	15	1.5 cm	8.1 cm	3.9 cm	1.5 cm
1+3	15	1.4 cm	9.2 cm	5.2 cm	2.5 cm
1+4	21	1.0 cm	10.0 cm	4.7 cm	2.4 cm
2+3	17	1.0 cm	7.1 cm	4.0 cm	1.8 cm
2+4	16	1.2 cm	7.9 cm	4.1 cm	1.6 cm
3+4	18	1.3 cm	8.0 cm	4.2 cm	1.9 cm
Average:	17	1.2 cm	8.4 cm	4.4 cm	2.0 cm

Table 4. Tag mapping errors of maps obtained after two consecutive merging operations

Maps joined	No. of Tags	Min. error	Max. error	Mean error	Std. dev. of mean error
(1+2)+(3+4)	21	0.5 cm	7.6 cm	3.8 cm	1.8 cm
(1+3)+(2+4)	21	1.6 cm	7.6 cm	4.2 cm	1.6 cm
(1+4)+(2+3)	21	0.8 cm	7.7 cm	3.9 cm	1.8 cm
Average:	21	1.0 cm	7.6 cm	4.0 cm	1.7 cm

Evaluation of map merging procedure. To assess the robustness of our map merging procedure with regard to the order in which overlapping maps are merged, we have joined the four partial maps in different sequential orders and compared the resulting minimum, mean, and maximum tag mapping errors.

In a first step, we merged the individual maps pairwise. The results show a slight increase of the mean tag mapping error to 4.4 cm, with a higher variability ($\sigma = 2.0$ cm), as shown in Table 3. The mean absolute tag mapping error increased slightly to 8.4 cm, with a new overall maximum error of 10.0 cm. The results differ significantly for each combined pair of partial maps. An explanation for this observation is that – at this stage – a better map merging result can be expected for maps that have more tags in common.

In a second step, we merged the previously paired maps. The resulting errors are shown in Table 4. We can see that the mean tag mapping error stabilized at 4.0 cm, with a lower standard deviation than in the case of the original partial maps. A stabilization can also be observed with respect to the minimum and maximum errors. The maximum tag mapping error after two consecutive map merging operations has even dropped below the initial values to 7.7 cm. Apparently, independently from the merging order, the errors with opposite signs tend to partially cancel each other out as the estimated tag positions of all available partial maps are eventually combined.

6 Conclusion

Based on an existing service middleware architecture for super-distributed smart entity infrastructures, we prototypically implemented basic middleware layers and services with the help of RFID technology: the Hardware Layer, the Hardware Abstraction Layer, and the three essential core services Local Data Sharing, Location Manager, and Position Manager. We demonstrated the application of these services by developing and evaluating systems for tracing and tracking, positioning, and collaborative map-making.

The SDRI-based tracking and positioning system we implemented on top of two core middleware services is fault-tolerant with respect to individual tag failures: (1) it redundantly stores trace data objects in physical places using the Local Data Sharing service, and (2) it exploits the data fusion capabilities of the Position Manager, which allows the service to tolerate the unavailability of single tags by interpolating the position coordinates of the MUD at a physical location. By means of experimental evaluation we demonstrated that our positioning service provides an average accuracy of approx. ± 15 cm at walking speed in our prototypical SDRI with a tag density of 39 tags/m^2. We consider this a promising result and a strong indication for the practicability and effectiveness of our approach, in particular considering that we used off-the-shelf RFID equipment that was not optimized for use in mobile environments.

The prototype system for the collaborative mapping of super-distributed smart entity infrastructures used mu-chip RFID tags as smart entities and low-cost rotation sensors for implementing the dead reckoning system. We experimentally evaluated an application for merging partial SDRI mappings created independently by autonomous MUDs. We observed that the mean tag mapping error stabilized on the level of the corresponding errors of the original individual mappings, independent from the order in which the mappings were combined. The maximum and particularly the minimum tag mapping errors were even reduced in the process, which we consider evidence for the feasibility of our approach. We conclude that the collaborative mapping prototype provides an encouraging example for the general idea of employing super-distributed smart entities as a substrate for the realization of collaborative activities.

Currently we are in the process of investigating means for performing the dead reckoning itself with the help of a pure SDRI-based middleware service, to free the MUD from its dependence on the rotation sensors. Besides, we intend to further develop our mapping system to make use of the *Location* abstraction provided by our Location Manager implementation to improve the robustness against individual tag failures.

Acknowledgements

We wish to thank Vito Piraino for his work on the implementation of the SDRI middleware prototype [13]. We further wish to acknowledge Nicola Oprecht for his work on the implementation of the SDRI Tracking and Positioning prototype [14], and Marco Bär for his work on the Collaborative SDRI Mapping system.

References

1. Bohn, J., Mattern, F.: Super-Distributed RFID Tag Infrastructures. In: Proc. 2nd European Symp. on Ambient Intelligence (EUSAI 2004). Number 3295 in LNCS, Eindhoven, The Netherlands, Springer-Verlag (2004) 1–12
2. Vorwerk & Co. Teppichwerke GmbH & Co. KG: Vorwerk is presenting the first carpet containing integrated RFID technology (2005) Press release, Hamlin, Germany.
3. Bohn, J., Mattern, F.: A Fault-Tolerant Middleware for Location-Aware Systems based on Super-Distributed Smart Entities (2005) Submitted for publication.
4. Philips Semiconductors: Identification – I·CODE. Homepage at www.semiconductors.philips.com/markets/identification/products/icode/ (2004)
5. Flörkemeier, C., Lampe, M.: RFID middleware design – addressing application requirements and RFID. In: Proc. sOc-EUSAI 2005, Grenoble, France (2005)
6. Flörkemeier, C., Lampe, M.: Issues with RFID usage in ubiquitous computing applications. In: Proc. PERVASIVE 2004. Number 3001 in LNCS, Linz/Vienna, Austria, Springer-Verlag (2004) 188–193
7. Burgard, W., Moors, M., Fox, D., Simmons, R., Thrun, S.: Collaborative multi-robot exploration. In: Proc. of the IEEE Int. Conf. on Robotics and Automation (ICRA). (2000)
8. Fox, D., Burgard, W., Kruppa, H., Thrun, S.: A Probabilistic Approach to Collaborative Multi-Robot Localization. Autonomous Robots 8(3) (2000) 325–344
9. Hähnel, D., Burgard, W., Fox, D., Fishkin, K., Philipose, M.: Mapping and localization with RFID technology. In: Proc. IEEE Int. Conf. on Robotics and Automation (ICRA), New Orleans, LA, USA (2004)
10. Kubitz, O., Berger, M., Perlick, M., Dumoulin, R.: Application of radio frequency identification devices to support navigation of autonomous mobile robots. In: IEEE 47th Vehicular Technology Conference. Volume 1. (1997) 126–130
11. Ni, L., Liu, Y., Lau, Y., Patil, A.: Landmarc: indoor location sensing using active RFID. In: Proc. 1st IEEE Int. Conf. on Pervasive Computing and Communications. (2003) 407–415
12. LEGO Mindstorms: Homepage at http://mindstorms.lego.com (2005)
13. Piraino, V.: A Middleware for Robust Self-Organizing Services Based on Highly Redundant RFID Tag Infrastructures. Master's thesis, Distributed Systems Group, ETH Zürich, Switzerland (2004)
14. Oprecht, N.: Positioning and Object Tracking based on Super-Distributed RFID Tag Infrastructures. Master's thesis, Distributed Systems Group, ETH Zürich, Switzerland (2005)

Combined Resource and Context Model
for QoS-Aware Mobile Middleware

Sten Lundesgaard Amundsen and Frank Eliassen

Simula Research Laboratory, Network and Distributed Systems,
P.O. Box 134, N-1325 Lysaker, Norway
{stena, frank}@simula.no
http://www.simula.no/departments/networks/

Abstract. Mobile computing systems are increasingly difficult to configure,
operate, and manage. To reduce operation and maintenance cost plus meet
user's expectation with respect to QoS, the computing system and its building
blocks should be self-managed. When addressing the challenges associated with
architecting self-managed mobile computing systems, one must take a holistic
view on QoS management and the heterogonous entities in the mobile environment. This paper presents a novel model that combines resources and context
elements. It helps us in modelling the environment and design resource and
context managers that support functions for adapting the application to changes
in the environment. The model is applied on a video streaming application for
mobile terminals: i) resource and context elements are classified, ii) their QoS
characteristics and context properties are modelled, and iii) weakly integrated
resource and context managers are presented and validated.

1 Introduction

System developers have embraced components as the most suitable software entity
for developing mobile computing systems. The focus within component-based software engineering has been on modelling the functional properties and developing
suitable execution environments [1]. The research community, on the other hand, has
worked on architectures, principles and mechanisms for dynamic adaptation of content, middleware services, and applications, e.g., the mobile middleware platforms
ANSAware [2], Odysse [3], BARWAN [4], ReMMoC [5], MobiPADS [6], and
MADAM [7]. Researches have also started to take a more holistic view on computing
systems to address the increasing complexity system administrators face as computing
systems are becoming tighter interconnected and opened up for connections from
Internet and wireless systems. The vision is to make the computing system and its
building blocks self-managed [8], and free system administrators from the details of
configuration, operations, and maintenance, plus provide users with services that meet
their expectations to performance and reliability. A self-managed system maintains
and adjusts itself in the face of changing components, loads, system failures, and user
demands. Properties of such a system are: self-configuration, self-optimisation, self-
healing, and self-protection. To achieve this existing concepts and technologies must

W. Grass et al. (Eds.): ARCS 2006, LNCS 3894, pp. 84–98, 2006.
© Springer-Verlag Berlin Heidelberg 2006

be combined to a system architecture that has the desired self-management properties [9][10]. One also needs to develop generic models and mechanisms that apply across all building blocks. The reflectiveness of dynamic middleware platforms is such a mechanism (see research on a reflective J2EE server [11]).

We argue that quality of service (QoS) management of component based applications is part of the self-configuration and -optimisation properties. Hence, the need for taking a holistic view on technologies and mechanisms also applies to QoS management support in middleware. Our work addresses this problem, which has resulted in a new reflective component based architecture that integrates QoS-specific elements [12][13]. Mobile terminals and wireless communication systems available today offer no QoS guarantees, so adaptation mechanisms are needed to maintain QoS. Work on dynamic mobile middleware have either used resource information (e.g., [2][3][24]) or context information (e.g., [5][6][16]) to decide the correct adaptation of the application and middleware. In more recent work [7], both resource and context managers have been included in the mobile middleware. The result is powerful designs, but since the holistic view is missing, the resource and context managers are designed as two enclosed entities with different interfaces, separate wrappers to sensors and monitors, and two repositories for storing of resource and context information. In sum, existing architectures and designs limit the QoS management mechanisms to adapt the application to either changes in context or fluctuations in resource availability, and not according to a larger picture of the environment.

Hence, the remaining *research problem* is: how to combine resource management and context awareness mechanisms and handle resource and context information in way that contributes towards the self-management vision? In this paper, we apply the scenario analysis *method* to identify the requirements to and validate the design of resource and context managers for a QoS-aware mobile middleware. We choose to combine the streaming application domain and the mobile technical domain, since this gives a scenario where QoS mechanisms and dynamic middleware are particularly useful. The implementation of the resource and context managers are used in our prototype; QUality of service aware component Architecture for MOBILE computing (QuAMobile). A combined resource and context model is a *contribution* towards the vision of self-managed systems, in particular the QoS management aspects of self-configuration and -optimisation, for two reasons. Firstly the model defines concepts useful in analysis models of the environment and the resource and context management mechanisms. Secondly the resulting resource and context managers provide a complete and consistent data set, which ensures that the middleware makes available the most suitable application configurations to the users.

In the following we start by discussing related work, followed by, in Sect. 3, a description of our QoS-aware mobile middleware prototype. Sect. 4 presents a combined resource and context model, which in Sect. 5 is applied to a scenario with a video streaming application for mobile terminals. Validation and qualitative assessment of the combined model and the resource and context manager implementations is presented in Sect. 6. Lastly, Sect. 7 gives some conclusions and directions for our future research.

2 Related Work

Mobile middleware platforms that adapt middleware services, applications, or support self-adaptive applications, must have processing and delivering mechanisms of either resource or context information. For instance Odysse [3] delivers resource information about changes in the mobile network to interested applications. Similarly the architecture in CARISMA [16] defines wrappers, to sensors and monitors, which encompass post-processing with filters and event messages that deliver context information to the applications according to triggers/policies set by the applications. ReMMoC [5] also gather context information about available services (detected by standard service discovery protocol) without aggregation. It uses the information to trigger the (re)configuration of the binding protocol. MobiPADS [6] is taking this a step further and has an event notification model that supports hierarchical composition of events, i.e., a particular combination of information about CPU, memory, and network. The BARWAN project [4] adds aggregation to the basic processing and delivery mechanisms, and combines context information about the execution environment with resource information about the wireless network. This highlights the importance of combining both resource and context information for controlling the adaptation in the mobile domain.

None of these mentioned mobile middleware platforms employ a general model of resources and context elements. The result is inflexible applications and middleware services that can not use new resource and context elements as they appear in the environment. Furthermore, without a common data model for resource and context information, it is difficult to integrate resource and context managers with other QoS management mechanisms.

A general resource model has been implemented in OpenORB, an enterprise middleware platform [20]. The resource model positions resource representatives in a hierarchy, physical resources are at the bottom and logical resources that encompass several resources at the top. The strength of a hierarchical resource model is that resource requirements can be expressed at the granularity level suitable for the application, but the model does not easily lend itself to analysis models of the environment or resource management mechanisms. This is, however, addressed in the general resource model (GRM) specified by the object management group (OMG) [19]. Due to the generality of the model and the support for new extensions, GRM is chosen as the starting point for the common resource and context model presented in this paper. Work that has utilised a general context model is the two context-aware middleware platforms AmbiSense [21] and Contextfab [26], designed for ubiquitous computing. Their implementation of a context model can store context information for any context type. Another context model is presented by the MADAM project [7], which also adopts a resource model from the object management group (OMG). The result is a powerful and flexible design, but since the applications are (re)configured to a combination of user and system context, it lacks resource QoS characteristics modelling and mechanisms for processing, delivering and storing resource QoS characteristics.

In sum related work highlights the need for a combined resource and context model that can be applied on analysis models of the environment plus resource and context managers. This will ensure that the middleware has the appropriate wrappers to sensors and monitors, and that the resource and context managers can handle the required resource and context information. In addition, the middleware can provide QoS management mechanisms with a complete data set of both resource and context information.

3 QuAMobile –A QoS-Aware Mobile Prototype

A new domain independent QoS-aware middleware platform has been developed, which is based on an open reflective component architecture, called QuA (Quality of service-aware component Architecture). To study the suitability of the architecture for the mobile domain, the baseline (see code and platform independent model in [25]) is extended with domain specific concepts and mechanisms. The result is QuAMobile. If the prototyping of the platform is encouraging, the gained insight will enable us to generalise and extend QuA accordingly. To make QuAMobile executable on mobile terminals and large servers, the architecture has a small core, with hooks where QoS management mechanisms are inserted as plug-ins [13][14] (see Figure 1).

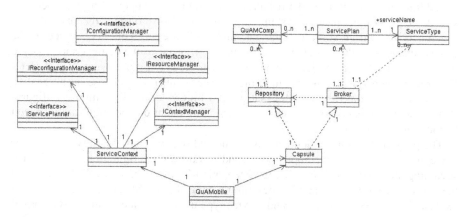

Fig. 1. Middleware overview

QuAMobile makes QoS decisions that take advantage of runtime information, to select the service configuration suitable for the current context and resource availability and that meets the user's QoS requirements. Fundamental in this approach is to model the application as service types and at runtime let the middleware select among alternative implementations of these types. The alternative implementations, each with different QoS characteristics, are provided by application developers and deployed in a repository, together with associated *service plans*. Service plans play a central role in QuAMobile and serve four purposes: i) provide the link between a service type and an implementation of the type; ii) specify service composition and parameter configuration of the implementation; iii) specify dependencies to context elements; and iv) describe the QoS characteristics of the implementation.

Users specify their QoS requirements in a user QoS specification using *dimensional utility functions*, which give users the means to specify their preferences at a high abstraction level. When a user requests a service, QuAMobile invokes the *service planner* plug-in (see Figure 1) with the service type name and the dimensional utility functions. The planner asks the *broker* to provide plans that implement the requested type, and the broker searches the *repository* for relevant plans. The results are one or more plans being returned to the service planner, each with different resource requirements and QoS characteristics. The returned plans specify composition of components and their parameter configurations, which the service planner combines into *service configurations*. The service planner now uses the dimensional utility functions from the user and the QoS prediction functions in the service plans [14] to assess the suitability of each service configuration. Since the *context manager* and *resource manager* plug-ins implements a combined resource and context model, the service planner retrieves from the context manager a data set with context and resource information. This enables the service planner to select the service configuration that provides the highest utility for the user in the current context and resource situation [12]. For each dependency the service configuration has to context elements in the environment, the service planner sets triggers in the context manager. Similarly, triggers are set in the resource manager for relevant resource QoS dimensions. The service planner also uses the resource manager to check if the resources can sustain the additional load and to make resource reservations, if supported by the operating system or the communication system. Next, the *configuration manager* uses the selected service configuration to instantiate and configure the requested service. If the context changes or the resource load fluctuates, triggers, in the context and resource managers, send to the service planner a message describing the event. If the user's QoS requirements are no longer met, the service planner will choose an alternative service configuration (if available) that gives a higher utility. Dynamic reconfiguration of the components configurations and the component compositions are managed by the *adaptation manager*.

The plug-ins like QuAMobile, are implemented in Java (JDK 5). Service plans for the components, service compositions, and parameter configuration of the video streaming application are deployed in eXtensible Markup Language (XML) files, and the service types in Web-service description language (WSDL) files. User service requests, with QoS requirements and service type name, are entered into a Web-based presentation layer, which through an applet and a user datagram protocol (UDP) socket interact with the business layer where QuAMobile components are created and executed.

4   Combined Resource and Context Model

The overall objective with a context and resource model is to define concepts and their relationships that are useful in analysis models of the environment and the resource and context management mechanisms. To achieve this objective the combined model shall: i) allow for classification of resources and context element in the environment according to their behaviour, ii) support quantification of the QoS characteristics and properties of resources and context elements, and iii) lend itself to models of resource and context managers.

During our research we have identified two resource models for middleware platforms [19][20], where the general resource model (GRM) [19] from OMG is considered most suitable for the combined model. It meets our three requirements and is the most comprehensive resource model. GRM includes a core model (see Figure 2) which has extensions for modelling of resource types, resource usage, and resource management. The core model is a general model that can be applied to all resources and it makes a distinction between resource types and their runtime instances, enabling designers to model unknown resources at design time. *Resource* is the basis element, which represents a physical or logical resource that offers one or more services; *ResourceService*. Each service is associated with both functional and nonfunctional properties, where *QoSCharacteristic* represents the quantifiable quality properties of the service. The runtime representation of the basis element resource is *ResourceInstance*, of the resource service is *ResourceServiceInstance*, and *QoSValue* is the quantification of the QoS characteristic.

For the context model we seek a model that, as stated in the beginning of this section, supports classification of the different entities in the environment. This covers entities with static and dynamic properties plus logical and physical entities that offer services. Hence, a resource is part of an entity in the context, establishing a relationship that connects the resource and context models together.

Existing context models, e.g., [21][22][23][26], do not meet our requirements, as they tend to be designed for location information and presence of resources at the different locations. Furthermore, properties of the entities are not included in the models. Therefore, a new context model must be defined. First, we make a distinction between general entities in the environment and those that are relevant for QoS management. Second, a general entity may consist of parts where one or more of these parts are relevant for QoS management. Therefore, in the model a *ContextElement* is the relevant aspect of an *Entity* in the environment. Each *Entity* has some *ContextProperties*, where the *ContextValues* are the quantification of these *ContextProperties* for the *ContextElement*. Lastly, since *ResourceInstances* also exists in the environment, a *Resource* is modelled as part of an *Entity* (see Figure 2).

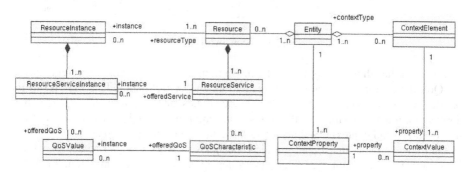

Fig. 2. Combined resource and context model

5 Applying the Combined Resource and Context Model

The concepts defined in the combined resource and context model provides a suitable framework for i) defining resource and context types according to their functional properties, ii) specifying resource QoS characteristics and context properties to instances of the resource and context types, and iii) designing resource and context management mechanisms, e.g., gather, process, deliver & store data about the environment, admission control, and resource reservation. To illustrate the usefulness of the combined model, it is applied to a scenario of a video streaming application for the mobile domain.

5.1 Video Streaming Scenario

Recent advances in wireless networking technologies have enabled the deployment of video streaming applications in the mobile domain, which raises several new challenges in order to achieve best possible playback at the terminal. Only aspects of the scenario that are relevant to resource and context management is presented here. For a detailed description of the scenario, please refer to our technical report [17].

Clients access the video server from different terminals types: home theatres, laptops, and personal digital assistants (PDAs), which are connected to the Internet over the access networks: fixed local area network (LAN), wireless LAN (WLAN), and general packet radio service (GPRS) in GSM (see Figure 3). IP mobility management enables the mobile terminals, PDA and laptop, to roam seamlessly between the access networks. The main challenge, with respect to QoS, is to satisfy user preference and efficiently exploit available resources in different contexts: home theatre-LAN, laptop-LAN, laptop-WLAN, PDA-WLAN, PDA-GPRS, when network conditions are changing and terminals roam between access networks.

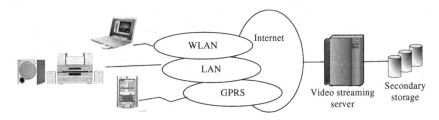

Fig. 3. System overview

Each user has their own opinion of what high quality video is, e.g., different values for QoS dimensions like frame rate, resolution, and colour depth. This may result in parallel video streams with different characteristics and requirements. Hence, the application must be adapted to the user's QoS requirements and the capabilities of all the resources and context elements along the data path from server to client.

QoS management and reconfiguration mechanisms work together to decide when, what, and how to adapt the video streaming application. The foundation for QoS management is end-to-end QoS prediction and allocation. In our approach QoS is a calculated by a set of functions that establish relationships between QoS at different abstraction levels (context-resource ←→ application ←→ user). QoS prediction and allocation functions for the components, service compositions, and parameter configurations (to the video streaming application) are described in the technical report [20]. These functions take data about resources and context elements as arguments. The basis for this is a model of the QoS characteristics and properties of the context. This again requires that the resources and context types for classification of the entities in the environment to the video streaming application are defined, corresponding to the *ResourceInstances* and *ContextElements* of Figure 2.

5.2 Resource and Context Types

OMG has in [19] (the standard that specifies the core resource model) defined three resource types, which are both general enough and sufficient for classifying the resources in the video streaming scenario. The three resource types are i) *Processor:* physical computational resource that is capable of storing and using code and data; ii) *Communication:* logical resource that provide connectivity and transport of bits between two locations; and iii) *Device:* logical or physical resource that is not classified as processor or communication resources. Figure 4 shows the three resource types including the *ResourceInstance* interface that all types implement and setter/getter methods for *QoSValues*.

Likewise, one must have context types for classification of entities in the system context. We have not found any general definitions of context types in related work, and therefore choose to define our own context types for video streaming scenario. The result is seven context types, illustrated in Figure 5: i) *LocalComputation:* local physical entity for computing and temporarily storing of data and code, i.e., CPU and memory; ii) *PermanentStorage:* logical entity for storing and retrieving permanent data and content, i.e., disc; iii) *RemoteStorage:* remote logical entity for storing and retrieving permanent data and content, i.e., streaming server; iv) *Network:* logical entity representing a data bearer service provided by the access network, such as GPRS packet switched; v) *LocalDisplay:* physical entity for presenting computation result or content, e.g., screen or ASCII display; vi) *LocalInput:* physical entity for entering of user data and QoS requirements, like a touch screen and keyboard; vii) *ExecutionEnvironment:* logical entity the application and middleware is running on, i.e., the combination of the operating system, virtual machine, and interpreters.

The notion of context and resource types is included in the combined resource and context model (see Figure 2). Furthermore, since the model specifies that a resource instance is part of a context element, a resource type must also be part of a context type. Thus, the three context types *LocalComputation*, *Network*, and *RemoteStorage* inherit the resource types *Processor*, *Device*, and *Communication*.

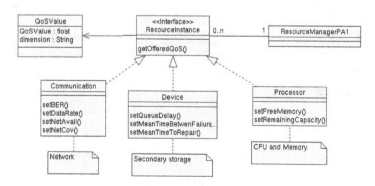

Fig. 4. Resource types

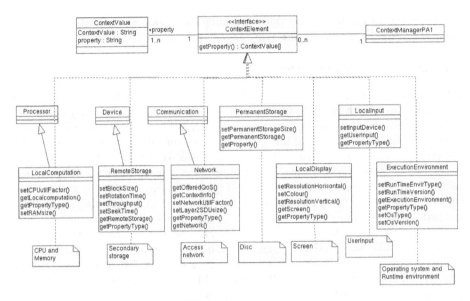

Fig. 5. Context types

5.3 Resource QoS Characteristics and Context Properties

To model the *QoSCharacteristics* and *ContextProperties* of the classified *ResourceIn-stances* and *ContextElements*, we adhere to the uniform modelling language (UML) profile for QoS modelling [18]. Because it is a formal specification that defines the required terms and meta-models, and it ensures that models can be integrated into other UML compliant design models, software development methods, and tools. First the resource QoS characteristics are modelled, which covers resource instances on both the mobile terminal and the server (see Figure 6). The QoS characteristics are quantified by QoS values along QoS dimensions.

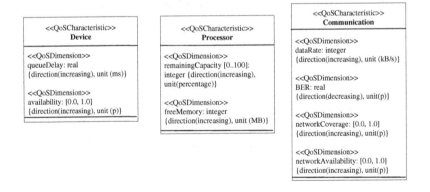

Fig. 6. Resource QoS characteristics

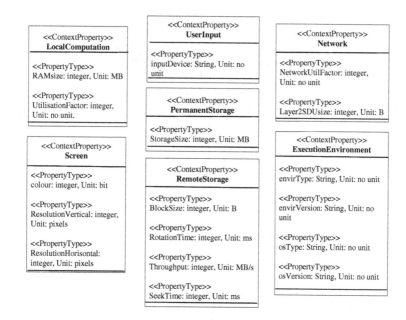

Fig. 7. Context properties

In general, context information is data about the environment that the user is in, but in the video streaming scenario only data about the technical context is required for QoS management. Figure 7 shows the resulting model of all seven context property types identified in the video streaming scenario. The model introduces two new UML stereotypes. *ContextProperty* represents a quantifiable property of the environment, and *PropertyType* is the quantification of the context property. The context properties specify what in the system context that the mobile middleware must gather and process data about. For the terminal this includes the memory, CPU, screen, execution environment, input devices available to the user, and disk for local permanent storage. On the server side there is no need for collecting data about the screen or user input devices. Instead data about the secondary storage server is required.

5.4   Resource and Context Management Plug-Ins for QuAMobile

QuAMobile has only one requirement to the design of the resource and context manager plug-ins (see Figure 1); all operations specified by the (core) interface classes shall be implemented. Design decisions like tight or weak integration of resource and context management mechanisms are left to the plug-in designer(s), who have the knowledge about the *QoSCharacteristics* of the resources and *ContextProperties* of the context elements in the environment.

For our video streaming scenario the resource and context manager must gather, process, trigger notifications, and store QoS and context values according to the resource QoS dimension and property type (see Figure 6 and 7) of the resource and context types (see Figure 5). Furthermore, aggregation of context values before triggering a notification plus admission control of resources, are functional requirements

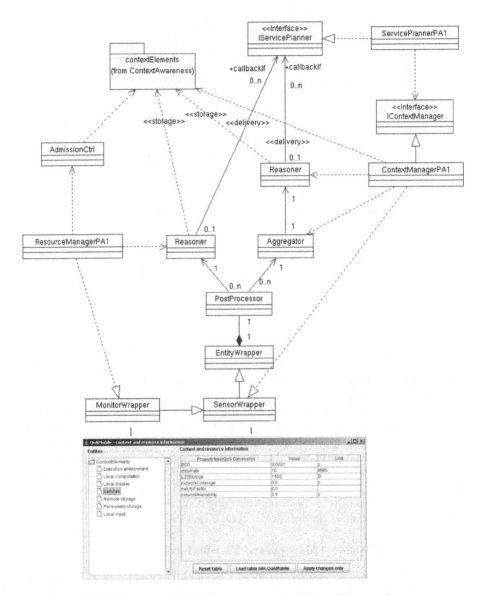

Fig. 8. Resource and context management design with test tool

from the service planner plug-in. To meet these requirements, the integration of resource and context managers is limited to gathering, post-processing, and storage. Remaining functionality in the two managers is kept separate.

Figure 8 shows the design of the resource and context management plug-ins. To avoid strong dependencies between the classes, only the context plug-in has dependencies to the other plug-in. The storage objects for QoS and context values are in the package *contextElements*, which contains instances of the classes shown in Figure 5, i.e., values are stored according to resource and context types. These objects form a context repository that can be extended with statistical analysis tools, for trends and quality estimation of the values. Wrappers and post-processing are configured by the resource and context managers to pass through the *QoSDimensions* and *PropertyTypes* specified in the model of the resource QoS characteristics and context properties, previously shown in Figure 6 and 7.

Triggers for delivery of notification messages about changes in the environment are set by invoking the *setTrigger()* operation, with the resource QoS dimension on the resource manager or context property on the context managers, together with a call-back reference of type *IServicePlanner*.

For simulating changes in the environment, data about each entity are fed into the wrappers using a test tool. The tool's graphical user interface (GUI), depicted in Figure 8, includes text, values, and unit fields for all property types and resource QoS dimensions in the video streaming scenario. Even though the design of the resource and context managers was easy to implement, one should not underestimate the technical challenges associated with developing sensor and monitoring software.

6 Validation and Assessment

Tests of the implementation were limited to validating the behaviour. Since all classes in the resource and context manager plug-ins are instantiated at load time and the signal path goes through maximum four classes, there was no need to test the performance of the design. Instead the test tool was used to insert data directly into the wrappers, and the resulting data set in the storage objects and notification messages was validated. This included filtering of data along unknown QoS dimensions and property types. The storage objects were accessed by the service planner and used to perform QoS prediction, and the triggers were set according to the user QoS requirements, dependencies to properties of the context, and minimum resource QoS requirements.

The combined resource and context model is designed to answer the research problem stated in Sect. 1: how to combine resource and context management mechanisms and handle context and resource information in way that contributes towards the self-management vision? This problem is based on the argument that the self-management vision [8] is achieved by applying generic models and mechanisms across all the building blocks in the computing system [9][10]. From applying the generic model and validating the implementation we make the following observations. The combined model helps designers with classification of all entities in the environment and modelling of both resource QoS characteristic and context properties. It simplifies the design of the resource and context managers by allowing for a weak integration between resource and context managers. Most importantly the resulting resource and context manager provide during runtime a complete data set of all relevant resources and context elements in the environment. This ensures that the mobile middleware has a holistic view of the environment and can find suitable configurations and optimise according to the context and resource availability. One possible weakness in the validation is that the model is applied to only one scenario. We believe that this weakness is limited, since the mobile domain is associated with a broad range of different resource and context elements and the streaming domain has stringent QoS requirements. Furthermore, there are no limits to the definition of an entity in the combined resource and context model. An entity can range from traditional hardware related resources to more abstract entities like other applications. As long as the entities can be classified and the non-functional properties quantified, the model can be utilised. Hence, it is our assessment that the combined model successfully answers the research problem and contributes towards the self-management vision and in particular QoS management aspects of self-configuration and –optimisation.

7 Conclusions

This paper argues that there is the need to take a holistic view on technologies and mechanisms to achieve the goal of self-configuration and -optimisation. The scope was limited to QoS-awareness, which we argue is central in achieving the self-management property. To answer the defined research problem, we use a combined resource and context model that specify concepts needed in analysis models of the environment and the resource and context managers. The essence of the proposed model is that resources are provided by the same entities as the context elements are part of. Thus, analysis models of the environment and resource and context managers include both the QoS characteristics of the resources and properties of the context elements.

The implementation and tests of the resource and context management mechanisms showed that the design was both useful and easy to apply on an application with dependencies to context elements and QoS requirements. It is also evident that the presented resource and context management design is only one possible solution. One can design other solutions that also will work. Though, our assessment is that a QoS-aware mobile middleware platform will benefit from applying a combined resource and context information, since this gave the QoS mechanisms a complete overview of all relevant entities in the environment and their non-function properties.

For a fully self-configurable middleware one need to have a central mechanism that can plan and re-plan the service configuration and make decision on which configuration that is best suited. Future work will look more into the architectural implications of such a centralisation, and the framework needed for supporting service planning.

Acknowledgements

The video streaming scenario that is used to define (realistic) requirements to a QoS-aware mobile middleware platform, have been developed in collaboration with Associate Professors Pål Halvorsen, and Carsten Griwodz from the Informatics department at the University of Oslo, and Post Doc. Ketil Lund from Simula Research Laboratory.

References

1. Emmerich, W.: Distributed Component Technologies and their Software Engineering Implications, Proceedings of the 24th International Conference on Software Engineering, (2002) 537-546
2. Davis, N., Friday, A., Blair, G.S., and Cheverst, K.: Distributed systems support for adaptive mobile applications, ACM-Baltzer Mobile Networks and Applications, Vol. 1, Issue 4 (1996) 399-408
3. Noble, B.D., Satynarayanan, Narayanan, D., Tilton, J.E., and Walker, K.R.: Agile application-aware adaptation for mobility, Proceedings of the sixteenth ACM symposium on Operating systems principles, Vol. 31, Issue 5, (1997) 276-287
4. Brewer, E.A., Katz, R.H., Chawathe, Y., Gribble, S.D., Hodes, T., Nguyen, G., Stemm, M., Henderson, T., Amir, E., Balakrishnan, H., Fox, A., Padmanabhan, V.N., Seshan, S., Personal Communications, IEEE Vol. 5, Issue 5, (1998) 8-24
5. Grace, P., Blair, G.S., and Samuel, S.: A Reflective Framework for Discovery and Interaction in Heterogeneous Mobile Environments, ACM SIGMOBILE Mobile Computing and Communications Review, Vol. 9, No. 1, (2005) 2-14
6. Chan, A.T.S., and Chuang, S.: MobiPADS: A Reflective Middleware for Context-Aware Mobile Computing, IEEE Transactions on software engineering, Vol. 29, No. 12, (2003) 1072-1085
7. The EU project -Madam, Theory of Adaptation –Specification of the MADAM Core Architecture and Middleware Services, Sixth Framework Programme, (2005) D2.1
8. Kephart, J. O., and Chess, D.E.: The Vision of Autonomic Computing, IEEE Computer, Vol. 36, (2003) 41-52
9. Kephart, J. O.: Research Challenges of Autonomic Computing, In Proceedings of the 27th international conference on Software engineering, (2005) 15-22
10. Parashar, M., and Hariri, S.: Autonomic Computing: An Overview, Lecture Notes in Computer Science, Vol. 3566, Springer-Verlag, (2005) 247-259
11. Huang, G, Liu, T, Mei, H, Zheng, Z., Liu, Z., and Fan, G.: Towards autonomic computing middleware via reflection, In Proceedings of the 28th International Computer Software and Applications Conference, (2004) 135-140
12. Amundsen, S., Lund, K., Eliassen, F., and Staehli, R.: QuA: Platform-Managed QoS for component architecture, In Proceedings from Norwegian Informatics Conference, (2004) 55-66
13. Staehli, R., Eliassen, F., and Amundsen, S.: Designing Adaptive Middleware for Reuse, In Proceedings of 3rd international Workshop on Reflective and Adaptive Middleware, (2004) 189-194
14. Solberg, A., Amundsen, S. Aagedal, J.Ø., and Eliassen, F.: A Framework for QoS-aware Service Composition, In Proceedings of 2nd ACM International Conference on Service Oriented Computing, (2004)
15. Amundsen, S., Lund, K., Griwodz, C., and Halvorsen, P.: QoS-aware Mobile Middleware for Video Streaming, In Proceedings of the 31st EUROMICRO conference on Software Engineering and Advanced Applications, (2005) 54-61
16. Capra, L.: CARISMA: Context-aware reflective middleware system for mobile applications, PhD thesis, University College London, University of London, (2003)
17. Amundsen, S., Lund, K., Griwodz, C., and Halvorsen, P: Scenario description –video streaming in the mobile domain, http://home.simula.no:8888/QuA/uploads/2/techVScenA1.1.pdf, (2005)

18. Object Management Group: UML profile for modelling Quality of Service and Fault tolerant characteristics and mechanisms, OMG adapted specification, (2004)
19. Object Management Group: UML profile for schedulability, performance, and time specification, v1.1, formal/05-01-02 (2005)
20. Duran-Limon, H.A., and Blair, G.S.: The importance of resource management in engineering distributed objects, Lecture Notes in Computer Science, Vol. 1999/2001, Springer (2003) 44-60
21. Watt, S., Myrhaug, H.I., Whitehead, N., Yakici, M., Bierig, R., Nuti, S.K., Cumming, H.: Demonstration: An ambient, personalised, and context-sensitive information system for mobile user, Proceedings of the 2nd European Union symposium on Ambient intelligence, (2004) 19-24
22. Chen, G., and Kotz, D.: A survey of context-aware mobile computing research, Technical report TR2000-381, Darthmouth Computer Science (2000)
23. Corradi, A., Montanari, R., and Tibaldi, D.: Context-based access control for ubiquitous service provisioning, Proceedings of the 28th international computer software and applications conference, (2004) 444-451
24. Lu, S., Bharghavan, V.: Adaptive resource management algorithms for indoor mobile computing environments, Proceedings of the ACM SIGCOMM '96 Conference on Applications, Technologies, Architectures, and Protocols for Computer Communication, (1996) 231-242
25. Simula Research Laboratory, QuA, http://www.simula.no:8888/QuA/55, (2005)
26. Hong, J.I., Landay, J.A.: An architecture for privacy-sensitive ubiquitous computing, In Proceedings of the 2nd international conference on Mobile systems, applications, and services, (2004) 177-189

Distributed Modular Toolbox for Multi-modal Context Recognition

David Bannach[1], Kai Kunze[1], Paul Lukowicz[1,2], and Oliver Amft[2]

[1] Institute for Computer Systems and Networks, UMIT, Hall in Tyrol, Austria
[2] Wearable Computing Lab, ETH Zurich, Switzerland

Abstract. We present a GUI-based $C++$ toolbox that allows for building distributed, multi-modal context recognition systems by plugging together reusable, parameterizable components. The goals of the toolbox are to simplify the steps from prototypes to online implementations on low-power mobile devices, facilitate portability between platforms and foster easy adaptation and extensibility. The main features of the toolbox we focus on here are a set of parameterizable algorithms including different filters, feature computations and classifiers, a runtime environment that supports complex synchronous and asynchronous data flows, encapsulation of hardware-specific aspects including sensors and data types (e.g., int vs. float), and the ability to outsource parts of the computation to remote devices. In addition, components are provided for group-wise, event-based sensor synchronization and data labeling. We describe the architecture of the toolbox and illustrate its functionality on two case studies that are part of the downloadable distribution.

1 Introduction

As context awareness gains popularity and moves towards applications, tools for the efficient implementation of context recognition systems become even more important. Such tools need to address a broad range of issues from sensor management middleware through low-level signal processing and pattern recognition to high-level context modeling and utilization. We focus on the signal processing and recognition part. Motivated by the needs of two large industrial projects sponsored by the European Union (WearIT@Work [1] and MyHeart [2]) we have developed the *Context Recognition Network (CRN) Toolbox* for development, prototyping, and implementation of multi-modal, distributed context recognition systems. The emphasis of the CRN Toolbox is on three issues:

1. simplifying the step from prototyping (often done with tools such as MATLAB) to real life implementation,
2. easy portability between different devices and sensor systems with a particular focus on low-power mobile devices, and
3. facilitating the reuse of components and easy extensibility/adaptation of existing recognition systems.

W. Grass et al. (Eds.): ARCS 2006, LNCS 3894, pp. 99–113, 2006.

Problem Description. The design of the CRN Toolbox is based on a system model that has been studied by our groups on a theoretical level in [3]. We assume a set of sensors distributed on the user's body and in the environment, each with its own data rate and format. A typical context recognition application consists of a series of filters, feature extractions, and classifications successively applied to the sensor data. In general, the processing follows a feed-forward hierarchical data-flow model with initial computations being applied to the data stream of each single sensor. Then, the individual data streams are successively fused in joint features and possible partial classifications until, at the final classifier stage, a decision is made based on all or most of the gathered data.

From previous experience with context recognition and the requirements of the abovementioned EU projects we have found the following issues to reoccur in most implementations:

1. Most applications rely on components from a relatively limited set of filters, features, and classifiers. The differences between the applications are (1) the specific combination of such components, (2) the data-flow path, and (3) component-specific parameters such as sliding window sizes, filter frequencies, and – last but not least – classifier training.
2. In general, system development begins with data collection followed by offline experiments with rapid development tools like MATLAB or WEKA [4]. In advance of any online experiments, the algorithms have to be hard- or re-coded for the specific platform. If problems occur or some sort of adaptation is required, the whole cycle restarts from the beginning because experiments tend to be difficult to conduct with optimized production code.
3. Porting complex context recognition tasks to mobile platforms, such as PDAs or phones, often requires parts of the implementation to be converted from floating point to integer because of hardware restrictions. In addition, it might be desirable to outsource the more computation-intensive higher-level algorithms to a remote server.
4. The synchronization of data from different sensors can be a major problem. This involves the merging of data streams with different sampling rates, finding a common start point for all sensors, and compensating for clock drifts and other sources of jitter to retain synchronization over longer periods of time.

Paper Contributions. Based on the above considerations, the central idea behind the CRN Toolbox is to provide a development environment offering (1) a set of parameterizable filter, feature, and classifier components, (2) a runtime system that controls the required data flow and handles synchronization, (3) parameterizable sensor interfaces, and (4) an easy-to-use GUI. With this system, a specific recognition application can be constructed by selecting the appropriate components from the GUI, specifying the component parameters and classifier training data, and connecting the components according to the required data paths. Extension and adaptation of the application are just a matter of adding/exchanging components in the GUI. Since sensor details are encapsulated in the interfaces, sensor changes are also easy to incorporate (as long as the classifiers are not affected). Different parts of the application can be made to run on different systems using special TCP/IP-based interface components, enabling the outsourcing of computationally intensive parts to external servers. Interfaces are also provided for tools like MATLAB and WEKA. By basing all computations on an abstract 'Value' data type equipped with arithmetic, any application may switch between floating point, fixed point, and integer without any recoding. Finally, special components are provided for group-wise sensor synchronization through events and for data labeling.

Related Work. Several research groups have already addressed the issue of on-line sensor data processing and have proposed modular extensible architectures. However, none of them cover all the problems specific to wearable and ubiquitous computing.

Sicheneder et al. [5] from the University of Passau presented a framework that facilitates the graphical specification and execution of complex signal processing applications with focus on industrial monitoring. In contrast to our toolbox, this framework does not address the specific requirements of wearable computing environments such as portability between different devices, outsourcing of computationally expensive tasks, or abstraction from actual data type. Furthermore, there is no explanation or validation of how distributed processing and synchronization of multiple sources work.

The Lancaster CommonSense ToolKit [6] is a collection of tools that assist in the communication, abstraction, visualization, and processing of sensor data. CSTK's core qualities are its real-time facilities and embedded systems-friendly implementation. However, it does not support a flexible composition of the processing entities, synchronization, embedding of tools like MATLAB, or distributed execution which are all key features of the CRN Toolbox and are needed for most real-world applications.

IU SENSE [7] is a Java-based approach to a toolkit that allows for real-time processing, visualization, and analysis of data generated by multiple sensors. Despite its modular and extensible design it is not suited to run on wearable devices, mainly because of performance issues.

OSIRIS-SE [8], developed at Umit, is the stream-enabled version of the hyperdatabase infrastructure for process management that was initially developed at ETH Zurich. It is focused on reliable data-stream processing in distributed environments where mobile devices interoperate with stationary computers. It utilizes Peer-to-Peer techniques and is implemented in Java. Due to the overhead coming from the high-level approach, it can only process simple algorithms on mobile devices and is not able to adapt optimally to different hardware.

Triana [9] is a GUI-based data analysis tool developed at Cardiff University. It is written in Java and provides a large library of analysis algorithms mainly targeted for particle physics, but also useful for other signal processing applications. Triana is focused on distributed computing using Grid and Peer-to-Peer techniques. It lacks most of the features specific for the wearable/ubiquitous environment described above.

Another well-known tool is the Context Toolkit [10] from Georgia Tech. Unlike our CRN Toolbox, it focuses on the application level. Thus, we view it as complementary rather than a competition to our system.

The area of sensor networks and associated middleware contains a lot of work that could be useful together with or as an extension to our system. The EU-funded RUNES project [11] is targeted towards flexible distribution of data processing tasks in heterogeneous sensor networks. The TinyDB [12] lets the sensor network appear as a database which can be queried with an SQL-like syntax. SensorWare [13] uses mobile agents that can replicate themselves throughout the network to gain information. With DSWare [14], applications can subscribe for events that occur on certain groups of sensor nodes.

2   Toolbox Concept and Implementation

The aim of the CRN Toolbox is to allow distributed multi-sensor context recognition to be implemented by simply plugging together standard, parameterizable components. Thus, with the CRN Toolbox, the implementation of a multi-modal context recognition system distributed over several platforms consists of:

1. compiling the toolbox for all platforms that it needs to run on,
2. using the GUI to select and configure the algorithms and data flow that the toolbox needs to execute on each platform, and
3. starting the toolbox on each platform with the configuration files created by the GUI.

Custom code and extensions are easily added to the toolbox by means of new classes compiled and linked in with the rest as desired. A detailed description of the toolbox implementation is beyond the scope of this text. Instead, we focus on the concepts behind the main features elaborated on in the previous section: component reusability and parameterization, flexible data flow, handling of synchronization events, encapsulation of hardware-specific aspects including sensors and data types (e.g., int vs. float), the ability to run and communicate across devices, and the configuration GUI. A detailed documentation of the implementation is contained within the source code.

Parameterizable, Reusable Components. The basic building blocks of the CRN Toolbox are *StreamTasks*, or *tasks* for short. Each algorithm (filter, classifier, etc.) available in the toolbox is implemented as such a task. The abstract `StreamTask` class shown in Figure 1 is based on POSIX threads. It serves as the superclass for all other tasks. Therefore, each task is a separate thread executing concurrently. A task has $0 \ldots n$ `InPorts` and $0 \ldots m$ `OutPorts`. It continuously processes the data received at its in-ports and puts the results on its out-ports.

Each task has a number of startup arguments that correspond to the parameters of the respective algorithm. The KNN classifier task for instance, requires KNNs "k", the filename of the training data, and an optional step size as its parameters.

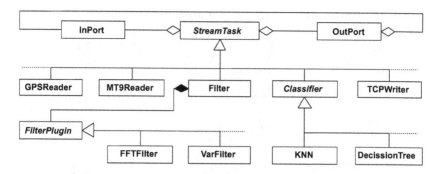

Fig. 1. Static structure of components

```
configuration = taskConf connectionConf [timeoutConf].
taskConf = taskKeyword "=" taskList.
connectionConf = connKeyword "=" connList.
timeoutConf = timeoutKeyword "=" number.
taskList = "[" [taskDef {"," taskDef}] "]".
taskDef = taskName "(" [param {"," param}] ")".
connList = "[" [connDef {"," connDef}] "]".
connDef = "Connection(" number "," number "," number "," number ")".
taskKeyword = "t" ["a" ["s" ["k" ["s"]]]].
connKeyword = "c" ["o" ["n" ["n" ["e" ["c" ["t" ["i" ["o" ["n"
    ["s"]]]]]]]]]].
timeoutKeyword = "s" ["e" ["c" ["o" ["n" ["d" ["s"]]]]]].
taskName = unquoted.
param = unquoted | quoted.
unquoted = letter | digit {letter | digit}.
quoted = '"' {character} '"'.
number = digit {digit}.
letter = "A" .. "Z" | "a" .. "z".
digit = "0" .. "9".
character = ( any ASCII character excluding " )
```

Listing 1.1. EBNF definition of the toolbox configuration language

The CRN Toolbox makes use of the Xparam library (http://xparam.sf.net/) for the de-serialization of objects. This allows the toolbox to be configured by a text file at runtime. See Listing 1.1 for the syntax definition of the configuration language in EBNF format. The 'tasks' section of the configuration file lists the class names and parameters of the `StreamTasks` that are instantiated and run in the toolbox. The connections between these tasks are defined in the 'connections' section.

Table 1 lists the algorithms currently existing in the toolbox. Customized algorithms can be added to the toolbox by creating a subclass of `StreamTask` and implementing the `run()` method as shown in Listing 1.2 for a sample task. The desired number of in- and out-ports must explicitly be allocated by the task constructor. If multiple in-ports are used, the task itself needs to take care in the `run()` method to avoid starvation problems. The `InPort` class provides both blocking and non-blocking access methods. For filter algorithms, there is a dedicated `Filter` class with a plug-in mechanism to support extended reusability of code. The `Filter` task handles packet I/O and calls the `filter()` method of the `FilterPlugIn` for each value. We recommend and prefer to implement filter

Table 1. List of existing algorithms in the CRN Toolbox

Reader Tasks:		
KeyboardReader	Keyboard reader task	available
MT9Reader	Reader for Xsens MT9-B sensors	available
XbusRawReader	Raw reader for Xsens Xbus	available
XSensLogFileReader	Reader for Xsens logfiles	available
NMEAReader	GPS reader task	available
ARSBReader	A reader for the ARSB	available
CricketReader	Cricket reader task	available
FileReader	Generic file reader	available
SerialReader	Generic serial port reader	available
BTnodeReader	BTnode reader	available
HexamiteReader	Hexamite reader	available
PhilipsReader	Reader for Philips protocol	available
RFIDReader	Reader task for ID-10 RFID reader	testing

Organizing Tasks:		
SelectiveSplitterTask	Splits a data stream into several streams	available
Synchronizer	Event based synchronizer	available
SyncMerger	Synchronizing merger task	available
SimpleMerger	Simple merger task	available
TransitionDetector	Transition detector	available

Filter Task and Plug-Ins:		
FilterTask	Configurable filter task	available
MaxFilter	Max filter plugin for FilterTask	available
MeanFilter	Mean filter plugin for FilterTask	available
MedianFilter	Median filter plugin for FilterTask	available
VarFilter	Variance filter plugin for FilterTask	available
SlopeFilter	Slope filter plugin for FilterTask	available
ScaleFilter	Scale filter plugin for FilterTask	available
ThresholdFilter	A two-thresholds filter	testing
FFTFilter	FFT filter plugin for FilterTask	testing
ASEFilter	Average signal energy filter	testing
BERFilter	Band energy ratio filter	testing
BWFilter	Bandwidth filter	testing
CGFilter	Center of gravity filter	testing
FlucFilter	Fluctuation filter (freq. and time domain)	testing
PeakFilter	Peak filter	testing
SFRFilter	Spectral rolloff frequency filter	testing

Classifier Tasks:		
ClassifierTask	Base class for classifier tasks	available
KNN	KNN classifier	available
RangeChecker	Very simple classifier	available
Hexamite2D	Very simple classifier	available
Distance2Position	Very simple position calculation	available
SimpleHexSensClassification	Simple Classifier using xsens and hexamite	available
SequenceDetector	Detects specified sequences	testing

Writer Tasks:		
TCPWriter	Write data to TCP port	available
TCPClientWriter	Write data to a server via TCP	available
SerialWriter	Multifunction serial writer	available
LoggerTask	Data logger task (FileWriter)	available
ConsoleWriter	Console logger	available
PhilipsWriter	Philips serial writer	available
Nothing	Data repeater (e.g. for debugging)	available
Nirvana	Quiet data sink	available

algorithms within such filter plug-ins. Finally, the use of the Xparam library makes it necessary to implement a copy-constructor for each task and to register all other constructors with special Xparam macros (not shown in sample code).

Parameterizable Engine with Data-Flow Control. The data streams between tasks are created by *directed connections* from out-ports to in-ports. The according section of the configuration file specifies the connections between tasks by indexing their corresponding out- and in-ports. A stream consists of a continuous sequence of `DataPackets`. The `DataPackets`, or *packets* for short, are the data entities that contain the sampled values belonging to a single time instant. Each packet bears its own time stamp and sequence number plus a vector of sampled values represented by the abstract data type `Value` (see Figure 2). The elements of this vector may be viewed as channels with equal sampling frequency. They are passed through the streaming network from task to task along the

```cpp
class CustomizedTask : public StreamTask {
    public:
        CustomizedTask( Value *offset );
    private:
        Value *offsetVal;
        void run();
};

CustomizedTask::CustomizedTask( Value *offset ) {
    // initialize parameters
    offsetVal = offset;
    // create as many in- and out-ports as needed
    inPorts.push_back( new InPort() );
    outPorts.push_back( new OutPort() );
}

void CustomizedTask::run() {
    DataPacket *p = NULL;
    InPort *inPort = inPorts[0];
    OutPort *outPort = outPorts[0];

    while( running ) {
        p = inPort->receive();
        if( p ) {
            // get the value(s) from the data packet
            Value *val = p->dataVector.at(0);
            // process the value(s) here
            log( "processing the value:" ) << val;
            *val += offsetVal;
            // send the modified packet
            outPort->send( p );
            p = NULL;
        }
    }
}
```

Listing 1.2. Sample code for customized tasks

internal connections. Actually, only a pointer is passed around while the object data itself stays in place for better performance. When multiple receivers are connected to the same out-port of a task, the packet is cloned. If several streams need to be merged (e.g., to create a feature vector containing data from multiple sensors), a special `Merger` tasks must be used. As described below, `Merger` tasks may include synchronization of data streams with different sampling rates.

Synchronization. Ideally, sensors would have an exact clock to timestamp each data sample with the exact global time. Several methods for network time synchronization exist that are relying on smart sensors. In the real world, however, we have to cope also with simple sensor devices that send data samples with either internal sequence numbers or just a specified sampling rate. Therefore, when working with several sensors, their data streams must be synchronized to a common starting point. Such synchronization often needs to be repeated at runtime as the sampling rates are not reliably exact and might be jittered by communication delays. A well known method for this type of synchronization is the use of events that occur simultaneously at all involved sensors (e.g., jumping up to synchronize a set of acceleration sensors). Our system supports such synchronization through **Synchronizer** and **SyncMerger** tasks.

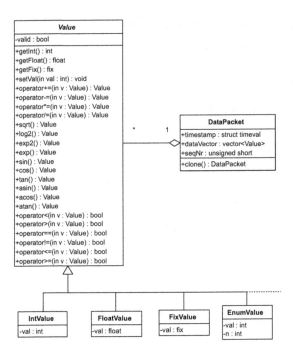

Fig. 2. Static structure of data packets

An example of such synchronization is shown in Figure 3. The `Synchronizer` searches for a distinct event[1] in the data received on the first in-port. The search is limited to a specified time-window which is triggered by a non-zero value on the second in-port. The time stamp t_e of the event is stored by the `Synchronizer`. The `Synchronizer` subtracts t_e from the time stamp of every data packet received later on. Hence, the time stamps of packets on the out-port will be relative to the event: $t_{out} = t_{in} - t_e$. Data streams synchronized this way can then be easily merged according to the time stamp to form one synchronized stream. The `SyncMerger` task merges two data streams that are synchronized to the same event. Packets on the second in-port are merged to matching packets from the first in-port. The matching criteria is the time stamp difference with a tolerance threshold. The data rate from the first in-port is maintained on the out-port, i.e., no packet from the first in-port is discarded. If the data packet P_a on the first in-port is older than the next available packet P_b at the second in-port (i.e., $t_a < (t_b - t_{tolerance})$), packet P_a is merged with a cached copy of the last packet from the second in-port to maintain the data rate. The copied values will be marked invalid. Otherwise, if P_b is older than P_a, P_b is discarded and merging continues with the next packet from the second in-port. The signals in Figure 3 stem from two MT9 acceleration sensors as configured in the GUI.

---

[1] We apply a variance filter with a sliding window of size 2 and take the maximal value as 'event'.

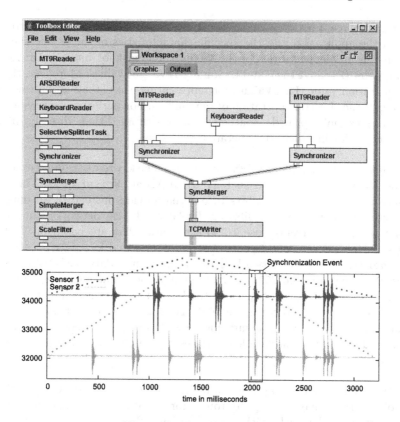

Fig. 3. Display of Sync event

Both sensors are moved at the same time but the signals are not synchronized at the beginning. After a short synchronization period, triggered by pressing a key, the toolbox is able to adjust the timestamps and merge the streams accordingly.

Sensor Hardware Encapsulation. Sensor interfaces are implemented as tasks with no in-ports and are called `Reader` tasks. They create a `DataPacket` for new sampling data as acquired from sensors (or other sources) and provide it on their out-ports. Our architecture supports multiple implementations of reader tasks that read from different sensors or even from other sources of information (e.g., web pages, other applications, files, etc.). We use a keyboard reader for online labeling of sensor data.

Data Type Encapsulation. The sampled values contained within data packets are all of the abstract data type `Value`. All mathematical operations and access methods are declared in the abstract `Value` class (see Figure 2). They are coded in the subclasses of `Value`. This allows algorithms to be implemented completely independent of the actual sampling data type when using the generic interface of the `Value` class. Such algorithms can process floating-point values on one machine and integer values on another without any recoding. The data type of each stream (or even channel) can be configured to optimally match the needs of the application and the specific characteristics of the device the toolbox runs on. Implementations of the `Value` class exist for integer (`IntValue`), floating-point (`FloatValue`), and fixpoint (`FixValue`) values. Moreover, there is an enumeration value (`EnumValue`) for representing class labels and a raw value (`ByteBufValue`) for transportation of raw buffers. For performance reasons, the `Value` classes only provide mathematical operations that directly modify the object as, for instance, the operator '+=' does.

Distributed Execution and Tools Encapsulation. The key to distributed execution and the usage of external tools such as MATLAB are `Writer` tasks. They send the data received at their in-ports to external devices instead of an out-port. Such external devices can be files or displays but also network connections. For the latter, we currently use `TCPWriter` tasks that are based on TCP/IP sockets. Such tasks can send `DataPackets` in a serialized form to corresponding `TCPReader` tasks over the network. The serialization of data packets is done by an `Encoder` plug-in in the `TCPWriter`. Similarly, the `TCPReader` uses a `Decoder` plug-in for de-serialization. Thus, two toolboxes running on different machines can work as a single toolbox using a `TCPWriter` to transport `DataPackets`. In a similar way, the toolbox can communicate with any other program augmented by `TCPReader`/`Writer` compatible interfaces. Currently, such interfaces exist for MATLAB and WEKA.

GUI. We implemented a graphical editor (see Figure 3) for easy configuration of the toolbox. Tasks may be dragged from a library into the workspace where they are connected to other tasks with just a few mouse clicks. The editor is written in Java and automatically produces the configuration files for the toolbox according to the language definition shown in Listing 1.1.

3   Case Studies

Although still being work in progress, we already use the CRN Toolbox for in the WearIT@Work and MyHeart projects as well as in a variety of student works and demonstrators. The toolbox code including different sample applications can be downloaded from `http://csn.umit.at/download/toolbox/`. This section provides two case studies that show how to apply our toolbox to context recognition problems. The first is based on the demonstrators included in the software distribution. The second is a real-life example from the WearIT@Work project. The examples illustrate how distributed multi-modal context recognition systems can incrementally be constructed and adapted with the help of the CRN Toolbox.

3.1   Assembly Activity Recognition

We begin this case study with an explanation of how to use the toolbox to gather and save experimental data from a sensor. The real-time sensor data from an

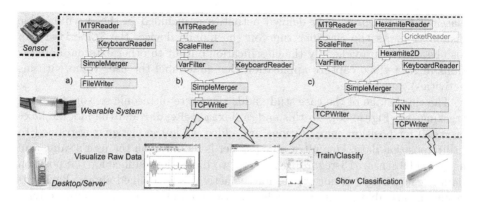

Fig. 4. Toolbox application schematics and MATLAB script reading sensor data

Xsens MT9 motion sensor is labeled by hand using a keyboard during the experimental trials. The sensor is mounted on the back of the user's hand. This setup resembles an initial stage in the development of an assembly activity recognition system for the WearIT@Work project. As shown in Figure 4a, the configuration consists of a `Reader` for the MT9 sensor, a `KeyboardReader` for labeling, a `SimpleMerger`, and a `FileWriter`, all executed on the wearable device. The `MT9Reader` acquires the data from the sensor while the experiment conductor can operate the keyboard and label the user's actions accordingly. The labels for the demonstrator included in the downloadable distribution mark the following activities: to hammer, to screw drive, to sandpaper, and to saw. The `Simple-Merger`, in turn, combines the sensor data with the labels and pipes them to the `FileWriter` which logs the labeled data to a file. In the same manner as the rest of the case study, this happens in perceived real-time.

In the next stage, the system is extended to include feature extraction using scaling (`ScaleFilter`) and a variance filter (`VarFilter`) on the signal processing side. Another component changed is the `TCPWriter` instead of the `FileWriter` to transmit the data to a remote server (see Figure 4b). The remote computer runs a MATLAB visualization application and/or our *SensServe* interface to the WEKA machine-learning software extended by a toolbox-compatible `TCPReader` module. Thus, the labeled data is forwarded to both applications. The MATLAB visualization application is able to display the sensor data in perceived real-time. This is a fast and easy way to ensure the correct operation of the sensors. It also proves to be a valuable help to get a first glimpse on characteristic features of the context recognition tasks. The *SensServe* interface can either be used to train a classifier or to do online tests and demonstrations. Naturally, as it interfaces to WEKA, it provides access to all classifiers and analysis algorithms implemented by this machine learning library. This eases the search for suitable features and classifiers dependent on the inference task.

Once the experimental stage of development is finished, the classification is moved from the server to a toolbox KNN classification component able to run on the mobile device. An already trained version of the toolbox KNN classifier for the previously defined activities is included in the downloadable distribution. As the classifier runs on the mobile device, the `TCPWriter` can also be used to provide only the classification output to other external applications (e.g., a video capture application that may label the user video with his activities).

The third stage of the case study adds Hexamite ultrasonic sensors for hand tracking (see Figure 4c). To this end, a `HexamiteReader` and the module `Hexamite2D` for position computations are added while the classifier is trained to utilize position data. One ultrasonic listener is mounted on the user's same arm as the MT9 sensor. Disregarding height, two dimensions suffice for the position data because height is not crucial for the activities we defined above. Thus, the system is now able to differentiate between where in the room a specific activity is performed. This in turn can be used to determine regions of interest or to improve the activity recognition rate as certain activities happen at a specific places only. The analysis and training is done using WEKA in a setup similar to Figure 4b. The training can also be done on the mobile device. Finally, the trained classifier running on the mobile device transmits the resulting classifications using the `TCPWriter` to a desktop machine. The desktop simply visualizes the results.

To underline the flexibility of the toolbox, the Hexamite sensors may be replaced by Cricket ultrasonic sensors with hardly any effort. The operation of both sensors is very similar. We only had to write a `CricketReader` that outputs the data in the same format as the `HexamiteReader`, and insert it into the system using our GUI. This underlines that sensors with similar outputs can easily be interchanged by only using different readers in the toolbox and by adapting some filter parameters. The CRN Toolbox also supports readers with several output formats to enhance reuse. For example, the `MT9Reader` can either provide raw (int) or calibrated (float) data. Any application using the MT9 accelerometer data can easily be adjusted to use other accelerometers, simply by adding appropriate readers.

For systems with no sensors attached, the toolbox offers a `FileReader`. The `FileReader` reads previously recorded sensor data from a file and sends it to other components of the system in the same way as if the data originated from a real sensor. Thus, it is possible to re-run any experiment in real-time to fine-tune the toolbox components or debug a more complex application.

3.2   Gesture Recognition for Controlling a Document Browser

As mentioned before, the toolbox is currently used in the WearIT@Work project. One scenario in this project takes place during a doctor's ward round in a hospital. One problem of the ward round is the extremely limited time available per patient. Accessing each patient's documents on-site is important but operating a computer or PDA tends to be time-consuming and distracting. In the solution investigated in the WearIT@Work project, we apply context- and gesture recognition to automate and simplify the access to the patient's documents. The doctor is equipped with a QBIC [15] wearable computer, and an MT9 motion

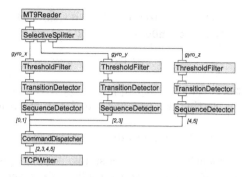

Fig. 5. Toolbox configuration for the gesture recognition

sensor plus an RFID reader at the right arm. The patient wears an RFID tag and the nurse carries a PDA. At each patient's bed, there is a bed-side monitor to display documents from the hospital database system. The QBIC connects wirelessly to both the PDA and the bed-side system. When the doctor approaches the patient's bed, the bed-side monitor automatically shows the specific patients list of documents. The doctor can then browse these documents by pointing at the monitor and swivel the forearm up and down or left and right. The following gestures are defined:

Forearm Gesture	Command
swivel up, then down	scroll up
swivel down, then up	scroll down
swivel left, then right	open document
swivel right, then left	close document
roll right, then left	activate gesture recognition
roll left, then right	deactivate gesture recognition

In the following, we briefly describe how the CRN Toolbox is extended with only three simple classes to deal with this gesture recognition and the controlling of the document browser. The configuration is shown in Figure 5. We use the 3–axis gyroscope of the MT9 motion sensor to detect the swiveling and rolling of the forearm. The x–axis of the gyroscope is aligned in parallel to the main axis of the forearm, and the y–axis in parallel to the plane of the hand. Rolling the forearm leads to either a positive or negative deviation of the angular velocity on the x–axis, depending on the roll direction. Similarly, swivel left/right is measured on the y–axis and swivel up/down on the z–axis.

We implemented a `ThresholdFilter` by extending the `FilterPlugin` class. The `ThresholdFilter` has two thresholds. All values greater than the upper threshold are set to 1, all value less than the lower threshold are set to 2, and all others are set to 0. With the appropriate thresholds, this filter applied to the x–axis gyroscope signal will output a sequence of values similar to

$$...00000011111111000022222222200000...$$

when rolling the hand and forearm to the right and then back immediately. Then, we apply the existing `TransitionDetector` task and get the sequence below.

$$\ldots 01020 \ldots$$

The `TransitionDetector` allows for skipping sequences of equal values shorter than a specified length. Setting this parameter to 4, we get the following sequence instead.

$$\ldots 0120 \ldots$$

Now, we only need to identify exactly this simple sequence in the filtered data stream in order to tell that the *activate*-gesture has been executed. Similarly, all other gestures can be recognized. Therefore, we implemented the `SequenceDetector` task which accepts a list of value-sequences as its parameter. If one such sequence is detected in the data stream, the `SequenceDetector` sends the index of that sequence on the out-port. We apply these three algorithms on every axis of the gyroscope in parallel. We insert pseudo-sequences that never occur (e.g., [-1]) in the parameters passed to the `SequenceDetector` for the y- and z-axis to ensure that every gesture is assigned a unique index value.

The third class that had to be implemented for this scenario is the `Command-Dispatcher` task. It simply forwards the gesture indices to its out-port if in *active* state and discards them otherwise. The state is set by the `activate-` and `deactivate` commands. This task is actually extended (but not shown here) with additional in- and out-ports to support RFID input and wireless connectivity to the nurse's PDA. The output of this task is sent to a `TCPClientWriter` that connects to the document browser of the hospital database system. The document browser can interpret the commands like real mouse and keyboard input.

4   Conclusion and Future Work

The CRN Toolbox is currently used in different projects. At the same time it is still evolving. In addition to the implementation of further components, the main directions are support for dynamic (re-) configuration of applications at runtime including ad-hoc cooperation between devices and better support for resource management. The later will include the back propagation of control messages through the processing network. Another immediate improvement of the CRN Toolbox that goes along with (re-) configuration is to provide a tighter coupling between runtime and GUI than just over configuration files. Furthermore, we envision extensions for ad-hoc cooperation of multiple toolboxes and a meta-model for sensors and context information.

References

1. WearIT@Work EU IST project http://www.wearitatwork.com/.
2. MyHeart EU IST project http://www.hitech-projects.com/euprojects/myheart/.

3. Anliker, U., Beutel, J., Dyer, M., Enzler, R., Lukowicz, P., Thiele, L., Troester, G.: A systematic approach to the design of distributed wearable systems. IEEE Transactions on Computers **53**(8) (2004) 1017–1033

4. Witten, I., Frank, E.: Data Mining: Practical machine learning tools and techniques. 2nd edn. Morgan Kaufmann, San Francisco (2005)

5. Sicheneder, A., Bender, A., Fuchs, E., Mandl, R., Sick, B.: A framework for the graphical specification and execution of complex signal processing applications. In: Proc. of ICASSP, Seattle, WA, USA (1998) 1757–1760

6. CSTK (CommonSense ToolKit) http://cstk.sourceforge.net/.

7. Caracas, A., Heinz, E., Robbel, P., Singh, A., Walter, F., Lukowicz, P.: Real-time sensor processing with graphical data display in java. In: Proc. of ISSPIT. (2003) 62–65

8. Brettlecker, G., Schuldt, H., Schek, H.: Towards reliable data stream processing with osiris-se. In: Proc. of BTW Conf., Karlsruhe, Germany (2005) 405–414

9. Taylor, I., Schutz, B.: Triana - A Quicklook Data Analysis System for Gravitational Wave Detectors. In: Second Workshop on Gravitational Wave Data Analysis, Editions Frontières (1998) 229–237

10. Dey, A., Salber, D., Abowd, G.: A conceptual framework and a toolkit for supporting the rapid prototyping of context-aware applications. Human-Computer Interaction (HCI) Journal **16**(2-4) (2001) 97–166

11. Runes project, EU IST http://www.ist-runes.org/.

12. Madden, S., Franklin, M., Hellerstein, J., Hong, W.: Tag: a tiny aggregation service for ad-hoc sensor networks. In: OSDI 2002, Boston, USA. (2002)

13. Boulis, A., Han, C.C., Srivastava, M.B.: Design and implementation of a framework for efficient and programmable sensor networks. In: The First International Conference on Mobile Systems, Applications, and Services (MobiSys 2003) San Francisco, CA. (2003)

14. Li, S., Lin, Y., Son, S., Stankovic, J., Wei, Y.: Event detection using data service middleware in distributed sensor networks. special issue on Wireless Sensor Networks of Telecommunications Systems, Kluwer **26:2-4** (2004) 351–368

15. QBIC - Belt Integrated Computer http://www.ife.ee.ethz.ch/qbic/index.htm.

Dynamic Dictionary-Based Data Compression
for Level-1 Caches

Georgios Keramidas, Konstantinos Aisopos, and Stefanos Kaxiras

Department of Electrical and Computer Engineering, University of Patras,
26500 Patras, Greece
Tel.: +302610 996441; Fax: + 302610997 333
{keramidas, aisopos, kaxiras}@ee.upatras.gr

Abstract. Data cache compression is actively studied as a venue to make better use of on-chip transistors, increase apparent capacity of caches, and hide the long memory latencies. While several techniques have been proposed for L2 compression, L1 compression is an elusive goal. This is due to L1's sensitivity to latency and the inability to create compression schemes that are both *fast* and *adaptable* to program behavior, i.e. dynamic. In this paper, we propose the first dynamic dictionary-based compression mechanism for L1 data caches. Our design solves the problem of keeping the compressed contents of the cache and the dictionary entries consistent, using a timekeeping decay technique. A dynamic compression dictionary adapts to program behavior without the need of profiling techniques and/or training phases. We compare our approach to previously proposed static dictionary techniques and we show that we surpass them in terms of power, hit ratio and energy delay product.

1 Introduction

Cache compression increases the apparent capacity of the cache and reduces the miss-rate at the expense of increased access latency associated with compression and decompression. As long as the cost of accessing a compressed datum in the cache does not exceed the cost of servicing a miss from the lower level of the memory hierarchy, cache compression is a wining proposition. This is easily attainable in the L2 or L3 caches where the compression/decompression costs compare favourably (i.e. are much lower) to the cost of going to main memory [1,11,14,15]. The same is true for main memory with respect to the long disc delays and this is why many proposals consider main memory compression [6].

But why would one consider compression in an age of excessively large transistor budgets? The reason is that it almost always pays to have a "bigger" cache: Alameldeen and Wood [1] show that in commercial applications where the miss rate is relatively high, compression of the L2, regardless of its size, is beneficial. Furthermore, we are fast moving towards multiple cores on a chip, which will exacerbate the problem of adequate cache capacity since the cache will have to be shared by many applications or threads. L2/L3 compression is therefore a useful technique for the foreseeable future and especially for future CMP architectures. Alternatively, compression can be used to free space in the cache which can then be translated to power savings [13,22,23,25].

W. Grass et al. (Eds.): ARCS 2006, LNCS 3894, pp. 114 – 129, 2006.

Of course this reasoning can be extended to include the L1 if it were not for a serious issue. L1 is typically very fast —single-digit number of cycles when pipelined— and therefore latency-sensitive: a few additional cycles for compression/decompression can more than double its latency and hurt system performance. In addition, at the top level of the hierarchy, compression/decompression costs of the order of 10 to 15 cycles approach L2 access latencies, which means that accessing a compressed L1 datum (that would be a miss) has little difference from going directly to the L2. Thus, latency alone rules out all complex compression/decompression schemes such as those used in L2 compression [1,11,14,15]. Power consumption is also becoming a critical issue in L1. The L1 is accessed much more frequently than the L2, rendering complex and power-hungry L1 compression mechanisms undesirable.

This leaves at our disposal only the simplest mechanisms for compression. One such simple, yet effective, mechanism is the *dictionary* (or *directory*) for frequent values [20,23,25,26]. A frequent-value dictionary stores the program's frequent values (e.g., the 32-bit value "0") and replaces all their occurrences in the cache with the respective dictionary indices (e.g., 8-bit indices for a 256-entry dictionary). However, until now, no mechanism has been proposed to implement a dynamic dictionary for caches [23,24]; in other words, a dictionary whose contents can adapt to the requirements of the running program. The dictionaries proposed so far for caches are loaded statically via profiling or are "trained" for a small period of time to detect and store frequent values for the remainder of a program's run [23,25,26]. In practice, such a static approach is avoided by designers since it is cumbersome in real systems. There, we would like adaptivity under different workloads without needing to resort to profiling or training. Moreover, a static approach is incompatible with multiprogrammed/multithreaded environments since the contents of the dictionary are part of program state and need to be changed accordingly with context switches. The need for dynamic dictonaries was also reported by Yang and Gupta [24] in the context of bus compression.

On the other hand, a straightforward dynamic dictionary is impractical. The difficulty in building a dynamic dictionary lies in that we cannot delete an entry from the dictionary unless we are certain that no cache line is compressed with it —otherwise the line cannot be decompressed with the correct dictionary index leading to consistency problems. It is far too expensive, unfortunately, to keep track of the all the cache lines that are compressed with any particular entry in the dictionary.

Contribution. The contribution of our work is the first mechanism for a dynamic L1 dictionary resulting from coupling a decay cache [12] to a decaying dictionary. The principle of cache decay is the identification of cache lines which are unlikely to be accessed in the future (before their replacement). Such lines can be safely discarded with minimal impact on performance. We apply the same principal to the dictionary and discard entries which are unlikely to be used in the future. By decaying the cache and the dictionary in exactly the same way, we are guaranteeing that when a dictionary entry is decayed no live line in the cache can possibly refer to this entry. This allows us to replace dead entries in the dictionary with new frequent values, thus adapting the dictionary contents to the requirements of the running programs.

In this paper, we exploit this mechanism for two compressed L1 schemes: i) a low-power, and ii) a high-performance cache. We study the proposed mechanism and we present our comparisons with static dictionaries (using either profiling or training) and with uncompressed caches of larger capacity. Our evaluation shows that our cache compression design can improve the Energy-Delay Product by 10% (on average) compared to the static and the training approaches. When high performance is the issue, our proposal shows 45% reduction in miss ratio compared to a conventional cache of the same capacity and up to 27% improvement compared to the static case.

Structure of this paper. We begin by motivating the need for dynamic dictionaries dictated by the behavior of frequent values in Section 2. In Section 3 we show how cache decay leads to a solution for dynamic dictionaries and describe our proposal in detail while in Section 4 we delve into design issues for our approach. We continue in Section 5 by presenting the evaluation of our proposal. In Section 6 we survey related work and in Section 7 we offer our conclusions.

2 The Dynamic Behavior of Frequent Values

Many algorithms for compression of the memory subsystem have been proposed in the literature. Such techniques try to exploit different characteristics of the address/data streams to achieve high compression ratios [1,11,14,15]. One direction concentrates on exploiting the well known phenomenon of locality and especially value locality. Value locality has been initially utilized in the design of value reuse and value prediction mechanisms for superscalar processors [8,16].

The main motivation of this work is *frequent value locality* introduced by Zhang et al. [26]. Zhang et al. showed that such locality is quite prevalent in programs. They applied their observations in the design of L1 cache compression schemes and bus encoding schemes. These approaches are based on a small number of distinct values, that are very frequently accessed and are found by profiling the application or by training the dictionary during a small initial phase of the program. These approaches are limited by the static nature of the dictionaries: only a small fraction of the frequent values are accommodated and this is not optimal for all program execution. Excluding a small set of values (e.g., 0, 1, -1) that are universally useful, other values which are frequent in one part of the program may not occur as frequently in other parts and vice versa. A dictionary whose content changes dynamically, not only frees the designers from the burden of initializing it properly, but has the potential for better performance and lower power.

To show the need for a dynamic dictionary we conduct the following experiment. We choose two benchmarks from the SPEC2000 suite, one from the integer suite — *vpr*— and one from the floating point suite —*galgel*. For each program, we divide its execution into smaller time intervals and for each of these intervals we find its top N frequent values. We then examine the commonality between each interval's set of N frequent values and the fixed set of N frequent values of a static dictionary (i.e., the set of N for the whole program).

The results of this experiment are presented in Fig. 1. In both graphs, the horizontal axis represents the number of time intervals that fit in the execution of the program (200 to 2), and the vertical axis represents the overlap (as a percentage of values) between the dynamically created dictionary and a fixed dictionary. The four curves in

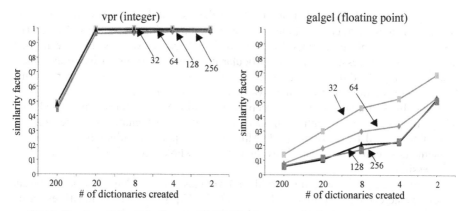

Fig. 1. Overlap of dynamically created dictionaries vs. static dictionary for various sizes

each graph plot the overlap of the dynamically created dictionaries of various sizes (32, 64, 128, and 256) to a "static" dictionary of equal size for the whole program run.

For both programs, the more frequent is the creation of dictionaries (smaller time interval), the smaller is the overlap with the "static" dictionary. This signifies the need to change the contents of the dictionary continuously. For *vpr* dictionary overlap is least with the smallest time intervals but reaches 100% when the dynamic directories are created less frequently (showing *vpr*'s highly dynamic nature at small time scales). *Galgel* on the other hand shows a more gradual change in the overlap at various time scales and even in the far right case of only two dynamically created dictionaries, their overlap with a single dynamic barely reaches 68%. With respect to dictionary size, smaller dictionaries have more overlap (because the topmost frequent values do tend to be the same) while larger dictionaries have more room to accommodate a more diverse set of values. At the largest time scales the overlap for the large dictionaries converges to about 50% for *galgel*, meaning that a full half of the dynamic dictionaries is different than the corresponding static dictionary —of course, *the absolute number of values that differ from the static dictionary is a function of size.*

Having described the need to create a dictionary whose context must be able to change on the fly, let us now discuss our proposal for keeping the dictionary and the cache context consistent. The next section presents the first mechanism —to the best of our knowledge— for a dynamic dictionary for cache compression.

3   Dynamic Dictionary and Compressed Data Consistency

As of yet, no mechanism has been proposed to implement a dynamic dictionary for caches; instead the dictionaries proposed so far are loaded statically via profiling or are "trained" for a small period of time but remain static once they are loaded with values [1,14,23,25,26]. Dynamic (adaptive) dictonaries are reported in the context of *bus compression* [2,7,17,19,20,24]. What makes dynamic dictionaries possible for bus compression is that there is no need to keep them consistent with any other state. Data are compressed on the fly as they enter the bus and are decompressed as they are delivered at the other end —there is no storage of compressed state to worry about. But, this is the main impediment for dynamic dictionaries when it comes to cache compression.

The problem of dynamic dictionaries for caches is that the compressed cache state (data) needs to be kept consistent at all times with the dictionary contents. This makes it very hard to replace an entry in the dictionary because we must be sure that no cache line is compressed using the particular dictionary entry under eviction. Otherwise, the compressed data are going to be decompressed with the new (wrong) value that enters the dictionary, rather than with the old (correct) one.

A possible solution would be to keep track of all the cache lines compressed with any particular dictionary entry. Upon replacement of that entry the corresponding cache lines would be decompressed. Although this approach solves the consistency problem, it is extremely costly, invalidating the whole premise of efficient cache compression.

Our technique to attack this problem leverages on a leakage-saving proposal, namely cache decay, proposed by Kaxiras et al. [12]. Cache decay identifies cache lines which are unlikely to be accessed in the future (before their replacement). In [12] such cache lines (deemed to be "useless") are switched off in order to save leakage power. About 70% of the L1 can be discarded this way with minimal performance loss. The main idea of our work is to apply decay both in the cache and in the dictionary, discarding both unneeded compressed cache lines *and* their corresponding "frequent values" that are no longer needed by the remaining live cache lines. By decaying the cache and the dictionary in exactly the same way —in concert— we are guaranteeing that when a dictionary entry is decayed no live line in the cache can possibly refer to this entry.

Decay is implemented by measuring time since the last access to a cache line/dictionary entry. If a specified time interval (called the *decay interval*) passes without any access, the cache line/dictionary entry is discarded. We assume that as in [12], power to the cache line is switched off to save leakage power but the dictionary entry is simply marked as empty (available for replacement).

To measure the decay interval we use counters in each line/entry. The counters are reset with every access but advance when the line/entry is idle. When a counter reaches the decay interval the corresponding cache line/dictionary entry is decayed. Since reasonable decay intervals for the cache are in the range of a few thousand cycles [12], we use a hierarchical counter scheme where a global cycle counter advances every few hundred cycles small (e.g., 2-bit) local counters in each line/entry.

To show that decay keeps the compressed cache and the decaying dictionary consistent let us walk trough an example:

- Initially the dictionary and the cache are empty.
- When a cache line is brought into the cache, all its words are checked against the contents of the dictionary; if a word matches a value in the directory it is compressed; otherwise if there are empty slots in the dictionary the word is entered as a new frequent value. Thus, when a cache line is brought into the cache all of its frequent values in the dictionary are accessed and kept live.
- Similarly, when a compressed cache line is accessed (and therefore live) all its frequent values should be kept live too. Besides the requested word which is decompressed if needed (accessing the corresponding frequent value), all other compressed words in the cache line are used to reset the decay counters of the corresponding frequent values. This is a lightweight operation since we just reset decay counters —not access the frequent values.

Thus far we have established that any live line will keep its frequent values live in the dictionary for at least a decay interval after the line's last access. Consequently, when a frequent value decays in the dictionary, it means that *no cache line that uses this frequent value for its compression has been accessed for at least a full decay interval* (otherwise the frequent value would not have a chance to decay). But this last condition means that *all cache lines copressed with this frequent value have also decayed.* This allows us to replace decayed entries in the dictionary with new frequent values, thus adapting the contents of the dictionary to the set of frequent values that are most relevant during different phases of execution. An important characteristic of our proposal is that we do not replace entries on demand —as we would do with an LRU algorithm —but simply replace according to the availability of dead (decayed) entries.

4   Design Issues

L1 cache compression techniques must be designed in a very cautious manner since this level of hierarchy lies on the most critical path of the processor-memory model. In this Section, we use the XCACTI 2.0 [10] to estimate all the design issues of our *Dynamic Frequent Value Cache* (DFVC) in terms of access time and power.

4.1   Design Issues of Decaying Dictionaries

The decaying dictionary is a critical part of the design, because it must be accessed/ updated every time a read/write operation is performed in the DFVC. As we will see in the rest of this section, the decode/encode operation is in the critical path of the cache. Therefore, having an efficient dictionary design is very important. Our solution, shown in Fig. 2.a, resembles a dual port register file design. In addition to the registers (holding the frequent values), there is an extra column that encapsulates the decaying functionality. This column contains the local decay counter and a decay status bit per entry showing its "liveliness" state. Collectively, the counter and the status bit are referred to as "decaying" bits since their overall functionality (and indeed their implementation) is captured by decaying 4-transistor (4T) memory cells.

We have modified XCACTI to estimate the access time required for a read/write operation in the dynamic dictionary. We adopted the register file model proposed in

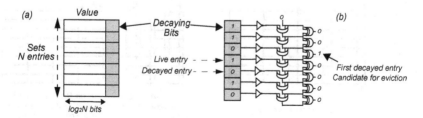

Fig. 2. (a) The dynamic decaying dictionary, (b) circuit to indetify the first decayed entry

Wattch [3], using process parameters for a 130 nm technology. Our XCACTI estimates showed that the decode/encode operation of the register file is quite small varying from 0.39 ns for decoding 4 bits (16 entries) to 0.629 ns for decoding 7 bits (128 entries).

The decaying hardware (counter and status bit) comes at   a negligible cost (in terms of time and power). We refer the reader to the work of Kaxiras et al. for this analysis [12]. From the other hand, to insert a new entry in the dictionary is not so trivial. A new frequent value must be inserted in the first decayed entry of the dictionary (considering a top-down ordering). Searching sequentially the dictionary for the first decayed entry (if any) is unacceptable since it will make the insertion of a new value extremely slow and costly. To alleviate this problem, we use a simple combinatorial circuit, shown in Fig. 2.b, which identifies the first decayed dictionary entry at the cost of a few gates.

Having discussed the design issues of the decaying dictionary, let us now demonstrate our proposals for a *Power-Aware DFVC* (PA-DFVC) and a *High-Performance DFVC* (HP-DFVC). The hope is to create an efficient design where the time spent on encoding/decoding of the values has little impact —if any— in the cache access time.

4.2 Design Issues of Power-Aware DFVC (PA-DFVC)

In this section, we will show how the dynamic behavior of the frequent values, explained in Section 2, can be exploited in a power-aware compressed cache proposed by Yang and Gupta [23,26]. In contrast to their proposal, our dynamic compression scheme is able to adapt to changes of the frequent values for different parts of the execution during the execution of a program. Fig. 3 shows the partitioning of the data array of the PA-DFVC —no changes required in the tag array in this case.

In the PA-DVFC cache, the data values are divided in two categories: a small number of N frequent values (N reflects the number of the dictionary entries) and all the remaining values that are marked as nonfrequent values. The frequent values are stored in encoded form, and therefore can be stored in log_2N number of bits, while the nonfrequent values are stored in unencoded form in 32-bit words.

As we can see from Fig. 3, the cache data array is partitioned so that one array contains log_2N bits corresponding to each word (4 words in this example) and the other

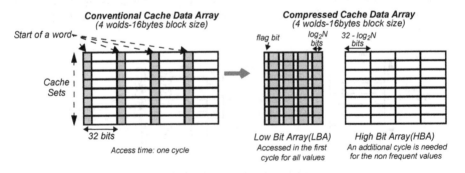

Fig. 3. PA-DFVC: data array partitioning

contains the remaining $32-\log_2 N$ bits. Frequent values are stored in encoded form in the Low Bit Array (LBA), while non-frequent values fill both data arrays. An additional bit (flag bit) corresponding to each word in a cache line is needed to indicate whether the word contains an encoded frequent value or an unencoded nonfrequent value.

The overall approach is as follows: when reading a word from the cache, initially we read from the LBA. Since the bits read out contain a flag bit, we examine it to determine what comes next. If the bit is set, which means the value was stored in encoded form, we do not need to read the HBA and must proceed to decode the value. In this case, the power consumption of the cache is reduced. However, if the value is stored in unencoded form, we proceed to access the remainder of the word from the HBA. Since the read from the LBA and the read from the HBA is serialized, it takes longer to read a non-frequent value than it would have taken to read the same value from a conventional cache.

The hope is to reduce the energy consumed in the data array by accessing as much as possible the LBA. The reduction in energy comes at a cost of an additional cycle needed to access non-frequent values. Thus, the PA-DFVC design trades power for performance.

In this design, we assume that the $\log_2 N$ bits from the LBA are accessed in one cycle and we account for an additional cycle when the HBA is accessed. Recall that we account for one cycle for the conventional cache. In fact, this is true only if the time spent to encode/decode a value does not impact the overall latency. In order to meet this condition, we turn our attention to set-associative caches. In other words, the target for comparison are the cache architectures whose (pipelined) access time is defined by the tag-array and not the data array. As long as the time spent to perform tag matching is greater than the time spent to read the data plus the time to do the encoding/decoding, no additional overhead will be introduced in our PA-DFVC compared to a conventional cache.

Our XCACTI experiments show that the access times of a conventional cache and the PA-DFVC are the same for a $\log_2 N$ range up 7 bits. In our XCACTI experiments, we use the cache model adopted by Yang and Gupta [23,26]. This cache model, initially presented by Ghose and Kamble [9], is based in a subbanking scheme and has the advantage that each word (within a cache line) can be read independently without the need to read the whole cache line. The same model was used by Villa et al. [22] in their dynamic zero compression scheme. The results of the PA-DFVC, in terms of Energy-Delay Product and power reduction, are presented in Section 5.2.

4.3 Design Issues of High-Performance DFVC (HP-DFVC)

Our dynamic cache compression technique can be used to improve the behavior of the L1 cache by increasing its effective capacity. Cache/Memory compression has been proposed for better utilization of the available transistor budgets [1,13,22]. The idea behind this approach is to store cache lines in a compressed form so a greater number of cache lines can reside in the cache at any given time, lowering the miss rate.

Yang and Gupta [25] proposed a compressed L1 cache design where each set can store either one uncompressed line or two compressed lines. A static dictionary was used in their design. We solve the problem of keeping the cache and the dictionary

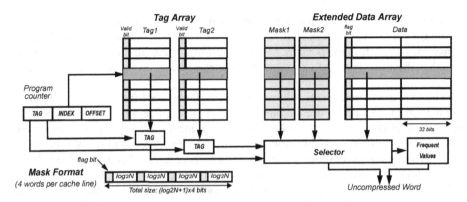

Fig. 4. HP-DFVC: detailed design

contexts consistent, and we evaluate our approach using their framework. The overall scheme works as follows: we assume that each cache line of $2L$ words can store either one uncompressed line or two compressed cache lines. If the line cannot be compressed to L words we keep it in uncompressed form. However, if two lines, each of which has been compressed to L words, map to the same cache line, they can reside in that line simultaneously. The architecture of the design is shown in Fig. 4.

As we can see, the cache entries must be accordingly modified to indicate whether or not they contain compressed lines. A flag bit is used for this purpose. We must also modify the entries so that they can hold the relevant information for the two compressed cache lines. Each line has its own tag (Tag1, Tag2) and a valid bit. In addition, the mask fields (Mask1, Mask2) provide useful information for the compressed lines. The determination of a cache hit is as follows: if there is a tag match and the valid bit is set, we have a hit. The retrieval of a word requires examining the mask. If the mask indicates that the word is compressed, then the mask provides the index of the dictionary entry that holds the value in a compressed form. Conversely, if the mask indicates that the value is not compressed, it specifies the location of the word in the cache line where it is stored in uncompressed form. We refer the reader to the work of Yang and Gupta [25] for more details about this design. The results of our evaluation for the HP-DFVC are presented in Section 5.3. The target for comparison is an uncompressed cache of larger capacity.

4.4 Compression/Decompression of Already Cached Data

Compression techniques have been initially used for instructions because code is not modified by a running program. Data compression techniques are harder to design because data values change as the program runs. This means that when cached data are modified, opportunities may arise to compress a previously uncompressed line. Our experiments show that compression opportunities for already cached data are rare for most benchmarks used in this paper. Thus, to simplify our designs we do not support compression of cached data —this can happen only when they are brought in the cache.

Furthermore, if an infrequent value is written on a compressed word, the need to uncompress the line may arise. In this case we immediately uncompress the whole cache line, possibly evicting its neighboring compressed line in the case of HP-DFVC.

5 Dynamic Frequent Value Cache Evaluation

5.1 Evaluation Methodology

To evaluate the effectiveness of our proposals, we perform simulations using Wattch [3], a detailed cycle level simulator which tracks dynamic power for each CPU structure. The processor model is based on the Alpha 21264. The execution core is 4-wide superscalar. The memory hierarchy includes a unified, 8-way set-associative, 1MB L2 cache. The latency of the main memory is 120 cycles. This configuration reflects prior work that examines the trade-off between power and performance using a static dictionary [23,25,26]. We use process parameters for a 130 nm technology and XCACTI 2.0 [10] to estimate all the modifications required by the proposed design. For the L1 data cache, we assume a decay interval of 8K cycles [12]. The same decay interval is used for the dictionary as explained in Section 3. We do not count leakage reduction from decay in our power consumption results —only dynamic power— since this would obscure the power benefit of compression.

The benchmarks suite for this study consists of a set of six SPEC2000 benchmarks (4 integer and 2 floating-point): *gzip*, *vpr*, *mesa*, *galgel*, *mcf* and *parser*, compiled for the Alpha ISA. For each program, we skip the first billion committed instructions to avoid unrepresentative startup behavior at the beginning of the program's execution, and then we simulate 200 million committed instructions using the reference input set.

5.2 Evaluation of the Power-Aware DFVC (PA-DFVC)

The main result of this Section is that cache compression using a dynamic dictionary leads to a more power efficient solution compared to the static/training dictionary approach. We conduct experiments using two cache configurations: an 8KB, 16-bytes-per-line, 4-way set associative cache and a 64KB, 32-bytes-per-line, 8-way set associative cache. Recall that the requirement for set-associativity is dictated by the need to hide the compression/decompression latency, as explained in Section 4.2.

Fig. 5 depicts the percent of hits in the frequent value dictionary (the left graph shows the results for the 8K cache configuration, while the right graph depicts the results for the 64K case). We compare our dynamic approach with static (referred as ideal in [24]) and training dictionaries of equal sizes. The static dictionary is created by profiling the benchmarks. The training dictionary is created by snooping at run time the values accessed during the first 10% of the program's execution, which are then used for the reminder of the run. The vertical bars in both graphs represent the static, training, and the dynamic techniques respectively. The light (bottom) bars stand for a dictionary size of 32 entries; every additional darker segment on top shows the increase in the dictionary hit ratio when a 64, 128 and 256 (darkest bar) entry dictionary is used.

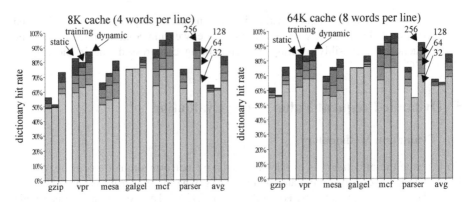

Fig. 5. Dictionary hit ratio using static, training and dynamic dictionary

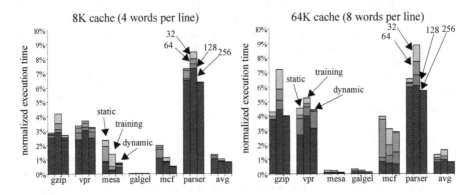

Fig. 6. Execution time for the static, training and the dynamic dictionary (normalized to non-decayed cache)

As we can see from Fig. 5, the static and the training approaches are fairly close. The static approach yields better results for *gzip*, *vpr*, and *parser*, while the training dictionary seems a better solution for *mesa* and *mcf*. Both approaches have almost the same behavior in *galgel*. The dynamic dictionary technique outperforms the other two techniques in all benchmarks independently of the dictionary size. The improvement (average for both cache configurations) for a 256-entry dictionary is 18% and 21% compared to the static and to the training dictionary approaches respectively. In fact, the hit ratio in *mcf* of the 256-entry dynamic dictionary reaches the 99%. The results are analogous with dictionaries of smaller sizes.

The superiority of our approach can be seen when another metric is used for comparison: the execution time of the program. Recall that we account for one cycle when a hit takes place in a compressed word and two cycles when a hit occurs in an uncompressed word. As a consequence, smaller dictionaries increase the program's execution time, since more cache accesses follow the slow path (touch nonfrequent values). The slow down in execution time decreases as the size of the dictionary increases. Fig. 6 shows this trend. The darkest (bottom) bars represent a dictionary size of 256

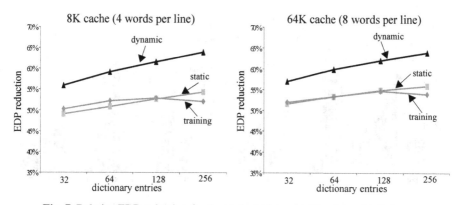

Fig. 7. Relative EDP reduction for the static, training and the dynamic dictionary

entries (minimal slow down) and every additional darker segment on top shows the increase in the execution time when a 128-, 64-, and 32- (lighter bar) entry dictionary is used.

Fig. 6 shows that our approach results in an increase in execution time less than 1% (average) even when a dictionary of 32 entries is used. In *parser*, which experiences the largest increases in execution time, the difference in execution time of the dynamic technique and the training technique is almost 3%.

We also use Wattch and XCACTI to estimate the relative Energy-Delay Product (EDP) reduction for the cache and for the three approaches we examine. The savings in the relative EDP, shown in Fig. 7, are substantial for the two cache configurations we examine. As we can see, our solution achieves up to 64% reduction in EDP compared to a non-decayed cache and nearly 10% reduction relative to the two other approaches, indicating that our solution is better for power-sensitive systems (i.e. portable devices).

5.3 Evaluation of the High-Performance DFVC (HP-DFVC)

In this section, we evaluate the effectiveness of the dynamic dictionary as opposed to increasing the effective capacity of the L1 data cache. As we explain in Section 4.3, the idea in this case is to store a cache line in a compressed form so that a greater number of cache lines can fit in the cache simultaneously and thus lower the miss rate.

Again, we consider two compressed cache configurations: a 4KB, 16-byte-per-line, and a 16KB, 32-byte-per-line. The compressed caches can accommodate up to two compressed lines per cache line. The targets for comparison are a conventional direct-mapped cache (DM) of equal size and a conventional 2-way cache of double size. Recall that, in the high-performance case, the design of the compressed cache necessities a doubling of the tag array and an increase of the data array by 2 bytes per cache line. We assume 3 cycles for the compressed cache, because in this case the compression/ decompression latency cannot be hidden by the tag comparison. We validated this model using the XCACTI simulator. Thus, in the first configuration the comparison is among a 4K, 2-cycle, direct mapped cache, our 3-cycle compressed cache (which yields an effective capacity of about 5K) and an 8K, 2-way, 3 cycle uncompressed cache.

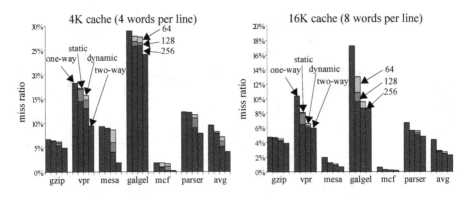

Fig. 8. Reduction in miss rates using static and dynamic dictionary

The cache miss rates (absolute numbers) for the six benchmarks are shown in Fig. 8. The right graph shows the results for the 4KB cache, while in the left graph presents the results for the 16KB cache. There are four bars per benchmark: the leftmost bar shows the miss rate for the DM cache, the next two bars represent the compressed cache using the static and the dynamic dictionary respectively, and the rightmost bar represents the 2-way uncompressed cache (of larger capacity). Similarly to previous graphs, for the compressed caches, the darkest (bottom) bars correspond to the 256-entry dictionaries and the two additional darker segments above show the increase in miss ratio with 128- and a 64-entry dictionaries.

For the majority of the benchmarks, the compressed-cache miss rate —for both the static and the dynamic dictionaries— is very close to the 2-way cache and is clearly better than the DM cache. Of course, our approach offers better improvements over the static case especially for the 4KB cache (left graph). For example, in *parser*, the compression using a static dictionary offers only a slight drop in miss ratio (< 0.2%) compared to the DM cache, while the dynamic approach manages to lower the miss ratio by 3%. This is a relative improvement of 26.5%. On average the DFVC improves the miss ratio by 45% for the 4KB cache and 44% for the 16KB cache, while the static approach achieves a 18% and 36% improvement for the two configurations we examined.

6   Related Work

Compression in Memory Components. Most schemes for cache compression are proposed for power/energy savings rather than performance. The idea behind such schemes is simple: unused storage cells and wires provide a benefit simply by not consuming power. In the Dynamic Zero Compression scheme [22], each zero valued byte is represented by a single bit. Another approach for power/energy reduction was by Kim et al. [13]. The authors exploit small sign-extended values by compressing the upper portion of a word to a single bit if it is all 1s or all 0s. Recently, the idea of compressing the sign-extended values was further refined [18]. The goal in this case was to increase the apparent capacity of the L1 data caches.

As we have already mentioned, our work is inspired by frequent value locality shown by Zhang et al. [26] and subsequently by Yang et al. [23,25]. This value locality motivates their initial approach to increase the effective capacity of the L1 cache [23] and their latter approach to reduce the power consumption of the cache [25]. Alameldeen and Wood exploit value locality in their Frequent Pattern Compression algorithm applied to L2 caches [1]. They observe that some data patterns, are frequent and compressible. This work can be considered as the only adaptive compression mechanism for hardware caches but relies on a compression mechanism that is too slow, expensive, and power-consuming for L1.

Lee et al. [14,15] propose a compressed memory hierarchy, called Selective Compressed Memory System (SCMS), that selectively compresses L2 cache and memory blocks that can be reduced to half their original size. The idea of the SCMS was recently further investigated by Hallnor and Reindardt [11]. Their design allows blocks to be compressed in variable amounts of storage according to their compressability. Their results show a significant benefit from this flexibility. Chen et al. [4] propose a scheme that dynamically partitions the cache into sections of different compressability.

The compression technique was applied in many commercial products too. In IBM's Memory Expansion Technology (MXT) [21], all main-memory data is stored in compressed form. A hardware engine built into the memory controller manages compression/decompression transparently to software. However, to reduce decompression latency for misses in the on-chip caches, the MXT memory controller includes a large (32 MB) off-chip uncompressed cache. Recently, Ekman and Stenstrom [6], attacked the problem of the long decompression latency in main memory compression schemes by using a simple but very effective compression technique. Their mechanism (inspired by the frequent value approach) introduces negligible decompression latency. Thus, their method does not rely on huge caches.

Compression in Communication Channels. There has been a significant amount of research on reducing address/data bus swithching activity. Work dedicated to address buses such as Bus Expander [5], Dynamic Base Register Caching [7], and Working Zone Encoding [17], is based on the sequentiality of program counters and regularity of memory accesses . These techniques have been re-evaluated for data buses. In this case, the benefits were significantly reduced, since these schemes fail to exploit locality in non-contiguous bit positions.

The work that applies to data buses includes variants of directory-based solutions. Frequent Value Encoding [24] is a data bus encoding scheme capable of encoding entire data values. FVMSBLSB [20] stores the MSB portions and the LSB portions of values in separate tables. While encoding MSB/LSB portions alone, the remaining portion of the data are sent unencoded. Recently, Suruch et al. [19] proposed a scheme, called TUBE, which captures chunks of varying widths from data values. Finally, Basu et al. [2] proposed a value cache at both ends of a memory channel. During a hit, the index to the cache entry is sent instead of the whole word.

7 Conclusions

In this paper, we propose the first mechanism —to best the of our knowledge— for dynamic dictionary-based compression for L1 data caches. Our approach relies on the frequent value locality. In contrast to the previously proposed dictionaries for cache compression, the context of our dictionary dynamically adjusts to the requirements of a running program. We solve the problem of keeping the cache state and the dictionary state consistent by decaying the cache/dictionary in exactly the same way. Decayed entries in the dictionary are available for replacement by new frequent values without worrying about dependencies with the cache compressed data (no live cache line can possible refer to a decayed dictionary entry). Thus, we adapt the contents of the directory to the set of frequent values that are most relevant at any point in the execution.

We evaluate our adaptive compression technique using full system simulation and a range of benchmarks. Our dynamic scheme provides an improvement in the relative EDP of the cache up to 10% compared to the static and training approaches leading to a more power-efficient solution. When high performance is the target for optimization, our proposal yields 45% reduction in miss rate compared to a conventional cache of the same capacity and up to 27% improvement over the static dictionary technique.

References

1. A. Alameldeen and D. Wood. Adaptive Cache Compression for High-Performance Processors. 31st International Symposium on Computer Architecture, 2004.
2. K. Basu, et al. Power protocol: Reducing Power Dissipation on Off-Chip Data Buses. 35th International Symposium on Microarchitecture, 2002.
3. D. Brooks, et al. Wattch: A framework for Architectural-level power analysis and optimizations. 27th International Symposium on Computer Architecture, 2000.
4. D. Chen, et al. A Dynamically Partitionable Compressed Cache. Singapore -MIT Alliance Symposium, 2003.
5. D. Citron and L. Rudolph. Creating a Wider Bus using Caching Techniques. 1st Symposium on High Performance Computer Architecture, 1995.
6. M. Ekman and P. Stenstrom. A Robust Main-Memory Compression Scheme. 32nd International Symposium on Computer Architecture, 2005.
7. M. Farrens and A. Park. Dynamic Base Register Caching: A technique for Reducing Address Bus width. 18th International Symposium on Computer Architecture, 1991.
8. F. Gabbay and A. Mendelson. Can Program Profiling Support Value Prediction?. 30th International Symposium on Microarchitecture, 1997.
9. K. Ghose and M. B. Kamble. Reducing Power in Superscalar Processor Caches using Subbanking, Multiple Line Buffers, and Bit Line Segmentation. International Symposium on Low Power Electronics and Design, 1999.
10. M. Huang, et al. L1 Data Cache Decomposition for Energy Efficiency. International Symposium on Low Power Electronics and Design, 2001.
11. E. Hallnor and S. Reinhardt. A Unified Compressed Memory Hierarchy. 11th Symposium on High Performance Computer Architecture, 2005.
12. S. Kaxiras, et al. Cache Decay: Exploiting Generational Behavior to Reduce Cache Leakage Power. 28th International Symposium on Computer Architecture, 2001.
13. D. Kim, et al. Low-Energy Data Cache using Sign Compression and Cache Line Bisection. Workshop on Memory Performance Issues, 2002.
14. J.S. Lee, et al. An On-chip Cache Compression Technique to Reduce Decompression Overhead and Design Complexity. Journal of Systems Architecture, 2000.

15. J.S. Lee, et al. Adaptive Methods to Minimize Decompression Overhead for Compressed On-chip Cache. International Journal of Computers and Application, 2003.
16. M. Lipasti, et al. Value Locality and Load Value Prediction. 7th International Conference on Architectural Support for Programming Languages and Operating Systems, 1996.
17. E. Musoll, et al. Working Zone Encoding for Reducing the Energy in Microprocessor Address Buses. Transaction on VLSI Systems, 1998.
18. P. Pujara and A. Aggarwal. Restrictive Compression Techniques to Increase Level 1 Cache Capacity. International Conference on Computer Design, 2005.
19. D. Suresh, et al. Tunable Bus Encoder for Off-Chip Data Buses. International Symposium on Low Power Electronics and Design, 2001.
20. D. Suresh, et al. Power Efficient Encoding Techniques for Off-Chip Data Buses. International Conference on Compilers, Architecture, and Synthesis for Embedded Systems, 2003.
21. R. Tremaine, et al. Pinnacle: IBM MXT in a Memory Controller Chip. IEEE Micro, 2001.
22. L. Villa, et al. Dynamic Zero Compression for Cache Energy Reduction. 33rd International Symposium on Microarchitecture, 2000.
23. J. Yang and R. Gupta. Frequent Value Locality and its Applications. Transactions on Embedded Computing Systems, 2002.
24. J. Yang and R. Gupta. Frequent Value Encoding for Low Power Buses. Transanctions on Embedded Computing Systems, 2004.
25. J. Yang, et al. Frequent Value Compression in Data Caches. 33rd International Symposium on Microarchitecture, 2000.
26. Y. Zhang, et al. Frequent Value Locality and Value-centric Data Cache Design. 9th International Conference on Architectural Support for Programming Languages and Operating Systems, 2000.

A Case for Dual-Mapping One-Way Caches

Arul Sandeep Gade and Yul Chu

Department of Electrical and Computer Engineering,
Mississippi State University,
P. O. Box 9571, Mississippi State, MS 39762-9571, USA
{asg41, chu}@ece.msstate.edu

Abstract. This paper proposes a dual-mapping function for one-way data cache to reduce cache misses, write-back rates, and access time for single-core or multi-core computing processors. Our simulation results show that it reduces cache misses significantly compared to any conventional L1 caches. Simple Scalar simulator has been used for these simulations with SPEC95FP and Minne SPEC2000FP benchmark programs. In addition, it has a simple hardware complexity similar to that of a 2-way SAC (set-associative cache). The proposed cache has good AMAT (average memory access time) compared to a 2-way cache and also uses fewer execution cycles. Simulations over CACTI were performed to evaluate the hardware implications as well.

1 Introduction

For an application program, there are two types of memory references: instruction references and data references. Much of the processor execution time is wasted if it has to wait a long time for data from slow memory (DRAM). An analysis of the simulations performed by Mowry *et al.* [1] reveals that the programs for scientific applications spend nearly one-fourth to one-half of the total processor execution time in waiting to fetch the data from the memory.

The need for a fast and efficient data cache is essential not only for single-core (or multi-core) processors to perform scientific applications but also for network routers (or switches) to store and retrieve large routing tables [2]. Though the existing small-sized (8KB to 64 KB) fast L1 caches provide fairly good access times, they fail to exploit the spatial and temporal localities associated with the data references [3][4]. In addition, they suffer from high conflict misses causing frequent thrashing of data.

Table 1 shows L1 (Level one) on-chip caches of current microprocessors, including the following: 1) 2-way and 4-way mapping functions are popular for the L1 data cache; 2) L1 cache sizes are in between 8KB and 64 KB; 3) Multi-level on-chip caches (L1 to L3) can be popular for future multiprocessors.

In general, since the L1 cache needs to be matched with the CPU clock speed, a small-sized and fast L1 cache is a must: 1-way (direct-mapped) is better than 2-way or 4-way from a cost and speed point of view. However, its cache misses are much higher than those of 2-way or 4-way. Therefore, most current processors have used 2-way or 4-way instead of 1-way, as you see in the Table 1.

W. Grass et al. (Eds.): ARCS 2006, LNCS 3894, pp. 130–144, 2006.
© Springer-Verlag Berlin Heidelberg 2006

Table 1. Cache schemes for current microprocessors. 12KB*: 12 KB Trace cache.

	L1 (Level one) cache		L2 cache	L3 cache
	Instruction	Data		
Intel Itanium II	16KB, 4-way	*16KB, 4-way*	256KB	3-6 MB
Intel P4	12KB*	*8KB, 4-way*	256KB	
Intel PIII	16KB, 4-way	*16KB, 4-way*	256KB	
AMD Athlon	64KB, 2-way	*64KB, 2-way*	256KB	
PowerPC G5	64KB, 1-way	*32KB, 2-way*	512KB	
Alpha 21364	64KB, 2-way	*64KB, 2-way*	1.5MB	

There are two main factors to consider in designing cache architecture such as mapping function and replacement policy [5]. Conventional mapping schemes map an address onto a cache location with a fixed number of bits (index) extracted from the address. The index can point to a single location in Direct-mapped caches or to a set of locations in SACs (set-associative caches) [5]. Due to the numerous cache misses encountered in these conventional caches, researchers have begun to develop different mapping schemes such as Pseudo-3way Set-associative and Skewed-associative schemes to reduce conflict misses. For a small-sized cache, conflict misses (caused by competing for the same location of a cache) is the most critical to the system performance. All these mapping functions greatly depend on their replacement policies to deliver a lower cache miss-rate.

After designing a cache memory, performance of the cache architecture can be evaluated by using ET (execution time) and AMAT (average memory access time) [5]. ET and AMAT mainly depend on miss-rate, miss-penalty, and write-back rate (refer to section 5).

Therefore, our motivation has been in designing a *data cache* that can effectively reduce the miss-rate, write-back rate, and access time by exploiting the data in spatial and temporal localities.

The remainder of this paper is organized as follows: Section 2 introduces Pseudo 3-way Set-associative cache, Skewed-associative cache, and Dual-port memories; Section 3 explains the operation and architecture of the proposed cache; Section 4 briefly describes simulation methodology; Section 5 analyzes the simulation results and Section 6 provides conclusions of the paper.

2   Related Works

The *access time* and *miss-rate* might be two main factors in determining the data cache performance. However, it is difficult to reduce the access time and miss-rate simultaneously because the extra hardware components to reduce the miss-rate may come into the critical path in accessing the cache. Therefore, the major research over the cache memories has been on developing cache memory architectures to achieve lower miss-rates and less access times, and several cache architectures such as Pseudo 3-way set-associative (P3-way) cache [3] and Skewed-associative (Skew) cache [6] have been proposed to adapt memory-access behaviors [7].

The P3-way cache is developed based on the Multiple Access Cache (MAC) [3]. The miss-rate of a 2-way MAC has the same limitation as that of a 2-way SAC.

The similarity is due to the fixed alternative locations determined by hashing functions that use static methods to compute indexes. To overcome this limitation, P3-way cache was proposed. In this cache, when a reference is not found in a direct mapped location, one of the two different hashing functions is used to access an alternative location. The selection between the two functions depends on dynamic reference pattern. A bit-array table is used to indicate the hashing function that is to be used to determine an alternative location [3].

The miss-rates achieved by the P3-way cache are slightly better than 2-way SAC [3]. This achievement is due to the reduction in the conflicts between two more recently used cache locations by being able to access different alternative locations. However, the Skew cache outperforms this improvement since Skew cache works similar to 4-way SAC [3][6].

Even though the P3-way cache showed improvement in achieving lower miss-rates, it still determines the alternative locations in a static manner. This static nature may cause the P3-way cache fail to resolve conflict misses when three or more references index to the same location.

Conflict misses, as seen in conventional SACs and P3-way caches, are mainly caused due to statically-determined alternative locations. To eliminate such conflict misses, Seznec [6] introduced the Skew cache, which maps each address onto different cache lines using *XOR mapping functions* on separate banks. Fig. 1 shows the mapping in a 2-way Skew cache. The XOR mapping functions can decrease conflict misses by dispersing conflict-references onto a broad range of inter-bank and local locations in a bank.

An example showing the XOR functions used in a 2-way Skew cache is as follows: Each referenced address is split into certain parts, as shown in Fig. 1. Consider that the cache has 64 lines on each bank; consequently A1 and A2 have 6 bits each.

Let '$f_0(R) = A2 \oplus$ shuffle $(A1)$, and $f_1(R) = A2 \oplus \phi^1[$shuffle $(A1)]$' be the two XOR mapping functions chosen for mapping [8]. ϕ^1 [shuffle (A1)] gives the circular shifted value of the shuffled bits of A1. The shuffling can be done by accumulating even bits towards the most significant locations and odd bits towards the least

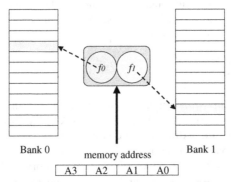

Bank 0   memory address   Bank 1

| A3 | A2 | A1 | A0 |

Each bank has different cache index because of two different mapping functions ($f0$ and $f1$).

Fig. 1. Address division and mapping in a 2-way skew-cache

significant locations. For instance, the shuffling of $A1 = (b_0\ b_1\ b_2\ b_3\ b_4\ b_5)$ by this method would generate a new bit sequence $A1' = (b_0\ b_2\ b_4\ b_1\ b_3\ b_5)$.

When both the mapping functions (f_0 and f_1) experience a cache-miss, a *pseudo-LRU replacement policy* is followed [6].

It is important to note that the access time of the Skew cache is fairly small since neither shuffling operations nor circular shift operations need any hardware logic to implement. The only hardware requirement is a little extra routing to extend the incoming bits from *A1 and A2* to *XOR gates* and then to *the memory*. All these XOR gates operate in parallel and account to only 1 XOR gate delay. Also, a 2-way Skew cache is shown to have hardware complexity similar to a 2-way SAC and obtains a miss-rate similar to a 4-way SAC [6].

However, the Skew cache has its own drawbacks: First, the ability of the Skew cache to map data to well-dispersed locations is limited by the size of banks. For example, for a Skew cache with $N \times L$ (index $\times$ cache line size) KB, each XOR function is free to disperse the conflicting addresses onto $N/2$ locations only. Thus, multiple small banks might make a Skew cache fail to minimize the conflict misses. Second, the LRU replacement policy in a Skew cache is hard to implement at a reasonable hardware cost [9]. Also, the replacement policy lacks the ability to provide equal preferences for all the blocks in bank1 compared to those in bank0.

A *dual-port cache* inherits its architecture from multi-port SRAMs. Multi-port SRAMs are generally used with multi-processors, which are capable of processing more than one instruction at a time. According to [10][11], the benefits/drawbacks of using a dual-port cache over a single-port cache are as follows:

1) Performance/Improved Bandwidth: Two locations in a dual-port cache can be simultaneously accessed which effectively doubles the bandwidth (benefit); and
2) Area and logic savings: A dual-port cache could save some extra logic requirements and area compared to *duplicated single-port caches* (benefit). However, the area of dual-port cache is bigger than *a (instead of duplicated) single-port cache* (drawback); and
3) Power savings: The dual-port cache power depends on how complex the support logic around the single-port SRAM array is. If the support logic is designed to implement full address arbitration and/or any other logic functions such as semaphore logic, then the *duplicated single-port (not dual-port cache) memories* consume significant power (benefit); and
4) Accesses: The second port of a dual-port cache might be accessed less than the primary port (drawback).

Therefore, the dual-port cache would work effectively for improving system performance if the above drawbacks, 2 and 4, are resolved. In this paper, we propose Pseudo-Direct Cache (PDC) that uses Dual-Mapping Function (DMF) to reduce drawbacks of dual-port cache and power consumption.

3 1-Way Cache with DMF

This paper proposes a 1-way cache memory called PDC (Pseudo-Direct Cache) that successfully exploits more data localities and attains lower miss-rates. The proposed

Pseudo-Direct Cache (PDC) works like a 1-way cache except for accessing two locations simultaneously with two different XOR mapping functions, which is called DMF (Dual-Mapping Function). These functions index a data reference onto two separate cache lines over the entire cache space. Also, unlike SAC, PDC can dynamically map each reference in a set of conflicting addresses to different locations depending on the address bits. According to our simulation results, *it is rare for two XOR mapping functions to access to the same locations simultaneously in a cache memory (much less than 0.001%).* Therefore, PDC enables conflicting references to map well-dispersed locations; thereby reducing the number of conflict misses. The dispersion space available for these mapping functions is double in PDC than in 2-way Skew cache. For example, each mapping function of the 32-KB PDC with a block size of 32 bytes can index onto any of the available 1024 lines. On the other hand, each function of the 2-way Skew cache can index onto only 512 lines. Thus, PDC is more effective in reducing the number of conflict misses than both Skew cache and SAC. To keep the conflict misses low, the PDC uses a Pseudo-Direct LRU (PDLRU) replacement policy that effectively selects the least recently used line for replacement. In this section, we present the working of the PDC, along with flow-chart for PDLRU, followed by hardware architecture and effects on hit-time and miss-penalty.

The PDC works as follows: On each reference, the PDC probes two distinct cache lines simultaneously to search for a referenced data. Each line is made to hold two 1-bit flags (*mapfn* and *altmap*) that are initially set as 1 (set (1)):

1) '*mapfn*' is used to recognize the mapping function that is responsible for the data stored in a cache line;
2) When a cache-line mapped by f_0 causes a cache-hit, *altmap* flag on that line is reset as 0 (reset (0)), and *altmap* flag on the line mapped by f_1 is set (1) and vice-versa. A cache line having *altmap*=0 indicates that the line is recently used.

The PDC uses the PDLRU replacement policy, developed to give equal preference to all the lines in the cache. This policy overcomes the biased nature of the replacement policy used in a Skew cache. The major functioning of the PDLRU policy is described as follows as shown in Fig. 2:

-   When a cache-miss occurs, if the *altmap* in f_0 indexed cache line (*altmap-f_0*) is found as reset (0), the PDLRU policy selects the line indexed by f_1 for replacement. It then resets the *altmap* in f_1 indexed cache line (*altmap-f_1*) and sets *altmap-f_0* flag. Setting the *altmap* bit indicates that the corresponding cache line is the least recently used among the current pair of cache lines.
-   On the contrary, if the *altmap-f_0* flag is found as *set (1)*, the PDLRU policy chooses the line mapped by f_0 for replacement. Here, it sets *altmap-f_1* and resets *altmap-f_0*.
-   For each replacement, the flag *mapfn* is as set (1) when the cache line is mapped with the first function (f_0) and as reset (0) otherwise.

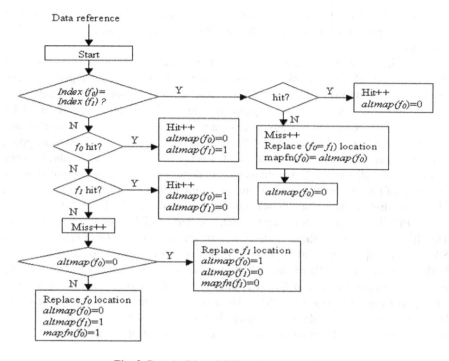

Fig. 2. Pseudo-Direct LRU replacement policy

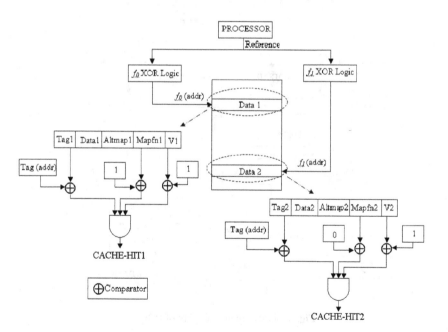

Fig. 3. PDC Architecture for checking cache hit and miss

According to the experimental results, the Pseudo-Direct LRU policy works well in giving equal preference to all the cache lines by exploiting the random nature of data references.

In Fig. 3, the hardware implementation of PDC needs slightly more extra resources than conventional cache implementations. As we discussed, a dual-port (SRAM) memory is used by the PDC to access two cache lines simultaneously on each reference. Additional extra hardware required by the PDC includes bit-XORs used for XOR mapping computation, comparators and multiplexers used with *mapfn* and *altmap* control bits, and certain AND/OR gates as shown in Fig. 3. The XOR mapping functions f_0 and $f1$ require computation of several XOR operations to obtain cache indexes. Since all the XOR operations can be done in parallel, this computation has the delay of only a single 2-input XOR gate. This makes the cache access time of a PDC to be slightly more, but almost equal to the access time of a 2-way SAC.

The PDLRU replacement policy is similar to that of LRU policy in a 2-way SAC. The difference between these policies lies in the LRU-bit update cycle. A 2-way SAC requires updating a single LRU bit in only one of the two cache lines on a two-bank memory. On the other hand, a PDC requires updating of LRU bits in both the cache lines mapped by f_0 and f_1 over a single bank of memory. Thus, when a single write port memory is used for a PDC, the miss-penalty increases by one write cycle. However, using a two-write port memory eliminates this increase. Therefore, a trade-off exits in the form of memory complexity versus miss-penalty in a PDC.

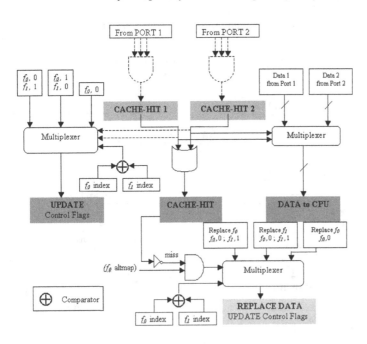

Fig. 4. Hardware architecture of PDC

Additionally, the 3-input AND gate and the 3-input Multiplexer in the replacement determination path slightly increases the miss-penalty of a PDC as compared to a 2-way SAC. The 2-way SAC uses both these gates, but each has only two inputs. This similarity in the replacement determination path makes the miss-penalty of PDC very close to the miss-penalty of a 2-way SAC. However, the exact amount of time by which the miss-penalty differs depends on implementation technology. As we discussed, Figures 3 and 4 show the overall hardware architecture of the PDC. In these figures, $(f_0, 0)$ implies f_0 location's *altmap* is '0' and $(f_0, 1)$ implies f_0 location's *altmap* is '1'. So is $(f_1, 0)$ and $(f_1, 1)$.

4 Simulation Methodology

This paper evaluates the Pseudo-Direct mapping scheme for an on-chip, first-level (L1) data cache. The conventional caches including the 2-way Skew cache are also evaluated and compared with the Pseudo-Direct cache.

These evaluations were done based on execution-driven simulations of the SPEC95FP and MinneSPEC2000FP benchmarks [12][16]. These benchmarks are compiled for the SimpleScalar PISA instruction set with no optimizations. A second-level direct mapped data cache that can only affect the overall miss-penalty is assumed to be present.

Simulations are performed for different cache sizes that ranged from 8 to 32 KB. For each cache size, different line sizes ranging from 8 to 32 bytes were employed. SimpleScalar Toolset (3.0 version) is used to perform these simulations. Fig. 5 gives a detailed evaluation methodology of a cache design using a SimpleScalar simulator and SPEC95/SPEC2000 benchmarks.

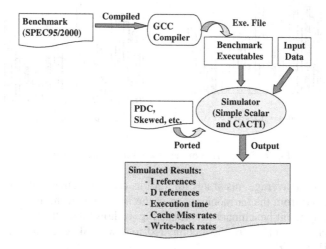

Fig. 5. Simulation Methodology

Out of the variety of simulators that SimpleScalar offers, sim-cache is used for evaluating the different cache designs. Sim-cache is a functional simulator that is ideal for fast simulation of caches [13].

CACTI 3.0 simulator is also used to obtain the access times and delays of different components for various cache organizations [14]. For a given cache organization, CACTI will detail all possible internal configurations and chooses the one with the best-weighted value. Simulations were performed giving equal consideration to latency, energy, and area. The simulations used 0.1um and 0.2um technologies for implementing different cache organizations.

The *miss-rates and write-back rates* obtained from SimpleScalar, and *the access times and delays* obtained from CACTI are used to calculate the performance metrics.

5   Simulation Results

This section presents the simulation results of different cache organizations along with performance improvement of PDC. Since the miss-rates of Skew cache [6] are lower than that of P3–way cache [3], only the former is implemented for simulation verification and comparison. Due to limited space, only the results for those caches with a block size of 16 bytes and 32 bytes are presented.

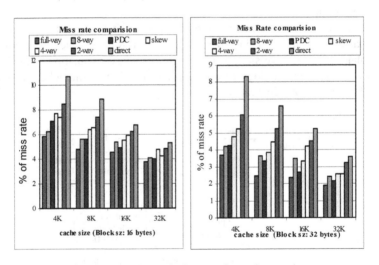

Fig. 6. Comparison of miss rates for various caches

Fig. 6 shows the average miss-rates for various cache schemes. The average miss-rates are obtained from the harmonic mean of the miss-rates from the results with the SPEC95 floating-point benchmark programs. Fig. 6 shows that PDC can reduce miss-rates more than 10% (10% to 20%) compared to 2-way Skew cache for 4 different cache sizes (4K to 32K).

Fig. 7 gives the conflict miss-rates for various cache schemes. These conflict miss-rates are computed as '*miss-rate of a cache – miss-rate of a full-way cache*'

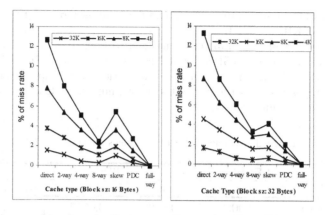

Fig. 7. Conflict miss rates for various caches

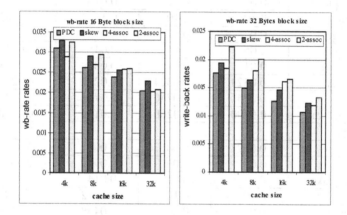

Fig. 8. Write-back rates for various caches

since we consider there is no conflict miss in a full-way set-associative (full-way) cache. In Fig. 7, PDC can reduce conflict misses significantly compared to other caches, and its conflict miss-rates are almost close to an 8-way SAC. Fig. 7 also shows that the conflict miss-rates of a 2-way Skew cache are close to that of a 4-way SAC and are higher than a PDC.

One of the ways to reduce the cache miss-penalty is to reduce the traffic amount between cache and main memory. The frequency of this traffic depends on the number of write-backs performed by the cache. Thus, a reduction in the write-back rate not only improves the CPU execution times but also reduces the power consumption. In general, a cache that causes lower power consumption is ideal for embedded processors. Fig. 8 shows the average write-back rates for 4 different cache schemes. The average write-back rates are obtained from the harmonic mean of the simulation results from all SPEC95 floating-point benchmark programs. Fig. 8 shows that, on an average, PDC can reduce write-back rates 6%-15% more than 2-way Skew cache.

Fig. 8 illustrates this comparative reduction in the write-back rates for the cache sizes of 4KB, 8KB, 16KB, and 32KB.

Similar type of reduction in the miss-rates and write-back rates by the PDC (over Skew) are seen for the MinneSPEC2000FP benchmarks as well. Since these benchmarks have relatively less number of associated spatial and temporal localities, the reduction of miss-rates and write-back rates is not eminent. Table 2 shows the results for these benchmark simulations in detail.

Table 2. Detailed miss-rates and write-back rates for MinneSPEC2000FP

	SKEW		PDC	
4K	miss-rate	wb-rate	miss-rate	wb-rate
wupwise	0.0088	0.0088	0.0072	0.0072
swim	0.10	0.10	0.0953	0.0953
equake	0.02	0.02	0.018	0.018
ammp	0.10	0.10	0.1042	0.1042
mgrid	0.07	0.07	0.0577	0.0576
applu	0.05	0.05	0.0455	0.0455
mesa	0.01	0.01	0.0058	0.0058
apsi	0.0324	0.0324	0.0297	0.0297
art	0.0746	0.0746	0.0741	0.0741
HMean	**0.0200**	**0.0200**	**0.0190**	**0.0190**
8K				
wupwise	0.0077	0.0077	0.006	0.006
swim	0.09	0.09	0.094	0.094
equake	0.01	0.01	0.014	0.014
ammp	0.10	0.10	0.0992	0.0991
mgrid	0.06	0.06	0.0458	0.0458
applu	0.04	0.04	0.0421	0.0421
mesa	0.00	0.00	0.0042	0.0042
apsi	0.0247	0.0247	0.0223	0.0223
art	0.0736	0.0736	0.0738	0.0738
HMean	**0.0166**	**0.0166**	**0.0150**	**0.0150**
16K				
wupwise	0.0061	0.0061	0.0056	0.0056
swim	0.09	0.09	0.0927	0.0927
equake	0.01	0.01	0.0116	0.0116
ammp	0.09	0.09	0.0834	0.0833
mgrid	0.04	0.04	0.0401	0.0401
applu	0.04	0.04	0.0401	0.0401
mesa	0.00	0.00	0.0031	0.0031
apsi	0.0213	0.0213	0.0203	0.0203
art	0.0733	0.0733	0.0735	0.0735
HMean	**0.0127**	**0.0127**	**0.0125**	**0.0124**

	SKEW		PDC	
32K	miss-rate	wb-rate	miss-rate	wb-rate
wupwise	0.0063	0.0063	0.0054	0.0054
swim	0.09	0.09	0.088	0.088
equake	0.01	0.01	0.0104	0.0104
ammp	0.08	0.08	0.0957	0.0956
mgrid	0.04	0.04	0.0334	0.0334
applu	0.04	0.04	0.038	0.038
mesa	0.00	0.00	0.0028	0.0028
apsi	0.0204	0.0204	0.0191	0.0191
art	0.0731	0.0731	0.0734	0.0734
HMean	**0.0121**	**0.0121**	**0.0115**	**0.0115**
64K				
wupwise	0.0054	0.0054	0.0052	0.0052
swim	0.09	0.09	0.0808	0.0808
equake	0.01	0.01	0.0095	0.0095
ammp	0.10	0.10	0.0949	0.0949
mgrid	0.03	0.03	0.0278	0.0278
applu	0.04	0.04	0.0352	0.0352
mesa	0.00	0.00	0.0027	0.0027
apsi	0.0189	0.0189	0.0175	0.0175
art	0.0729	0.0729	0.0732	0.0732
HMean	**0.0112**	**0.0112**	**0.0109**	**0.0109**

The CPU execution time for a cache scheme can be computed by using the following equations [5]:

$$\text{CPU time} = (\text{CPU clock cycles} + \text{Memory\_stall cycles}) \times T,$$

$$\text{CPU clock cycles} = IC \times CPI,$$

Memory_stall cycles

$$= IC \times \{RPI \times [1 + Rmr \times MMAT \times (wbrate + 1)] + WPI \times [1 + Wmr \times MMAT \times (wbrate + 1)]\}$$

where T is the Time period of CPU clock, IC is Instruction Count, CPI is Cycles Per Instruction, Rmr is Read miss rate, $MMAT$ is main memory access time, $wbrate$ is write-back rate, RPI = (Reads/Instructions), and WPI = (Writes/Instructions).

We computed the execution times for turb3d benchmark program for PDC and 2-way skew cache separately and then compared. For these calculations, a single level split-cache memory is assumed to be present. A second level L2 cache is not considered, as its effect on both PDC and Skew would be the same. Also, the delay along the critical path for a PDC is assumed to be almost equal to that of a skew cache. Our computation results from turb3d benchmark program show that PDC performs approximately 1.1 times better than 2-way Skew cache.

The AMAT for PDC and Skew cache is computed for both 0.1um and 0.2um technologies. The Skew cache architecture is implemented in CACTI using the single port 2-bank memory. Similarly, the PDC architecture is implemented in CACTI using a two-port 1-bank memory. The total access delay for a single XOR gate in both PDC and Skew cache is assumed to be negligible. The additional delay due to the data

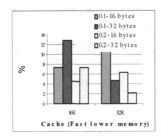 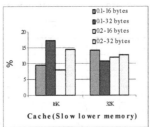

Fig. 9. Percentage reduction in AMAT for both memories

selection multiplexer (Dmux) in PDC is assumed the same as the Dmux delay in 2-way Skew cache.

In computing the AMAT, the hit times are obtained from the CACTI and the miss-rates get from the average miss-rates from our simulation results. These calculations were performed through typical fast memory types (Level 2 (L2): 20ns, main memory: 100ns) and typical slow memory types (L2: 60ns, main memory: 250ns) separately. Fig. 9 shows that PDC has 2-18 % lesser AMAT than Skew cache. This reduction in AMAT by PDC is better when slow lower level memories are used in the memory hierarchy. Therefore, PDC provides an advantage over Skew cache in applications that use slow lower level memories, which is cheaper than fast lower ones.

For a memory system consisting of L1 and L2 caches, where the miss rate in L2 cache (large size ≈ 1MB) is assumed to be negligible, the energy consumption (nano Joules) is given by the following equations:

- *Average energy consumed per instruction (nJ)*

$$= (Energy\ consumed\ on\ a\ hit + Energy\ consumed\ on\ a\ miss)$$

- *Average energy consumed on a hit = Hit rate × L1 energy*

$$= (1 - Miss\ rate) \times L1\ energy$$

- *Average energy consumed on a miss*

$$= Miss\ rate \times (L1\ energy + L2\ energy \times (1 + wbrate))$$

L1 and L2 energies are the energies required to access and check a location in L1 cache and L2 cache respectively. These energies are measured by using the CACTI simulator [14].

Our simulation results show that PDC consumes 30-50 % more energy than 1-way and 2-way SAC. In case of 4-way SAC, the PDC is observed to consume 4 % less energy for a 32 KB cache but 10% more energy for a 16 KB cache. When compared to 8-way SACs, the PDC is observed to consume 35-45 % less energy.

In order to reduce the increase in energy consumptions by PDC, the numbers of cache accesses are to be reduced. Since 90 % of the references are found on an L1 cache a small register buffer can eliminate the repeated accesses belonging to a spatial locality. The buffer can have a size of about 2 to 4 times of the block size of L1 cache. A similar idea is proposed in Caching on Cache (CoC) architecture developed for embedded systems [15]. The CoC is proposed as a small sub-cache in L1 caches. Simulations performed to evaluate the CoC energy consumption show that the CoC effectively reduces the energy consumption by about 45 % over a 1-way cache [15]. The results also show that the overhead on the performance (delay) is only 5.6% compared to 1-way cache. Therefore, PDC can make the energy consumption almost equal to 1-way and better than any of the SACs without much loss to its performance improvement. Currently, we are working on reducing power consumption by adding a small buffer and we expect 40 to 50% power savings for programs with high spatial locality.

6 Conclusions

The goal of this research is to develop an efficient cache scheme that could reduce access time, write-back rates, and cache misses for single-core or multi-core processors. An optimal cache scheme would be the one that can effectively keep the miss-rates to a minimum and also maintain fast access times. Efficient cache schemes such as P3-way and Skew cache were introduced. Although some performance gain is achieved by these schemes, both have certain drawbacks. The performance of the P3-way cache is limited by static methods employed in reducing the conflict misses. The performance of the Skew cache is limited by its restricted dispersing ability. Also, the replacement policy used in a Skew cache does not give equal preference to all the blocks in the cache.

This paper proposed a new cache architecture called PDC that effectively counters the drawbacks of both P3-way and Skew cache architectures. PDC reduces the number of conflict misses effectively by allowing conflicting addresses to be dynamically mapped over the entire cache space.

The simulation results over SPEC95FP and Minne SPEC2000FP benchmarks show that the PDC is successful in achieving an improvement of 10-20% reduction in the cache miss-rates compared to 2-way Skew cache. In addition, PDC has better miss-rates than 4-way SAC, has better execution times than Skew cache, and is expected to have data access time close to 2-way SAC. Finally, there would be a slight increase in the hardware cost to implement the design. However, the effect of the extra hardware on critical path delays is negligibly small.

Currently, we are working on reducing the power consumption for the PDC by adding a buffer. It can be expected to save energy by 40 to 50% for application programs with high spatial locality. The performance of this cache can be evaluated in shared memory environments, especially in network routers as well.

References

1. T. Mowry, M. Lam, and A. Gupta, Design and evaluation of a compiler algorithm for prefetching, *the Fifth International Conference on Architectural Support for Programming Languages and Operating Systems (ASPLOS-V)*, pages 62–73, Boston, MA, October 1992.
2. T. Wolf and J.S. Turner, Design Issues for High-Performance Active Routers, *IEEE Journal on Selected Areas in Communication*, vol. 19, no.3, pp. 404-409, March 2001
3. Yongjoon Lee, and Byung-Kwon Chung, Pseudo 3-way Set Associative Cache: A Way of Reducing Miss Ratio with Fast Access Time, *IEEE Canadian Conference on Electrical and Computer Engineering*, Edmonton, Alberta, Canada, May 9-12 1999.
4. Koji Inoue, Vasily G. Moshnyaga, *and* Kazuaki Murakami, Trends in High-Performance, Low-Power Cache Memory Architectures, *IEICE Trans. Electron*, vol. E85-C, no.2, pp.304-314, Feb. 2002.

5. David A. Patterson A. & John L. Hennessy, Computer organization and design: the hardware/software interface, *third edition, Elsevier Inc.,* San Francisco, California, USA, 2005.
6. A. Seznec, A case for two-way skewed-associative cache, *the 20th International Symposium on Computer Architecture (IEEE-ACM),* San Diego, May 1993.
7. Agarwal, A., and Pudar, S.D., Column-associative Caches: A Technique For Reducing The Miss Rate Of Direct-mapped Caches, *the 20th Annual International Symposium on Computer Architecture,* 16-19 May 1993, pp. 179-190.
8. A. Seznec and J. Hedouin, The CACHESKEW simulator, *http://www.irisa.fr/caps/ PROJECTS/Architecture/CACHESKEW.html,* Sept. 1997.
9. F. Bodin, A. Seznec, Skewed-associativity improves performance and enhances predictability, *IEEE Transactions on Computers,* May 1997.
10. Cheryl Brennan, Application Note AN-254, Integrated Device Technology, March 2000.
11. H. Peter Hofstee, "Power Efficient Processor Architecture and The Cell Processor", the 11th Int'l Symposium on High-Performance Computer Architecture (HPCA-11), San Francisco, CA, USA, February 2005.
12. SPEC official website: http://www.specbench.org/osg/cpu95, Aug 2004.
13. Todd Austin, Eric Larson, Dan Ernst, "SimpleScalar: An Infrastructure for computer system modeling," IEEE Computer, 35(2): 56-67, Feb 2002.
14. P. Shivakumar and N. Jouppi, "An integrated cache timing, power, and area model," http://www.research.compaq.com/wrl/people/jouppi/CACTI.html, Research Report 2000/7, February 2000.
15. Hung-Cheng Wu, Tien-Fu Chen, Hung-Yu Li, "Energy efficient caching-on-cache architectures for embedded systems", Journal of Information Science and Engineering, November 2002.
16. A. J. KleinOsowski and D. J. Lilja, "MinneSPEC: A New SPEC Benchmark Workload for Simulation-Based Computer Architecture Research," Computer Architecture Letters, June 2002, pp. 10-13.

Cache Write-Back Schemes for Embedded Destructive-Read DRAM

Haakon Dybdahl, Marius Grannæs, and Lasse Natvig

Department of Computer and Information Science,
Faculty of Information Technology, Mathematics and Electrical Engineering,
Norwegian University of Science and Technology
{dybdahl, grannas, lasse}@idi.ntnu.no

Abstract. Much of the chip area and power in a modern processor are used by mechanisms that compensate for slow main memory such as caches, out-of-order execution and prefetching. We attack this problem by utilizing a DRAM macro made by Hwang et. al that is faster than conventional DRAM macros, but does not conserve data in the DRAM cells after reading. Their prototype included a large write-back buffer for conserving data without degrading performance of read accesses. We eliminate this buffer by utilizing the already existing cache in processor designs at the cost of potential memory bank congestion. Two implementable and one theoretic upper-bound scheme for cache write-back are evaluated. We find that the size of the cache can be highly reduced without degrading performance when utilizing destructive-read DRAM. The large write-back buffer can be omitted when destructive-read DRAM is used with a processor with cache without significant degradation of performance.

1 Introduction

The pipeline of a processor is now running at a higher frequency than main memory. Caches are used to reduce the number of memory accesses that require data from main memory and hence reduce the effect of the slow main memory. However, caches have several disadvantages, they require substantial chip area, increase power consumption and do not work equally well for all applications. Other mechanisms are out-of-order execution, prefetching and thread switching. These techniques increase the complexity of the processor, power consumption and chip area as well. Increasing the chip area increases the cost of manufacturing the chip as the yield and number of chips per wafer are reduced. Increasing the power consumption increases the cost of packaging for the chip due to increased cooling requirements and reduces the operation time when powered by batteries.

By reducing the latency of the main memory itself the processor core and cache system can be simplified without degrading performance. The latency of main memory can be decomposed into different parts: Cache miss latency, latency of bus to main memory and memory bank latency. The latency of the off-chip bus to main memory can be eliminated by integrating the memory bank and

W. Grass et al. (Eds.): ARCS 2006, LNCS 3894, pp. 145–159, 2006.
© Springer-Verlag Berlin Heidelberg 2006

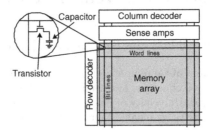

Fig. 1. A logical sketch of a DRAM macro

processor on the same chip. Dense main memory is made with DRAM technology. DRAM chips are highly optimized for storing data and a large amount of the design is analog. Capacitors are used to store data (see Figure 1) which fills a large area of the chip. Logic circuits on the other hand are optimized for speed and power distribution. Merging these technologies results in compromises. Several projects have researched into merging processors and memory over a long period of time ([1, 2, 3, 4, 5, 6, 7, 8, 9, 10]). Chips with DRAM and processors are now in mass production for example Sony's Playstation 2, EZchip's NP-1c network processor[11] and Nintendo's GameCube. Embedded DRAM is still not as dense (bits per area) as pure DRAM chips (typically 50% less bits per area), but this is claimed to be better with denser technologies [12].

Embedding DRAM does not reduce the latency of the DRAM bank itself, and even with the off-chip bus latency eliminated the DRAM is much slower than the pipeline of the processor. Hwang et. al[13] made a DRAM macro called *destructive-read DRAM* where access time was reduced with 50%, but where data in memory is deleted when read. In order to understand how destructive-read DRAM works, we will start with describing the conventional DRAM bank and such a bank is shown in Figure 1. The row decoder is the first component activated in a read access. It enables one *word line* and causes all transistors in that row to be activated. These transistors connect the capacitors in the memory array to the *sense amplifiers* through *bit lines*. The sense amplifiers work in three phases as shown in Figure 2a. In the first phase the charge from the capacitor drives the sense amplifier into a logic state. In the second phase that logic state is locked. In Figure 3a the locking works as a buffer. From this buffer the data is sent to the processor and written back to memory. In the final phase the bit lines are pre-charged so they are ready for the next access. Destructive-read DRAM memory works differently. The read operation of conventional DRAM (see Figure 2a) is split into two cycles (see Figure 2b and c) Destructive-read DRAM does not lock the data after reading (as shown in Figure 3b). Instead the data are sent directly out of the cell, in this case to cache memory. Since data is not sent back to memory, data is destroyed after reading. Data is conserved by writing it back to DRAM after use as shown in 2c. However, write-back can be done later in contrast to conventional DRAM where read and write-back are one single operation. The prototype had four independent memory banks and large write back buffer (WBB) that was the same size as one memory bank. The purpose

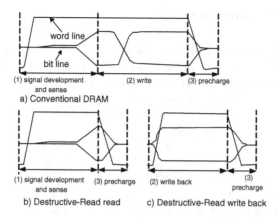

Fig. 2. Conceptual waveform diagrams of conv. DRAM architecture vs. destructive-read[13]

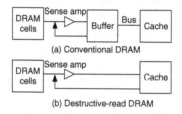

Fig. 3. Conceptual view of DRAM

of the WWB was to hide write-backs, not to reduce latency. The WBB could write to several banks simultaneously and required significant chip area. Later a new scheme was made where the WBB was implemented with destructive-read DRAM[14]. Both designs guaranteed that write-backs never conflicted with read operations.

We have earlier studied the effect on power consumption by using destructive-read DRAM [15]. The findings were only a small increase in system power consumption (0.5% and 3% for 16kbyte and 2kbyte caches respectively). This paper studies writing back data without using large explicit WBB. The baseline architecture is a small processor with small caches and embedded DRAM. This represents an embedded system. We compare performance by utilizing the modification proposed by Hwang et. al and compare the performance in terms of instructions per clock cycle (IPC). We propose two new schemes for write-backs based on the existing cache in a processor. The cache architecture is modified in different ways so data are conserved.

Our findings are that the cache can be much smaller without degrading instructions per clock cycle (IPC) with destructive-read DRAM compared to conventional main memory. The large write-back buffer in the prototype can be omitted by using the cache for this purpose.

2   New Write-Back Schemes

The design by Hwang et. al included a large write-back buffer and in this work we utilize the cache of the system to do this task so the write-back buffer can be removed. However, it is not obvious when data should be written back from the cache and how this will impact performance since the cache is much smaller than the original write-back buffer. As shown in the evaluation section, simulations show that these schemes work well.

We call the first scheme the *delayed write-back scheme*. It can be compared to a cache that always has dirty cache lines. This implies that all data that are read into the cache have to be written back when replaced. A different approach is to write back data immediately after reading and we call this the *immediate write-back scheme*. The differences between conventional DRAM and destructive-read DRAM with the immediate write-back scheme can be clarified by examining the steps in a read operation. For conventional DRAM a read operation is completed with the bit line not being changed. There is only one access on the memory bus. For destructive-read with immediate write-back scheme, the data is first transferred to the cache and then written back to main memory. Two accesses are executed on the bus to perform one read operation. One intuitive idea might be to insert a buffer inside the conventional DRAM macro so data becomes available earlier. An important factor is that the DRAM is embedded. Insertion of extra latches for each DRAM bank will require substantial chip area. Each independent memory bank seen from the processor can have several sub banks. In this case the sense amplifiers have to drive both the extra latch and data to the cache and will therefore have to be more powerful. By centralizing these latches fewer are needed at the cost of extra (on-chip) bus traffic. This enables

Cache content before instruction is executed

Immediate	1	2	3	4	5	6	7	8	9	10	11	12	13	14	15	16	17	18	19	Line 0	Line 1
1 ADR[0]→R1	LO	LO	LO																	x	y
2 ADR[1]→R2				SO	SO	SO	L1	L1	L1											0	y
3 R1+R2→ADR[0]											S1									0	1
4 ADR[2]→R2												S1	S1	SO	SO	SO	L2	L2	L2	0 *	1

Delayed	1	2	3	4	5	6	7	8	9	10	11	12	13	14	15	16	17	18	19	Line 0	Line 1
5 ADR[0]→R1	Sx	Sx	Sx	LO	LO	LO														x	y
6 ADR[1]→R2							Sy	Sy	Sy	L1	L1	L1								0	y
7 R1+R2→ADR[0]																				0	1
8 ADR[2]→R2														SO	SO	SO	L2	L2	L2	0	1

Fig. 4. Example of execution with the two different write-back schemes. DRAM bus activity is shown with *L*A for reading and *S*A for writing address *A*. The addresses that are kept in the cache(i.e. the state of the cache) before the instruction is executed are shown to the right. The cache is initialized with addresses *X* and *Y* which are not address 0, 1 or 2. Addresses 0, 2 map into the first cache line, while address 1 maps into the second cache line. * indicates a modified cache line. In all cases the delayed write-back scheme has to write data back to DRAM on replacement, so cache lines can always be considered to be dirty.

buffering of write-backs for subsequent accesses which will improve performance. In a system with non-embedded DRAM, the situation is different as bus traffic is slow, limited and energy expensive.

In the delayed write-back scheme data in the cache has to be written back to make space before a read operation can start. If the data to be written and the data to be read belong to different DRAM banks, the two operations can be executed in parallel. The advantage with this scheme is that data is only written back to DRAM once. With the immediate write-back scheme, data might be written back to DRAM twice. First, the data is written back right after reading. Then, if the data is modified, it is written a second time when it is thrown out of the cache.

A simple program (see Figure 4) illustrates the difference between the two write-back schemes. The program is executed on hardware with the following properties: There is only one DRAM bank, and a read or write operation to DRAM takes 3 clock cycles. The read operations are destructive, the content of the loaded addresses are erased in DRAM. The data cache has two cache lines and each line can store one word. The cache has a 1 cycle latency and is *not* write-through. The cache is initialized with unmodified cache lines for addresses x and y. The example shows the difference in access patterns (number refers to lines in Figure 4):

1. Address 0 is loaded into the cache and address x is thrown out. This line is clean and there is no need for a write-back.
2. Address 1 is about to be loaded into cache, but the bus is busy with the write-back from the previous instruction and this has to finish before loading can start.
3. The result of an addition is written in address 0. Since this address is in the cache, it is a cache hit, and no activity on the bus is needed. The write-back from the previous instruction starts as well.
4. Data from address 2 is loaded into the cache. However, before any DRAM accesses can start, the write-back from instruction in line 2 has to finish (2 clock cycles). Then, the data in the cache has to be written back since it has become dirty (address 0 and address 2 map to the same cache line). Finally the load operation can start.
5. In the delayed write-back scheme data in cache is always treated as dirty. Therefore before loading data for address 0, data in the cache has to be written back.
6. Same as line 5.
7. Cache hit, no activity on the system bus.
8. Data in the cache has to be written back before loading can start.

In the delayed write-back scheme data for address 0 is only written once, while in the immediate write-back scheme it is written twice for address 0. A load instruction with the delayed write-back scheme takes 3 or 6 cycles; if the data in the cache line that is replaced is on the same memory bank as the data that is loaded, it takes 6 cycles. Otherwise, when the data in the cache line and the data to be read are on different banks, it takes 3 cycles. Load instructions with the immediate write-back scheme takes 3 to 9 cycles. The first 3 clock cycles might be needed to wait for the bus to become available due to earlier background writing operations. 3 additional cycles are needed when the data in the cache line is dirty and have to be written back to the same memory bank. Finally, 3 cycles are always needed for reading data.

One important question is which of the two schemes has the highest performance. With the immediate write-back scheme the result from a load operation is available after only 3 cycles when the cache line is clean. The strength of the delayed write-back scheme is the reduced traffic on the memory bus. In cases where data in the cache is modified, the number of transactions on the bus is reduced to only one.

The advantage of the immediate write-back scheme depends on unmodified cache lines while the advantage of the delayed write-back scheme depends on a modified cache lines. Smaller caches will have a lower ratio of modified cache lines that are replaced because data are swapped out before they are written to, while larger caches will have a higher ratio of modified cache lines. The ratio of modified cache lines that are replaced depends on the program as well.

3   Methodology

The purpose of our simulation is to study the performance of different write-back schemes with destructive-read DRAM and compare this to conventional embedded DRAM and to a theoretical write-back scheme with free write-backs for data conservation. The simulator is based on SimpleScalar version 3 [16]. It is extended to simulate a configurable number of DRAM banks and a configurable stand alone write-back buffer in addition to the two write-back schemes and Hwang's original scheme.

A logical sketch of the simulated computer is shown in Figure 5. The target is a computer with embedded memory and one level of cache. The processor is simple to save area and power. The configuration for the baseline of the simulations is:

- Cycle-true simulation.
- Alpha processor with a five stage pipeline running at 1 GHz.

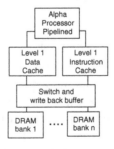

Fig. 5. The simulated computer

- Single issue, no branch prediction buffer, no translation look-aside buffer, in-order execution, single decode, single commit width, single ALU.
- Two independent caches, one instruction cache and one data cache. Both are one kbyte, two way set associative caches with 64 bytes cache lines. Latency is 1 ns.
- Four independent memory banks with simulation of congestion. Memory bus width is the same as cache line width (64 bytes).
- Latency of DRAM is 6 ns for a read operation. For destructive-read, this is 3 ns for reading and 3 ns for writing based on the prototype made by Hwang. DRAM Refresh is not simulated as it is presumed to have little effect on the result.
- In simulations of Hwang's original scheme, the latency of the memory system is always 3 ns (write-backs are perfectly hidden in the large write-back buffer).
- A write-back buffer is implemented for each memory bank capable of storing one cache line.

SPEC2000 applications were used as benchmark with *lgred* (large reduced input dataset)[17] as the data set. One of the 26 applications found in the *SPEC2000* did not work with the simulator (*vortex* application). In order to reduce computation time experiments that return average values are based on a subset of the applications (*gzip, gcc, crafty, mcf, swim, mgrid* and *equake*). Sample tests show that the subset represents the total average values within +/- 2%.

Four different configurations were simulated:

- *Conventional* represents the conventional DRAM scheme. Access latency is double the latency of destructive-read DRAM (i.e. 6 ns), but no write-back is required.
- *Immediate* is the immediate write-back scheme. Data is written back immediately or put in the write-back buffer if enabled. Access time is 3 ns.
- *Delay* is the delayed write-back scheme. The cache behaves like a normal cache, but the lines are always written back on replacement. Access time is 3 ns.
- *No cost* represents an ideal DRAM, combining the speed of destructive-read and the data integrity of conventional DRAM. The intention is to study the performance degradation imposed by the extra write-backs for conserving data. Access time is 3 ns.
- *Hwang* represents the original scheme from Hwang. Access time is 3 ns. The accesses are guaranteed to be congestion free. No fast cache is included.

4   Evaluation

4.1   Initial Experiment

An initial experiment was run to verify the predictions regarding performance (see Figure 4) of the two write-back schemes. The experiment has two test programs, one that reads data and one that reads and writes data into a data

```
/* Code for read experiment */
for(x=0;x<30000;x++) {
    y=y+data[x];
    z=z+data[x];
}
/* Code for read/write experiment */
for(x=0;x<30000;x++) {
    data[x]=data[x]+y;
    data[x]=data[x]+z;
}
```

Fig. 6. Source code for the initial experiment

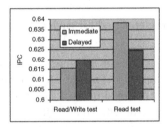

Fig. 7. Results from the initial experiment

structure as shown in Figure 6. To reduce the effect of instruction cache misses, the experiment was run with a very large instruction cache. The data cache was limited (128 bytes) in the same way as in the example. There was only one memory bank with 10 ns latency. The latency was set high so the effect of memory latency becomes dominant. This configuration does not reflect a real system, but is used to illustrate the differences between the two write-back schemes. The immediate write-back scheme should suit the read experiment as the second line in the loop can execute while write-back from the first line is executed in the background. The delayed write-back scheme should suit the read/write experiment as the number of write-backs to DRAM is reduced compared to the immediate write-back scheme. The results from the experiment are summarized in Figure 7 and are according to predictions.

4.2   IPC for Different Write-Back Schemes

Simulation of the different write-back schemes for the baseline architecture is shown in Figure 8. Average values are shown to the right. First of all we see that all applications benefit from destructive-read DRAM except for *art* where the Hwang scheme degrades performance. Secondly we see that the schemes with free write-backs for data conservation, *no cost*, do not perform much better than the *delayed* and *immediate* schemes. This indicates that the write-backs are well hidden in both the *delayed* and *immediate* schemes. Even though Hwang

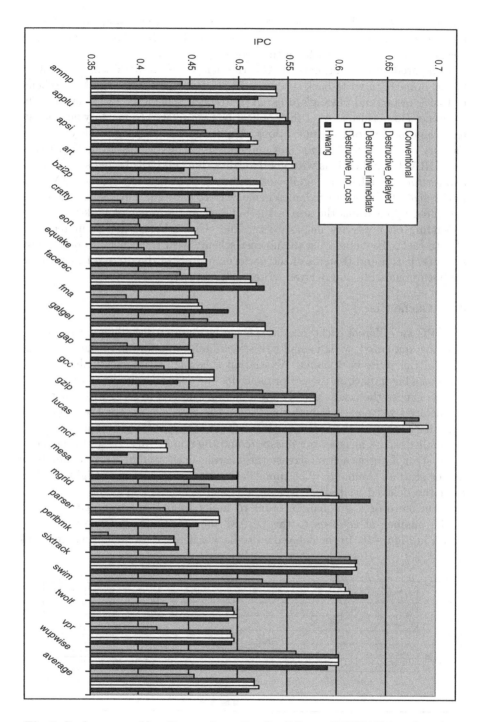

Fig. 8. Performance of baseline configuration for different SPEC2000 benchmarks

scheme perform well for some applications such as *mgrid* and *crafty* due to less congestion, the overall performance is lower than the other scheme. This is because there is no fast cache in this scheme.

Compared to conventional DRAM, the delayed write-back scheme is 13.2% faster, immediate write-back scheme is 13.5% faster, no cost write-back scheme is 14.4% faster and Hwang's original write-back scheme is 12.1% faster. The differences in performance of the applications are related to memory access patterns and locality of the applications. Applications with poor locality that are memory bound such as *ammp, mcf* and *crafty* benefit the most from destructive-read DRAM. Applications with good locality that are CPU bound such as *lucas* and *sixtrack* have less but significant advantage of destructive-read DRAM. The buffer size of Hwang's original scheme was 25% of the DRAM size. For the simulated applications the size of the buffer is in the range of 170k-5714kbyte, depending on necessary memory size. The other schemes are simulated with 1kbyte cache. By comparing the no cost scheme with the other two destructive schemes, it is found that 1% of the performance is lost due to extra write-backs for both immediate and delayed write-back schemes.

4.3 Cache Size

The IPC for different cache sizes are shown in Figure 9. Two different configurations are simulated, with a small write-back buffer in addition to the cache, and without this write-back buffer. We see that this small write-back buffer (one entry) has a big impact on the performance for the delayed write-back scheme. The buffer changes the access pattern for a memory access; in cases with congestion the delayed write-back is performed after the read access. For the immediate write-back schemes the buffer has less impact, but is still significant.

Smaller caches increase the *miss rate* and the number of accesses to the memory system. Larger caches increase the *hit rate* until a point where compulsory misses start to dominate. The immediate write-back scheme is slightly better than the delayed write-back scheme for small caches. For larger caches they perform more or less equal. In order to understand this advantage, the ratio of the number of accesses to the DRAM subsystems for the two schemes is shown in Figure 10. In the delayed write-back scheme, data are not written back

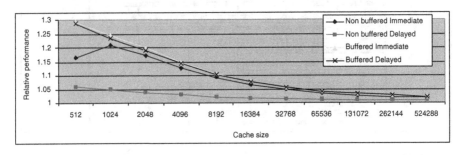

Fig. 9. Speedup in terms of increased IPC compared to conventional architecture

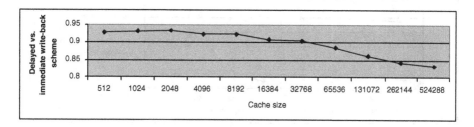

Fig. 10. Comparison of the total number of accesses to DRAM from caches for the two different write-back schemes

immediately. For modified data (by the CPU), the total number of accesses is reduced compared to immediate write-back scheme where data are written twice in this case. Larger caches improve the probability of data being modified before being replaced for data caches. The advantage of the immediate write-back scheme is that data is available earlier in cases where there is a conflict between writing and reading data. Even though the two models are different, performance is similar except for small caches where the immediate write-back scheme is better.

4.4   Latency and Number of DRAM Banks

Simulation of different DRAM-latencies is shown in Figure 11. As latency increases, performance degrades as the CPU is stalled. Even though the IPC is degraded by increasing the latency of the memory, the speedup of using destructive-read memory increases with increasing cache size. The delayed and immediate schemes degrade faster than the no cost scheme due to conflicts between reading and writing. Increasing the number of memory banks reduces the

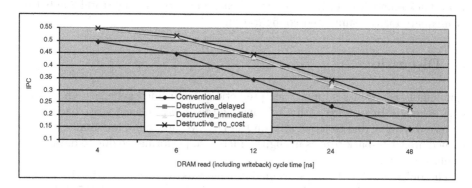

Fig. 11. Average IPC as a function of latency. Write-backs become blocking as latency is increased. The values on the x-axis are non-linear, the first value is increased from 3 to 4 ns to match the cycle time of the CPU.

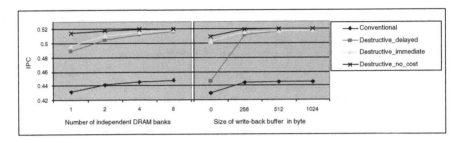

Fig. 12. (a) To the left, average IPC as a function of the number of DRAM banks. For a small number of DRAM banks, write-backs blocks performance. (b) To the right, average IPC as function of number of buffer size. By turning off the write-back buffer, the delayed write-back model has to wait for the data in the cache to be written back before a new line can be loaded in cases where these two line are mapped to the same memory bank.

probability of congestion. The effect of increasing (or decreasing) the number of DRAM banks is shown in Figure 12a. In this configuration each bank is independent and can handle one memory access each simultaneously. In addition to increasing the maximum number of parallel accesses, increasing bank count decreases the probability that two accesses are to the same memory bank as data are spread out to more banks.

4.5   Write-Back Buffer Size

The write-back buffer is complementary to the cache and each memory bank has its own small fully associative write-back buffer. They are important for performance of the delayed write-back scheme as shown in Figure 12b. In this scheme data has to be written back when the cache line is replaced. Without a buffer the processor has to wait for both operations to finish before data becomes available. In the immediate write-back scheme this buffer is less important. A write-back buffer with only one entry for each memory channel (total 256 bytes) is adequate for the simulated configuration.

5   Discussion

The simulated results support our predictions regarding cache size and write-back schemes. In systems with a relatively large cache, delayed write-back is the preferred scheme due to less traffic on the DRAM bus, while for smaller caches, immediate write-back results in slightly increased performance due to data being available earlier.

The buffer size of Hwang's original scheme was 25% of the DRAM size. For the simulated applications this buffer will be in the range of 170k-5714k byte, and this is outperformed with the new schemes with a smaller 1kbyte cache.

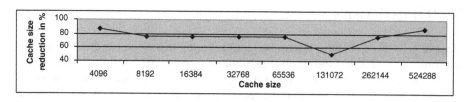

Fig. 13. Cache size saving in % by using destructive-read DRAM compared to conventional DRAM for equal or better performance. This figure is based on Figure 9.

The simulations show that the process of writing back data is hidden quite well (about 1% of IPC is lost due to write-backs in the baseline scheme), this is true for both write-back schemes. This is shown to be connected to the number of independent memory banks and the write-back buffers for each memory bank. More banks reduces the probability of congestion. Write-back buffers change the delayed write-back scheme to first read data before the existing cache line is written, and therefore data becomes available earlier and performance is increased. For longer memory latencies, congestion is increasing as a write operation has to finish before a read operation can start.

By comparing the performance of different configurations it can be seen that by replacing conventional DRAM with destructive-read DRAM, cache sizes can be reduced without degrading performance. The savings in cache size is shown in Figure 13. Even though the baseline for the simulation has small caches, we have found that the cache size can be reduced with median 75% for cache size in the range 4kbytes to 512 kbytes when applying destructive-read DRAM without degrading performance. Reducing cache size has a positive impact on power consumption and less chip area is needed.

The bus between DRAM and cache has to run at double the speed with destructive-read DRAM compared to conventional DRAM. Since the bus is on-chip this should result in only slightly higher power consumption. DRAM contributes to just a small portion to the total power consumption in most computers (not including off-chip buses).

We have used a constant latency for the caches in our simulation. In real caches the latency of the cache is a function of the size of the cache. Smaller caches are faster than larger caches. A more accurate model would be to reduce the latency of the cache for smaller caches. This would be an advantage for the destructive-read DRAM schemes, and by using a constant cache access time we introduce an error that is a disadvantage for our schemes.

We have simulated a factor two difference in latency for destructive-read compared to conventional read from DRAM. This was based on the number from a prototype. However, we have shown that the write-backs are hidden very well. Less than 1% of the performance is lost due to congstion for the baseline scheme. Therefore, even a small decrease in latency for destructive-read DRAM will increase IPC.

We have not evaluated SRAM as technology for on-chip memory technology since DRAM stores data much denser.

6   Related Work

Most of projects that have researched into merging processors and memory have not looked into DRAM design, but presume a conventional design. The C*RAM project[2] is an exception that integrated small processing elements into the sense amplifiers and utilized the parallelism available at that level. A scaled down prototype was made. It was a SIMD computer with single bit processors. This architecture was mainly suitable for problems with high data locality because of limited communication between the single bit processing elements.

Many other projects use SIMD architectures to utilize the extra bandwidth: the IRAM project [18], Yukon [5], Terasys [3] and Execube [19]. The Mitsubishi M32R/D [7] chip uses the bandwidth to increase the number of bits in the data bus between main memory and cache. The use of FPGA technology and independent processors have also been proposed to utilize the bandwidth ([6, 1]).

7   Conclusion

By using destructive-read DRAM the cache size can be reduced without degrading system performance. In our schemes the caches are responsible for conserving data read from DRAM memories. We have shown that this does not infer any bottlenecks and that the cache size can be reduced by median 75% compared to a conventional architecture without degrading performance in terms of IPC. The large write-back buffer used in the prototype by Hwang et. al can be eliminated without significant performance degradation. The possible reduction in cache size reduces both dynamic and static power consumption as well as system size. The chip area made available by reducing cache size can be used to increase the number of processors or memory size.

References

1. Draper, J., Kang, C.W., Kim, I., Daglikoca, G., Chame, J., Hall, M., Steele, C., Barrett, T., LaCoss, J., Granacki, J., Shin, J., Chen, C.: The architecture of the DIVA processing-in-memory chip. Proc. 16th ACM Int'l Conf. Supercomp. (2002)
2. Elliott, D.G., Snelgrove, W.M., Stumm, M.: Computational RAM: A memory-SIMD hybrid and its application to DSP. In CICC, Boston, MA (1992)
3. Gokhale, M., Holmes, B., Iobst, K.: Processing in memory; the Terasys massively parallel PIM array. IEEE Computer, p:23-31 (1995)
4. Kang, Y., Huang, W., Yoo, S.M., Keen, D., Ge, Z., Lam, V., Patnaik, P., Torellas, J.: FlexRAM: Towards an advanced intelligent memory system. ICCD (1999)
5. Kirsch, G.: Active memory: Micron's Yukon. Parallel and Distributed Processing Symposium, Proceedings. International, number of p:11 (2003)
6. Mai, K., Paaske, T., Jayasena, N., R. Ho, W., Dally, Horowitz, M.: Smart Memories: A modular reconfigurable architecture. ISCA (2000)
7. Nunomura, Y., Shimizu, T., Tomisawa, O.: M32R/D-integrating DRAM and microprocessor. Micro, IEEE, Volume: 17, Issue: 6, p:40-48 (1997)

8. Oskin, M., Chong, F., Sherwood, T.: Active Pages: A model of computation for intelligent memory. Int. Symp. on Computer Arch., Barcelona, Spain (1998)
9. Saulsbury, A., Pong, F., Nowatzyk, A.: Missing the memory wall: the case for processor/memory integration. In: ISCA '96: Proc. of the 23rd annual int. symp. on Computer architecture, New York, NY, USA, ACM Press (1996) 90–101
10. Yerosheva, L., Kuntz, S., Brockman, J., Kogge, P.: A microserver view of HTMT. Parallel and Distributed Processing Symposium, Proc. 15th Int (2001)
11. Gwennap, L.: Embedded DRAM use rises. Nikkei Electronics Asia, June (2003)
12. Furuyama, T.: Trends and challenges of large scale embedded memories. Custom Integrated Circuits Conference, 2004. Proceedings of the IEEE 2004, Page(s):449 - 456 (2004)
13. Hwang, C.L., Kirihata, T., et.al, M.W.: A 2.9ns random access cycle embedded DRAM with a destructive-read architecture. VLSI Circ., Digest of Tech. Pap., IEEE Symp. on, p:174-175 (2002)
14. Ji, B., Munetoh, S., Hwang, C.L., Wordeman, M., Kirihata, T.: Destructive-read random access memory system buffered with destructive-read memory cache for SoC applications. VLSI Circuits, Dig. of Tech. Papers. Symp. on (2003)
15. Dybdahl, H., Kjeldsberg, P., Granns, M., Natvig, L.: Destructive-read in embedded DRAM, impact on power consumption. Journal of Embedded Computing, Special Issue on Embedded Single-Chip Multicore Architectures, Issue 2 (2006)
16. Austin, T., Larson, E., Ernst, D.: SimpleScalar: an infrastructure for computer system modeling. IEEE Computer, Volume 35, Issue 2 (2002)
17. KleinOsowski, A., Lilja, D.J.: MinneSPEC: A new SPEC benchmark workload for simulation-based computer architecture research. Comp. Archi. Letters 1 (2002)
18. Patterson, D., Anderson, T., Yelick, K.: A case for intelligent DRAM: IRAM. Presented at Hot Chips VIII, Palo Alto CA, p:18-20 (1996)
19. Kogge, P., Sunaga, T., Miyataka, H., Kitamura, K., Retter, E.: Combined DRAM and logic chip for massively parallel systems. IEEE, Adv. Research in VLSI (1995)

A Processor Architecture with Effective Memory System for Sort-Last Parallel Rendering

Woo-Chan Park[1], Duk-Ki Yoon[1], Kil-Whan Lee[2], Il-San Kim[2],
Kyung-Su Kim[1], Won-Jong Lee[2], Tack-Don Han[2], and Sung-Bong Yang[2]

[1] Department of Internet Engineering, Sejong University, 98 Kunjadong,
KwangjinKu, Seoul 143-747, Korea
pwchan@sejong.ac.kr, {dkyoon, kimks}@rayman.sejong.ac.kr
[2] Department of Computer Science, Yonsei University, 134 Shinchon-Dong,
Seodaemun-Ku, Seoul 120-749, Korea
{kiwh, sany, hantack}@kurene.yonsei.ac.kr
{airtight, yang}@cs.yonsei.ac.kr

Abstract. In this paper, a consistency-free memory architecture for sort-last parallel rendering processors with a single frame buffer is proposed to resolve the consistency problem which may occur when more than one rasterizer try to access the data at the same address. Also, the proposed architecture reduces the latency due to pixel cache misses because the rasterizer does not wait until cache miss handling is completed when the pixel cache miss occurs. For these goals, a consistency-free pixel cache architecture and three effective memory systems with consistency-test units are presented. The experimental results show that the proposed architecture can achieve almost linear speedup up to four rasterizers with a single frame buffer.

1 Introduction

Recently high-performance rendering processors have been introduced by almost all of the PC manufacturers. These rendering processors should process triangles (or primitives) one at a time with their multiple pixel pipelines. As the semiconductor technology advances, it is possible to produce a parallel rendering processor by integrating several rasterizers into a single chip. The Sony's GScube includes 16 graphics processing units (GPUs) integrated with 256-Mb embedded DRAMs [1]. Because the outputs of 16 GPUs are fed into a pixel merge unit which drives the data stream to a video display, each GPU must have its own frame buffer. Thus a large amount of embedded DRAMs should be integrated into a rendering processor. Note that such an organization is similar to that of the sort-last parallel rendering machine classified in [2].

The sort-last architecture performs both geometry calculation and rasterization in object-level parallel. This architecture is scalable because the required bandwidth of its communication network is almost constant with respect to the number of polygons [2,3]. Though the sort-last architecture is quite suitable for a large-scale rendering system, as mentioned in [2], it constraints the choice of

W. Grass et al. (Eds.): ARCS 2006, LNCS 3894, pp. 160–175, 2006.

rendering algorithms because visibility is determined strictly by composition. Some rendering systems allow rendering order to determine visibility as well as depth values (for effects like stencil, blending for transparency, and multi-pass rendering).

In SAGA [4], which is a recent sort-last rendering machine, there are two execution modes: *the unordered rendering mode* and *the ordered rendering mode*. In the ordered rendering mode, special control tokens enforce various render-order constraints. For example, when a special synchronization token marking a hard ordering constraint is encountered, then no more fragment from that rasterizer will be processed until other rasterizers have also encountered the synchronization token. We denote the primitive data to be kept ordering strictly in the ordered rendering mode as *the order-dependent data*, otherwise in the unordered rendering mode as *the order-free data*. The sort-last architecture is the most suitable for processing order-free data in parallel.

In this paper, a consistency-free memory architecture for sort-last parallel rendering processors on the order-free data is proposed to resolve the consistency problem and reduce the latency due to pixel cache misses significantly. In the proposed parallel rendering processor, called *DAVID II*, only a single frame buffer exists and each rasterizer executes a conventional rasterization pipeline with its local pixel cache. Parallel rendering with a single frame buffer causes a consistency problem when more than one rasterizer access the data at the same address. We allow the consistency problem to occur in each pixel cache. But we maintain the consistency in the frame buffer by performing additional *consistency-tests (C-tests)* for all the pixels within each pixel cache block, whenever it is written into the frame buffer. A C-test performs z-test and *color*-write operations for each pixel. The proposed architecture also reduces significantly the latency due to pixel cache misses by executing the rasterization pipeline immediately after transmitting the cache block on which a miss was generated into the memory interface unit (MIU).

To evaluate the proposed architecture, various simulation results with three benchmarks are given. A trace-driven simulator has been built for the proposed architecture. We first perform the pixel cache simulations as the number of rasterizers increases. We also calculate the memory latency reduction rates with increasing the number of rasterizers. We can achieve up to 90% zero-latency memory system even with four rasterizers.

2   Background and Related Work

2.1   Background

A conventional pixel rasterization pipeline is shown in Fig. 1. In the z-test pipeline, a z-value from the depth cache is retrieved and is compared with that of the current fragment, and a new z-value is written into the depth cache at the z-write stage if z-test is successful. Observe that the pixel cache consists of the depth cache and the color cache, as shown by a dotted box in Fig. 1.

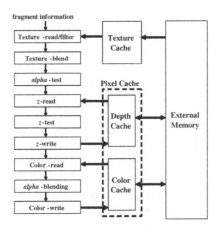

Fig. 1. A conventional pixel rasterization pipeline

In the color-write pipeline, we read the color data from the color cache of the pixel cache, *alpha*-blend them with the result of texture blending, and then write the final color data back to the color cache. If order-independent transparency technique is used, color-read and *alpha*-blending stages can be moved into order-independent transparency unit [5,6]. In [5], for each pixel the closest opaque fragment is placed into the frame buffer and all transparent fragments that could not be culled are stored into a separate R-buffer. Because no transparent fragments exist in the frame buffer, the operation of the color-write pipeline is only writing a color-value of the current fragment into the color cache if z-test is successful. Therefore, we assume in this paper that only a color-write stage exist in the color-write pipeline.

2.2   Sort-Last Architecture

The sort-last architecture can be divided into two classes based on which set of data is transmitted via communication network [2,3]. The first class is the image composition architecture, in which case each rasterizer outputs all the pixels on the screen [1,3]. Fig. 2 shows the overall structure of an image composition architecture. A pixel cache is locally placed on each rasterizer and can be omitted on occasions. Texture cache is not provided in Fig. 2 because it is not interested in this paper.

In the first class, all polygonal model data are distributed into each rasterizer which generates a sub-image with its own full-screen frame buffer, called a local frame buffer. The contents of all the local frame buffers are merged periodically by the image merger at the speed of CRT scan. During image merging, the depth comparisons with the contents of the same screen address for each local frame buffer should be performed to accomplish hidden surface removal. The final merged image is then transmitted into the global frame buffer.

In the second class, as our proposed rendering processor and [4], each rasterizer sends only the pixel generated. Thus each rasertizer does not require the

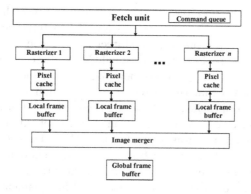

Fig. 2. Conventional image composition architecture

full-screen frame buffer in the local frame buffer. In [4], sample buffer composed of a number of 3D-RAMs[9,10] acts as the local frame buffers. In our proposed architecture, local frame buffers are even removed because the proposed pixel cache acts as a buffer.

3   The Proposed Architecture

Fig. 3 illustrates the parallel rendering processor, called David II, with proposed consistency-free memory architecture. Compared with the conventional image composition architecture in Fig. 2, David II does not require local frame buffers. Instead of the image merger of Fig.2, the ALUs for C-tests are inserted in between MIU and the frame buffer to perform image merging with consistency-test.

One of the main ideas of our architecture is that we allow the consistency problem to occur in each pixel cache, yet we maintain the consistency strictly in the frame buffer. The data in a pixel cache are transmitted into the frame buffer

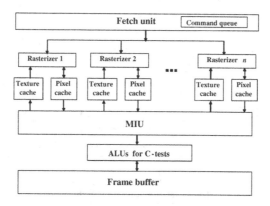

Fig. 3. David II: the proposed parallel rendering processor

whenever a pixel cache miss occurs. The transmission into the frame buffer is also generated in flushing the pixel cache when the rasterization for the current frame is completed. In the proposed architecture, the consistency of the frame buffer is maintained by performing additional C-tests for each transmitted block from the pixel cache against the corresponding block in the frame buffer.

Another main idea is that the rasterizer, even though a pixel cache miss occurs, does not wait until cache miss handling is completed. Rather, the rasterizer rather continues to execute the rasterization immediately after transmitting the cache block on which a miss was generated into MIU. Thus, the latency due to a cache miss, including the time to transfer the corresponding block from the pixel cache into the frame buffer, can be significantly reduced. By doing so, the rasterization pipeline and C-tests can be executed independently. We introduce a new pixel cache architecture for this purpose.

3.1   The Proposed Pixel Cache Architecture

The proposed pixel cache in Fig. 4 consists of the data memory, the tag memory, and the initialization logics. The data memory has the depth cache and the color cache. The tag memory comprises three fields: the valid bit (V), the *Depth tag* for the depth cache and the *Color tag* for color cache. The depth cache and the color cache are coupled in such a way that both a depth block and the neighboring color block with the same screen position are transmitted into MIU in case of a cache miss. Because z-read is performed before color-write as shown in Fig. 1, the tag comparison only with the depth tag needs to be performed to determine

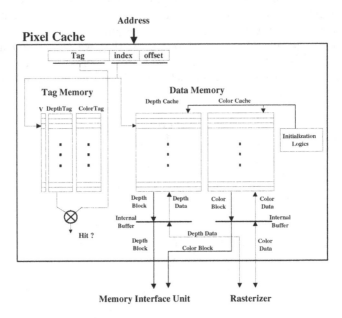

Fig. 4. The proposed pixel cache architecture

whether a cache miss has occurred or not. The color tag stores only the color addresses of the color blocks in the frame buffer. Thus, one bit is enough for V to indicate the validity of a pixel cache block, rather than having two bits; one for each of a depth cache block and a color cache block.

There are two types of data transmissions with respect to the pixel cache. The first type is the transmission between the pixel cache and the rasterizer. As in a conventional cache system, z-read operation retrieves a depth block from the depth cache and stores it into the internal buffer if it is not in the internal buffer. Then the depth data is read from the internal buffer. Z-write operation stores a depth data into the internal buffer. The processing flow of color-write operation is similar to that of z-write operation.

The second type is the transmission from the pixel cache into the frame buffer. Unlike a conventional cache system, a write-only operation is enough. That is, no information is required from the frame buffer. When a cache miss occurs, the pixel block that caused a cache miss, called a replaced cache block, is transferred into MIU. The cache block previously occupied by the replaced cache block, denoted as a usable cache block, is initialized into the maximum value (i.e., all 1 bits), which represents the farthest position from any viewpoint and the background black color in case of the depth value and the color value, respectively. This initialization is also used to initiate the pixel cache at the start of a new frame.

In the second type of the transmission, the critical path includes the tag comparison, the cache block transmission, and the initialization operation. The initialization operation after tag comparison is similar to the operation when the cache write hits; it is the data write into the cache after tag comparison. In general, we can allow it to be executed within a single cycle because it can be performed in a pipelined fashion. Thus, we can determine the critical path of the second type of the data transmission as the cache block transmission, because both the cache block transmission and the initialization operation can be executed simultaneously. If the buffer queue of MIU is not full, the second type of the data transmission can be done within a single cycle. Otherwise, the rasterizer should wait until any entry of the buffer queue is available.

3.2   The Processing Flow of the Rasterizer

When a new frame starts, all V bits of the pixel cache are set to zeros to indicate the invalid states for all the pixel cache blocks. Both the depth cache and the color cache are also initialized into the maximum values. When a depth cache block is accessed for the first time at the z-read stage, the V bit of the depth cache block is changed into 1, the tag field of the depth address is fed into the depth tag of the depth cache block, and a depth value is retrieved from the depth cache block. When a color cache block is accessed at the color-write stage for the first time, the tag field of the color address is fed into the color tag of the color cache block and a color value is written into the color cache block. These two types of initial accesses imply that a cold-start cache miss never occurs.

When a hit occurs in the pixel cache, the rasterizer continues to execute without any pipeline stall. In case of a pixel cache miss, the replaced cache block is sent to MIU and the usable cache block is initialized. Thus, the replaced cache block holds the rasterization results from the time when it is initiated as a usable cache block until it is sent to MIU due to a cache miss.

The replaced cache block goes through C-tests and then the final result cache block is written into the frame buffer. When the rasterization of the current frame buffer is completed, each block in the pixel cache should undergo the same processing flow of a replace cache block. The detailed architectures for the memory system are described in Section 4.

4   The Memory Systems of the Proposed Architecture

A unified memory system is widely adopted by recent rendering processors. As mentioned in [11], the biggest advantage of a single graphics memory system is the dynamic reallocation of memory bandwidth. The external bus width of a current rendering processor is either 128 bits or 256 bits. It is expected that a wider bus will be announced in the next generation rendering processors. The pixel cache and the texture cache are essentially included into a rendering processor to use a wide external bus effectively and to run the rasterization pipeline as high a rate as possible.

A conventional MIU has several queues to buffer the data transmissions between the processor and the external memory. For example, each memory controller in [11] has five request queues. The replaced cache blocks transmitted from the pixel cache are fed into the pixel output queue in MIU and then each of them is written into the frame buffer after C-tests. It is desirable for an effective memory system that the input rate of MIU should match well with the output rate of MIU.

Fig. 5 shows the three memory systems for the proposed architecture: *conventional DRAMs for the frame buffer (CDFB), C-RAMs for the frame buffer (CRFB)*, and *embedded DRAMs for the frame buffer (EDFB)*. The shaded blocks reside within a rendering processor chip. The non-shaded blocks can be organized as separate chips. The three figures in Fig. 5 are arranged according to the output rate of MIU; that is, conventional DRAMs in Fig. 5(a) have the

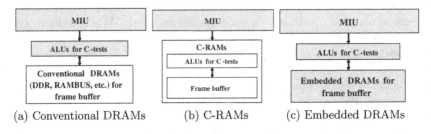

(a) Conventional DRAMs   (b) C-RAMs   (c) Embedded DRAMs

Fig. 5. The three memory systems

lowest output rate, C-RAMs in Fig. 5(b) are the next, and embedded DRAMs in Fig. 5(c) have the highest rate.

In CDFB, conventional DRAMs are used for the frame buffer and the ALUs for C-tests are included within the rendering processor. On the other hand in CRFB, C-RAMs are used for the frame buffer and the ALUs for C-tests are included within C-RAMs. Note that the relationship between the processor and the frame buffer in CDFB is read-modify-write, while that in CRFB is write-only. Thus, in accessing the frame buffer for rasterization, CRFB requires only a half amount of the memory bandwidth of CDFB. However, CDFB has an overwhelming advantage over CRFB in terms of the cost-effectiveness, because C-RAMs are too expensive to develop.

Because C-tests are performed per cache block, the processing style of C-RAMs is similar to that of current DRAMs. Thus, C-RAMs can be implemented by adding simple hardware logics into current DRAMs, while 3D-RAMs include an internal cache and other complex schemes to improve the performance of the internal cache.

In EDFB, because both the ALUs for C-tests and the frame buffer are included in the rendering processor, a very wide bus width, for example more than 1024 bits, between MIU and the frame buffer is available and the latency to access the frame buffer is also reduced. Note that Sony's PlayStation® 2 and GScube are typical rendering processors with embedded DRAMs for the frame buffer.

4.1   The Internal Architecture of CDFB

Fig. 6 shows the block diagram of CDFB. The pixel output queue in Fig. 6 contains the replaced cache blocks transmitted from the pixel cache. The ALU pool consists of several ALUs, each of which performs a C-test for a fragment (or a pixel). We illustrate the execution flow of CDFB in Fig. 6 when the data bus width between MIU and the external DRAM is 256 bits and a replaced cache block size is k256 bits. The first 256 bits (four 32-bit depth data and four 32-bit color data) of a replaced cache block at the head entry indicated by the head pointer are sent to the ALU pool and at the same time the first 256 bits of a target block are fetched from the frame buffer. After C-tests, the resulting four pixel data are then written into the frame buffer through the output buffer. After the k-th iteration of the above steps, C-tests for the replaced cache block are completed.

Both the burst data read operation from the frame buffer and the burst data write operation into the frame buffer are performed for the pipelined execution of C-tests. It is desirable to execute the burst write operation immediately after the burst read operation is completed. We assume that the number of the pipeline stages of the ALU is $(k+l)$. It is not difficult to adjust the number of pipeline stages because the z-test pipeline and the color-write pipeline can be connected either sequentially or in parallel. The burst data read operation followed by the burst data write operation requires a setup latency between these two operations. This latency is assumed to be l. Then the ALU pipeline executions can be performed simultaneously during $k256$-bit read operations from the frame buffer.

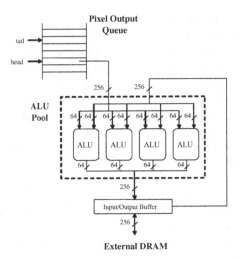

Fig. 6. A block diagram of CDFB

The first 256 bits after C-tests have completed appear in the output buffer after $(k+l)$ cycles. Thus the final 256 bits appear after $(2k+l)$ cycles.

4.2 The Memory Organization with C-RAMs

Fig. 7 shows the memory organization with a 256-bit external bus width in the proposed parallel rendering processor. Both the frame data and the texture data reside in C-RAMs harmoniously, while only the frame data reside in 3D-RAMs[9,10]. As in 3D-RAMs, the depth data and the color data are stored separately into the color C-RAMs and the depth C-RAMs, respectively. Thus, the overall ALU's performance of the architecture in Fig. 7 is the same as that of the architecture in Fig. 6, even though the number of ALUs in the architecture in Fig. 6 is only a half of that in architecture in Fig. 7. The other buffers in the C-RAMs

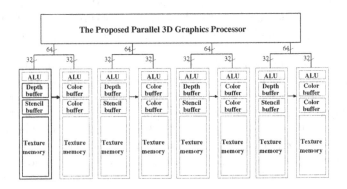

Fig. 7. Memory organization with 256-bit bus width

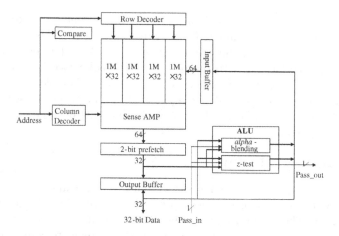

Fig. 8. A brief block diagram of an example of C-RAM

include the stencil buffer for stencil effect, R-buffer for order-independent transparency, etc.

Four 32 bits of the depth data and four 32 bits of the color data are transferred at a time from the rendering processor into four depth C-RAMs and four color C-RAMs, respectively, which is similar to the case of 3D-RAMs. The next 256-bit data into C-RAMs are transmitted at the next cycle and such transmission is repeated until all the data of a given replaced cache block are completely transferred. However, this type of execution is not guaranteed in 3D-RAMs.

During C-tests, z-test operations are accomplished in the ALU of the depth C-RAMs. The result of each z-test operation is then forwarded into the ALU of the connected color C-RAM via a separate path. Finally, the color-write operations are executed in the ALU of the color C-RAMs. A detailed example for the C-RAM architecture is illustrated in the next Fig. 8.

4.3   A Detailed Example of C-RAM

A brief block diagram of an example of a C-RAM chip is shown in Fig. 8. It is designed by modifying a 128-Mb DDR graphics DRAM that is widely used in current rendering processors. The internal data bus width is 64 bits and hence 32-bit data can be transferred into the output buffer at a time. The texture memory and the frame buffer occupy respective memory spaces within a chip. By checking the row address fed into the row decoder, we could determine which part of the memory is being accessed.

If the texture memory is being accessed, C-RAM acts as a conventional DDR DRAM. When a pixel cache block is transmitted from MIU, the execution flow of C-RAM is converted to perform C-tests. In this case, the pipeline organization and the execution flow of the ALU are similar to those of 3D-RAM.

The ALU consists of the z-test and the color-write pipelines. Each pipeline has multiple stages; for example, two stages each for z-test and color-write. At first, a z-value from MIU and that from the frame buffer are tested at the z-test pipeline of each depth C-RAM. If it is a success, the former is sent to the input buffer to be stored into the frame buffer and the pass_out signal is activated into 1. This signal is passed into the connected color C-RAM. The pass_out of the depth C-RAM is connected with the pass_in of the color C-RAM. If the value of the pass_in is 1, color-write is then accomplished in the color C-RAM with the color data from MIU. Because the input data can be transmitted from MIU into the C-RAMs synchronously with the clock, the ALU pipeline is able to run fully without any stall.

4.4   The Latency in EDFB

Compared with the previous two memory systems, EDFB can reduce the latency to complete C-tests for a pixel cache block. We assume that the internal bus width is equal to the size of a pixel cache block and the ALUs execute C-tests for a pixel cache block at each cycle. Then the overall latency to complete C-tests for a pixel cache is the latencies both to read from and to write into the frame buffer plus one cycle to execute C-tests.

5   Experimental Simulation Results

In this section, various simulation results are given to evaluate the proposed architecture. A trace-driven simulator has been built for the proposed architecture. The traces are generated with three benchmarks, *Quake3*[14] demo I, *Quake3* demo II, and *Lightscape* [15] for 1600×1200 screen resolution by modifying the Mesa OpenGL compatible API. We assume that the traces consist of order-free data only.

For each benchmark, 100 frames are used to generate each trace. The model data of each benchmark are evenly distributed into a given number of rasterizers by a round-robin fashion. For example, if the number of the rasterizers is n, $(mn+1)$-th triangles, $m=0,1,2,$, are fed into the first rasterizer. We assume that one order-free pixel is generated per cycle for each rasterizer. With these traces, the pixel cache simulations are performed by modifying the well-known Dinero III cache simulator [12].

Fig. 9 shows some captured scenes for the benchmarks. *Quake3* in particular is one of many typical current video games on the market and is frequently used

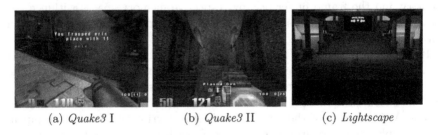

(a) *Quake3* I   (b) *Quake3* II   (c) *Lightscape*

Fig. 9. The three benchmarks

as a benchmark in other related work for the simulation. *Lightscape* is a product of the SPECviewperf^{TM} and is used as a benchmark in this paper because of its high scene complexity compared with other SPECviewperf^{TM} products and its distinct pixel cache miss distributions ,as provided in [8], compared with other benchmarks.

5.1   The Pixel Cache Simulations

In [8], the cache miss rates of a conventional pixel cache architecture for various cache sizes with different block sizes and set associativities are provided. The simulation results show that the miss rate varies according to the block size, but not to the cache size and the associativity. It also shows that as the block size increases, the miss rate decreases. As mentioned in [9], these results imply that graphics hardware rendering does not exhibit much temporal locality, but does exhibit spatial locality. Thus we perform the pixel cache simulation only for various block sizes.

Fig. 10 shows the pixel cache miss rates for direct-mapped 16 KB depth cache with three different block sizes as the number of rasterizers increases, where the miss rates for multiple rasterizers are averaged over all the pixel caches. Because triangles are distributed into multiple rasterizers with a round-robin fashion, the locality of each pixel cache with multiple rasterizers seems to decrease more than that of the pixel cache with a single rasterizer. The simulation results show that the miss rates increase quite slowly as the number of rasterizers increases for *Quake3* I and *Quake3* II. But the miss rates for *Lightscape* increase somewhat rapidly compared with those of *Quake3* I and *Quake3* II.

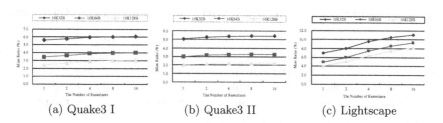

(a) Quake3 I   (b) Quake3 II   (c) Lightscape

Fig. 10. The pixel cache miss rates

5.2   The Memory Latency Reduction Rates

A replaced cache block from the pixel cache is stored into the tail entry of a pixel output queue indicated by the tail pointer. When the replaced block reaches the head entry indicated by the head pointer, it is written into the frame buffer. The overall pipeline does not stall as long as the pixel output queue is not full. Thus, with a buffer of infinite size, the proposed architecture is able to achieve a zero-latency memory system.

Fig. 11 shows the memory latency reduction rates for the three memory systems and the other one, *Modified*, discussed at Section 5.4. Note that the reduction rate of 100% represents a zero-latency memory system. If the reduction

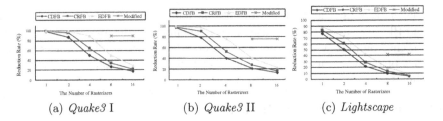

(a) *Quake3* I   (b) *Quake3* II   (c) *Lightscape*

Fig. 11. The memory latency reduction rates

rate is 0%, the full memory latency is required for a pixel cache miss. We assume that the numbers of cycles to complete C-tests for a pixel cache block for CDFB, CRFB, and EDFB are 16, 12, and 8, respectively. The number of cycles can be determined according to the block size of a pixel cache, the number of ALUs, the DRAM performance, etc. We also assume that the number of entries in a pixel output queue is fixed to 128, because the simulation results on the reduction rates for various numbers of entries, which is not provided in this paper, show that the numbers of entries from 4 up to 1024 affect the reduction rates under 8%.

The simulation results show that an almost zero-latency memory system can be achieved with CRFB and EDFB with one rasterizer and two rasterizers. With four rasterizers, significant reduction rates are achieved for EDFB. Because the number of replaced blocks fed into MIU at the same time increases as the number of the rasterizers increases, the reduction rates decrease as the number of rasterizers increases. The reduction rates are not sufficient when the number of rasterizers is eight or sixteen.

5.3   Enhancing the Performance with More Than Eight Rasterizers

The performance of the proposed architecture in Fig. 3 can be enhanced by modifying it to utilize the scalability of a sort-last rendering machine. Fig. 12 shows the modified architecture with sixteen rasterizers. Because an effective memory system seems to be maintained until we deploy four rasterizers, we integrate four rasterizers into one group. Each group is equivalent to the proposed architecture in Fig. 3 with four rasterizers.

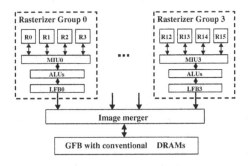

Fig. 12. The modified architecture with sixteen rasterizer

The overall structure and the execution flow of the modified architecture in Fig. 12 are similar to those of a sort-last rendering machine. Each rasterizer group generates a subimage with its own full-screen frame buffer, called the local frame buffer (LFB). The contents of all LFBs are merged periodically by the image merger at the speed of a CRT scan with a pipelined fashion. The final merged image is then transmitted into the global frame buffer (GFB). By double buffering for LFB and GFB, the rasterization can be executed simultaneously with the image merging.

Because each rasterizer group can be performed independently, the memory latency reduction rates for eight and sixteen rasterizers, denoted by *Modified* in Fig. 11, are equal to that with four rasterizer. However, LFBs (two for eight rasterizers and four for sixteen rasterizers) and the image merger should be embedded in the rendering processor.

5.4   Performance Evaluation

To evaluate the performance analytically, we calculate the average fragments per cycle (*AFPC*) with a rasterizer. In [8], the miss penalties due to both the pixel cache and the texture cache are assumed to degrade the overall performance. In this paper, we assume that only the memory latency due to the pixel cache can degrade the performance. Hence, *AFPC* can be calculated as follows.

$$AFPC = 1/(1 + Miss\_Rate \times Latency \times (1 - Reduction)), \qquad (1)$$

where *Miss_Rate* is the miss rate of the pixel cache, *Latency* is the cycle times of the memory latency due to a pixel cache miss, and *Reduction* is the reduction rates shown in Fig. 11. The denominator of the above equation represents the average cycles per fragment with a rasterizer.

Fig. 13 shows AFPCs for the proposed architecture with different numbers of rasterizers and five different configurations. *EDFB0* represents the embedded DRAMs for n frame buffers with 0% reduction rate, where n frame buffers are equal to n local frame buffers of n rasterizers for conventional sort-last architecture provided in Fig. 2. The AFPC of EDFB0 is provided to compare it with those of other four proposed configurations. For example, for four rasterizers in Fig. 13 (a), the AFPC of EDFB0 is almost the same as that of CDFB. The performance increment for n rasterizers can be calculated easily by multiplying

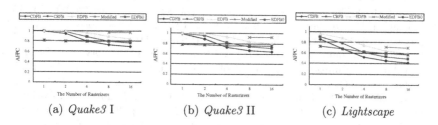

(a) *Quake3* I   (b) *Quake3* II   (c) *Lightscape*

Fig. 13. AFPCs of the proposed architecture

n with *AFPC* of the architecture with n rasterizers. Thus, the *AFPC* of the modified architecture in Fig. 13 (a) shows that the modified architecture achieves an almost linear speedup even with sixteen rasterizers.

6   Conclusions

This paper has proposed a new parallel rendering processor architecture to solve the consistency problem of the pixel cache and reduce significantly the memory latency due to pixel cache misses. One of current works on David II is to implement effectively the order-independent transparency unit, such as R-buffer. Also, a prototype for David II will be developed in the near future.

Acknowledgement

This work was supported by the Korea Research Foundation Grant (KRF-2004-041-D00560).

References

1. Khan, A.K., et al.: A 150-MHz graphics rendering processor with 256-Mb embedded DRAM. IEEE Journal of Solid-State Circuits, Vol. 36, No. 11, Nov (2001) 1775-1783
2. Molnar, S.,Cox, M., Ellsworth, M.,Fuchs, H.:A sorting classification of parallel rendering. IEEE Computer Graphics and Applications, Vol. 14, No. 4, July (1994) 23-32
3. Nishimura, S., Kunii, T. : VC-1: A scalable graphics computer with virtual local frame buffers, In Proc. of SIGGRAPH '96, Aug (1996) 365-372
4. Deering, M., Naegle, D.: The SAGE Architecture, In Proc. of SIGGRAPH 2002, July (2002) 683-692
5. Wittenbrink, G.M. : R-buffer: A pointerless A-buffer hardware architecture. In Proc. SIGGRAPH/Eurographics Workshop on Graphics Hardware, Aug (2001) 73-80
6. Aila, Timo., Miettinen, Ville., Nordlund, Petri.: Delay streams for graphics hardware, In Proc. SIGGRAPH 2003, Aug (2003) 792-880
7. Carpenter, L.: The A-Buffer, an antialiased hidden surface method, In Proc. SIGGRAPH, (1984) 103-108
8. Park, Woo-Chan., Lee, Kil-Whan., Kim, Il-San., Han, Tack-Don., Yang, Sung-Bong.: An effective pixel rasterization pipeline architecture for 3D rendering processors, IEEE Transactions on Computers, Vol. 52, No. 11, Nov (2003) 1501-1508
9. Michael, F.D., Stephen, A.S., Michael, G.L.: FBRAM: A new form memory optimized for 3D Graphics, In Proc SIGGRAPH'94, (1994) 167-174
10. Inoue, K., Nakamura, H., Kawai,H.: A 10b Frame buffer memory with Z-compare and A-bending units, IEEE Journal of Solid-State Circuits, vol. 30, No. 12, Dec (1995) 1563-1568
11. McCormack, J., McNamara, H., Gianos, C., Seiler, L., Jouppi, N.P., Correl, K., Dutton, T., Zurawski, J.: Neon: a (big) (fast) single-chip 3D workstation graphics accelerator, Research Report 98/1, Western Research Laboratory, Compaq Corporation, Aug. (1998) revised July (1999)

12. Hill, M.D., Larus, J.R., Lebeck, A.R, Talluri, M., Wood, D.A.: Wisconsin architectural research tool set, ACM SIGARCH Computer Architecture News, vol 21, Sep. (1993) 8-10

13. Patterson, D.A., Hennessy, J.L.: Computer organization & design: The hardware/software interface, Morgan Kaufmann Publisher Inc., Second edition (1998)

14. http://www.idsoftware.com/games/quake/quake3-arena

15. http://www.spec.org/gpc/opc.static/opcview70.html

Controller Synthesis for Mapping Partitioned Programs on Array Architectures

Hritam Dutta, Frank Hannig, and Jürgen Teich

Department of Computer Science 12, Hardware-Software-Co-Design,
University of Erlangen-Nuremberg, Germany
{dutta, hannig, teich}@cs.fau.de

Abstract. Processor arrays can be used as accelerators for a plenty of dataflow-dominant applications. Innately these applications have almost no control flow, but the application of sophisticated partitioning and scheduling techniques in order to handle large scale problems and to balance local memory requirements with I/O-bandwidth has the disadvantage of a more complex control flow. Thus, efficient control path synthesis is one of the greatest challenges when compiling algorithms onto processor arrays. This paper presents an efficient methodology for the automated control path synthesis for the mapping of partitioned algorithms onto processor arrays. The major advantages observed in the presented methodology are seen in, (a) control generation for different partitioning techniques and arbitrary parallelepiped tiles, (b) combined use of a global and a local control strategy in order to reduce the control overhead, (c) up to 90 percent reduction in control path area and resources compared to existing approaches.

1 Introduction and Related Work

In the last decade, there has been a dramatic growth in research and development of massively parallel processor arrays both in academia and industry. The trends in lithography and process integration technology allow the implementation of hundreds of 32-bit microprocessors on a single die. Furthermore, the expensive design process for ASICs calls for an automated synthesis of such accelerators in form of array architectures. Also, the introduction of reconfigurable architectures allows to exploit the flexibility of software along with the performance of processor arrays. Processor array architectures provide an optimal platform for the parallel execution of number crunching loop programs from fields of digital signal processing, image processing, linear algebra, etc. However, due to a lack of mapping tools, these massively parallel processor architectures are not able to realize their full potential. The ultimate aim of such mapping tools is to map software loops, such as *for* or *while* loops in C programs, onto a hardware target subject to the performance constraints in latency, area, or power. The example of state of the art mapping tools are PICO-Express [1], and MMalpha [2].

The polytope model [3] is an intuitive methodology for loop parallelization and mapping of loop nests onto massively parallel architectures. The architectures in form of processor array may be implemented on FPGAs or coarse-grained programmable array architectures. The *space-time mapping* is an important transformation for obtaining full-size processor array descriptions from a given nested loop program. *Partitioning*

W. Grass et al. (Eds.): ARCS 2006, LNCS 3894, pp. 176–190, 2006.

is another necessary transformation for mapping loops onto reduced-size arrays in order to meet the resource constraints. Well known partitioning techniques are *Tiling* and *Clustering*. *Control generation* is a transformation which is responsible for the control path synthesis, which produces control signals to orchestrate the correct execution of the loop program. The systematic design of control units of full-size processor arrays was first introduced in [4]. Another procedure for the systematic definition of control signals for the class of conditional uniform recurrence equations (CUREs) was introduced in [5]. The first method is characterized by local control flow, problem size independence, and optimization of the number of required control variables. However, both the methodologies are restricted to simple space-time mappings obtained by a projection. Darte et al.[6] introduced a method for the automatic generation of control code in case of clustering with rectangular tiles and tight linear schedules. The main contribution of this paper is the introduction of a general methodology for control path generation on loop partitioning with congruent tiles with maximum reuse of control predicates in massively parallel architectures. But first in Section 2, we briefly introduce some definitions and important transformations. Afterwards in Section 3, our novel control generation methodology is presented. Finally, in Section 4 and 5, a case study of our methodology and conclusions are presented, respectively.

2   Background

2.1   Definitions, Notations, and Transformations

In this paper, the class of algorithms we are dealing with is a class of recurrence equations defined as follows:

Definition 1. *(PLA). A piecewise linear algorithm consists of a set of N quantified equations, $S_1[I], \ldots, S_i[I], \ldots, S_N[I]$. Each equation $S_i[I]$ is of the form*

$$\forall I \in \mathcal{I}_i \; : \; x_i[P_i I + f_i] \; = \; \mathcal{F}_i(\ldots, x_j[Q_j I - d_{ji}], \ldots) \; \text{if} \; C_i^I(I)$$

P_i, Q_j are constant rational indexing matrices and f_i, d_{ji} are constant rational vectors of corresponding dimension.

The domains $\mathcal{I}_i$ are defined as *Linearly Bounded Lattices*[7]. With these definitions, several combinations of parallelizing transformations like *embedding* of variables, *localization* (vectorization), or *operator splitting* in the polytope model can be applied, for the sake of brevity we refer to [8].

Example 1. The matrix multiplication is taken as an example to illustrate our methodology. The product $C = A \cdot B$ of two square matrices $A, B \in \mathbb{Z}^{N \times N}$ is defined as $c_{ij} = \sum_{k=1}^{N} a_{ik} b_{kj} \; \forall 1 \leq i \leq N \wedge 1 \leq j \leq N$. Let $N = 8$, then after application of the above mentioned transformations the following PLA (satisfying Definition 1) is obtained.

$$
\begin{aligned}
a[i,j,k] &= a[i,0,k] \\
b[i,j,k] &= b[0,j,k] \\
z[i,j,k] &= a[i,j,k] \cdot b[i,j,k] \\
c[i,j,k] &= \begin{cases} c[i,j,k-1] + z[i,j,k] & \text{if} \quad k > 0 \\ z[i,j,k] & \text{if} \quad k = 0 \end{cases} \\
C_{out}[i,j,k] &= c[i,j,k] \qquad\qquad\qquad\; \text{if} \quad k = 7
\end{aligned}
$$

The matrices A and B are embedded into the arrays as follows, $a[i,0,k] = a_{ik}$, $b[0,j,k] = b_{kj}$. The index space is given by $\mathcal{I} = \{I = (i\ j\ k)^T \in \mathbb{Z}^3 \mid 0 \le i,j,k \le 7\}$.

2.2 Partitioning

Partitioning is a well known transformation which covers the index space of computation using congruent hyperplanes, hyperquaders, or parallelepipeds called *tiles*[9],[10]. For processor arrays (PAs), it is carried out in order to match a loop nest implementation to resource constraints in terms of available number of processing elements (PEs), local memory, and communication bandwidth. Well known partitioning techniques are multiprojection, LSGP (local sequential global parallel, often also referred as clustering or blocking) and LPGS (local parallel global sequential, also referred as tiling). Formally, partitioning divides the index space $\mathcal{I}$ using congruent tiles such that it is decomposed into spaces $\mathcal{J}$ and $\mathcal{K}$, i.e., $\mathcal{I} \mapsto \mathcal{J} \oplus \mathcal{K}$, where tiles may be defined by tiling matrix, P [1]. $\mathcal{J} \in \mathbb{Z}^n$ represents the points within the tile and $\mathcal{K} \in \mathbb{Z}^n$ accounts for regular repetition of the tiles, i.e., the origin of each tile. Hierarchical partitioning (often referred to as multi-blocking) methods use different hierarchies of tiling matrices to divide the index

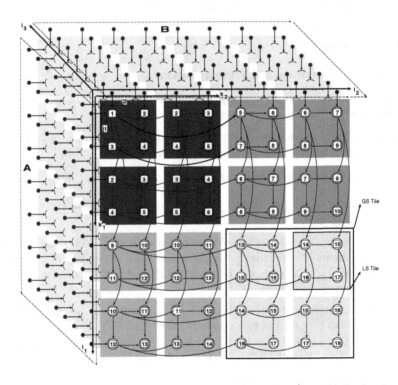

Fig. 1. The iteration space of the partial localized co-partitioned matrix multiplication 8×8 example. Each arc denotes a data dependency. The numbers correspond to the time step of execution as specified by the space-time mapping in Eq. (3).

---

[1] $\mathcal{J} \oplus \mathcal{K} = \{i = j + P \cdot k \mid j \in \mathcal{J} \wedge k \in \mathcal{K} \wedge P \in \mathbb{Z}^{n \times n}\}$.

space. Co-partitioning is such an example of a 2-level hierarchical partitioning[11], where the index space is first partitioned into LS (local sequential) tiles, this tiled index space is tiled once more using GS (global sequential) tiles as shown in Fig. 1. Co-partitioning uses both LSGP and LPGS methods in order to balance local memory requirements with I/O bandwidth with the advantage of problem size independence. Formally, it is defined as splitting of an index space into spaces $\mathcal{J}$, $\mathcal{K}$ and $\mathcal{L}$, i.e., $\mathcal{I} \mapsto \mathcal{J} \oplus \mathcal{K} \oplus \mathcal{L}$ [2] using two congruent tiles defined by tiling matrices, P_{LS} and P_{GS}. $\mathcal{J} \in \mathbb{Z}^n$ represents the points within the LS tiles and $\mathcal{K} \in \mathbb{Z}^n$ accounts for the regular repetition of the origin of LS tiles (i.e., tiles marked with same shade in Fig. 1). $\mathcal{L} \in \mathbb{Z}^n$ accounts for the regular repetition of the GS tiles (i.e., bigger tiles marked with different shade in Fig. 1).

Example 2. Co-partitioning and subsequent partial localization[12] of the matrix multiplication example is shown in Fig. 1. The PLA obtained on application of above mentioned transformations is given in Eq. (2) and is shown in Fig. 1. The matrices used for tiling are

$$P_{GS} = \begin{pmatrix} 4 & 0 & 0 \\ 0 & 4 & 0 \\ 0 & 0 & 1 \end{pmatrix} \qquad P_{LS} = \begin{pmatrix} 2 & 0 & 0 \\ 0 & 2 & 0 \\ 0 & 0 & 1 \end{pmatrix}$$

One can verify that the index point $I = (5,7,0)$ is uniquely mapped to $J = (1,1)$, $K = (0,1)$ and $L = (1,1,0)$ after co-partitioning[3].

$$a[j_1,j_2,k_1,k_2,l_1,l_2,l_3] = \begin{cases} a[j_1,j_2-1,k_1,k_2,l_1,l_2,l_3] & \text{if} \quad j_2 > 0 \\ a[j_1,j_1,k_1,k_2-1,l_1,l_2,l_3] & \text{if} \quad j_2+k_2 > 0 \wedge j_2 = 0 \\ a[j_1,j_1,k_1,k_2,l_1,l_2-1,l_3] & \text{if} \quad j_2+k_2+l_2 > 0 \wedge \\ & \qquad j_2+k_2 = 0 \wedge j_2 = 0 \\ A_{j_1+2 \cdot k_1+4 \cdot l_1, l_3} & \text{if} \quad j_2+k_2+l_2 = 0 \wedge \\ & \qquad j_2+k_2 = 0 \wedge j_2 = 0 \end{cases}$$

$$b[j_1,j_2,k_1,k_2,l_1,l_2,l_3] = \begin{cases} b[j_1-1,j_2,k_1,k_2,l_1,l_2,l_3] & \text{if} \quad j_1 > 0 \\ b[j_1,j_2,k_1-1,k_2,l_1,l_2,l_3] & \text{if} \quad j_1+k_1 > 0 \wedge j_1 = 0 \\ b[j_1,j_2,k_1,k_2,l_1-1,l_2,l_3] & \text{if} \quad j_1+k_1+l_1 > 0 \wedge \\ & \qquad j_1+k_1 = 0 \wedge j_1 = 0 \\ B_{l_3,j_2+2 \cdot k_2+4 \cdot l_2} & \text{if} \quad j_1+k_1+l_1 = 0 \wedge \\ & \qquad j_1+k_1 = 0 \wedge j_1 = 0 \end{cases} \qquad (1)$$

$$z[j_1,j_2,k_1,k_2,l_1,l_2,l_3] = a[j_1,j_2,k_1,k_2,l_1,l_2,l_3]$$

$$\cdot b[j_1,j_2,k_1,k_2,l_1,l_2,l_3]$$

$$c[j_1,j_2,k_1,k_2,l_1,l_2,l_3] = \begin{cases} c[j_1,j_2,k_1,k_2,l_1,l_2,l_3-1] & \text{if} \quad l_3 > 0 \\ + z[j_1,j_2,k_1,k_2,l_1,l_2,l_3] \\ z[j_1,j_2,k_1,k_2,l_1,l_2,l_3] & \text{if} \quad l_3 = 0 \end{cases}$$

$$C[j_1,j_2,k_1,k_2,l_1,l_2,l_3] = c[j_1,j_2,k_1,k_2,l_1,l_2,l_3] \qquad \text{if} \quad l_3 = 7$$

---

[2] $\mathcal{J} \oplus \mathcal{K} \oplus \mathcal{L} = \{i = j + P_{LS} \cdot k + P_{GS} \cdot l \mid j \in \mathcal{J} \wedge k \in \mathcal{K} \wedge l \in \mathcal{L} \wedge P_{LS}, P_{GS} \in \mathbb{Z}^{n \times n}\}$.

[3] j_3, k_3 are removed from the description as $j_3 = 0$, and $k_3 = 0$.

for all $J = (j_1 \ j_2)^T \in \mathcal{J}$, $K = (k_1 \ k_2)^T \in \mathcal{K}$, and $L = (l_1 \ l_2 \ l_3)^T \in \mathcal{L}$, with
$\mathcal{J} = \{J \in \mathbb{Z}^2 \mid 0 \le j_1, j_2 \le 1\}$, $\mathcal{K} = \{K \in \mathbb{Z}^2 \mid 0 \le k_1, k_2 \le 1\}$, and
$\mathcal{L} = \{L \in \mathbb{Z}^3 \mid 0 \le l_1, l_2 \le 1 \wedge 0 \le l_3 \le 7\}$

2.3   Allocation and Scheduling

Linear transformations are used as *space-time mappings* in order to assign a processor p (space) and a sequencing index t (time) to index vectors [8]. In co-partitioning, the index points within the LS tiles are executed sequentially. All LS tiles within a GS tile are executed in parallel by the processor array. Therefore, the number of PEs is equal to the number of LS tiles within a GS tile. The GS tiles are executed sequentially.

Definition 2. *(Space-time mapping for co-partitioning). A space-time mapping in case of co-partitioning is an affine transformation of the form*

$$\begin{pmatrix} p \\ t \end{pmatrix} = \begin{pmatrix} 0 & E & 0 \\ \lambda_J & \lambda_K & \lambda_L \end{pmatrix} \begin{pmatrix} J \\ K \\ L \end{pmatrix} \tag{2}$$

where $E \in \mathbb{Z}^{n_K \times n_K}$ is the identity matrix, $\lambda_J \in \mathbb{Z}^{1 \times n_J}$, $\lambda_K \in \mathbb{Z}^{1 \times n_K}$, $\lambda_L \in \mathbb{Z}^{1 \times n_L}$.

Other hierarchical partitioning schemes can be realized using an appropriate selection of an affine transformation characterizing scheduling and allocation of the index points. The problem of determining an optimal sequencing index (i.e., $\lambda_J, \lambda_K, \dots$) might be solved by Mixed Integer Linear Programming similar as in [13].

Example 3. An optimal space-time mapping for Ex. 2 on co-partitioning according to Def. 2 is

$$\begin{pmatrix} p_1 \\ p_2 \\ t \end{pmatrix} = \begin{pmatrix} 0 & 0 & 1 & 0 & 0 & 0 & 0 \\ 0 & 0 & 0 & 1 & 0 & 0 & 0 \\ 2 & 1 & 1 & 1 & 8 & 4 & 16 \end{pmatrix} \begin{pmatrix} J \\ K \\ L \end{pmatrix} + \begin{pmatrix} 0 \\ 0 \\ 1 \end{pmatrix}, \text{where } J = \begin{pmatrix} j_1 \\ j_2 \end{pmatrix}, K = \begin{pmatrix} k_1 \\ k_2 \end{pmatrix}, L = \begin{pmatrix} l_1 \\ l_2 \\ l_3 \end{pmatrix}$$

Therefore, a 2×2 processor array is obtained which executes the LS tiles in parallel and GS tiles sequentially. The PLA obtained after space-time mapping is shown in Eq. (3).

$$
\begin{aligned}
a[p_1, p_2, t] &= \begin{cases}
a[p_1, p_2, t-1] & \text{if } j_2 > 0 \\
a[p_1, p_2-1, t-1] & \text{if } j_2 + p_2 > 0 \wedge j_2 = 0 \\
a[p_1, p_2, t-4] & \text{if } j_2 + p_2 + l_2 > 0 \wedge j_2 + p_2 = 0 \wedge j_2 = 0 \\
A_{2p_1+j_1+4l_1, l_3} & \text{if } j_2 + p_2 + l_2 = 0 \wedge j_2 + p_2 = 0 \wedge j_2 = 0
\end{cases} \\
b[p_1, p_2, t] &= \begin{cases}
b[p_1, p_2, t-2] & \text{if } j_1 > 0 \\
b[p_1 - 1, p_2, t-1] & \text{if } j_1 + p_1 > 0 \wedge j_1 = 0 \\
b[p_1, p_2, t-8] & \text{if } j_1 + p_1 + l_1 > 0 \wedge j_1 + p_1 = 0 \wedge j_1 = 0 \\
B_{l_3, 2p_2+j_2+4l_2} & \text{if } j_1 + p_1 + l_1 = 0 \wedge j_1 + p_1 = 0 \wedge j_1 = 0
\end{cases} \\
z[p_1, p_2, t] &= a[p_1, p_2, t] \cdot b[p_1, p_2, t] \\
c[p_1, p_2, t] &= \begin{cases}
c[p_1, p_2, t - 16] + z[p_1, p_2, t] & \text{if } l_3 > 0 \\
z[p_1, p_2, t] & \text{if } l_3 = 0
\end{cases} \\
C[p_1, p_2, t] &= c[p_1, p_2, t] \quad\quad\quad\;\; \text{if } l_3 = 7
\end{aligned}
\tag{3}
$$

3   Control Generation

The control path generation is an intrinsic part for the automated generation of PAs. The data path synthesis can be easily obtained from the assignment statements in a PLA (see Eq. (3)) as they are only processor p and time t dependent. The control path synthesis is more complicated as the control predicates depend on variables other than p and t. The iteration dependent if-conditionals occurring in a given PLA (see Eq. (1) and Eq. (3)) have to be replaced by control variables for efficient parallelization. Furthermore, scheduling and allocation of operations on a resource constrained architecture requires the generation of control signals. Therefore, a step for control generation is needed that specifies the control units and the signals of the processor array. All the iteration dependent conditionals after co-partitioning can be represented in one of the following forms[4]:

$$A_J \cdot J \geq b_J \quad \wedge \quad A_K \cdot p \geq b_K \quad \wedge \quad A_L \cdot L \geq b_L \tag{4}$$

$$A_J \cdot J + A_K \cdot p + A_L \cdot L \geq b \tag{5}$$

The original iteration space co-ordinates, I are obtained as $J \oplus K \oplus L$. Therefore, the calculation of memory addresses and control predicates which are affine functions of I or other index variables can be done only if the following values are available.

- LS tile co-ordinates, J: For each given time step t and processor p, the LS co-ordinates J of the index points being executed have to be known.
- Processor co-ordinates, K or p: as defined by the space-time mapping.
- GS tile co-ordinates, L: For each time step t and processor p, the GS co-ordinate L of the index point being executed is required.

The rigidity of the problem stems from the fact that given $(p\,t)^{\mathrm{T}}$, the space $(J\,p\,L)^{\mathrm{T}}$ is to be calculated for the predicate computation from following linear Diophantine equation

$$t - \lambda_K \cdot p = \lambda_J \cdot J + \lambda_L \cdot L \tag{6}$$

The direct approach for finding a solution of Eq. (6) is the usage of the *Smith Normal Form* [14]. However the direct approach is computationally inefficient and is associated with high hardware costs. For sake of brevity, we refer to [15].

3.1   Control Design Flow: Methodology

The methodology for control generation introduced in this section is not based on a direct solution approach, but based on the scanning of the index space in the order as given by the space-time mapping. The methodology proposed in this section encompasses all possible partitioning techniques (i.e., LPGS, LSGP, co-partitioning and other hierarchical partitioning methods) using congruent parallelepiped tiles. The only major assumption is the application of linear affine scheduling. Fig. 2 shows a 2×2 processor array realization of the co-partitioned matrix multiplication example, where the

---

[4] Note, $p = K$ directly follows from the definition of the space-time mapping for co-partitioning, cp. Definition 2.

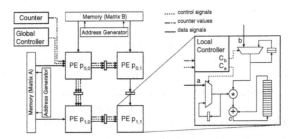

Fig. 2. An example 2×2 processor array implementation of a co-partitioned matrix multiplication

iterative conditionals which depend on the processor index are implemented by a *local controller*. The conditionals (usually common over a group of processors) and counter (generating index variables) independent of the processor index are implemented in a *global controller* and *counter*, respectively. To determine these described components, our approach for control path generation is constituted of the following four steps.

Determination of PE types. This step finds processor regions of same type. This helps in classification of control predicates for local and global controllers.

Scanning of the partitioned polytope. In this step, a global counter (see Fig. 2) for producing values of the index space variables is determined.

Initialization of local and global control signals. In this step, local and global controllers (see Fig. 2) for the execution of control predicates are generated.

Propagation of control and iteration variables. The requisite delays and directions (see Fig. 2) required for the propagation of global counter and global control signals in the processor array are determined.

3.1.1 Determination of PE Type

The main aim of the determination of PE types is to separate as many predicates as possible which can be executed by a global controller from those which must be locally computed. Without the determination of different PE types, the methodology would implement the local control model, i.e., all predicates would be computed in a local controller inside each PE. Secondly, It classifies processor regions executing the same functions. The advantage appears in customizing local control units and therefore customized hardware synthesis of data paths of PEs. The following strategy is used for the separation of predicates to be implemented in a local or a global controller. Processor p based iteration dependent conditionals of the form as in Eq. (5) have to be implemented by a local controller in each PE, if $A_K \neq 0$. Control conditions of types as in Eq. (4) and in Eq. (5) if $A_K = 0$ may be implemented in a global controller. However, processor regions associated with global control signals have to be identified. This is done by an orthogonal projection of the set of inequalities defining the corresponding control space onto the subspace defined by processor variables, p [5].

---

[5] $(A_s \cdot p \geq b_s = \text{Proj}_p(\begin{pmatrix} A_J & A_K & A_L \\ A_J & 0 & 0 \\ 0 & A_K & 0 \\ 0 & 0 & A_L \end{pmatrix} \begin{pmatrix} J \\ p \\ L \end{pmatrix} \geq \begin{pmatrix} b \\ b_J \\ b_K \\ b_L \end{pmatrix}))$.

Let Q be the number of statements having conditionals of type Eq. (4) or Eq. (5) (if $A_K = 0$). The statement S_q is associated with polyhedron $\mathcal{P}_q$ as defined by $A_q \cdot p \geq b_q$ for $q = 1, \ldots, Q$. The problem of identifying processor regions is now reduced to finding a non-intersecting set of k polyhedra, whose union covers the set $\bigcup_{q=1}^{Q} \mathcal{P}_q$. This is similar to the problem of code generation for multiple statements each defined over a different polyhedron [16]. The Q statements are then reallocated to the k processor regions. Therefore, we obtain a PLA description (as in Eq. (3)) for each of the k PE types. The PLA in Eq. (3) for matrix multiplication has four PE region types: PE1($p_1 = 0 \wedge p_2 = 0$), PE2($p_1 > 0 \wedge p_2 = 0$), PE3($p_1 = 0 \wedge p_2 > 0$), and PE4($p_1 > 0 \wedge p_2 > 0$).

3.1.2 Determination of Scanning Code

The purpose of this section is to synthesize a global counter which produces values of the required index variables (e.g., J, L for co-partitioning, J for LSGP, or K for LPGS) as specified by the schedule vector. The schedule vector is defined by a *loop matrix*[7].

Definition 3. *A loop matrix $R = (r_1 \ r_2 \ \ldots \ r_s) \in \mathbb{Z}^{s \times s}$ determines the ordering of index points J within a tile at time t. Index points in direction of r_1 are mapped side by side onto t, index points in direction of r_2 are separated by blocks of points in direction r_1 and so on. The ordering is similar to a sequential nested loop program where the loop index i_k corresponds to iterations in direction of r_k. The inner loop index is i_1, and the outermost loop index is i_s.*

To find a suitable schedule vector for co-partitioning, two loop matrices are required for J and L, respectively. However, for the sake of brevity, the following example illustrates our methodology for the counter generation of a LSGP tile using a single loop matrix.

Example 4. Fig. 3 (a) shows for a tile the relationship between the chosen loop matrix $R = \begin{pmatrix} -3 & 3 \\ 3 & 6 \end{pmatrix}$ and the derived schedule vector λ_J, $t = \lambda_J J = (3 \ 4)\begin{pmatrix} j_1 \\ j_2 \end{pmatrix}$. The lexicographic scanning in j_1, j_2 cannot lead to an execution order as defined by the loop matrix R. Therefore, a transformation to the orthogonal domain defined by y_1, y_2 as depicted in Fig. 3 (b) has to be defined. Let the vectors $Y = (y_1 \ y_2)^T$ and $J = (j_1 \ j_2)^T$ represent the transformed orthogonal domain and the initial domain, respectively. The transformation is defined by $E \cdot Y = T \cdot J$, where E is the identity matrix and T is an *appropriate* transformation matrix (in this example $T = \begin{pmatrix} -2 & 1 \\ 1 & 1 \end{pmatrix}$). Subsequently, a lexicographic scanning in the transformed domain is implemented. In Fig. 3 (b), the transformed domain isshown where a lexicographic scanning of black points (images of index points in

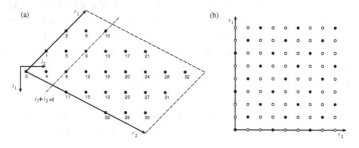

Fig. 3. (a) Execution of index points within a tile (b) Transformed domain

$$
\begin{pmatrix} E & -T \\ -E & T \\ 0 & A \end{pmatrix} \begin{pmatrix} Y \\ J \end{pmatrix} \geq \begin{pmatrix} 0 \\ 0 \\ b \end{pmatrix}
\quad \Leftrightarrow \quad
\begin{pmatrix} 1 & 0 & 2 & -1 \\ 0 & 1 & -1 & -1 \\ -1 & 0 & -2 & 1 \\ 0 & -1 & 1 & 1 \\ 0 & 0 & -6 & 3 \\ 0 & 0 & 3 & 3 \\ 0 & 0 & 6 & -3 \\ 0 & 0 & -3 & -3 \end{pmatrix}
\begin{pmatrix} y_1 \\ y_2 \\ j_1 \\ j_2 \end{pmatrix} \geq
\begin{pmatrix} 0 \\ 0 \\ 0 \\ 0 \\ 0 \\ 0 \\ -26 \\ -26 \end{pmatrix} \quad (7)
$$

original domain) needs to be carried out. Therefore, a counter has to be obtained in terms of a **FOR** loop which counts in the transformed domain the image points and skips the *holes* (i.e., the white points in Fig. 3 (b)). The strides of the loop variables y_1, y_2 can be determined by finding the diagonal elements of the Hermite Normal Form (HNF) [14] of the transformation matrix T (here, $S = \text{HNF}\left(\begin{smallmatrix} 1 & 0 \\ -2 & 3 \end{smallmatrix}\right)$). The outer counter variables depend on the loop matrix which in turn determines the scheduling vector. The lower bounds (i.e., initialization values) of the loop variables is the lexicographic minimum of the loop variables in the system of inequalities (see Eq. 7) under the context of the outer loop variables [17]. The set of inequalities $AJ \geq b$ defines the given initial tile whose points are to be scanned. Using *Parametric Integer Programming* (PIP) [18], Eq. (7) can be used to find the lexicographic minimum of the inner loop variables (i.e., in this example y_1) under the context of the outermost loop as obtained from the corresponding row in $AT^{-1} \cdot y \geq b$ (i.e., $0 \leq 3y_2 \leq 26$). The variable *lower* in the following pseudocode[6] is the lexicographic minimum of y_1. Finally, the inverse of the transformation matrix obtains the index variables in the original domain to give following pseudo-code for counter.

```
FOR (y₂ = 0; y₂ ≤ 8; y₂ = y₂ + 1)
    lower = y₂ − 3(((2y₂) ÷ 3) ÷ 2)
        FOR (y₁ = lower; y₁ ≤ 8; y₁ = y₁ + 3)
            j₁ = (−y₁ + y₂) ÷ 3;
            j₂ = (y₁ + 2y₂) ÷ 3;
        ENDFOR
ENDFOR
```

The pseudocode is implemented as a ScanCounter which produces the index variables.

The questions that remain to be answered are: How can the above scanning code be synchronized with the time as determined by the schedule vector? Also, how can the transformation matrix, T be determined? The scanning code needs to be synchronized with the time as determined by the schedule vector. In this example, this corresponds to generating no values (stall states) at time steps $t = 3, 7, 14, 18, 25, 29$ as shown in Fig. 3 (a) and Table 1. This is accomplished by providing an enable signal to the Scan-Counter which stops it at the requisite time steps. The enable mechanism's concept is shown in Fig. 4. The index points as determined by the loop matrix are output of the ScanCounter. The second counter counts over the time, which runs from 0 to t_{tile}, the

---

[6] The symbol "÷" denotes a modulo division.

Table 1. Counter output for Fig. 3(a). En, Res, "x" are the enable signal, reset signal, and stall states, respectively

t	0	1	2	3	4	5	6	7	8	9	10	11	12	13	14	15	16	17	18	19	20	21	22	23	24	25	26	27	28	29	30	31	32
y_1	0	3	6	x	1	4	7	x	2	5	8	0	3	6	x	1	4	7	x	2	5	8	0	3	6	x	1	4	7	x	2	5	8
y_2	0	0	0	x	1	1	1	x	2	2	2	3	3	3	x	4	4	4	x	5	5	5	6	6	6	x	7	7	7	x	8	8	8
j_1	0	-1	-2	x	0	-1	-2	x	0	-1	-2	1	0	-1	x	1	0	-1	x	1	0	-1	2	1	0	x	2	1	0	x	2	1	0
j_2	0	1	2	x	1	2	3	x	2	3	4	2	3	4	x	3	4	5	x	4	5	6	4	5	6	x	5	6	7	x	6	7	8
s	0	1	2	4	4	5	6	8	8	9	10	11	12	13	15	15	16	17	19	19	20	21	22	23	24	26	26	27	28	30	30	31	32
En	1	1	1	0	1	1	1	0	1	1	1	1	1	1	0	1	1	1	0	1	1	1	1	1	1	0	1	1	1	0	1	1	1
Res	0	0	0	0	0	0	0	0	0	0	0	0	0	0	0	0	0	0	0	0	0	0	0	0	0	0	0	0	0	0	0	0	1

last execution time of an index point within the tile. If at time t, $s = 3j_1 + 4j_2 \neq t$, then the ScanCounter is halted. If an enable mechanism is required or not can be determined by considering if the total time taken to compute a tile is a multiple of the number of points within the tile. The transformation matrix is given by

$$T = \frac{\sigma \cdot \mathrm{adj}(R)}{\gcd(r_{i,j})} \tag{8}$$

where $\sigma = |\det(R)|/\det(R)$ and $\gcd(r_{i,j})$ is the greatest common divisor of all elements of the loop matrix. The methodology can be extended to LPGS, co-partitioning and other hierarchical partitioning methods by passing the relevant loop matrices and schedule vectors in Algorithm 1. For instance, for co-partitioning λ_J, λ_L and two corresponding loop matrices. Therefore, for co-partitioning we obtain two counters producing J and L independently.

Algorithm 1: Counter generation

INPUT: Loop matrix R, Schedule vector λ, A, b.
OUTPUT: ScanCounter (as a FOR loop for J), Enable logic.

- Step 1: Determination of the transformation matrix T: If $\mathrm{adj}(R) \neq R$, the transformation matrix is determined using Eq. (8), else $T = E$ where E is the identity matrix.
- Step 2: Generation of scanning code:
  - Step 2.1: Determine the strides from the HNF of the transformation matrix T, i.e., $S = \mathrm{HNF}(T)$.
  - Step 2.2: Determine upper and lower bounds of variables in the transformed domain defined by Y. The lower bounds are found as lexicographic minimum of the system of inequalities (7) under the context of the outermost loop. The upper bounds are found from $(AT^{-1})Y \geq b$.
  - Step 2.3: Determine values of counter variables in $\mathcal{J}$ by inverse transformation, i.e., $J = T^{-1}Y$.
  - Step 2.4: Write down the counter description in terms of a FOR loop.
- Step 3: If the total time taken to compute a tile is not a multiple of the number of index points in the tile then generate an enable mechanism to synchronize the scanning code:
  - Step 3.1: Calculate $t_{tile} = \max_{J \in \mathcal{J}}\{\lambda_J J\}$, time needed to execute the tile.
  - Step 3.2: Generate the TimeCounter as in Fig. 4 with 0 as lower bound and t_{tile} as upper bound.
  - Step 3.3: The conditional unit as in Fig. 4 is configured, producing enable as true if and only if the time ($S = \lambda J$) corresponding to the ScanCounter matches the time t as specified by Time-Counter. The reset signal is produced when the TimeCounter reaches the upper bound t_{tile}.
- Step 4: Update the ScanCounter every δ cycles, where δ is the iteration interval.

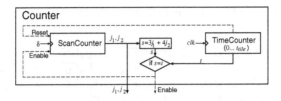

Fig. 4. Enable mechanism: The ScanCounter implements the scanning pseudocode. The enable signal is turned off if $s \neq t$. The TimeCounter is incremented each clock cycle *clk* from zero to the time of execution of the last index point. The scan counter is incremented only every δ clock cycle, where δ denotes the *iteration interval* which is the number of time instances between the evaluation of two successive instances of a variable within one processing element.

3.1.3 Control Unit Generation

This section deals with the automated control unit generation given the requisite predicates. After PE classification, each PE of different type has an individual behavioral specification. The behavioral specification of an example PE of qth PE type ($p \in P_q$ (say)) can be the PLA in Eq. (9).

$$
\begin{aligned}
x_1[I] &= \begin{cases} \mathcal{F}_1^1(\ldots,x_j[I-d_{1,1}]\ldots) & \text{if } \tilde{I} \in \tilde{\mathcal{I}}_1^1 \ \text{(L)} \wedge \hat{I} \in \hat{\mathcal{I}}_1^1 \ \text{(G)} \\ \vdots & \vdots \\ \mathcal{F}_1^{W_1}(\ldots,x_j[I-d_{W_1,1}],\ldots) & \text{if } \tilde{I} \in \tilde{\mathcal{I}}_1^{W_1} \ \text{(L)} \wedge \hat{I} \in \hat{\mathcal{I}}_1^{W_1} \ \text{(G)} \end{cases} \\
&\ \ \vdots \qquad\qquad\qquad\qquad\qquad\qquad\qquad \vdots \\
x_K[I] &= \begin{cases} \mathcal{F}_K^1(\ldots,x_j[I-d_{1,K}],\ldots) & \text{if } \tilde{I} \in \tilde{\mathcal{I}}_K^1 \ \text{(L)} \wedge \hat{I} \in \hat{\mathcal{I}}_K^1 \ \text{(G)} \\ \vdots & \vdots \\ \mathcal{F}_K^{W_K}(\ldots,x_j[I-d_{W_K,K}],\ldots) & \text{if } \tilde{I} \in \tilde{\mathcal{I}}_K^{W_K} \ \text{(L)} \wedge \hat{I} \in \hat{\mathcal{I}}_K^{W_K} \ \text{(G)} \end{cases}
\end{aligned} \tag{9}
$$

with the index vector $I = (p\ t)^{\mathrm{T}}$, where t is the time and $p = (p_1\ p_2 \ldots\ p_n)^{\mathrm{T}}$ is the processor index, where normally $n = 1$ or 2 due to physical limitations. The "if" conditionals also known as *Housekeeping* code, describe the conditional execution of the recurrence equations. The "if" conditional for co-partitioning under type (L) are characterized by a processor index dependent equation (given $A_K \neq 0$) as in following Eq. (10) and therefore must be implemented in the local controller.

$$\text{if } \ \tilde{I} \in \tilde{\mathcal{I}} = \{\tilde{I} = (J\ p\ L)^{\mathrm{T}} \in \mathbb{Z}^{3 \cdot n} \mid G\tilde{I} \geq g \ \Leftrightarrow A_J \cdot J + A_K \cdot p + A_L \cdot L \geq b\} \tag{10}$$

The "if" conditional under type (G) is described in the space $\hat{I} = (J\ L)^{\mathrm{T}}$, explicitly describes those iterative conditionals that are independent of processor index p as shown in Eq. (11) and can therefore be implemented by a global controller.

$$\text{if } \ \hat{I} \in \hat{\mathcal{I}} = \{\hat{I} = (J\ L)^{\mathrm{T}} \in \mathbb{Z}^{2 \cdot n} \mid G\hat{I} \geq g \Leftrightarrow A_J \cdot J \geq b_J \wedge A_L \cdot L \geq b_L\} \tag{11}$$

Let $G\tilde{I} \geq g$ be simplified so that it can be defined by a minimal number of m inequalities. Then the control needs to check whether the vector $\tilde{I}$ is inside the polyhedron defined by the m inequalities. This is done by introducing m boolean variables $lctr^i$, which are '1' only if $G_i \tilde{I} \geq g_i$. The control signals are generated for all LHS variables, x_k, $k = 1, \ldots, K$. The following pseudo-code is the behavioral description of the generation of local control path and signals for processor p of type PE_q.

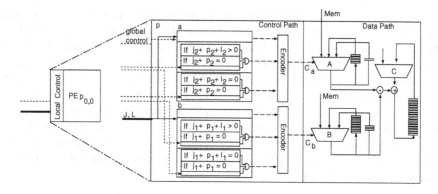

Fig. 5. An example of a local control path of a PE as derived from the PLA in Eq. (12)

$$lctr^l_{r,i}[I] = \begin{cases} 1 & \text{if} \quad G^l_{r,i} \cdot \tilde{I} \geq g^l_{r,i} \\ 0 & \text{else otherwise} \end{cases} \quad \forall \begin{matrix} r = 1,\ldots,K \wedge i = 1,\ldots,W_r \\ \wedge l = 1,\ldots,m_{r,i} \end{matrix}$$

$$lctr_{r,i} = lctr^1_{r,i} \wedge \ldots \wedge lctr^m_{r,i} \quad \forall \begin{matrix} r = 1,\ldots,K \wedge i = 1,\ldots,W_r \\ \wedge m = m_{r,i} \end{matrix}$$

$$C_1[I] = \begin{cases} 0 & \text{if} \quad lctr_{1,1} = 1 \wedge gctr_{1,1} = 1 \\ \vdots & \vdots \\ W_1 - 1 & \text{if} \quad lctr_{1,W_1} = 1 \wedge gctr_{1,W_1} = 1 \end{cases}$$

$$\vdots$$

$$C_K[I] = \begin{cases} 0 & \text{if} \quad lctr_{K,1} = 1 \wedge gctr_{K,1} = 1 \\ \vdots & \vdots \\ W_K - 1 & \text{if} \quad lctr_{K,W_K} = 1 \wedge gctr_{K,W_K} = 1 \end{cases}$$

$$x_1[I] = \text{SWITCH}(C_1[I] == 0, \mathcal{F}^1_1(\ldots,x_j[I - d_{1,1}],\ldots), \\ \ldots, C_1[I] == W_1 - 1, \mathcal{F}^{W_1}_1(\ldots,x_j[I - d_{W_1,1},\ldots]))$$

$$\vdots$$

$$x_K[I] = \text{SWITCH}(C_K[I] == 0, \mathcal{F}^1_K(\ldots,x_j[I - d_{1,K}],\ldots), \\ \ldots, C_K[I] == W_K - 1, \mathcal{F}^{W_K}_K(\ldots,x_j[I - d_{W_K,K},\ldots]))$$

$I = (p\ t)^T$, where $p \in PE_q$ and $\tilde{I} = (J\ p\ L)^T$. J and L are index variables obtained from a global counter. $lctr_{r,i}$ denotes the local control signal for the ith iterative conditional for variable x_r, which is obtained by AND relation of the m corresponding local control bits $lctr^l_{r,i}$. The mutual exclusivity of conditionals within a variable allows to encode the control variables in minimal bit encoding form in control variable $C_k[I]$. The global control signals, $gctr$ originating from the global controller are obtained by propagation from neighboring processors. The control signal is responsible for the selection of the appropriate input as dictated by the "if" statement. The local controller for PE1(i.e. $p_1 = 0 \wedge p_2 = 0$) is illustrated in Fig. 5 is defined by the following program. The construction of global control units is derived from the Type G as shown in Eq. (11). The transformation for construction of global control units collects the Type

G conditionals (processor independent conditionals) from all PE definitions in a single program. The computation of global control pursues the same methodology of checking whether the index vector, $\hat{I} = (J\,L)^{\mathrm{T}}$ lies in the polyhedron defined by inequalities. The global controller propagates the control signals from the border of the processor array as shown in Fig. 2. Unlike the memory resources, the size of control unit is independent of the partitioning parameters. The local and global control units are problem size independent as the number of control variables are independent of the number of index points in any index space. The discussion in this section can be similarly modified for control generation of LSGP, LPGS, and other hierarchical partitioning methods. The propagation of the global control signals and counter variables to the individual PEs is discussed in the next section.

3.1.4   Propagation of Global Control Signals and Counter Values

The counter variables and the control signals are propagated through the processor array (see Fig. 2) instead of being broadcasted to the respective processor elements. *Localization* (a transformation for converting global data dependencies into local dependencies) of control signals follows from $gctr(p,t) = gctr(0, t - \lambda_d)$ where λ_d is the number of delay registers or the number of time steps required by the global signals to travel to processor p. The equation is brought to a form where each PE receives the global signal from neighboring PEs as defined by $gctr(p,t) = gctr(p - d_p, t - \lambda_K \cdot d_p)$. The propagation vector, d_p is limited to $\{(1,0),(0,1),(1,1),(-1,0),$ $(0,-1),(-1,1)(1,-1),(-1,-1)\}$ for 2-d processor array. The selection of a propagation vector d_p for a PE(p) is obtained by looking at the start time of execution λ_s for each neighboring processor, $(p - d_p)$. The neighboring PE with λ_s less than start time of (p) and the difference being smallest is selected and the communication link is the propagation vector d_p. In case of a tie, the propagation vector is the same as the propagation vector for the neighboring PE if they are of same PE type. Otherwise the selection is done at random. This leads to regular circuit structure. Once the propagation vector d_p is found, the number of delay registers is found as $\lambda_K \cdot d_p$. For PE$(0,0)$ the index variables and the global control signals are directly taken from the counter and global controller, respectively. The program for a PE after application of following algorithm incorporates the delay registers and propagation vectors.

Algorithm 2: Delay and propagation determination

INPUT: Processor space $(\mathcal{P})$, schedule vector (λ).

OUTPUT: Propagation vector (d_p), delay (λ_d).   For all processing elements, $p \in \mathcal{P}$

    For all possible propagation vectors, d_p,

        determine $\lambda_{(p-d_p)}$ (start time) using the schedule vector, i.e., $\lambda_{(p-d_p)} = \lambda_K \cdot (p - d_p)$.

        Select d_p, s.t $\lambda_{p-d_p} < \lambda_p$ and $\lambda_{p-d_p} \geq \lambda_{p-s} \, \forall \lambda_{p-s} < \lambda_p$, where $s \in d_p$.

        In case of tie, if p and $p - d_p$ are of the same PE type, then the propagation vector of p is the same

        as the propagation vector of PE $p - d_p$ else d_p is selected randomly.

    ENDFOR

ENDFOR

---

4   A Case Study

Matrix multiplication was used as a case study for testing our methodology. The processor array specification is interpreted from the PLA after *control generation*. Afterwards, a VHDL implementation of the example co-partitioned matrix multiplication was carried out. The target FPGA architecture is a Xilinx Virtex XCV800. Table 2 summarizes the comparison of results from a multi-dimensional time implementation of matrix multiplication [19] and our implementation of co-partitioned matrix multiplication. The methodology for the generation of a controller for multi-dimensional time implementation includes an automaton (counter) for scanning the space-time polyhedron within each PE thus accounting for the high cost of the control path as seen in Table 2. As compared, our methodology has a global counter which generates the iteration co-ordinates and the some of the common predicates thus leading to reduced area costs. Therefore, a control path area reduction of 90% is obtained. The absence of RAM blocks is explained by use of slices as registers to realize the local memory. That accounts for the large size of the data path. The global counter takes up 209 slices. The high cost of the global counter and controller is however an offset as by increasing the number of processor elements it is almost a constant cost.

Table 2. Comparison of implementation for resource use by a single PE. Area complexity is expressed in terms of slices(4 LUTs).

Implementation	Control	Memory	Datapath	Clock
Multidimensional time	65 slices	2 RAM Blocks	26 slices	60 Mhz
Co-partitioned MM	12 slices	-	153 slices	58 Mhz

5   Conclusions and Future Work

Our scheduling methodology for partitioning techniques enables the update of iteration co-ordinates in a global counter synchronous to the implementation as specified by the space-time mapping. Therefore, a considerable cost reduction in area of the control path is obtained as compared to the methodologies suggested in [6],[19] where a FSM (Finite State Machine) local to every PE is responsible for the generation of iteration co-ordinates. Furthermore, the control generation methodology can deal not only with LSGP, LPGS, multi-projection but also co-partitioning and other hierarchical partitioning methods with added advantage of using parallelepiped tiles of arbitrary shape. The area and speed trade-off obtained between calculation of control signals from predicates or storage in a circular buffer needs to be studied with respect to resource constraints. The hardware interpretation of the program can be tuned to the architectures. For example, the propagation of global control signals can be optimized by having one global controller for each PE type in case of limited routing resources. Also, the optimal generation of address generation units and control units for PEs can be optimized by using an update scheme instead of re-computation. The results of our work are currently implemented in our design system [20].

References

1. Synfora, Inc.: (www.synfora.com)
2. Derrien, S., Risset, T.: Interfacing Compiled FPGA Programs: The MMAlpha Approach. In: PDPTA. (2000)
3. Lengauer, C.: Loop Parallelization in the Polytope Model. In Best, E., ed.: CONCUR'93. Lecture Notes in Computer Science 715, Springer-Verlag (1993) 398–416
4. Teich, J., Thiele, L.: Control Generation in the Design of Processor Arrays. Int. Journal on VLSI and Signal Processing 3(2) (1991) 77–92
5. Xue, J.: The Formal Synthesis of Control Signals for Systolic Arrays. PhD thesis, University of Edinburgh (1992)
6. Darte, A., Schreiber, R., Rau, B., Vivien, F.: Constructing and Exploiting Linear Schedules with Prescribed Parallelism. ACM Transactions on Design Automation of Electronic Systems 7(1) (2002) 159–172
7. Teich, J., Thiele, L., Zhang, L.: Scheduling of Partitioned Regular Algorithms on Processor Arrays with Constrained Resources. Journal of VLSI Signal Processing 17(1) (1997) 5–20
8. Hannig, F., Dutta, H., Teich, J.: Regular Mapping for Coarse-grained Reconfigurable Architectures. In: Proceedings of the 2004 IEEE International Conference on Acoustics, Speech, and Signal Processing (ICASSP 2004). Volume V., Montréal, Quebec, Canada, IEEE Signal Processing Society (2004) 57–60
9. Wolfe, M.: High Performance Compilers for Parallel Computing. Addison-Wesley Inc. (1996)
10. Oldfield, J., Dorf, R.: Field Programmable Gate Arrays: Reconfigurable Logic for Rapid Prototyping and Implementation of Digital Systems. John Wiley & Sons, Chichester, New York (1995)
11. Eckhardt, U., Merker, R.: Hierarchical Algorithm Partitioning at System Level for an Improved Utilization of Memory Structures. IEEE Transactions on Computer-Aided Design of Integrated Circuits and Systems 18(1) (1999) 14–24
12. Teich, J., Thiele, L.: Exact Partitioning of Affine Dependence Algorithms. In Deprettere, E.F., Teich, J., Vassiliadis, S., eds.: Embedded Processor Design Challenges. Volume 2268 of Lecture Notes in Computer Science (LNCS)., Springer, Berlin (2002) 135–153
13. Hannig, F., Teich, J.: Design Space Exploration for Massively Parallel Processor Arrays. In Malyshkin, V., ed.: Parallel Computing Technologies, 6th International Conference, PaCT 2001, Proceedings. Volume 2127 of Lecture Notes in Computer Science (LNCS)., Novosibirsk, Russia, Springer (2001) 51–65
14. Schrijver, A.: Theory of Linear and Integer Programming. Wiley – Interscience series in discrete mathematics. John Wiley & Sons, Chichester, New York (1986)
15. Dutta, F., Hannig, F., Teich, J.: Control Path Generation for Mapping Partitioned Dataflow-dominant Algorithms onto Array Architectures. Technical Report 03-2005, University of Erlangen-Nuremberg, Department of CS 12, Hardware-Software-Co-Design (2005)
16. Quillere, F., Rajopadhye, S., Wilde, D.: Generation of Efficient Nested Loops from Polyhedra. International Journal of Parallel Programming 28(5) (2000) 469–498
17. Bastoul, C.: Efficient Code Generation for Automatic Parallelization and Optimization. In: Int. Symposium on Parallel and Distributed Computing (ISPDC'03). (2003) 23–30
18. Feautrier, P.: Parametric Integer Programming. RAIRO Recherche Operationnelle 22 (1988) 243–268
19. Guillou, A., Quinton, P., Risset, T.: Hardware Synthesis for Multi-Dimensional Time,. IEEE computer Society, ASAP'2003 (2003)
20. PARO Design System Project: (www12.informatik.uni-erlangen.de/research/paro)

M²E: A Multiple-Input, Multiple-Output Function Extension for RISC-Based Extensible Processors

Xiaoyong Chen and Douglas L. Maskell

School of Computer Engineering, Nanyang Technological University,
Block N4, Nanyang Avenue, Singapore 639798
{y030068, asdouglas}@ntu.edu.sg

Abstract. Recent study shows that a further speedup can be achieved by RISC-based extensible processors if the incorporated custom functional units (CFUs) can execute functions with more than two inputs and one output. However, mechanisms to execute multiple-input, multiple-output (MIMO) custom functions in a RISC processor have not been addressed. This paper proposes an extension for single-issue RISC processors based on a CFU that can execute custom functions with up to six inputs and three outputs. To minimize the change to the core processor, we maintain the operand bandwidth of two inputs, one output per cycle and transfer the extra operands and results using repeated custom instructions. While keeping such an limit sacrifices some speedup, our experiments show that the MIMO extension can still achieve an average 51% increase in speedup compared to a dual-input, single-output (DISO) extension and an average 27% increase in speedup compared to a multiple-input, single-output (MISO) extension.

1 Introduction

RISC-based extensible processors, which combine the speedup and power/area savings offered by application-specific hardware in addition to the simplicity and flexibility offered by a RISC processor, have emerged as a promising solution to high performance embedded systems. Generally there are two extension schemes in such processors. The first scheme uses the custom logic as coprocessors, which are loosely coupled with the datapath of the core processor. Examples of this scheme include Garp [4], MicroBlaze [17] and Molen [13]. In this scheme, complicated computation tasks such as a loop can be performed on the custom logic without the intervention of the core processor. This results in significant performance improvement; however, the implementation of a complicated task requires considerable hardware resources and design effort. Additionally not all operations are suited to be implemented into custom logic. The second scheme integrates the custom logic into the datapath of the core processor, where the custom logic serves as additional function units. PRISC [11], ConCISe [5], and NIOS II [16] are examples of this scheme. The CFUs in such extensions contain little state or control logic and cost less in communicating with the core processor's instruction pipeline, making them easy to design and economic for small and frequently executed program patterns.

W. Grass et al. (Eds.): ARCS 2006, LNCS 3894, pp. 191–201, 2006.

Nevertheless, the attainable speedup of such an extension is limited by some practical constraints [3] [6] [10]. One of them is the number of inputs and outputs of the custom functions[1]. By relaxing the constraints on the number of inputs and outputs of a custom function, a larger cluster of operations can be fitted into it, resulting in a lot more speedup [9] [6] [10]. Ideally, a MIMO custom function can be executed like a core instruction with all its operands encoded in one instruction and transferred in a single cycle. But the practical 32-bit or 16-bit instruction length of RISC processors restricts the number of operands that can be encoded in one instruction. Moreover this approach generally requires increasing the number of input and output ports of the core processor's register file to provide higher operand bandwidth. Such a modification may impair the resource efficiency of the core processor which has been deliberately designed to execute DISO instructions.

A more back-compatible extension is to maintain the operand bandwidth of the core processor and transfer the extra operands of the custom functions using additional instructions. We observe that such an extension, though requiring a few more cycles to transfer the inputs and outputs, can still bring about a significant speedup compared to a DISO or MISO extension. We use the following code sequence to illustrate this.

```
I1. Add    r8, r2, r3     #op output, input, input
I2. Mult   r9, r4, r8
I3. Mult   r10, r2, r5
I4. Add    r2, r9, r10
I5. Mult   r11, r3, r6
I6. Add    r3, r9, r11
```

Assuming that each multiply instruction takes 5 cycles and each add instruction takes 1 cycle, this code sequence will cost 18 cycles on a single-issue RISC processor with an unpipelined multiplier. With a MIMO extension and the ideal operand bandwidth, this code sequence costs 7 cycles: the operand r2, r3, r4, r5, and r6 are put into CFU in the first cycle and the result r2 and r3 can be read out in the 7th cycle. If we still use a MIMO extension but limit the operand bandwidth to be two inputs and one output per cycle, this code sequence costs 8 cycles: the operand and r2 and r3 are put into the CFU in the first cycle; the operand r4 and r5 are put into the CFU in the second cycle; the operand r6 is put into the CFU in the third cycle; the result r2 can be read out in the 7th cycle and the result r3 can be read out in the 8th cycle. If we keep the operand bandwidth limit but use a MISO CFU, this code sequence costs 14 cycles. This is because the operation I3 and I4 cannot be concurrently evaluated with I5 and I6 due to the output limit. Certainly we could add a CFU to exploit the parallelism here. However, in that case more issue slots need to be spent in transferring the operand r2, r3, r4 and r6 to the second CFU. Therefore, the MIMO extension achieves additional speedup even with the operand bandwidth limits.

---

[1] For the sake of clarity, in this text we define a custom function as a group of operations in a program that are implemented in a CFU while defining custom instructions as the processor instructions used to invoke custom functions.

Encouraged by the above observation, we propose a processor extension based on a CFU that can execute custom functions with up to six inputs and three outputs. Using the SimpleScalar toolset [12], we developed a cycle-accurate simulator for a MIPS R3000 like processor with the proposed extension. We obtained a tool chain for this extensible processor by modifying GCC and GNU binutils. Using these tools, we evaluated the performance of our MIMO extension over a selection of MediaBench [14] applications.

In the rest of this paper, Section 2 discusses other research efforts in this area. Section 3 introduces the proposed MIMO processor extension. Section 4 presents experimental analysis of the proposed extension. Section 5 concludes this paper and describes our future work.

2 Related Work

PRISC [11] augments a RISC processor with a single hardware-programmable function unit that evaluates combinational functions. The delay of these combinational functions is restricted to be equal to the delay of the ALU in the core processor. PRISC only supports DISO custom functions. The ConCISe [5] system is a RISC processor enhanced by a CPLD-based reconfigurable functional unit. Multiple custom functions are encoded in a single reconfigurable unit to save resources. Like PRISC, ConCISe supports only DISO custom functions. The commercial soft-core processor NIOS II [16], allows users to choose different custom instruction architectural types that range from a simple, single-cycle combinatorial architecture to an extended variable-length, multi-cycle custom instruction architecture. Though flexible, NIOS II's custom logic interface is also designed for DISO custom functions since each custom function is invoked by a single custom instruction [1].

Many automatic instruction-set customization algorithms [2] [3] [8] proposed recently are capable of identifying MIMO custom functions from applications. With these algorithms, some researchers investigated the theoretical speedup by relaxing the constraints on the inputs and outputs of custom functions. Cong et al [9] quantitatively analyzed the operand bandwidth limitation on the performance of the extensible processors and concluded that the four inputs per cycle constraint can achieve an 80% speedup over the two inputs per cycle constraint. They also proposed a solution to improve the operand bandwidth. However this solution needs to modify many instructions' format to address the shadow registers. Ienne et al [6] studied the maximum potential speedup of specialized processors by mapping only data flow sections of code to the custom logic. According to their results, more than 60% of the potential gain comes from basic blocks with more than two inputs and about 50% from basic blocks with a single output. Yu and Mitra [10] studied the effect of more constraints and concluded that 4 inputs, 3 outputs could achieve a speedup of close to the theoretical limit. Kubilay et al [3] and Partha et al [8] also considered the effect of different input/output constraints in their work. These studies [3] [6] [8] [10] assumed an ideal operand bandwidth and focused on the theoretical speedup potential rather than the architectural consequences of MIMO extensions.

3 M²E Architecture Extension

As alluded to in previous sections, our aim is to improve the processor performance by developing an architectural extension which exploits the advantages of MIMO solutions without resorting to complicated structural changes to the core processors' ISA and micro-architecture. With this aim in mind, we propose a relatively simple architectural extension, named M²E (MIMO extension), which enhances the micro-architecture of a classical single-issue pipelined RISC processor. Our extension consists of only one or two CFUs, although it could be quite easily changed to include more CFUs. The operation of the CFUs is controlled by a single custom instruction and can involve from 1 to 16 custom functions per CFU. Figure 1 shows the architecture of our proposed M²E extension with a single CFU. Like PRISC and NIOS II, the CFUs are inserted in parallel with the ALU so that only minor changes to the existing datapath are needed. The ALU and CFUs operate independently of each other. A multiplexer selects the appropriate output from the ALU or the CFUs as the result to be forwarded to the next stage.

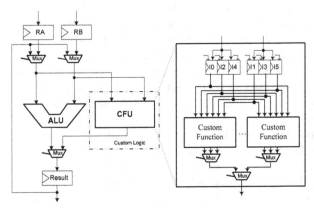

Fig. 1. The architecture of M²E

3.1 M²E CFU

As illustrated in Figure 1, a M²E CFU implements a number of (1-16) custom functions. Each custom function can have up to six inputs and three outputs. A multiplexer is used to select the requested output of a custom function. To provide inputs for the custom functions, six 32-bit transparent D-Type latches (I0-I5) are used. These latches (called input latches) are divided into two groups, with each group controlled by a 2-bit signal. The signal selects the latch that will be enabled from the clock edge used by the pipeline registers to the opposite one. When an input latch is enabled, it becomes transparent so that the CFU input can propagate across it. When it is disabled, the latch holds the last state of the input. Therefore, the inputs of a custom function can be used as early as possible and held in multiple cycles. The custom functions in the same CFU share the input latches and can also share part of their logic. Hence, unlike the custom functions residing in different CFUs, the execution of them cannot overlap. A multiplexer decides which custom function is being executed and whose output is valid.

Like in PRISC, our custom functions are implemented using combinational logic. We define I_j ($0 \leq j \leq 5$) and O_k ($0 \leq k \leq 2$) as the jth input and the kth output of a custom function respectively. If a change to the input I_j can result in a change of output O_k, we say I_j and O_k are *related* and use D_{jk} to represent the delay between them. We use D_{ri} to represent the maximum delay from the operand registers (RA & RB) to the inputs of the custom functions. We use D_{or} to represent the maximum delay from an output of a custom function to the result register in Figure 1. We further define the total delay (D_{rjkr}) associated with a *related* input-output pair (I_j, O_k) as the sum of D_{ri}, D_{jk} and D_{or}, $D_{rjkr} = D_{ri} + D_{jk} + D_{or}$. We assume D_{rjkr} has been translated into cycles and rounded up if necessary.

For each output O_k, we have a valid signal V_k. V_k is set false if any *related* input of O_k changes (more accurately, the input latch is enabled). V_k is set true after each *related* input of O_k has remained unchanged for D_{rjkr} -1 cycles. We employ a number of cycle counters to achieve this. Each cycle counter corresponds to one *related* input-output pair (I_j, O_k) whose associated D_{rjkr} is greater than 1. Once I_j changes the cycle counter is reset to the value D_{rjkr} -1. The cycle counter counts down in each cycle until zero. When all the counters relevant to O_k become zero, V_k is set valid. For most custom functions, the number of *related* input-output pairs is below 8 (4 inputs, 2 outputs). And some of the input-output pairs can share a cycle counter if they have the same input and symmetric outputs (the delay between the input and the two outputs are equal) or vice versa. Thus the hardware resource needed by the cycle counters is quite small.

3.2 Instruction Set Extension

We use the MIPS I instruction set architecture [15] to demonstrate our extension. A single custom instruction, *cust*, is added to execute the custom functions. The format of this instruction is shown in Figure 2. Each instruction field is briefly described in Table 1.To a large extent, it resembles a MIPS R-type instruction with two input operands and one output operand. The *s, t, d* fields in this instruction are used to control the inputs and outputs of the custom function. Different combinations of them may put operands in or get results from a custom function or do both of them. The *fn* and *cn* fields tell which custom function in which CFU is being operated. Currently we allow for 2 CFUs and up to 16 custom functions. A slight change to the instruction format will allow different combinations of CFUs and custom functions if needed. Like other instructions in the MIPS I instruction set, each *cust* instruction takes one cycle unless it is interlocked. A *cust* instruction is interlocked only when it requests an output (the *d* field is not zero) but the output is not valid at that time. The pipeline will be stalled until the output is ready.

Fig. 2. Custom instruction format

Table 1. Fields of custom instruction

Field	Size (bits)	Description
opcode	6	instruction opcode
rs	5	source operand register
rt	5	target operand register
rd	5	destination register
cn	1	CFU number
fn	4	custom function number
s	2	0: source operand is ignored 1: put source operand in I0 2: put source operand in I2 3: put source operand in I4
t	2	0: target operand is ignored 1: put target operand in I1 2: put target operand in I3 3: put target operand in I5
d	2	0: no output 1: get output 0 into destination register 2: get output 1 into destination register 3: get output 2 into destination register

Invocation of a custom function is achieved by using a sequence of *cust* instructions. For example, assuming the code fragment in section 1 is implemented as custom function 0 in CFU 0, it can be invoked by the following instruction sequence (using the format in Figure 2):

```
cust r2, r3, $0, 0(cn), 0(fn), 1(s), 1(t), 0(d)

cust r4, r5, $0, 0(cn), 0(fn), 2(s), 2(t), 0(d)

cust r6, $0, $0, 0(cn), 0(fn), 3(s), 0(t), 0(d)

cust $0, $0, r2, 0(cn), 0(fn), 0(s), 0(t), 1(d)

cust $0, $0, r3, 0(cn), 0(fn), 0(s), 0(t), 2(d)
```

To ensure correctness, the instructions in the sequence must be in the proper order. And in order to reduce code generation complexity, we enforce the additional constraint that instructions that transfer inputs must be issued before the instructions that transfer outputs in one invocation of a custom function. Nevertheless, these instructions don't need to be consecutive. In fact, to reduce possible interlocking, we usually insert other ALU operations into the sequence. This is detailed in section 4.2.

4   Evaluation

In this section, we present our experimental evaluation of M^2E. In Section 4.1, we describe the performance model we used for our evaluation. In Section 4.2, we introduce the process to map an application to the extended instruction set architecture. In Section 4.3, we present the experimental results and a discussion of them.

4.1 Performance Model

We measure the relative performance of an extensible processor with M^{2}E extension against the core processor by comparing the execution cycles of a range of applications executing on them. The relative performance, or speedup, is computed as [10]:

$$speedup(s) = \frac{exec.\ cycles\ on\ core.\ processor}{exec.\ cycles\ on\ ext.\ processor} - 1$$

The execution cycles are derived from a performance simulator developed using the SimpleScalar toolsuit [12]. The instruction set used in the simulator is MIPS I. The simulator models an enhanced micro-architecture of the MIPS R3000 processor [15] and an M^{2}E extension to it. Like the MIPS R3000, the modeled processor has 5 pipeline stages: IF, RD, ALU, MEM and WB, and two forwarding paths: from MEM to ALU and from WB to ALU. The modeled processor includes a one-cycle ALU and a separate multiplier unit. The multiplier unit can execute concurrently with the ALU.

As the core processor for the M^{2}E extension may be either a soft core processor such as NIOS II [16], or a more advanced hard core processor such as PowerPC 405 [7], we added some additional features (shown in Table 2) to the MIPS R3000 memory hierarchy. This makes the modified configuration better than NIOS II and comparable to a PowerPC 405. All instructions have one-cycle latency except when interlocked. When interlock occurs, the previous stages are stalled and the following stages are fed NOP instructions. The instructions that may cause an interlock include: MFLO/MFHI, load instructions, and the *cust* instruction. A multiplication operation costs 4 cycles and a division operation costs 8 cycles. The processor has no branch prediction unit but each branch instruction has a one-cycle delay slot. Many of the delay slots can be filled by the compiler with useful instructions. So on average the branch instruction latency is between one and two, which is better than what most embedded processors' branch architecture can achieve.

Altera's Quartus II software was used to measure the custom function delay. Balanced, medium optimization options and the Stratix II device ep2s15f484c3 were used in the experiments. The Stratix II device uses 90 nm copper technology with a maximum frequency of up to 500 MHz. In the simulation, the measured delays are translated into processor cycles based on the assumed frequency of the processor core.

Table 2. Memory hierarchy parameters

Instruction L1 cache	16K, directly mapped, 1-cycle hit latency
Data L1 cache	16K, 4 associativity, 1-cycle hit latency
Unified L2 cache	256K, 4 associativity, 6-cycle hit latency
Memory latency	32 cycles
Instruction TLB	64-entry fully associative
Data TLB	64-entry fully associative
TLB hit latency	1 cycle
TLB miss latency	32 cycles

4.2 Mapping Applications

We use the algorithm proposed in [3] to identify MIMO instruction clusters which are suited to be implemented as custom functions. Memory operations are precluded from our custom functions because of their variable latency. After an instruction cluster is identified and synthesized as a custom function, we replace the instruction cluster with the appropriate invocation of the custom function. This is done in an extra optimization phase inserted into the compiler. As mentioned previously, a MIMO custom function is usually invoked by a sequence of the same custom instruction (*cust*). According to our experience, most MIMO custom functions need 3-20 cycles to complete their computation. In some situations the pipeline has to be stalled to wait for the output of the custom function to be ready. To avoid this, some ALU instructions that precede or follow the *cust* instruction sequence are moved into the *cust* instruction sequence based on the analysis of the latency of the custom function together with the data dependence between the custom function and the ALU instructions. This process is similar to rescheduling instructions to exploit the empty issue slots between instruction MULT and instruction MFLO/MFHI in MIPS processors [15].

4.3 Experimental Results

Five applications from MediaBench [14] were used in our experiments. Integer fdct functions were used in the benchmark *mpegenc* for we modeled only an embedded processor without floating point unit. All the applications were compiled using GCC with option -O2 and –funroll-loops. The tool chain used in our compilation process is MIPS 32-bit little-endian GCC 3.4.3 with glibc 2.3.5 and GNU binutils 2.15.91. In all experiments we assume a single CFU.

In the first experiment, we compare the proposed M^2E to a DISO extension, a MISO extension as well as a MIMO extension with ideal operand bandwidth (IMIMO) in terms of the speedup achieved. In this experiment, we assume a hard-core processor running at 500 MHz. The input-output delays were translated under

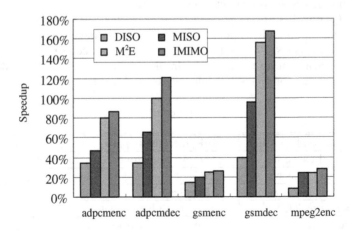

Fig. 3. Compare M^2E with DISO, MISO, and IMIMO in terms of the speedup achieved when using a hard core (500 MHz) and a single CFU

this assumption. The results shown in Figure 3 indicate that M²E on average can achieve roughly 77% speedup over the core processor, while the DISO and MISO extension can only achieve about 26% and 50% respectively. There are three principal reasons for the differences. First, compared to a DISO or MISO custom function, a MIMO custom function allow more operations to benefit from the speedup advantages of FPGA [18]. Second, even though the custom logic needs the same time to execute the custom functions as the core processor does, putting more operations into it will save more issue slots. These issue slots can be used to issue other ALU instructions, which will possibly cause a reduction of the program's critical path. The third reason is that DISO & MISO extensions usually need more custom functions to approach the maximum speedup than M²E. This can be seen in Figure 4, which shows the speedup for two benchmarks (*adpcmenc* & *adpcmdec*) for different numbers of custom functions. When a large custom function is broken into several small custom functions, the total number of outputs of all custom functions may increase as some intermediate variables need to be passed between the ALU and the custom functions. The increase in the total number of outputs will cause the delay between any output of the custom functions and the result register (D_{or}) to grow. As a result, the outputs of custom functions may need more cycles to become available. Certainly, in some situations a MIMO custom function that satisfies all constraints may not be available. And sometimes a DISO or MISO custom function may get more speedup than a MIMO custom function as a smaller custom function usually has a greater chance to repeat itself in elsewhere in a program. Our extension has the flexibility to employ custom functions with 1-6 inputs and 1-3 outputs.

From Figure 3, we can also observe that generally IMIMO achieves more speedup than M²E. However, the difference between them is not large (about 9% on the average). One reason is that compared to the latency of the custom functions, the number of cycles spent in transferring operands or results is usually small. Another reason is that increasing operand bandwidth does not necessarily reduce the custom functions' latency especially when there is data dependence between the operations.

In the second experiment, we studied the speedup difference between using a soft core and a hard core assuming that the CFU is implemented on the same reconfigurable fabric. Again, the hard core is assumed to run at 500 MHz [7] while the soft core is assumed to run at 150 MHz [16]. From the results shown in Figure 5, we can see that the speedup achieved with a hard core is smaller than with a soft core. This is

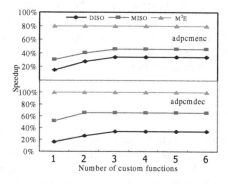

Fig. 4. The relationship between speedup and the total number of custom functions

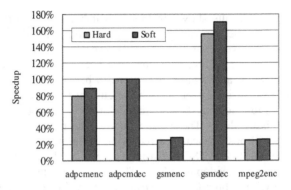

Fig. 5. Speedup difference when extending a hard core (500 MHz) and a soft core (150 MHz) with single-CFU M^{2}E

because the same latency of custom logic is translated into fewer processor cycles in a soft core situation. However, the difference (about 6% on the average) is not as large as the processor frequencies suggest. There is even no difference for the benchmark *adpcmdec*. This is because the instructions that are executed in the ALU are the critical path (in *adpcmdec* situation) or will become the critical path when the latency of the custom function is reduced.

5 Conclusions and Future Work

RISC-based extensible processors have emerged as a promising solution for high performance embedded systems. The attainable performance of such processors is limited by the number of inputs and outputs of the custom functions. In this paper we proposed a very simple MIMO processor extension for classical single-issue pipelined RISC processors. To minimize the change to the core processors' ISA and micro-architecture, we use only a single custom instruction and maintain the operand bandwidth of two inputs, one output per cycle. The extra operands and results of the custom functions are transferred using a repeated sequence of the same custom instruction. While keeping such an operand bandwidth limit does sacrifice some speedup, the experiments show that our M^{2}E extension can still achieve an average speedup 51% more than a DISO extension and 27% more than a MISO extension, and approaches the theoretical limit for MIMO extensions. Our current M^{2}E extension is limited to fixed-point operations and in-order single issue processors. Adding support for floating-point operations and out-of-order processors as well as implementing a prototype of the extension on a NIOS II development board are areas for future work.

References

1. Altera Corp., NIOS II Custom Instruction User Guide, 2005.
2. Pan Yu and Tulika Mitra: Scalable Custom Instructions Identification for Instruction-Set Extensible Processors. Proceedings of the International Conference on Compilers, Architectures, and Synthesis for Embedded Systems, Washington, D.C., Sept. 2004.

3. K. Atasu, L. Pozzi, and P. Ienne: Automatic Application-Specific Instruction-Set Extensions Under Microarchitectural constraints. 40st ACM/IEEE Design Automation Conference (DAC), 2003

4. John R. Hauser and John Wawrzynek: Grap: A MIPS Processor with A Reconfigurable Coprocessor. Proceedings of the 5th IEEE Symposium on Field-Programmable Custom Computing Machines, Napa Valley, Calif., April 1997.

5. B.Kastrup, A. Bink, and J. Hoogerbrugge: ConCISe: A Compiler-Driven CPLD-based Instruction Set Accelerator. Proceedings of the 7th IEEE Symposium on Field-Programmable Custom Computing Machines, Napa Valley, Calif., Apr. 1999.

6. P.Ienne, L. Pozzi, and M. Vuletic: On the Limits of Processor Specialisation by Mapping Dataflow Sections on Ad-hoc Functional Units. Technical Report 01/376, Swiss Federal Institute of Technology Lausanne, Computer Science Department, Dec. 2001.

7. Xilinx Inc., PowerPC Processor Reference Guide, 2003

8. Partha Biswas, Sudarshan Banerjee, Nikil D. Dutt, Laura Pozzi, Paolo Ienne: ISEGEN: Generation of High-Quality Instruction Set Extensions by Iterative Improvement. Design Automation and Test in Europe (DATE), 2005.

9. J. Cong, Y. Fan, G. Han, A. Jagannathan, G. Reinman and Z. Zhang: Instruction Set Extension with Shadow Registers for Configurable Processors. Proceedings of the ACM International Symposium on Field-Programmable Gate Arrays, Feb. 2005.

10. Pan Yu and Tulika Mitra: Characterizing Embedded Applications for Instruction-Set Extensible Processors. 41st ACM/IEEE Design Automation Conference (DAC), June 2004.

11. Rahul Razdan and Michael D. Smith: A High-Performance Microarchitecture with Hardware-Programmable Functional Units. Proceedings of the 27th Annual International Symposium on Microarchitecture (MICRO-27), November, 1994.

12. SimpleScalar LLC, http://www.simplescalar.com.

13. Georgi Kuzmanov, Georgi Gaydadjiev, and Stamatis Vassiliadis: The MOLEN Processor Prototype. FCCM 2004.

14. MediaBench, http://cares.icsl.ucla.edu/MediaBench/.

15. G. Kane and J. Heinrich: MIPS RISC Architecture. Prentice-Hall, 1992.

16. Altera Corp.: Nios II Processor Reference Handbook, 2005.

17. Xilinx Inc.: MicroBlaze Processor Reference Guide, 2005.

18. Zhi Guo, Walid Najjar, Frank Vahid, Kees Vissers: A Quantitative Analysis of The Speedup Factors of FPGAs over Processors. Proceeding of the 2004 ACM/SIGDA 12th international Symposium on Field programmable Gate Arrays, Monterey, California, USA, February 2004.

An Operating System Infrastructure for Fault-Tolerant Reconfigurable Networks

Dirk Koch, Thilo Streichert, Steffen Dittrich, Christian Strengert,
Christian D. Haubelt, and Jürgen Teich

Department of Computer Science, 12,
University of Erlangen-Nuremberg, Germany

Abstract. Dynamic hardware reconfiguration is becoming a key technology in embedded system design that offers among others new potentials in dependable computing. To make system designers benefit from this new technology, powerful infrastructures and programming environments are needed. In this paper, we will propose new concepts of an operating system (OS) infrastructure for reconfigurable networks that allow to efficiently design fault-tolerant systems. For this purpose, we consider a hardware/software solution that supports *dynamic rerouting, hardware* and *software task migration, hardware/software task morphing,* and *online partitioning.* Finally, we will present an implementation of such a reconfigurable network providing this OS infrastructure.

1 Introduction

Nowadays, embedded systems are typically networked at different levels of granularity. This can be either at system level, where different controllers cooperate with each other, like in sensor networks or body area networks, or at chip level where different processor cores and dedicated hardware modules are implemented on a single die. The motivation to design such a networked embedded system can be found in automotive and avionic industries where system requirements range from high computational power to reliability and flexibility aspects.

In this paper, we will present the possibilities that distributed dynamic hardware reconfiguration offers in the context of fault tolerance and flexibility. In the following, we will use the term *reconfigurable network* to denote a networked embedded system consisting of hardware reconfigurable nodes (FPGAs). In such a reconfigurable network, it becomes possible to migrate hardware and software tasks from one node to another at run time. Thus, resource faults can be compensated by *rebinding* tasks to fully functional nodes of the network. This task of rebinding is also known as *online partitioning* [1, 2]. However, in order to allow system designers to benefit from this new technology, powerful infrastructures and programming environments are needed.

Recent research focuses on operating systems for single FPGA solutions [3, 4, 5, 6] where hardware tasks are dynamically assigned to FPGAs. On the other hand, architectures for networked reconfigurable solutions like PACT [7], Chameleon [8], HoneyComb [9], and dynamically reconfigurable networks on chips (DyNoCs) [10] were investigated intensively. Nevertheless, the former omits

W. Grass et al. (Eds.): ARCS 2006, LNCS 3894, pp. 202–216, 2006.

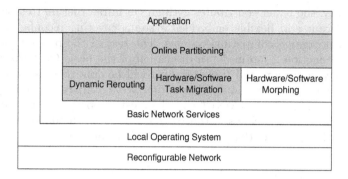

Fig. 1. Basic OS features provided by a RECONET. On each node in the reconfigurable network a local OS is needed. Based on these local OSs, basic network services can be implemented. On top of the basic network services, the basic OS features *dynamic rerouting, task migration*, and *morphing* are defined. In order to increase the fault tolerance of a RECONET, *online partitioning* must be supported as well. Finally, an application can be build on top of all these layers.

the fact that more and more embedded systems become networked, whereas the latter does not account the support of basic hardware task management for *online scheduling* and *online placement*. Moreover, only by considering both aspects simultaneously, the problem of designing fault-tolerant and flexible or even self-optimizing embedded systems can be solved.

In this contribution, we close this gap by proposing new concepts for an operating system (OS) infrastructure for reconfigurable networks that allow for designing dependable computing systems efficiently. This operating system provides an efficient infrastructure and programming environment by providing the basic tasks known as *dynamic rerouting, hardware* and *software task migration, hardware/software task morphing*, and *online partitioning*. This is shown in Fig. 1. In this paper, we focus on dynamic rerouting, task migration, and online partitioning. Whereas hardware/software task morphing is covered only briefly. In the following, we denote a reconfigurable network as RECONET.

The first three features that are provided by the OS in a RECONET are (1) *dynamic rerouting*, (2) *task migration*, and (3) *task morphing*. Note that these features that deal with erroneous resources have to be implemented on each reconfigurable node such that they run in a distributed manner in the network. Thus, we are able to compensate line errors by computing a new route for broken communications and we can migrate tasks from one node in the network to another at run time. Moreover, we are able to morph the implementation style of a task. Especially the task of fault tolerant communication in networked reconfigurable systems is of outer importance and will be discussed in this paper comprehensively. This communication protocol is the basis for an efficient rerouting algorithm for a RECONET. Based on the three tasks *dynamic rerouting, task migration*, and *task morphing*, we define feature (4) called *online partitioning* as the process of optimally binding tasks to nodes in the network. Feature (4) guarantees the fault tolerance of the RECONET.

In summary, the paper contributes with an OS infrastructure to design modern fault-tolerant and flexible embedded systems covering reconfigurable networks or even organic computing systems. The rest of the paper is organized as follows: In Section 2, an in depth discussion of the basic OS tasks *dynamic rebinding*, *task migration*, and *task morphing* will be done. Section 3 is devoted to the topic of *fault tolerance* and *online optimization*. Finally, Section 4 presents our implementation of a RECONET and the most important figures related to this implementation. The focus in this section will be on the implementation of a communication protocol that supports dynamic rerouting.

2   Basic OS Features

This section describes the basic features needed for running a RECONET. Before defining these features, we will take a closer look on the underlying architecture. The main aspects of the architecture are:

- small: Each node in the network is able, but is not necessarily required, to store the current state of the entire network. The state of a network is given by its current topology consisting of all available nodes, of available links, and of the distribution of the tasks in the network.
- dynamic hardware reconfiguration: Allows the implementation of arbitrary functions in hardware. Thus, it accelerates the computation of the corresponding functions required in the network.
- embedded: requires the optimization of different objectives, like power consumption, cost, etc. simultaneously.

These are the fundamental properties of a reconfigurable network that we call a RECONET. Furthermore, in order to increase the degree of fault tolerance and flexibility of a RECONET, it must support *online partitioning* of tasks in the network. For this purpose, we have to implement four basic OS features. In order to compensate errors in the hardware infrastructure, we implemented the OS features *dynamic rerouting, hardware* and *software task migration*, and *hardware/software task morphing*. Network connectivity faults are compensated by the computation of a new routing and faults of a complete node are compensated by migrating tasks to other nodes. Finally, the task morphing allows for changing the implementation style of a task from hardware to software and vice versa at run time. On top of these features, we implemented an additional, fourth OS feature named *online partitioning* which will be discussed in Section 3. This online partitioning uses task migration and morphing due to optimality reasons.

In order to describe these OS features formally, we need an appropriate model. The application implemented by the reconfigurable network is given by n tasks $T = \{t_1, t_2, \ldots, t_n\}$ running on m possible nodes $R = \{r_1, r_2, \ldots, r_m\}$. Tasks may communicate with each other modeled by so-called *data dependencies* $D = \{d_1, d_2, \ldots, d_k\} \subseteq T \times T$. Moreover, the RECONET structure is given by l links $C = \{c_1, c_2, \ldots, c_l\}$ between the nodes where $C \subseteq R \times R$. Each task $t_i \in T$ can be mapped onto an arbitrary set of nodes. Moreover, a task can be implemented in either hardware (HW) or software (SW). We therefore model all possible bindings as a set M, where $M \subseteq T \times R \times \{hw, sw\}$. The actual binding of tasks to resources is called $\beta \subseteq M$. A task t_i bound to hardware $(t_i, r_j, hw) \in \beta$ produces a hardware load (number of resources occupied on the FPGA) of $w^H(t_i)$. The same task implemented in software produces a software load (CPU utilization) of $w^S(t_i)$. The OS features are triggered if a resource fault is detected. In the following, we reveal the basic OS features *dynamic rerouting*, *task migration*, and *task morphing* in detail. Online partitioning will be discussed in Section 3 in the scope of fault tolerance.

2.1   Rerouting

The first OS feature to be defined is the task of *dynamic rerouting*. Rerouting is required if a connection $(c_f \in C)$ in the network fails. All data dependencies routed over this connection have to be redirected. There are several publications dealing with this issue where recent work was mainly focused on probabilistic approaches [11]. Here, we consider a high-level fault tolerant approach. Dynamic rerouting itself can be decomposed in three subproblems:

1. Line detection: Is a link $c_i = (r_j, r_k)$ between two nodes r_j and r_k available?
2. Network state distribution: If a connection between two nodes (r_j, r_k) fails, all nodes using link c_f must be informed.
3. Routing of broken communications (data dependencies).

Note that communication takes place between tasks and the binding of a task to a network node can change at run-time. Therefore, the rerouting is much more complex as in static networks where communication takes place between nodes. This will be discussed comprehensively in Section 4 where we present an efficient algorithm for dynamic rerouting.

2.2   Hardware and Software Task Migration

Task migration describes the rebinding of hardware and software tasks $t_i \in T$ from one node r_j in the network to another node r_k. If t_i is implemented in hardware, i.e., $(t_i, r_j, hw) \in \beta$ the rebinding leads to $(t_i, r_k, hw) \in \beta$. To perform this step, we need $\{(t_i, r_j, hw), (t_i, r_k, hw)\} \in M$. Note, that if we configure the reconfigurable nodes r_i, r_k with a processor, it may be possible to morph a hardware task $((t_i, r_j, hw) \in \beta)$ to a software task $((t_i, r_j, sw) \in \beta)$ and vice versa, too. For a node r_j this will further need $\{(t_i, r_j, hw), (t_i, r_j, sw)\} \in M$.

Task migration is applied to compensate resource faults, i.e., if a node r_f in the network fails, all tasks running on r_f must be migrated to other nodes. Thus, task migration can be divided into two subproblems: 1) detection of resource errors and 2) rebinding of tasks to nodes. The first subproblem can be solved by observing if a node r_f has at least one working connection to any of its neighbors $(\{r_i \mid (r_f, r_i) \in C\})$. Otherwise, this node is called *isolated*. An isolated node cannot be used for process execution any longer and all tasks bound to this node must be migrated.

An important question is how to perform a save task migration, i.e., how to keep track on the current state of a task. For this purpose, we use so-called *checkpoints* as discussed in the following section. Moreover, we must answer the question of how to optimally bind a task t_i after some resource fault. This is especially necessary in the context of embedded systems where multiple objectives have to be optimized simultaneously while meeting several constraints. This topic will also be discussed in the subsequent section in the context of fault tolerance.

2.3   Hardware/Software Task Morphing

Hardware/software task morphing describes the switching of the implementation style of a task from hardware to software or vice versa. Assuming that functionality can be implemented for the available hardware and software resources, the morphing phase needs several steps, e.g., for extracting states of the functionality implemented in either hardware or software and transforming these states such that they can be loaded in their functional counterpart. Due to space limitations, we will omit an in depth discussion.

3   Fault Tolerance

With the above presented methods for *dynamic rerouting, task migration,* and *task morphing,* we are now able to investigate new concepts for increasing the fault tolerance in a RECONET. The problem we face is the following: Suppose a node r_f in the reconfigurable network fails and with this node all its functionality will be lost. All tasks $t_i \in T$ with $(t_i, r_f, \{hw, sw\}) \in \beta$ must be migrated to a fully functional node $r \in R \backslash \{r_f\}$. Obviously, this should be done quickly in order to compensate the resource fault. However, the new task binding β' might be suboptimal or even miss some constraints imposed on the system, such that we have to perform an optimization of the system at run time.

The described scenario is sketched in Fig. 2. The *online partitioning* basically consists of two phases: (i) a *fast repair phase* that reestablishes the functionality of a defect node and (ii) a *repartitioning phase* that optimizes the binding of tasks in the network.

In order to guarantee a *fast repair*, we propose the use of *self replication of tasks* in combination with *checkpointing*. Checkpointing is responsible for saving a task's state in order to recover this state, whereas replicating tasks assures that a fast migration decision can be made in case of some node fault. Hence, after a resource fault, the replicated tasks take over control of the computation and restore the last state saved from this computation. In a second step, the task is replicated as well in order to guarantee a fast migration step in case of an additional node failure.

During the replication of tasks, we might step into another problem, which will be solved by so-called *dynamic repartitioning*. The new tasks that will be produced during the replication phase has to be bound to free resources. Unfortunately, it cannot be guaranteed at design time, that exactly the resource for binding either a task implemented in hardware or software is free at run time. Hence, a novel strategy for dynamic repartitioning needs to be investigated that decides whether a tasks will be implemented in hardware or software and on

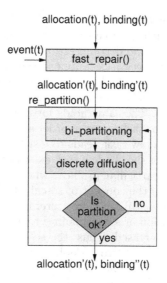

Fig. 2. Phases of the online partitioning. In case of certain events, indicating e.g., temporary or permanent resource and link faults, a fast reassignment of tasks to available resources is found by *fast_repair()*. In the second phase, a diffusion-based *dynamic repartitioning* is applied where an actual temporal bi-partition is iteratively improved by migrating tasks to other active resources and by possibly changing their implementation style.

which node a task will be executed. In the following, we will discuss the three aspects *self replication, checkpointing*, and *dynamic repartitioning* separately.

3.1 Self Replication

For the purpose of redundancy, a *regular task* replicates itself on another node, such that an execution of a task can be continued if one of these nodes fails. Self replication is task migration to an adjacent node without stopping/removing the regular task. This replicated and migrated task will be called *shadow task* subsequently. Thus, there exists a shadow task for each regular task in the reconfigurable network. A regular task and its corresponding shadow task observe each other by periodically sending and requesting so-called *keep alive messages* from each other. To permit this mutual monitoring a task to task communication protocol (Task2Task) must be supported by a RECONET (cf. Sec. 4.2). In Task2Task communication so-called *task addresses* (TAD) are resolved to physical *node addresses* (NAD) such that messages can be routed between nodes in the network.

To avoid confusions during the resolution of a TAD to a NAD, TADs must be unique in a RECONET. Thus, a designer has to define unique TADs for a regular task and the corresponding shadow task at design time.

If a shadow task becomes a regular task, i.e., if the former regular task is not available any longer, it takes the TAD of the former regular task. On the other hand, if the shadow task fails, a new shadow task is created by the regular task and the TAD of the shadow task will be assigned. This shadow task is bound on the first adjacent node, which has free capacities for an additional task.

A problematic scenario is the decomposition of a network in two parts and the reconnection of two subnetworks. Suppose the regular task is running in one part of the network and its shadow task is running in the other part. The regular task does not receive any keep alive messages from its shadow task and therefore creates a new one. The same holds for the shadow task. This task in turn assumes that the regular task is out of order and sets itself to be the regular task. Producing another shadow task, leads to a situation in which two TADs of the regular and two TADs of the shadow task exist in the decomposed network.

In order to resolve this particular problem when two parts of a network are reconnected, we make use of the concept of so-called *checkpoint sessions*, which will be introduced in more detail later on. Here, it is only important to understand, that after each creation of a checkpoint or each rollback to a checkpoint, a session number will be increased. Thus, the session number is representative for the lifetime of a task. Now, if two tasks have the same TAD, the tasks with the shortest lifetime survives. If they have the same lifetime, the task on the node with the lowest NAD will be removed.

With this concept, it can be ensured that always one regular and one shadow task exist, if an adjacent node provides the necessary resources for execution.

3.2   Checkpointing

Without an efficient mechanism for saving and restoring states of processes, the migration and replication of tasks is not applicable. For this purpose, *checkpointing* mechanisms are integrated which contain a context of a task and are periodically updated.

The checkpointing mechanisms can be used in order to keep the shadow task in an actual state. Every time a task generates or updates its checkpoint, it transmits this checkpoint also to the shadow task. When the shadow task takes control and becomes a regular task, it detects that its local data is inconsistent and causes a rollback. Note that it is applicatory not possible to hold consistent local data at a shadow task. This would otherwise result in a multiplication of communicated messages in the network. Each task of a checkpoint group would have to duplicate its messages and send them to the receiving task and to its shadow task. For further information about checkpointing mechanisms, [12] provides a good survey.

3.3   Dynamic Repartitioning

After a node fails in a network, new shadow tasks are started and restored, such that they are in a consistent state with their corresponding regular tasks. In [2], this phase has been called *fast repair* phase and aims at a network with full functionality and the same redundancy as before the failure. This phase has to be passed in a certain time, so that we can make assumptions about the real-time behavior.

The second phase, described in this section, tries to find an optimal binding of processes to nodes with respect to certain objectives. In this phase, the decision whether a task will be implemented on hardware resources or software resources as well as the distribution of tasks in the network will be done iteratively until a satisfying binding β concerning the objectives is found. Note that due to reasons of fault tolerance this approach has to run in a distributed manner in the network.

Our overall approach to *dynamic repartitioning* tries to find a binding of tasks to nodes such that the load reserves of hardware as well as of software resources are maximized on all nodes. Optimizing the binding of tasks to resources in this way, increases the probability that a shadow task can be bound onto an adjacent node. In [13], we proposed a two step methodology consisting of a *diffusion phase* and a local *hardware/software partitioning phase*:

Diffusion Phase: During the diffusion phase nodes exchange tasks according to their load differences on the nodes. Characteristic to a diffusion-based algorithm, introduced first by Cybenko [14], is that iteratively each node is allowed to move any size of load to each of its neighbors. Communication is only allowed along point-to-point connections. The quality of such an algorithm may be measured in terms of the number of iterations that are required in order to achieve a balanced state and in terms of the amount of load moved over the edges of the graph. In [2], we have presented an extended diffusion algorithm, that exchanges only whole tasks between nodes and thus, only discrete load entities. Anyway, it has been shown theoretically and by experiment that our proposed version of the diffusion algorithm does not exceed optimality constraints concerning the optimization flow of its continuous counterpart and moreover, we are able to show theoretically maximal deviations with respect to the quality of the load balance. Note that the diffusion phase makes use of the OS feature *hardware* and *software task migration*.

Local Bi-Partitioning: The local bi-partitioning supposes that each task $t_i \in T$ can be either implemented in hardware or software. Each implementation style causes certain costs or load on the node's resources $w^{H/S}(t_i)$ and upon these costs a ratio is determined for each task: $w^H(t_i)/w^S(t_i)$. According to this ratio the bi-partitioning algorithm selects one task and implements it either in hardware or software. Due to such a local strategy, we can guarantee that the total load will be minimized, but to reach an optimal hardware/software balance, we calculate the total software load and the total hardware load on one node. If the hardware load is less than the software load, the algorithm selects a task which will be implemented in hardware, and the other way round. Due to these competing objectives (balanced hardware/software load and minimization of total load), tasks with a ratio larger than one can be assigned to hardware and tasks with a ratio less than one are assigned to software. Of course it is possible that tasks are assigned to a resource such that they are implemented suboptimal. But during the diffusion phase, we diffuse these tasks at first. Therefore, we introduce two priority lists, one for software and one for hardware tasks. In these lists, we collect all tasks in the reverse order as they are assigned to a hardware or software resource. Thus, the last task which was, e.g., assigned to software is the first task which will be diffused if the node has to send tasks via the network. Therefore, suboptimal partitioned tasks will have a higher mobility, which leads to an improvement concerning the convergence speed. Note that the implementation of the local bi-partitioning needs the OS feature *hardware/software task morphing.*

4   Prototype Implementation

In this section, we will present our implementation of a RECONET. Here, we will focus on the *communication infrastructure* and *dynamic rerouting* algorithm.

4.1   Architecture and Local OS

Our prototype implementation of a RECONET consists of four fully connected Altera Cyclone FPGA boards [15]. Each Board is configured with a NIOS soft-core CPU [16] running microC/OS-II [17] as local operating system. The local OS permits, multi-tasking by priority-based preemptive scheduling. We extend the microC/OS-II, by a new C++-API for task creation and an Inter Process Communication (IPC) infrastructure based on message passing. As Altera FP-GAs do not support dynamic hardware reconfiguration, we configure each node with a set of hardware modules implementing selected tasks. These hardware modules can be activated during run time to emulate dynamic reconfiguration. Beside the NIOS processor and the application dependent hardware modules, each Cyclone board is configured with a number of new designed communication ports. These communication ports permit line detection which is a basic functionality for *dynamic rerouting.* Moreover, a novel communication protocol was developed providing many features to support *dynamic rerouting* and *task migration.* This communication protocol will be discussed in detail next.

4.2   Communication

Our RECONET approach demands a specialized network infrastructure. In order to obtain a high degree of fault tolerance, we cannot allow busses that are based on a shared physical medium. Even a doubling of the bus medium in order to get a parallel redundant communication path is based on a too restricted fault model. One faulty node can prohibit the communication inside the entire network by randomly sending unintentional data.

Point-to-point (P2P) networks on the other side demand some routing over-head to channel packages through the network. In the case of a faulty link, data can be sent via alternative paths.

Beside the fault tolerance, P2P networks have the advantage of an extreme high total bandwidth. Thus, RECONET uses P2P communication.

For our RECONET we implemented a new communication protocol which supports dynamic rerouting as well as hardware and software task migration. The communication protocol works on different layers. Firstly, a node-to-node (N2N) protocol at the transport layer is defined. The N2N protocol is responsible for reliable communication between nodes (multi-hop). Secondly, a task-to-task (T2T) protocol is implemented that handles the task resolution in the network. The most important features of the communication protocol can be summarized as follows:

- *Priorities* are used to achieve different service levels in the network in order to prevent low priority messages blocking high priority messages.
- *Different sizes* are supported to allow the efficient transfer of simple sensor values as well as the efficient transfer of large binary (configuration) data. The size of the payload field can vary between 4 and 20 bytes per cell.
- *Celling* is used by the network driver to determine if the cell is a fraction of a multi-cell package or not.
- *Cut through* for small multi-hop communication latencies.
- *Data transfer rate* of $12.5Mb/s$.

Task2Task Communication. One of the major design goals of the RECoNET is to decouple structure from functionality. This means that a task is not forced to run on a predefined resource in the network if it does not demand special resources that are only available on specific nodes (e. g., a sensor). Thus, a *task resolution* mechanism has been integrated with the following requirements:

- Fast assignment of task addresses (TADs) to node addresses (NADs). Note, due to the rapid change of the TAD to NAD assignment, the resolution has to take place after each reconfiguration.
- Resolution of conflicts in case of multiple TADs which can occur in the context of task replication.
- Task resolution is an operating system task which is not visible to the user and does not affect the design style.

Line Detection. If we want to compensate failures, we have to build failure detection mechanisms into a RECoNET. In the case of links, we have to distinguish between intermediate and long term failures. A single bit flip for example is an intermediate failure that will not demand additional care with respect to the routing, while a link down should be recognized as fast as possible in order to determine a new route for packages to be transferred over this link. As the link state is recognized in the transceiver ports of our implementation we chose the advantageous variant to perform the line detection completely in hardware.

All links of a RECoNET support full duplex mode. If for example one transceiver port fails the failure is recognized in the adjacent node and not in the faulty one itself. Hence, the recognizing node needs to send its receive link state back to the adjacent node with the faulty transceiver. If this happens the hardware tries to reestablish the link by itself. If this was not successful, the hardware generates an interrupt to the CPU to switch over to an alternative routing. This will be described in the following section. The complete process takes place in less then a millisecond. In case that both lines will go down at the same time, this is recognized by an inactivity on the link. If no traffic is demanded by the application the transceivers generate keep alive message for their adjacent neighbors. If a link is down, the hardware tries to setup the connection periodically. This allows to include new links at run time (e. g., after the repair of a faulty link).

Routing and Rerouting. The main design objective described in this paper is to achieve a high degree of fault tolerance by self-optimizing network components. Consequently, we demand that the self-optimizing process itself has to be fault-tolerant. Hence, all network management processes have to operate distributed without global knowledge and robust with respect to faulty nodes.

The routing is based on a hierarchical approach and has some similarities to distance vector routing (also known as Bellman-Ford algorithm). Routing is defined as the problem of finding an output port for an associated node specified by its address. In our approach we have hardware routers each with a local routing table evaluating the primary routing function by a lookup. This permits routing with a small latency. In addition, every node maintains a second routing function that determines an alternative port in software that has to differ from the port selected by the primary routing function. As a consequence, this allows for a fast reaction on link failures when packages have to be sent over alternative routes. In the case of a fault, it is mandatory to determine new routes as fast as possible. In this phase it is not important to find the best alternative route. The secondary routing function determines the alternative port before the fault occurs. For this purpose, we need the so-called *reachability set* (RS_p) for each output port p that contains the nodes that can be reached from p.

The routing is based on a special addressing scheme allowing a node to send a package to a neighbor node without knowing the target address. With UP being the set of ports connected to active nodes and $cost_r$ the cost function defined as the distance given by the number of hops to reach a node $r \in R$, then the routing algorithm initializes each node $\bar{r}$ as follows:

```
1:   UP := ∅              \\at the beginning there is no port available
2:   ∀r ∈ R\{r̄} : ROUTE_1st(r) := −1    \\we have no primary route
3:   ∀r ∈ R\{r̄} : ROUTE_2nd(r) := −1        \\we have no 2nd route
4:   ∀p ∈ outputs(r̄) : RS_p := ∅                    \\no neighbors
5:   ∀r ∈ R\{r̄} : cost_r := −1   \\we don't know the cost to any node
```

If a link to a neighbor node $\tilde{r}$ is established, we do the following in node $\bar{r}$:

```
1:   UP := UP ∪ {p}       \\put new link to set of connected ports
2:   HELLO(p, r̄, 1)                     \\send via port p that r̄
                                        \\is reachable with cost 1
```

The incoming $HELLO(p, \bar{r}, cost)$ message on port $\tilde{p}$ then starts an update of the primary routing function on the neighbor node $\tilde{r}$:

```
1:   RS_p̃ := RS_p̃ ∪ {r̄}                    \\put neighbor node r̄ into the
                                           \\reachability set of port p̃
2:   ROUTE_1st(r̄) := p̃           \\set route on port p̃ for node r̄
3:   cost_r̄ := cost                        \\update cost function
4:   ∀q ∈ UP\{p̃} : ROUTE(q, r̄, cost + 1, r̃)      \\propagate routing
5:   ROUTE(p̃, r̃, 1))              \\inform new node with own identity
6:   ∀r ∈ R|_ROUTE_1st(r)≠−1 : ROUTE(p̃, r, cost_r + 1, r̃)
                                 \\inform new node with all known routes
```

In line 4 we propagate the new route to node $\bar{r}$ to all connected neighbor ports different from the new one. The value of the cost function has to be incremented by 1 if the traffic is routed through node $\tilde{r}$. If these nodes receive a route with lower cost they will update their own table and only in this case the routing information is propagated further through the network until all routing tables can be updated with a better route. In line 5 we set the new route in backward direction whereas in line 6 we inform the new neighbor about the complete routing information we know until now. As a result, the neighbor will test for each route if there was a better one or not. In the former case the local routing table is updated and the result is propagated further.

Because of the optimality principle, the route written to the primary routing table is optimal with respect to the number of hops. The secondary routing function stores the port with the second best cost function and is used when the hardware detects that the link of a specific port is down. Note that this algorithm needs no information about the network topology. Even the ports of a single router can be used in any order.

In the case of a link failure the primary routing table gets the values from the second routing table for all nodes that were originally routed through the now faulty port. This alternative table has usually a higher cost. Therefore, we have to propagate the new cost to the remaining neighbor ports that can locally decide whenever to update a routing table or not. Every node only has to store locally the two best routing alternatives. In the worst case, we have to propagate the routing information over the complete network. This can take up to $|R| - 1$ time steps with $|R|$ being the number of nodes in the RECoNET. An additional delay can only occur if the node degree k is larger than two. But a node with degree $2+k$ will reduce the longest possible path in a RECoNET at least by k. Therefore, the sum of links passed by a package will always be less than $|R| - 1$. The proposed routing algorithm will not execute more than two consecutive commands (e.g., $HELLO$ and $ROUTE$) in a single node to update all routing tables. As a consequence, the routing is finished in $O(2 \cdot (|R| - 1)) = O(|R|)$ time steps.

Fig. 3 gives an example of the rerouting algorithm for the case that node A sends a package to node D. In the error free case I), the message will pass node

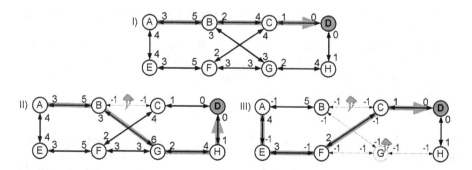

Fig. 3. Rerouting of a route $A \rightarrow D$ in the case of a link failure II) or the failure of a complete node III). The numbers specify the cost for each transceiver port to reach port D. If a transceiver port is not capable to reach D then the cost is set to -1.

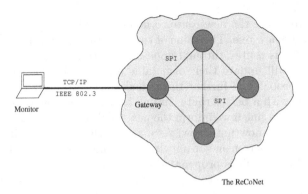

Fig. 4. In a network of several nodes, one node is acting as the gateway to the network monitor. The gateway collects all data and sends them via a TCP/IP connection to a host computer.

B and C. If the link from B to C fails, node B will look into the second routing table guiding the package via the nodes G and H instead of node C. The route is invalidated by writing -1 into the cost function table for the broken ports. If next node G fails its neighbor node B will have the only possibility to reach D via A. As a consequence node A will invalidate its port to node B and a new route is established via the nodes E, F, C.

4.3   Online Analysis and Experimental Results

For analyzing the performance of the presented methods, a network monitoring system has been designed and integrated. It basically consists of a gateway collecting the data of the nodes in the network and a host computer for interpreting and displaying the collected data (see Fig. 4). The gateway is integrated into one dedicated node and each other node sends periodically its own status to the gateway. The information displayed by the monitoring system contains

- the binding of tasks to nodes in the network and the implementation style (hardware/software),
- a time line for each task, such that it can be analyzed when a task has been started on a node and when it migrated to another node,
- the data traffic on a link over the time,
- the topology of the network and
- the content of routing tables.

Routing: The routing algorithm has been tested with different network topologies. Initially, the nodes had to discover routes after start-up. Then, at run-time links are disconnected and reestablished. In order to compare the results of the routing time after start-up T_S and in case of an error T_F with the theoretical upper bound $\hat{T} = 2(n-1)$, the results in Fig. 5 are presented in time steps. Note that the number of nodes in the network is denoted with n.

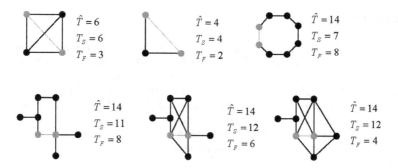

Fig. 5. Several scenarios are presented containing one broken link each. The given time steps denote a theoretical upper bound of routing time $\hat{T}$, the measured time after startup T_S and the measured time after a link defect T_F, respectively.

Performance of Task2Task Messaging: As presented in Sec. 4.2 the data transfer rate depends on the message type which is chosen. Remember that dedicated messages are intended for e.g. sensor values with a good ratio between protocol data and small data entities. Another message type is intended for high volume data transfers having again a good ratio between protocol data and large data entities. With the constraint of a 50MHz CPU and a physical layer that supports a data transfer rate of $12.5Mb/s$, a data transfer rate of

- $1MB/s$ is reached for multi cell packets and
- $400KB/s$ could be transfered for single cell data packets during task to task communication.

5 Conclusion and Future Work

In this paper, we presented a new operating system infrastructure for reconfigurable networks which allow for the efficient design of dependable computing systems. The scope of this paper is on fault tolerance and a novel strategy was presented which deals with permanent faults or defects of communication links and computational resources. To establish this task, the basic OS features *dynamic rerouting, hardware* and *software task migration, hardware/software task morphing,* and *online partitioning* were discussed and implemented. In particular, the online partitioning that consists of a fast repair phase and an optimization phase is a key contribution in the area of modern embedded system design covering *reconfigurable networks* as well as *organic computing systems.*

In future work, we will present an application from the automotive industry running on our RECONET. Moreover, in order to support dynamic hardware reconfiguration at full scale, we consider the integration of state-of-the-art Xilinx FPGAs into our RECONET.

References

1. Lysecky, R., Vahid, F.: A Configurable Logic Architecture for Dynamic Hardware/Software Partitioning. In: Proceedings of the Conference on Design, Automation and Test in Europe, Paris, France (2004) 480–485
2. Streichert, T., Haubelt, C., Teich, J.: Online HW/SW-Partitioning in Networked Embedded Systems. In: Proceedings of Asia and South Pacific Design Automation Conference (ASP-DAC'05), Shanghai, China (2005) 982–985
3. Walder, H., Platzner, M.: Online Scheduling for Block-partitioned Reconfigurable Devices. In: Proc. of Design, Automation and Test in Europe (DATE03). (2003) 290–295
4. Ahmadinia, A., Bobda, C., Koch, D., Majer, M., Teich, J.: Task Scheduling for Heterogeneous Reconfigurable Computers. In: Proceedings of the 17th Symposium on Integrated Circuits and Systems Design (SBCCI), Pernambuco, Brazil (2004) 22–27
5. Ahmadinia, A., Bobda, C., Teich, J.: On-line Placement for Dynamic Reconfigurable Devices. Int. Journal of Embedded Systems (IJES) (2005)
6. Hecht, R., Timmermann, D., Kubisch, S., Zeeb, E.: Network-on-Chip basierende Laufzeitsysteme für dynamisch rekonfigurierbare Hardware. In: Proceedings of ARCS 2004, Augsburg, Germany (2004) 185–194
7. Baumgarte, V., May, F., Nückel, A., Vorbach, M., Weinhardt, M.: PACT XPP - A Self-Reconfigurable Data Processing Architecture. In: ERSA, Nevada (2001)
8. Chameleon Systems: CS2000 Reconfigurable Communications Processor, Family Product Brief. (2000)
9. Thomas, A., Becker, J.: Aufbau- und Strukturkonzepte einer multigranularen rekonfigurierbaren Hardwarearchitektur. In: Proceedings of ARCS 2004, Augsburg, Germany (2004) 165–174
10. Bobda, C., Koch, D., Majer, M., Ahmadinia, A., Teich, J.: A Dynamic NoC Approach for Communication in Reconfigurable Devices. In: Proceedings of International Conference on Field-Programmable Logic and Applications (FPL), Antwerp, Belgium (2004) 1032–1036
11. Dumitraş, T., Kerner, S., Mărculescu, R.: Towards On-Chip Fault-Tolerant Communication. In: Proceedings of the Asia and South Pacific Design Automation Conference 2003, Kitakyushu, Japan (2003)
12. Elnozahy, E.N.M., Alvisi, L., Wang, Y.M., Johnson, D.: A Survey of Rollback-Recovery Protocols in Message-Passing Systems. ACM Comput. Surv. **34**(3) (2002)
13. Streichert, T., Haubelt, C., Teich, J.: Distributed HW/SW-Partitioning for Embedded Reconfigurable Systems. In: Proc. of DATE05, Munich, Germany (2005)
14. Cybenko, G.: Dynamic Load Balancing for Distributed Memory Multiprocessors. Journal of Parallel and Distributed Computing **7** (1989) 279–301
15. Altera: Nios Development Board - Reference Manual,Cyclone Edition (2005) http://www.altera.com.
16. Altera: Nios II Processor Reference Handbook (2005)
17. Jean Labrosse: micro-C/OS-II Second Edition (2002)

Architectural Tradeoffs in Wearable Systems

Nagendra Bhargava Bharatula[1], Urs Anliker[1],
Paul Lukowicz[2], and Gerhard Tröster[1]

[1] Wearable Computing Lab, ETH Zürich, Switzerland
[2] Institute for Computer Systems and Networks, UMIT Hall, Austria
{bharatula, uanliker, troester}@ife.ee.ethz.ch, paul.lukowicz@umit.at
http://www.wearable.ethz.ch

Abstract. Wearable computing places tighter constraints on architecture design than traditional mobile computing. The architecture is described in terms of; miniaturization, power-awareness, global low-power design and flexibility or suitability for an application. In this article we present a new methodology based on four metrics that represent different properties. Flexibility, Electronic Packaging, Relative Recognition Performance and Energy Consumption metrics are proposed and evaluated on practical design examples to study different trade-offs. The proof of concept case study is analyzed by studying (a) walking behavior with acceleration sensors (b) office-worker activities with a combination of acceleration and light sensors and (c) a computational task. The results show that the proposed metrics and methodology assists in selecting an optimal architecture for a given application in the domain of wearable computing.

1 Context Aware Wearable Systems

Wearable computing as defined by [1, 2] envisions personal, mobile computing systems that are always on, useful in all situations, and most of all, easy to use. Thus whereas a conventional mobile device would only be used for an occasional schedule check or address lookup, a wearable device would constantly provide the user with useful information such as nearby shops and special offers, transport delays, or health and lifestyle-related reminders (taking medicine, diet etc). Such systems are particularity important in professional applications such as emergency response units, manufacturing and maintanance. Thus a wearable system might constantly provide a fireman with hints and warning about hazards related to his environment, his physiological state and his current actions.

A key component of the wearable computing vision is the ability of the system to model and recognize user activity and the situation around him. This so called context awareness [3] allows the system to proactively provide the user with the right information at the right time, reduces the complexity of the user interface, and allows new modes of information recording. One of the most popular approaches to context awareness in a mobile environment is based on simple on-body sensors. Thus an accelerometer, light sensor and a microphone placed on the wrist could be

W. Grass et al. (Eds.): ARCS 2006, LNCS 3894, pp. 217–231, 2006.
© Springer-Verlag Berlin Heidelberg 2006

used to track interaction with household appliances [4] or the use of tools [5]. In a similar way an accelerometer and/or gyroscope on the upper leg can differentiate between level walking, going upstairs, going downstairs and running.

1.1 Basis Architecture

Overall, a context aware wearable system consists of several interconnected modules placed at different body locations . Each module consists of sensors, computing elements, RF circuitry and hybrid power supplies (batteries and energy scavenging generator) (see figure 1). When designing such systems one has to take into account not only the usual computer performance measures but also the limitations imposed by the human body. One key aspect of such a system is 'Wearability'. 'Wearability' is defined as the interaction between the human body and the wearable object. It can be improved by designing low-power miniaturized systems with a comfortable form-factor suitable to be worn on the body as unobtrusively as possible. Miniaturization can be achieved by designing smaller individual components and integrating them as one functional unit with suitable electronic packaging technologies. Power consumption can be minimized by duty cycling, reducing the active energy per operation and implementing power-aware algorithms on the processor. At the same time, the performance of the wearable system should not be affected and should offer high suitability for different tasks. Here, a tradeoff is faced by designers between; flexibility (suitability for a given task), efficiency or performance, Wearability and energy. Commercial micro controllers and processors are flexible enough due to their versatile instruction sets that allow the implementation of different wearable tasks. Dedicated processors (ASICs) on the other hand execute the given task faster, require less silicon area and consume lower power than general-purpose architectures. However, they lack the flexibility. If the wearable scenario changes, a redesign of the ASIC is required. Reconfigurable devices combine the flexibility of general processors and the performance of ASICs, but they do not meet the strict demands of power consumption.

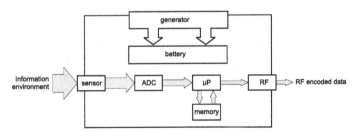

Fig. 1. Proposed Wearable System Architecture

1.2 Paper Scope

As sketched above, the design of a wearable system can be viewed as a multi dimensional problem with conflicting optimization criteria. This paper is dedicated to formalizing the tradeoffs involved in solving this problem. In doing so we focus on an individual module as shown by figure 1. We propose to describe such a module by four parameters that are either orthogonal to each other or represent different properties. They are 'Electronic Packaging parameters'(routing area, volume) and 'Flexibility of the processor/ASIC', both regarded as hardware metrics; 'Relative recognition performance' in a task and 'Normalized Energy/Power consumption' which are both regarded as application oriented metrics. We propose a methodology based on these four metrics to study the architectural trade-offs to answer the following questions. Which architecture is ideal/suitable in a context recognition scenario offering high flexibility, recognition performance and lowest energy consumption?. Which wearable architecture provides high Wearability and low- packaging costs?. This methodology is applied to practical design examples implemented at the *'ETH Wearable Computing Lab'*. The results show that the proposed methodology assists in selecting an optimal architecture for solving a given context recognition task. It will also be shown that, it is not possible to optimize all the four metrics at the same time. We will prove that the proposed metrics are orthogonal to each other.

2   Related Work and Paper Contribution

The main aspect which sets us aside from the work done by other groups in the field of computer architecture is the focus on *context aware wearable systems*. Design space exploration studies of computer architecture has been widely investigated by several researchers. Here we quote few examples, as it is not the purpose of the paper to advance the state-of-the-art in this area in general. Design studies of computer architectures consisting of heterogeneous systems with different hardware components was investigated by [6, 7, 8, 9]. However, they have not been applied to design nor to evaluate context aware wearable systems. System-level design approaches specific to power-performance optimization, speech processing in wearable computing was proposed by[10, 11], Systematic design approaches in wearable computing, were proposed by [12, 13]. Here, wearable systems do not necessarily include sensors and are not evaluated in activity context recognition tasks. They also do not deal with the aspect of miniaturization with electronic packaging and evaluating the flexibility. Developing new electronic packaging technologies such as SOP (System-On-Package) for achieving the goals of miniaturization, long-term performance and low productions costs have been the interest of several packaging research groups with more emphasis on technology. They did not focus on wearable system architectures and an evaluation of different tasks [14].

A detailed systematic approach considering wearability and power consumption in the design space was investigated by [15]. The methodologies for context-aware system design were proposed by [16] for selecting optimized architectures with respect to power consumption and classification performance. Evaluation of different context recognition algorithms with low-power wearable systems were investigated by [17, 4]. Electronic packaging aspects of an ultra-miniaturized wearable micro-system [18] was investigated by our group in the earlier studies.

In this paper, we present an advanced methodology purely applied to wearable systems by deriving the metrics from the different areas such as electronic packaging, processor architecture and context recognition algorithms. This evaluation methodology is based on four different metrics, viz; flexibility, packaging, relative recognition rate and normalized active energy consumption. Our methodology aims at investigating the architectural tradeoffs and finding optimized architecture for solving a wearable computing task. To the best of our knowledge this paper provides the following novelties.

– Proposing a new methodology by deriving the metrics from system design aspects such as 'flexibility' and 'electronic packaging' and combining them with task/application oriented 'relative recognition rate' and 'energy consumption' metrics to evaluate wearable systems.
– Evaluation of the methodology by applying to practical design examples as a proof-of-concept to find an optimal architecture.
– It is also shown that the proposed metrics are orthogonal to each other. i.e Optimizing all the four metrics at the same time is not feasible.

In Chapter 3, we propose the metrics, methodology and introduce different categories of tasks. In Chapter 4 we present different wearable systems and explain the hardware. Chapter 5 consists of a case study where wearable systems are evaluated. Finally we state our conclusions and proposed work for the future.

3   Proposed Metrics-Methodology

Considering the hardware aspects and application oriented aspects we have derived four metrics to represent the trade-offs. A task is defined as a set of isolated or continuous activities in a wearable scenario which needs to be recognized. eg: sitting-standing-walking, recognizing wood-workshop sounds

3.1   Proposed Metrics

(a) **Flexibility:** Flexibility is defined as suitability for solving different tasks. Suitability of the processor, is restricted by it's internal memory and operating frequency. Commercial processors have different instruction sets which also determines it's suitability in solving the given task. By Combining these three important properties we derive the Flexibility metric. It is specified by the device/processor maximum operating frequency (f_{max}), internal program memory in kb (M_p) and number of core instructions 'I', normalized on a logarithmic scale. In order to represent a wide range of processor families, a logarithmic scale would be imperative. Often ASIC (Application-Specific-Integrated-Circuits) and FPGA (Field-Programmable-Gate-Arrays) are custom designed for a specific application and do not rely on the instruction-set, so the number of CPU states or the number of outputs from the ASIC can be taken as a similar measure. With the proposed metric, different families of processors used in context recognition tasks are evaluated as shown in Table 1. Here, for ASICs we have calculated the number of outputs in two different scenarios (walking, arc$_A$ is 3 and office-worker, arc$_B$ is 5) (See chapter 5). ASICs show the lowest flexibility followed by low-performance micro-controllers. If the scenario changes a redesign would be required in the case of an ASIC, whereas less memory and lower operating frequencies restrict the flexibility of micro-controllers. The calculated values are shown in Table 1, proving that this metric holds true for a wide range of processor families.

Table 1. Flexibility Metric applied to Processors used in context recognition

Processor	$f_{max}(MHz)$	$M_p(kb)$	Inst	Pin Count	Flex.
MSP430F123	8	4	27	32	2.15
MSP430c33x	3.8	24	27	100	3.20
MSP430F1611	8	48	27	64	4.64
PIC18Fx480	10	16	75	44	4.78
PIC18Fx580	10	24	75	44	5.19
μPD78082	5	16	66	44	3.96
μPD78083	5	24	66	44	4.37
SA-1110	251	24	110	256	8.79
x-scale	400	32	80	544	13.83
AT91M40807	21	128	40	100	6.98
TMS320c55xx	200	24	85	144	8.31
ASIC$_{arcA}$	8	30	3	84	1.97
ASIC$_{arcB}$	8	30	5	84	2.48

$$Flexibility = log(\frac{f_{max} * M_p * I}{100 * 1MHz * 1kb}). \tag{1}$$

f_{max} = maximum operating frequency in MHz
M_p = program memory in kb
I = No. of core instructions

Modern FPGAs offer to combine the flexibility of digital signal processors and performance of ASICs to improve the suitability. However, they consume very high-power compared to an ASIC, that is designed to solve the similar application. One such example can be quoted to justify the reason, not to consider them in the current investigation. Mencer et. al[19] compared the implementation of the IDEA cryptography algorithm to comapre SA-1000 (RISC), DSP, FPGA and ASIC architectures. Although, it's possible to achieve high performance,but they can not achieve power savings compared to an ASIC which is intend to do the same task.

(b) Electronic Packaging Metrics: The wearable systems should be compact and light. The electronic packaging technology and scheme in which the systems are designed with sensors, a processor and signal conditioning circuitry, dominates the agenda since it directly affects the Wearability. Area in the x-y space (area occupied on the human-body when placed) and volume of the

Table 2. Comparision Between RISC, DSP, FPGA and ASIC

Type	Technology	clock	Performance	Power	Efficiency .
	μm	(MHz)	(MBit/s)	(W)	(MBit/J)
RISC SA-110	0.35	200	32.0	1.0	32.0
DSP TMS320C6x	0.25	200	53.1	6.0	8.9
FPGA XC4020XL	0.35	33	528.0	3.2	167.6
ASIC (VINCI)	1.20	25	177.8	1.5	118.7

system represents comfort and miniaturization. Based on the ITRS road map [20], the projections for processor pin-count follows a scale of power 2. In order to compensate for this growth and emphasize the 'packaging effort' within the system, ($\sqrt{(Pin_{proc})}$ * vol.) metric with usage of a logarithmic scale is imperative. For a wearable system, using a processor with a higher pin-count does not affect it's wearability but the packaging effort does ('effort in system-integration').

$$Pkg_a = log[\frac{Area * \sqrt{(Pin_{proc})}}{1mm^2 * 1000}]. \tag{2}$$

$$Pkg_b = log[\frac{Vol. * \sqrt{(Pin_{proc})}}{1mm^3 * 1000}]. \tag{3}$$

Area = Area of the Wearable-System after Packaging in mm^2
Vol. = Volume of the Wearable-System after packaging in mm^3
Pin$_{proc}$ = Number of pins of the processor

(c) Normalized Active Power or Energy Consumption: The active power or energy consumption of a processor is defined as the energy/power consumed in performing a number of classifications (N) in a time 't' to solve a context recognition task. The energy/power values of the processor are measured and normalized to a logarithmic scale. The proposed power-consumption metric serves to represent a wide range of power values (from a few micro watts to several watts), which would not be feasible with linear representation. The normalized power consumption P$_{norm}$ of the processor is defined as

$$P_{norm} = log(\frac{P_{proc}}{1m.W}). \tag{4}$$

The number of classifications per second depends on the architecture of the processor, the complexity of the algorithm and the task to be recognized. In order to compare different architectures, active classification energy for performing 'N' classifications in time 't' sec can also be used as a metric .

$$E_N = log(\frac{E_{proc}}{1m.J}). \tag{5}$$

E_N = Normalized Classification Energy consumption
E_{proc} = Energy consumption of the processor in mJ

If the task is a computational job such as calculating a particular set of features or a single feature then execution time T_{ex} normalized on a logarithmic scale can be considered as a suitable metric(T_N).

$$T_N = log(\frac{T_{ex}}{1ms.}). \tag{6}$$

(d) **Relative Recognition Performance (R.R.P):** Isolated actions or continuous activities can be recognized by using features from single or multiple sensors together with a classifier algorithm. Implementation of the complex features and algorithms is restricted by the available hardware resources, which influences the recognition rates. The proposed metric normalizes the recognition rates of different tasks on a scale of 0.1 to 1. We define the limits of recognition performance based on the task. A task is deemed successful if it meets the stipulated 'higher limit or above' and unsuccessful if it does not meet the lower limit with respect to the recognition rates.

 - R.R.P = 1 (completion of the task)
 - R.R.P = 0.1 (un successful completion of the task)
 - R.R.P = W_p (partial completion of the task) where W_p= weights assigned

$$W_p = \frac{R_s - R_{low}}{R_{high} - R_{low}} * x. \tag{7}$$

R_s = Recognition Rate achieved during the task
R_{low} = Lower limit of Recognition rate (scenario specific)
R_{high} = Upper limit of Recognition rate (scenario specific)
x = 0.9 (for the R.R.P scale (1.0 - 0.1 = 0.9))

This metric serves as a performance-measure of a system for solving a context recognition task considering the effect of features and classifier algorithms. Also the task can be a computational job such as calculation of a feature, set of features towards application in context recognition. It can be termed as Relative Task Solvability (R.T.S). R.T.S can only be rated as either 1.0 or 0.0 for successful and unsuccessful completion. All the four metrics: costs of flexibility,packaging,energy, recognition performance can be calculated in a combined form for a given architecture. It will also be shown that, these metrics help in selecting optimal wearable architecture.

3.2   Tasks

A task is recognition of a single or set of activities in a wearable computing scenario, using information from sensors. Tasks are divided into three categories (table 2) based on the computational complexity (No. of Instructions per sec.)& minimum memory size (M_{min}) It is assumed that we have a priori knowledge about what sensors are required in each activity. The features and the classifier algorithms are known [17, 4] . They range from simple daily-life activities detection using 'mean' feature with a C 4.5 decision tree classifier algorithm to solving a complex health monitoring task using Hidden Markov models

Table 3. Categories of tasks based on the complexity

Task	Category	Features -*Classifier*	Inst./sec (MIPS)	M_{min} (Kb)
low	household activities[4]	mean, mcr, max., min. - *C4.5*	< 1	< 2
medium	Walking [21, 22] Kitchenette [17] Workshop[5]	mean, std, fluc variance, cg, rpt, LDA FFT- *K-NN, Bayes*	$\geq 1\ \&$ ≤ 10	$\geq 2\ \&$ ≤ 100
high	Eating Habits Sign Language[23]	- *HMM, Vision Algorithms*	> 10	> 100

(HMM). For low level tasks the features are simple time-domain features such as 'mean','maximum', 'minimum' and 'slope' with a C 4.5 decision tree classifier algorithm. For medium level tasks, a combination of time and frequency domain features ('FFT', 'roll-off-point', 'center of gravity', 'band width' etc.) or time domain features ('variance' and 'fluctuation' which requires a multiplication or division operation) with classifier algorithms such as K-Nearest Neighbor and Naive Bayes. High-level tasks deal with much more complex algorithms such as Hidden Markov Models and wearable vision algorithms.

- std - standard deviation, rpt - roll off point, fluc- fluctuation
- cg - center of gravity, mcr - mean crossing rate, LDA - Linear Discriminant Analysis
- FFT - Fast Fourier Transformation

4   Wearable Systems Architecture

In order to evaluate the proposed Metrics we have implemented the following wearable systems. The systems A,B and C consists of accelerometers (ADXL311 from Analog Devices), microphone (SPO103 from Knowles Acoustics) and visible light sensor (SFH3410 from Osram Semiconductors) as sensors together with MSP430 family processors and an nRF 2401 Transceiver from Nordic Semiconductors. In 'A'(WSpack 1.0) an external ADC, 12 bit and 8 channel AD7888 from Analog devices is used, where as 'MSP430F1611' already includes a 12-bit AD converter. The clock for the micro-controller, is generated by an internal digital controlled oscillator (DCO). The DCO is stabilized by an external 32kHz quartz crystal. The data from the micro-controllers is forwarded to an nRF2401 transceiver for wireless transmission.They are powered by a small lithium-polymer battery (VPP402025 from Varta) which has a capacity of 130 mAh. The entire systems are fabricated on a 4 layer FR-4 substrate. 'A' has overall size of 27 x 32 mm^2 with a thickness of 9 mm, where as B has a size of 41.5 x 27.5 mm ^{2} with a thickness of 9 mm due to slightly bigger micro-controller. A detailed hardware explanation for A, B is given in [4, 24] System 'C' additionally includes a hybrid power supply (a DC-DC converter with solar cell). The entire

Fig. 2. Hardware Architecture of Autonomous Sensor Button

system is divided into three modules. Sensors and the RF transceiver are on the top module, the micro-controller with hybrid power supply are in the second module which in turn is connected to a third module: a solar cell for energy harvesting. The system has a radius of 15 mm with 1 mm holes for sewing it to the clothing for wearability.

We also have implemented an ASIC (0.25 μm UMC L250) for detecting walking behavior. It can process the input data from accelerometers, pressure sensors and a GPS sensor. The chip is designed to calculate; 'mean', 'variance', 'maximum', 'high-band', 'low-band', 'slope', 'entropy' features together with FFT (64, 128, 256 pt) with an option to by-pass certain features. The K-Nearest Neighbor algorithm is implemented in the chip to detect walking behavior. The activity recognition chip is used for simple-walking behavior (idle, walking straight, walking up/down) using only acceleration data and detailed level-walking (elevator up, down) using the additional data from the pressure sensor. The entire area occupied by the chip is 2.435 mm * 2.435 mm with a core area of 3.204 mm^2 The chip is designed to have a maximum operating frequency of 8 MHz. The supply voltage to the core is 2.5 V and the I/O : max is 3.3 V The final system that we have considered in the study is the QBIC, this consists of an x-scale processor from the 'Intel' family. The QBIC has a belt form factor and can be used for field trials. The friendly user-interface allows different sensors to be connected without major modifications in the design.

5   Case Study - Discussion

The proposed four metrics are evaluated in two tasks with the systems introduced in section 4. In Task A, 'walking behavior', three activities are required to be detected using accelerometers. 'Idle', 'walking', and 'walking up/down' using the features shown in Table. 4, it is possible to achieve recognition rates of around 90% [22, 21]. In Task B, 'office-worker' activities such as ' sitting at the desk', 'typing on the keyboard', 'moving the mouse', 'taking a nap', 'lifting a cup and drinking from it' are to be recognized. Simple feature with a C 4.5 decision tree classifier algorithm is sufficient in this case as recommended in [27]. In Task C a 32- bit FFT is implemented and tested on the systems to calculate the execution time.

Table 4. Practical Design Examples

System	Processor
A. WSpack 1.0[4]	MSP430F123(Texas Instruments)
B. WSPack 2.0[24]	MSP430F1611(Texas Instruments)
C. Wearable Sensor Button	MSP430F1611(Texas Instruments)
D. ARC chip [25]	ASIC (0.25 μm UMC L250 technology)
E. QBIC[26]	x-scale(Intel)

Table 5. Evaluated Tasks

Evaluated Tasks	Sensors	Feat.- *Classifier*	Recogn.
A. Walking	accl. - (12-bit, 100 Hz)- above knee	'mean','max','var'- *K-NN*	$\geq$80 %
B. Office- Worker	accl.,light (12-bit, 32 Hz) on the wrist	'mean', 'MCR', 'fluc' or only 'mean' - *C 4.5*	$\geq$75 %
C. FFT	64,128,256 pt (16, 32-bit)	FFT	1.0 or 0.0

The test results of ARC chip power consumption, using the acceleration test vectors calculating 'mean', 'variance', 'maximum' and fast fourier transform (256 pt FFT) with the K-NN algorithm is shown in Fig.3. Also the measured active power-consumption results of the MSP430F1611 processor at different supply voltages are shown in Fig.4. These measurements allow us to estimate the energy consumption values in the current case study. For task A, the MSP430F123 processor could not complete the recognition task. It does not have a hardware multiplier and due to limited memory, during the distance matrices calculations of the K-NN algorithm with 5-9 neighbours, buffer-overflow problems occur. The

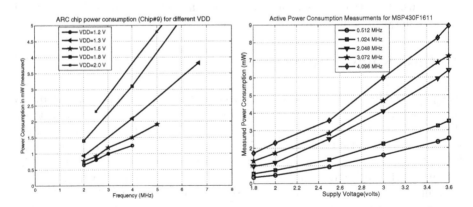

Fig. 3. ASIC   **Fig. 4.** MSP430F1611

'ARC chip' performed 200 classifications@ 2 MHz, the behavior with frequency is linear. The x-scale processor performed 10 classifications/sec @400 MHz using 'mean', 'variance' features and running a K-NN classifier algorithm with a data input of 100 samples/sec. K-NN requires calculation of eucledian distances to the training vectors in the memory and classifies the activities using sorting. Here a sorting algorithm such as bubble sort would be required, which takes 390 ms at 1 MHz sorting 32 bytes of data (32 vectors) on the MSP430F1611 or similar processors [28]. This can be roughly translated so that sorting 100 feature vectors can take 1.17 seconds. Therefore at 4MHz around 3 classifications are possible. The active energy costs (E_{Na}) of all the systems are calculated to perform 10 classifications of task A.

For task B, the expected recognition performance (80-83%) can be achieved by using all the processors and slightly lower recognition rates for MSP430F123 can be attributed due to it's limited memory size. The calculation of 'mean' feature and classification with decision tree classifier (6-7 decisions) is possible on all the four processors. Using MCR, fluctuation even higher recognition rates can be ahieved. In this scenario, a complete redesign of ASIC would be required, hence we have emulated an ASIC, similar to the ARC chip used in the walking behavior task. Using MSP430 processors 3 classifications @1MHz were achieved. For the ASIC, it would be above 100 classifications@ 1MHz, whilst on an x-scale processor performing around more than 100 classifications @150 MHz (minimum clock frequency) can be achieved. This can be attributed due to the lower complexity of the decision tree classifier in comparison to a K-NN classifier algorithm [17, 4]. The active energy costs (E_{Nb}) of all the systems are calculated to perform 100 classifications for task B. The measured and calculated metrics for all wearable systems for both tasks are shown in Table 4.

Discussion: From the behavior of the diagrams the ideal system is that which is centralized. For task A, only WSPack1.0 (F123) failed to complete the task but scores the lowest packaging costs. ARC (ASIC) shows best energy costs with respect to other systems but lacks the flexibility, whilst QBIC/x-scale combination showed best flexibility, R.R.P but higher packaging and energy costs. WSPack2.0 has medium flexibility and packaging costs. It fails to score above QBIC in flexibility and lower energy costs than the ARC chip. Task B has a lower complexity than Task A and all the systems could complete it. The distribution of metrics moves closer to the center in case of WSPack1.0. For this task too, ASIC scored the lowest energy costs. It also scores better flexibility only comparision (see

Table 6. Evaluation of Metrics to Design Examples

System/ Processor	Flex.	Pkg_a	E_{Na}	$R.R.P_a$	E_{Nb}	$R.R.P_b$
(a) WSPack1.0/MSP430F123	2.15	1.58	2.17	0.1	3.37	0.72
(b) WSPack2.0/MSP430F1611	4.64	2.21	2.54	1.0	3.41	1.0
(c) ARC/ASIC$_{arcA}$	1.97	1.86	-3.21	1.0	-0.79	1.0
(d) QBIC/X-Scale	13.83	4.58	6.90	1.0	5.92	1.0
(e) SensorButton/MSP430F1611	4.64	1.73	2.54	1.0	3.41	1.0

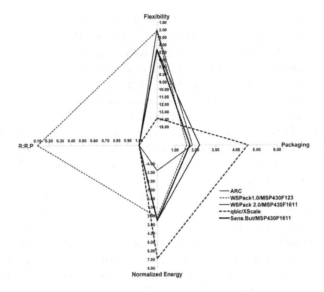

Fig. 5. Architectural tradeoffs for task A

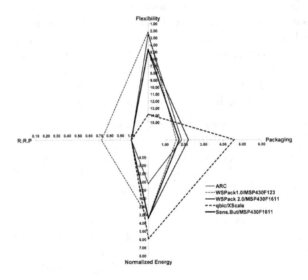

Fig. 6. Architectural tradeoffs for task B

Tab.1) to WSPack1.0. WSPack2.0 scores medium packaging, energy, flexibility costs with best R.R.P. QBIC/x-scale, meanwhile has poor performance considering high packaging and power costs but scores best flexibility and R.R.P. None of the systems score best performance for all the proposed metrics in both of the tasks. From the case study it can be inferred that it's not possible to optimize the four metrics, to have the best centralized distribution.

High flexibility is characterized by high memory and operating frequencies. This contradicts achieving lowest energy consumption as well as lower packaging costs (higher pin-count corresponds to higher packaging effort and more area). At the same time, commercial processors which consume lower energy might not achieve better recognition performance or cannot complete the tasks at all. This implies it's not feasible to optimize all the four metrics at the same time to design an architecture to have centralized distribution. This implies, that these four metrics are orthogonal to each other and that they represent four different system properties. The proposed orthogonality can also be verified by search algorithms such PISA [29]. Due to the current design space, instead of a complete search algorithm we have applied dominance-non domiance algorithm *(for minima)*[29]. This approach is useful, to check the dependency of solutions, where automaticly solutions can be identified as shown in solution dependecies in Case (A),(B) and (C). In the case of 32-bit 64 pt FFT, using the R.T.S metrics such behavior can be osberved, where XScale processor is faster than its F1611 (both scoring 1), where as F123 fails to complete the task scoring 0. But in this case also all the metrics are orthogonal to each other.

$$Min.Sol(A) = \begin{pmatrix} -2.15 & 1.58 & 2.17 & -0.10 \\ -1.97 & 1.86 & -3.21 & -1.00 \\ -13.83 & 4.58 & 6.90 & -1.00 \\ -4.64 & 1.73 & 2.54 & -1.00 \end{pmatrix}$$

$$Min.Sol(B) = \begin{pmatrix} -2.15 & 1.58 & 3.37 & -0.72 \\ -1.97 & 1.86 & -0.79 & -1.00 \\ -13.83 & 4.58 & 5.92 & -1.00 \\ -4.64 & 1.73 & 3.41 & -1.00 \end{pmatrix}$$

$$Min.Sol(C) = \begin{pmatrix} -2.15 & +1.58 & \pm\infty & 0 \\ -13.83 & +4.58 & -5.92 & -1 \\ -4.64 & +1.73 & +4.56 & -1 \end{pmatrix}$$

It can be seen from the results of dominance(non) algorithm that no solution dominates and it is not possible to optimize all the four metrics at the same time. With in the family of systems, between WSPack2.0 and Sensor Button (using the similar processor), the Sensor Button dominates only in terms of electronic packaging metric due to smaller size. Hence the solutions of architecture 2 are ruled out in the design space and rest of the solutions output is executed.

6   Conclusions and Future Work

We have presented a new methodology to study the architectural tradeoffs in wearable systems. From the evaluation of the proposed metrics it was concluded that all the four metrics cannot be optimized at the same time. This implies that; flexibility, packaging, energy and relative recognition performance, are orthogonal to each other. Also it can be concluded that ASICs can not be optimized for achieving highest flexibility. Medium Performance processors are more suitable for solving both low and medium level tasks showing medium overall costs.

However, they cannot be optimized for lowest energy and highest flexibility and are not suitable for high level tasks just as low performance micro controllers are not suitable for medium level tasks. In our future work, we would like to consider even more complex scenarios for evaluation.

Acknowledgements. Special thanks to Mathias Stäger for the valuable discussions and suggestions. Thanks to Thomas Stiefmeier for allowing us to explore ARC and Veronica Housen for proof reading.

The Wearable Sensor Button concept is patented under ETH Technology transfer number 04-013-01.

References

1. Pentland, A.: Wearable intelligence. Scientific American **276**(1es1) (1998)
2. Mann, S.: Wearable computing as means for personal empowerment. In: Proc. 3rd Int. Conf. on Wearable Computing (ICWC). (1998)
3. Abowd, D., Dey, A., Orr, R., Brotherton, J.: Context-awareness in wearable and ubiquitous computing. Virtual Reality **3**(3) (1998) 200–211
4. Bharatula, N.B., Stäger, M., Lukowicz, P., Tröster, G.: Empirical study of design choices in multi-sensor context recognition systems. In: In Proc. of 2 nd International Forum on Applied Wearable Computing, IFAWC 05. (2005) 79–93
5. Lukowicz, P., Ward, J.A., Junker, H., Stäger, M., Tröster, G., Atrash, A., Starner, T.: Recognizing workshop activity using body worn microphones and accelerometers. In: Pervasive Computing: Proc. of the 2nd Int'l Conference. (2004) 18–22
6. Thiele, L., Chakraborty, S., Gries, M., Künzli, S.: Design space exploration of network processor architectures. In: Network Processor Design 2002: Design Principles and Practices. Morgan Kaufmann Publishers (2002)
7. Wolf, W.: Computers as Components: Principles of Embedded Computing System Design. Morgan Kaufman Publishers (2002)
8. Austin, T., Larson, E., Ernst, D.: SimpleScalar: An infrastructure for computer system modeling. **35**(2) (2002) 59–67
9. Sinha, A., Chandrakasan, A.P.: JouleTrack – a web based tool for software energy profiling. (2001) 220–225
10. Smailagic, A., Reilly, D., Siewiorek, D.P.: A system-level approach to power/performance optimization in wearable computers. In: Proc. IEEE Computer Society Workshop on VLSI (WVLSI). (2000) 15–20
11. Smailagic, A., Ettus, M.: System design and power optimization for mobile computers. In: Proc. of the IEEE Computer Society Annual Symposium on VLSI, IVLSI. (2002) 10–14
12. Warren, J., Martin, T., Smailagic, A., Siewiorek, D.: System design approach to power aware mobile computers. In: Proc. of the IEEE Computer Society Annual Symposium on VLSI. (2003) 101–106
13. Smailagic, A., Siewiorek, D.: System level design as applied to CMU wearable computers. J. VLSI Signal Processing Systems for Signal, Image, and Video Technology **21**(3) (1999) 251–263
14. Tummala, R., Madisetti, V.: System on chip or system on package. IEEE Design and Test of Computers (1999) 48–56
15. Anliker, U., Beutel, J., Dyer, M., Enzler, R., Lukowicz, P., Thiele, L., Tröster, G.: A systematic approach to the design of distributed wearable systems. IEEE Transactions on Computers **53**(3) (2004) 1017–1033

16. Anliker, U., Junker, H., Lukowicz, P., Tröster, G.: Design methodology for context-aware wearable sensor systems. In: Proceedings of the 3 rd International Conference on Pervasive Computing. (2005) 220–236
17. Stäger, M., Lukowicz, P., Tröster, G.: Implementation and Evaluation of a Low-Power Sound-Based User Activity Recognition System. In: ISWC 2004: Proc. of the 8th IEEE Int'l Symposium on Wearable Computers. (2004) 138–141
18. Bharatula, N.B., Ossevoort, S., Stäger, M., Tröster, G.: Towards wearable autonomous microsystems. In: Pervasive Computing: Procc of the 2nd Int'l Conference. (2004) 225–237
19. Mencer, O., Morf, M., Flynn, M.: Hardware software tri-design of encryption for mobile communication units. In: IEEE Int. Conf. on Acoustics, Speech, and Signal Processing. (1998) 3045–3048
20. Homepage of the ITRS RoadMap: Itrs roadmap. http://public.itrs.net (2004)
21. Randell, C., Muller, H.: Context awareness by analysing accelerometer data. In: ISWC 2000: Proc. of the 4th Int'l Symposium on Wearable Computers. (2000) 175–176
22. Sekine, M., Tamura, T., Fujimoto, T., Fukui, Y.: Classification of walking pattern using acceleration waveform in elderly people. In: Proc. of the 22nd Annual Int'l Conference of the IEEE Engineering in Medicine and Biology Society. Volume 2. (2000) 1356–1359
23. Starner, T., Weaver, J., Pentland, A.: Real-time american sign language recognition using desk and wearable computer based video. IEEE Transactions on Pattern Analysis and Machine Intelligence 20(12) (1998) 1371–1375
24. Bharatula, N.B., Stäger, M., Lukowicz, P., Tröster, G.: Power and size optimized multi-sensor context recognition platform. In: In ' 9 th IEEE International Symposium on Wearable Computers, ISWC 05'. (2005) 195–196
25. T.Stiefmeier, G.Tröster: Activity Recognition Chip(arc) (2005)
26. Amft, O., Lauffer, M., Ossevoort, S., Macaluso, F., Lukowicz, P., Tröster, G.: Design of the qbic wearable computing platform. In: 15 the IEEE conference on Application-Specific Systems, Architectures and Processors. (2004)
27. Bao, L., Intille, S.S.: Activity recognition from user-annotated acceleration data. In: Pervasive Computing: Proc. of the 2nd Int'l Conference. (2004) 1–17
28. MAXIM Dallas Semiconductor. http://www.maxim-ic.com/appnotes.cfm/ (2004)
29. PISA. http://www.tik.ee.ethz.ch/pisa/ (2005)

Do Trace Cache, Value Prediction and Prefetching Improve SMT Throughput?

Chen-Yong Cher[1,*], Il Park[1,*], and T.N. VijayKumar

ECE, Purdue University, IN 47907, USA
{chenyong, ilpark, vijay}@ecn.purdue.edu

Abstract. While trace cache, value prediction, and prefetching have been shown to be effective in the single-threaded superscalar, there has been no analysis of these techniques in a Simultaneously Multithreaded (SMT) processor. SMT brings new factors both for and against these techniques, and it is not known how these techniques would fare in SMT. We evaluate these techniques in an SMT to provide recommendations for future SMT designs. Our key contributions are: (1) we identify a fundamental interaction between the techniques and SMT's sharing of resources among multiple threads, and (2) we quantify the impact of this interaction on SMT throughput. SMT's sharing of the instruction storage (i.e., trace cache or i-cache), physical registers, and issue queue impacts the effectiveness of trace cache, value prediction, and prefetching, respectively.

1 Introduction

Simultaneous Multithreading (SMT) has been proposed for improving processor throughput by overlapping multiple threads in a wide-issue superscalar processor. Three techniques which are used to exploit more instruction-level parallelism (ILP) and to improve single-thread performance in superscalar are: 1) trace cache to increase fetch bandwidth, 2) value prediction to break data dependences, and 3) prefetching to hide memory latency. While these techniques have been shown to be effective in the single-threaded superscalar, there has been no analysis of their effectiveness in SMT. which is becoming the microarchitecture of choice for high-performance microprocessors (e.g., Intel's Hyperthreading, Sun's Niagara, IBM's POWER5). Compared to superscalar, SMT brings new factors both for and against these techniques, and it is not known how these techniques would fare in SMT. Some of these techniques are implemented in superscalars today, and they will be included automatically in SMT when the superscalars are converted to SMT. Therefore, it is important to know how they fare in SMT.

This paper fills this important gap by evaluating these techniques in the context of an out-of-order issue SMT and provides recommendations for future SMT designs.

---

[1] Chen-Yong Cher and Il Park completed all the work in this paper during their PhD studies at Purdue University. After graduation, Chen-Yong Cher and Il Park joined IBM TJ Watson Researcher Center. This paper is not affiliated with IBM.

* Current Address: IBM T. J. Watson, P.O. Box 218, Yorktown Heights, NY 10598, USA
{chenyong, ilpark}@us.ibm.com

W. Grass et al. (Eds.): ARCS 2006, LNCS 3894, pp. 232–251, 2006.

Because SMT's goal is to improve throughput, which is also an important performance metric for server-class machines which increasingly use SMT, we evaluate the techniques in terms of processor throughput.

Our novelty is not in the techniques we study, but in their evaluation in the context of SMT. Our key contributions are: (1) we identify a fundamental interaction between the techniques and SMT's sharing of resources among multiple threads, and (2) we quantify the impact of this interaction on SMT throughput. This interaction is the key issue and common theme in our evaluation of the three techniques.

Previous studies showed that trace cache increases fetch bandwidth [22,20,19,8,3]. Trace cache creates traces from dynamic instruction sequences and allows an entire trace to be fetched in one access. A key motivation for trace cache is that increasing fetch bandwidth in superscalar is complicated and involves more than merely using many fetch ports. To utilize multiple fetch ports, superscalar needs multiple branch prediction, which is not straightforward. Implementing multiple branch prediction involves both (1) maintaining high accuracy of prediction and (2) providing multiple, contiguous fetch PCs for the same thread. Trace cache handles these issues effectively and achieves better performance than multiple branch prediction.

Unfortunately, trace cache introduces multiple copies of instructions in different traces, despite the most efficient implementation [3]. This redundancy reduces the effective size of the cache. Increasing the cache size is difficult due to latency, area, and power considerations. This trade-off of space for bandwidth seems reasonable for superscalar because a single thread may not need a large instruction cache. However, SMT needs a larger instruction storage (i.e., trace cache or i-cache) because multiple threads share the storage. In contrast to superscalar, SMT can supply multiple fetch PCs from different threads and utilize extra fetch ports effectively without needing multiple branch prediction. Therefore, it is not clear whether trace cache's trade-off of space for bandwidth will improve SMT throughput.

Value prediction predicts values instead of waiting for long-latency dependences to be resolved, speeding up computation even beyond data-flow limits [16,1,23,17,5]. Prediction accuracy can be increased and the benefit of the technique can be sustained by trading off coverage and predicting only highly-predictable long-latency operations (e.g., cache misses) [5]. In contrast to value prediction in superscalar, SMT simply tolerates L1 misses. Upon L2 misses, SMT squashes the thread [27], releasing the thread's shared resources (i.e., physical registers and issue queue slots), and over-laps the L2 miss with other threads.

Applying value prediction to SMT raises a key but subtle issue related to sharing of registers. Value prediction holds up physical registers even when the prediction is correct! Due to program-order commit, instructions that follow a correctly-value-predicted, long-latency instruction hold up registers even after completing execution. These instructions can release their registers only after the long-latency instruction completes, confirms the prediction, and commits. Building larger register file to alleviate such hold-up is not easy due to latency, area, and power considerations [2,4,18]. While this hold-up of registers may be acceptable for superscalar, it may not be profitable for SMT, in which multiple threads create a higher demand for the shared registers. It is not clear whether SMT throughput is improved more by value-predicting long-latency instructions and holding up registers; or by squashing the instructions and releasing registers so other threads can use the registers and overlap the latency.

Prefetching predicts future memory references and brings data into caches before the data is actually needed [24,14,25,6,10,13,32,9]. Recent proposals for aggressive hardware prefetching, such as Dead-block predictor[13] and its successor Time-Keeping predictor [32], are highly successful even with non-strided access patterns. SMT has two opposing effects on the opportunity available from prefetching. On one hand, because SMT can tolerate cache misses, it may present less opportunity to prefetching. On the other hand, because SMT issues memory references from multiple threads, it increases the pressure on the memory hierarchy and may present more opportunity.

Prefetching in SMT achieves coverage and accuracy comparable to those of a single thread. However, prefetching raises a subtle issue related to sharing of the issue queue. While prefetching into L2 achieves most of the benefit of prefetching into L1 without incurring L1's contention problems for a single thread [9], prefetching only into L2 causes a problem for SMT. Prefetching into L2 converts slow L2 misses into fast L2 hits; however, the L2 hits still miss in L1, resulting in the same L1 misses occurring in fewer cycles. L1 misses clog the issue queue with dependent instructions, even though L1 misses are short. While SMT without prefetching is also clogged for the L1-miss duration, it eventually incurs an L2 miss and squashes the thread [5], unclogging the issue queue to allow other threads to progress. Because prefetching causes L1 misses to occur in fewer cycles, the issue queue is clogged more often with prefetching than without. Thus, even correct prefetching may hurt SMT throughput! Unfortunately, neither removing L1 misses nor circumventing them to avoid the clogging is easy; removing L1 misses by prefetching into L1 is difficult due to L1's high contention [9], which is worse in SMT. Circumventing L1 misses is also difficult because L1 misses are known too late in the pipeline to prevent dependent instructions from entering the pipeline. Thus, in addition to the uncertainty in opportunity, the question of whether issue-queue clogging or latency hiding will impact SMT throughput more is unclear. Table 1 summarizes the trade-offs of the techniques when they are implemented in SMT.

The main results of our simulations using a subset of the SPEC2000 benchmarks are:

- Trace cache, value prediction and prefetching significantly improve single-thread performance. This result agrees with previous papers and validates our implementations.
- Given similar size for the duo of trace cache and backup i-cache as the conventional i-cache, trace cache degrades SMT throughput compared to the conventional i-cache (throughput improves for 2 threads, agreeing with the two-threaded Pentium IV's use of a trace cache). This result shows that trace cache's space-for-bandwidth trade-off hurts SMT. Giving considerable extra size to the trace cache results in the trace cache performing only marginally better than the conventional i-cache, showing that trace cache is not effective in SMT.
- Given a typical number of physical registers, value prediction degrades SMT throughput, showing that holding up registers under value prediction hurts SMT. While value prediction does improve individual threads that have long-latency misses, it does so at the cost of the other threads, defeating SMT's purpose. Using infinite physical registers and perfect confidence prediction results in value prediction performing only marginally better than conventional SMT, showing that value prediction is not effective in SMT.

- For memory-intensive workloads, there is substantial opportunity for prefetching even with many threads, showing that not all long-latency misses can be hidden by SMT. We found that prefetch coverage can be reduced to balance prefetching and issue queue clogging, improving throughput for this workload. For workloads with mixed memory demand, SMT significantly reduces opportunity. Despite reducing the coverage, prefetching slightly degrades throughput for this workload due to issue queue clogging. Like value prediction, prefetching also improves individual threads at the cost of the other threads in this workload, degrading overall throughput.
- Our findings create a new responsibility for the OS: Because the techniques improve single-thread performance, we recommend that the OS disable the techniques when running multi-programmed workload, and enable them for single-threaded workload and for high-priority threads in a multi-programmed workload.

Section 2 gives the background of the techniques. Section 3 describes our methodology. Section 4 shows our results, and Section 5 concludes the paper.

Table 1. Trade-offs of each techniques

	Trace Cache	Value Prediction	Prefetching
Pros	- satisfies SMT's high demand of fetch bandwidth	- breaks the data dependences of individual threads	- fulfills SMT's high demand on memory access
Cons	- causes redundancy in instruction storage while SMT demands high instruction storage capacity - SMT provides high fetch bandwidth without needing multiple branch prediction	- Data dependence delay can be hidden by other threads. - holds up resources even when predictions are correct	- Opportunity may drop because of thread-level parallelism. - may cause issue queue clogging even when prefetches are correct

2   A Brief Background of the Techniques

2.1   Trace Cache

Before trace cache was introduced, Tyson et al. [31] increased fetch bandwidth by predicting multiple branches every cycle with Branch Address Cache. Rotenberg et al. [22] introduced trace cache, and compared it with other high-bandwidth instruction fetch schemes. Others [20,21,8] studied important issues concerning trace cache performance such as partial matching, cache associativity, fill unit, and multiple branch prediction. Patel et al. [19] proposed branch promotion and trace packing for improving trace cache bandwidth. To achieve better utilization of trace cache space, Black et al. [3] suggested the block-based trace cache, which stores pointers to blocks constituting a trace, instead of storing instructions. Any repetition of the traces results in only the pointers being repeated instead of the entire trace, reducing space requirements.

Because we wish to study the effectiveness of trace cache's space-for-bandwidth trade-off, and because the block-based trace cache is the most space-efficient implementation that also achieves high bandwidth, we use the block-based trace cache in our evaluations. We discuss the details of this specific trace cache later in Section 4.1.1.

2.2 Value Prediction

Lipasti et al. [16] proposed last-value prediction with saturating confidence counters. Mendelson et al. [1] added a stride prediction scheme, and Farkas et al. [23] studied the implementation details for the context-based prediction scheme. Others predict load values by using recent store information [17,30]. However, without accurate prediction, value prediction may hurt performance due to misprediction penalties unless there is hardware support, such as selective recovery, to reduce the penalty. Calder et al. [5] showed the importance of confidence prediction to perform selective value prediction to avoid mispredictions and achieve good speedup even without the complicated machinery of selective recovery.

In addition to avoiding complicated selective recovery, reducing mispredictions is important for SMT so that processor resources are not wasted on incorrect execution. Therefore, we use [5]'s selective value prediction, which combines confidence prediction and value prediction, in our evaluations and discuss their details in Section 4.2.1.

2.3 Prefetching

While prefetching can be implemented in either software [24,14] or hardware, we focus on hardware prefetching in this study. Chen et al. [25] proposed the stride prefetcher, and others [11,7] used a stream buffer for prefetching. Markov prefetching uses address correlation (i.e., correlation among addresses in the cache miss stream) to improve the accuracy of prefetching arbitrary, non-strided access patterns [6,10]. These proposals focused on *what* to prefetch but do not pinpoint *when* to prefetch.

Lai et al. [13] first proposed to consider the timing of memory access patterns to determine when to prefetch and improves accuracy over [10]. They introduced Dead-Block Predictors to predict the dead blocks — i.e., the blocks that will be evicted without any use — in L1. When a block dies, the prefetcher predicts the next access to the block's set and prefetches the next access into the dead block's frame. Kaxiras et al. [12] also proposed a scheme to predict dead blocks, but they used the prediction for reducing cache leakage power and not for prefetching data. Hu et al. [32] applied [12] to prefetching and used smaller prediction tables than [13] for both dead-block predicition and next-address prediction while achieving better performance.

Lastly, Hu, et al. [9] simplified [32] by showing that when prefetching into a large highly-associative L2 cache, dead-block prediction was not necessary. [9] also showed that prefetching into L2 can achieve most of the benefit of prefetching into L1 without disrupting the highly contentious L1 with untimely or incorrect prefetches. Because SMT's multiple threads cause even higher contention on L1 than that of superscalar, we implement the latest, best-performing tag-correlating prefetching of [9] to prefetch into L2 without disrupting L1. We discuss the prefetcher implementation details in Section 4.3.1.

3 Methodology

We modified simplescalar-3.0 for our evaluation. Our simulator carefully models SMT pipeline details, including out-of-order issue, memory-bus occupancy, multiple contexts, virtual-to-physical address translation, per-thread load/store queues and active lists, and shared physical register file and issue queue. The simulator models a pipeline that supports thread-level squashing on branch misprediction. To improve instruction throughput in SMT, we apply squashing on L2 misses [27], except for special cases that we will mention later. Because the L1 caches are virtually indexed, we use address offsetting described in [15] to spread out accesses of different threads in the cache. We also use the Bin-Hop page allocation policy to spread out accesses in the L2 cache [15].

Our simulator runs *Alpha* binaries that are compiled with *peak* setting. We fast-forward the first two billion instructions of each thread. The fast-forwarding warms up branch predictor, the L2 and L1 caches, but do not gather statistics. We then simulate until one of the threads reaches 100 million instructions. For four or eight threads this method simulates more than 100 million instructions. Therefore, our results are unlikely to be biased by individual programs. Recently [26] proposes clustering phases to reduce simulation time while minimizing errors for simulating single program. However, clustering for a multi-programmed workload is more complicated and involves mixing phases of several programs. Because [26] does not show clustering for SMT simulations, we do not use such approach.

Table 2. Applications and workloads

Category	Benchmarks		
1T.ILP	**mesa, crafty, fma3d, eon, facerec, equake, sixtrack, galgel**		
1T.MEM	*vpr, apsi, art, applu, swim, lucas, mcf, ammp*		
1T.MIX	1T.ILP + 1T.MEM		
Workload	**Composition**	**Workload**	**Composition**
2T.ILP.1	**mesa, crafty**	2T.MIX.1	*vpr,* **mesa**
2T.ILP.2	**fma3d, eon**	2T.MIX.2	*apsi,* **crafty**
2T.ILP.3	**facerec, equake**	2T.MIX.3	*art,* **fma3d**
2T.ILP.4	**sixtrack, galgel**	2T.MIX.4	*applu,* **eon**
2T.MEM.1	*vpr, apsi*	2T.MIX.5	*swim,* **facerec**
2T.MEM.2	*art, applu*	2T.MIX.6	*lucas,* **equake**
2T.MEM.3	*swim, lucas*	2T.MIX.7	*mcf,* **sixtrack**
2T.MEM.4	*mcf, ammp*	2T.MIX.8	*ammp,* **galgel**
4T.ILP.1	2T.ILP.{1,2}	4T.MIX.1	2T.MIX.{1,2}
4T.ILP.2	2T.ILP.{3,4}	4T.MIX.2	2T.MIX.{3,4}
4T.MEM.1	2T.MEM.{1,2}	4T.MIX.3	2T.MIX.{5,6}
4T.MEM.2	2T.MEM.{3,4}	4T.MIX.4	2T.MIX.{7,8}
8T.ILP.1	4T.ILP.{1,2}	8T.MIX.1	4T.MIX.{1,2}
8T.MEM.2	4T.MEM.{1,2}	8T.MIX.2	4T.MIX.{3,4}

Multi-programmed workload is one of the most important workloads for SMT. To simulate real-world workloads, we choose sixteen benchmarks from SPEC2000 to compose workloads that have two, four and eight threads. Out of these sixteen benchmarks, eight achieve the highest IPCs (shown in bold) and the other eight have the most L2 cache misses per instruction (shown in italics). We mixed these benchmarks to create three representative workloads of different ILP and memory demand. Table 2 lists the SPEC2000 benchmarks and multi-programmed workloads we use in this study. The first set, called *ILP,* consists of the high-ILP programs; the second set, called *MEM,* consists of the high-miss-rate programs; and the third set, called *MIX,* combines programs from both ILP and MEM. Within a set, there are four groups (*1T, 2T, 4T, and 8T*) and each group indicates the workloads for a given number of threads. We use the ref input for all benchmarks.

Table 3. Base Configuration

Issue Width	8
L1 I-cache	64KB, 2-way, pipelined
L1 D-cache	64KB, 4-way, 3-cycle hit latency
L2 Cache	4MB, 8-way, 15-cycle hit latency
Memory	150 cycle latency, 4-cycle pipelined, split-transaction bus
Branch Predictor	16k/16k/16k spec-update, 8-cycle misprediction penalty
Physical Registers	$100+T*32$ INT , $100+T*32$ FP for T threads
Active List	128/context
Load-Store Queue	64/context
Issue Queue	32 INT, 32 FP
MSHR	32

Table 3 lists the configuration for the basic SMT in our study. We carefully choose an aggressive SMT core such that our results are representative of many different SMT configurations in the foreseeable future; a less aggressive SMT would handicap the techniques we study because of less headroom for improvements. We use an issue width of eight as other SMT-related previous studies do [29,27,28], unless otherwise specified. For branch prediction, we use a hybrid of local and *gshare* predictors. Each context uses a 128-entry return address stack and maintains its own branch history for the gshare predictor. The SMT in this study has two fetch ports and fills up fetch bandwidth from up to two threads. We use *ICOUNT* as our SMT fetch policy as recommended in [28].

We will describe the implementation details of trace cache, value prediction and prefetching, in Section 4.1.1, Section 4.2.1, and Section 4.3.1, respectively.

4 Results

We present our results for trace cache, value prediction, and prefetching in Section 4.1, Section 4.2, and Section 4.3, respectively. As stated in Section 1, because SMT's goal is to improve throughput, which is also an important performance metric for server-class machines which increasingly use SMT, we evaluate these techniques in terms of instruction throughput.

We find that (1) given similar size for the duo of trace cache and backup i-cache as the conventional i-cache, trace cache degrades SMT throughput compared to the conventional i-cache; (2) given a typical number of physical registers, value prediction degrades throughput; (3) prefetching improves throughput for memory-intensive workloads but degrades throughput for workloads with mixed memory demand.

4.1 Trace Cache

4.1.1 Trace Cache Implementation

We implement the latest, most space-efficient block-based trace cache (TC) described in [3]. The TC is implemented using a block cache and a trace table. Each block of a block cache stores a small subtrace (e.g., a few consecutive basic blocks up to six instructions) and the trace table stores pointers to the block cache. To provide high bandwidth, the block cache is multi-ported (implemented via true ports and/or copies). The trace table provides n pointers which are used to pull out n subtraces from the block cache, and the subtraces together form the fetch unit of one trace. The subtraces are formed by observing past instances of the instruction stream. The trace table is updated with pointers to the subtraces. Because the subtraces are small, there is less repetition than trace cache using full-blown traces [22,21,20,8,19]. Furthermore, only the pointers to subtraces, but not subtraces themselves, are repeated in the full traces, achieving further compaction.

Because our results show that TC is ineffective for SMT, we make the following assumptions to ensure that our results are not due to insufficient resources or inefficient implementation: 1) Our TC uses an ideal, sequential, atomic multiple-branch predictor that accurately updates branch history even for branches predicted in the same cycle. In contrast, the base case SMT's i-cache uses a conventional, speculatively-updated predictor which predicts up to one taken branch or up to two branches per thread. The TC uses infinite branch-prediction bandwidth, therefore the branch promotion optimization in [19] is irrelevant. 2) The TC uses perfect target prediction for direct branches. 3) The TC has zero-cycle fill latency.

We implement the following key optimizations from [3]: 1) For termination, a subtrace ends upon encountering a branch, a jump, a call or a return instruction near the end of the subtrace. 2) Our TC employs partial matching which allows a substring of a trace, instead of restricting to complete traces, to be supplied. 3) We use a two-way associative "rename table" to map PCs to trace pointers. The table determines whether a trace is present in the block cache on every TC access and handles replacement in the block cache. The table's associativity effectively makes each copy of block cache two-way associative. 4) On fetching, the processor sends a request to both TC and i-cache simultaneously. If the request misses in the TC but hits in the i-cache, there is a one-cycle penalty, as in [22,21,20,19,8,3]. 5) To compensate for block-level fragmentation, the TC provides more instructions than the processor's front-end width. The front end picks the number of instructions requested to send into the pipeline and buffers any excess instructions to be combined with the next trace. Our TC has a six-instruction block size, as recommended in [3]. 6) We update the block cache speculatively on misses, as opposed to updating at commit. Other simulations (not shown) reveal that speculative update performs better.

When using the TC in SMT, we do the following to ensure that our SMT adaptation of the scheme is not disadvantaged by easily solvable problems: 1) We employ address offsetting in the TC and its accompanying i-cache. 2) Each cycle, two threads access the TC and each thread gets half the TC bandwidth. Our simulations (not shown) reveal that this policy achieves better performance than giving the full TC's bandwidth to only one thread.

4.1.2   Trace Cache Results

Recall from Section 1 that TC trades off space for bandwidth and that the sharing of instruction storage among SMT's threads impacts this trade-off. In this section, we evaluate this trade-off in SMT. Because we found that TC benefits little with an 8-issue pipeline even for single-thread workloads (not shown), we use 16-issue width for the TC as in [22,21,20,19,8,3]. Accordingly, we also double the pipeline resources listed in Table 3, such as rename registers, issue queue, active list, load-store queue, and execution units.

Figure 1 shows the throughput improvements of TC over the base case, which has 64KB i-cache and no TC. We show three sets of workloads: ILP, MEM, and MIX, as defined in Section 3. For each set, there are four groups of bars (*1T, 2T, 4T, and 8T*) varying the number of threads as one, two, four, and eight. Each bar indicates the geometric mean of throughput improvements for the workloads in the set.

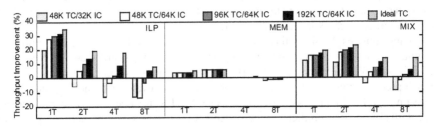

Fig. 1. Trace Cache Throughput Improvements

Because we are interested in TC's space-for-bandwidth trade-off, we vary TC size. Within each group of bars for a given number of threads, the first bar shows a 48K TC using two copies of dual-ported block cache backed up by a dual-ported 32K i-cache, for a total size of 80K, compared to the base case of a dual-ported 64K i-cache. Thus, the first bar represents our comparison using a similar total size. The next three bars from left to right show a 64K i-cache combined with TC of 48K, 96K, and 192K (1-cycle latency). These bars represent the cases where the TC configurations use extra space compared to the base case of a 64K i-cache.

To examine the upper limit of improvement through enhancing TC, by increasing size/associativity or using per-thread TC, we simulate *Ideal TC* which is an oracle configuration that has infinite size and always supplies as many instructions as the fetch bandwidth from two threads every cycle. Ideal TC does not suffer from fetch fragmentation or capacity/conflict miss, and subsumes enhancements. Ideal TC uses the same ideal multiple branch predictor as other TCs mentioned in Section 4.1.1. The last bar shows Ideal TC's throughput improvement.

Figure 1 shows two clear trends. First, TC benefits ILP and MIX but not MEM. While ILP and MIX have enough parallelism that fetch bandwidth is important for performance, MEM is dominated by data cache misses that fetch bandwidth is not important.

Second, for similar-size configurations, TC offers no benefit to SMT, and can lead to throughput degradation as the number of threads increases. This similar-size comparison is important because increasing the size of the level-1 instruction storage is difficult due to latency, area, and power considerations, as mention in Section 1. When we add an extra TC to the base 64K i-cache, TC is effective for single threads. This result agrees with previous papers [22,21,20,19,8,3] ([3] also gives extra space to TC), indicating that our TC implementation is correct. For two threads, TC improves SMT throughput; this results agrees with the two-threaded Pentium IV's use of a trace cache. However, when threads increase to more than two, TC's advantage rapidly diminishes. The *base case throughput*, shown in the first row of Table 4, continues to improve as we increase the number of threads to eight, showing that TC's diminishing returns are *not* due to pipeline saturation. Even with a large, 192K TC with single-cycle latency, TC shows only modest improvement over the base case for four or more threads. These results are no surprise when we look at the last bar, which shows the throughput improvement with an ideal TC. The last bar clearly shows that TC's potential drops rapidly as thread increases. Thus, we see that SMT's sharing of instruction storage makes TC's space-for-bandwidth trade-off unprofitable.

In SMT, applying a technique may impact low-IPC threads and high-IPC threads differently. With the goal of maximizing throughput, SMT distributes resources (fetch and front-end bandwidth, issue queue slots, etc.) among threads proportional to each thread's individual IPC (e.g., using ICOUNT). However, applying a technique may improve a low-IPC thread, fooling SMT into allocating more resources to the improved-but-still-low-IPC thread at the cost of other high-IPC threads, reducing overall throughput. That is, one thread may improve but the overall throughput may reduce. To capture such cases, [27] introduces *weighted speedup*, which is the geometric mean of IPC improvements of each thread. If the weighted speedup is more than throughput improvement, then the technique impacts (positively or negatively) low-IPC threads more than high-IPC threads; if the weighted speedup is less than throughput improvement, then the reverse is true. If the two metrics are similar, then the impact on low- and high-IPC threads are similar. Although our goal is to evaluate processor throughput, we show weighted speedup for 48K TC with 64K i-cache in the second row in Table 4. We see that weighted speedup follows the same trend as throughput, confirming that TC's advantage diminishes as the number of threads increases.

To explain TC's downward trend with an increasing number of threads, we compare base case i-cache miss rates with TC miss rates. The third row in Table 4 shows the

Table 4. Trace cache statistics

	ILP workload				MEM workload				MIX workload			
	1T	2T	3T	4T	1T	2T	3T	4T	1T	2T	3T	4T
Base case IPC	4.3	6.9	8.2	9.2	1.4	2.0	3.1	3.5	2.6	4.8	6.9	7.6
Weighted Speedup (%)	28.5	5.2	-2.3	-12.7	4.3	6.1	4.4	0.0	15.7	13.6	4.2	-1.2
64K IC miss rate (%)	0.1	0.0	0.2	0.2	0.0	0.0	0.0	0.0	0.0	0.1	0.1	0.2
48K TC miss rate (%)	10.5	20.1	31.2	41.9	0.2	0.8	2.5	6.8	5.2	8.6	17.2	29.0
192K TC miss rate (%)	1.2	4.2	10.8	19.7	0.0	0.1	0.3	0.7	0.6	1.0	4.2	10.0
64K IC avg Insts	5.2	8.5	9.4	9.8	1.6	2.9	4.8	5.3	3.1	6.2	8.8	9.2
48K TC avg insts	8.5	9.2	9.0	8.4	2.0	3.5	5.1	5.4	4.4	7.9	9.3	8.9
Ideal TC avg insts	8.7	10.8	11.3	10.9	2.0	3.5	5.1	5.4	4.4	8.5	10.4	10.6

i-cache *miss rate* in the base case, and the fourth and fifth rows show the *miss rates* for the 48K and 192K TCs, respectively. The significantly-higher TC miss rates show that the efficiency of the TC rapidly decreases as the number of threads increases.

Table 4 also shows the average number of instructions supplied by a 64K i-cache (*64K IC avg insts*), a 48K TC with its accompanying 64K i-cache (*48K TC avg insts*), and an ideal TC (*Ideal TC avg insts*) to the pipeline. On average, TC can supply 8.5 instructions per cycle in a single thread, which is 63% more than an i-cache can supply. When multiple threads are available, SMT uses the second fetch port to fetch from another thread. Therefore, SMT sustains high instruction throughput without the complication of a TC. With eight threads, the base i-cache with two ports achieves 9.8 IPC, which is higher than TC's. The base case's higher bandwidth combined with the large, diverging gap between the base case's and TC's miss rates as the number of threads increases, clearly shows that TC's space-for-bandwidth trade-off is not effective in SMT.

There is an interesting observation in Figure 1: MIX gets more benefit from TC than ILP and MEM as threads increase. As expected, ILP gets the most benefit of TC in single-thread runs. As threads increase, the pressure on the TC greatly increases and the miss rate in the TC increases quickly. When we put ILP and MEM together (MIX), the ILP threads experience less pressure in the TC compared to the ILP threads in the ILP workload because ILP threads in MIX take up the slack of the TC space created by MEM threads in MIX. This argument is supported by TC's miss rate shown in Table 4. For instance, TC's miss rate for 8 threads in MIX is similar or lower than TC's miss rate for 4 threads in ILP.

Some processors use TC to hold pre-decoded instructions (e.g. Pentium IV). If such a cache holds merely decoded individual instructions but not traces spanning multiple branches, we consider such a cache to be an i-cache and not a TC, and our results are not applicable to it.

Our experiments favor TC by giving it unrealistic advantages and an aggressive, 16-issue processor which gives TC much headroom for improvement. Nevertheless, we find that TC degrades SMT throughput. Using miss latencies longer than our numbers to model future technology will shift the performance bottleneck to the back-end and reduce opportunity for the front-end, further discouraging the use of TC. We also show that an ideal TC only marginally improves throughput. Therefore, our results unequivocally prove that TC hurts SMT running more than two threads, and there is no need to vary other parameters.

4.2 Value Prediction

4.2.1 Value Prediction Implementation
We implement the latest, best-performing selective value predictor (VP) described in [5]. The value predictor uses a confidence predictor to select when to predict and a hybrid of stride and context predictors to predict values.

Because our results show that VP is ineffective for SMT, we make the following assumption to ensure that our results are not due to inefficient implementation: we assume that VP's value history is updated correctly by an oracle in the decode stage.

We implement the following key optimizations described in [5]: 1) To minimize mispredictions, we implement a history-based confidence predictor. 2) We employ warm-up counters so that instructions with insufficient history do not update predictors. 3) To reduce mispredictions and maximize the benefit, we allow the predicted value to be used only for load instructions that incur L1 misses. According to our evaluations, this scheme has better performance than one that predicts all instructions. While we use the predictions only on misses, we predict and update on all loads regardless of a hit or a miss to accelerate the predictor's warm-up. 4) Instructions that directly or indirectly consume predicted values are assigned lower priority and can execute only on otherwise-idle execution units. These instructions resume their normal priority when the prediction outcome is known. When a misprediction is detected, the pipeline squashes the thread's instructions that are subsequent to the producer. To avoid unnecessary squashing, squash does not happen if the mispredicted value has not been consumed.

When using VP in SMT, we do the following to ensure that our SMT adaptation of the scheme is not disadvantaged by easily solvable problems: 1) Because VP benefits mostly from L2 misses, SMT's squashing on L2 misses would nullify much of the benefit of VP. Therefore, we modify the squashing policy on L2 misses in SMT. If an L2-missing load is value-predicted, we do not squash the pipeline. This mechanism allows dependent instructions to consume predicted values and later release issue queue entries. When a thread fills up its active list or load/store queue on an value-predicted L2 miss, we squash the thread's instructions only in the front end and stall fetching from the thread until the miss returns. Otherwise, fetched instructions from the thread would clog the front end preventing other threads from making progress. This squashing of the front end is not extra because the base case already squashes the pipeline on all L2 misses, regardless of whether resources fill up. 2) To reduce aliasing in prediction tables, we add tags to all prediction table entries. 3) To avoid inter-thread interference in the prediction tables, we use per-thread prediction tables.

4.2.2 Value Prediction Results

Recall from Section 1 that value-predicting a long-latency operation causes hold-up of registers until the operation completes and the prediction is confirmed. This hold-up occurs even with correct value prediction. In contrast, SMT simply squashes the thread containing the operation, releasing the resources held by the thread and allowing other threads to progress. Thus, there is a choice of value-predicting and holding up registers, versus squashing and overlapping the latency with other threads. SMT's sharing of registers among its threads impacts this choice. In this section, we evaluate this choice in SMT.

Each thread has two four-way, 8K-entry tables, one each for stride prediction and context prediction. To minimize mispredictions, each of these table also has its own 2KB confidence tables. The total size of the VP tables in an eight-thread SMT is a generous 5MB, ensuring that our results are not limited by small tables.

Figure 2 shows VP's throughput improvements compared to an SMT without VP. Similar to Section 4.1.2, Figure 2 shows three sets of workloads, ILP, MEM, and MIX, and varies the number of threads as one, two, four, and eight. Each bar indicates the geometric mean of throughput improvements for the workloads in the set.

Because we are interested in register pressure in the presence of VP, we show two configurations with different number of physical registers. One configuration, called *VP-finite*, contains $(100 + T * 32)$ integer registers and $(100 + T * 32)$ floating-point

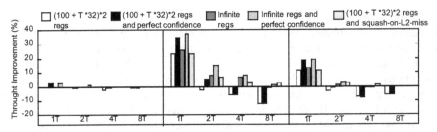

Fig. 2. Value prediction throughput improvements

registers, where *T* is the number of threads. The number 32 in this expression is the minimum number required for per-thread architectural registers, and 100 is the number of registers for renaming. This configuration represents a realistic number of registers, and it has also been used in [28]. The other configuration, called *VP-infinite*, has infinite physical registers. To examine if VP can benefit SMT by overlapping only L1 misses, we show a configuration called *VP-squash*. *VP-squash* uses VP if a load misses in L1 but squashes (mentioned in Section 3) if the load also misses in L2. *VP-squash* has the same number of physical registers as *VP-finite*.

Figure 2 shows a group of five bars for a given number of threads. The first bar shows *VP-finite*. The second bar shows *VP-finite* with perfect confidence prediction. The third and fourth bars show *VP-infinite* without and with perfect confidence prediction, respectively, quantifying VP's potential if register pressure were absent. The base case for the first and second bars is an SMT with as many physical registers as *VP-finite*. The base case for the third and fourth bars is an SMT with an infinite number of physical registers. The last bar shows *VP-squash* normalized to the base case for *VP-finite*.

Figure 2 shows that VP benefits MEM and MIX but not ILP. This result is hardly surprising because VP is triggered only for L1 misses, and ILP has low L1 miss rates. On the other hand, VP hides the penalties of the misses present in MEM and MIX.

Looking at MEM and MIX, this figure shows a interesting trend: VP significantly improves single-thread performance, especially for MEM. This result agrees with the results from previous VP papers [16,1,23,17,5], indicating that our value predictor is implemented correctly. However, *VP-finite*'s throughput improvements decrease significantly and become negative as the number of threads increases in both MEM and MIX. Note that the *base case throughput*, shown in the first row of Table 6, continues to improve as we increase the number of threads to eight, showing that VP's diminishing returns are *not* due to pipeline saturation. *VP-finite* with perfect confidence (second bar) shows the same trend, showing that the degradation exists even when VP is 100% accurate (albeit at non-perfect coverage). Thus, the second bars rule out mispredictions as the cause of the degradation trend.

Two reasons contribute to VP's degradation with multiple threads, even with large VP tables. First, VP's holding up of registers degrades throughput with two or more threads. Figure 2 support this observation by showing that *VP-finite*'s degradation largely disappears when infinite registers are available, as shown by *VP-infinite* (third and fourth bars). Second, SMT's latency tolerance reduces VP's opportunity. Figure 2 supports this argument by showing that even using *VP-infinite* with perfect confidence, VP's opportunity diminishes and eventually disappears, as the number of threads increases. Near-zero opportunity combined with register pressure forces *VP-finite* to incur degradation at more than two threads. The near-zero opportunity also shows that VP's benefit would be marginal, even if the VP implements selective recovery (mentioned in Section 2.2) to reduce misprediction penalty.

The four-thread *VP-infinite* bars for MIX show a small degradation despite having infinite registers. Because MIX has high-ILP and low-ILP threads, VP's impact is not uniform (this point is also made in Section 4.1.2). VP helps low-ILP threads more than high-ILP threads to the point that SMT allocates resources to the improved-but-still-low-ILP threads at the cost of the high-ILP threads. Such allocation causes a slight overall throughput degradation. *VP-squash* improves two-thread MEM by 6%, but improves little for other workloads (0-3%). This result shows that implementing VP to overlap only L1 misses is not profitable for SMT.

Table 5 shows important statistics for VP. *Coverage* is the ratio of the number of predictions over the number of L1 load misses. WP in the table means Weighted Speedup. *Squash Rate* is the ratio of the number of squashes caused by value mispredictions over the number of predictions. We see that coverage and squash rate are fairly stable across threads, and the squash rate is low. The stability of these metrics clearly indicates that VP's degradation with two or more threads is not due to worse coverage or more value mispredictions.

The fourth, fifth and sixth rows show the *weighted speedup* (explained in Section 4.1.2) for *VP-finite, VP-infinite and VP-squash. VP-finite's* weighted speedups are positive for two or more MEM and MIX threads while the overall throughput degrades. Because there is a large variance in the individual predictability and IPCs of these MEM and MIX threads, VP's impact is uneven among the threads, causing weighted speedup to deviate from overall throughput (as explained in Section 4.1.2). VP fools SMT into allocating more registers to the improved-but-still-low-ILP threads which hold up the registers from the high-ILP threads, degrading overall throughput. Because SMT's goal is to improve processor throughput, techniques which improve individual threads while degrading processor throughput defeat SMT's purpose. In fact, SMT does the reverse: SMT employs several optimizations which improve processor throughput at the cost of individual threads. For example, (1) because the SMT pipeline is typically deeper than a superscalar pipeline [29], single-thread performance slightly worsens on SMT. (2) SMT's ICOUNT, which optimizes processor throughput, may worsen a low-IPC thread by fetching more often from higher-IPC threads [28]. (3) Squashing a thread on L2 misses improves processor throughput while slightly worsening the thread's IPC [27].

Table 5. Value prediction statistics

	ILP workload				MEM workload				MIX workload			
	1T	2T	3T	4T	1T	2T	3T	4T	1T	2T	3T	4T
Base case IPC	3.5	4.6	5.1	5.3	1.1	1.8	2.9	3.9	2.1	3.8	4.7	5.2
Coverage (%)	15.0	22.6	27.9	42.2	34.4	28.4	24.0	31.0	24.3	30.6	28.7	31.3
Squash rate (%)	0.3	0.2	0.2	0.2	0.6	0.5	0.4	0.4	0.4	0.3	0.2	0.2
VP-finite WP (%)	0.5	-1.5	-1.6	-1.9	23.0	8.8	8.5	7.5	11.2	6.0	0.7	1.6
VP-infinite WP (%)	0.5	-0.4	-0.2	-0.4	26.0	18.2	19.3	14.7	12.5	10.6	7.1	6.9
VP-squash WP (%)	0.5	-0.4	-0.3	-0.4	23.0	12.2	4.4	2.9	11.3	4.5	2.3	0.9

Our experiments favor VP by giving it unrealistic advantages and an aggressive processor which gives VP much headroom for improvement. Still, VP degrades SMT throughput. Because VP holds up physical registers during an L2 miss, using longer miss latencies to model future technology will further degrade throughput. We also show that VP does not improve throughput even with infinite registers. Therefore, our results unequivocally prove that VP hurts SMT and there is no need to vary other parameters.

4.3 Prefetching

4.3.1 Prefetching Implementation

We implement the latest, best-performing tag-correlating prefetching (PF) [9]. The prefetcher decides what to prefetch by using the L1 miss stream as history to predict the next miss. The predictor is a two-level scheme, where the first level stores per-set miss stream history, and the second level stores the tag of next-misses. Upon an L1 miss, the prefetcher triggers prefetch to the predicted next miss. Instead of using dead-time prediction to trigger prefetches, this simplified prefetcher uses L1 misses as the triggers.

Because our results show that PF is effective for SMT, we do not give any undue advantage to the prefetcher to ensure that our results are not due to unjustifiable implementation assumptions. Specifically, because PF uses additional space for prediction tables, we compensate the base case by running it with a larger L2. Because the largest predictor size we use is 498KB (in an eight-thread SMT), we use a 4.5 MB L2 for all base case runs, while using only a 4MB L2 for all the PF runs. We enlarge the base case's L2 with no penalty to the L2 hit latency.

We implement the following key optimizations in the two-level predictor: 1) The predictor uses eleven bits of the L1 tag and one bit of the L1 index from the previous three misses, together with the full L1 tag from the previous miss, to form indexes into the second-level table as in [9]. 2) The first level uses per-set history as recommended in [32]. 3) The prefetcher uses 32 extra MSHRs to hold in-flight prefetch status and a 128-entry prefetch queue to hold pending prefetch requests, as recommended in [32].

When using PF in SMT, we do the following to ensure that our SMT adaptation of the scheme is not disadvantaged by easily solvable problems: 1) While [32] prefetches data into L1, [9] argues that prefetching into L1 is difficult due to L1 contention. [9] shows that prefetching data only into L2 achieves most of the benefit of prefetching into L1 while entirely eliminating dead-block prediction. This effect is seen because L1 miss latency can be overlapped easily with ILP. While prefetching into L2 in SMT introduces the issue queue clogging described in Section 1, we could reduce prefetch coverage to balance prefetching and issue queue clogging and improve overall throughput. Therefore, we evaluate prefetching into L2. 2) The second-level table is accessed with the previous L1 miss and history, that is also made of L1 misses. Because the L1 is physically tagged, the L1 miss stream has physical addresses which are already randomized by bin-hopping (Section 3). Consequently, the second-level table does not need any offsetting to reduce conflicts. 3) Each level of prediction tables may be configured to be shared across threads or to be private to each thread. Because there is not much difference between shared or private for the second level, we use a shared second-level table. We show both private and shared configurations for the first-level table. 4) We increase the second-level shared table size with the number of threads (the table size is $T * 120KB$ for T threads, except for eight-thread SMT we use T=4 to keep the size under 512KB). We increase the size with no change in the associativity, keeping the implementation reasonable. Although the table is shared among threads, no major conflicts among the threads occur because the table is accessed using physical addresses, which are unique across the threads.

4.3.2 Prefetching Results

Recall from Section 1 that because SMT tolerates latency but at the same time increases pressure on the memory hierarchy by overlapping multiple threads, the opportunity for PF is unknown. While PF reduces memory latency, prefetching into L2 encourages L1 misses in fewer cycles, which causes clogging of the issue queue and slows down the other threads. Ironically, only correct prefetches cause this clogging. Thus, SMT's sharing of the issue queue across multiple threads impacts PF's effectiveness. In this section, we evaluate these opposing effects of PF in SMT.

While we showed that TC and VP do not improve SMT throughput; in this section, we will show that PF improves throughput for MEM, but has limited opportunity for MIX.

Figure 3 shows PF's throughput improvements compared to the SMT without PF. As before, Figure 3 shows the three sets of workloads, ILP, MEM, and MIX, and varies the number of threads as one, two, four, and eight. Each bar indicates the geometric mean of throughput improvements for the workloads in the set. Note that the Y-axis scale has changed from the previous graphs.

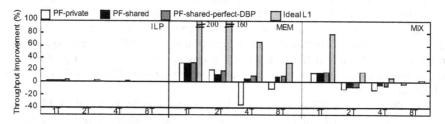

Fig. 3. Prefetching throughput improvements

Because prefetching into L2 causes the issue queue clogging problem, we studied ways to reduce this clogging. First, we experimented with prefetching into L1. Unlike prefetching into L2, prefetching into L1 cannot use L1 misses as triggers (prefetched block will displace useful data) and needs dead-block prediction [32]. We found that because of high pressure on L1 in SMT, the dead time is shorter in SMT than that in a single thread. The shorter dead time makes dead block prediction harder. Second, we resumed prefetching into L2 and tried to avoid clogging by preventing instructions which are past an L1 miss that hits in a prefetched L2 block from entering the pipeline. To this end, we used an L1 miss predictor which stops fetching past a predicted L1 miss. The predictor essentially needs to balance accuracy (avoid incorrectly stopping fetch due to mispredictions) and coverage (identify all the misses). Unfortunately, achieving this balance proved to be difficult. Therefore, we looked into other ways to reduce the clogging. Taking a hint from VP, which reduces coverage to reduce mispredictions, we tried to reduce prefetch coverage to prevent too many L2 misses from being converted to L1 misses, which cause clogging. Reasoning that a shared first-level history would have less coverage than a private first-level history due to inter-thread interference, we experimented with these two configurations. We found that the shared first-level history works better and achieves throughput improvements. Because PF already shows throughput improvement for MEM and little opportunity for MIX, further enhancements through either prefetching into L1 or using a better L1 miss predictor will improve MEM's throughput more and will not improve MIX. Any such further enhancement will only reinforce our conclusions.

Figure 3 shows a group of four bars for a given number of threads. The first bar shows PF-private, which uses a private first-level history. The second bar shows PF-shared, which uses a shared first-level history. To confirm that the absence of dead-block prediction does not affect PF (as previously shown in [9]), the third bar, PF-shared-prefect-DBP, shows PF with perfect L2-dead-block prediction. To show the potential of PF, the last bar shows Ideal L1, which lets every access from the processor hit in L1.

From Figure 3, we see that PF does not benefit ILP much with multiple threads, because ILP has low L1 miss rates. Looking at MEM, PF significantly improves single-thread performance. This result agrees with the results from previous PF papers [32,9], indicating that our prefetcher is implemented correctly. With multiple threads, we see that while PF-private degrades throughput, PF-shared improves throughput. PF-private's poor performance is due to issue queue clogging, as can be seen in the second and third rows in Table 6 by the larger fraction of time the Issue Queue (*IQ*) stays clogged (*IQ clog frac.*) with PF-private (*PF-p*) than with PF-shared (*PF-s*). Note that the base case throughput, shown in the first row of Table 6, continues to improve as we increase the number of threads to eight, showing that PF-private's diminishing returns are not due to pipeline saturation. Thus we see that SMT's sharing of the issue queue among its threads accounts for the difference between PF-private's failure and PF-shared's success.

We also see that PF-shared-perfect-DBP is marginally better than PF-shared, showing that using L1 misses as triggers is a good dead-block predictor, as also claimed by [9]. Ideal L1 shows that though the opportunity reduces with more threads, there is still substantial opportunity even with eight threads. PF-shared captures some

Table 6. Prefetching statistics

	ILP workload				MEM workload				MIX workload			
	1T	2T	3T	4T	1T	2T	3T	4T	1T	2T	3T	4T
Base case IPC	3.5	4.6	5.1	5.3	1.2	1.8	3.1	4.0	2.1	3.8	4.7	5.2
PF-p IQ clog frac. (%)	2.5	1.0	0.3	0.3	37.7	25.2	36.8	18.2	18.8	10.3	7.2	1.7
PF-s IQ clog frac. (%)	2.5	1.0	0.5	0.4	37.7	24.8	11.5	6.1	18.8	9.6	3.9	1.1
Base case L2 miss (%)	9.8	7.5	9.1	4.8	26.8	25.3	26.7	32.6	18.0	24.8	21.9	21.9
PF-p L2 miss (%)	7.9	5.0	4.9	3.4	12.2	9.1	12.0	15.8	10.0	11.1	9.5	10.8
PF-s L2 miss (%)	7.9	5.0	7.5	4.6	12.2	16.9	19.9	26.5	10.0	12.4	17.1	18.6
PF-p accuracy (%)	22.7	24.6	46.6	68.2	66.1	85.1	83.7	86.9	42.7	63.2	81.3	80.5
PF-s accuracy (%)	22.7	24.0	34.7	30.5	66.1	73.6	67.6	62.2	42.7	59.3	66.5	55.9
PF-p WP (%)	2.0	1.2	0.5	0.3	30.7	53.0	22.3	20.9	15.5	19.7	26.0	12.4
PF-s WP (%)	2.0	1.0	0.2	0.0	30.7	21.7	14.7	10.7	15.5	16.7	7.2	2.4

of this opportunity, achieving 7% improvement with four threads and 9% with eight threads. These results show that when memory latency is a major bottleneck, even multiple threads cannot tolerate all L2 misses, and PF is effective.

For MIX, PF-shared suffers 6% and 4% degradation with two and four threads, respectively. Despite using a shared configuration, this workload causes issue queue clogging, resulting in slight throughput degradation. This result is not surprising when we look at Ideal L1, which shows little opportunity for PF with increasing threads. This limited opportunity combined with issue queue clogging forces PF-shared to degrade with two or more threads.

Table 6 presents important statistics for PF. The fourth, fifth, and sixth rows show the L2 miss rates in the base case and PF-private and PF-shared, respectively. These miss rates confirm that PF is effective in reducing L2 misses. PF-private's miss rates are lower than those of PF-shared, indicating that PF-private has higher coverage than PF-shared. This higher coverage causes clogging problems that result in throughput degradation. The next two rows show that the accuracy of PF-private and PF-shared behave similarly to coverage and have the same effect. Finally, we show weighted speedup for PF-private and PF-shared. PF-private has positive weighted speedups for MEM and MIX while it degrades throughput, showing that PF-private improves low-IPC threads with high miss rates at the cost of overall throughput. PF-shared has positive weighted speedups but lower than those of PF-private due to lower coverage. For MEM, PF-shared has both positive weighted speedups and improved throughput, indicating that PF-shared improves low-IPC threads without hurting the other threads.

Our experiments do not give PF any undue advantage and yet show that PF improves SMT throughput for MEM. Because PF hides L2-miss latencies, using longer latencies will further improve throughput. For MIX workload, we showed that PF does not improve even with an ideal L1. Therefore, our results unequivocally prove that PF improves MEM and does not improve MIX, and there is no need to vary other parameters.

5 Conclusions

In this paper, we evaluated trace cache, value prediction and prefetching in SMT. We found that SMT's sharing of the instruction storage (i.e., trace cache or i-cache), physical registers, and issue queue impacts the effectiveness of trace cache, value prediction, and prefetching, respectively.

We found that: (1) Trace cache introduces multiple copies of the same instructions in different traces, trading off space for bandwidth. However, SMT needs a large instruction storage because multiple threads share the storage. Furthermore, trace cache's benefit of supplying many instructions in one fetch diminishes in SMT because SMT can do so by fetching from multiple threads. Our simulations showed that when compared to a similar-sized i-cache, trace cache's space-for-bandwidth trade-off degrades SMT throughput (for 2 threads, throughput improves, supporting Intel's decision to use a trace cache in the two-threaded P4). (2) Value prediction causes hold-up of physical registers and cannot release them until after the predicted instruction completes and commits. Because SMT's multiple threads share physical registers, this hold-up stalls progress in other threads. Thus, unlike superscalar, SMT incurs throughput degradation even with correct value predictions. Our simulations showed that with a typical number of physical registers, value prediction degrades SMT throughput; and with unlimited registers, value prediction's benefit disappears with an increasing number of threads. (3) Prefetching into L2 converts slow L2 misses into fast L2 hits. However, the L2 hits still miss in L1, resulting in the same L1 misses occurring in fewer cycles. Because instructions dependent on the L1 misses clog the issue queue and because SMT's multiple threads share the issue queue, this clogging stalls progress in other threads. With prefetching, L1 misses occur in fewer cycles, clogging the issue queue more often. Thus, unlike superscalar, SMT incurs throughput degradation even with correct prefetches. Therefore, SMT needs to balance prefetching and issue queue clogging. Our simulations showed that prefetch coverage can be reduced to achieve such balance, improving throughput for memory-intensive workloads. However, for workloads with mixed memory demand (high-ILP and memory-intensive threads), prefetching has little opportunity and slightly degrades throughput.

On one hand, the techniques are ineffective for multi-programmed workloads and in many cases hurt throughput; on the other hand, the techniques significantly improve single-thread performance, and disabling them to improve multi-programmed throughput would hurt single-thread performance. In an SMT with thread priority, these techniques may also hurt high-priority threads in a multi-programmed workload. Thus, our findings create a new responsibility for the OS: We recommend that the OS disable the techniques when running multi-programmed workload, and enable them for single-threaded workload and for high-priority threads in a multi-programmed workload.

References

1. A.Mendelson and F.Gabbay. Speculative execution based on value prediction. Technical report, Technion, 1997.
2. R. Balasubramonian, S. Dwarkadas, and D. H. Albonesi. Reducing the complexity of the register file in dynamic superscalar processors. In *Proc. of the 34th MICRO*, Nov. 2001.
3. B. Black, B. Rychlik, and J. P. Shen. The block-based trace cache. In *Proc. of the 26th ISCA*, Oct. 1999.
4. E. Borch, E. Tune, S. Manne, and J. Emer. Loose loops sink chips. In *Proc. of 8th HPCA*, Feb. 2002.
5. B. Calder, G. Reinman, and D. M. Tullsen. Selective value prediction. In *Proc. of the 26th ISCA*, May 1999.
6. M. J. Charney and A. P. Reeves. Generalized correlation-based hardware prefetching. Technical Report EE-CEG-95-1, Cornell University, Feb. 1995.
7. K. I. Farkas and N. P. Jouppi. Complexity/performance tradeoffs with non-blocking loads. In *Proceedings of the 21st Annual International Symposium on Computer Architecture*, pages 211–222, Apr. 1994.
8. D. H. Friendly, S. J. Patel, and Y. N. Patt. Alternative fetch and issue policies for the trace cache fetch mechanism. In *Proc. of the 30th MICRO*, Nov. 1997.
9. Z. Hu, M. Martonosi, and S. Kaxiras. Tcp: Tag correlating prefetchers. In *Proc. of 9th HPCA*, Feb. 2003.
10. D. Joseph and D. Grunwald. Prefetching using markov predictors. In *Proc. of the 24th ISCA*, June 1997.
11. N. P. Jouppi. Improving direct-mapped cache performance by the addition of a small fully-associative cache and prefetch buffers. In *Proc. of the 17th ISCA*, May 1990.

12. S. Kaxiras, Z. Hu, and M. Martonosi. Cache decay: Exploiting generational behaviour to reduce cache leakage power. In *Proc. of the 28th ISCA*, June 2001.
13. A.-C. Lai, C. Fide, and B. Falsafi. Dead-block prediction and dead-block correlating prefetchers. In *Proc. of the 28th ISCA*, June 2001.
14. M. H. Lipasti, W. J. Schmidt, S. R. Kunkel, and R. R. Roediger. Spaid:software prefetching in pointer and call intensive environments. In *Proc. of the 28th MICRO*, Nov. 1995.
15. J. Lo, L. Barroso, S. Eggers, K. Gharachorloo, H. Levy, and S. Parekh. An analysis of database workload performance on simultaneous multithreaded processors. In *Proc. of the 25th ISCA*, June 1998.
16. M.H.Lipasti, C.B.Wilkerson, and J.P.Shen. Value locality and data speculation. In *Proc. of the 7th ASPLOS*, Oct. 1996.
17. A. Moshovos and G. S. Sohi. Streamlining inter-operation memory communication via data dependence prediction. In *Proc. of the 30th MICRO*, Dec. 1997.
18. I. Park, M. D. Powell, and T. N. Vijaykumar. Reducing register ports for higher speed and lower energy. In *Proc. of the 35th MICRO*, Nov. 2002.
19. S. J. Patel, M. Evers, and Y. N. Patt. Improving trace cache effectiveness with branch promotion and trace packing. In *Proc. of the 25th ISCA*, June 1998.
20. S. J. Patel, D. H. Friendly, and Y. N. Patt. Evaluation of design options for the trace cache fetch mechanism. In *IEEE Transactions on Computers, Special Issue on Cache Memory and Related Problems*.
21. S. J. Patel, D. H. Friendly, and Y. N. Patt. Critical issues regarding the trace cache fetch mechanism. Technical Report CSE-TR-335-97, University of Michigan, May 1997.
22. E. Rotenberg, S. Bennett, and J. E. Smith. Trace cache: A low latency approach to high bandwidth instruction fetching. In *Proc. of the 29th MICRO*, Dec. 1996.
23. Y. Sazeides and J. E. Smith. Implementations of context based value predictors. Technical Report ECE-97-8, University of Wisconsin-Madison, Dec. 1997.
24. T.C.Mowry, M.S.Lam, and A.Gupta. Design and evaluation of a compiler algorithm for prefetching. In *Proc. of the 5th ASPLOS*, Oct. 1992.
25. T.F.Chen and J.L.Baer. Reducing memory latency via non-blocking and prefetching caches. In *Proc. of the 5th ASPLOS*, Oct. 1992.
26. G. H. Timothy Sherwood, Erez Perelman and B. Calder. Automatically characterizing large scale program behavior. In *Proc. of the 10th ASPLOS*, Oct. 2002.
27. D. M. Tullsen and J. A. Brown. Handling long-latency loads in a simultaneous multithreading processor. In *Proc. of the 34th MICRO*, Dec. 2001.
28. D. M. Tullsen, S. J. Eggers, J. S. Emer, H. M. Levy, J. L. Lo, and R. L. Stamm. Exploiting choice: instruction fetch and issue on an implementable simultaneous multithreading processor. In *Proc. of the 23rd ISCA*, May 1996.
29. D. M. Tullsen, S. J. Eggers, and H. M. Levy. Simultaneous multithreading: maximizing on-chip parallelism. In *Proc. of the 22nd ISCA*, June 1995.
30. G. S. Tyson and T. M. Austin. Improving the accuracy and performance of memory communication through renaming. In *Proc. of the 30th MICRO*, Dec. 1997.
31. T.-Y. Yeh, D. Marr, and Y. Patt. Increasing instruction fetch rate via multiple branch prediction and a branch address cache,. In *In Proc. of the 7th ACM Int. Conf. on Supercomputing*, July 1993.
32. S. K. Zhigang Hu and M. Martonosi. Timekeeping in the memory system: Predicting and optimizing memory behavior. In *Proc. of the 29th ISCA*, May 2002.

Scalable and Partitionable Asynchronous Arbiter for Micro-threaded Chip Multiprocessors

Nabil Hasasneh[1], Ian Bell[1], and Chris Jesshope[2]

[1] Department of Electronic Engineering, University of Hull, UK
N.Hasasneh@eng.hull.ac.uk, I.M.Bell@hull.ac.uk
[2] Institute for Informatics, University of Amsterdam, The Netherlands
jesshope@science.uva.nl

Abstract. This paper presents a scalable and partitionable asynchronous bus arbiter for use with chip multiprocessors *(CMP)* and its corresponding pre-layout simulation results using *VHDL*. The arbiter exploits the advantage of a concurrency control instruction *(Brk)* provided by the micro-threaded microprocessor model to set the priority processor and move the circulated arbitration token at the most likely processor to issue the create instruction. This mechanism provides latency hiding during token circulation by decoupling the micro-threaded processor from the ring's timing. It is shown that this arbiter can be extended easily to support large numbers of processors and can be used for chip multiprocessor arbitration purposes.

1 Introduction

The history of the IBM Power PC *(PPC)* processor shows that clock speed has increased at twice the predicted rate, i.e. from 33MHz to 1GHz over the last twelve years, but increases in system-level concurrency have not tracked the packing density [1]. With some processors using 2 Billion transistors, we may ask if these transistors are being effectively used. Evidence that all is not well is provided by the fact that Intel has cancelled its 4GHz Pentium 4 [2], because this processor has effectively reached the limit of its performance and has poor scaling properties. Simply increasing the clock speed and using more and more transistors (enabled by smaller feature sizes) is a poor strategy for future generations of processors and does not guarantee better performance.

Chip multiprocessors (CMPs) are becoming an increasingly attractive for obtaining high performance and low power consumption and we expect that many new microprocessor designs will be based on this approach. However if CMP architectures are based on a single clock domain with global synchronization and control signals system performance and prevent overall system scalability will be severely restricted.

The Globally Asynchronous Locally Synchronous *(GALS)* design style is an approach to VLSI system design that holds the promise of combining the advantages of both synchronous and asynchronous operation [3]. Eliminating the need for a centralized clock minimizes the clock-skew problem and opens the

W. Grass et al. (Eds.): ARCS 2006, LNCS 3894, pp. 252–267, 2006.

door wide for system scalability and functional portioning, which both are the requirements for future CMP designs. The Semiconductor Industry Association *(SIA)* Roadmap recognizes that, by 2007, asynchronous techniques will be used in many designs [4].

The micro-threaded CMP architecture [1], exploits the advantages of a GALS design by using a set of global buses all of which are fully asynchronous. One of these buses is the *broadcast bus*, which each processor uses in order to create a new family of micro-threads. The broadcast bus is also used to broadcast the global state to all processors. To avoid processor contention and to take the advantages of asynchronous communication, this paper introduces an asynchronous arbiter design. The arbiter exploits the advantage of a concurrency control instruction *Brk*, provided by the micro-threaded microprocessor to set a priority policy and to hide the token circulation time by decoupling the micro-threaded pipeline from the ring's timing. It provides useful features, such as modularity, partitioning organization, and is starvation free.

The rest of the paper organized as follows: In the next section, we present a brief background and related work. Section 3 explains the micro-threaded approach, its concurrency controls and the micro-threaded chip multiprocessor architecture model. In section 4, the asynchronous arbiter organization and its mechanism are presented. The arbiter pre-layout simulation results using VHDL is described in section 5. Finally, we present a conclusion in section 6.

2   Background and Related Work

GALS systems not only mitigate the clock distribution, power consumption, and clock skew problems, but also simplify design reuse [5]. Recently, Hemani et.al. [6] compare the GALS architecture with the globally synchronous (GS) case. The results show that 70% power savings in clock distribution with negligible overheads can be achieved using GALS architecture design compared to the GS design case.

Delay modelling is one of the most significant elements of validating asynchronous design. One popular well-known approach that gives unbounded delays to both wire and gate elements is the delay-insensitive design approach. This avoids the need for timing analysis, providing designs that operate correctly whatever the delay in the interconnecting wires [7]. It also has some benefits over bounded-delay methodologies in that the former delay model forces the designs to use conventions such as completion signals and transition signalling which are both important to good asynchronous circuit structure [8]. Furthermore, the delay-insensitive model facilitates the exploitation of average-case delay rather than the worst case, providing significant saving with long interconnections [7]. There have been some processors that have used a delay-insensitive design technique such as [9, 10].

Asynchronous-synchronous interfaces using point to point GALS interconnect as described in [11] represent a very efficient and a suitable way to synchronize asynchronous and synchronous clock domains. The design described in this paper uses a point to point connection between arbiter modules. A delay-insensitive methodology is used giving unbounded delays to both wires and logic gates.

It is well-known that access to shared resources by two or more processors requires an arbitration mechanism to prevent contentions. Many arbitration schemes have been proposed [12, 13, 14] with different characteristics. Arbiters can be centralized, decentralized, daisy chained, tree, round-robin with fixed or dynamic priority. Comparison between these mechanisms concerns a set of factors including reusability, modularity, fairness, avoidance of starvation, power consumption and area. Most of the arbitration mechanisms are only suitable for some cases and none of them is optimal for all cases.

Macii and Poncino [15] described a synchronous scalable multiprocessor bus arbiter using a ring architecture. The priority of each processor is reduced by one at every arbitration cycle to rotate priority between the processors. Two signals (Bus_Busy and Token_Out) are propagated through the ring to circulate the token. Our arbiter also uses a ring structure but is fully asynchronous with one grant signal (Gout) rather than two. Furthermore, we exploit the concurrency control instruction (Brk) provided by the micro-threaded microprocessor to hide the token circulation time and to set a priority processor based on the processor that has succeed in executing this instruction.

Bellido et. al. [12] presents a modular asynchronous design for an n-user linear array arbiter. A centralized control signal drives all the modules in the array. When this signal is 0, the arbitration process takes place in such a way that this signal is not 1 until the requests have been granted in the same order as the modules in the array. Priority is dependent on the relative position of the modules. This mechanism is not fair and may cause starvation if a large number of modules are used. Our approach has the advantage that each arbiter can decide locally to access the bus or to wait. Also, our priority policy provides fair communication and avoids processor starvation.

Moore et. al. [11] proposed an asynchronous-synchronous interface for a point to point communication channel with independent clock domain. The authors suggested an asynchronous FIFO between producer and consumer modules to hide the waiting time during request and acknowledge synchronization. This mechanism requires a complex control scheme, and in some cases, if the FIFO is deep, the performance will be significantly degraded.

Rigaud et. al. [13] describes an asynchronous arbiter for on-chip communication, proposing both a fixed and dynamic arbiter priority configuration. In the fixed approach three blocks are used to handle the arbitration mechanism. These blocks are the loop control block to reactivate the arbiter after serving requests, the synchronizer block to sample the input requests and the fixed-priority block to determine the priority value based on a hardware coded priority mechanism. Dynamic priority design also has the same complexity of blocks, where n-request analyzer blocks and n-priority comparator blocks are required to handle n-requests. This arbiter has a complex design with a centralized structure, which prevents partitioning. Also, many comparisons may be required to determine the priority values if the previous comparison failed. In contrast, our arbiter has less complexity and provides a simple arbitration mechanism for a large number of processors on-chip.

Villiger et. al. [16] proposes a mechanism for transferring data between GALS modules using a self-timed ring topology. This configuration provides a point-to-point communication between two adjacent GALS modules and provides modular connectivity, with full scalability in both bandwidth and area for increasing numbers of GALS modules. The design we described in this paper has the advantage of a ring organization that connects GALS micro-threaded processors with the broadcast bus in a circular fashion.

3 Micro-threaded Chip Multiprocessor Architecture Model

3.1 Micro-threaded Microprocessor Model

The CMP model was first introduced in 1996 [17], then extended in a set of papers e.g. [1, 18] to support systems with multiple processors on-chip. It combines the advantages of blocked multi threading and interleaved multi-threading by interleaving the threads when one thread is blocked on a cycle-by-cycle basis using an explicit context switch instruction or tag, which is required when the compiler cannot guarantee that data will be available. The model exploits instruction level parallelism primarily across loop bodies, as the families of threads are defined on loops.

Threads are reactivated after being suspended by a context switch when the data they were waiting for becomes available. Indeed the thread is suspended and awaits its data in the register that the compiler determined was non-deterministic. There is one other situation where the compiler may flag a context switch and that is following a branch instruction. In this case the thread is reactivated upon the computation of the branch target address. The concurrency controls used in this model provide a flexible and efficient mechanism for thread creation, context switching and synchronization. Context switching is compiler controlled by recognizing and tagging instructions which could fail synchronization.

The micro-threaded model provides instructions to create families of threads *(Cre)*, to explicitly context switch between threads *(Swch)*, to kill a thread *(Kill)* and two instructions for global synchronization, one a barrier synchronization *(Bsync)*, the other a form of a break instruction *(Brk)*, which forces a break from a loop executed concurrently. The Brk instruction terminates all other threads and leaves the issuing thread as the main thread. This instruction gives a hint that the processor needs to create a new family of micro-threads after a few cycles. Thus, a processor that has succeed in executing this instruction can assert a high request signal through the Brk wire line to its arbiter to inform it that this processor will be requesting the broadcast bus. Based on this prediction, our asynchronous arbiters moves the grant token until it has reached the requesting module. This mechanism provides latency hiding and deadlock freedom during token circulation time.

3.2   Micro-threaded Chip Multiprocessor Model

A block diagram of a micro-threaded chip multiprocessor is shown in figure 1. A set of shared components are used in this model to support the micro-threaded CMP. These components are the *Broadcast Bus* which enables one processor to create a family of identical threads. This bus arbitrates between multiple processors and at any time one processor can access this bus to create a descriptor of a new family of micro-threads. Descriptors are processed by the scheduler to determine the subset of the family of threads the processor will execute.

The broadcast bus is also used to replicate what the compiler defines as global state to each processor's local register file instead of using a centralized register file for global variables. It is one of two mechanisms that allow the register file in micro-threaded model to be fully distributed between the processors. The other is the *Shared Registers Ring Network*, which allows compiler-specified communications between pairs of threads, one of which produces data and the other which consumes it. This communication between the *shared* and *dependent thread* will be performed by the ring network if the threads are allocated to different processors. The justification for using a ring network is that it is scalable and, given sufficient resources, the model, can adopt a schedule which ensures that any constant-strided, loop-carried dependency be mapped to a neighboring processor.The distribution of threads to pipelines is deterministic and based on a simple scheduling algorithm. It is dynamic as it is determined by resource allocation and release (the concurrency exposed is parametric and not limited by the hardware resources). The instruction issue schedule is also dynamic and is scalable. Instructions can be issued from any micro-thread already allocated and active. The concurrency is limited only by the linearly growing hardware cost for a given

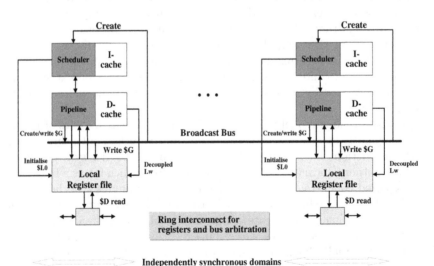

Fig. 1. A chip multi-processor based on an asynchronous collection of microthreaded pipelines

chip area. Clearly if such a system could also give linear performance increases, then it can provide a solution to both CMP and ILP scalability [18].

4   Arbiter Organization

Figure 2 shows the arbiter organization. Each processor has its own local control and a separate arbiter module in order to allow processor partitioning. Each arbiter module is linked to the next one in a ring arrangement and the processors are arranged in a grid layout as shown in figure 3a. Thus, each arbiter can be linked to two physically adjacent ones to reduce propagation delays. Our arbiter has the optional capability of being usable in a dynamically partitionable processor array, assuming a suitable routing architecture is available. For example a possible reconfiguration of the processors in figure 3a onto two independent groups is also shown in figure 3b. However, a detailed description of the partitioning architecture is beyond the scope of this paper.

Figure 4 shows the arbiter input and output signals. Each arbiter are linked by four lines comprising the request high (RH_i), which is the highest priority request, request low (RL_i), which is the lowest priority request, an acknowledgement signal (Ack_i) to release the bus, and the grant line (G_i) to grant requests and move the grant token towards the requesting module. The request and grant signals propagate in opposite directions around the ring. Also, one output wire $(Wout_i)$ is required from each arbiter module to give processor P_i permission to access the broadcast bus.

There are three signals from each processor to its arbiter. The first is to inform the arbiter that the current processor has succeed in executing the Brk_i instruction, the next signal (D_i) is used to assert a demand request. The third is the local acknowledgement $(Ackl_i)$ signal to inform the arbiter that a receiving processor has finished with the bus. The Brk_i signal is assigned to the RH_i signal line with highest priority and the D_i signal assigned to RL_i line with low priority. An initial (init) signal is also required to determine the initial location of the token. One arbiter is initialized with the token, the others without.

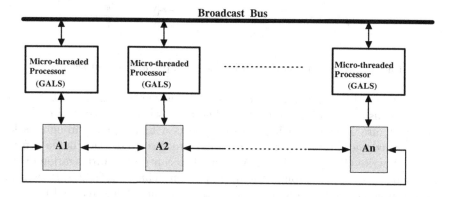

Fig. 2. Asynchronous Arbiter Block Diagram

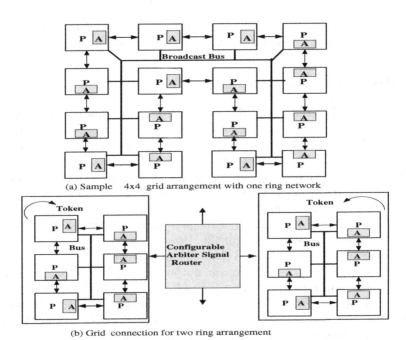

(a) Sample   4x4 grid arrangement with one ring network

(b) Grid connection for two ring arrangement

Fig. 3. Asynchronous Arbiters with Different Partitioning. a)Grid Organization. b)Independent Group Organization.

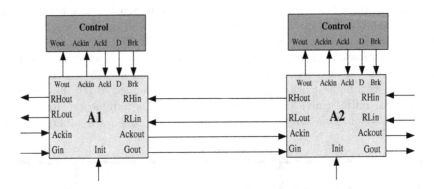

Fig. 4. Asynchronous arbiter with require input and output signals

Once a processor has responded to a grant acknowledgement is sent back to the grantee using the ring connectivity The acknowledgment control circuit is shown in figure 5, where each processor asserts a high signal through its local acknowledgment ($ACKl_i$) line when that processor has read the data from the bus. A write (WR) signal is also required to control the propagation of the acknowledgment signal through the arbiter chain. Thus, the acknowledgement signal is propagated from one module to another until it has reached the processor that has reserved the broadcast bus. When that processor received an

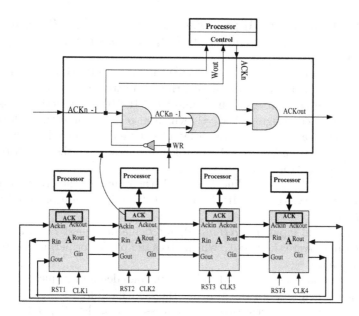

Fig. 5. Released Control Circuit

input acknowledgment ($Ackin_{i-1}$) signal from the previous arbiter module the processor releases the token and the arbiter responds by deasserting Wout.

Instead of just assigning current priority based on position in the ring as described in [12] higher priority is given to a processor executing the Brk instruction, while the lower priority is assigned to a processor that making a demand request. The Brk instruction always occurs before executing the Cre instruction, thus providing latency hiding. In our CMP only one processor can succeed in executing the Brk instruction at a given time, so there is no need for many levels of priority. However, the mechanism we described in this paper can be easily extended for many levels of priority and can be used to support any CMP arbitration model.

The arbiters operations can be described as follows, where we have N arbiter modules and only one processor can succeed in executing the Brk instruction at a given time.

- The arbiter are labelled using modulo arithmetic so for M arbiters A_{i+1} is A_0 for $i = M - 1$ and A_{i-1} is A_{m-1} for M=0.
- Note that $init_0 = 1$ and $init_1$ to $init_{m-1} = 0$. This means that processor 1 would have a request acknowledged immediately after system initialization (reset) but other processors must wait for the grant to propagate ($A_1 to A_2 \ldots \ldots to A_m$).
- If $Brk_i = 1$, A_i outputs a high request to the next arbiter via $RHout_i$. The rest of the modules can also generate a demand request via $RLout_k$ where k can be any number from 1..N except i ($k \neq i$). If all Brk=0 any module can assert RLout.

- If $Brk_i=0$ and $D_i=0$, A_i propagates $RHin_i$ to $RHout_i$, $RLin_i$ to $RLout_i$ and Gin_i to $Gout_i$. This propagate RH_i and RL_i from A_i to A_{i-1} and G_i from A_i to A_{i+1}.
- If $Brk_i=1$ and $Gin_i=1$, and $Ackin_i=0$ then A_i asserts $Wout_i$ (read), which gives processor permission to access the broadcast bus.
- When a receiving processor has completed the bus transaction it asserts a local acknowledge signal $Ackl_i=1$, which also propagated through the ring until it has reached the module that has currently reserved the bus. Thus, when $Ackin_i=1$ and $Wout_i=1$, the token is released and the arbiter responds by deasserting Wout.
- If $Brk_i=0$, and the input line $RHin_i=1$, then forward the grant to the next module irrespective of D. If $D_i=1$ assert $RLout_i=1$, else propagate $RLin_i$ to $RLout_i$.
- If $Brk_i=0$, and input line $RHin_i=0$, and demand request $D_i=1$ and $Ackin_i = 0$, then activate the $Wout_i$, which gives the processor permission to access the broadcast bus.
- If $Brk_i=0$, and $Gin_i=1$ and $RHin_i=0$, and demand request $D_i=0$, and $RLin_i=1$, then forward the grant to the next module.
- When there is no request from any processor, then the RH_i, RL_i, G_i, Ack_i, and $Wout_i$ will all be 0.

It is clear from this mechanism that the highest priority is given always to the processor that asserts a high signal through its Brk output.

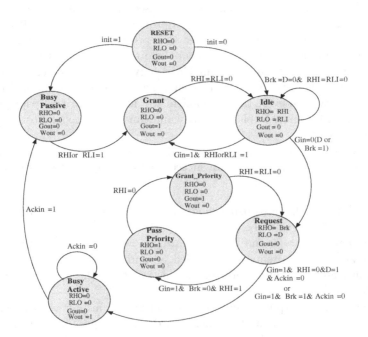

Fig. 6. Arbiter State Transition Diagram

The state machine diagram for the arbiter module is shown in figure 6. As shown, there are eight states, however an asynchronous version of this machine can be minimized. Two states reset and grant priority can be eliminated, where the elimination of redundant stable states allows us to draw a simplified and minimized state machine. The idle state receives the input requests from $RHin_i or RLin_i$ and if there is no input grant $Gin_i = 0$, it propagates the input requests to the next arbiter module via output request lines $RHout_i or RLout_i$. The request must be propagated until it reaches the module that currently holds the token. The token is stored in the busy passive state, from which high input requests from RHi or RLi cause a change to the grant state. In the grant state the machine waits for removal of the incoming request before returning to the idle state.

From the idle state an incoming bus demand from the processor (D=1 or Brk=1) causes a change to the request state. In the request state, if the input grant $Gin_i = 1$, and $Brk_i = 1$, and $(Ackin_{i-1} = 0)$, then the state changes to busy active, which gives the processor permission to access the broadcast bus by activating the $Wout_i$ wire line. When the input acknowledge $Ackin_{i-1} = 1$ is received, this means that all processors complete accessing the bus and the state changes to busy passive. While if the input grant $Gin_i = 1$, $Brk_i = 0$ and the input request $Rh_i=1$, then the pass priority state is used to pass the request, ignoring the lower priority demand from this processor.

Our arbiter is both starvation free and provides deadlock freedom. If we assume that the token is initially in module one and a demand requests to access the broadcast bus is encountered from all modules, then the token is given first to module one, which gives it access to the bus. When this module finished, it passes the token towards to the next module i.e. module two and so on. Thus, as described above the highest priority is given first to the module that has succeed in executing the Brk instruction, then the rest of the modules that have requested the bus are served based on the position in the ring and in sequential order. It is clear that this mechanism provides a fairness and is starvation free. As soon as the processor releases the bus the next module will be served directly. Also, in the microthreaded model [1], only the main thread has triggered a bus request and these have been performed in sequence and hence there will be virtually no delay in arbitration, as there is no contention.

4.1   Arbiter Partitioning

A partitionable design methodology will become one of the design requirements, which ensures low power and high performance in future processors [19, 20]. It also offers a promising approach to fault tolerance problems and provides an independent communication between different system blocks. Each arbiter connects to two other arbiters associated with adjacent processors to form an arbitration ring as shown in fig 3a. This arrangement could be hardwired, however, by providing a routing architecture as shown in figure 7 each arbiter and their associated global resources can be dynamically partitioned into groups, where each group has a separate token.

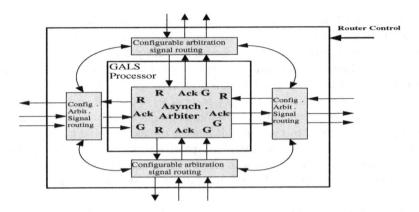

Fig. 7. Asynchronous Arbiter with programmable routing for partitionable processor arrays

4.2   Arbiter with N-Levels of Priority

Figure 8 shows a block diagram for a scalable asynchronous arbiter design with n-levels of priority. As illustrated, three blocks are required to handle n requests, which comprise the processor bus access controller block, request logic block and the state machine block. The function of the first block is to control and manipulate different levels of priority, where the priority levels can be determined by the compiler.

The second block determines whether the demand input signal has a high or low priority compared with the incoming requests. Thus if the demand line D has low priority, then a high signal is asserted to the state machine through PP wire line. Otherwise, if the demand has high priority, then PP=0 is asserted. The state machine uses the input signals from the request logic block to decide

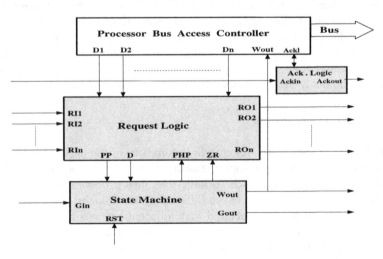

Fig. 8. A block diagram for a scalable asynchronous arbiter design

whether to pass the grant line to the next module via Gout if the current module has a lowest priority; or to activate the Wout line, which allows the processor to access the bus. So, if the current module has the highest priority, then the pass-high-priority (PHP) signal is activated by the state machine to inform the request logic block that the bus access is given to the current module. Otherwise PHP=0 is asserted. The zero request line (ZR) can be used to control all output request RO, which block the propagation of output request RO if ZR=0, or to pass the request to the next module if ZR=1.

5   Simulation Results

We simulated the arbiter using VHDL, exploiting the generate statement to create networks of N processors/arbiters in the test bench. The simulations used processors with different clock phases and frequencies in order to model their globally asynchronous nature. The arbiter modules were linked using arbitrary delay elements as shown in figure 9 to model interconnect delays. Simulations using this approach verified correct operation of the arbiter with up to 64 processors. The processors were modelled using a high level description of the continuation queue and scheduling system, which will be reported elsewhere and whose details are not critical to the current discussion. In effect the sequencing of bus requests in these simulations were manually controlled by the test bench set up.

We are investigating the performance of our arbiter with respect to the request-to-grant delay by replacing the processor model with a simple state machine and generated requests at delays determined by a sequence of random numbers. The state machine is shown in figure 10. The state machine first generates a request (*local* state) then changed to *wait bus* state. When a grant is received the state changes to *bus in use*. When the bus access is complete the state changes to *acknowledge* informing the rest of the processors in the ring that bus is free again. The simulation includes a different sizes of processors i.e. 4, 8, 16, 32, and 64.

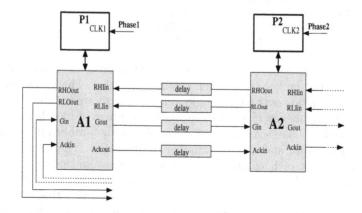

Fig. 9. Asynchronous Arbiter Simulation Model

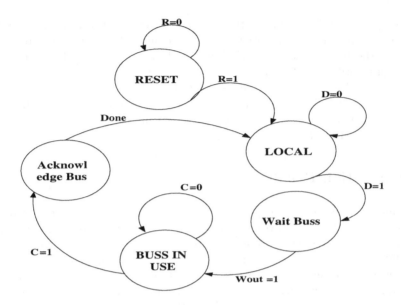

Fig. 10. Processor state machine

Table 1. Relative frequency of create instruction over a range of loop kernels

Loop	Create instruction rate compared to other instructions
A: Partial Product	0.3333
B: 2-D SOR	0.2
L3: inner Product	0.25
L4: Banded Linear Equation	0.2
L5: Tri-Diagonal Elimination	0.25
L6: General Linear Recurrence	0.1429
C:Pointer Chasing	0.0714
L1: Hydro Fragment	0.1111
L2: ICCG	0.0909
L7: Equation of State Fragment	0.0385

The rate of requests to the arbiter within the context of the microthreaded CMP depends on the behavior of the create instruction. The frequency of executing this instruction over a range of loop kernels as shown in table 1. Figure 11 also shows the frequency create executing over a range of loop kernels against the normalised problem size, where m is the size of the problem in terms of the number of iterations, and n is the number of processors. The loops considered included a number of livemore kernels, some that are independent and some that contain loop carried-dependencies. As shown, the frequency of executing this instruction is very low, and the percentage of executing this instruction is less than 17% over all loop kernels considered in this analysis. Thus, the bus is used infrequently hence the delay in arbitration will primarily depend on the ring

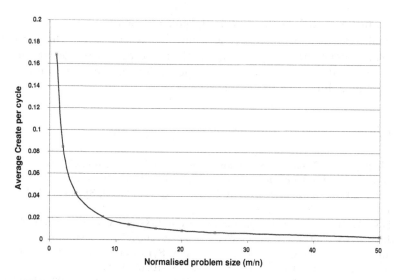

Fig. 11. Frequency of executing create instruction over a range of loop kernels, m= problem size

delay, as there is very little or no contention. Furthermore, the microthreaded processors are tolerant to latency when they have created threads, so it does not matter how long it takes to create the next family of microthreads.

6 Conclusion

In this paper we have discussed the design and the pre-layout simulation using VHDL of an asynchronous arbiter. The arbiter provides a very simple system architecture, where each module has a few wires connecting the next one and the last is connected to the first module in a circular fashion. Delay-insensitive methodologies with unbounded wire and gate delays were considered in the arbiter simulation procedures. The arbiter also has the advantages of GALS communication design and include the following features:

- The ring configuration to arbiter modules and the point-to-point communication between two adjacent arbiter modules provide a modular connectivity, which has full scalability in both bandwidth and area with increasing numbers of micro-threaded processors GALS modules.
- Each arbiter module has its own control signals and implements a self-timed model. Therefore, there is no need to propagate the control signals throughout all the arbiter modules.
- There are four wires connecting every arbiter module in the chain to the next one and the last to the first in a circular fashion. The latency of the wire delay is very small. Thus the decision is made locally by each arbiter module instead of using large wire delay, which gives it a partitioning properties.

– Each processor arbiter has a priority policy dependent on a processor successfully executing the concurrency control instruction Brk. This mechanism provides latency hiding by decoupling the micro-threaded processor from the token circulation time. It also, offer a fairness communication between processors and eliminates processors starvation.

References

1. Jesshope, C. R.: Scalable Instruction-level Parallelism. In Proc. Computer Systems: Architectures, Modeling and Simulation, 3rd and 4th International Workshops, SAMOS 2004, Samos, Greece, July 19-21, LNCS Vol. 3133, Springer-Verlag (2004) 383-392

2. Shilov, A.: Intel to Cancel NetBurst Pentium 4 Xeon Evolution.(2004). Available at http:/www.xbitlabs.com/news/cpu/ display/20040507000306.html.

3. Shapiro, D.: Globally Asynchronous Locally Synchronous Circuits. PhD Thesis, Stanford University, Report No. STAN-CS-84-1026, (1984)

4. International Technology Roadmap for Semiconductors: ITRS (2003). Available at http://public.itrs.net.

5. Shengxian, Z., Li, W., Carlsson, J., Palmkvist, K. and Wanhammar, L.: An Asynchronous Wrapper with Novel Handshake Circuits for GALS Systems. In Proc. IEEE 2002 Int. Conf. on Communication, Circuits and Systems, Cheungdu, China, June 29- July 1 (2002) 1521-1525

6. Hemani, A., Meincke, T., Kumar, S., Postula, A., Olsson, T., Nilsson, P.. Oberg, J., Ellervee, P. and Lundqvist, D.: Lowering Power Consumption in Clock by using Globally Asynchronous Locally Synchronous Design Style. In Proc. of ACM/IEEE design Automation Conference, New Orleans, Louisiana, United States (1999) 873-878

7. Bainbridge, W. J. and Furber, S. B.: Delay Insensitive System-on-Chip Interconnect Using 1-of-4 Data Encoding. Proc. of the Seventh International Symposium on Asynchronous Circuits and Systems (2001) 118

8. Hauck, S.: Asynchronous Design Methodologies: An Overview. Proc. of the IEEE, Vol. 83, January (1995) 69-93

9. Takamura, A., Kuwako, M., Imai, M., Fujii, T., Ozawa, M., Fukasaku, I., Ueno, Y. and Nanya, T.: TITAC-2: An Asynchronous 32-bit Microprocessor based on Scalable-Delay-Insensitive Model. Proc. of the 1997 International Conference on Computer Design (ICCD'97), Austin, TX, USA (1997) 288-294

10. Martin, A. et al.: The Design of an Asynchronous MIPS R3000 Microprocessor. In Advanced Research in VLSI (1997) 164-181

11. Moore, S., Taylor, G., Mullins, R. and Robinson, P.: Point to Point GALS Interconnect. Proc. of the Eighth International Symposium on Asynchronous Circuits and Systems (ASYNC'02) (2002) 69-75

12. Bellido, M. J., Valencia, M., Huertas, J. I., Acosta, A. J. and Sanchez-Solano, S.: Modular Asynchronous Arbiter Insensitive to Metastability. IEEE Computer Society, Vol. 44, Washington, DC, USA (1995) 1456-1461

13. Rigaud, J-B., Quartana, J., Fesquet, L. and Renaudin, M.: High-Level Modeling and Design of Asynchronous Arbiters for On-Chip Communication Systems. Proc. of the IEEE 2002 Design, Automation and test in Europe Conference and Exhibition, (2002) 1090

14. Josephs, M. and Yantchev, J.: CMOS Design of the Tree Arbiter Element. Proc. of the IEEE Trans. on VLSI Systems **4** (1996) 472-476
15. Macii, E. and Poncino, M.: The Design of Easily Scalable Bus Arbiters with Different Dynamic Priority Schemes. Proc. of 29th Asilomar Conference on Signals, Systems and Computers, Vol. **1**, Pacific Grove, California (1995) 211-213
16. Villiger, T., Kaslin, H., Gurkaynak, F. K., Oetiker, S. and Fichtner, W.: Self-timed Ring for Globally-Asynchronous Locally-Synchronous Systems. Proc. of the Ninth International Symposium on Asynchronous Circuits and Systems (ASYNC'03), Vancouver, BC, Canada (2003)
17. Bolychevsky, A., Jesshope, C. R. and Muchnick, V. Dynamic Scheduling in RISC Architectures. IEE Proc. Computer Digital Techniques, Vol. **143** (1996) 309-317
18. Jesshope, C. R.: Multi-Threaded Microprocessors Evolution or Revolution. Proc. of the 8th Asia-Pacific Conference, September 23-26, ACSAC'2003, Aizu, Japan (2003) 21-45
19. Yingmin, L., Brooks, D., Zhigang, H. and Skadron, K.: Performance, Energy, and Thermal Considerations for SMT and CMP Architectures. Proc. of the 11th IEEE International Symposium on high performance computer architecture (HPCA), San Francisco, CA, USA (2005) 71-82
20. El-Moursy, A., Garg, R., Albonesi, D. and Dwarkadas, S.: Partitioning Multi-threaded Processor with a Large Number of Threads. International Symposium on Performance Analysis of Systems and Software (2005)

GigaNetIC – A Scalable Embedded On-Chip Multiprocessor Architecture for Network Applications

Jörg-Christian Niemann, Christoph Puttmann, Mario Porrmann, and Ulrich Rückert

Heinz Nixdorf Institute, University of Paderborn, Germany
{niemann, puttmann, porrmann, rueckert}@hni.upb.de

Abstract. In this paper, we present the prototypical implementation of the scalable GigaNetIC chip multiprocessor architecture. We use an FPGA-based rapid prototyping system to verify the functionality of our architecture in a network application scenario before we are going to fabricate the ASIC in a modern CMOS standard cell technology. The rapid prototyping environment gives us the opportunity to test our multiprocessor architecture with Ethernet-based data streams in a real network scenario. Our system concept is based on a massively parallel processor structure. Due to its regularity, our architecture can be easily scaled to accommodate a wide range of packet processing applications with disparate performance and throughput requirements at high reliability. Furthermore, the composition from predefined building blocks guarantees fast design cycles and simplifies system verification. We present standard cell synthesis results as well as a performance analysis for a firewall application with various couplings of hardware accelerators.

1 Introduction

Embedded multiprocessor systems can efficiently meet the ever-growing performance requirements of network applications. The scalable GigaNetIC architecture is a novel approach to flexibly meet the disparate performance requirements of different network application scenarios. The backbone of our architecture is a powerful and yet flexible network on-chip (NoC) – the GigaNoC. Like other network on-chip architectures, e.g., [1][2][3] the GigaNoC offers the possibility to easily extended SoC designs to new application requirements by additional components (cf. Sec. 2.4). Differently coupled hardware accelerators can easily be integrated in the GigaNetIC system to improve the performance for specialized tasks. Not only as a proof of concept, but to speed up the simulation and verification process, we implemented a prototype of the GigaNetIC system using a reconfigurable FPGA platform. For this PCI-bus-based system we have developed a graphical user interface (GUI), which allows a convenient interaction with the FPGA hardware. Because our embedded multiprocessor architecture is highly suitable for packet processing purposes, we consider a network application scenario to evaluate the system performance.

The paper is organized as follows. In the next section, we describe the architecture of our system-on-chip multiprocessor concept. Furthermore, three different ways of

W. Grass et al. (Eds.): ARCS 2006, LNCS 3894, pp. 268–282, 2006.

coupling hardware accelerators with the system will be discussed. Section 3 explains the implementation of system components in detail and shows the synthesis results for an FPGA mapping as well as for a semi custom standard cell design. The performance evaluation for a network application is discussed in Section 4, revealing the capability of the GigaNetIC approach. Finally, the paper is concluded in Section 5.

2 Architectural Concept

The GigaNetIC approach focuses on a scalable architecture for universal coprocessors and for network processors in particular. Our platform is scalable in respect to the number of the clusters, the processors instantiated per cluster, the provided hardware accelerators, and the available bandwidth of the on-chip communication channels. By this, a high reusability of our architecture can be guaranteed. Further advantages of such a uniform system architecture lie in the simplified testability and verification of the circuit and in a homogeneous programming model. The proposed architecture is structured into the following three domains: *PE level*, *Cluster level*, and *SoC level*. The programmer is relieved from specifically handling the on-chip communication protocol since routing, memory management, and I/O are transparently controlled by the switch boxes (SBs). At the cluster level, the programming model is based on a proprietary parallelizing ANSI C compiler. A preceding tool partitions and schedules the tasks for the individual processor clusters.

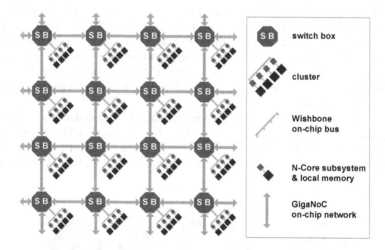

Fig. 1. Scalable parallel GigaNetIC SoC architecture based on hierarchical IP blocks

2.1 PE Level

At the processing element (PE) level, we use our 32 bit RISC processor N-Core, as processing element [4][5]. The core is a softmacro and can be adapted to the needs of the respective area of application. Instructions have a fixed width of 16 bit, providing a high code density, which is of special importance for embedded systems with limited memory resources. The instruction set can be extended through additional operations due to 11% free opcode space. Therefore, it is possible to optimize the architecture for specific application domains, e.g., the networking area. In this field, we have already implemented several new instructions for header modification and for encryption algorithms used in IPsec protocols [6][5]. These instruction set extensions can be seen as the smallest hardware blocks used in our architecture. Additionally, the N-Core provides a coprocessor interface for hardware accelerators, facilitating further acceleration by adding larger HW blocks. The processor core has been verified in silicon successfully. It is also possible to connect other embedded general purpose CPUs than the N-Core to the local bus due to the standardized bus interfaces. Even specialized hardware accelerators can be easily integrated (cf. section 2.4). Each PE has a local memory, which is used for program code as well as for local data. There is also a shared memory belonging to the cluster level that is used as a packet buffer for all PEs connected to the local bus.

2.2 Cluster Level

At the cluster level, switch boxes act as high speed routing nodes, which combine the individual processor clusters with each other. The on-chip communication is based on a packet switched network-on-chip [7][8]. Data is transmitted by means of Flits (Flow Control Digits) – packet fragments that represent the atomic on-chip data transmission unit [9]. A locally connected processor cluster consists of a multitude of processors or other intellectual property (IP) blocks, which are connected to the SB by the Wishbone on-chip bus. We also have the opportunity to use an AMBA high-speed interconnection matrix together with a multiprocessor cache. However, in this paper, we focus on applications for which such a complex cache system is not necessary due to independent data streams and applications with very few inter-process communications thus making a complex cache coherency protocol useless. Therefore, we focus on the Wishbone implementation, which is much smaller in terms of chip area requirements.

The number of SB communication ports is variable and depends on the desired on-chip network topology. Despite its simplicity, this architecture allows parallel operation and a pipelining of the processor fields. Additionally, it guarantees almost equal link lengths and thus an identical and short propagation delay of the signals

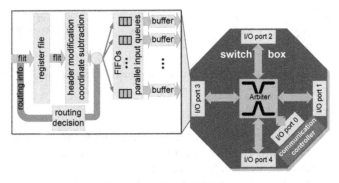

Fig. 2. Switch box HW block

between SBs. Each SB can be connected to a multiprocessor array by an additional input/output port (port 0 in Fig. 2) that interfaces a communication controller (CC). The CC transfers data to and from the local clusters. The SB consists of two main parts. The first part combines the I/O port and the crossbar to form the communication structure that ensures that the data packets are rapidly transmitted and reach the correct switch box output port on the basis of the routing strategy. The second part of the SB comprises the control structures, which serve as an interface between the processor field and the on-chip network. This task is performed by the communication controller, which is located between port 0 and the bus of the local cluster. The communication controller performs the following tasks: It receives the flits, reorders them if necessary, and forwards them to the connected HW blocks, e.g., processors or hardware accelerators. Another important function is the initialization of the PE code memories at system startup.

2.3 SoC Level

The coarse-grained level of our architecture is the SoC level. For integrating a huge amount of processors on a single chip, it has to be ensured that these units are able to communicate efficiently over an on-chip interconnection network. To support the software engineer, we have developed special programming models and libraries. Following this programming paradigm, our chip will speed up many network applications in a cost and power saving way. Despite its simplicity, our architecture allows parallel operation and a pipelining of the processor fields. Additionally, it guarantees almost equal link lengths and thus an identical and short propagation delay of the signals between SBs. Furthermore, the parallel structure of the SB concept allows a high fault tolerance: if the software detects a malfunctioning processor unit, others can take over the pending tasks.

2.4 Hardware Accelerators and Other HW Blocks

Besides the processor cores and the local memories, further HW blocks can be integrated in several ways. The processor supports the tight connection of hardware accelerators via a coprocessor interface (cf. Fig. 3a). If these units should be available to a number of processors, they can be coupled via the local bus at cluster level. Coupled closely to the processor field, these HW blocks are integrated through additional master/slave interfaces of the local bus system and addressed via memory-mapped I/O ports (cf. Fig. 3b). Besides hardware accelerators, additional modules, such as UARTs for debugging purposes, can also be integrated.

At the SoC level, more independent units can be connected to any SB and are addressable via the on-chip network. These units can be loosely coupled hardware accelerators enqueued in the data path, such as encryption modules, or units that realize outwards connections such as memory controllers for external memory or Ethernet controllers that take over the connection to external networks (cf. Fig. 3c). To connect a unit to the GigaNoC, a CC is connected to the respective component and to a SB port. The CC performs the conversion of the data into the flit protocol and the termination of the protocol, respectively. Due to this connection mode, the units are

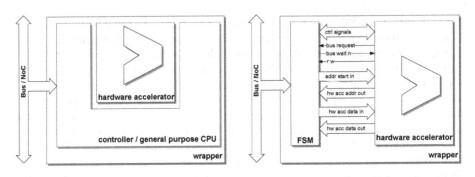

a) tight controller / CPU coupling to bus / NoC   b) coupling to bus / NoC without own memory

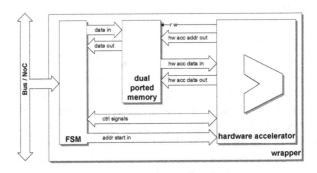

c) coupling to bus / NoC with own memory (dual ported)

Fig. 3. Different variants of hardware accelerator couplings

universally suited and offer a simple adaptation of the system to new application areas. In this case, the units normally need an own memory as a packet buffer.

3   Implementation

Despite an already available SystemC simulation model [10], the GigaNetIC system is implemented at Register Transfer Level (RTL) using VHDL and Verilog. As mentioned in Section 2, the structure of our architecture consists of three domains: PE level, Cluster level, and SoC level. In the following we will describe the implementation of these three levels and their core components in more detail. From a bottom-up view of the GigaNetIC system, the N-Core is the core component at PE level. As already mentioned, the N-Core represents a 32 bit RISC microprocessor with a common load/store architecture. The implemented three-stage pipelined architecture delivers reasonable performance for embedded systems [4]. Two independent banks of sixteen 32 bit registers allow fast program context switching, e.g., for fast interrupt handling.

Additional HW blocks extend the microprocessor core to an embedded processor subsystem environment (cf.). The HW blocks are very tightly coupled to the PE by using the 32 bit wide processor system bus. The bus controller acts as a wrapper,

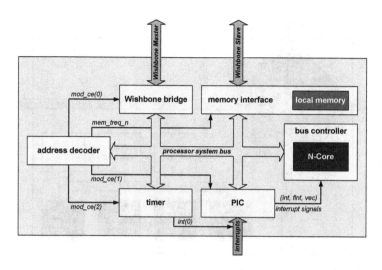

Fig. 4. Architecture of the processor subsystem environment

which connects the N-Core to the processor system bus. All HW blocks can be accessedfrom the PE using memory mapped I/O and are arbitrated by the address decoder. The programmable interrupt controller (PIC) handles up to 32 interrupt sources, which are prioritized and can be assigned to normal or fast interrupts. Fast interrupts use the alternative register banks of the N-Core, whereas normal interrupts have to save the register contents at the stack before performing the interrupt service routine. One interrupt input signal is connected to the programmable timer module, which allows creating periodic interrupts. Furthermore, the timer module features a programmable counter, which can be used for cycle accurate timing purpose (e.g., benchmarking and system optimization). The memory interface block offers dual port access to the local memory of the processor subsystem. The N-Core can access instructions or data via the processor subsystem bus. In order to access the local memory from other components, e.g., for initialization or shared variables, the second memory port is implemented as a Wishbone slave interface. Via the Wishbone bridge module the processor subsystem is connected to the next higher level of our hierarchal architecture: the cluster level (cf. Fig. 2). On cluster level every N-Core subsystem can access the 32 bit wide Wishbone bus as a master and supports byte granular data transfer. The implemented Wishbone standard [11] uses a multiplexed master-slave bus protocol with a round-robin arbiter assuring uniform access distribution. Once again, additional HW blocks can be connected to the Wishbone bus at cluster level. In contrast to HW extensions at PE level, those modules can not only be addressed by the associated processor element, but are accessible by every N-Core subsystem connected to the local bus. The serial interface module (UART) is intended to connect I/O components, e.g., touch screens, which are used for debugging purposes and for user interaction. Via the SRAM interface external memory can be attached to the Wishbone bus, in order to store large or shared data structures. However, the packet memory block features on-chip dual-ported memory space to store data packets of the

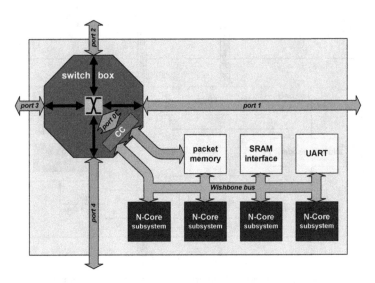

Fig. 5. GigaNetIC architecture at cluster level

on-chip network. The N-Core subsystems can access the packet memory via the Wishbone bus, whereas the other port is connected to the memory interface of the switch box's communication controller.

On the SoC level of the GigaNetIC hierarchy several cluster components are connected to a powerful grid network (cf.), the GigaNoC [10]. Furthermore, every switch box port can be used to connect loosely coupled HW blocks, which are addressable via the on-chip network from every PE in the system. In order to communicate with other network devices, we implemented an Ethernet controller HW block. Every Ethernet controller has up to four fast Ethernet ports to send and receive network packets.

3.1 Synthesis Results

The target technology for the GigaNetIC architecture will be a semi custom ASIC design. As shown in the first tapeout will consist of eight switch boxes and 32 processing elements. However, since all components are specified in a hardware description language, the GigaNetIC architecture can also easily be synthesized for FPGAs. Therefore, we have the opportunity to map a GigaNetIC demonstrator system to a hardware emulation platform. For this purpose we use the FPGA-based rapid prototyping system called RAPTOR2000 [12] (cf. Sect. 3.2), which has been developed at our research group. When using the RAPTOR2000 system for hardware verification we can achieve a speed-up of about 100,000 compared to HDL simulation on a 3 GHz Pentium 4. In the following, the synthesis results for an FPGA implementation are presented as well as for a semi custom ASIC design.

FPGA Prototype. Not only to accelerate simulation speed, but also as a proof of concept, we mapped a GigaNetIC demonstrator system on our FPGA-based rapid prototyping platform RAPTOR2000. The architecture of the demonstrator system is shown in Fig. 6 and its functionality will be explained in Sect. 4.1 in detail. In this section we want to focus on the synthesis results of individual system components. The following results are based on Xilinx Virtex-II FPGAs:

Table 1. Synthesis results for FPGA implementation

HW block	Slices	RAM16s
address decoder	121	-
bus controller incl. N-Core	3,206	-
memory interface incl. 32 KB RAM	71	16
programmable interrupt controller	6	-
timer	163	-
Wishbone bridge	95	-
∑(N-Core subsystem)	3,662	16

HW block	Slices	RAM16s
4 x N-Core subsystem	14,648	64
packet memory (32 KB)	53	16
SRAM interface	22	-
UART	626	-
Wishbone arbiter	13	-
∑(cluster)	15,362	80

a) PE level components   b) cluster level components

The demonstrator system comprises two switch boxes, which are used to connect two clusters at SoC level. A single switch box with an integrated communication controller and four external data ports occupies 14,133 slices. Hence, a switch box is the most resource intense component of the system and requires almost as much slices as four N-Core subsystems. The reason for this is because a switch box buffers data in FIFO structures, which are currently realized as registers. About 59 % of the switch box slices are used for implementing FIFO registers. In order to communicate with external network devices, additional Ethernet controllers are connected to open switch box ports (cf. Fig. 6). An Ethernet controller with two implemented Ethernet ports occupies 5,544 slices and 32 RAM16 memory blocks, used as packet buffers. On each Virtex-II FPGA a switch box, with a cluster and Ethernet controller attached, is mapped. Adding all component resources separately results in a total of 35,309 slices and 112 RAM16 memory blocks for the whole SoC level implementation. However, the synthesized FPGA design only requires 29,288 slices and 112 RAM16 components. The resource variation is caused by optimization reasons, since, e.g., we only use two of the four switch box ports (cf. Fig. 6). The final utilization ratio for a Xilinx Virtex-II 8000 is 63% of FPGA slices and 67% of BlockRAM resources. A maximum clock frequency of 12.5 MHz is achieved.

ASIC Realization. The synthesis results for the semi custom standard cell process are based on a modern 90nm CMOS technology. The results in Table 2 are based on typical operating conditions, which mean a chip core voltage of 1.20 V and a temperature of 27 °C. A cluster including a switch box (cf. Fig. 5) occupies 5.78 mm² chip area and runs at a maximum clock frequency of 263 MHz. The critical path runs through the N-Core and the respective memory interface (cf. Fig. 4). The local memory of each PE as well as the packet memory inside the cluster architecture is based on SRAM blocks. Adding the 32 KB packet memory and the 32 KB local memory of all four N-Core subsystems results in a total of 160 KB memory space per cluster. The chip area for the corresponding SRAM structures adds up to 4.43 mm², which equals 77 % of the whole cluster chip area. Considering the 2x4 grid structure according to, the required chip area for 8 clusters will be 46.22 mm². Additional chip area

Table 2. Synthesis results for 90nm CMOS technology

	frequency [MHz]	chip area [mm²]	power consumption [mW]	power consumption [mW / MHz]
N-Core	278	0.127	414.98	1.49
switch box	714	0.530	1510.30	2.12
cluster (incl. SB)	263	5.777	737.57	2.80
ethernet controller	435	2.181	957.30	2.20

may be consumed by loosely coupled hardware accelerators (cf. Fig. 3c) as well as by Ethernet controllers connected to the open switch box ports. An Ethernet controller with four Ethernet ports implemented covers 2.18 mm² chip area, whereof 70 % is again occupied by SRAM.

3.2 System Integration

The RAPTOR2000 platform is used for the system integration of the GigaNetIC demonstrator. RAPTOR2000 is a modular FPGA-based rapid prototyping system, which has been developed by our research group [12]. The prototyping system consists of the RAPTOR2000 motherboard, which can be equipped with up to six application specific daughterboard modules. Based on FPGA daughterboard modules, RAPTOR2000 is able to emulate circuits with a complexity of more than 100 million gates. The host computer can communicate via a PCI bus interface with the RAPTOR2000 board and each attached daughterboard, respectively.

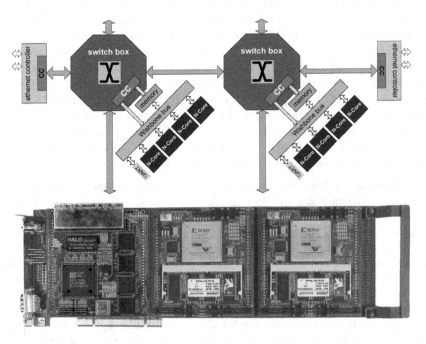

Fig. 6. RAPTOR2000 Rapid Prototyping System with Ethernet- and FPGA-modules

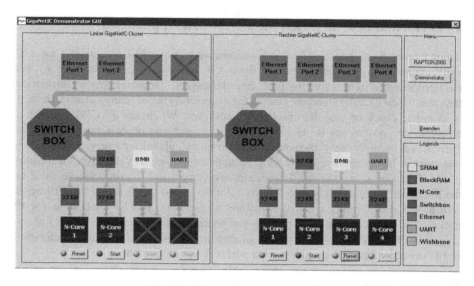

Fig. 7. GigaNetIC demonstrator GUI

To implement the GigaNetIC demonstrator, we used two Xilinx Virtex-II 8000 FPGA modules and an Ethernet transceiver module (cf. Fig. 6). The Ethernet daughterboard features four independent Ethernet ports for network communication working with either 10 Mbps or 100 Mbps.

For user convenience, we have developed a Graphical User Interface (GUI) for the GigaNetIC demonstrator, which allows comfortable initialisation, controlling and debugging of the prototype. By using RAPTOR2000 dynamic link library (DLL) functions, which provide a user-friendly API for hardware access, the software is able to read and write all necessary register contents. After starting the GUI program the user can select a configuration file for each FPGA module on the RAPTOR2000 board. When the FPGAs are initialized the GUI automatically detects the system setup in terms of processor elements per cluster, memory sizes and available Ethernet ports. In order to initialize the code memory, the user can assign a program file to each N-Core subsystem. As soon as the initialization is finished, each processor system can individually be started and reset, respectively. The status of each processor element is visualized by colored circles underneath the corresponding N-Core symbol. Gray color symbolizes that the processor has not been initialized yet, whereas a red circle indicates that the processor has not been started or stopped due to a reset. A green symbol indicates that a processor is executing the assigned program code. In order to debug the demonstrator system, the user can access additional status information of every hardware component by selecting the corresponding GUI symbol. For example, the content of each memory component can be displayed as easily as the connection status of an Ethernet port. In this way we are able to verify our system architecture and evaluate software algorithms at satisfactory speed compared to simulation models. Furthermore, new hardware blocks can easily be integrated in the system and can be tested in a real world environment. This ensures fast design cycles and a high reliability of the system.

4   Performance Evaluation for a Network Application

Among other domains, the GigaNetIC architecture is particularly suitable for network applications. Incoherent packet flows can be processed concurrently by our multiprocessor system achieving high data throughput. However, when considering the established TCP/IP standard, one of the core functions of many network devices is to either check or calculate protocol checksums. Whenever a TCP/IP packet is received, the system has to decide whether to accept and process the packet or to drop it. Accordingly, new checksums have to be calculated for every packet that is transmitted. In our application scenario packets are defined as valid if the checksums of the IP header as well as the TCP header are correct and the time-to-live value of the IP header is greater than zero. We have implemented this function in software as well as using differently coupled hardware accelerators. Header checksums for IP packets, TCP packets and UDP packets can be checked or calculated. In the following, we will first describe the system setup with all types of hardware accelerators and afterwards present the results of our performance evaluation.

4.1   System Setup

As described in section 3.2, we use the RAPTOR2000 system to realize a GigaNetIC demonstrator. Fig. 6 shows the basic architecture of the demonstrator system, consisting of two clusters. Each cluster includes four processor subsystems, wherein every N-Core has 32 KB local memory (cf. Fig. 4) for program code and local data. Two switch boxes interconnect the clusters and also connect Ethernet controllers to the system. Every time an Ethernet packet is received the Ethernet Controller sends the packet to the connected cluster. The communication controller stores the incoming data in the 32 KB packet memory. Subsequently, one of the processor elements can access the received packet. As mentioned earlier, the packet has first to be checked for correctness, before processing the actual packet data. This compute-intensive packet header verification can be done in software by the corresponding N-Core itself, as well as by a hardware accelerator. We have implemented three different interfaces for our hardware accelerators. For this system setup a hardware accelerator has been developed, which can check and calculate header checksums for TCP/IP or UDP/IP packets. The accelerator requires a chip area of 28.3 µm² and achieves a clock frequency of 575 MHz at typical conditions (90nm technology). The closest coupling of the hardware accelerator is called PE coupled coprocessor (PE coprocessor). In this case the accelerator is connected directly to the processor system bus of one N-Core subsystem (cf. Fig. 4). Therefore, the hardware accelerator can only be used by the corresponding processor. In the second case, the hardware accelerator (WB HW acc) is connected to the Wishbone bus at cluster level (cf. Fig. 5). This accelerator is more loosely coupled and can be used by every N-Core subsystem of one cluster. The third implementation is the open switch most independent one: the hardware accelerator (*CC HW acc*) can be attached to every box port. Hence, it can be used by every CPU in the system.

Once all headers of a received packet are verified, either by a processor or by a hardware accelerator, the packet itself can be processed. For our demonstrator system we have developed packet parsing algorithms, which search the packet data for specific key words. If a TCP/IP packet contains one of those key words, the packet data can be altered or the packet may even be dropped. After processing the packet, new header checksums are calculated. Again, this can be done in software or by one of the hardware accelerators. At the end, the packet is send to the Ethernet controller and transmitted to its final destination.

The application scenario may be used in packet parsing network devices, e.g., firewalls or spam filters. When the software validates every packet and searches for specific key words a packet can be dropped (firewall) or marked as potentially not relevant (spam filter).

4.2 Analysis Results

In this section, we introduce the results of a test series with software-based and hardware-accelerated packet processing, and evaluate these in respect to the various coupling possibilities of the hardware accelerators (cf. Fig. 2.4). When evaluating the performance results, the number of active processing units at the local bus must be taken into account. We will concentrate on two extreme cases, that is, one processing unit is exclusively active, or all four processing units are occupied with packet processing (cf. Fig 8). Hybrid cases of software processing and hardware-accelerated processing are also neglected. For the superior NoC, the numbers of active units are also of relevance. As we initially base our survey on a 32 PE system with a number of hardware accelerators adapted to the application scenario, there will be no noteworthy impairment of the system [13].

For the processing, packets of characteristic size according to the Internet MIX (iMIX), i.e., Ethernet packets of 64, 570 and 1518 bytes, have been used. The proposed hardware accelerator is about an order of magnitude faster than the processor element when both operate at the same clock frequency. The fact that a significantly higher clock frequency of the hardware accelerator would be possible is not taken into account here. With large packets the acceleration is higher than with smaller ones since the share of fixed operations in the total workload decreases in comparison to the data-dependent share.

In this analysis, we differentiate between communication and calculation. Communication includes the addressing of the hardware accelerator, the delivery of control words and address pointers as well as additional data that may be required. When using the software-based variant, this part is omitted since the CPU does not have to perform additional communication with other hardware blocks. Calculation means the part of cycles that is required for the actual checking of the packet data.

It becomes evident that the bus-related communication is no bottleneck for the software-based processing with four processing units. Only with more than four processors, we can determine a reduction of the processing speed, which is due to competing bus accesses. This is different for the hardware accelerator that is connected to the local bus (*WB HW acc*). Here, the clearly higher processing speed becomes noticeable. Accordingly, the number of required cycles increases from 27 (64 bytes packet / 1518 bytes packet) with one active processor to 72 (64 bytes packet) and 477 (1518 bytes packet) with four active processors, respectively. This is caused by delays arising through the bus arbitration and corresponds to an increase of the communication costs of 267 % and 1767 %. The costs of the communication with

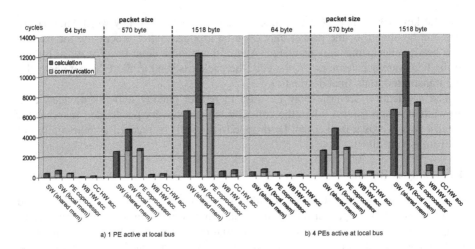

Fig. 8. Comparison of software-based packet processing and HW accelerator-supported packet processing with various system couplings

four active processors at the bus are in the same order of magnitude as the costs of calculation. This is also the case when using the accelerator connected to a switch-box-port (*CC HW acc*). However, in this case, the local bus is relieved far more, and the wait cycles arise through the NoC. Therefore, this solution is offered especially for large systems where a multitude of CPUs target the compute-intensive tasks to a few specialized hardware accelerators that are accessible through the NoC.

Two variants of the software-based processing can be distinguished. On the one hand, there is the variant, which works on the data in the shared memory of the cluster, meaning every time this data is to be accessed by the corresponding CPU the bus is occupied. On the other hand, we provide a solution with which the data is copied into the local processor memory (local memory). The communication costs of this variant are in the same order of magnitude as the costs for calculation, whereas the costs for communication of the shared memory approach are zero. From that, this form of processing is worthwhile only if further operations occur on the packets such as any additional packet parsing as described in Sect. 4.1. This would relieve the bus after the usual packet examination and could finally lead to a speed-up in processing. Using a multiprocessor cache, also developed by us, instead of the normal local processor memory, the transfer of new packets could be accelerated by prefetching. This would also increase the throughput of the system.

The operating time of the software-based calculation ranges from 6.1 cycles/byte (64 bytes packet) to 4.3 cycles/byte (1518 bytes packet), whereas the hardware accelerator approach requires only 0.4 cycles/byte (64 bytes packet) and 0.3 cycles/byte (1518 bytes packet), respectively.

Fig 9 shows the maximum amount of packets that can be processed by a cluster with one and with four active CPUs for the three different packet sizes. This shows that maximum throughput can be achieved with the bus and NoC-coupled variants. The highest throughput with one active CPU is achieved by the bus-coupled hardware accelerator. Here, a throughput of 2.82 MByte/MHz is reached for 1518 bytes packets whereas the four processor variant reaches a maximum throughput of 6.9 MByte/MHz

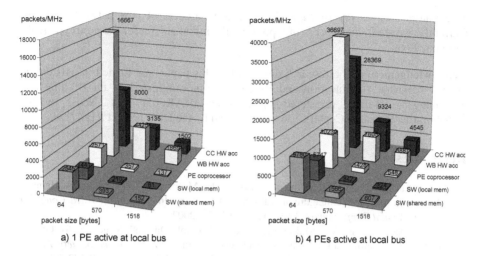

a) 1 PE active at local bus   b) 4 PEs active at local bus

Fig. 9. Possible processed packets per MHz for each processing variant

in the NoC based solution (*CC HW acc*). In relation to our synthesis results this corresponds to a maximum throughput of 1.814 GB per cluster at an operating frequency of 263 MHz. This, in turn, allows an examination of packets on Layer 3 and Layer 4, e.g., of approx. 900 ADSL2+ (16 MBit/s, Downstream) connections. With the software-based variant in about 120 of these DSL connections could be processed under full load. Despite of the reduced clock frequency, the introduced demonstrator is able to process more than 86 MByte/s at 12.5 MHz.

5 Conclusion

In this paper, we have presented a scalable, IP (Intellectual Property)-based network processor architecture, which is adaptable to different application domains in respect to performance, power consumption and area requirements. We have characterized this architecture by key figures for achievable performance and area requirements based on elementary tasks for a firewall scenario.

Our FPGA-based emulation environment RAPTOR2000 facilitates an early verification of the application software and of the entire multiprocessor system in a real world network scenario. With this environment, we determine key architectural parameters for a broad range of networking applications and verify the functionality of our system early in the design phase. Especially for compute-intensive tasks, hardware accelerators can simply be integrated at various architectural levels of the SoC.

Concluding this work, we found that with the aid of our powerful GigaNoC, application-specific architectures can be designed in a resource-efficient way. The coupling takes place either at the local bus or, with the presented communication controller, on an arbitrary port of a switch box. The system is easily adaptable to dedicated application scenarios, can be optimized, and is scalable to other domains of network processing. By using coprocessors, we achieved substantial increases in performance. The embedded PEs could be strongly relieved and are thus available for additional tasks. Our future work comprises the integration of additional hardware accelerators such as crypto engines for security aspects of new network services. Currently, we are in the process of taping out the initial silicon for the prototype realization in 90nm.

Acknowledgements. The research described in this paper was funded in part by the Federal Ministry of Education and Research (Bundesministerium für Bildung und Forschung - BMBF), registered there under 01AK065F - PlaNetS, by the Collaborative Research Centers 376 and 614, and by the DFG project RU 477/8.

References

1. S. Kumar, A. Jantsch, J.-P. Soinien, M. Forsell, M. Millberg, J. Tiensyrjä and A. Hemani. A network on chip architecture and design methodology. In *Proc. of the IEEE Computer Society Annual Symposium on VLSI*, pages 117-124, 2002.
2. A. Thomas and J. Becker. Multi-Grained Reconfigurable Datapath Structures for Online-Adaptive Reconfigurable Hardware Architectures. In *IEEE Computer Society Annual Symposium on VLSI: New Frontiers in VLSI Design (ISVLSI'05)*, pages 118-123, 2005.
3. T. Hollstein, H. Zimmer, T. Murgan and M. Glesner. Flexible Communication-centric System-on-Chip Platforms for Ambient Appliances. In *ITG-Fachtagung Ambient Intelligence*, pages 127-132, October 2004.
4. D. Langen, J.-C. Niemann, M. Porrmann, H. Kalte and U. Rückert. Implementation of a RISC Processor Core for SoC Designs FPGA Prototype vs. ASIC Implementation. In *Proc. of the IEEE-Workshop: Heterogeneous reconfigurable Systems on Chip (SoC)*, Hamburg, Germany, 2002.
5. M. Grünewald, U. Kastens, D. K. Le, J. Niemann, M. Porrmann, U. Rückert, M. Thies and A. Slowik. Network Application Driven Instruction Set Extensions for Embedded Processing Clusters. In *PARELEC 2004, International Conference on Parallel Computing in Electrical Engineering, Dresden, Germany*, pages 209-214, 2004.
6. U. Kastens, D. K. Le, A. Slowik and M. Thies. Feedback Driven Instruction-Set Extension. In *Proceedings of ACM SIGPLAN/SIGBED 2004 Conference on Languages, Compilers, and Tools for Embedded Systems (LCTES'04)*, Washington, D.C., USA, June 2004.
7. W. J. Dally and B. Towles. Route Packets, Not Wires: On-Chip Interconnection Networks. In *Proceedings of the Design Automation Conference*, pages 684-689, Las Vegas, Nevada, USA, 2001.
8. J. Duato, S. Yalamanchili and L. Ni. *Interconnection Networks: An Engineering Approach*. IEEE Computer Society Press, Los Alamitos, CA, USA, 1997.
9. L. Zhonghai and A. Jantsch. Flit admission in on-chip wormhole-switched networks with virtual channels. In *Proc. of the International Symposium on Systems-on-Chip*, 2003.
10. J. Niemann, M. Porrmann and U. Rückert. A Scalable Parallel SoC Architecture for Network Processors. In *IEEE Computer Society Annual Symposium on VLSI (ISVLSI), Tampa, FL., USA*, 2005.
11. Silicore Inc. *WISHBONE System-on-Chip (SoC) Interconnection Architecture for Portable IP Cores*. B.3 Edition, September 2002.
12. H. Kalte, M. Porrmann and U. Rückert. A Prototyping Platform for Dynamically Reconfigurable System on Chip Designs. In *Proceedings of the IEEE Workshop Heterogeneous reconfigurable Systems on Chip (SoC)*, Hamburg, Germany, 2002.
13. J. Niemann, M. Porrmann, C. Sauer and U. Rückert. An Evaluation of the Scalable GigaNetIC Architecture for Access Networks. In *Advanced Networking and Communications Hardware Workshop (ANCHOR), held in conjunction with the ISCA 2005*, 2005.

Efficient System-on-Chip Energy Management
with a Segmented Bloom Filter

Mrinmoy Ghosh[1], Emre Özer[1], Stuart Biles[1], and Hsien-Hsin S. Lee[2]

[1] ARM Ltd.
{mrinmoy.ghosh, emre.ozer, stuart.biles}@arm.com
[2] School of Electrical and Computer Engineering, Georgia Institute of Technology
leehs@ece.gatech.edu

Abstract. As applications tend to grow more complex and use more memory, the demand for cache space increases. Thus embedded processors are inclined to use larger caches. Predicting a miss in a long-latency cache becomes crucial in an embedded system-on-chip(SOC) platform to perform microarchitecture-level energy management. Counting Bloom filters are simple and fast structures that can eliminate associative lookup in a huge lookup space. This paper presents an innovative segmented design of the counting Bloom filter which can save SOC energy by detecting misses aiming at a cache level before the memory. The filter presented is successful in filtering out 89% of L2 cache misses and thus helps in reducing L2 accesses by upto 30%. This reduction in L2 Cache accesses and early triggering of energy management processes lead to an overall SOC energy savings by up to 9%.

1 Introduction

The increasing complexity and shrinking feature size of present day microprocessors has led to energy becoming an important design constraint. Energy is more of an issue in embedded cores that are a part of System-on-chips (SoCs) for handheld devices, where the prime concern is battery life. However, also due to shrinking feature size designers have more transistors per die at their disposal. This has led to large caches, which are major consumer of both static and dynamic power in embedded SoCs. This paper presents an innovative design to help reduce energy consumption in caches and also the SoC platform comprising of the CPU and multi-level caches.

The memory hierarchy of most processors contains single or multi-level caches designed as SRAM memories followed by a large DRAM backstore. Since an access to DRAM memory may take 100s of cycles,therefore in in-order processors, and in some cases for out of order processors, severe stalls may occur on a cache miss in the cache-level before the DRAM. Hence, the cache miss event can be used as a trigger for several microarchitectural energy management processes in the SoC. The energy management processes may include but are not limited to putting all caches in a state preserving low power drowsy mode and for power gating all or part of the processor core.

W. Grass et al. (Eds.): ARCS 2006, LNCS 3894, pp. 283–297, 2006.
© Springer-Verlag Berlin Heidelberg 2006

Bloom filters are simple and fast structures that can eliminate associative lookup when the lookup address space is huge. They can replace associative tables with a simple bit vector that can precisely identify addresses that have not been observed before. This mechanism provides early detection of events without resorting to the associative lookup buffers. This has significant implications on the performance and power consumption considering the fact that Bloom filters are very efficient hardware structures in terms of area, power consumption and speed.

This paper presents an innovative segmented design of the counting Bloom filter that saves energy by detecting a miss in the cache level before the memory. The detection of the miss happens much earlier than the actual request reaches the particular cache. The early detection would allow the processor to make the energy management processes quite early in the memory hierarchy. Starting energy saving measures early provides more energy saving opportunities than in the case where the measures are taken after a miss in the lowest cache level is detected.

The rest of this paper is arranged as follows. Section 2 explains the basics of Bloom filters. Section 3 describes the novel segmented Bloom filter design and elucidates how it aids in saving energy. Then, Section 4 describes the simulation methodology and the energy savings obtained using the segmented Bloom filter and presents the experimental results. Section 5 discusses prior art. Finally, Section 6 concludes the paper.

2   Bloom Filters

The structure of the original Bloom filter idea as described by Bloom [1] is shown in Figure 1a. It consists of several hash functions and a bit vector. A given N-bit address is hashed into k hash values using k different random hash functions. The output of each hash function is an m-bit index value that addresses the Bloom filter bit vector of 2^m where m is much smaller than N.

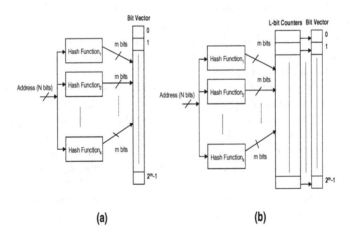

Fig. 1. (a) Original Bloom filter, (b) counting Bloom filter

Each element of the Bloom filter bit vector contains only 1 bit that can be set. Initially, the Bloom filter bit vector is zero. Whenever an N-bit address is observed, it is hashed to the bit vector and the bit value hashed by each m-bit index is set. When a query is to be made whether a given N-bit address has been observed before, the N-bit address is hashed using the same hash functions and the bit values are read from the locations indexed by the m-bit hash values. If at least one of the bit values is 0, this means that this address has definitely not been observed before. This is called a *true miss*. On the other hand, if all of the bit values are 1, then the address may have been observed but cannot guarantee it. If the address has not been observed but the bit vector indicates it does, this is called a *false hit*.

As the number of hash functions increases, the Bloom filter bit vector is polluted much faster. On the other hand, the probability of finding a zero during a query increases if more hash functions are used. The major drawback of the original Bloom filter is the high false hit rate because the filter can get polluted quickly and filled up with all 1s and it starts signalling false hits.

The original Bloom filter has to be quite large to reduce the false hit rate since once a bit is set in the filter there is no way we may reset it. So as more bits are set in the filter, the number of false hits increase. To improve performance of this kind of filter a mechanism for resetting entries set to one is needed. The counting Bloom filter as shown in Figure 1b is proposed by *Fan et al.* in [2], which aims at wcb cache sharing, provides the capability of resetting entries in the filter. For a counting Bloom Filter, an array of counters is added along with the bit vectors of the classical Bloom Filter. When a new address is observed for addition to the Bloom filter, each m-bit hash index addresses to a specific counter in an L-bit counter array. Then, the counter is incremented by one. Similarly, when a new address is observed for deletion from the Bloom filter, each m-bit hash index addresses to a counter, and the counter is decremented by one. If more than one hash index addresses to the same location for a given address, the counter is incremented or decremented only once. If the counter becomes non-zero, the bit in the Bloom filter bit vector addressed by the same m-bit index is set. If the counter becomes zero, then the bit is reset. Queries to a counting Bloom filter are similar to the original Bloom filter.

3   Segmented Bloom Filter Design

We propose an innovative segmented counting Bloom filter as shown in Figure 2 where the counter array of L bits per counter is decoupled from the bit vector and the hash function is duplicated on the bit vector side. The cache line allocation/de-allocation addresses are sent to the counter array using one hash function while the cache request address from the CPU is sent to the bit vector using the copy of the same hash function. The segmented Bloom filter design allows the counter array and bit vector to be in separate physical locations.

A single duplicated hash function is sufficient as our experiments show that the filtering rate of a Bloom filter with a single hash function is as good as the

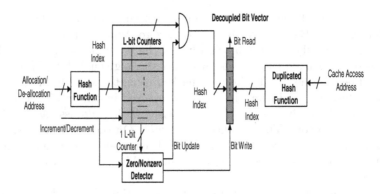

Fig. 2. Segmented Bloom filter

one with two or more hash functions. The implemented hash function chops the physical address into several chunks of hash index long and bitwise XOR them to obtain a single hash index. The number of bits needed per counter (L) depends on how the hash function distributes indeces across the Bloom filter. In the worst case, if all cache lines map to the same counter, the bit-width of the counter must be at most $log_2(Numofcachelines)$ to prevent overflows. In reality, the required number of bits per counter is much smaller than the worst-case.

The counter array is updated with cache line allocation and de-allocation operations. Whenever a new cache line is allocated, the address of the allocated line is hashed into the counter array and the associated counter is incremented. Similarly, when a cache line is evicted from the cache, its associated counter is decremented.

The counter array is responsible for keeping the bit vector up-to-date. The update from the counter array to the bit vector is done only for a single bit location if and only if the counter becomes zero from one during decrement operation or one from zero during increment operation. The following are the steps taken for updating the bit vector:

1) The L-bit counter value is read from the counter array prior to an increment or decrement operation.
2) The counter value is checked for a zero boundary condition by the zero/nonzero detector whether it will become non-zero from zero or zero from non-zero inferred by the increment/decrement line.
3) If a zero boundary condition is detected, the bit update line is asserted, which forwards the hash index to the bit vector.
4) Finally, the bit write line is made 1 to set the bit vector location if the counter will become non-zero. Otherwise, the bit write line is made 0 to reset the bit vector location.
5) If there is no zero boundary condition, then the bit update is not activated, which disables the hash index forwarding to the bit vector.

When the CPU issues a lookup in the cache, the cache address is also sent to the bit vector through the duplicated hash function. The hash function generates an index and reads the single bit value from the vector. If the value is 0, this is a safe indication that this address has never been observed before. If it is 1, it is an indefinite response, i.e. can be either miss or hit.

There are several reasons for designing a segmented Bloom filter: 1) We only need the bit vector, whose size is smaller than the counter, to know the outcome of a query to the Bloom filter. Decoupling the bit vector enables faster and low power accesses to the Bloom Filter. So, the result of a query issued from the core can be obtained by just looking at the bit vector. 2) The update to the counters is not time critical with respect to the core. So, the segmented design allows the counter array to run at a much lower frequency than the bit vector. The vector part being smaller provides a fast access time, whereas the larger counter part runs at a lower frequency to save energy. The only additional overhead of this segmented design is the duplication of the hash function hardware. Using a single hash function in the Bloom filter also simplifies the implementation and duplication of the hash function. 3) The decoupled bit vector can sit between the L1 and L2 caches or can also be integrated into the core. For systems in which the L1 and L2 caches are inclusive, the integrated bit vector can also filter out the L1 instruction and data caches if an L2 cache miss is detected.

3.1   SoC Energy Management

This section explains how the segmented Bloom Filter detects L2 Cache misses, and saves the overall system energy without losing performance in an in-order processor. In an in-order processor with two cache levels, severe stalls may occur due to an L2 Cache miss. This is because after a data access misses the L2 cache, it accesses the DRAM memory, which may take more than 100 cycles, depending on the processor frequency before the data returns.

By detecting an L2 cache read miss early with a segmented Bloom filter, we can save static energy of the system by turning off all or part of the core and by putting the L1 and L2 caches into drowsy or low-power state-preserving mode until the data returns. The overhead incurred by this technique is turning on and

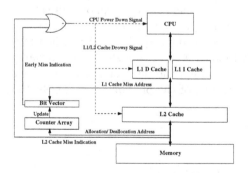
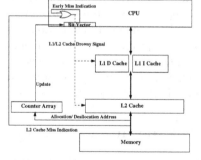

Fig. 3. SOC with caches not assumed to be inclusive and the bit vector below the L1 Cache

Fig. 4. SOC with inclusive caches and the bit-vector inside the CPU

turning off of the core and caches. This overhead is not much of a concern because the turn-off period overlaps with the memory access, which may take hundreds of cycles. Also, since it is known exactly when the data returns from memory, the turned-off units can be turned on in stages to save power. In addition to reducing static energy, dynamic energy of the system can also be reduced by preventing an L2 Cache access. Not only does this save the dynamic energy of the L2 but also reduces the bus energy consumption due to reduction in bus switching activity.

The segmented Bloom filter is shown in Figure 3 for a SOC in which the L1 and L2 caches which are not assumed to exhibit inclusive behaviour. In such a system, the bit vector is located just below the L1 caches. The CPU issues a cache address to the L1 data cache. On a miss, the bit vector snoops the address and signals in a cycle if the L2 cache does not have the cache line. On receiving the signal, the CPU is powered down and the L1 I and D and L2 caches can be put into the drowsy mode. The access to the L2 cache is also stopped.

Figure 4 shows a system where the L2 cache is inclusive with the L1 caches. Here, the bit vector is placed inside the core and can detect L2 cache misses before they are sent to the L1 caches. In a cache system using inclusion property, an L2 miss is also a miss in the L1 cache. Thus, a cache request address can be sent to directly to memory when a miss is detected by the bit vector inside the core.

For both systems, the bit vector may not be 100% consistent with the counter array as there is some delay occuring between the counter array and bit vector. This situation happens if incrementing the counter in the counter array is deferred till the time of a linefill. At that moment, the corresponding bit location in the bit vector might be 0. So, if the counter changes from 0 to 1, the counter array sends an update to the bit vector to set the bit location in the vector. Before this update reaches the bit vector, if the CPU accesses to the same bit location, then it reads 0 and assumes that this line is not in the cache and therefore forwards the request to memory. This drawback is eliminated if the counter is incremented at the time of the miss, rather than the linefill. By the time the actual linefill occurs, the bit vector will have been updated by the counter array. We see that segmenting the Bloom Filter allows the bit vector to be placed in a different physical location leading to more energy saving opportunities. This concept may be extended to cases where there are more than two levels of caches and the segmented bloom filter is used to filter out requests to the cache that is accessed just before DRAM memory. In such a case, though the counter array would be updated for the cache before memory, the bit vector may be kept at a place where it would be accessible with any of the previous cache levels, thus providing early miss indication.

4   Experimental Results

4.1   Experimental Framework and Benchmarks

We use SimpleScalar [3] to model the behavior of caches and segmented Bloom filter. The CPU is an in-order processor that stalls on a load operation, which is a typical behavior of many embedded processors. We compute the total energy consumption of the on-chip system including the CPU, caches and the Bloom filter. Our baseline model is the system with no Bloom filter. We use a total of eight applications, *bzip2, gcc, gzip, mcf, parser, vortex* and *vpr* from *SPECint2000*, *lame* MP3 player application from *MiBench* [4]. 2 billion instructions are simulated in the SPECint benchmarks while *lame* runs to completion. SPECInt benchmarks were chosen because they are known to stress the L2 cache. Only a few embedded applications such as *lame* could stress the L2 cache.

Table 1. Architectural assumptions

Drowsy-mode in/out time = 10 cycles
CPU turn-on/off time = 10 cycles
Shutdown Penalty = 20 cycles
Bit vector access time = 1 cycle
Memory access time = 100 cycles
CPU Energy = 2 x L1 Cache Energy
Cache Drowsy Energy = 1/6 x Cache Leakage Energy

Other pertinent architectural assumptions or fixed-parameters are listed in Table 1. The following assumptions are made to estimate the energy consumption of the baseline system (i.e. system without the Bloom filter) and a low-power system with the segmented Bloom filter. The time taken to put the caches in drowsy mode is 10 cycles, and it also takes another 10 cycles to put them into the normal mode. Similarly, the time taken to turn the CPU components off is also assumed to be 10 cycles. The total time for turning on and turning off, that is 20 cycles is called the *shutdown penalty*. The access time to the bit vector takes one cycle while the memory access time is 100 cycles. We also assume that the CPU energy consumption is twice the total L1 instruction and data cache energy consumption. This is a realistic assumption as embedded processors tend to have this trend as illustrated in [5]. The cache leakage energy in the drowsy mode is taken to be one sixth of the cache leakage energy as estimated by *Flautner et al* in [6].

We experiment two different cache architecture configurations as shown in Table 2. The first configuration has 2-way set-associative 8KB L1 instruction and data caches, 4-way 64KB L2 cache, a 8192-bit Bloom filter bit vector and a

Table 2. Architectural configurations

Description	Configuration 1	Configuration 2
L1 I and D cache	2-way 8KB	2-way 32KB
L2 cache	4-way 64 unified	4-way 256 unified
Bit vector size	8192 bits	32768 bits
Counter array size	8192 3-bit counters	32768 3-bit counters
L1 latency (cycles)	1	4
L2 latency (cycles)	10	30

Bloom filter counter array of 8192 entries with 3-bit[1] counter per entry. The line size is 32B for both L1 and L2 caches. The latencies of the L1 instruction and data caches and L2 cache are 1 and 10 cycles, respectively. This configuration represents low-end market such as industrial and automative applications in the embedded domain.

The second configuration includes 2-way set-associative 32KB L1 instruction and data caches, 4-way 256KB L2 cache, each has a 32B line size. The Bloom filter consists of a 32768-bit bit vector and a counter array of 32768 entries with 3-bit counter per entry.

The latencies of the L1 instruction and data caches and L2 cache are 4 and 30 cycles, respectively. This configuration represents the domain where slightly larger scale applications are targeted, e.g. consumer and wireless applications.

We have chosen the number of Bloom Filter entries to be around four times the number of cache lines. We experimented with different BF sizes and found this emperical ratio to provide best results. The area overhead for the Bloom Filters is about 6% of the L2 Cache area for both the configurations.

4.2 Energy Modeling

The L1 caches, L2 cache, bit vector and the counter array were designed using the *Artisan* 90nm SRAM library [7] in order to get an estimate on the dynamic and static energy consumption of the caches and the segmented Bloom filter. The Artisan SRAM generator is capable of generating synthesizable verilog code for SRAMs in 90nm technology. The generated datasheet gives an estimate of the read and write power of the generated SRAM. The datasheet also provides a standby current from which we can estimate the leakage power of the SRAM.

We have two system energy models. The first model is the baseline model in which the dynamic and static energy consumption of the CPU, L1 instruction and data caches and the L2 cache are calculated. The second system model is the low-power system model in which the dynamic and static energy consumption of the bit vector and counter array is also added to the rest of the system components. Table 3 shows the abbreviation of the variables used in the formulation to evaluate the system energy of the baseline and low-power system models.

Baseline System Energy Model.

$$Cyc_{off} = Num_{L2readmiss} * (Lat_{mem} - SP)$$
$$Cyc_{con} = Cyc_{tot} - Cyc_{off}$$
$$E_{cpu}^{base} = Cyc_{con} * CPU_{dyn} + Cyc_{off} * CPU_{leak}$$
$$E_{\$}^{base}(type) = Num_{cacheaccess} * \$_{dyn} + Cyc_{con} * \$_{leak} + Cyc_{off} * \$_{dr}$$
$$E_{sys}^{base} = E_{cpu}^{base} + E_{\$}^{base}(I) + E_{\$}^{base}(D)$$
$$+ E_{\$}^{base}(L2) \tag{1}$$

---

[1] Although the worst case number of bits required per counter is 12, we observe in our experiments that the value of each counter never exceeds 4. Thus we use 3 bits per counter to save energy and have a policy of disabling a particular counter if it saturates.

Table 3. Abbreviations and their descriptions

Abbreviation	Description
Cyc_{tot}	Total Number of Cycles
Cyc_{off}	Number of Idle Cycles
Cyc_{on}	Number of Active Cycles
$Num_{cacheaccess}$	Number of Cache Accesses
$Num_{L2readmiss}$	Number of L2 Read Misses
$Num_{L2access}$	Number of L2 Accesses without filtering
$Num_{L1access}$	Num of L1 Accesses
Num_{L2filt}	Number of Filtered L2 Misses
Lat_{mem}	Memory Latency
SP	Shutdown Penalty
Lat_{L2}	L2 latency
Lat_{vector}	Bit vector latency
CPU_{dyn}	CPU Dynamic Energy per Cycle
CPU_{leak}	CPU Leakage Energy per Cycle
$\$_{dyn}$	Cache Dynamic Energy per Cycle
$\$_{leak}$	Cache Leakage Energy per Cycle
$Cache_{dr}$	Cache Drowsy Energy per Cycle
BV_{dyn}	Bit Vector Dynamic Energy per Cycle
BV_{leak}	Bit Vector Leakage Energy per Cycle
BV_{dr}	Bit Vector Drowsy Energy per Cycle
$Counter_{dyn}$	Counter Array Dynamic Energy per Cycle
$Counter_{leak}$	Counter Array Leakage Energy per Cycle
$Counter_{dr}$	Counter Array Drowsy Energy per Cycle

Low-Power System Energy Model. We now estimate the energy consumption of the low-power system model having L1 and L2 caches which are assumed to exhibit inclusive behaviour with the segmented Bloom filter as follows:

$$Cyc_{off} = Num_{L2readmiss} * (Lat_{mem} - SP) + Num_{L2filt} * (Lat_{L2} - Lat_{vector})$$
$$Cyc_{on} = Cyc_{tot} - Cyc_{off}$$
$$E_{cpu}^{low} = Cyc_{on} * CPU_{dyn} + Cyc_{off} * CPU_{leak}$$
$$E_{L2}^{low} = (Num_{L2access} - Num_{L2filt}) * L2_{dyn} + Cyc_{on} * L2_{leak} + Cyc_{off} * L2_{dr}$$
$$E_{L1}^{low}(type) = Num_{L1access} * L1_{dyn} + Cyc_{on} * L1_{leak} + Cyc_{off} * L1_{dr}$$
$$E_{vector}^{low} = Num_{L2access} * BV_{dyn} + Cyc_{on} * BV_{leak} + Cyc_{off} * BV_{dr}$$
$$E_{counter}^{low} = Num_{L2access} * Counter_{dyn} + Cyc_{on} * Counter_{leak} + Cyc_{off} * Counter_{dr}$$
$$E_{sys}^{low} = E_{cpu} + E_{L1}^{low}(I) + E_{L1}^{low}(D) + E_{L2}^{low} + E_{vector}^{low} + E_{counter}^{low}$$

If the L1 and L2 caches are inclusive, then the energy consumption of the L1 cache is determined by the total number of L1 accesses less the number of filtered L2 misses. Also, the number of L2 accesses is replaced by the number of L1 accesses in the bit vector energy equation.

$$E_{L1}^{low}(type) = Num_{L1access} - Num_{L2filt} * L1_{dyn} + Cyc_{on} * L1_{leak} + Cyc_{off} * L1_{dr}$$
$$E_{vector}^{low} = Num_{L1access} * BV_{dyn} + Cyc_{on} * BV_{leak} + Cyc_{off} * BV_{dr}$$

Finally, the percentage savings in the total system(Dynamic + Leakage) energy is defined by the following equation:

$$\% \text{ Savings} = \frac{E_{sys}^{base} - E_{sys}^{low}}{E_{sys}^{base}} \tag{2}$$

4.3   Cache and Bloom Filter Statistics

The cache miss rates for the L1 instruction and data caches and L2 cache and the miss filter rates of the Bloom filter for the two configurations are provided in Table 4 and Table 5. The miss filter rates in the last column of the tables are the percentage of the L2 misses that the Bloom filter can detect. For instance, 94% of the L2 misses can be detected by the Bloom filter in *gcc* for the first configuration. The remaining 6% of them cannot be detected, i.e. false hit rate. The average miss filter rates across all benchmarks are 86% and 88% for both configurations. These rates imply that a great majority of the L2 misses can be caught by the Bloom filter. An 88% filtering of L2 misses also implies that the Bloom Filter is able to reduce accesses to the L2 cache by more than 30%.

Table 4. Cache miss and miss filtering rates for configuration 1

Benchmark	L1 I	L1 D	L2	Bloom Filter
bzip2	4.82%	0.002%	45.55%	83.21%
gcc	10.52%	4.19%	48.56%	94%
gzip	5.66%	0.01%	45.99%	96.12%
mcf	26.21%	1.24%	58.07%	87.60%
parser	6.08%	0.68%	36.68%	82.76%
vortex	3.84%	13.24%	21.41%	84.49%
vpr	3.64%	2.14%	13.35%	81.47%
lame	2.76%	0.78%	27.61%	81%
MEAN	**7.84%**	**2.78%**	**37.15%**	**86.33%**

Table 5. Cache miss and miss filtering rates for configuration 2

Benchmark	L1 I	L1 D	L2	Bloom Filter
bzip2	3.54%	0.0002%	48.90%	88.36%
gcc	10.01%	1.55%	55.92%	99.07%
gzip	4.72%	0.001%	12.45%	95.25%
mcf	25.12%	0.0001%	63.74%	83.43%
parser	3.60%	0.05%	31.81%	86.38%
vortex	1.36%	4.84%	5.88%	77.96%
vpr	1.71%	0.21%	39.19%	83%
lame	0.99%	0.30%	12.36%	93.88%
MEAN	**6.38%**	**0.87%**	**33.78%**	**88.42%**

4.4   Energy Consumption Results

Table 6 shows the L2 dynamic energy savings for the two configurations with respect to the L2 cache in the baseline model. *gzip*, *parser*, *vortex* and *lame* suffer a drop in L2 dynamic energy savings in the second configuration because of improvements in L2 miss rates for using a much larger L2 cache. As the L2 miss rate improves, the number of misses of which the Bloom filter can take advantage to shutdown the CPU and caches diminishes. The L2 energy savings drop rates in *gzip*, *vortex* and *lame* are more dramatic because their miss filtering rates also drop in the second configuration except for *lame* where it actually improves. However, this increase in the miss filtering rate is not sufficient to boost the L2 energy savings for *lame*. The miss filtering rate for *parser* also improves in the second configuration. This explains why the drop in L2 energy savings in the second configuration for *parser* is not as significant as the others.

In summary, using the segmented Bloom filter provides an average of 33% and 30% savings in the L2 dynamic energy respectively for the two configurations.

Figure 5 plots the SoC static energy savings. The SoC static energy includes the leakage energy of the CPU, L1 and L2 caches in the baseline model, and

Table 6. L2 cache energy savings

Benchmark	Configuration 1	Configuration 2
bzip2	37.90%	43.21%
gcc	45.65%	55.40%
gzip	44.21%	11.85%
mcf	50.87%	53.18%
parser	30.35%	27.47%
vortex	18.09%	4.59%
vpr	10.88%	32.53%
lame	22.37%	11.60%
MEAN	**32.54%**	**29.98%**

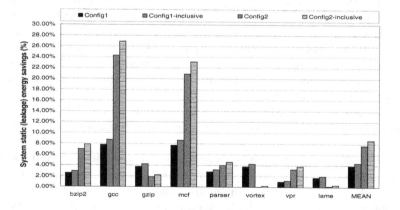

Fig. 5. Static SoC energy results

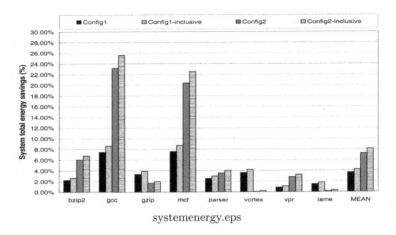

systemenergy.eps

Fig. 6. Total SoC energy results

the leakage energy of the bit vector and the counter array are accounted for the low-power SoC model. In addition to the two configurations, we also show the results of the inclusive versions for each configuration. In the inclusive version, the bit vector is embedded within the core and filters out the L1 instruction and data cache accesses as well.

The percentage increases in the system static energy savings are quite significant for *gcc* and *mcf* from a smaller configuration to larger one. In configuration 2, 24% and 21% of the static energy consumption can be saved by using the segmented Bloom filter for *gcc* and *mcf*, respectively. The percentage increase in *gcc* is higher than *mcf* because the L2 miss rate increases and the miss filtering rate improves in *gcc* . Similar to the L2 dynamic energy results, when switching from a smaller configuration to a larger one, *gzip*, *vortex* and *lame* benchmarks observe some percentage loss in the static energy savings due to lower L2 miss rates. However, the static energy savings of *parser* in configuration 2 is slightly higher than that of configuration 1 even though its L2 miss rate is lower. This is because the high miss filtering rate in configuration 2 is sufficient to boost the energy savings.

The inclusive versions for both configurations show slightly better savings than the cases where inclusion is not assumed, for all benchmarks because the inclusive configuration allows early turning off the system components, which reduces the system static energy consumption.

The average system static energy savings are 3.9%, 4.4%, 7.7% and 8.7% for configuration 1, its inclusive version, configuration 2 and its inclusive version, respectively.

Figure 6 plots the total SoC energy savings in percentage. The total SoC energy is defined as the total dynamic and static energy consumed by the CPU, L1 caches, L2 cache for the baseline model. This also includes the dynamic and static energy consumption of the bit vector and the counter array for the low-power SoC model. Here, we see a very similar trend to the system static energy savings graph above in terms of rise and falls in the system total energy savings when changing to a larger configuration from a smaller one.

Similar to the SoC static energy reduction, the inclusive versions for both configurations reduces the total energy more than the cases where inclusion property is not assumed, for all benchmarks because of reductions in the number of L1 cache accesses, which reduces the dynamic as well as the static energy consumption.

The average total SoC energy savings for the first configuration and its inclusive version are 3.6% and 4.2%, respectively. These rates go up to 7.2% and 8.1% for the second configuration and its inclusive version. The reason for the additional improvement is due to much higher the L2 latency in the second configuration. A large amount of static energy can be saved during the long-latency L2 accesses by turning off the CPU, caches and also the counter array. Since the bit vector access time is constant, the effective gain in the total energy with increasing L2 latencies (i.e. larger L2 caches) also rises.

5   Related Work

The initial purpose of Bloom Filters was to build memory efficient database applications. Bloom filters have found numerous applications in networking and database areas [8] [9] [10] [11] [12] [13]. Bloom filters are also used as microarchitectural blocks for tracking load/store addresses in load/store queues. For instance, *Akkary et al.* [14] uses one to detect the load-store conflicts in the store queue. *Sethumadhvan et al.* [15] improve the scalability for load store queues with a Bloom filter. More recently, *Roth* [16] uses a Bloom filter to reduce the number of load re-executions for load/store queue optimizations.

The earliest example of tracking cache misses with a counting Bloom filter is given by *Moshovos et al.* [17], which proposes a hardware structure called *Jetty* to filter out cache snoops in SMP systems. Each processing node has a *Jetty* that tracks its own L2 cache accesses, and snoop requests are first checked in the *Jetty* before searching the cache. This is reported to reduce snoop energy consumption in SMP systems. A *Jetty*-like filter is also used by *Peir et al.* [18] for detecting load misses early in the pipeline so as to initiate speculative execution. Similarly, *Mehta et al.* [19] also uses a *Jetty*-like filter to detect L2 misses early so that they can stall the instruction fetch to save processor energy. We, on the other hand, propose a decoupled Bloom filter structure where the small bit vector can potentially be kept within the processor core to perform system dynamic and static energy conservation of L1 and L2 caches and the core itself.

Memik et al. [20] proposes some early cache miss detection hardware techniques encapsulated as *Mostly No Machine(MNM)* to detect misses early in the multi-level caches below L1 (i.e. L2, L3 and etc). Their goal is to reduce dynamic cache energy and to improve the performance by bypassing the caches that will miss. The MNM is a multi-ported hardware structure that collects block replacement and allocation addresses from these caches and can be accessed after the L1 access or in parallel with it. In comparison to the MNM, the segmented

Bloom filter design allows the processor to access only the bit vector, which is smaller and much faster. Potentially, it can run at the processor frequency. Since the counter array is located at the L2 cache, it can run at the same clock frequency as the slower L2 cache. This is a more energy-efficient design than the MNM. Besides, the bit vector can also be located inside the processor so that the L1 instruction and data cache misses can also be filtered out in the case of an inclusion between the L1s and L2. This way, we can save L1 I and D cache dynamic energy by not accessing them at all, and static energy by putting them into a drowsy mode. The *MNM* did not discuss static energy consumption in the caches, CPU or filters.

6   Conclusion

This paper introduces a segmented counting Bloom filter to perform microarchitectural energy management in an embedded SoC environment and evaluates its energy saving capabilities. We have shown that the segmented Bloom filter technique can be an efficient microarchitectural mechnanism for reducing the total SoC energy consumption. A significant part of the total SoC energy including L2 dynamic cache energy, L1, L2 and CPU static static energy can be saved in a system where the cache hierarchy is not assumed to exhibit inclusive behaviour. However, the segmented design is shown to be particularly more energy-efficient if the cache hierarchy exhibits inclusive behaviour. This is because the segmented design provides the opportunity to make the bit vector accesible before the L1 Cache access and allows for detection of misses much earlier in the memory hierarchy. The segmented counting bloom filter has been shown to filter out more than 89% of L2 misses, causing a 30% reduction in accesses to the L2 Cache. This results in a saving of more than 33% of L2 Dynamic Energy. The results also demonstrated that the overall SoC energy can be reduced by up to 9% using the proposed segmented Bloom filter.

As future embedded applications demand more memory and shrinking feature sizes allow more transistors on a die, embedded processors would be inclined to have larger caches. Having these longer latency caches would provide more opportunities for the segmented design to facilitate microarchitectural energy management earlier in the memory hierarchy. Therefore cache miss detection in general and the segmented filter design presented in this paper would play a key role in energy management for future embedded processors.

References

1. Bloom, B.H.: Space/time trade-offs in hash coding with allowable errors. Communications of the ACM **13**(4) (1970)
2. Fan, L., Cao, P., Almeida, J., Broder, A.: Summary cache: A scalable wide-area web cache sharing protocol. IEEE/ACM Transactions on Networking **8**(3) (2000) 281–293

3. Burger, D., Austin, T.M.: The simplescalar tool set, version 2.0. Technical Report 1342, Computer Science Department, University of Wisconsin-Madison and MicroComputer Research Labs, Intel Corporation (1997)
4. Guthaus, M.R., Ringenberg, J.S., Ernst, D., Austin, T.M., Mudge, T., Brown, R.B.: MiBench: A Free, Commercially Representative Embedded Benchmark Suite. In: the IEEE 4th Annual Workshop on Workload Characterization, Austin, TX (2001)
5. Fan, D., Tang, Z., Huang, H., Gao, G.R.: An energy efficient tlb design methodology. In: Proceedings of the International Symposium on Low Power Electronics and Design. (2005)
6. Flautner, K., Kim, N.S., Martin, S., Blaauw, D., Mudge, T.: Drowsy caches: Simple techniques for reducing leakage power. In: Proceedings of the 29th Annual International Symposium on Computer Architecture. (2002)
7. Artisan: Sram libraries. http://www.artisan.com (2005)
8. Border, A., Mitzenmacher, M.: Network application of bloom filters: A Survey. In: 40th Annual Allerton Conference on Communication, Control, and Computing. (2002)
9. Rhea, S., Kubiatowicz, J.: Probabilistic location and routing. In: IEEE INFOCOM'02. (2002)
10. Dharmapurikar, S., Krishnamurthy, P., Sproull, T., Lockwood, J.: Deep packet inspection using parallel bloom filters. In: IEEE Hot Interconnects 12. (2003)
11. Kumar, A., Xu, J., Wang, J., Spatschek, O., Li, L.: Space-code bloom filter for efficient per-flow traffic measurement. In: Proc. IEEE INFOCOM. (2004)
12. Chang, F., Feng, W., Li, K.: Approximate caches for packet classification. In: Proc. IEEE INFOCOM. (2004)
13. Cohen, S., Matias, Y.: Spectral bloom filters. In: Proceedings of the 2003 ACM SIGMOD International Conference on Management of Data. (2003)
14. Akkary, H., Rajwar, R., Srinivasan, S.T.: Checkpoint processing and recovery: Towards scalable large instruction window processors. In: Proceedings of the 36th International Symposium for Microarchitecture. (2003)
15. Sethumadhavan, S., Desikan, R., Burger, D., Moore, C.R., Keckler, S.W.: Scalable hardware memory disambiguation for high ilp processors. In: Proceedings of the 36th International Symposium for Microarchitecture. (2003)
16. Roth, A.: Store vulnerability window (svw): Re-execution filtering for enhanced load optimization. In: Proceedings of the 32th International Symposium on Computer Architecture (ISCA-05). (2005)
17. Moshovos, A., Memik, G., Falsafi, B., Choudhary, A.: Jetty: Snoop filtering for reduced power in smp servers. In: Proceedings of International Symposium on High Performance Computer Architecture (HPCA-7). (2001)
18. Peir, J.K., Lai, S.C., Lu, S.L., Stark, J., Lai, K.: Bloom filtering cache misses for accurate data speculation and prefetching. In: Proceedings of the 16th International Conference of Supercomputing. (2002) 189–198
19. Mehta, N., Singer, B., Bahar, R.I., Leuchtenburg, M., Weiss, R.: Fetch halting on critical load misses. In: Proceedings of the The 22nd International Conference on Computer Design. (2004)
20. Memik, G., Reinman, G., Mangione-Smith, W.H.: Just say no: Benefits of early cache miss determination. In: Proceedings of the Ninth International Symposium on High Performance Computer Architecture. (2003)

Estimating Energy Consumption for an MPSoC Architectural Exploration

Rabie Ben Atitallah[1], Smail Niar[1], Alain Greiner[2],
Samy Meftali[1], and Jean Luc Dekeyser[1]

[1] Laboratoire d'informatique fondamentale de Lille,
Université des sciences et technologies de Lille, France
{benatita, niar, meftali, dekeyser}@lifl.fr
[2] Laboratoire d'informatique de Paris6,
Université Pierre et Murie Curie, France
alain.greiner@lip6.fr

Abstract. Early energy estimation is increasingly important in MultiProcessor System-On-Chip (MPSoC) design. Applying traditional approaches, which consist in delaying the estimation until the architectural layout has been produced, is inefficient and prevents the rapid exploration of alternative architectures. In this paper, we present a framework for architectural exploration as part of MPSoC design. Our framework allows configurations that offer a good performance/energy tradeoffs to be found early in the design flow. The hardware components, described at the Cycle-Accurate Bit-Accurate (CABA) level of SystemC, were taken from the SoCLib library. For each component in the library, we developed an energy model using both physical measurements and analytical models of energy consumption. These models indicate a good accuracy/speed tradeoffs. Plugging the energy models into the SoCLib architectural simulator makes it easy to estimate the application's performance and energy consumption. The effectiveness of our method is illustrated through design space exploration (DSE) for a parallel signal processing application.

1 Introduction

As advances in technology lead to smaller and smaller feature sizes, in accordance with Moore's law, more and more transistors will be integrated on a single die. Such huge transistor budgets stress designers' capacity to design and verify the resulting very complex chips, making the gap between chip complexity and the productivity of the logic design wider and wider. Thus, the multiprocessor system-on-chip (MPSoC) architecture becomes an incontrovertible solution for the embedded systems designed for applications that require intensive parallel computations. MPSoC are generally very heterogeneous, that can, for example, contain memories (Cache, SRAM, FIFO...), processors (MCU, DSP...), interconnecting elements (Bus, Crossbar, NoC...), I/O peripherals and FPGA [8]. This heterogeneity makes the DSE of such systems one of the most important design challenges. Increases in clock frequency, IP multiplicity and silicon integration are accompanied by a dramatic increase in energy consumption. Thus, in addition to traditional performance criteria, such as area and execution speed, it has become imperative to take energy consumption into account when designing MPSoC.

W. Grass et al. (Eds.): ARCS 2006, LNCS 3894, pp. 298–310, 2006.

In any MPSoC design flow, an efficient architectural exploration requires a set of tools capable of estimating performance and energy consumption at different abstraction levels. The availability of such estimators at different levels allows designers to make fast decisions at several design stages, which reduces the exploration space, shortens the time to market and increases the design team's productivity. Unfortunately, to our knowledge, there are very few tools that allow rapid and accurate energy consumption evaluation for MPSoC. To remedy this problem, we have developed a flexible architectural exploration environment that allows energy consumption to be estimated at the cycle-accurate bit-accurate (CABA) level. This framework provides accurate estimates within a reasonable simulation time. It will be used in our future research to allow performance and enrgy consumption to be estimated at higher levels.

This paper in organized as follows. An overview of related work on system performance and energy consumption estimation at different abstraction levels is given in section 2. Section 3 describes the major estimation techniques at the CABA level. Details about our energy consumption models are presented in section 4. Section 5 presents experimental results for a parallel version of the DCT application, and section 6 offers our conclusions and prospects for future research.

2 Related Work

Significant research efforts have been devoted to developing tools for evaluating performance and energy consumption at the different abstraction levels in embedded system design. In the existing tools, performance and energy consumption are generally evaluated at four different levels:

- the functional level, at which system behaviour is inaccurate and un-timed;
- the TLM (Transactional Level Model) level, at which time is introduced approximately;
- the CABA (Cycle Accurate-Bit Accurate) level, at which the system is described in detail with respect to time; and
- the Register Transfer Level or RTL (i.e. the physical level), at which the description is given at a low level that corresponds precisely to physical module's structure and behaviour.

Among the existing tools for low abstraction levels we can mention, SPICE [4], Diesel [12] and PETROL [11], which operate at the RTL level. These tools are fairly accurate, but require significant amount of simulation time, because each component must be estimated at very low levels. At such low level, it is very hard to explore different complex architecture alternatives because many details must be set.

To reduce the simulation time, several studies have proposed evaluating system performance at higher abstraction levels. These tools use an architectural level simulator to evaluate system performance and an analytic power model to estimate consumption for each platform component. Wattch [7] and Simplepower [15] are two of the tools available for this level. With these two tools, the power consumption of the main internal units is estimated using power macro-models, produced during lower-level simulations. The contributions of the internal unit activities are calculated and added together during the execution of the program on a micro-architectural simulator. In our approach, the functional unit activities are also added together to evaluate the dynamic part of the energy consumption.

For the functional level, Tiwari et al. [14] have introduced the concept of Instruction Level Power Analysis (ILPA). They associate a power consumption model with instructions or instruction pairs, which are characterized using measurements on a real chip. The power consumed by a program running on the processor can then be estimated by using a standard instruction-set simulator to extract instruction traces, and then adding up the total cost of the instructions. Estimation at high levels reduces the simulation time and thus permits a rapid exploration. However, the higher the description level, the more difficult it is to produce sufficiently accurate estimates. In this paper, we propose an approach that solves the problem of the accuracy/speed trade-off.

All the studies mentioned above concern single-processor Systems-on-Chip (SoC). To our knowledge, little research has been devoted to performance and energy consumption estimations for architectural exploration in MPSoC design. In fact, we are aware of only one recently published approach that allows cycle-accurate power estimation for multiprocessor systems [10]. That approach, called MPARM, focus on the exploration for the cache components. This approach is limited because the authors used in-house low level energy models. Our approach does not have this limitation as we provide an open and flexible environment for performance and power consumption estimation at the CABA level of MPSoC design.

3   Energy Consumption Estimation at CABA Level

Compared to lower levels, estimations done at the CABA level are sufficiently rapid to allow the entire multiprocessor system to be analyzed in a reasonable time. Doing the estimations at this level permits flexibility in the choice of performance or energy model parameters for each component, which makes it possible to separately evaluate the processing part (processor and memory activities) and the communication part (interconnection network activity).

The total energy consumption of a given system is obtained by adding the consumption of each system component together. Two types of energy consumption can be distinguished: dynamic consumption, which corresponds to component activity (e.g., internal circuit switching), and static consumption, which corresponds to leakage currents. For a long time, dynamic power consumption has been considered more significant than static consumption. However, this point of view changed with the advent of new sub-micron technologies, for which the two types of consumption both have their degree of importance. For this reason, real measurements with low level tools remain the most accurate solution.

For this study, we developed energy models for the main components in the SoCLib MPSoC architecture: the processor, the cache memory, the shared SRAM memory and the interconnection network. We integrated these models into the SoCLib simulator, taking the architectural and technological parameters into account. Our energy estimation strategy is based on identifying each component's pertinent activities. For this, a counter is allotted to each kind of activity, and these counters are incremented during the simulation if the corresponding activity occurs during the current cycle. Thus, the

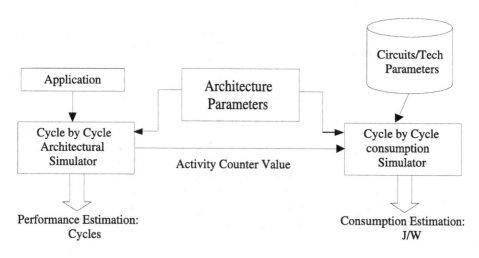

Fig. 1. Performances and energy estimation at CABA level

number of activity occurrences is obtained for each component. An energy consumption cost is also evaluated for each activity, calculated from the developed power models and from physical measurements.

The application's total energy consumption is calculated using the following equation:

$$E = \sum_i N_i \times C_i \tag{1}$$

N_i: Number of times where the activity i is executed
C_i: Energy consumption for one occurrence of activity i

Figure 1 shows our estimation strategy in detail. First, the architectural parameters (e.g., number of processors, cache size) are specified. Interval by interval, or at the end of the simulation, the values on the activity counters are transmitted to the energy consumption models to calculate the energy dissipation per interval or the total dissipation. The consumption simulator contains energy models for each component. This approach was applied to a multiprocessor architecture composed of several R3000 MIPS processors, data and instructions caches, shared instructions and data SRAM memory, a timer and locks engine. These locks are used to ensure inter-processor synchronization. All these components, which are reused from SoCLib library [6], are described in SystemC [5] at the CABA level and are VCI compliant.

4   Energy Modeling for the SoCLib

The energy consumed by a circuit depends on its physical implementation and its technological parameters. To estimate activity consumption, the most accurate approach works with the component at the physical level, taking measurements directly on the component. However, this solution requires a lot of time and effort to design the circuit and to handle low level tools. In our study, we used low level simulations for the

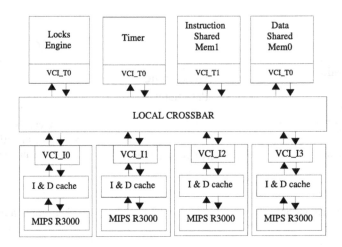

Fig. 2. Example of SoCLib MPSoC [6]

activity energy consumption evaluation when possible. The values estimated at the physical level are injected into the energy model at the CABA level. Consequently, our approach is a hybrid technique, relying on both physical measurement and analytic modeling. This hybrid approach yields acceptable levels of precision and speed. Still, measuring the activities with low level CAD tools is not always possible for all the MPSoC components. For instance, such a characterization is not possible for the interconnection network, the crossbar, which is not a preexisting component like the processor or the memory. In fact, the connection (or the wire) length in the crossbar depends on the structure of the MPSoC and the mapping of the components on the die. For this reason, we chose to use an analytical model to evaluate the activity energy cost.

4.1 SRAM Memory Energy Model

For an SRAM, three main activities consume energy: *Read*, *Write* and *Idle*. These activities correspond respectively to the read access mode, the write access mode and the waiting state. This approach is similar to the approach proposed by Loghi et Al. [10]. To estimate an activity's energy cost, different SRAM sizes are simulated at the physical level using the ELDO analog simulator [3]. The logical synthesis, the placement, the routing and the layout extraction is carried out using CAD tools in the ALLIANCE VLSI design environment [1]. The objective is to produce a parameterized energy model for estimating the cost of SRAM activities, according to the number of words (M) and number of bits per word (N). This model facilitates the architectural exploration. The simulation results show that the energy costs change linearly according to the number of words and number of bits per word. This is presented in figure 3 for a read access.

From the simulation results, the following equations can be written:

$$
\begin{aligned}
E_{read} &= (R_0 + R_1 \cdot N) \cdot (R_2 + R_3 \cdot M) \\
E_{write} &= (W_0 + W_1 \cdot N) \cdot (W_2 + W_3 \cdot M) \\
E_{idle} &= (I_0 + I_1 \cdot N) \cdot (I_2 + I_3 \cdot M)
\end{aligned}
\tag{2}
$$

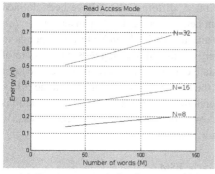

(a) Energy cost variation in terms of M

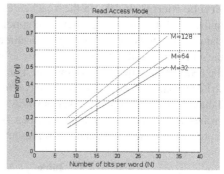

(b) Energy cost variation in terms of N

Fig. 3. Energy cost variation in terms of M (the number of words) and N (the number of bits per word)

Using the experimental values, these equations must be solved in order to find the coefficients R_i, W_i and I_i and to obtain a simple estimation model for the SRAM activities. However, these parameters are only valid for a given technology process. To obtain a general model, it is necessary to find the weighting coefficient α to move from the parameters of technology λ_0 to another technology λ:

$$R_i = R_{i0} \cdot (\lambda/\lambda_0)^\alpha$$
$$W_i = W_{i0} \cdot (\lambda/\lambda_0)^\alpha \qquad (3)$$
$$I_i = I_{i0} \cdot (\lambda/\lambda_0)^\alpha$$

Using 2 and 3 the following model is deduced for energy consumption calculation in the SRAM:

$$E_{SRAM} = n_{read} \cdot E_{read} + n_{write} \cdot E_{write} + n_{idle} \cdot E_{idle} \qquad (4)$$

n_read, n_write and n_idle are respectively the counter values of read access, write access and waiting cycles.

4.2 Cache Memory Energy Model

Xcache component description. In the SoCLib library, the xcache component contains the instruction cache and the data cache. These two caches share the same VCI interface with the crossbar. Each cache is controlled by an independent FSM. Instructions and data are represented on 32 bits. The size and the shape (e.g., block size, associativity) of each cache are parameterized. In the example presented in the next section, the two caches are direct mapped caches, and they use the "write through" policy to handle write hits. The xcache has a FIFO buffer to store read and write requests for missed data and un-cached data. The VCI interface controller reads the FIFO buffer and constructs a request packet for several addresses on the same page (4Kbytes). The xcache is designed to answer to the processor request in one cycle.

Xcache energy model. In the xcache description, different states have been defined in the SoCLib to guarantee that the component behaves correctly. For instance, the *Init* state corresponds to the cache initialization, and the *Write_Updt* state corresponds to the data loading of the cache. The xcache energy consumption depends on the state of the FSM that controls the component. Each state corresponds to one or several read or write operations. These operations may affect the tag array, the data array and the FIFO. Tables 1 and 2 represent the various FSM states that control the data and instructions caches and their corresponding activities. In these tables, *R* represents a read access, *W* represents a write access and "–" represents a wait state.

Table 1. DATA cache FSM

	Activity Type		
DATA cache FSM	TAG	DATA	FIFO
DCACHE_INIT	W	–	–
DCACHE_IDLE	R	R	–
DCACHE_WRITE_UPDT	–	W	–
DCACHE_WRITE_REQ	R	R	W
DCACHE_MISS_REQ	–	–	W
DCACHE_MISS_WAIT	–	–	–
DCACHE_MISS_UPDT	W	W	–
DCACHE_UNC_REQ	–	–	W
DCACHE_UNC_WAIT	–	–	–

Table 2. Instructions cache FSM

	Activity Type	
INST cache FSM	TAG	DATA
ICACHE_INIT	W	–
ICACHE_IDLE	R	R
ICACHE_WAIT	–	–
DCACHE_UPDT	W	W
DCACHE_UNC_WAIT	–	–

Therefore, estimating the energy consumption of an FSM state is equivalent to evaluating the energy cost of a write or read access to the SRAM memory (tag array or data array) and evaluating the energy cost of a write access to the FIFO buffer. The procedure for the SRAM has already been explained in the preceding section, and the procedure for the FIFO buffer is the same as for the SRAM. We conducted several simulations with different FIFO buffer sizes using the ELDO tool to find a parameterized model.

We defined a complete set of cache access modes, with different power models: *Write_Tag*, *Read_Tag*, *Write_Data*, *Read_Data*, *Write_Fifo* and *Idle*. For each access mode, we declared a counter in the SystemC description of the component. These counters correspond to the number of different access modes and states of the SRAM arrays. At the end of the simulation, the values of these counters are read, and then they are multiplied by the activity energy costs to find the overall consumption of the xcache component. Note, it is also possible to read these counters on interval basis.

4.3   Processor Energy Model

Energy consumption at the processor level depends not only on the application to be executed, but also on the processor's architecture. For this reason, this architecture must be adapted to the system specifications in terms of performance, size and consumption. In our study, we used the Mips R3000 processor. This scalar processor has a 5-stage pipeline. In our simplified power consumption model for the Mips R3000, we considered two states: *Running* (execution of an instruction) and *Waiting* for data or instruction (due to a data or instruction cache miss). The energy consumptions for these two states are different.

The processor's energy consumption in the active state depends on the instruction to be executed. The set of all the instructions' energies will constitute the processor energy model, and the cost of each instruction can be determined from low level measurements. This approach has been used by several other authors [10] [13]. For instance Sinha [13] demonstrated that for the StrongARM SA-1100 processor, the maximum current variation between instructions during the execution of a program is only 8%. The Hitachi HS-4 processor behaves in the same way [13]. Consequently, for a processor with a relatively simple architecture, like the Mips R3000, a consumption model that considers only the average current per instruction is sufficient. Thus, we adopted the following energy model for estimating processor energy consumption:

$$E_{processor} = n_{running} \cdot E_{running} + n_{idle} \cdot E_{idle} \qquad (5)$$

Where $n_{running}$ represents the number of cycles during which the processor is in the running state and n_{idle} represents the number of cycles during which the processor is in an idle state.

4.4   Crossbar Energy Model

The crossbar interconnection network connects one processor and its caches to one of the shared components (e.g., RAMs, timer or lock engine). In the connection protocol, the processor is called the *initiator*, and the component with which the connection is made is called the *target*. The crossbar in our MPSoC architecture was chosen for performance reasons, specifically for the large bandwidth constraint. However, the physical implementation constraints allow only a limited number of processors (8 or less) to be embedded in the SoC. The main activity of the crossbar is to transfer data between two VCI ports, and its most significant consumption is at the wire level. The energy dissipation of these wire connections depends on their length and the used process technology. Thus, to estimate the crossbar consumption accurately, the connection lengths between components must first be estimated, and these lengths depend on the final organization of the components on the chip. For our study, we supposed a particular component structure in order to obtain approximate wire lengths, using the Graal tool (Layout editor) in the Alliance environment to measure the size of each component according to the process technology. The following equation yields the energy consumption during a data transfer from the initiator i to the target j:

$$E = \sum_{N} E_{i,j} \qquad (6)$$

i and *j*: *Number of ports*

N: *Number of transmitted words in the packet*

$E_{i,j}$: *Energy transfer cost of a word from i to j.*

A word transfer from an initiator *i* to a target *j* (request word) or vice versa (response word) corresponds to several wire activation along the VCI request interface (93 bits) or the VCI response interface (46 bits). The energy cost $E_{i,j}$ for transferring one word depends on the number of bits on the interface that commutated between 0 towards 1 or conversely (noted α)and on the bit energy cost transfer E_0.

$$E_{i,j} = \alpha \cdot E_0(L_{i,j}) \tag{7}$$

α can be calculated in the crossbar component description, though this will slow the simulation down, or it can be estimated to be half the number of wires of the request or response interface. E_0 which depends on the wire length between *i* and *j* (noted $L_{i,j}$) is calculated as follows:

$$E_0 = WirePower(L_{i,j}) \cdot Wiredelay(L_{i,j})$$

$$WirePower = \frac{1}{2} \cdot C(L_{i,j}) \cdot V^2 \tag{8}$$

Where wireDelay is the data propagation time between i and j and $C(L_{i,j})$ is the capacitance of the wire $C(L_{i,j})$. These two parameters are deduced from the wire model used in the Cacti Tool [2].

5   Experimental Results

The previously developed energy models were integrated into the SoCLib architectural simulator in order to benefit from a fast architectural exploration environment for MP-SoC design. To validate our approach, we used a Visiophony application for the UMTS network. For this application, we chose a minimal resolution using the QCIF format (144*176 pixels). The coding standard chosen was the H.263, adapted for Visiophony and Videoconference applications. For this paper, we evaluated only the DCT task to validate our approach of DSE.

To evaluate the impact of the number of processors on the performance and the total consumption of the system, we executed the DCT task on QCIF image macroblocs, using systems with 1 up to 8 processors. The size of the instruction and data cache was set to 4 KB, and the MIPS frequency was set at 50MHz. All the processors execute the same DCT task but on different image macroblocs. Figure 4 reports the execution time in cycles and the total energy consumption in mJ.

Given these results, it seems that adding processors to the system decreases execution time, which improves system performance. This variation is not linear because the processors share resources, and sometimes they cannot reach the same target simultaneously, which necessitates waiting cycles and diminishes system performance. In terms of energy consumption, up to a certain number of processors, the total system energy consumption decreases as the number of execution cycles is reduced, and then it tends to stabilize as the system performance improves. But increasing the number of processors

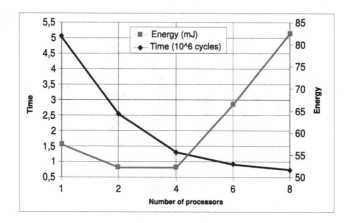

Fig. 4. Performance and energy variation in terms of the number of processors

over a certain limit tends to be ineffective, as it just adds new conflicts at the crossbar, leading to more waiting cycles. More conflicts at the crossbar and more waiting cycles dramatically alter overall performances, especially in terms of power consumption.

Next, we used a 4-processor configuration to examine the impact of varying instruction and data cache size on the performance and energy consumption of the whole system. We executed the DCT-parallelized algorithm using instruction and data caches of increasing size; from 2 KB up to 16KB. Our results are presented in figure 5.

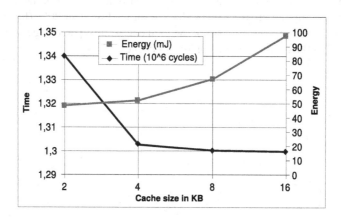

Fig. 5. Variations in performance and energy consumption in terms of cache size with 4 processors

The increase in the cache size significantly increases overall system energy consumption. In general, larger caches improve system performance; however, this depends on the size of the task or of the data to be handled. In our example, the move from 4KB to 8 KB, for instance, improved performance by 0.2%, but also increased energy consumption by 29%. For the 8 KB and 16 KB caches, the performance did not change but energy consumption increased by 45%.

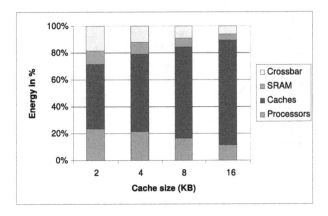

Fig. 6. Consumption of energy in the various components

Figure 6 presents the energy consumption (expressed in percentages) of the system components for the different caches sizes. In our multiprocessor system, caches constitute the primary source of consumption. In fact, instruction and data caches are responsible for 50% to 80% of the entire system's energy consumption. It is interesting to note that the increase in cache size decreases the number of caches misses, which reduces processor execution time and minimizes the traffic on the interconnection network and the access to the different memories. Consequently, except for the caches, the energy percentage of the all components decreases significantly as cache size increases. The processors are responsible for between 10% and 23% of the overall energy consumption, while the crossbar generally consumes less than 20% (for 2 KB). The shared SRAM consumes a small part of the total energy, this percentage varies between 10.09% (for 2 KB caches) and 7% (for 16 KB caches).

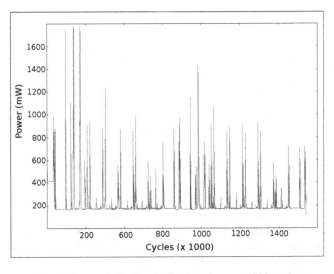

Fig. 7. Power dissipation in the Crossbar per 1000 cycles

Up to this point, we have focused on the advantages of estimating performance and energy consumption on the CABA level to allow design exploration for MPSoC. Our approach may be also useful for managing the power dissipated by the system. In fact, in a circuit, power consumption is responsible for thermal dissipation, which must be taken into account for reliability reasons. This heat problem is worsened on multiprocessor systems-on-chips, which tend to heat up, which in turn accelerates the functional degradation of the silicon. This dissipated power can be calculated directly from the energy and the execution time, given by the number of cycles. Our environment permits the power consumption to be calculated cycle by cycle or over n consecutive cycles (interval) for each component. This makes it easier to control overall thermal dissipation and power peaks, thus making batteries last longer.

Figure 7 represents the power consumption in the crossbar per 1000-cycle interval. This information can be used to verify that the circuit operated correctly during the execution of the application.

6   Conclusion

A reliable DSE for multiprocessor systems-on-chip requires well-developed simulation techniques. MPSoC design also requires rapid and accurate tools for estimating performance and energy consumption. In this study, we enhanced the SoCLib CABA-level architecture simulator with an energy consumption estimator. The designed environment is flexible and allows rapid and accurate performance estimations. Future research will focus on several areas. First, we plan to apply the same methodology to more complex architectures, including other types of processors and interconnection networks. Second, we hope to adapt this approach for higher abstraction levels, such as the TLM level. Finally, we are planning to integrate this framework into our complete design flow, Gaspard[9].

References

1. ALLIANCE home page. http://www-asim.lip6.fr/recherche/alliance/.
2. CACTI home page.   http://research.compaq.com/wrl/people/jouppi/ CACTI.
3. Mentor home page. http://www.mentor.com.
4. SPICE manual. University of Berkeley (USA), URL: http://bwrc.eecs.berkeley. edu/Classes/IcBook/SPICE/.
5. Systemc. World Wide Web document, URL: http://www.systemc.org/.
6. SoCLib project: An integrated system-on-chip modeling and simulation platform, 2003. Technical report, CNRS, URL: http://soclib.lip6.fr/.
7. D. Brooks, V. Tiwari, and M. Martonosi. Wattch: a framework for architectural-level power analysis and optimizations. In *Proceedings of the 27th annual international symposium on Computer architecture*, pages 83–94, 2000.
8. Ahmed A. Jerraya and Wayne Wolf. *Multiprocessor Systems-on-Chips*, chapter 1. Elsevier, September 2004.
9. Laboratoire d'informatique fondamentale de Lille, Université des sciences et technologies de Lille. Gaspard home page. http://www.lifl.fr/west/gaspard/, 2005.

10. M. Loghi, M. Poncino, and L. Benini. Cycle-accurate power analysis for multiprocessor Systems-on-a-Chip. In *GLSVLSI*, Boston, Massachusetts, USA, April 2004.

11. R. Peset-Llopis and K. Goossens. The petrol approach to high-level power estimation. In *Proceedings of the ISLPED*, Monterey, California, USA, August 1998.

12. Philips Electronic Design and Tools Group. DIESEL User Manual. Technical report, Philips Research, June 2001.

13. A. Sinha and A.P. Chandrakasan. Jouletrack - a web based tool for software energy profiling. In *Proceedings of the 38th DAC Conference*, 2000.

14. V. Tiwari, S. Malik, and A. Wolfe. Power analysis of embedded software: A first step towards software power minimization. In *Transactions on VLSI Systems*, 1994.

15. W. Ye, N. Vijaykrishnan, M. Kandemir, and M.J. Irwin. The Design and Use of SimplePower: A Cycle Accurate Energy Estimation Tool. In *Design Automation Conf*, June 2000.

An Energy Consumption Model for an Embedded Java Virtual Machine

Sébastien Lafond[1] and Johan Lilius[2]

[1] Turku Centre for Computer Science, Embedded Systems Laboratory,
Lemminkäisenkatu 14A, FIN-20520 Turku, Finland
sebastien.lafond@abo.fi

[2] Åbo Akademi University, Department of Computer Science,
Lemminkäinengatan 14A, FIN-20520 Åbo, Finland
johan.lilius@abo.fi

Abstract. In this paper we establish a general framework for estimating the energy consumption of an embedded Java virtual machine (JVM). We have designed a number of experiments to find the constant overhead of the Virtual Machine and establish an energy consumption cost for individual Java Opcodes. The results show that there is a basic constant overhead for every Java program, and that a subset of Java opcodes have an almost constant energy cost. We also show that memory access is a crucial energy consumption component.

1 Introduction

In recent years we have seen an explosion of markets for portable electronic devices such as PDAs, personal communicators and mobile phones. These battery-operated devices provide more and more functionalities and as a consequence become more and more complex. They have in common strong constraints on energy consumption, and thus maximizing battery life for such devices is crucial.

Several techniques have been developed to optimize the energy consumption of embedded systems. Those techniques can be hardware based solutions, as well as software or co-design solutions [1]. Techniques for low power optimization of software have been mostly applied on processor instructions level [2, 3] by mainly using processor specific instructions [4, 5]. Techniques on memory management have also been widely applied for optimizing energy consumption [6, 7].

At the same time, the size and complexity of applications and development constraints like getting the product to market on time, make necessary the use of high-level languages. Due to the wide diversity of hardware and OS used in the world of handheld devices, portability across systems is not easy and needs efforts. Java language eases portability by allowing application developments with an abstraction of the target platform, making the concept "write once, run it anywhere" possible.

In this paper we establish a general framework for estimating the energy consumption of an embedded Java virtual machine. We present a number of experiments to estimate the constant overhead of the JVM energy consumption and establishe an energy consumption cost for individual Java Opcodes.

W. Grass et al. (Eds.): ARCS 2006, LNCS 3894, pp. 311–325, 2006.

The major contributions of this paper are a better understanding of the energy consumption distribution of an embedded Java virtual machine (JVM) and the definition of the energy cost for the Java bytecodes.

The remainder of this paper is organized as follows. Section 2 proposes a methodology scheme used to characterize the energy consumption of an embedded Java Virtual Machine. Section 3 presents several experiments in order to define some constant overheads of the JVM and comments the repartition of the JVM energy consumption. Section 4 presents a measurement methodology used to define the energy cost of Java bytecode by cost comparison between two appropriate class files. Finally, section 5 concludes the paper and suggests future possible work. This paper is presenting the main results of [8] where more example graphs and results can be found.

2   An Energy Consumption Model of Java Applications

The Java Virtual machine is an abstract machine, making the interface between platform independent applications and the hardware, through a possible operating system. Thus the use of Java language can be seen as adding one more layer, the Java virtual machine, between the hardware and software layers. We want to study how well applying estimation techniques on the virtual machine opcodes level can be done, similarly to what has been done on processor instructions level. Figure 1 shows a simple view of the JVM life cycle. An efficient energy model should characterize each stage of the life cycle model, and thus shows in which stage(s) effort needs to be concentrated to achieve energy optimization. It seems obvious that such model needs to consider the system's hardware and software configuration and therefore is not directly portable. But the methodology used to build it can easily be applied on different configurations by changing the platform configuration parameters.

As shown in [9] the memory consumption must also be included in the model, as the memory might represent the biggest source of energy consumption on a typical embedded system. This is even more important to take into account as the JVM is a stack machine and will therefore have a relatively high memory activity.

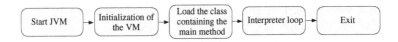

Fig. 1. Simple view of the JVM life cycle

2.1   Measurements Methodology

We chose to use the Sun Microsystems K Virtual Machine (KVM), CLDC v1.0.3, as it has been developed for a resource-constrained platform and has its source code freely available. KVM is a small virtual machine containing about 50-80 Kb of object code in its standard configuration and has a total memory footprint in the range of 128-256 Kb. KVM can run on a 16-bit or 32-bit RISC/CISC processor clocked from 25MHz.

To build an energy model of the KVM we adapted the energy profiler *enprofiler* [10] developed by the Embedded Systems Groups at Dortmund University. The adaptation was done in order to integrate the Java environment in the results provided by the energy profiler. With the adaptation, when summing up the energy cost for each instruction execution or memory access the *enprofiler* checks in which KVM stage the event occurred and increments the corresponding costs variable. Enprofiler is a processor instructions level energy profiler for ARM7TDMI processor cores operating in Thumb mode [11] and integrating the consumption of memory accesses. It has been built from physical measurements done on an Atmel AT91EB01 evaluation board consisting of a AT91M40400 processor clocked at 33MHz and an external 512K bytes SRAM. A detailed description of the energy model used by *enprofiler* is given in [12]. According to [12] *enprofiler* shows a precision of 1.7% for the cost measurement of 12 instructions in an endless loop.

Figure 2 shows the measurements methodology scheme used to characterize each stage of the KVM life cycle. The Java class generator generates, from template classes, Java applications with the possibility to modify parameters inside the class source code. With the Java Code Compact (JCC) we compile and link together the JVM source code and the generated Java application. The executable code is run on the ARM7TDMI emulator ARMulator, which traces instructions, memory accesses and events that occur during the application execution. From this trace, we extract all information concerning the memory access addresses, size and type (read, write, sequential, non-sequential), the instructions addresses and their corresponding processor opcodes. The energy profiler *enprofiler* reads the emulator trace and accesses databases providing processor instruction costs and the cost of a memory access depending of its address, size

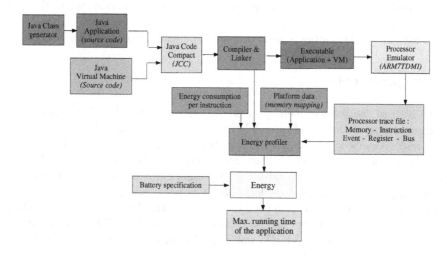

Fig. 2. Measurements methodology scheme

and type. The energy profiler estimates the energy consumed by the application and provides information on how the energy is distributed between the processor and memories for each KVM stage.

2.2 Energy Profiler

The energy profiler provides the number of instructions, memory accesses and garbage collections that occur during each KVM stage. It needs as input information on the JVM stage addresses inside the emulator trace. These addresses are provided by the linker from which eight useful address symbols are collected:

- main: this symbol represents the *main()* function of KVM, and is used by the energy profiler to detect the start of the KVM execution.
- StartJVM: represents the *StartJVM(argc, argv)* function (in StartJVM.c source file). This function only checks if the user gave a class name as argument, and then calls the *KVM_Start()* function.
- KVM_Start: represents the *KVM_Start()* function (in StartJVM.c source file). This function initializes the VM, the global variables, the profiling variables, the memory system, the hashtable, the class loading interface, the Java system classes, the class file verifier and the event handling system. It also initializes the multithreading system after loading the main application class.
- garbageCollect: represents the *garbageCollect()* function (in garbage.c source file) that performs a mark-and-sweep garbage collection.
- ExitGarbage : the ExitGarbage symbol was added into the KVM source code in order to detect the end of the garbage collector.
- Interpret : represents the *Interpret()* function (in execute.c source file) that runs the interpreter loop.
- KVM_Cleanup : KVM_Cleanup represents the *KVM_Cleanup()* function (in StartJVM.c source file). It runs several finalization functions when the VM is shut down.
- ExitVM : This symbol is used to detect the end of the KVM execution.

3 Experiments

We have run the measurement process over several representative benchmarks to characterize each stage of the KVM life cycle and determine if some stages are dominant. The benchmarks used are: a) the dhrystone benchmark, b) parts of The Java Grande Forum Benchmark Suite and the DHPC Java Grande Benchmarks. In addition to these established benchmarks we also used as reference an empty application in order to reflect the KVM basic costs. Dedicated intensive allocation applications was also used in order to study the behavior of the KVM stage costs. All benchmarks can be retrieve from [13]. For all measurements, if not explicitly expressed the KVM was compiled with an heap size of 256 Kb.

3.1 Benchmarks

Empty application: We run the empty application through the measurement process in order to find out if overhead constants in the KVM energy consumption can be determined. We can predict that one or several stage(s), like StartJVM, will have a constant energy consumption, as they have an application independent behavior. Its source code is the following:

```
public class HelloWord {
 public static void main(String arg[])
  {
  //nothing to do
  }
}
```

Intensive allocation applications: Two intensive allocation applications were used in order to study a possible application related evolutions in the KVM costs. The first application, called alloc1, instantiates inside a loop one object of class MyClass. This class doesn't contain any field and has just one *main* method. Each new class MyClass created by main is stored in the heap, and will contain only a reference to the class definitions area. Each instantiation will create a new stack frame and call the MyClass constructor which by default will only call java/lang/Object constructor method. The stack frame created by the main method contains two operand stacks and three local variables to store the object reference, the length and the loop index. This application is used to observe the evolution of different KVM stage costs with the length of the loop. The source code for alloc1 is the following:

```
public class MyClass {
  public static void main(String arg[])
  {
   int length = X;
   for(int i=0; i<=length ; i++) {
   new Myclass();
   }
  }
}
```

The second intensive allocation application, called alloc2, is similar to the precedent one with the difference that MyClass contain one field define by an integer array of size 500. Alloc2 is used to observe the weight that can take the garbage collector in comparison to the other KVM stages in extreme allocation rate. As each new instance takes approximatively 2Kb, with an heap size of 128Kb the garbage collector needs to be triggered every 64th objects created in the loop to reclaim the heap space occupied by the unreferenced objects. The source code for alloc2 is the following:

```
public class MyClass {
int[] tab = new int[500];
  public static void main(String arg[])
  {
   int length = X ;
   for(int i=0; i<=length ; i++) {
   new Myclass();
   }
  }
}
```

Dhrystone: Dhrystone tests the system's integer performance. It is a well established benchmark for performance measurement of general purpose system. We conducted the measurement process with two test executions of 50 and 250 benchmark runs.

Table 1. Benchmarks used from Java Grande Forum Benchmark suite

Low level operation benchmarks	
Name	Short description
Arith	Execution of arithmetic operations
Assign	Variable assignment
Create	Creating objects and arrays
Exception	Exception handling
Loop	Loop overheads
Math	Execution of maths library operations
Method	Method invocation
Generic	Local and Static variable handling

Java Grande Benchmarks: We used the sequential benchmarks which are the one suitable for single processor execution. Several low level operation benchmarks was used from the Java Grande Forum Benchmark Suite and the DHPC Java Grande Benchmarks. Table 1 summarize all benchmarks used for our study.

3.2 Results

This section presents the results obtained by the introduced applications and benchmarks through the measurement process.

Empty application: The empty application has been used in order to find out if overhead constants in the KVM energy consumption can be determined.

Table 2 shows the obtained results and figure 3 presents the energy consumption distribution among all KVM stages and also the distribution between the energy consumed by memory accesses and processor instruction execution.

We can make some remarks from figure 3. Even if this application does absolutely nothing, it has to be noticed that the interpreter stage represents about

Table 2. Empty application - Energy consumption of KVM's stages in μJ

StartJVM Inst.	StartJVM Mem.	KVMStart Inst.	KVMStart Mem.	Interpr. Inst.	Interpr. Mem.
9,42	20,08,	748,81	1639,18	3552,28	8273,34
		KVM Clean Inst.	KVM Clean Mem.		
		144,92	326,38		

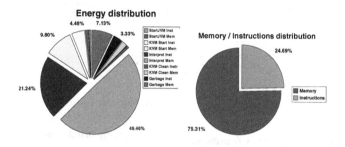

Fig. 3. Empty Application - Energy consumption distributions

70 % of the consumed energy from all stages, and memory accesses represent 75% of the total consumed energy. As the application was *'empty'* the values in table 2 represent the KVM basic costs or the minimal overhead energy cost that any application will have to dissipate.

Intensive allocation applications: From the alloc1 results in figure 4 we note that only the energy consumed by the interpreter is dependent on the loop length value. All other stages of the KVM consume a constant energy including the garbage collector, as the maximum number of created object was not enough to fill up the Java heap and trigger off a garbage collection. It is also important to notice that the energy consumed by the interpreter stage is linear and proportional to the loop length. This can be explain by the fact that the interpreter is looping over a number of constant Java opcodes. These opcodes are:

```
4 goto 18
7 new\#2  -> create a new 'MyClass' object in the heap
10 dup     -> duplicate new object reference in the operand stack
11 invokespecial \#3 -> call the constructor
14 pop -> remove the top of the operand stack
17 iinc 2 1 -> increment the second local variable by 1
18 iload\_2 -> load 2nd local variable in operand stack (i)
19 iload\_1 -> load 1st local variable in operand stack (length)
20 if\_icmple 65543
```

As the energy profiler evaluates the cost of a memory access according to the memory technology, i.e. have for each memory type (RAM, ROM, Flash, etc.) an average cost for each access type regardless of its address, and as the *new* opcode allocates the same amount of memory for all created (and already resolved) objects, it will have an identical cost for each execution.

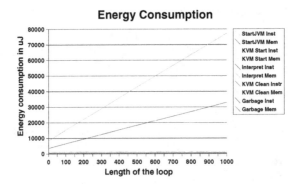

Fig. 4. Alloc1 - KVM's stages energy consumption depending of the loop length

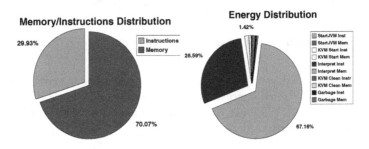

Fig. 5. Alloc1 - Energy distribution for loop length equal to 1000

The energy distribution for a loop length of 1000 presented in figure 5, is similar to the first experiment with an interpreter stage even more dominant, representing over 95% of the total energy consumed.

Alloc2 application was used to observe the garbage collector weight in comparison to other KVM stages. Several factors can influence the garbage collection behavior and thus its energy consumption: the size of the heap, the sizes and numbers of live or dead objects, and heap fragmentation. However, as shown on figure 6, the garbage collection stage will hardly exceed more than 15% of the total energy consumed even for application with intensive allocation rate. Table 3 shows the energy values consumed by the interpreter and garbage collector for alloc2 application with a loop length of 1000 where the garbage collection represent 13,65% of the interpreter stage energy consumption.

Benchmarks: Table 4 and 5 gather the results for all benchmarks. Table 4 shows for the used benchmarks the energy values in μJ for StartJVM, KVMStart and KVMClean stages. We can notice that the obtained values for each stage are very similar for all benchmarks, and there values and variations extremely small compare to the interpreter stage values show in table 5 (in mJ). We can say that with an average of 98% of the total energy consumption the interpreter stage is fare ahead the stage where the energy consumption is dissipated inside the KVM, and that StartJVM, KVMStart and KVMClean have an almost

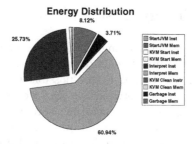

Fig. 6. Garbage collection weight

Table 3. Energy consumption values for a loop length of 1000 in μJ

Interpreter Inst.	Interpreter Mem.	Garb. Collect. Inst.	Garb. Collect. Mem.
54 035	127 949	7 789	17 057

Table 4. Stable energy costs for StartJVM ,KVMStart and KVMClean stages in μJ

	StartJvm		KVMStart		KVMClean	
Benchmark	Instuction	Memory	Instuction	Memory	Instruction	Memory
Dhrystone250	9,42	20,08	857,74	1868,40	155,41	350,31
Dhrystone50	9,42	20,08	849,82	1851,51	154,74	348,82
Arith	9,42	20,08	815,78	1776,04	145,67	328,40
Assign	9,42	20,08	823,32	1791,09	145,94	329
Create	9,42	20,08	807,81	1833,57	147,48	335,21
Exception	9,42	20,08	814,08	1772,99	145,94	329
Loop	9,42	20,08	810,01	1764,06	145,67	328,40
Method	9,42	20,08	823,89	1793,72	146,75	330,93
Generic	9,42	20,08	838,76	1828,55	152,78	344,39
Math	9,42	20,08	823,89	1793,72	146,75	330,93

Table 5. Interpreter stage energy cost and weight in mJ

	Dhrystone250	Dhrystone50	Arith	Assign	Create	Exception
Inst.	97-29.65%	88-29.30%	877-29.21%	2380-29,87%	1053-26,38%	2250-29,82%
Mem.	850-69.90%	207-68.92%	2121-70.62%	5584-70,05%	2779-69,61%	5475-70,04%

	Loop	Math	Method	Generic
Inst.	533-29,32%	2718-29,77%	533-29,86%	611-29,65%
Mem.	228-69,03%	6408-70,17%	1246-69,84%	1445-70,09%

constant and insignificant energy consumption. All measurements were done on an opteron 244 1.8GHz machine with 4Gb of RAM, and for the slowest benchmark JGFMathBench the measurement process took about 36 hours.

From all experiments done it is clear that the interpreter stage is far ahead the main source of energy consumption and a better comprehension of it is needed if someone wants to achieve energy optimization on the KVM. As the interpreter reads and executes the Java bytecode, having a closer view on the interpreter implies increasing the granularity of its energy consumption model by looking at the cost of each Java opcode interpreted.

4   Java Opcode Energy Cost

In order to get a better understanding of the interpreter energy consumption, an evaluation of each Java opcode energy cost is needed. As a strict class file structure needs to be respected, it is not possible to only execute one Java opcode. Thus a cost comparison between two class files is needed to estimate the cost difference between them. The general measurements methodology scheme used to characterize each KVM stage life cycle can be re-used with different inputs. Instead of using Java source code files we will use as input appropriate byte-code executable class files.

4.1   Measurements Methodology

Figure 7 shows an abstract view of the class files generator used to create two class files, named ClassFile and ClassFile_Ref. The opcode behavior towards the Java operand stack and the local variables array has to be defined for each studied Java opcode, i.e. provide the operand stack state needed before and re- sulting after the studied opcode execution as well as the number of local variables needed. Figure 8 shows an example of generated bytecode classes for the Java opcode *NOP (0x00)*. In this example ClassFile method 1, the *main* method, executes 256 *NOP* opcodes when the ClassFile_Ref method 1 executes only the

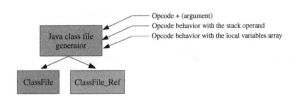

Fig. 7. Bytecode executable class file generator

	ClassFile			*ClassFile_Ref*	
Method 1:			Method 1:		
0000d8 0009	access flags = 9		0000d8 0009	access flags = 9	
0000da 0008	name = #8<main>		0000da 0008	name = #8<main>	
0000dc 0009	descriptor = #9<([Ljava/lang/String;)V>		0000dc 0009	descriptor = #9<([Ljava/lang/String;)V>	
0000de 0001	1 field/method attributes:		0000de 0001	1 field/method attributes:	
	field/method attribute 0			field/method attribute 0	
0000e0 0006	name = #6<Code>		0000e0 0006	name = #6<Code>	
0000e2 00000119	length = 281		0000e2 00000019	length = 25	
0000e6 0000	max stack: 0		0000e6 0000	max stack: 0	
0000e8 0001	max locals: 1		0000e8 0001	max locals: 1	
0000ea 00000101	code length: 257		0000ea 00000001	code length: 1	
0000ee 00	0 nop		0000ee b1	0 return	
0000ef 00	1 nop		0000ef 0000	0 exception table entries:	
0000f0 00	2 nop				
0000f1 00	3 nop				
....					
0001ed 00	255 nop				
0001ee b1	256 return				
0001ef 0000	0 exception table entries:				

Fig. 8. Example of generated byte-code class files

compulsory *return* opcode in order to return *void* from the main method. By comparing the interpreter energy consumption for both class files we can get the energy consumption estimation for 256 *NOP* executions and thus the energy cost of one *NOP* opcode.

To ensure the estimation quality for each opcode we generate several pairs of class files executing the studied opcode and also monitor the possible energy consumption differences between all other KVM stages. All measurements were done on a Linux 700Mhz Pentium III machine with 256MB of RAM, and on average the estimation of a Java opcode cost took 3 minutes.

4.2   Results

From all Java opcodes we will not study the 51 opcodes which handle floating point values as floating point is not supported by the CLDC specification. The opcode *athrow* was also omitted from this study, it is not possible to directly estimate its energy cost using this comparison method as its cost can not be extracted from the context cost. All the same, in table 5 in [13] we can see from the opcode *checkcast* the cost of throwing an *ClassCastExeption* exception and exiting the KVM.

Due to space requirement all obtained values for each studied opcode are published in [13], where the opcodes are divided in six functional groups:

Stack and local variable operations opcodes: Tables 2 and 3 in [13] show the results concerning opcodes that operate on the operand stack and local variable. We can notice that loading a value from the local variables array to the operand stack is lightly more expensive than storing the same value back to the local variable. It is also interesting to note that the opcode *bipush* consumes about 9% less energy than *iload* and 5% less than *ilaod_x*. Thus it is more energy efficient to load an constant integer lower than 256 into the operand stack using *bipush* than initializing the local variable array with the constant and use *iload* or *ilaod_x*. The same is true if a constant integer lower than 65536 has to be loaded into the operand stack, it will be more efficient to use the opcode *bipush* instead of *iload*. But in case the integer constant can be stored in the first 4 local variables then *iload_x* becomes the most efficient opcode.

Type conversion opcodes: Table 1 in [13] shows the results for opcodes that convert value from one primitive type to another. The costs are in the same range as the stack and local variable operations opcodes as the conversion opcodes pop a value from the stack, perform a right shift or truncate the popped value and push back the result.

Arithmetic opcodes: Table 4 in [13] shows the costs for arithmetic opcodes. As it was easy to predict, the cost of an arithmetic operation is dependent on the type of the operands and the operation. Operations on long types are about 50% more expensive than on integers, except for the division of types long which is about two times more expensive than to divide integers.

Logic opcodes: As for the arithmetic opcodes, the cost of logic opcodes is also depending of the type of the operand and operations on longs are from 23% to 37% more expensive than operation on integers. Table 9 in [13] shows the costs for logic opcodes.

Control flow opcodes: The control flow opcodes are the opcodes that implement the following Java language statements: *do-while, while, if, if-else, for* and *switch*. Table 8 in [13] shows the cost for the 25 control flow opcodes. For all conditional *if* opcodes (i.e. opcodes from 0x99 to 0xa6 and *ifnull, ifnonnull*) the energy cost depends on a two values comparison success. If the comparison success the VM jumps to a target defined by the opcode operands, in the other case the VM continues by executing the following opcodes. The KVM *lookupswitch* implementation uses the binary search algorithm to retrieve the branch offsets associated with the case values of the switch statement. In consequence, the *lookupswitch* cost depends on the number of needed iterations through the binary tree which is determined by the position of the researched case value in the tree. As on average for a binary tree of size n it takes $(\log_2 n - 1)$ iterations to found the researched value, it is possible to determine an *lookupswitch* average cost depending on the number of case values included in the switch statement. The *tableswitch* opcode performs the same task as *lookupswitch*, with the difference that it requires a consecutive list of case values contained between one low and high endpoint. Thus the VM knows in advance the position of all case values so that the retrieving cost is the same for all cases. Compared with *lookupswitch*, *tableswitch* has a lower energy cost but generates all the more bigger class file size as the gape between the case values is great.

Objects and arrays opcodes: Tables 5 and 6 in [13] show the cost of opcodes that create and manipulate arrays and objects. The creation cost, with *newarray*, of a single dimension array of primitive type integer, long, short, byte, char or boolean is not directly dependent on array type and size, but more on the memory size that needs to be allocated for its creation. That means that the creation cost is identical for an integers array of size 8, a shorts array of size 16, or a longs array of size 4. The creation cost, with *multiarray*, of multidimensional arrays is dependent on the array dimensions and dimensions indexes values. Each dimension adds a basic cost to the array creation cost, thus creating a 2*2*2 integers array will be 70% more expensive than creating a 2*4 integers array, and especially 18 times more expensive than creating a single dimension integers array of size 8. Moreover, in order to access to one multidimensional array value the JVM has to retrieve from the first dimension the second dimension address and so one until it reaches the last dimension.

The objects creation cost depends on the objects themselves, i.e on the type and size of their constant pool, interfaces, fields,methods and their super-classes, and also on their resolution flags inside each class constant pool. A new object is resolved only once within a same class, and its address is stored in the constant pool structure of the class. Table 5 in [13] shows as an example the creation cost of an object of type *java.lang.Object* and *java.lang.String*. In addition, table 5 in [13] refers to two objects called *Class* and *subClass* which is a empty (none interface,field nor method) sub class of *nonResolvedClass* itself empty sub class of *java.lang.Object*.

Method invocation and return opcodes: Because invoking a method implies returning from it at some point, table 7 in [13] shows the costs of different invoke/return pairs. They all invoke an empty 'already resolved' method within the same class or instance. We can notice from this table that calling a static, public or private method costs almost the same, and that the type of the returned value has not a great influence on the overall cost.

It is also important to compare all obtained values with the *NOP* energy consumption. As the opcode *NOP* is the first case statement in the interpreter switch and doesn't execute any instruction, its energy consumption represents the minimum overhead cost due to the interpreter mechanism. For the most of the stack and local variable operation opcodes the interpreter mechanism overhead represents about 70% of their energy consumption.

The obtained values allow us to get an estimation of how long the KVM will run for a given battery. If we suppose that on average the execution of one Java opcode consumes a total of $3.372\mu J$ and is executed in 200 cycles, the average power dissipated by the processor (clocked at 33MHz) to execute Java opcodes is 0.556 Watt. Thus for the processor supply voltage sets at 3.3 Volts, an ideal 3.3 Volts 500 mAh battery will allow the KVM to run for 200 minutes.

4.3   Opcode Costs Verification

In order to verify the obtained opcode costs we calculated for each benchmark execution the value $\sum(Opcodecost * OpcodeOccurrence)$. The computed value was then compared with the cost given by the energy profiler for the interpreter stage. The occurrence for each opcode was calculated thanks to the KVM tracing ability. For control flow opcodes we checked if the branch was taken or not to attribute the correct opcode cost, but to keep the verification simple we didn't looked at the type of variable handled by *putfield, getfield, putstatic* and *getstatic*. There respective cost for handling integer was used for all occurrences. In addition for all other none static opcode costs only the respective basic cost was used. The benchmark *Exception* from the Java Grande Forum Benchmark Suite was not used as we didn't studied the cost for the opcode *athrow*.

Table 6 presents the normalized verification results where the value 100 represent for each benchmark the energy cost given by the energy profiler for the interpreter stage. For each benchmark the accuracy obtained by calculating the value $\sum(Opcodecost * OpcodeOccurrence)$ is staying between -5 and +10% of the cost given by the energy profiler. But this lost in precision has to be balance with the time needed to compute it. It takes only few seconds to calculate the occurrence

Table 6. Verification results

Dhrystone50	Arith	Assign	Loop	Create	Method	Math	Generic
103,99	105,31	95,55	100,30	97,95	102,51	96,74	109,43

for each opcode and compute the value $\sum(Opcodecost * OpcodeOccurrence)$, compare to several hours needed by the energy profiler.

5 Conclusion

Several observations have been done in this paper concerning the energy consumption of the KVM. For the hardware configuration fixed by the energy profiler, the distribution between the processor and memories is constant over the KVM execution with 70% of the energy consumed by memory accesses. This shows the major importance of the memories for embedded system runtime performance.

This paper can also guide developers to produce energy-aware java application by limiting the use of long data type, avoiding multidimentional array and trying to use consecutive case values inside a switch statement. Furthermore, the opcodes energy cost can be helpful for developing a energy-aware Java compiler as well as optimizing the JVM by pointing out the expensive opcodes. This paper shows the first steps toward an energy aware performance analysis tool for Java application, as a such tool would ask a more detailed model for a subset of opcodes.

Also as the interpreter mechanism overhead cost is a predominant factor in opcode execution cost, it will be interesting in the future to look at the cost differences between the two possible Java execution modes: interpreted or JIT compilation. JIT compilation increases significantly the execution speed, but in the same time increases memory footprint. A trade-off between execution time and memory footprint size will certainly have to be found to reach the optimum optimization point for energy consumption.

References

1. F. Parain, M. Banatre, G.C.T.H.V.I.J.P.L.: Techniques de reduction de la consommation dans les systemes embarques temps-reel. Technical report, INRIA Rennes (2000)
2. Vivek Tiwari and Sharad Malik and Andrew Wolfe: Power Analysis of Embedded Software. In: International Conference on Computer-Aided Design, San Jose CA. (1994)
3. Anil Seth, Ravindra B Keskar, R.: Algorithms for energy optimization using processor instructions. In: International conference on Compilers, architecture, and synthesis for embedded systems- Atlanta, Georgia, USA. (2001)
4. Wen-Tsong Shiue: Retargetable Compilation for Low Power. Technical report, (Silicon Metrics Corporation)
5. Mike Tien-Chien Lee, Vivek Tiwari, S.: Power analysis and low-power scheduling. In: International Symposium on System Synthesis. (1995)
6. Catherine H. Gebotys: Low Energy Memory and Register Allocation Using Network Flow. In: Design Automation Conference. (1997) 435–440
7. Fan, X., Ellis, C., Lebeck, A.: Memory controller policies for DRAM power management. International Symposium on Low Power Electronics and Design (ISLPED) (2001)

8. Lafond, S., Lilius, J.: An energy consumption model for java vitual machine. Technical Report 597, Turku Centre for Computer Science (2004)
9. Kaushik Roy, M.C.J.: Software design for low power. In: Low Power Design in Deep Submicron Electronics. (1997) 433–460
10. Enprofiler: (http://ls12-www.cs.uni-dortmund.de/research/encc/)
11. An introduction to thumb. Technical report, Advenced RISC Machines Ltd (1995)
12. Stefan Steinke, Markus Knauer, L.W.P.M.: An accurate fine grain instruction-level energy model supporting software optimization. In: PATMOS 01. (2001)
13. (http://www.abo.fi/~slafond/javacosts)

PASCOM: Power Model for Supercomputers

Arrvindh Shriraman[1], Nagarajan Venkateswaran[2],
and Niranjan Soundararajan[3]

[1] Department of Computer Science, University of Rochester, Rochester, USA
`ashriram@cs.rochester.edu`
[2] WARAN Research Foundation, Chennai, India
`waran@warftindia.org`
[3] Department of Computer Science, Pennsylvania State University, State Park, USA
`soundara@cse.psu.edu`

Abstract. The onset of Deep Sub Micron (DSM) technology has driven the computing world towards billion device multi-GHz processor architectures leading to a stiff upward curve in power consumption and power density (W/cm^2). In this paper we develop a graph-based power model for multiprocessors that predicts power requirements across the components of the cluster (Compute node, Memory and Network system) at various hierarchical levels when applications are run. PASCOM proposes new metrics for power measurement that integrates execution module characteristics with power dissipation metrics. The PASCOM model is applied to Memory In Processor chip and we study power consumption for parallel scientific applications from SPLASH2 and NAS Parallel suite. Total power dissipated varies by 15%. However, the static and dynamic power dissipation exhibit up to 33% and 60% variation respectively due to workload characteristics.

1 Introduction

The advent of Deep Sub Micron (DSM) [2] technology has begun to pose some serious questions for the chip designers. Even with 50% percent more transistor integration the leakage power will be a few hundred watts beyond 90 nm [1]. Sub-threshold leakage is approaching the practical limit of 50% of overall power. Over the technology generations, interconnect designs have not kept up with the scaling trends of the devices. The parasitic resistance, capacitance and inductance associated with interconnections and contacts are now beginning to influence circuit performance and power. The global clock and bus lines consume up to 25% [3] of overall processor power consumption while the local interconnects consume up to 15% of overall power consumption [2] [4]. Interconnect limitations will be one of the primary factors in the evolution of deep sub micron technology.

Supercomputers with focus on performance and performance-density are constrained by power dissipation density. From the CRAY C90 [6] to the ASCI Q [5] machine performance has increased by a factor of 2000 but the performance/watt by stark contrast has increased by just 200 fold.

W. Grass et al. (Eds.): ARCS 2006, LNCS 3894, pp. 326–340, 2006.

Scaling conventional processor models to multiprocessor systems result in considerable loss of accuracy and require long prediction time. The error in power estimation increases due to influence of workload and other components (i.e. system interconnects, remote latency induced stalls). Processor power estimations can be applied at various levels of abstraction namely gate level [19][20], architectural level [21] and behavioral levels [22] [23]. The processor power estimation techniques are slow and preclude online runtime usage. They also require a complex accurate description of the structure of micro-architecture components.

This research paper brings out a novel Power-Aware-SuperCOMputing (PASCOM) paradigm that leads to hardware-software co-design introducing power awareness at all levels (i.e hardware and software), into multiprocessor systems. The paper proposes a power model for supercomputers. In this paper we develop a graph based power model that parameterizes architecture, layout, technology and measures power based on workload influence on various hardware components of the system. We put forth the concept of hierarchical power libraries to estimate and predict the power requirements when an application is run on the supercomputer. We have developed application mapping based hierarchical power metrics help in introducing power awareness systems to all stages in the system.

The MIP (Memory In Processor) [7][8] architecture is used as a case study for the PASCOM power model. The device and interconnect technology was fixed up for the MIP processor. The interconnect R-C-L parameters and device specifications were obtained from the ITRS 2003 specifications. The PDIP tool [13] was extended and used to predict the interconnect distribution and area for the MIP processor. The OCEAN, BARNE's Hut, Embarrassingly parallel, Integer Sort applications were used to perform a power analysis of the MIP S.C.O.C (SuperComputer On a Chip).

We believe that the hardware-software co-design approach holds the most promise for introducing power awareness. PASCOM's interface between the hardware and software will enable the designers to integrate the system software with hardware level power aware techniques. PASCOM power model will enable the operating system to utilize the power-libraries of applications to initiate actions for effective power management both at the node and system levels. The paper discusses primarily the power estimation techniques while it proposes to use power saving techniques such as multiple V_{DD}, clock gating and other node hardware dependent approaches.

2   PASCOM Power Model

The PASCOM Power (PASCOMP) model employs power estimation methodologies at various levels of the task mapping process across the nodes of the supercomputer. The PASCOMP model encompasses (1) Multiprocessor hardware specifications (i.e node architecture, interconnect topology, memory hierarchy) (2) Application task mapping and scheduling characteristics. The application and algorithm mapping have been factored into the power estimation methodology since the computation mapping and communication characteristics have a critical impact on the power requirements at various components in a multiprocessor system, as we show in our results.

The PASCOMP model integrates the application execution hierarchy with the corresponding architecture hierarchy. It engages a set of analytical models to predict the power associated with the various architecture components of the system (processor, on-chip cache,network processor and network interconnects). There are two design phases for the PASCOMP model. (1) Development of architecture level power models for the various architecture components (2) Framework design for developing power-libraries The PASCOMP models the Supercomputing system using (1) SUPERARCH (SUPERcomputer Architecture) power models (2) APPLIB (APplication Power LIBraries).

Fig. 1 shows the integration of SUPERcomputer ARCHitecture (SUPERARCH) power model and APplication Power LIBraries(APPLIB) into the schema of the PASCOM model. The SUPERARCH power model employs power estimation models for the various architecture components. It is designed hierarchically and integrates the power models at every level (i.e node, board, cluster) based on the components that participate in co-ordinating execution (i.e. data transfer and computation). The APPLIB design is closely coupled with the mapping libraries of the application. It was designed hierarchically to provide power prediction for the various execution-module levels (Instruction,..Algorithm, ..Application). The execution-module levels are created based on complexity of the task, scheduling granularity and hardware components employed. The PASCOM model binds the execution module with the architecture system that runs the module to estimate power. It then employs the SUPERARCH power models to predict the power dissipation during the execution. PASCOMP estimates the influence of task-graph characteristics and hardware

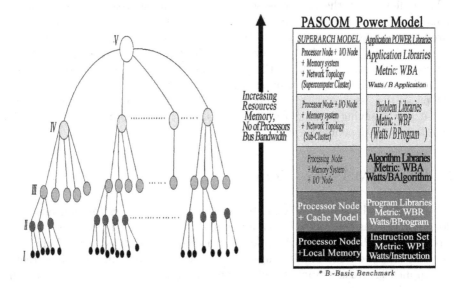

Fig. 1. PASCOM Design paradigm. Integration of the SUPERARCH & APPLIB.

on power dissipation. Conventional power models take into consideration only hardware characteristics and approximate workload to simple component on/off activity factors.

Figure 1 shows the correspondence between the various PASCOM model levels and the hierarchical build up of the supercomputer. The PASCOM model evolved, models the multiprocessor architecture at various levels (I-V) and will use the execution library modules to predict the power consumption at all the levels as shown in the Fig. 1. This allows us to estimate the power consumption at every level (WBA (watts/ basic algorithm),WBP (watts/ basic program)....WBI(watts/basic instruction)),see Fig. 1. The term "basic" refers to primary execution tasks which are used to synthesize applications.

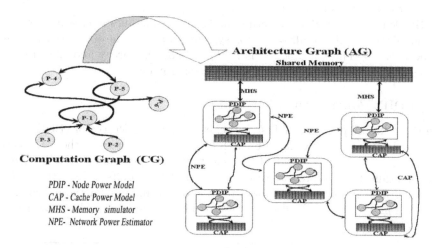

Fig. 2. Embedding a Computation Graph on an Architecture Graph

Fig. 2 shows interaction of PASCOM components. PASCOM models application execution as a graph embedding problem and estimates power dissipated with a graph traversal. The AG in Fig. 2 represents the architecture graph or the cluster structure and the various elements in the cluster. The CG in Fig. 2 represents the computation graph which represents the interaction between the various mapping libraries. The arrow illustrates the embedding of the CG onto the AG. Following this process, the various nodes in the CG will be scheduled for execution on specific nodes of the AG. The nodes are generic and represent various components in a multiprocessor system (eg: I/O processor, processor, or memory bank). Power involved in the execution of a mapping library is evaluated as a graph traversal problem. Based on architecture and technology the corresponding analytical model is incorporated in respective nodes to evaluate power consumed. The appropriate network power model is applied to the hyperedge during the course of data transfer across the network.

3   SUPERARCH Components

The SUPERARCH employs a set of power models that parameterizes the
architecture, layout, technology metric influences on the various components
of the cluster. The various power models involved in the SUPERARCH Power
model are .

PDIP: An parameterized graph-theory based power model that parameterizes
architecture-layout-technology factors that influence power dissipation in
processors.

CAP: A cache power model that parameterizes the influence of floor-plan and
technology on power. Includes the power dissipated in wordline, bitline and
other datapath components.

MHS: Defines generic data structures and software modules to create the memory hierarchy of a multiprocessor system. Captures the data transactions
between (1) The multiple levels in the memory hierarchy and (2) The dependent data transfer between the processing nodes.

3.1   PDIP: Power Estimation Tool

The Power Delay product for Instruction execution in a Processor (PDIP) tool
[13] was developed at WARAN Research Foundation as a part of the PASCOM
project. In [13] we have studied the sensitivity and accuracy of PDIP model
using Pentium-III as representative design. The PDIP tool(see Fig. 3) was developed primarily to provide a power-delay product analysis for the instruction
execution in a processor. It also has the capability to provide ad-hoc power and

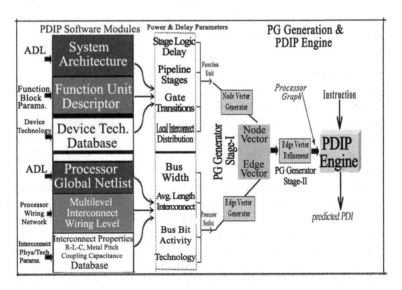

Fig. 3. Integrated schema of PDIP showing the Software modules, Processor Hyper-
graph generation and PDIP engine

delay analysis. The processor is modeled as a PG (Processor hyperGraph), the function blocks of the processor map into the nodes of the graph while the hyper-edges map the interconnect structure. The instruction execution is modelled as a graph traversal problem. Instruction execution flows(i.e. data/address/control bus flows) is mapped onto the hyperedges. Based upon the paths traced in the PG the weight vectors assigned to nodes and edges will provide the parameters for predicting the power for instruction. An integrated schema of the functional modules, corresponding PG parameter generation, PG extraction and generation is shown in Fig. 3a. Parameterized power models have been developed for functional units based on [15]. Interconnect power estimation is a two stage process. The first stage involves Interconnect Distribution (ID) prediction for the processor. The interconnect distribution prediction is adopted from [24][25]. The second stage involves application of distributed R-C power models [14] to the various interconnect levels.

The architecture details and technology specification of the functional unit are specified as a weight vector 'N' assigned to the node. N is a 4 tuple specified as $< n1, n2, n3, n4 >$. These indicate the propagation delay (n1), pipeline rate (n2), average number of gate transitions (n3), local interconnect distribution (n4). We model interconnects in all three tiers (1) Local (2) Semi-Tier (i.e Inter-function unit) and (3) Global (i.e Bus, Clock). In PDIP we model influence of the local nets (i.e internal to function unit) with node weight vector parameter n4. Semi-Tier Global nets are mapped onto the edges of the hypergraph. The weight vector generated for an edge is used to evaluate the delay and power associated with the inter-function unit interconnects. An edge weight vector E is defined as a 4 tuple $< e1, e2, e3, e4 >$. Edge weights vector elements represent the bus-width (e1),average length(e2), average transition along the interconnects(e3) and the technology parameters(e4). In Fig. 3 we also show the inputs used to calculate the vectors. Architecture-Descriptor-Language (ADL) is used to provide a class description of the components of the processor and their network.

The instruction initiates execution at a node of the PG(Processor hyper-Graph). The path traced in the graph by the various data, address and control flows of the instruction is defined as the IEP(Instruction Execution Path). The power associated with an instruction is evaluated as a summation of power prediction associated with nodes and edges of the IEP. The simulator stages of PDIP is illustrated in Fig. 3.

The PDIP integrates the processor unit's power prediction with instruction execution trace in the processor and thereby measures power as a function of the instruction execution. PDIP parameterizes architecture-technology-layout details and does not suffer from limitations of conventional processor power models that do not take into consideration the DSM effect of multi-level interconnect and crosstalk effects on power.

3.2   CAche Power Estimator (CAP)

CAche Power Estimator (CAP) [16] was developed to predict the power consumption on on-chip cache memory structures. CAP bridges the divide between the functional and micro-architecture simulators. Similar to the PDIP in construction, it uses a set of parameterized power models to predict the power dissipation of various cache components. Currently CAP has been developed only for SRAM based caches. CAP is an extension of [27][18] cache power models. The various input parameters of CAP is listed in Table 1. As shown in Table 1, the parameter vector consists of terms that are used to model architecture, technology and layout dependent features. The sub-banking and block buffering strategies have not been taken into consideration for power prediction. The Data and Tag arrays in a cache basically employ the same structure. The dynamic switching power and the static leakage current power of all gates, interconnects, and sense amplifiers are modelled.

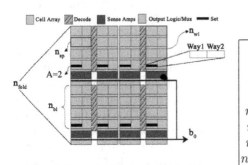

Fig. 4. Generic Cache Architecture

Table 1. Cache Parameters

b_o	Processor-Cache bus width(bits)
C	the size of the cache in bytes
B	the block or line size of the cache
A	the associativity of the cache
n_{wl}	number of word line divisions
n_{bl}	number of bit line divisions
n_{sp}	number of sets per physical row
n_{fold}	number of folds in cache array.

The power dissipation estimation follows the critical path modelling. Equations 1,2 list the power equation for the data and tag array respectively. Table 2 lists the terms associated with power estimation.

The dynamic power is estimated by calculating the total switched capacitance. Additionally, each gate and SRAM cell is modelled as a leakage component. Critical Path average interconnect length was predicted and distributed R-L-C model was applied. The interconnect R-C parameters, the device parasitic capacitance values and V_{dd} values for a given technology have been obtained from [17]. The CAP power analytical models was compared with Hspice results [16] and it was found that up to 1MB cache positive error was within 10% limit, beyond which the prediction deviated to up to 30% for 6MB caches. With supercomputers and DSM processors driving towards larger cache structures this will not be acceptable. Currently we have overcome this problem by employing CAP to predict power for cache partitions and then scaling it up.

$$P_{data} = P_{addrd} + P_{predecoded} + P_{fdecoded} + P_{wld} + P_{bld} + P_{sensed} + P_{outd} \quad (1)$$

$$P_{tag} = P_{addrt} + P_{predecod} + P_{wlt} + P_{blt} + P_{senset} + P_{outt} \quad (2)$$

Memory hierarchy in a multiprocessor is more complex than that of a processor since there are more levels in the hierarchy and complex coherence protocol interactions. The CAP power model primarily seeks to incorporate the effects of Cache and DRAM memory banks. The Memory-Hierarchy-Simulator(MHS) is

Table 2. Power Dissipation Terms

P_{addr}	Driving Address Bus
$P_{predecode}$	Non-Shutdown Pre-Decoder(synthesized using NAND gates)
$P_{fdecode}$	Final Decoder (synthesized using NOR gates)
P_{wl}	Word Line Driver
P_{bl}	Global/Local Bit Line (SRAM Access Dynamic power + Leakage power)
P_{sense}	Sense Amplifier (Clocked nFET Analog unit)
P_{out}	Output Driver

used to simulate the traffic pattern of memory transactions on the inter-node bus network and the various memory architectures such as Shared Memory, COMA and NUMA-UMA's. All memory architectures vary, primarily based on the number of memory levels, off-chip /on-chip characteristics, and the type of memory cell employed. Main memory DRAM power has been obtained and scaling factors were employed to estimate power for various memory blocks. PASCOMP model also currently does not include the power factors of the secondary disks.

4   APPLIB Hierarchy

Application execution on a multiprocessor, is hierarchically decomposed in to mapping libraries. The mapping library is an execution module which specifies application decomposition, task assignment, scheduling and synchronization. The PASCOM model integrates the power prediction for architecture components and mapping libraries. The mapping process is hierarchical. In this hierarchy, at every level the execution process is represented using a computation graph. The nodes of this graph are of varying complexity (Instruction/.. Application) based on the level in the hierarchical task-mapping process. The graph nodes in Fig. 2 are of varying complexity based on the system which is going to execute the corresponding execution module in the mapping hierarchy level. The PASCOM graph based model enables us to map various programming model, since we express every programming model as combination of basic messages and sources/sinks. The hierarchical power library model provides a schema to express this process conveniently. A monolithic model will not scale with the problem size and complexity.

The POWer LIBraries (POWLIBs) are constructed at various levels in the execution hierarchy of the multiprocessor as shown in Fig. 1. The POWLIB at a particular level consists of only a specific class of execution module (Instruction/ Program/ Algorithm/ Problem/ Application). The POWLIB(POWER Library) consists of Basic-Execution-Modules (BEM) that are developed based on an analysis of mapping techniques (i.e inherent parallelism, and process flow). Currently this is a combination of manual call-graph analysis and automated trace extraction. The POWLIBs for a particular application is constructed during the process of mapping the application onto the supercomputer. The model is built bottom up to reverse engineer the application mapping process. A bottom-up construction for the power libraries will enable us to proceed from a micro to

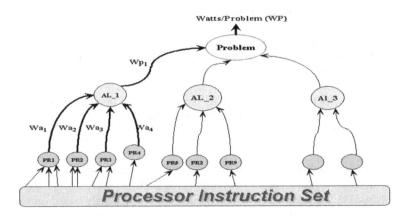

Fig. 5. Power Tree for a problem execution. The bold tree edges show synthesis of root from branches.

macro execution module. This will give rise to a detailed, more accurate analysis of the power.

The Fig. 5 shows the evaluation of power at different levels during the execution of an application. Power is calculated for an application by constructing a power-tree. The power-tree is a weighted tree that illustrates the synthesis of the application from the ISA of the processor.The power requirement of the application is computed by traversing the tree bottom-up integration power factors up the various sub-trees. Every node involves a weighted summation of the power calculated in its sub-trees. Every level in the power-tree corresponds to a particular level in the APPLIB model shown in Fig. 1. The conventional metric of *Watts* for expressing power, is replaced with hierarchical metric schema which express power requirements of execution libraries. This provides us with a lucid and in depth figure of merit for power that takes into consideration the application mapping on the cluster.

5 Experimental Case Study: Memory-In-Processor

The Memory In Processor(MIP) SuperComputer On a Chip(S.C.O.C) [7][8] is a current project of the Vishwakarma group at WARAN Research Foundation. PASCOM applied on the MIP S.C.O.C will provide us with a definitive indication for power requirements of future billion device architectures. The MIP S.C.O.C was designed to overcome the memory bottleneck and develop massive on-chip parallelism to achieve Teraflop scale single chip performance. We case study here a specific 2 MB MIP node that has a 128 bit datapath. The overall organization of the MIP node is discussed in [8] [9] and the Processor-hyperGraph (PG) used in PDIP is shown in Fig. 6b . In [9] we discuss the resource specifications, performance analysis and develop scheduler support for the architecture.

The technology for the MIP S.C.O.C has been fixed up for two generations as shown in Table 3. Two feature sizes of 75nm and 45nm were chosen based on maximum transistors/die supported by the technologies. The preliminary

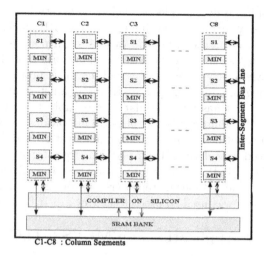

Fig. 6. 2MB MIP S.C.O.C organization

analysis based on [17] indicate that fine-grain bit level logic-SRAM integration [8] is possible with aggressive technology scaling although there are certain creases in the manufacturing process. The objectives during the chip design for memory is density whereas for logic transistors it's been the scaling and switching abilities. Table 3 shows the long term(45nm) and short term(75nm) manufacturing prospects of the MIP S.C.O.C. The device and interconnect parameters have been obtained from ITRS 2003 [17]. These parameters have been used in estimation of static power and dynamic power consumption for processor.

Table 3. MIP S.C.O.C Technology

Year	2007	2010
Device Parameters		
Feature Size	75nm	45nm
Total No of Transistors	1.5 Billion	
Number of Metal Levels	10	12
V_{dd}	1.1	1.0
V_{th}	0.21	0.15
Parasitic Source/Drain Resistance (Ohm-m)	162	135
Ideal NMOS device gate Capacitance (F/μm)	6.64E-16	5.6E-16
Interconnect Parameters		
Number of Metal Levels (Local:3 Global:5 Clock:2)		
Total Interconnect length (m/cm^2)	1002	1784
Metal 1 wiring pitch (nm)	191	108
RC delay(ps) for M1 (1mm)	46	616
Intermediate wiring pitch (nm)	215	135
Interlevel Insulator(k)	3.3-3.6	2.3-2.6

Table 4. Processor Die specifications

C4 Flip-Chip Packaging		
Technology	75nm	45nm
Die Area	$720mm^2$	$550mm^2$
Ground Pin Count	1000	780
V_{cc} Pin Count	450	300
Data I/0 pins	2000	2000
Pad Pitch(μm)	120	80
Pin Voltage(V)	0.92	0.78
Power Specifications		
Clock Distribution Power	75W	50W
I/O Pad Power	120W	110W

The PDIP tool has been extended to include area estimation techniques from [25] to provide us with an area estimate for the MIP shown in Fig. 6. The interconnect length estimations for the various segments has also been shown in Table 3. Due to the 2D array structured organization of the MIP S.C.O.C the global lines are of lower complexity and length is proportional to number of segments sharing the line. The processor die parameters have been shown in Table 4. The pin count has been estimated (see Table 4) for the MIP S.C.O.C based on bandwidth requirements and physical limitations of the packaging and die area. The pin count has been partitioned amongst ground, V_{cc} and I/O data pins. The data feed rate derived from performance estimates in [8] is fixed at 125 GBytes/s. The PDIP tool was used to extract the critical length for the clock distribution. The number of repeaters was predicted using [14]. An R-C tree analytical model was used to predict the clock distribution power.

6   Benchmark Applications on MIP S.C.O.C

Five major parallel benchmark applications were chosen from NAS and SPLASH2 suite and mapped onto the MIP S.C.O.C. We capture the function

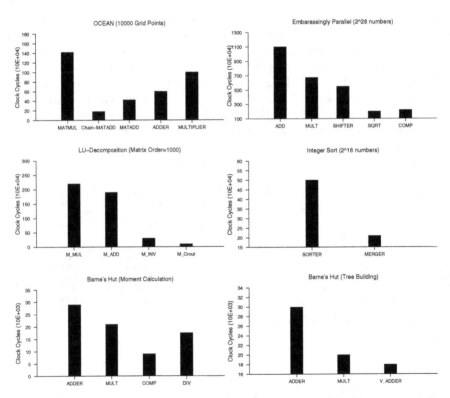

Fig. 7. Graphs plot the resource utilization of the MIP S.C.O.C for various applications. The X-Axis plot the function units used to map the application. The Y-Axis plots the clock cycle utilization.

calls, their execution points and the memory load/store traces to generate the application graph. Currently we generate the graphs from the traces manually. With more sophisticated call-graph analyzers and binary instrumentation this process can be automated. The resource utilization curves are shown in Fig. 7. We assume a 75nm process technology for deriving constants to estimate power. Table 5 shows the MIP S.C.O.C static and dynamic power under various workload conditions. We have integrated power consumed in interconnect transfers into the static power calculations. We define dynamic power as power consumed consumed for by function units when (1) performing computation and (2) used as memory storage. Since data transfer bus lines themselves are not involved with providing storage/computation we include them in static power calculations. Static power numbers shown in Table 5 include (1) Static power of devices (2) Static power of interconnects (3) Power consumed by interconnects during data transfer. We discuss in this section influence of workload on type of power dissipation.

Table 5. Power Estimation for Algorithms

Algorithm	Static Power	Dynamic Power
OCEAN (10000 Grid Points)	300W	250W
Barnes's Hut Tree(10000 Body)	320W	320W
LU-D(Matrix order=1000^2)	300W	400W
Integer Sort(2^18 numbers)	450W	150W
EP (2^{28} numbers)	350W	275W

Table 5 illustrates the influence of workload on power dissipation break-up. The dominant source of power dissipation will influence the power saving mechanism employed to save power. There is a difference of 33% between maximum and minimum static-power dissipation across the benchmarks (see Table 5 Integer-Sort and OCEAN). For dynamic power the disparity between maximum and minimum across the various workloads is even greater at 60%(see Table 5 Integer Sort and LU-D). The total average power varies between 600W-700W. However, they clearly indicate the influence of workload on power estimation, and demonstrate our short-sightedness if we only measure workload independent total power consumption. Conventional power model assumptions lead us to gross mis-estimations not in total power, but the power dissipation source.

Application kernels such as Barne's Hut, Ocean, and LU-D are primarily synthesized using matrix algorithm libraries and they have been mapped onto the matrix and vector cores [8]. The mapping statistics for LU-D indicate a normal trend with the dynamic power greater than the static power. But, important observation is that dynamic power is not significantly greater as in conventional processors. In Barne's hut which is primarily a tree building/traversal problem, Dynamic power=Static power. This is due to characteristics of balanced computation/communication ratio. In Barne's hut the two distinct phases of tree building and force estimation are complements of each other. The tree building is the communication intensive algorithm with close to no computation and it alternates with force estimation which employs $3 * N^2$ multiplication and N^2

divisions where 'N' is number of bodies in subtree. In Ocean we see the influence of communication bound workloads creating the situation of Dynamic power < Static power. Ocean is streams through large data structures and performs few computations at each point.

In MIP processor with functional units being of such distinct classes, mapping policies which entirely utilize only one core, the other cores and functional units act as only memory locations. The number of active function units, the SRAM leakage, and idle function units increase static power prohibitively. In application such as Integer Sort (IS) dominated by communication over the network bus $N_{perf}/N_{data\_transfer} < 1$. The static power dominates over the dynamic power since only the vector core is utilized while the and the scalar and matrix cores are idle. The Embarrassingly Parallel benchmark is dominated by small computation phases which have very little intra-dependency. This is reflected in the power numbers of Table 5 where static power dominates, but is due idle function units rather than communication.

We advocate a metric in the form of $N_{perf}/N_{data\_transfer}$ where 'N_{perf}' is computation performance (ie. communication time is not included) in FLOPS and $N_{data\_transfer}$ is the communication bound in MBytes/s would be appropriate measure for estimating power dissipation dominant factors. Due to simulation constraints we have evaluated a single-chip multiprocessor system. The quantitative results would change if we employ a multi-node system, however it would not change qualitative results since power would be lost on global system network rather than chip interconnects. We hope to validate our network power model and hope to analyze multiprocessor clusters in results work.

7   Conclusion

This paper presents a first ever workload based model targeted towards supercomputers and large multiprocessor systems. We presented a hierarchical hyper-graph based power model for uniprocessor and multiprocessor systems. We developed two schemas (1) SUPERARCH (2) APPLIB , to model the various architecture components, application task mapping and integrated them into our power estimation model. The novel concept of APPLIB was evolved to evaluate the power associated with the execution modules. The power library includes at every hierarchical level the respective characteristics of the application. Suitable power metrics were defined for mapping the levels in the hierarchy (see Fig. 1). In sections 3.1 and 3.2 we developed power models for processors (PDIP) and caches(CAP) that parameterize architecture, technology, and layout details and take into consideration sub-micron effects like interconnect dominance, and crosstalk. We demonstrated our system on a single-chip supercomputer MIP S.C.O.C. We presented our results for a subset of scientific applications from NAS and SPLASH suite and showed the influence of workload characteristics on static,dynamic power dissipation sources. The hierarchical power model, the concept of power library and new power metric definition will contribute greatly towards introducing power awareness in supercomputers. The application dependent power prediction will help supercomputer architects in proposing application specific power saving techniques for various runtime environments. This will aid in putting forth a hardware-software co-design for power estimation. Currently we are validating and estimating PASCOM's accuracy on multiprocessor systems.

References

1. Shekhar Borkar, *"Getting Gigascale Chips"*, ACM Queue magazine (October 2003)
2. D. Sylvester and K. Keutzer, *"Getting to the bottom of deep submicron,"*, Proc. of International Conference on Computer-Aided Design,1998.
3. A. Vittal and M. Marek-Sadowska, *"Low-power buffered clock tree design,"*, IEEE Transactions on Computer-Aided Design, vol. 16, pp. 965-975, September 1997.
4. M.K. Gowan, L.L. Biro, D.B. Jackson, *"Power considerations in the design of the Alpha 21264 microprocessor,"*, Proc. of Design Automation Conference, pp. 726-731, 1998.
5. Fabrizio Petrini, Darren J. Kerbyson, and Scott Pakin *"The Case of the Missing Supercomputer Performance: Achieving Optimal Performance on the 8,192 Processors of ASCI Q "*, Proceedings of Supercomputing Conference,Los Alamos National Laboratory,ACM, November 2003
6. Wu Chun Feng *"Making a Case for Efficient Supercomputing"*, ACM Queue, Oct 2003
7. N Venkateswaran , Arrvindh Shriraman, Aditya Krishnan, S. Niranjan, S.Srinivas *"Memory In Processor:Evolution of a novel Supercomputer Architecture"*, MEDEA Workshop PACT,IEEE and ACM SIGARCH, September 2003
8. N Venkateswaran, Aditya Krishnan, S. Niranjan, Arrvindh Shriraman, S.Srinivas, *"Memory In Processor:A novel design paradigm for Supercomputers,"*, ACM SIGARCH Computer Architecture News, June 2004
9. N Venkateswaran , Arrvindh Shriraman, S. Niranjan Kumar, *"Memory In Processor:A novel design paradigm for Supercomputers,"*, Workshop On Massively Parallel Processing (WMPP), IPDPS, April 2005
10. Synopsys Corporation *"Powermill Data Sheet"*, 1999.
11. Mentor Graphics Corporation *"Quickpower-Power estimation tool"*, 1999
12. David Brooks, Vivek Tiwari and Margaret Martonosi, *"Wattch: A Framework for Architectural-Level Power Analysis and Optimizations"*, Proc. of the 27th International Symposium on Computer Architecture, June 2000, pp 83-94.
13. Arrvindh Shriraman and N. Venkateswaran, *"Power-Delay product for Instruction Execution in a Processor"*, WARF Technical Report VTR_13, November 2003,Link:www.cs.rochester.edu/u/ashriram/pdip.pdf
14. T. Sakurai, *"Closed-form expressions for interconnection delay, coupling, and crosstalk in VLSI's"*, IEEE Transactions on Electron Devices, vol. 40, pp. 118-124, January 1993
15. R. Zimmermann and W. Fichtner, *"Low-power logic styles:CMOS versus pass-transistor logic."*, IEEE Journal of Solid-State Circuits,1997
16. Arrvindh Shriraman, *"CAP : CAche Power estimator"*, WARF Technical Report VTR_14, November 2003
17. Industry Consortium *"International Roadmap for Semiconductors"*, 2003
18. J.C.Eble III, *"A Generic System Simulator with Novel On-Chip Cache and Throughput Models for Gigascale Integration"*, Ph.D. Dissertation, Georgia Institute of Technology, Atlanta, Georgia, 1998

19. L.Benini, M.Favalli, P. Olivo, and B. Ricco, *"A novel approach to cost-effective estimate of power disipation in CMOS ICs"*, European Design Automation Conference, pp. 354-360, 1993

20. F. Dresig, Ph. Lanches, O. Rettig, and U.G. Baitinger, "Simulation and reduction of CMOS power dissipation at logic level," European Design Automation Conference, pp. 341-346, 1993

21. P. Landman and J. Rabaey, *"Black-Box Capacitance Models for Architectural Power Analysis"*, Proceedings of the 1994 International Workshop on Low Power Design, Napa Valley, CA, pp 165-170, April 1994

22. Anantha P. Chandrakasan et al., *"HYPER-LP: A System for Power Minimization UsingArchitectural Transformations"*,Proc. ICCAD, pp.300-303, November 1992

23. Paul Landman and Jan Rabaey, *"Power Estimation for High Level Synthesis"*, Proc. of EDAC-EUROASIC, pp 361-366, February 1993

24. Jeffery.A.Davis, James D. Meindl and Vivek K.De, "A Stochastic Wire-Length Distribution for Gigascale Integration(GSI)" *IEEE Transactions on Electron Devices*,Vol 45,Mar 1998

25. Jeffery.A.Davis, James D. Meindl and Prakash Zarkesh, "Prediction of Net Length Distribution for Global Interconnects" *IEEE Transactions on VLSI*,Dec 2000

26. Dirk Stoobandt and Jan Van Campenhout, "Accurate interconnect length estimation for predictions early in design cycle" *Dept of Electronics and Information Systems,University of Ghent-Belgium*,2000

27. S. Wilton and N. Jouppi, *"An enhanced access and cycle time model for on-chip caches"*, DEC Western Research Lab Technical Report 93/5, July 1994.

28. E. S. Tam et. al, *"mlcache: A Flexible Multi-Lateral Cache Simulator"*, International Symposium on Modeling, Analysis and Simulation of Computer and Telecommunication Systems Jul 1998 pp 19-26

29. T. Wada, S. Rajan, and S. A. Przybylski. *"An Analytical Access Time Model for On-chip Cache Memories"*, IEEE Journal of Solid-State Circuits, vol. 27,pp. 1147-1156, August 1992.

30. M. Zhang, K. Asanovic., *"Highly-associative caches for low-power processors"*, Kool Chips Workshop, 33rd International Symposium on Microarchitecture,December 2000

31. D. H. Bailey, E. Barszcz et.all *"THE NAS PARALLEL BENCHMARKS"* Intl. Journal of Supercomputer Applications, vol. 5, no. 3 (Fall 1991), pp 66.73

32. David E Culler, Jaswinder Pal Singh with Anoop Gupta, *"Parallel Computer Architecture"*, Morgan Kaufmann Publishers Inc., 1999

Power-Aware Collective Tree Exploration[*]

Miroslaw Dynia[1], Miroslaw Korzeniowski[2], and Christian Schindelhauer[3]

[1] DFG Graduate College "Automatic Configuration in Open Systems",
University of Paderborn, Germany
mdynia@uni-paderborn.de
[2] International Graduate School of Dynamic Intelligent Systems,
University of Paderborn, Germany
rudy@uni-paderborn.de
[3] Institute of Computer Science, University of Paderborn, Germany
schindel@uni-paderborn.de

Abstract. An n-node tree has to be explored by a group of k mobile robots deployed initially at the root. Robots traverse the edges of the tree until all nodes are visited. We would like to minimize maximal distance traveled by each robot (e.g. to preserve the battery power). First, we assume that a tree is known in advance. For this NP-hard problem we present a 2-approximation. Moreover, we present an optimal algorithm for a case where k is constant.

From the 2-approximation algorithm we develop a fast 8-competitive online algorithm, which does not require a previous knowledge of the tree and collects information during the exploration. Furthermore, our online algorithm is distributed and uses only a local communication. We show a lower bound of 1.5 for the competitive ratio of any deterministic online algorithm.

1 Introduction

Suppose, we conduct a Mars expedition by sending a group of robots to this distant planet. The team lands at the bottom of an unknown crater. Each mobile robot is equipped with a wireless communication device and batteries for energy supply. The goal of the first mission is to explore the unknown terrain minimizing the energy consumption of each robot.

Since it takes many minutes for a signal to reach the Earth, the remote coordination of the exploration is impossible. So the robots organize themselves as a team and using local distributed strategies complete the mission and return to the landing zone in order to send results (the map of the terrain) to the Earth.

In this paper we investigate the problem of exploring graphs by a group of wireless mobile robots. We assume that there is no central authority, which could coordinate the robots. So the team has to organize itself in order to jointly

---

[*] This research is partially supported by the DFG-Sonderforschungsbereich SPP 1183: "Organic Computing. Smart Teams: Local, Distributed Strategies for Self-Organizing Robotic Exploration Teams".

W. Grass et al. (Eds.): ARCS 2006, LNCS 3894, pp. 341–351, 2006.

explore the terrain. All decisions are made locally without any prior knowledge of the terrain's complexity, as it is always the case for such online problem. The global (optimal) solution emerges from decisions made locally by the robots.

We investigate a terrain with a tree topology. An n-node tree has to be explored by a group of k mobile robots initially deployed at the root. Robots traverse the edges of the tree until all nodes are visited. The goal is to minimize the maximal distance traveled by one robot.

The standard approach in the competitive analysis [1] is to compare results of our *online* algorithm to the results of the optimal *offline* algorithm which knows the tree in advance.

1.1   The Model

We assume we are given a tree T with a root r and D is the maximal distance (number of edges) from r to any node in T, i.e. the height of the tree. The team of k robots has to explore the tree in such a way that robots start and finish at r and jointly traverse all edges of the tree. We minimize the maximal distance traveled by each robot. This problem can be defined in the following way [2]:

Definition 1 (of k-MIN-RE problem).

Instance:	*an undirected tree $T = (V, E)$, $|V| = n$, a fixed node $r \in V$, an integer $k > 0$*
Solution:	*tours $C_1, C_2, \ldots C_k$, where $\bigcup_{i=1}^{k} C_i = E$ and each tour contains the node r*
Goal:	*minimize $c_{\max} = \max\{|C_i| : i = 1, \ldots k\}$*

For the *offline* approximation, we assume that the tree T is known in advance and we construct tours C_i in polynomial time, so that $c_{\max}$ is close to the optimal value.

In the *online* model we assume that robots initially have no knowledge of T and a robot in a node v of T sees only the outgoing *ports*, i.e. beginnings of edges adjacent to v. It does not see the other node adjacent to any edge leaving v. Moreover, we have discrete and synchronous time and each time step consists of the following events:

1. a robot placed at some node v gets the information on all outgoing ports of that node,
2. a robot can communicate with other robots at distance at most 1 (or it can read or write some information on the landmark at node v),
3. a robot may choose either to wait or to traverse an edge from the chosen port.

Waiting and communicating does not induce any energy cost, while traversing an edge costs one unit. The overall cost of the exploration is the maximal distance traveled by one robot, which describes maximal energy used by one robot. We compare this cost to the cost of the optimal algorithm, which knows T in advance.

1.2   Related Work

An exploration of unknown environments is widely studied (see [3] for a survey). The simplest case is when a mobile robot is initially placed at some node of a graph. If the graph is unlabeled, a robot cannot explore the graph alone. Hence, in [4] the robot marks the nodes of the graph with the *pebbles* in order to recognize visited nodes.

In [5] one robot traverses an arbitrary graph in a piecemeal manner and in [6] some natural exploration algorithms are presented (DFS) and lower bounds for exploration are established. In [7] the cost (*penalty*) is measured as a ratio between the number of edge traversals of an algorithm and the overall number of edges m in a graph. There, the authors develop an algorithm with penalty $O(m)$.

The single robot approach can be extended by introducing a larger number of robots and exploring the graph by a *group* of them. In [8] a team of two robots explores an unlabeled directed graph in time $O(d^2n^5)$ with high probability, where d is the maximal degree in the graph.

Profits from a collective exploration of trees are investigated in [2]. They prove $O(D + n/\log k)$ running time of their algorithm, which gives a multiplicative overhead of $O(k/\log k)$ for the time of exploration comparing to the time of an optimal algorithm which knows the tree. They also prove lower bound of $2 - 1/k$ for this ratio.

In [9] they present an $(2 - 2/(k+1))$-approximation algorithm for k-traveling salesman problem for edge-weighted trees with running time $O(k^{k-1} \cdot n^{k-1})$. In [10] the running time is improved to $O((k-1)! \cdot n)$. The k-traveling salesman problem is similar to our model, but it does not constrain the the starting positions of the robots.

The problem of minimizing the maximal distance traveled by a single robot in a collective exploration of an *unweighted* tree is shown to be NP-hard. For trees with *weighted edges* it is NP-hard too and remains NP-hard even for a constant number of robots [11].

1.3   Our Results

In this paper we focus on the exploration of an arbitrary, *unweighted* tree. Unlike in [9] and [10] we constrain positions of robots to one node in the tree (i.e. to the root). As a first result we show how to compute in polynomial time the optimal tours for the problem of the exploration with a fixed number of robots k.

Moreover, we show a 2-approximation algorithm for the problem with an arbitrary number of robots which runs in $O(k \cdot \max\{D, (n-1)/k\})$ time. This significantly improves the time comparing to results of [9] and [10].

Furthermore, from our 2-approximation we develop an 8-competitive algorithm with the same running time for the online problem (Sect. 1.1). We also prove a lower bound of 1.5 for the online problem.

2 The Complexity of *k-MIN-RE*

We start with an observation that *k-MIN-RE* is intractable [2]. The following remark is a result of a simple reduction of *k-MIN-RE* to the *3-PARTITION* problem.

Remark 1. The decision version of the *k-MIN-RE* problem is NP-hard.

We show that for unweighted trees the problem becomes easy when we assume that the number of robots is fixed. The algorithm *DPExplore* based on the dynamic programing technique constructs a k-dimensional array A_v of size n in a bottom-up fashion for each node v. The element $A_v(a_1, a_2, \ldots, a_k)$ of the array is the sequence $(T_1, T_2, \ldots, T_k)$ of subtrees, such that $\bigcup T_i = T_v$, $T_i \subset T_v$, $v \in T_i$ and $a_i = |T_i|$ is the number of edges in T_i. Each subtree defines a tour of a single robot.

The array A_v is capable of storing all possible *reasonable* traversals of T_v (and clearly includes the optimal one) by a group of k robots. The *reasonable* traversals are those, which are optimal or can be used to construct the optimal traversal. If there are many such traversals for fixed $a_1, a_2, \ldots, a_k$, then we take any of them.

The algorithm *DPExplore*(v, T) computes A_v for any v and thus after computing A_r, the *OptFixed*(v, T) algorithm can easily find the optimal solution for $T = T_r$ by finding the cell of an array A_r with the best content. Pseudo-codes for the algorithm and its subprocedures are depicted in Fig. 1, 2 and 3.

$Extend(v, A_s)$
  foreach $b_1, \ldots, b_k$ where $A_s(b_1, \ldots, b_k) \neq \emptyset$ do
    $(T_1, \ldots, T_k) \leftarrow A_s(b)$
    foreach $b_i > 0$ do
      $b_i' \leftarrow b_i + 1$
      $T_i' \leftarrow T_i \cup \{v\}$
      $A'(b') \leftarrow (T_1', \ldots, T_k')$
  return A'

$Combine(A_x, A_y)$
  foreach a, b where $A_x(a) \neq \emptyset$ and $A_y(b) \neq \emptyset$ do
    foreach $1 \leq i \leq k$ do $c_i \leftarrow a_i + b_i$
    $A'(c) \leftarrow A_x(a) \cup A_y(b)$
  return A'

Fig. 1. The *Extend* and *Combine* procedures

Lemma 1. *The algorithm* DPExplore(v, T_v) *computes in* $O(n^{2k+2})$ *time steps the array* A_v, *which contains all* reasonable *traversals of* T_v.

Proof. For $D = 0$ the algorithm computes A_r such that $A_r(0, \ldots, 0)$ is a set of k trees each containing only one node. Clearly this is an optimal solution for a tree in height of 0.

```
DPExplore(v, T)
    if v has no children
        A_v(0, ..., 0) ← the sequence of k trees consisting only of node v
    else
        foreach child s of v do A_s ← DPExplore(s, A_s)
        foreach child s of v do A'_s ← Extend(v, A_s)
        foreach child s of v do A_v ← Combine(A_v, A'_s)
    return A_v
```

Fig. 2. The *DPExplore* algorithm

```
OptFixed(v, T)
    A ← DPExplore(v, T)
    find (a_1, ..., a_k) minimizing max_i{a_i} for which A(a_1, ..., a_k) ≠ ∅
    (T_1, ..., T_k) ← A(a_1, ..., a_k)
    return sequence of C_i described by a tree T_i
```

Fig. 3. The optimal polynomial algorithm for *k-MIN-RE* and fixed k

Suppose that T is $h > 0$ in height and *DPExplore* computes properly arrays for all smaller subtrees. The root r of T has children $s_1, s_2, \ldots, s_d$ where d is the degree of r (clearly $d > 0$). Assume that $A_{s_1}, A_{s_2}, \ldots, A_{s_d}$ have already been computed and contain all *reasonable* traversals of subtrees T_{s_i}. The procedure *Extend*(v, A_{s_i}) builds an array A'_{s_i}, which contains all *reasonable* traversals of subtree $T_{s_i} \cup \{v\}$ for each i. The next d calls of procedure *Combine*(A_v, A_{s_i}) construct all *reasonable* traversals of T.

The upper bound for the number of nonempty elements in A_v is n^k. So, the procedure *Extend* needs $O(n^k)$ time steps. The procedure *Combine* needs $O(n^{2k})$ time steps for the same reason, thus the algorithm *DPExplore* terminates after $O(n^{2k+2})$ time steps.   □

Lemma 2. *The algorithm* OptFixed(r, T) *computes an optimal solution to the problem* k-MIN-RE *for a fixed k in a polynomial time.*

Proof. The first step of *OptFixed* is a call to subalgorithm *DPExplore* which computes in time $O(n^{2k+2})$ the array A containing all reasonable traversals of T (Lemma 1).

Then, the optimal traversal of T can be easily found in $O(n^k)$ time. This implies that the *OptFixed* finds an optimal solution in $O(n^{2k+2})$ time steps, which is polynomial in the size of the tree.   □

3   The Approximation

In this section we present the algorithm which produces tours C_i in such a way that $c_{\max}$ is only two times larger than the cost of the optimal tours. We need

---

LeftWalker(r,t)
    Perform $t/2$ steps of DFS using only unmarked edges and preferring ports with the smallest IDs and then return to r. Mark each traversed edge which does not lead to unmarked edges.

Fig. 4. The *LeftWalker* algorithm

the following simple procedure which is similar to the well-known Depth First Search algorithm. It traverses the tree and marks some edges, which is described in details on Fig. 4.

Let T_v denote the subtree rooted in v and S_v be the sequence of children of v, such that for each $s \in S_v$ the tree T_s contains an unmarked edge. We assume that S_v is sorted in increasing order of IDs.

Furthermore, $B_v = \{(v, w) : w \in S_v\}$ is a set of outgoing edges which lead to subtrees containing unexplored edges. The following fact is straight-forward for a DFS-kind algorithm.

Remark 2. For any v and $s_1, s_2 \in S_v$ where $id(s_1) < id(s_2)$ the *LeftWalker* will not enter the T_{s_2} before completely marking all edges of T_{s_1}

Let $t = 4 \cdot \max\{D, (n-1)/k\}$ and we sequentially run *LeftWalker(r,t)* on the same tree k times. We show two lemmas concerning subsequent calls of *LeftWalker(r,t)* (Fig. 5).

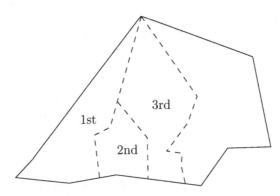

Fig. 5. Subsequential calls of *LeftWalker* algorithm

Lemma 3. *At the beginning of any subsequent call of* LeftWalker(r,t) *the following assertion holds. For each $v \in V$ at most one edge from the current set B_v has been traversed by a robot. If there is such an edge in B_v, it must be (v, w) where w is the node from the current S_v with the smallest ID.*

Proof. Assume that for some v we have two traversed edges in the current B_v. We denote these edges by (v, w_1) and (v, w_2) where $w_1, w_2 \in S_v$ and (w.l.o.g) the ID of the port connecting to w_1 is smaller than the ID of the port connecting to w_2. Then, there is an unexplored edge in both T_{w_1} and T_{w_2}. It means that in some round in the past, *LeftWalker* started to explore 'right' subtree T_{w_2} before finishing T_{w_1}, which contradicts the Remark 2.   □

Lemma 4. *If the next subsequent call of* LeftWalker(r,t) *does not finish the exploration of T, it discovers at least* $\max\{D, (n-1)/k\}$ *'new' edges which were not traversed by any robot before.*

Proof. Suppose that *LeftWalker*(r, t) explores the tree for the first time (first subsequent call) and it will not finish the exploration in this round. Before it starts returning to the root, its energy units are limited to $t/2$. It can traverse each edge at most twice, so it will traverse at least $t/4$ 'new' edges, before reaching the limit.

Suppose that it is a further subsequent call of *LeftWalker*, i.e. there was at least one call before. Assume that the exploration will not be finished in this round, so it will traverse exactly $t/2$ edges. We claim that at least $t/4$ of these edges are 'new', since at most $t/4$ of these edges were traversed before.

Indeed, from Lemma 3, we have that there is at most one such edge at arbitrary distance from the root r. This implies that there exist at most $D \leq t/4$ such edges which have been already traversed and are not marked.   □

Basing on the *LeftWalker* and its properties we define the algorithm depicted in Fig. 6, and in the following lemma we show that it produces a feasible solution.

2-ApproxAlg(T)
    t=max$\{D, (n-1)/k\}$
    for i=1 to k do
        $C_i \leftarrow$ *LeftWalker*$(r, 4t)$

Fig. 6. The approximation algorithm

Lemma 5. *For any tree $T(V, E)$ with root r the algorithm produces a sequence of paths C_i such that*

$$\bigcup C_i = E$$

and r belongs to each path described by C_i.

Proof. Clearly, r belongs to each path described by C_i, since *LeftWalker*$(r, 4t)$ starts and ends in the root. Furthermore, Lemma 4 guarantees that in each pass *LeftWalker*$(r, 4t)$ explores at least $\max\{D, (n-1)/k\}$ 'new' edges or finishes the exploration. This implies that k passes suffice to completely explore the tree ($k \cdot \max\{D, (n-1)/k\} \geq n - 1$ 'new' edges traversed).   □

In the next lemma we show that the algorithm is an approximation of an optimal solution, i.e. we show a lower bound of any feasible solution.

Lemma 6. *For every algorithm for* k-MIN-RE *there exists an index* i *such that* $|C_i| \geq 2 \cdot t$, *where* $t = \max\{D, (n-1)/k\}$.

Proof. Assume that for each i the size $|C_i| < 2D$. Then, the bottom of the tree cannot be reached and at least one leaf cannot be explored. In the case, where for each i, $|C_i| < (2n-2)/k$, we have $\sum_{i=1}^{k} |C_i| < 2n - 2$ steps made, which is not sufficient to explore any tree consisting of n nodes.   □

Our algorithm outputs in $O(k \cdot \max\{D, (n-1)/k\})$ time steps k feasible sequences C_i (Lemma 5), such that $|C_i| \leq 4 \cdot t$ and Lemma 6 states the lower bound of $2 \cdot t$ for the optimal algorithm, which proves the approximation factor of 2 for *k-MIN-RE*.

4   The Online Problem

As described in Sect. 1.1 in the online setting, we assume no previous knowledge of the tree. The robots have to gather information on the terrain's complexity during the exploration. First, we show that no deterministic online algorithm can be optimal and then, we develop the strategy which gives the close to optimal solution. We apply the standard approach and we search in a binary way for the appropriate value of s for the tree.

4.1   Lower Bound

The following lemma states a lower bound on the competitive ratio of any deterministic algorithm.

Lemma 7. *Any deterministic online algorithm for* k-MIN-RE *has the competitive ratio* $\delta \geq 1.5$.

Proof. For an arbitrary deterministic algorithm A we will present a tree for which A needs at least $6 \cdot p$ energy units to explore and for which the optimal offline solution needs only $4 \cdot p$ energy units.

We construct a tree T which is an union of $2k - 2$ paths of length p and one path of length $2p$. The tree $T = (V, E)$, depicted in Fig. 7, is such that:

$$V = \{r\} \cup \{v_{i,j} : 1 \leq i \leq p, 1 \leq j \leq 2k - 1\} \cup \{v_{i,q} : p + 1 \leq i \leq 2p + 2\}$$

and

$$E = \{(r, v_{1,j}) : 1 \leq j \leq 2k - 1\}$$
$$\cup \{(v_{i-1,j}, v_{i,j}) : 2 \leq i \leq p, 1 \leq j \leq 2k - 1\}$$
$$\cup \{(v_{i-1,q}, v_{i,q}) : p + 1 \leq i \leq 2p + 2\}$$

The parameter q is defined for A in such a way, that the node $v_{p,q}$ is visited by a robot which has already visited another node on level p (a node from the set $\{v_{p,j} : 1 \leq j \leq 2k - 1\}$). We assume that q is the smallest number with this property.

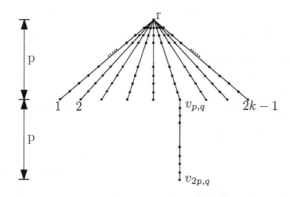

Fig. 7. The tree of lower bound

The offline algorithm may assign one robot to traverse the long path and all other robots to traverse two short paths each. Thus, the tree is explored with an energy of $4p$ per robot. Below we show that the deterministic online algorithm A will need at least $6p$ energy units for at least one robot.

By the definition of q, A uses $q - 1$ robots and $2p$ energy per robot to visit the first $q - 1$ dead ends and then return to r. Then one of these $q - 1$ robots is sent to explore the long path. After the robot reaches node $v_{p,q}$, it discovers that this is the long path. It can not decide to explore this path (its total energy consumption would grow up to $6p$). It comes back to the root, thus some other robot explores the long path. The yet unexplored long path has to be traversed by the robot which has explored no edge before.

Let us sum up the energy the robots used so far. We have three groups of robots:

2 robots with energy consumption of at least $4p$ (which are useless now),
$q - 1$ robots with energy consumption of at least $2p$,
$k - q - 1$ robots which have used no energy.

There are $2k - 1 - q$ unexplored dead ends left, and even if the second group explores $q - 1$ of them, there are still $2k - 2q$ unexplored short paths and only $k - q - 1$ robots which can explore them. Even if each robot takes two short paths, running out the whole available energy, there will be at least one unexplored path. Thus, the team will fail to explore the tree with an energy smaller than $6p$.
□

4.2 The Online Algorithm

Now we introduce a distributed online algorithm which uses *LeftWalker* routine and explores an unknown tree.

Assume that robots have unique IDs from set $[0, 1, \ldots, k - 1]$. The algorithm to explore the tree is depicted in Fig. 8. In the following two lemmas we prove the correctness and a good performance of the algorithm.

```
WarningBee(r,k)
    energy ← 1
    while (tree is not completely explored){
        energy ← energy · 2
        wait( id · energy )
        get list of the most left ports to unmarked edges from the robot id − 1
        LeftWalker( r, energy )
        wait( (k-id) · energy )
    }
```

Fig. 8. The online parallel algorithm for a group of robots

Lemma 8. WarningBee *terminates after* $\lceil \log(2t) \rceil + 1$ *rounds, and thus eventually it completely explores the tree with energy consumption of at most* $16t$ *units per robot.*

Proof. As we know from Sect. 3, running *LeftWalker*$(r, 4t)$ sequentially k times will completely explore the tree. This is the case in the $\lceil \log(2t) \rceil + 1$ round of *WarningBee*, where $energy = 2^{\lceil \log(t) \rceil + 2} \geq 4t$. After all robots have completed this round the whole tree is explored. This implies that *WarningBee* will terminate after $\lceil \log(2t) \rceil + 1$ rounds, where $energy \leq 8t$. Summing up the overall energy used in all rounds, we get at most $16t$ energy units per robot.   □

Lemma 9. *WarningBee is 8-competitive for the online model.*

Proof. Since the *WarningBee* uses at most $16t$ energy units (Lemma 8) and optimal algorithm uses at least $2t$ energy units (Lemma 6) we have the bound of 8 for the competitive ratio.   □

5   Conclusion

We have presented algorithms for exploration of trees with the goal of minimizing maximal energy used by each robot.

The first two algorithms deal with the situation where the tree is known in advance. The third one is online and it efficiently explores a tree not known in advance. The online algorithm is distributed and uses only local communication. Both algorithms are optimal up to a constant factor.

It turns out that the 8-competitive (energy) online algorithm, *WarningBee*, uses at most $O(k \cdot D + n)$ time steps. *WarningBee* moves only one robot at a time and therefore is not capable of optimizing the time of exploration, achieving k-competitiveness in this model (time).

It is known that there is $O(k/\log k)$ competitive online algorithm for optimizing time [2]. At the moment there is a lower bound of $2 − 1/k$, so there is a huge gap left for further research.

References

1. Borodin, A., El-Yaniv, R.: Online computation and competitive analysis. Cambridge University Press, New York, NY, USA (1998)
2. Fraigniaud, P., Gasieniec, L., Kowalski, D., Pelc, A.: Collective tree exploration. In: Proc. LATIN 2004. Volume 2976. (2004) 141–151
3. Rao, N., Kareti, S., Shi, W., Iyenagar, S.: Robot navigation in unknown terrains: Introductory survey of non-heuristic algorithms. Technical report (1993)
4. Bender, M., Fernández, A., Ron, D., Sahai, A., Vadhan, S.: The power of a pebble: exploring and mapping directed graphs. In: Proc. 30th Symp. Theory of Computing, ACM (1998) 269–278
5. Awerbuch, B., Betke, M., Rivest, R., Singh, M.: Piecemeal graph exploration by a mobile robot. Information and Computation **152**(2) (1999) 155–172
6. Dessmark, A., Pelc, A.: Optimal graph exploration without good maps. In: Proc. ESA 2002. Volume 2461. (2002) 374
7. Panaite, P., Pelc, A.: Exploring unknown undirected graphs. In: SODA '98: Proceedings of the ninth annual ACM-SIAM symposium on Discrete algorithms, Philadelphia, PA, USA, Society for Industrial and Applied Mathematics (1998) 316–322
8. Bender, M., Slonim, D.: The power of team exploration: two robots can learn unlabeleddirected graphs. In: Proc. FOCS 1994. (1994) 75–85
9. Averbakh, I., Berman, O.: (p - 1)/(p + 1)-approximate algorithms for p-traveling salesmen problems on a tree with minmax objective. Discrete Applied Mathematics **75**(3) (1997) 201–216
10. Nagamochi, H., Okada, K.: A faster 2-approximation algorithm for the minmax p-traveling salesmen problem on a tree. Discrete Applied Mathematics **140**(1-3) (2004) 103–114
11. Averbakh, I., Berman, O.: A heuristic with worst-case analysis for minimax routing of two traveling salesmen on a tree. Discrete Applied Mathematics **68** (1996) 17–32

Biologically-Inspired Optimization of Circuit Performance and Leakage: A Comparative Study

Ralf Salomon and Frank Sill

Faculty of Computer Science and Electrical Engineering,
University of Rostock, 18051 Rostock, Germany
{ralf.salomon, frank.sill}@uni-rostock.de

Abstract. State-of-the-art technologies in very large scale integration (VLSI) allow for the realization of gates with varying energy consumptions and hence delays (i.e., processing speeds) in the very same circuit. By considering this technological advent as an option, the design process can pursue two different goals: (1) making the circuit as fast as possible and (2) making non-time-critical gates slower in order minimize the circuit's overall energy consumption. This paper utilizes evolutionary algorithms, a population-based heuristic optimization technique, in order to find optimal solutions. From a technological point of view, this goal can be accomplished by varying the individual threshold voltages, which determine both the device's processing speed and its *leakage currents*. The experimental results indicate that evolutionary algorithms yield significantly better solutions than rather traditional optimization algorithms. By maintaining populations of candidate solutions, evolutionary algorithms are able to escape from sub-optimal designs, which contrasts traditional single-point optimization approaches.

1 Introduction

Off-the-shelf products offered virtually everywhere indicate that the processing speed of digital devices, such as personal computers, laptops, personal digital assistents, cellular phones, and the like, is of high importance to many end-users. In other words, end-users expect their devices to operate at a processing speed as *high* as possible. With respect to *mobile devices,* the markets today also suggest another trend: mobile devices are expected to yield times-of-operation as long as possible, probably in order to maximize the end-user's independence on electrical wires.

The issue of a suitable power supply, e.g., by means of rechargeable batteries, becomes even more important in *small* mobile devices, such as cellular phones and personal digital assistants. For example, it would probably be unacceptable for most end-users, if the battery was larger and/or heavier than the actual cellular phone. High processing speed and long time-of-operation are probably *the* driving forces for research on low-power technologies. Section 2 briefly reviews the technological background as well as the relation between energy consumption and processing speed. It turns out, unfortunately, that these two parameters compete with each other by their very nature.

W. Grass et al. (Eds.): ARCS 2006, LNCS 3894, pp. 352–366, 2006.

Among other aspects, current research on low-power [3, 9, 10, 18, 19] tries to minimize a circuit's energy consumption without tampering its processing speed. Normally, a circuit consists of very many interconnected gates. But as Section 2 argues, not all of these gates are equally responsible for the circuit's processing speed. Based on this observation, previous research has proposed to *simultaneously* use both fast high-energy-consuming and slow low-energy-consuming gates in the very same circuit. For this approach, the term dual-threshold CMOS (DTCMOS) has been coined.

It is obvious that all gates within the critical path must be implemented in fast high-energy-consuming technology, in order to obtain maximal processing speed. For all other gates, however, it remains to be determined, which technology is to be used in order to reach both *optimization goals*: fastest processing speed by paying minimal energy consumption.

Previous research [18, 19, 22, 24] has already reported on some encouraging results when applying special-purpose algorithms to the present optimization problem. This is also discussed in Section 2. However, a comparison with human-optimized designs indicates that these algorithms yield good but only sub-optimal solutions. Apparently, these algorithms got stuck at sub-optimal solutions, also known as diverting local optima in the pertinent literature on optimization.

Since the optimization procedures mentioned above do not reliably yield optimal solutions, this paper applies evolutionary algorithms to the problem at hand. Evolutionary algorithms are heuristic population-based search procedures that incorporate random variation and selection. This paper focuses on the application of evolutionary algorithms to the optimization problem at hand, since both numerous experiments and theoretical analyses [1, 6, 17] stress their superior global optimization performance, especially in the presence of unwanted local optima. Therefore, Section 3 presents a short description of this class of algorithms.

In order to allow for an evaluation, this paper applies selected evolutionary algorithms to some rather standard design problems, which are drawn from the ISCAS benchmark suite [7]. Section 4 provides a short description of these tasks, and also summarizes all the relevant parameter settings. The results presented in Section 5 suggest that the selected algorithms evolve designs better than previously reported. Finally, Section 6 concludes with a brief discussion.

2   The Circuit Model and Previous Research

The introduction has already indicated that a device's processing speed f as well as its energy consumption P_{total} are tightly coupled. From a technological point of view, this relation can be approximated by the sum of a static and a dynamic term P_{static} and P_{dynamic}, respectively:

$$P_{\text{total}} = P_{\text{static}} + P_{\text{dynamic}}$$

with

$$P_{\text{static}} \approx P_{leakage} \approx V_{DD} I_{DS} \quad \text{and} \quad P_{\text{dynamic}} \sim \alpha C_{\text{load}} f V_{DD}^2 , \qquad (1)$$

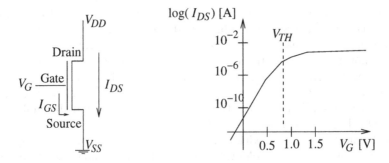

Fig. 1. A CMOS transistor with the main voltages and currents as well as the drain-to-source current $I_{DS} = f(V_G)$ as a function of the gate voltage V_G for a constant power supply V_{DD}. The voltage V_{TH} is called the threshold voltage.

with C_{load} denoting the sum of the device's dynamic capacities (e.g., the gate capacities), V_{DD} denoting the device's power supply, I_{DS} denoting the drain-to-source (static) current (see below), and $P_{leakage}$ denoting the static leakage energy consumption. The dynamic term, as equation (1) indicates, is proportional to the square of the power supply V_{DD}. Research on low-power has consequently reduced V_{DD} from $5V$ to approximately $1.4V$ in recent years. In order to make the CMOS devices still function properly, the gate threshold-voltage V_{TH} has similarly been reduced from approximately $0.7V$ to $0.4V$ [9, 25].

Figure 1 illustrates a CMOS transistor with some of its major voltages and currents. The figure also illustrates the drain-to-source current $I_{DS} = f(V_G)$ as a function of the gate voltage V_G for a constant power supply V_{DD}. It should be noted that the y-axis is in logarithmic scale, thus expressing that the drain-to-source current $I_{DS} \sim \exp(V_G)$ grows exponentialy with the gate voltage V_G. The term V_{TH} is called threshold (gate) voltage, and the regime $V_G < V_{TH}$ is called *sub-threshold*. In current VLSI technologies, the drain-to-source sub-threshold currents $I_{DS} \gg I_{GS}$ are much larger than the gate-to-source sub-threshold currents I_{GS} and thus dominate the static energy consumption $P_{leakage}$.

Unfortunately, the reduction of the gate threshold voltage to $V_{TH} \approx 0.4$ has led to a left-shift of the $I_{DS}(V_G)$ curve, and thus to a significant increase of the sub-threshold drain-to-source current. By contrast, technological advances in the development of new insulators, prevent other leakage currents, such as the gate-to-drain currents I_{GD}, from further increases. Currently available low-power technologies indicate that the static energy consumption $P_{leakage}$ is and will be dominated by the sub-threshold drain-to-source leakage current I_{DS}.

The particularly chosen value of the threshold voltage V_{TH} not only influences the sub-threshold drain-to-source leakage current I_{DS} but also the transistor's delay[1] and thus the device's processing speed: a higher threshold voltage V_{TH}, with a lower sub-threshold drain-to-source leakage current I_{DS} associated to it, requires more time to charge and discharge the transistor's capacitor. Hence,

---

[1] On the transistor as well as gate level, the term *delay* rather than processing speed is more commonly used.

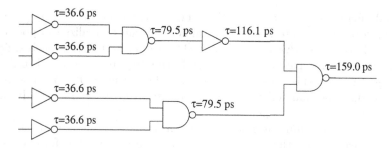

Fig. 2. A simple CMOS-circuit with different path delays, caused by different numbers of gates in each path. The lower path is non-critical, and thus may be subject to the implementation in slow high-voltage technology.

saving energy consumption by increasing the threshold voltage also increases a transistor's delay.

A digital VLSI circuit generally consists of very many gates of different types, such as NAND, NOR, inverters, etc., and varying numbers of inputs, which together realize the circuit's functionality, e.g., a network adapter or a microprocessor. It used to be that throughout the entire VLSI circuit, the very same threshold voltage V_{TH} was used for all transistors. But the simple example presented in Figure 2 allows for the observation that not all gates are equally important for the circuit's overall delay: the upper path has more gates in sequence and thus constitutes the circuit's critical path, since it determines its overall delay, whereas the lower path processes its signals faster anyhow. In other words, the gates residing in the non-critical path can be processing their signals slower without affecting the circuit's overall delay to some extent.

Based on the observation discussed above, dual-threshold CMOS (DTCMOS) design techniques [9, 10, 22, 24] have proposed to employ both slow high-threshold and fast low-threshold gate types in the very same circuit. These two gate types are obviously realized by high-threshold and low-threshold transistors, respectively. In addition, previous research [3, 18, 19, 23] has also generalized this idea by allowing a variable number of fast and slow transistors, thus providing a rather fine-grained differentiation of the gate's delay and its energy consumption. Table 1 provides three examples of three different realizations with their resulting delays and leakage currents. For further details, the interested reader is referred to [18, 19].

Table 1. This table shows three different realizations with their resulting delays and leakage currents for NOR-2, NAND-2, and an inverter

NOR-2		NAND-2		INV	
66.3 ps	86.0 nA	42.9 ps	135.0 nA	36.6 ps	92.8 nA
78.0 ps	36.6 nA	51.3 ps	46.5 nA	37.6 ps	62.5 nA
90.0 ps	10.6 nA	58.3 ps	20.3 nA	45.8 ps	12.6 nA

By offering p specific implementations, i.e., delay and energy consumption, per gate and a total of g gates, the very same circuit can be realized in potentially $n = g^p$ alternatives. Previous research [11] has suggested that $p=3$ different implementations per gate are optimal; unfortunately, no substantial indication was provided, why this choice is supposed to be optimal. One possible reason might be that the number of possible realizations grows exponentially in the number p implementations per gate.

For the task of finding optimal designs, previous research [10, 18, 19, 22] has employed various algorithms, from which two serve as a baseline for comparison purposes. The first algorithm [18], denoted as SFA-I (straight-forward algorithm, variant I) for short, starts off by using the slowest implementation for all gates. It then accelerates the critical path by substituting some of them with their fastest counterparts until either this path has turned into a non-critical one or no further gates can be accelerated. This step is repeated as long as it can change a critical path into a non-critical one. Finally, all fast gates are substituted by the medium ones as long as this does not affect the circuit's overall delay.

The second algorithm [19], denoted as SFA-II for short, is a modification of a previous development [12, 21]. It starts off by selecting the fastest alternatives for all gates. It then consecutively substitutes them with medium or slow alternatives by preferring gates with a high fan-out. The step is repeated until no further gate can be slowed down without affecting the circuit's overall delay. For further details, the interested reader is referred to the literature [18, 19].

3   The Evolutionary Approach

The term *evolutionary algorithms* refers to a class of heuristic population-based search procedures that incorporate random variation and selection, and provide a framework that mainly consists of genetic algorithms [6], evolutionary programming [4, 5], and evolution strategies [15, 17].

Even though all evolutionary algorithm have their own peculiarities, they share many common features. All evolutionary algorithms maintain a population of μ individuals, also called parents. In each generation, an evolutionary algorithm generates λ offspring by copying randomly selected parents and applying variation operators, such as mutation and recombination. It then assigns a fitness value (defined by a fitness or objective function) to each offspring. Depending on their fitness, each offspring is given a specific survival probability. The canonical form of an evolutionary algorithm can be "formally" described as follows:

Step 0: Initialization of the population's individuals and evaluation of the individuals' fitness

Step 1: Selection of the parents according to a preselected selection scheme (e.g., roulette wheel, linear ranking, truncation selection)

Step 2: Recombination of selected parents by exchanging parts of their genes

Step 3: Mutation of some genes by a pre-specified probability

Step 4: If not termination criterion met, go to Step 1

The Generic Evolutionary Algorithm

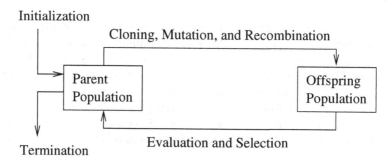

Fig. 3. A graphical visualization of an evolutionary algorithm in its canonical form

Figure 3 presents a graphical visualization of an evolutionary algorithm, and for a good overview as well as further details, the interested reader is referred to [1].

By selecting certain individuals as parents, an evolutionary algorithm advances from one generations to another. The two most-commonly used selection schemes are denoted as either (μ,λ) or $(\mu+\lambda)$. The first selection scheme, i.e., (μ,λ) indicates that the algorithm chooses the parents for the next generation *only* from the offspring, whereas the latter selection scheme selects from the union of the previous parents *and* the current offspring; the latter form is also known as μ-fold elitism.

As has been discussed above and exemplified in Table 1, all gates can be configured with three different leakage currents[2]. Therefore, the optimization problem at hand is *discrete* by its very nature for which the traditional form of genetic algorithms is particularly suited. In the experimental comparisons, these algorithms are denoted as $(\mu+\lambda)$-GA or (μ,λ)-GA for short. The other evolutionary algorithm variants, particularly evolutionary programming and evolution strategies, are *rather* tailored to continuous parameter optimization and are thus not further considered in this paper.

4   Methods

The first task of almost any optimization procedure is to find a proper machine coding, also called genome or genotype, for the problem at hand. Here, this paper adopts a direct coding in which every gate is represented by a particular allele, which codes for the particularly chosen leakage current I_{DS}. Thus, a device that consists of n gates is represented by a genome of n positions with each being able to assume three different values (see above and also [11]).

Since each gate can choose its leakage current only from three different values, the implementation of an appropriate mutation operator is straight forward: it

---

[2] It should be noted that the actual values of the leakage currents are not equivalent for all gates, but depend on their number of inputs, functionality, and other parameters.

chooses the next lower or higher value. In accordance with the literature [6, 16] a mutation probability $p_m = 1/n$ with n denoting the number of gates was chosen in all experiments.

The literature [1, 6, 15] offers a large selection of various recombination operators for evolutionary algorithms. But since recombination could not yield any performance advantage in the present task, non of these operators is been used in this paper. Furthermore, the literature [15] suggests that $\mu=1$ parent and $\lambda=6$ offspring yield the highest sequential efficiency.

As has been outlined above, the fitness function should incorporate both the network's delay and its energy consumption. Since the network's delay is of primary interest (by definition), the following fitness function has been used:

$$f = \text{delay} - \frac{1}{\text{leakage}} . \tag{2}$$

For the goal of doing a comparative study, this paper has selected the following five standard designs (for further details, see [7]):

C432 is a 27-channel interrupt controller [26] with a total of 36 inputs and 7 outputs. The controller has 27 interrupt request inputs, which are grouped into 3 buses with 9 lines each. It has further 9 control inputs, which activates/de-activates the associated interrupt lines. The implementation of such an interrupt controller, requires 160 gates.

C1355 is a 32-Bit single-error correcting circuit [27]. By utilizing a (40,32) Hamming code matrix, it generates a 8-bit long syndrom by reading the 32 input lines. The 41 input lines are forwarded along with the 8-bit syndrom to a correction unit. The implementation of this device requires 546 gates.

C3540 is a 8-bit arithmetic-logical-unit (ALU) [28] with 50 inputs and 22 outputs. It realizes various arithmetic, logical, BCD, shift, and other operations on 8 input lines, and its implementation requires 1669 gates.

C5315 is an extension of the C3540-circuit [29], in that it realizes a 9-bit ALU with 178 inputs and 123 outputs, which requires 2406 gates for its implementation.

C7552 is a device [30] that contains a 34-bit adder, a 34-bit comparator, which requires an additional 34-bit adder, and an 34-bit parity checker. The circuit requires 3512 gates to map the 207 inputs onto 108 outputs.

For the realization, this paper used a previously developed gate library [20], which is based on the 65 nm Berkeley predictive technology models (BPTM).

5   Results

Direct performance comparisons are not straight forward for the following two reasons: first, two quality measures are simultaneously subject to the optimization process, and second, the optimization procedures considered in this paper operate on different time scales. Therefore, this section starts off with a detailed

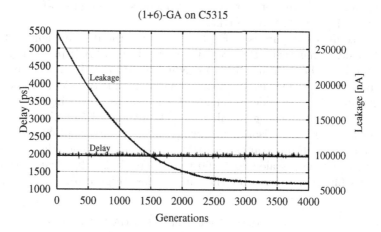

Fig. 4. The evolution of both the circuit's delay (y-axis on the left-hand-side) and leakage (y-axis on the right-hand-side) when using (1+6)-genetic algorithms for the C5315 problem

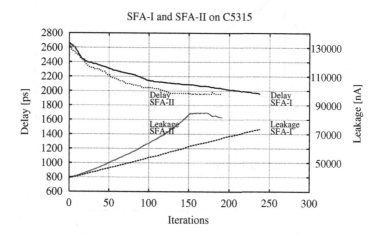

Fig. 5. The evolution of both the circuit's delay (y-axis on the left-hand-side) and leakage (y-axis on the right-hand-side) when applying a straight-forward optimization algorithm on the C5315 problem

discussion of Figures 4-7, which show various performance figures obtained on the ALU-design problem C5315.

Figure 4 shows the evolution of the both the delay and leakage when using both a (1+6)-GA and a (1,6)-GA. Since the genetic algorithms initialize all gates with the fastest realizations, the delay starts at 1955 ps and a (total) leakage of 272,600 nA. During the corse of evolution, then, the leakage drops to almost a fifth of that value, i.e., about 58,597 nA, without increasing the circuit's delay as requested. Since the performance graphs of both procedure are virtually identical, the remainder of this section focuses on the (1+6)-GA and does not consider the (1,6)-GA any further.

For comparison purposes, Figure 5 presents the development of both delay and leakage when using the procedures SFA-I and SFA-II previously developed [18, 19]. It can be seen that both procedures start off with a relatively large delay of about 2656 ps, but arrive at the same final value of 1955 ps after about 150 to 250 iterations. In order to attain this improved processing, both procedures have increased the leakage to about 73,443 nA and 81,580 nA, respectively.

For a better comparison of the two parameters under optimization, Figures 6 and 7 combine those graphs into two figures. To this end, the time scale, i.e., x-axis, has been rescaled to a 100 time units. It can be clearly seen that the circuit's final delay arrive at the same values (Figure 6), whereas the genetic

Delay on C5315 when using a (1+6)-GA, SFA-I, and SFA-II

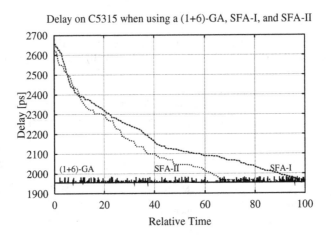

Fig. 6. The evolution of the delay for all algorithms

Leakage on C5315 when using a (1+6)-GA, SFA-I, and SFA-II

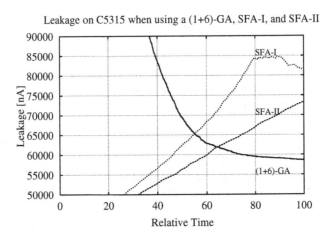

Fig. 7. The evolution of the leakage for all algorithms

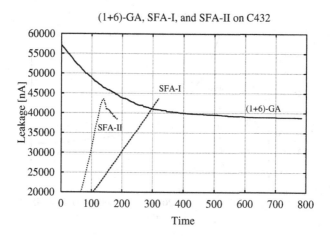

Fig. 8. The evolution of the leakage when applying a (1+6)-GA, SFA-I, and SFA-II to the C432 problem

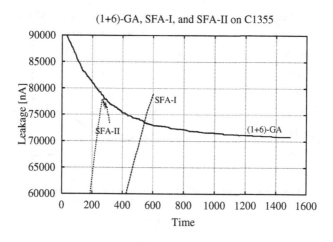

Fig. 9. The evolution of the leakage when applying a (1+6)-GA, SFA-I, and SFA-II to the C1355 problem

algorithms were able to improve the leakage by about 20-30% (Figure 7). This, however, came at the cost of a significant increase in the computational requirements. With respect to the end-users expectations on the time-of-operation, this additional optimization effort might by worth it, especially since this has to be done only once during the circuit's design process.

Figures 8 to 11 show how the optimization procedures under consideration evolve the leakage over time for the other four design problems C432, C1355, C3540, and C7552, respectively. As for the C5315 problem discussed first, all procedures exhibit a similar behavior. Furthermore, all procedures arrive at the same final delay (not shown in any figure) for each problem.

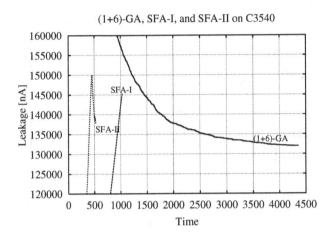

Fig. 10. The evolution of the leakage when applying a (1+6)-GA, SFA-I, and SFA-II to the C3540 problem

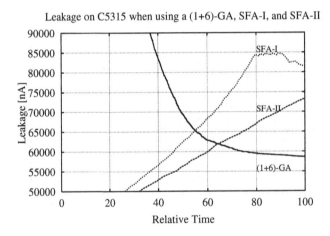

Fig. 11. The evolution of the leakage when applying a (1+6)-GA, SFA-I, and SFA-II to the C5315 problem

The performance graphs may be summarized as follows: In comparison to SFA-I, SFA-II constitutes a significant improvement in that it requires shorter optimization time and often yields lower leakage values. SFA-II increases the leakage by substituting slow high-voltage gates by their fastest counter parts, until the circuit has the shortest delay possible. It then reduces the resulting leakage by also considering medium-voltage gates.

The genetic algorithms by contrast, yielded the lowest overall leakage and thus energy consumption values, but required substantially more time. This observation goes in-line with the pertinent literature [15]: evolutionary algorithms are a general framework, which might be slower than special-purpose procedures

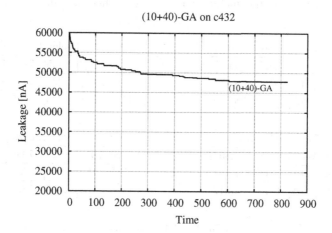

Fig. 12. The evolution of the leakage when applying a (10+40)-GA to the C432 problem

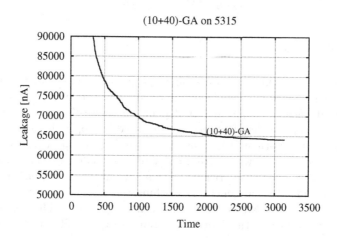

Fig. 13. The evolution of the leakage when applying a (10+40)-GA to the C5315 problem

in many cases but have the ability to escape from local optima, and are thus often able to yield superior results. For comparison purposes, Table 2 presents the final values for delay and leakage for all algorithms over all problems considered in this paper.

In order to assess the utility of large population sizes, Figures 12 and 13 illustrate the application of a (10+40)-GA to the C432 and C5315 problems, respectively. A comparison with Figures 8 and 11, respectively, indicates that a (10+40)-GA might be faster in terms of the number of generations but significantly slower in terms of the number of functions evaluations, which is the product of the number of generations and the number of offspring λ.

Table 2. Comparison of the final delay and leakage values over all procedures and all problems

C432	Delay	Leakage
SFA-I	1045	43,699
SFA-II	1045	38,482
(1+6)-GA	1045	38,779

C1335	Delay	Leakage
SFA-I	925	79,037
SFA-II	925	73,443
(1+6)-GA	925	70,781

C3540	Delay	Leakage
SFA-I	1618	145,504
SFA-II	1618	137,857
(1+6)-GA	1618	132,012

C5315	Delay	Leakage
SFA-I	1955	73,443
SFA-II	1955	81,580
(1+6)-GA	1955	58,597

C7552	Delay	Leakage
SFA-I	1198	180,714
SFA-II	1198	195,898
(1+6)-GA	1198	169,948

6   Conclusions

This paper has argued that processing speed and energy consumptions are properties, which end-users consider important for mobile devices. It has been discussed that these two parameters depend on each other due to technological reasons. This paper has furthermore reviewed two optimization procedures, which have been investigated in previous research. Since previous research has led to optimized designs, which are inferior to devices designed by humans, this paper has applied genetic algorithms to this optimization problem. The experimental results indicate that genetic algorithms were able to reduce the leakage by about 10-40% as compared to previously optimized designs. The results also indicate, however, that genetic algorithms require substantially more computation time.

Future research will be dedicated to the investigate of further optimization approaches, such as simulated annealing and other evolutionary algorithm variants, Furthermore, future research will be investigating to what extent an increase of the number p of different gate implementations can benificial for the overall energy consumption.

Acknowledgements

The authors gratefully thank Ralf Joost for fruitful discussions and many valuable comments on draft versions of this paper. The authors also thank Prof. Timmermann for his continuous support. Part of this research was supported by the German Research Foundation (DFG), grant number 466.

References

1. T. Bäck, U. Hammel, and H.-P. Schwefel, Evolutionary Computation: Comments on the History and Current State. *IEEE Transactions on Evolutionary Computation*, **1**(1):3-17, 1997.
2. Y.S. Borkar. VLSI Design Challenges for Gigascale Integration, keynote address at the 18th Conference on VLSI Design, Kolkata, India, 2005.
3. W. Chen, W. Hang, P. Kudva, G.D. Gristede, S. Kosonocky, and R.V. Joshi. Mixed Multi-Threshold Differential Cascode Voltage Switch (MT-DCVS) Circuit Styles and Strategies for Low Power VLSI Design, in E. Macii, V. De, and M.J. Irwin (Eds.) *Proceedings of the 2001 International Symposium on Low Power Electronics and Design (ISLPED'01)*, pp. 263-266, 2001.
4. Fogel, L.J., 1962. Autonomous Automata. *Industrial Research*, **4**:14-19.
5. D.B. Fogel. *Evolutionary Computation: Toward a New Philosophy of Machine Learning Intelligence.*. IEEE Press, NJ, 1995.
6. D.E. Goldberg. *Genetic Algorithms in Search, Optimization and Machine Learning.* Addison-Wesley, Reading, MA, 1989.
7. M. Hansen, H. Yalcin, and J. P. Hayes. Unveiling the ISCAS-85 Benchmarks: A Case Study in Reverse Engineering, in *IEEE Design and Test,* **16**(16):72-80, 1999.
8. J.K. Kao, A. Chandrakasan, and D. Antoniadis. Transistor sizing issues and tool for multi-threshold CMOS technology, in *Proceedings of the 34th Conference on Design Automation (DAC)*, pp. 409-414, 1997.
9. J.K. Kao and A. Chandrakasan. Dual-Threshold Voltage Techniques for Low-Power Digital Circuits, *IEEE Journal of Solid State Circuits*, **35**(7):1009-1018, 2000.
10. T. Karnik, Y. Ye, J. Tschanz, L. Wei, S. Burns, V. Govindarajulu, V. De, and S. Borkar, Total Power Optimization by Simultaneous Dual-Vt Allocation and Device Sizing in High Performance Microprocessors, in *Proceedings of the 39th Conference on Design Automation*, pp. 486-491, 2002.
11. T. Kuroda. Low-Power, High-Speed CMOS VLSI Design. In *Proceedings of the IEEE International Conference on Computer Design: VLSI in Computer and Processors (ICCD 2002)*, pp. 310-315, 2002.
12. M. Liu, W.S. Wang, and M. Orshansky. Leakage Power Reduction by Dual-Vth Designs under Probabilistic Analysis of V_{th} Variation, in R.V. Joshi, K. Choi, V. Tiwari, and K. Roy (Eds.), *Proceedings of the 2004 International Symposium on Low Power Electronics and Design (ISLPED 2004)*, pp. 2-7, 2004.
13. D.G. Luenberger. *Linear and Nonlinear Programming.* Addison-Wesley, Menlo Park, CA, 1984.
14. W.H. Press, B.P. Flannery, S.A. Teukolsky, and W.T. Vetterling. *Numerical Recipes.* Cambridge University Press, 1987.
15. I. Rechenberg, *Evolutionsstrategie* (Frommann-Holzboog, Stuttgart, 1994).
16. R. Salomon. Reevaluating Genetic Algorithm Performance under Coordinate Rotation of Benchmark Functions; A survey of some theoretical and practical aspects of genetic algorithms. *BioSystems*, **39**(3):263-278, 1996.
17. H.-P. Schwefel. *Evolution and Optimum Seeking.* John Wiley and Sons, NY. 1995.
18. F. Sill, F. Grassert, and D. Timmermann. Low Power Gate-level Design with Mixed-Vth (MVT) Techniques, in *Proceedings of the 17th Symposium on Integrated Circuits and Systems (SBCCI)*, 2004.
19. F. Sill, F. Grassert, and D. Timmermann. Reducing Leakage with Mixed-Vth (MVT), in *Proceedings of 18th Conference on VLSI Design*, pp. 874-877, 2005.

20. F. Sill, F. Grassert, and D. Timmermann. Total Leakage Power Optimization with Improved Mixed Gates, in *Proceedings of the 18th Symposium on Integrated Circuits and Systems Design (SBCCI 2005)*, 2005.

21. A. Srivastava, D. Sylvester, and D. Blaauw. Statistical Optimization of Leakage Power Considering Process Variations using Dual-V_{th} and Sizing, in S. Malik, L. Fix, and A.B. Kahng (Eds.), *Proceedings of the 41st Design Automation Conference (DAC 2004)*, pp. 773-778, 2004.

22. V. Sundararajan and K. Parhi. Low Power Synthesis of Dual Threshold Voltage CMOS VLSI Circuits, in *Proceedings of the IEEE International Symposium on Low Power Electronics and Design*, pp. 139-144, 1999.

23. L. Wei, Z. Chen, and K. Roy. Mixed-vth (MVT) CMOS Circuit Design Methodology for Low Power Applications. in *Proceedings of the 36th Design Automation Conference*, pp. 430-435, 1999.

24. L. Wei, K. Roy, and C. Koh. Power Minimization by Simultaneous Dual-Vth Assignment and Gate-sizing, in *Proceedings of the IEEE Custom Integrated Circuits Conference*, pp. 413-416, 2000.

25. N.H.E. Weste and D. Harris. *CMOS VLSI Design: A Circuits and Systems Perspective*, 3rd edition. Addison-Wesley. 2004.

26. http://www.eecs.umich.edu/~jhayes/iscas/c432.html

27. http://www.eecs.umich.edu/~jhayes/iscas/c499.html

28. http://www.eecs.umich.edu/~jhayes/iscas/c3540/c3540.html

29. http://www.eecs.umich.edu/~jhayes/iscas/c5315/c5315.html

30. http://www.eecs.umich.edu/~jhayes/iscas/c7552/c7552.html

A Synchronous Multicast Application for Asymmetric Intra-campus Networks: Definition, Analysis and Evaluation

Pilar Manzanares-Lopez, Juan Carlos Sanchez-Aarnoutse,
Josemaria Malgosa-Sanahuja, and Joan Garcia-Haro

Departament of Information Technologies and Communications,
Antiguo Cuartel de Antigones, E-30202, Cartagena, Spain
{pilar.manzanares, juanc.sanchez, josem.malgosa, joang.haro}@upct.es

Abstract. In this paper, we propose and analyze an application called SOMA (SynchrOnous Multicast Application) which offers multicast file transfer service in an asymmetric intra-campus environment. For efficient bandwidth utilization, SOMA uses IP multicasting. Since TCP cannot be used in multicast situations, we also propose a transport protocol involving a flow control algorithm. This algorithm adapts the protocol window size and the overall application transfer rate to the minimum network capacity, allowing synchronism and reacting quickly when congestion arises at any router. The protocol behavior has been intensively tested in a lab, using a mixture of wired and wireless networks. The paper also explains how to capture and post-process SOMA network traffic. In addition, we develop a mathematical model to validate the most important protocol parameters. The methodology employed to define, analyze and evaluate this protocol is, indeed, another contribution and can be easily extended to other multicast protocols.

1 Introduction

The use of multicasting within a network has many benefits. Multicast minimizes the link bandwidth consumption because no multiple unicast connections are needed to send the information. It also reduces the sender and router processing and the delivery delay.

In this paper we propose, analyze, implement and test a SynchrOnous Multicast Application called SOMA to transfer large amount of data from a server to a group of clients. It is specially featured to operate in an intra-campus environment (several interconnected LANs through few routers). We also describe how to capure and post-process its generated network traffic. In particular, we have used a Linux kernel architecture to improve the packet capture process (*BSD Packet Filter*) and we have modified the two well-known open-source sniffers (*tcpdump* and *ethereal*) to interpret our protocol packets.

Since TCP is a unicast (point-to-point) oriented protocol, it cannot be used in a multicast environment. Therefore, a key aspect associated to the application design is the definition and implementation of an appropriate multicast transport

W. Grass et al. (Eds.): ARCS 2006, LNCS 3894, pp. 367–381, 2006.

protocol. Although a large number of multicast transport protocols have been proposed in the literature, most of them are extremely complex and some of them move transport level tasks to network devices (for example, to provide NAK or ACK suppression).

Our main contribution in comparison with the related work in [1][2][3] is to define and code an efficient and extremely simple multicast transport protocol able to work in an asymmetric intra-campus scenario. Obviously, our solution requires multicast network facilities, but this is not a concern since involved routers are located into our administrative domain. In spite of its simplicity, our proposed protocol provides the main tasks of a transport protocol: Efficient and simple flow control, congestion control and error correction algorithms. In addition, it fairly shares network capacity with other flows.

SOMA protocol simplicity makes possible an easy codification and a feasible mathematical analysis of the main key features which enables the optimization of some parameter values. It has been described and validated using the SDL specification and description language and it has been written in C language using standard Linux kernel routines.

The rest of this paper is organized as follows. Section 2 describes the protocol. In section 3 the key protocol parameters are analytically characterized. Section 4 describes the methodology used to capture and process SOMA traffic. Section 5 presents our test results in a mixed wired and wireless LAN. Finally, section 6 concludes the paper.

2   SOMA Description

SOMA is a multicast application designed for transmitting synchronously large files and hard disk partitions to a set of clients. This protocol is an extension and enhancement of a previous work [4] to cover asymmetric intra-campus networks.

The application employs IP multicast addressing and implements its own multicast transport protocol over UDP. Thereby, port multiplexing and error checking facilities are automatically resolved by the kernel. However, due to the UDP simplicity, the flow control and error recovery mechanisms have to be implemented to fit the transport layer requirements of our application. For this reason we refer to SOMA alternatively as an application or as a transport protocol.

2.1   Overall Protocol Description

SOMA splits the transmission process into two phases. In the first one, the server multicasts a set of data packets (a window) to all clients. The clients store the payload and confirm the received packets by an ACK. Although in this phase the server never retransmits any data packet, a client issues a NACK packet when packet losses are detected and it also saves an error mark instead of the payload. The feedback information (ACK and NACK packets) received at the server are used to resize the window. The above procedure is repeated until the file is completely transferred.

The second phase, that is focused on error correction, starts when the entire file has been transmitted. Each receiver re-scan their file looking for error marks. If one of them is found, the client delivers a unicast Repair-Request packet towards the server. The server answers the client sending a unicast Repair-Response packet.

One of the main SOMA protocol features is synchronicity. The proposed flow control algorithm, that is explained and tested below, adapts the server transmission rate to the slowest bitrate of a participant network. Therefore, all the clients receive the information at the same time.

SOMA is mainly used to replicate a large amount of information. In this scenario, the reduction of packet flows to only one multicast data flow is the objective and synchronicity is a consequence. However, the syncronicity feature converts SOMA in a useful and simple multicast transport protocol also for real time applications.

Error correction tasks are relegated to a final phase since current network technologies offer low error rates. This assumption avoids a complex protocol design, solving unfrequent packet losses during the transmission. Furthermore, the protocol adaptation for real time applications only requires to disable the error correction phase.

2.2   Proposed Header

The SOMA packet header consists of 4 fields. The Sequence Number (SN, 4 bytes long) used mainly for packet loss detection. The Type Of Packet (TOP, 1 byte), which distinguishes a DATA, an ACK, a NACK, a Repair Request or a Repair Response packet. The Payload Length (PL, 2 bytes) indicates the total packet length in bytes. The Last Window Sequence Number (LWSN, 4 bytes) is used to indicate the last packet of a given window. The header is followed by the payload, which transports 512 information bytes.

2.3   Flow Control Algorithm

After the server sends a data packet window, it starts a timer called timeout and immediately waits until an ACK packet for each participating LAN acknowledges the window or until the timer expires. If the timer expires before the ACKs are received, its value is increased multiplying it by a factor of α ($\alpha > 1$). But if the window is confirmed in time, the timer value is decreased as denoted by expression (1)

$$T_{out} = max\{\frac{Tout}{\beta}, default\_Tout\}. \tag{1}$$

Where β is also greater than one ($\beta > 1$) and *default_Tout* is the bottom threshold value. The server repeats the above operation until the file is completely transferred.

The window is only confirmed when the server receives one ACK for each LAN, ensuring synchronism among all multicast clients. Therefore, if one of the networks suffers congestion, the timeout value is increased and therefore, the data transmission rate decreases. When congestion disappears, the timer redefinition allows to increase the transfer rate again.

To improve the flow control reaction, it is convenient that not only the timer but also the window size changes appropriately. To accomplish this, just before sending the next data window, the server modifies the window size as follows:

- If the expected ACKs associated to this window have been received before the timer expires, the server increases the window size in one unit.
- If the timeout expires, the server decreases in one unit the window size.
- For each NACK that indicates a different packet lost (only the first identical NACK is considered), the server decrements the window size in one unit.

On the other hand, the clients are waiting for data packets. When a packet arrives, each client extracts the SN and compares it with the expected value:

- If SN is the expected one, the client stores the payload and updates the sequence number.
- If SN is greater, the client detects packet losses and sends a NACK with the sequence number of the received data packet. Simultaneously, it finds out the number of packets lost and it stores an error mark for each one. Finally it also stores the data contained in the received packet.
- If SN is smaller, the data packet is discarded.

In addition, if the SN matches with the LWSN value, the client competes for sending an ACK to confirm the entire window issued by the server.

2.4   Feedback Implosion Reduction

To reduce the amount of ACK feedback packets in the network, a client must wait a random period called ARTP (ACK Random Time Period) before sending an ACK and simultaneously listens if other client is transmitting the same ACK. If the ARTP expires and the ACK has not been received, the client generates and multicasts its own ACK. The rest of clients will receive the ACK but only the clients at the ACK sender side will disable its own ACK transmission. The ARTP value is obtained from a uniform probability distribution function ranging between zero and $ARTP_{max}$. Thereby, only one ACK for each participant LAN is sent to the server, independently of the number of clients.

The effective ACK generation time is a random variable defined as: $ARTP = min(ARTP_1, \cdots, ARTP_n)$, where n is the number of clients. Therefore, the mean ARTP value is

$$\overline{ARTP} = \left(1 - \frac{n}{n+1}\right) \cdot ARTP_{max}. \tag{2}$$

It is clearly decreasing with the number of clients.

Figure 3 briefly shows the usual protocol operation. The server sends a set of data packets, increasing each time the window size until W_T size is reached. At this point, the timer expires just before the ACK is received, probably because

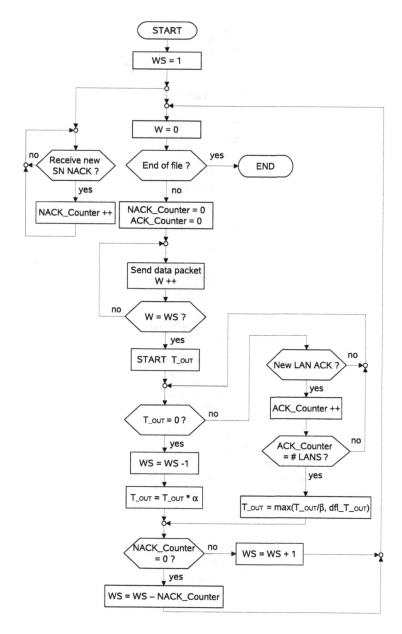

Fig. 1. Flowchart of the multicast stage of the server

at some network point congestion arises. The server reacts quickly increasing the timer value and decreasing the window size. It is clear that for protocol consistency, the timer (timeout) must be greater than the mean ARTP value $(\overline{ARTP})$.

Figures 1 and 2 summarize server and client behavior.

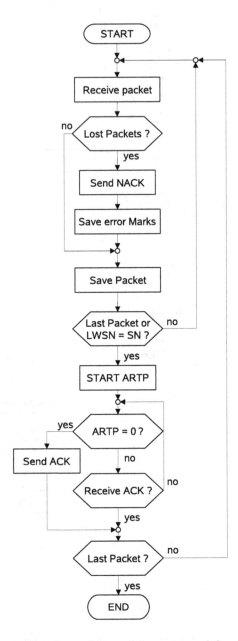

Fig. 2. Flowchart of the multicast stage of the client

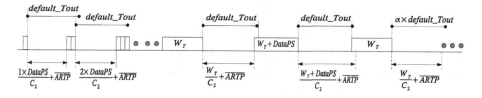

Fig. 3. Window size evolution in an asymmetric network environment. One of the networks (at C_1 Mbps) is slower than the other one (at C_2 Mbps). The window size (W) is expressed in bits.

3   Protocol Characterization

The protocol behavior is strongly correlated with the flow control algorithm performance. In particular, the maximum window size, the steady state window size and the maximum throughput values are the three most important protocol parameters.

3.1   Maximum Window Size

The transmission rate is determined by the network capacity, the timeout timer and the window size. The proposed flow control algorithm modifies the last two parameters to reach an optimum transfer rate.

If there is no congestion, the server increases the window size up to its maximum value (suppose also an error-free transmission channel). To simplify, but without loss of generality, suppose that there is only one LAN with capacity C bps. Suppose also that the file size is large enough to assume that the transmission is performed by the maximum window size. Under these conditions, the total transfer time can be calculated as

$$T = \frac{FileS}{PayloadS} \cdot \frac{DataPS}{C} + \frac{FileS}{PayloadS \cdot WindowS} \left(\overline{ARTP} + \frac{AckPS}{C} \right). \quad (3)$$

Where FileS is the file size, PayloadS is the data packet payload size, DataPS and AckPS are the data and ACK packet sizes respectively and WindowS is the maximum window size.

The first addend is the time needed for the server to transfer the file and the second one is the required time by the clients to issue the ACKs. It is obvious that a high maximum window value enables a faster transmission rate, but at the same time the protocol has fewer opportunities to react to network congestion.

By simply operating in (3), the transfer time reduction due to the use of a window size W_2 instead of W_1 ($W_2 > W_1$) is equal to

$$\frac{FileS}{PayloadS} \left(\overline{ARTP} + \frac{AckPS}{C} \right) \cdot \frac{W_2 - W_1}{W_1 W_2}. \quad (4)$$

If an appropriate window size W_1 is selected, an alternative window size W_2 (where $W_2 \gg W_1$) does not provide a remarkable transfer time reduction since

$$\lim_{W2 \to \infty} \frac{W_2 - W_1}{W_2 W_1} = \frac{1}{W_1}. \tag{5}$$

According to (4) and (5) we choose a maximum window size of 100 data packets (rule of thumb) since it achieves both, fast data transmission rate and a quick response when congestion arises.

3.2   Window Size Convergence

The window size during the transmission reaches a steady state value, which is strongly correlated with the throughput. In this section we find out a mathematical expression to this parameter.

In our analytical model, we must assume some simplifications to reduce the extremely complex general situation. We assume that the intra-campus network consists of two unequal capacity LAN networks (LAN_1 at C_1 Mbps and LAN_2 at C_2 Mbps, where $C_1 >> C_2$), both connected through a router (see figure 4). We also assume that there is not any other applications using the network and that the server is situated at the slowest LAN, the LAN_1 network.

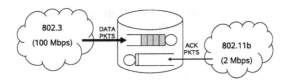

Fig. 4. Router model. Delay from LAN_2 to LAN_1 network is negligible.

Due to the network capacity difference, congestion may arise at the router, which can be modeled as a pair of buffers serving packets at C_2 and C_1 Mbps respectively. LAN_2 to LAN_1 buffer delay can be neglected because it is filled only with the ACK packets and the service rate at the other side is very high (C_1 Mbps).

Supposing an initial window size of one (see figure 3), the server sends only one data packet to the network and waits for ACKs (one for each LAN). The ACK packet from LAN_1 arrives early, since it does not need to go through the router. The ACK packet from the LAN_2 network arrives approximately at

$$\frac{DataPS}{C_1} + \frac{DataPS}{C_2} + \overline{ARTP} \approx \frac{DataPS}{C_2} + \overline{ARTP}, \quad where \ C_1 >> C_2. \tag{6}$$

When both ACKs have arrived, the window size is increased by one unit and the next data window is issued. For a W window size, the server will receive the ACK from the slowest network approximately at

$$\frac{W \cdot DataPS}{C_2} + \overline{ARTP}. \tag{7}$$

The window size just before congestion is detected (W_T) can be obtained when (7) slightly matches with $default\_Tout$ (see figure 3):

$$W_T = \frac{(default\_Tout - \overline{ARTP})}{DataPS} \cdot C_2. \tag{8}$$

At this time, the server increases again the window size and sends the next data block. But now, congestion is declared since the timer expires before the ACK packet from LAN_2 arrives. Therefore, the flow control multiplies the timer by α and decreases the window in one unit. In this new situation, it can be guaranteed that the server assumes that the congestion has disappeared since $\alpha > 1$. Once again, the window is increased and the timer is divided by β. But since $\beta > \alpha > 1$, the timer value reaches again its default value and then congestion is declared again.

This behavior is continuously repeated. Therefore, the window size reaches a steady-state value slightly oscillating around W_T. This study can be extrapolated to other intra-campus scenarios if it is satisfied that one of the networks has a lower capacity than the others.

3.3   Maximum Throughput

SOMA obtains the maximum throughput and the maximum window size (W_{max}) when it is the only running application and there is no congestion. In that situation, the time interval between two consecutive data windows is restricted by the ARTP mean value (2) and not by the timer ($default\_Tout >> ARTP_{max}$). Therefore, in this case the maximum throughput is bounded by

$$\frac{W_{max}}{\frac{W_{max}}{C} + \overline{ARTP}}. \tag{9}$$

Where C is the network capacity at the server side and W_{max} is expressed in bits.

But, if congestion arises at some network point, the timeout timer restricts the time between data blocks and the window size reaches its steady-state value. Therefore, the maximum throughput is bounded by

$$\frac{W_T + DataPS}{\frac{W_T + DataPS}{C} + default\_Tout}. \tag{10}$$

Where C is the network capacity at the server side and W_T is expressed in bits.

4   Capturing and Processing SOMA Traffic

There are several solutions to capture real traffic in a network. The first one is to use a hardware protocol analyzer. They are able to capture frames and to get some traffic figures in real time. The capture can also be stored in a file to obtain more statistical parameters by subsequent processing. The equipment price and a very limited adaptation to new emerging network technologies are the main drawbacks of this solution.

Other solution is to use a software network sniffer running in a computer. Many companies (Cisco, HP, Nortel Networks, etc.) add this feature to their network management tools. However, the software cost and the limited traffic analysis characteristics are the main drawbacks in this case. Finally, there is another solution: The freeware sniffers like *ethereal* [5] and *tcpdump* [6] (the first one is a GUI network sniffer and the second one is a line-oriented sniffer).

This is the best solution in most of the situations. Their features are comparable to hardware solutions and they require a low investment. Furthermore, this option can adapt to any network technology since, nowadays, there are many network interfaces (Frame Relay, ISDN, ATM) available to PC at competitive prices. We have chosen *tcpdump* and *ethereal* sniffers to evaluate our proposed protocol.

Working with open-source sniffers allows us to easily improve the protocol analysis capabilities. The software can be modified to be able to identify a SOMA packet and to show the packet fields in an adequate format. *Ethereal* is a multi-platform software written in C language. Amongst other libraries, *ethereal* uses the packet capture and filtering library *libpcap* (Packet CAPture LIBrary), the graphical user interface *gtk+* and the *glib* library which allows the sniffer to generate and manage a protocol stack similar to the recommended OSI model. Adding a new protocol to the protocol supported set requires the codification of a new dissector (a C language file which name must be *packet_soma.c*, that is, the reserved word *packet_* followed by the new protocol acronym). The dissector encodes the new protocol definition, its header fields, its names and the format they must be shown in the result window. Moreover, the new dissector must be registered to the lower level dissector, and then *glib* library is able to insert SOMA protocol into the global protocol stack. In our case, SOMA packets are encapsulated into UDP packets, and therefore, the lower dissector is the specific UDP dissector.

Like *ethereal*, *tcpdump* is an open-source sniffer written in C that uses the *libpcap* library. However, the capture information is shown in console mode. This feature allows to capture traffic using computers without a graphical interface (i.e. X Server). This fact allows to save system resources in limited computers and therefore to improve the traffic capture process.

Tcpdump adaptation implied different modifications. First, the predefined display format has been completely redefined. Original *tcpdump* displays the packet information in a tree structured format, where each protocol information is printed in a different line. Our customized *tcpdump* displays all the packet information in only one line (for post-processing purposes, as it is explained later). Second, as *ethereal*, *tcpdump* must be able to detect and interpret a SOMA packet. For that, the UDP protocol module (*print_udp.c*) has been modified to determine the port number associated to a SOMA packet. Then, if a UDP port number of a received packet matches the SOMA port number, *print_udp.c* calls the *print_soma()* function, coded in *print_soma.c* which analyzes and prints the SOMA header.

As well as adapting open-source sniffers to interpret our protocol, we use the Linux Packet Filter (LPF) inspired by the BSD Packet Filter (BPF)[7], a kernel architecture for packet capture. The BPF has two main components: The network tap and the packet filter. The network tap collects copies of packets from the network device drivers and delivers them to listening applications. The filter decides if a packet should be accepted and, if so, how much of it to copy to the listening application.

When a packet arrives at a network interface, the link level device driver normally sends it up to the system protocol stack. But when BPF is listening on this interface, the driver first calls BPF. BPF feeds the packet to each participating process filter. For each filter that accepts the packet, BPF copies the requested amount of data to the buffer associated with that filter. The device driver then regains control.

The main advantage of the BSD Packet Filter is that it discards unwanted packets as early as possible and therefore it minimizes the packet copies across the kernel buffers.

Once traffic is captured and stored, information from packet header must be processed to extract the desired statistical figures. For that, we have use *awk*, a powerful pattern scanning and processing language. *Awk* scans input lines, line by line, to see if a line matches a set of patterns or conditions specified in a program. If a line matches a certain pattern, a specified action is carried out.

The high processing rate offered by the *awk* language has determined this election. *Awk* functions and programming philosophy are very similar to C language. Multiple arithmetic calculations can be programmed in an extremely easy way, and therefore many protocol figures and parameters can be obtained efficiently and quickly.

5   Test Results Discussion

In this section, we evaluate SOMA in a real situation. It should be noticed that our analytical study is focused on a transport layer but test experiments are obviously the result of all OSI layers integration, from the physical layer up to the transport one. Concretely, in section 3 we have not made any consideration about the MAC, LLC, IP and UDP sub-layers. Moreover, SOMA runs over a multi-task OS, which has non real-time facilities. Therefore, although we try to minimize the computational load in each computer (unnecessary processes, like *cron*, are killed), sometimes the kernel may give priority to other processes instead of SOMA. Both effects, the OSI layers integration and the multi-task OS may cause that the test results reveal some smaller differences with the analytical ones.

The intra-campus environment is formed by two LANs of extremely unequal capacities, a wired Ethernet LAN operating at 100 Mbps and a wireless LAN 802.11b at 2 Mbps, both connected through a wireless access-point router. The

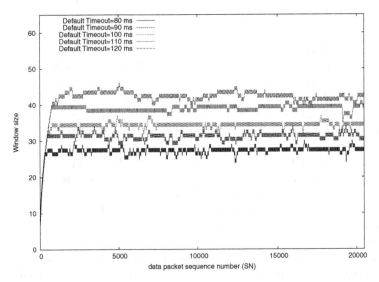

Fig. 5. Window size evolution for different *default_Tout* values: 80, 90, 100, 110 and 120 ms

access-point router is a Linksys WRT54G, co-sponsored by Cisco Systems. We changed its firmware by a stable and configurable Linux OS called OpenWrt [8].

To verify that the analytical results obtained in section 3 fit good enough with the test results, the same intra-campus environment is used: the clients are situated in both LANs and the server is situated in the wired network.

Our test intra-campus network forces congestion since the wireless LAN capacity (2 Mbps) is fifty times lower than the wired network capacity (100 Mbps).

Figure 5 shows the evolution of the window size for different *default_Tout* values: 80, 90, 100, 110 and 120 ms. According to expression (8) the window size should oscillate around 29, 32, 36, 39 and 43 packets respectively. To obtain these values it is assumed that: (a) The $\overline{ARTP}$ is 120 μs, which is calculated using (2) when n=4 and the $ARTP_{max}$ is 600 *mus*. (b) The effective wireless LAN capacity is around 1.6 Mbps instead of the theoretical 2 Mbps.

As it can be observed, the analytical values fit good enough with the experimental ones and the window size remains always around its steady state value (W_T). Sometimes the window size slightly decreases due to sporadic packet losses at the wireless LAN side and also by background control applications packets, like spanning-tree, that overload the access point buffer capacity.

Figure 6 represents the instantaneous throughput. Independently of the *default_Tout* value, the server throughput slightly oscillates around 1.6 Mbps. Therefore, the proposed flow control algorithm is able to adapt the server transmission rate to the slowest network capacity maintaining synchronism among all clients and avoiding congestion.

This test result can be corroborated analytically by introducing the value of W_T in (10). Assuming always that mean ARTP value is negligible, the throughput can be approximated by

$$\frac{default\_Tout \cdot C_2 + DataPS}{\frac{default\_Tout \cdot C_2 + DataPS}{C_1} + default\_Tout} \approx C_2. \qquad (11)$$

Where $C_2 << C_1$ and $DataPS << default\_Tout \cdot C_2$.

In the next experiment, our protocol is evaluated in a single congestionless wired LAN. Figure 7 depicts the window size evolution and the instantaneous throughput. Now, the window size reaches its maximum value limited by the protocol (W=100). The maximum theoretical throughput is 97.4 Mbps (9) which approximately fits in the experimental result. Again, the flow control is able to adapt the transmission to the maximum network capacity.

Finally, figure 8 illustrates the window size evolution in a different experiment. At the beginning only wired clients participate in the file replication process.

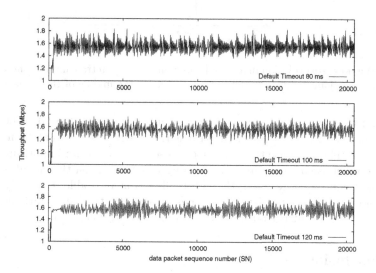

Fig. 6. Instantaneous throughput evolution for different *default_Tout* values: 80, 100 and 120 ms

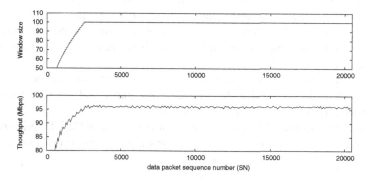

Fig. 7. Window size and instantaneous throughput evolution in a congentionless 100 Mbps wired LAN

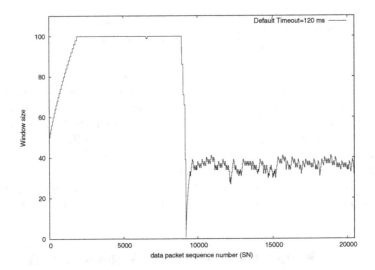

Fig. 8. Window size evolution in a mixed wired and wireless intra-campus. The wireless LAN terminals join the file transfer approximately in the middle of the transfer.

As it can be seen, the window size reaches its maximum value (W=100). But approximately in the middle of the transfer, the wireless terminals join to the file transfer. The response time of our proposed protocol is an important factor since the wireless channel capacity is strongly dependent on the signal to noise ratio. As it can be appreciated, the SOMA flow control is able to quickly adapt to the new situation by resizing the window (and also the timer, although it is not shown) synchronizing both networks and avoiding congestion.

6   Conclusions

SOMA is a multicast application for fast file replication. One of its most remarkable aspects is its own transport protocol definition focused mainly on flow control which is designed to work fine in an asymmetric intra-campus scenario. The proposed flow control algorithm is able to quickly react under congestion, resizing adequately the window size and the time between data blocks to maximize the throughput.

Some of the main protocol parameters have been also characterized analytically under certain constrains. In addition, the mathematical study has been validated with real traces in a test lab network.

Although the proposed transport protocol is used in SOMA for file transfer, its synchronicity and simplicity makes it interesting for other type of applications like real time video and audio streaming.

Acknowledgments

The Spanish Research Council under project ARPaq (TEC2004-05622- C04-02/TCM) has supported this work.

References

1. Obraczka, K.: Multicast Transport Protocols: A Survey and Taxonomy. IEEE Communications Magazine, Vol. 36, (Jan. 1998), 94-102
2. Levine, B.N., Garcia-Luna-Aceves, JJ.: A Comparison of Reliable Multicast Protocols. ACM Multimedia Systems Journal, Vol. 6, No. 5 (Sept. 1998), 334-348
3. Kirschberg, J., Delgado, M., Ribes, S: RCCMP: A TCP-Friendly Reliable Multicast Transport Protocol. In Proceedings of the 10th. ISCC, La Manga, Spain, (June 2005), 730-738
4. Manzanares-Lopez, P., Sanchez-Aarnoutse, J.C., Malgosa-Sanahuja, J., Garcia-Haro, J.: Empirical and Analytical Study of a Multicast Synchronous Transport Protocol for Intra-Campus Replications Services. In Proceedings of the International Conference on Communications (ICC'04), Paris, (June 2004)
5. http://www.ethereal.com
6. http://www.tcpdump.org
7. McCanne S., Jacobson V.: The BSD Packet Filter: A New Architecture for User-level Packet Capture. In the 1993 Winter USENIX conference, San Diego, CA, (January 1993), pp. 259-269.
8. http://openwrt.org

A Real-Time MAC Protocol for Wireless Sensor Networks: Virtual TDMA for Sensors (VTS)

Esteban Egea-López, Javier Vales-Alonso, Alejandro S. Martínez-Sala,
Joan García-Haro, Pablo Pavón-Mariño, and M. Victoria Bueno-Delgado

Department of Information Technologies and Communications,
Polytechnic University of Cartagena, Spain
{esteban.egea, javier.vales, alejandros.martinez, joang.haro,
pablo.pavon, mvictoria.bueno}@upct.es

Abstract. Wireless Sensor Networks (WSN) are designed for data gathering and processing, with particular requirements and constraints: low
hardware complexity, low energy consumption, special traffic pattern
support, scalability, and in some cases, real-time operation. In this paper we present the Virtual TDMA for Sensors (VTS) MAC protocol,
which intends to support the previous features, focusing particularly on
real-time operation. VTS adaptively creates a TDMA arrangement with
a number of timeslots equal to the actual number of nodes in range.
Thus, VTS achieves an optimal throughput performance compared to
TDMA protocols with fixed size of frame. The TDMA frame is set up
and maintained by a distributed procedure, which allows sensors to asyn-
chronously join and leave the frame. A major advantage of VTS is that it
guarantees a bounded latency, which allows soft real-time applications.
An expression for the upper latency bound is also provided in this paper.
VTS performance is evaluated by simulation. Results show less power
consumption than other proposals in the field. We also introduce a novel
multi-hop operation by coordinated sleep/awake cycles among clusters.

1 Introduction

Wireless Sensor Networks (WSNs) are a new paradigm of telecommunication
networks. WSNs are designed to perform efficient data collection and environment monitoring, among other applications. WSNs share key properties with
Mobile Ad-hoc NETworks (MANETs): decentralized control, wireless broadcast
nature, self-configuring capabilities, multi-hop routing and ephemeral topologies.
However, unlike MANETs, WSNs must support: (a) specific traffic patterns,
characterized by very long idle periods and sudden peak transmissions, (b) long
run battery-powered deployment, which yields to tight energy constraints, and
(c) device (hardware and software) simplicity. Therefore, two fundamental goals
of WSN protocols are energy saving and traffic/environment adaptivity. In addition, there are new incoming proposals of combined sensor and actors (devices
that act upon events) networks [1], yielding the so-called Wireless Sensor and
Actor Network (WSAN) model. WSANs are by nature alarm-driven systems,

W. Grass et al. (Eds.): ARCS 2006, LNCS 3894, pp. 382–396, 2006.

where the reaction time (from sensor detection to actor action) must usually be bounded. Thus, WSAN proposals must add real-time operation as a requirement for their associated protocols.

WSNs major sources of energy waste are related to radio communication issues [2]. Namely, *collisions, idle listening, overhearing* packets addressed to other nodes, and *packet overhead* (sending and receving too many control packets). Since nodes do not know when they will receive packets from their neighbors, they are always listening to the channel (idle listening) and the radio is kept in receiving mode, consuming energy. Reference [3] states that idle listening is the dominant factor. Thus, radios must be *turned off* during periods of inactivity to save energy. Besides, sudden trafffic peaks are likely to happen in WSNs. High loads may collapse the network, degrading its performance (throughput and latency) and raising power consumption. Consequently, adaptation to extreme situations is mandatory for WSN protocols. Device limitations (both hardware and software), additionally impose that algorithms and protocols be simple.

In this paper we propose the VTS (Virtual TDMA for Sensors) MAC protocol. VTS provides a TDMA-like access scheme, in which the number of available slots *dynamically* adjusts to the number of nodes present in a cell (cluster) of nodes. Such a mechanism, after a transient adjustment phase, leads to a *scalable* and collision-free MAC protocol that consumes *considerably less energy* than contention-based protocols and has a *bounded packet latency* (providing support for soft real-time services). VTS also addresses network setup and synchronization issues. The trade-off is the average latency, which is slightly worse than contention protocols under low/medium loads.

As most of the sensor network proposals [2, 5, 8], VTS periodically puts nodes to sleep to reduce power consumption, which results in *listen/sleep* cycles. Our protocol employs a synchronization procedure similar to S-MAC [2] to establish the *listen/sleep* schedule. However, unlike S-MAC, only one node can transmit in every *listen/sleep* cycle. Thus, every cycle becomes what in a TDMA context is called a *timeslot*[1]. By following an extremely simple procedure, the nodes in a cluster will transmit in different timeslots. Therefore, when each node is finally transmitting in a different timeslot, a *frame* of timeslots has been built in a *distributed way*. VTS allows frame adjustment, that is, to increase or reduce the number of timeslots, which improves throughput compared to a TDMA frame with a fixed number of timeslots. With this TDMA-like access there is no contention for data transmission and latency is guaranteed.

Besides, in a multi-hop network VTS achieves good performance. Border nodes maintain time-shifted TDMA arrangements for each cell they belong to. This assumption implies that separate clusters of nodes independently select listen periods which do not overlap. It is a reasonable assumption because the usual listen interval only lasts around 10% of the cycle time. We call this operation mode Awake Time Division Multiple Access (ATDMA).

---

[1] In this paper, we refer to a listen/sleep cycle as timeslot, cycle or frame, depending on the context. A set of listen/sleep cycles is called a superframe.

The rest of the paper is organized as follows: Section 2 contains related work on MAC protocols for WSNs. In Section 3 the basis of the S-MAC protocol is reviewed to introduce VTS synchronization procedure. Section 4 thoroughly describes the VTS protocol. A performance analysis of VTS is presented in section 5. Finally, section 6 concludes and suggests future work.

2 Related Work

A considerable research effort has been devoted to WSNs in the last few years. Many new protocols and applications are currently being proposed and tested. WSN MAC protocols focus mainly on energy efficiency. Latency in message delivery is not usually a metric to be optimized. Most of the proposals can be classified in one of the classical categories: contention or TDMA-based.

MAC contention protocols are simple, scalable and flexible. Their major drawback is a high idle listening time (the dominant factor of energy waste). WSN contention-based proposals presently extend the Carrier Sense Multiple Access/-Collision Avoidance (CSMA/CA) mechanism, applying additional schemes to reduce overhearing and idle listening: (1) Out-of-band signaling requires additional radio channels [4], and hardware is more complex and expensive. (2) Coordinated scheduling of listen time, which was first proposed by the Sensor-MAC (S-MAC) protocol [2]. S-MAC introduces a procedure to synchronize nodes on a common structure, that yields a shared listen/sleep cycle among neighbor nodes. This schedule reduces idle listening and, therefore, energy consumption. The Timeout-MAC (T-MAC) [5] protocol improves S-MAC by using an adaptive cycle length. The listen/sleep interval duration adapts to traffic fluctuations and obtains a better energy profile. This family of MAC protocols is relatively simple but does not guarantee latency. In contrast, with a similar complexity, *our protocol keeps latency bounded* (see section 4).

TDMA protocols assign timeslots to nodes, avoiding collisions and idle listening. However, in *ad-hoc* and sensor networks, establishing and maintaining a superframe of timeslots is a complex task. In addition, if the number of nodes dynamically changes, which is likely to occur in WSNs, scheduling must be readapted. *All* TDMA proposals for WSNs (and MANETs) utilize contention stages to setup and maintain a properly organized TDMA. Our protocol also belongs to this category. There is a number of these proposals for MANETs and WSNs: (1) The Five Phase Reservation Protocol (FPRF) [6], which provides a distributed algorithm to solve the problem of slot allocation in multi-hop networks. FPRF allocation procedure performs well at the expense of a great complexity, and does not implement any energy saving mechanism. (2) In Eyes MAC (EMAC) [7] a node can be active or passive. Active nodes own a timeslot and form a network backbone that performs routing tasks. Passive nodes use contention periods to send data. EMAC is focused on the increase of network lifetime, whereas latency or throughput are not addressed. (3) The Lightweight Medium Access Protocol (LMAC) protocol [8] is a modification of EMAC in which each node selects a timeslot using slot occupancy information from its one-hop neighbors. Its main limitations are that the number of available slots is fixed and the nodes listen to unused slots. Therefore, LMAC latency and throughput degrades at low loads [9]. In comparison with these proposals, VTS *is simpler and does not fix the number of timeslots*, therefore, it achieves a better performance.

3   S-MAC Overview

S-MAC [2] is a contention-based protocol that reduces energy consumption by means of several mechanisms.

Periodic listen and sleep forces nodes to activate periodically for a small time interval (the listen period); the rest of the time the nodes turn off their radio and sleep (the sleep period). A listen/sleep cycle is also called a frame (see Fig. 1). The ratio of the listen interval to the sleep interval is the *duty cycle*. Neighbors achieve and maintain a *coordinated sleeping* time, synchronizing their listen/sleep schedules by means of the short SYNChronization (SYNC) packet. SYNC packets correct clock drifts and are used to discover new neighbors. In a stationary situation, each node broadcasts a SYNC packet after a fixed number of frames (N_C) to maintain synchronization. Within a frame, the listen interval is subdivided into SYNC period (for SYNC packets) and Data period (for data packets), as shown in Fig. 1. Nodes perform carrier sense during a random number of slots (contention) before transmitting SYNC. If two nodes contend for transmitting a SYNC in the same cycle, it may happen that: (1) Nodes choose a different number of carrier sense slots. As a result, the node with a higher number defers its SYNC transmission (losing contention), and makes another attempt in the next synchronization cycle. (2) Both nodes select the same slot. A collision occurs which is not detected by any of them. After N_C cycles, both nodes contend again for SYNC transmission. Transmission of an information packet, occurs in the Data period inside the frame (see Fig. 1). Nodes can make use of the Data period in any frame: synchronization and Data periods operate independently.

Collision avoidance is based on CSMA/CA. It uses a RTS (Request To Send)-/CTS (Clear To Send)/Data/ACK sequence, with a fixed backoff contention window. Notice that S-MAC uses two independent periods of contention in every cycle, one for SYNC and one for Data transmission.

To avoid *overhearing*, all the nodes sleep either at the beginning of the sleep period or inmediately after receiving a RTS or a CTS not addressed to them, and they wake up when the next frame starts. This scheme (periodic listen and

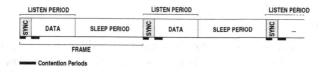

Fig. 1. S-MAC listen-sleep frame

sleep) significantly reduces idle listening. However, there is an undesirable effect on packet latency, because nodes must wait for the next listen period to send their data. To overcome this issue, S-MAC proposes a technique called *adaptive listening*: nodes which overhear a RTS or CTS packet wake up at the end of the transmission, instead of waiting for their next scheduled listen time. Thereby, if a node is the next-hop destination, its neighbor is able to immediately pass the data to it.

Summarizing, S-MAC reduces idle listening and provides an efficient mechanism to synchronize nodes. Nevertheless, it does not act upon the other major sources of energy waste: collisions and packet overhead. It even increases them: there are two contention intervals (SYNC and Data) every cycle, and a new control packet (SYNC). Moreover, S-MAC cannot guarantee packet latency.

3.1   S-MAC Synchronization

In S-MAC, when a node initializes, it keeps listening for a certain amount of time. If it receives a SYNC packet, it adopts its listen/sleep schedule and tries to send its own SYNC in the next available chance. Otherwise, the node chooses its own schedule and broadcasts it using a SYNC packet. After N_C listen/sleep cycles, nodes broadcast a new SYNC packet to maintain synchronization.

Figure 2 illustrates this effect for a network with M neighbor nodes, being node A_1 the first node sending a SYNC. Any other node will follow A_1 schedule. The rest of the nodes compete to send a SYNC packet in the next scheduled SYNC time. Nodes that lose contention compete again every cycle until they send a SYNC. Let the i-*th* listen/sleep cycle be called *timeslot i* (t_i), the evolution of the network is as follows:

- At t_1, node A_1 sends the first SYNC. A cycle counter is set to N_C, which decreases by one every cycle. When the cycle counter reaches 0 a new SYNC is delivered.
- At t_2, the rest of the nodes try to send a SYNC packet, but only the contention winner sends it. Let us assume that an arbitrary node A_2 wins contention and so it sets its cycle counter to N_C. We say that node A_2 has *captured* this timeslot.
- At t_3, the remaining nodes try to transmit their SYNC packet, but, again, only the contention winner actually sends it. Node A_3 wins the contention (captures timeslot) and sets its cycle counter to N_C.
- At t_M, the last present node sends its SYNC packet and sets its cycle counter to N_C.
- From t_{M+1} to t_{N_C}, there are timeslots without SYNC transmissions.
- At t_{N_C}, A_1 sends a SYNC again.
- At t_{N_C+1}, A_2 sends a SYNC again.
- And so on.

Let us notice that S-MAC implicitly defines a TDMA-like arrangement of N_C timeslots, even though, in fact, it is not used, because S-MAC allows *all* nodes to contend for sending data *every* listen period. On the contrary, *VTS takes advantage of this property to setup and maintain an adaptive TDMA frame.*

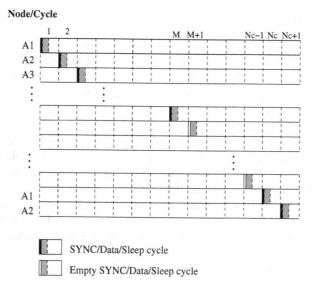

Fig. 2. S-MAC and VTS setup evolution

4   VTS Description

As stated in section 2, TDMA access schemes are the natural way to keep latency bounded and to reduce energy consumption, since there are neither contention nor collisions. VTS constructs a TDMA structure with the *exact number of timeslots needed*, that is, VTS dynamically adjusts the number of timeslots (N_C) in the TDMA frame to the number of nodes in the cell. In a stationary state, the protocol ensures that each node owns a single timeslot, not shared with any other node. In this situation, a *virtual superframe of timeslots* is created. The word *virtual* means that nodes do not know the superframe arrangement: neither its limits, nor their relative position in the superframe. They just *independently* keep a counter with the superframe length (N_C). VTS synchronization procedure works as S-MAC (Sect. 3.1), but, unlike S-MAC, VTS nodes are only allowed to send data in their captured cycle, i.e., *nodes only send packets, any kind of packet, every N_C cycles after their firstly sent SYNC packet*. It can be seen in Fig. 2 that a superframe of length N_C is virtually established.

Briefly, a VTS node contends every cycle until it captures a timeslot (wins the contention). From then on, the node only sends packets every N_C cycle. After a number of network setup (initialization) cycles, the nodes adjust their superframe length counter to their number of known neighbors. If nodes leave the cell, the superframe length is distributedly reduced. Finally, to allow new nodes to join the superframe, there is always a short contention period before packet transmission, where new nodes can contend with the owner of the timeslot.

In the following sections a detailed description of VTS operation is provided, starting with the single-hop network description and followed by the extension of VTS for multi-hop topologies.

4.1   Network Setup

The network setup phase lasts from nodes activation, to the definition of a (still of fixed size) virtual superframe. In VTS we prefer the name ConTroL (CTL) packet to SYNC packet, because the packet is used also for other purposes which are discussed in next sections. VTS setup stage behaves exactly as the S-MAC synchronization mechanism presented in section 3.1. That is, a node contends to send a CTL packet every listen cycle until it actually sends it. Then, the node only can send a new CTL packet after N_C cycles, and it *must* send it as a keep-alive beacon. When all the nodes have sent their first CTL packet, the virtual superframe of N_C timeslots is formed. Let us notice that nodes are not aware of the implicit timeslot allocation. They just know that they are only allowed to transmit packets every N_C cycle. Thus, the slot allocation procedure is simple and fully distributed. Let us also notice that nodes know who their neighbors are when they receive CTL packets. In the example of Fig. 2 it is assumed that all the nodes are initialized simultaneously and that they always capture timeslots consecutively. Let us see what would happen if these assumptions did not hold:

1. *If a node is initialized after the superframe has been formed.* It will wait for a CTL packet to join the listen/sleep schedule. Once it has been received, the new node tries to send its own CTL packet in the next scheduled timeslot. If this timeslot is owned by another node, both of them contend for the timeslot. The contention winner becomes the owner of the timeslot. The looser retries to send its CTL packet in the next timeslot. If this timeslot is also owned by a node, the contention winner will own the timeslot and the looser will keep trying. Eventually, an empty timeslot will be reached, which is captured by the only remaining node trying to access the medium at that moment. If more than one new node initialized, the only difference would be that the number of contending nodes for a timeslot would be higher. Eventually, every node would be assigned an empty timeslot. We call this process of multiple deallocation and reassignment "allocation loop" .

2. *If more than one node selects the same access instant during contention there is a collision.* In this case, two or more nodes send their CTL packets simultaneously. However, the contenders are not aware of the collision and each one considers that its own CTL has been correctly sent. After N_C cycles (the superframe length) they will try to send their CTL packet again, so there will be a new contention. The contention winner will own the timeslot. The looser will keep trying to send the packet, as discussed in the previous case. In the unlikely event of a new collision this sequence is repeated.

4.2   Adjustment of Virtual Superframe Length

With the previous setup procedure, a virtual superframe of fixed length N_C is created. If N_C were kept fix, protocol performance would be poor. On one hand, if N_C is less than the maximum number of neighbors, nodes cannot exclusively own a timeslot. In this case, there would always be contention between at least two nodes in every slot. On the other hand, if N_C is greater than the actual number of neighbors, VTS latency and throughput are negatively affected, since they are proportional to superframe length.

To overcome these situations, the number of timeslots should be adapted to the actual number of nodes. Therefore a node adjusts the initial cycle counter (set to N_C) to the real number of neighbors in the cell, that is, *to the number of received CTL packets from distinct nodes up to that moment*. This is done a number of timeslots (let it be N_S, a protocol parameter) after node initialization, From then on, the node dynamically adapts to the possibility of nodes joining and leaving the cell:

1. *New nodes join the cell*: anytime a node receives a CTL packet from an unknown neighbor, the superframe length is updated ($N_C = N_C + 1$).
2. *Nodes leave the cell*: within a superframe the mandatory CTL packet from the timeslot owner must be received. Therefore, CTL serves as a keep alive beacon, which allows to signal missing neighbors. However, a single CTL packet missed does not mean that its corresponding node has actually left the network: its CTL packet may have been corrupted or it may have been a collision with a new node joining the cell. Hence, a node is considered missed only after a certain number of inactivity timeslots (let it be N_I). On such event, the frame length and number of known nodes is updated ($N_C = N_C - 1$).

Let us note that in both cases there is a transient period before stability: in the first case the incoming node "steals" a slot, and it causes a new allocation loop. In the second case, nodes are not aware of the position of the lost node in the superframe, so they cannot properly adjust their cycle counter. To overcome it nodes randomly select a value within zero and the number of known neighbors. This solution requires a full reallocation of positions in the superframe. Since these events are supposed to be unlikely, this scheme was preferred because it keeps the protocol extremely simple. It should be remarked here that sensor nodes do not usually move, that is, networks are assumed to be static, and a node leaves the cell only when it has depleted its battery.

4.3   Data Exchange and Control Packets

At the beginning of each timeslot, all the nodes wake up and listen. The owner of the timeslot performs a carrier sense (choosing a random slot from a fixed

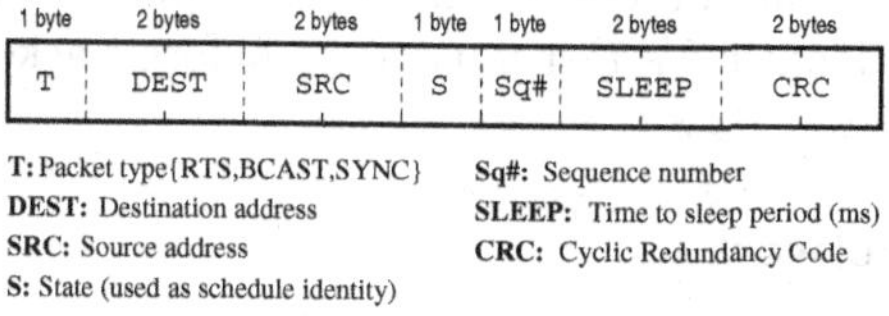

1 byte	2 bytes	2 bytes	1 byte	1 byte	2 bytes	2 bytes
T	DEST	SRC	S	Sq#	SLEEP	CRC

T: Packet type{RTS,BCAST,SYNC}   Sq#: Sequence number
DEST: Destination address   SLEEP: Time to sleep period (ms)
SRC: Source address   CRC: Cyclic Redundancy Code
S: State (used as schedule identity)

Fig. 3. CTL packet format

contention window), and broadcasts a single and short control packet (CTL), see Fig. 3. which is used as:

- Synchronization and schedule discovery (as S-MAC SYNC packet).
- Keep-alive beacon. It is mandatory for a node to send a CTL packet in its owned slot, since its neighbors must know that the node is active.
- New node discovery. CTL packets include source address. Thus, new nodes are added to the list of known neighbors as CTL packets arrive.
- Channel reservation: RTS information is included in CTL packets. This way, non-addressed nodes may go to sleep just after CTL packet reception.

VTS uses the CSMA/CA mechanism for data delivery. The following types of transmissions exist:

1. Unicast packet transmission. A $CTL_{\{RTS\}}$ packet is sent by the owner of the timeslot. Non addressed nodes change to the sleep state inmediately, avoiding overhearing. Destination node replies using a CTS. Transmission is finished after a Data/ACK sequence and both nodes go to sleep.
2. Broadcast packet transmission. A $CTL_{\{BCAST\}}$ packet is sent by the owner of the timeslot. Destination is a broadcast address. All the nodes keep listening. Inmediately, sender sends the broadcast packet, that is, without waiting for any CTS reply. After receiving the packet nodes go to sleep. No ACK is sent.
3. No data transmission. A $CTL_{\{SYNC\}}$ packet is sent. Nodes adjust the clock reference, clear sender inactivity counter and go to sleep.

Control packet overhearing is reduced this way. A single CTL packet performs synchronization and discovery, reservation and keep-alive functions.

4.4   Single-Hop Cluster Latency

Let T_C be timeslot duration. In a single-hop cluster in steady-state (i.e., all the nodes are the owners of a timeslot) any data transmission between two nodes has a maximum latency (L) given by:

$$L \leq N_C T_C \tag{1}$$

This is the maximum expected latency considering that MAC layer does not enqueue packets. Figure 4 illustrates this expression. Let us assume that the node A_1 generates a packet for any other node in cluster A. In the worst case, this packet arrives just at the end of the activity period (label T_0 in figure 4), so a superframe (of length $N_C T_C$) must pass before packet transmission ends (label T_1 in the figure).

4.5   Multi-hop Network

Large sensor networks are usually organized in *clusters* [10] , with the border nodes sharing coverage areas between adjacent clusters. Information coming from one cluster to another must hop among them. VTS proposes the Awake Time Division Multiple Access (ATDMA) scheme for multi-hop networks. That is, nodes coordinate awakening among clusters in order to have one-hop neighbor clusters never wake up at the same time, to avoid inter-cluster interferences. In other words, all the clusters except one are in their sleep period. When this active cluster goes to sleep, another one wakes up, and so on. Thus, a VTS border node forms different superframes with its neighbors in each cluster. The length of both superframes depends on the number of neighbors in each cluster and it may be different. Once superframes are created, packets can travel from one cluster to other during its corresponding listen interval. Hence, ATDMA satisfies cluster operation without interference. Combining VTS and inter-cluster ATDMA two goals are achieved: (1) Bounded multi-hop latency and (2) Spatial reuse of channel.

ATDMA is based on the assumption that clusters adopt different listen/sleep schedules, since they are independently initialized. Which means that virtual superframes in every cluster are time-shifted. In this case, border nodes see several schedules and adopt all of them. ATDMA operation is also depicted in the example of figure 4, where two neighborhoods share the media using ATDMA. Nodes in the first cluster are A_1, A_2, A_3 and A_4. Nodes in the second cluster are B_1 and B_2. To clarify ideas, let us assume that A_1 is a border node between the two clusters A and B, and therefore, it also owns a cycle in cluster B. Let us note that ATDMA seamlessly allows a different number of nodes in each cluster.

However, if there exists overlapping two problems arise: (1) A border node cannot know in which schedule each of its neighbors is. VTS still works because there is always a channel sense period before transmission, but the latency *cannot be guaranteed*. (2) The border node will suffer from hidden node collisions. Nodes in adjacent cells will own the same slot in pairs, causing collisions at the boder node.

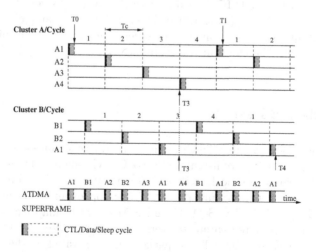

Fig. 4. ATDMA superframe evolution with two adjacent clusters (A and B) with 3 and 2 nodes respectively, plus one common border node A_1

Therefore, VTS must ensure non overlapping schedules. In any case, ATDMA can be easily achieved after running a network-layer clustering protocol like [10], that can shift sleep time between superframes. At the moment, we assume that border nodes always see non-overlapping schedules. In a clustered network, with random initialization, this is a reasonable assumption. With a 1-10% duty cycle, different schedules are likely to be in the 99-90% remaining time.

4.6 Multi-hop Cluster Latency

Using ATDMA, intra-cluster packets have a bounded latency of $L_{intra} \leq N_C T_C$ (the same as the single-hop operation). Inter-cluster latency is expressed by:

$$L_{inter} \leq \sum_{i \in \{clusters\}} L_{i-intra} \tag{2}$$

$L_{i-intra}$ denotes the intra latency of the i-th cluster in the path from source (first cluster) to destination (last cluster) (this route is determined by upper level protocols). Let N_H be the number of hops in the path (N_H is always the number of clusters in the path minus one) and N_{C_i} the TDMA frame length of the i-th cluster, then:

$$L_{inter} \leq (T_C \sum_i N_{C_i}) \leq (N_H + 1) T_C \max_i \{N_{C_i}\} \tag{3}$$

This relationship holds for any (inter or intra-cluster) data exchange.

For the sake of clarity, let us assume that node A_4 wants to send a packet to node B_2 in the scenario of figure 4. The packet must be delivered through the path $A_4 \rightarrow A_1 \rightarrow B_2$. Intra-cluster A transmission ($A_4 \rightarrow A_1$) maximum latency is given by eq. 1. In the worst case A_4 packet arrives at A_1 just after A_1 slot in the cluster B (as shown in label T3 in the example). Then, a full additional B superframe is required to complete the $A_1 \rightarrow B_2$ transmission (label T4 in the figure). Therefore, in this example, $L_{inter} \leq L_{A-intra} + L_{B-intra} = (4+3)T_C = 7T_C$.

5   Simulation Results

In this section we evaluate VTS through comparative simulations with S-MAC (with and without adaptive listening). S-MAC is chosen as reference because it is a general purpose protocol, it is well documented and previous results can be found in the open literature [2]. All single-hop experiments are evaluated in a 20 node cell for VTS, S-MAC and S-MAC with adaptive listening. All figures show the measured parameter versus the packet Inter Arrival time (IAt, where $IAt = 0$ means that all the packets are generated at the same time). Unicast packet destination is randomly chosen with equal probability among all the neighbors.

Table 1. VTS simulation parameters

Parameter	Value
Radio bandwith	20 Kbps
CTL packet	11 bytes
Listen period	130 ms
Duty cycle	10%
Contention window	31 slots, 1 ms/slot
Consumption in reception state	14.4 mW
Consumption in transmission state	36 mW
Consumption in sleep state	15 μW
Initial N_C counter	20
Inactivity counter (N_I)	5 superframes
Setup cycles (N_S)	20 cycles
T_C	1.3 s

Simulation Configuration. OMNET++ [2] is used as simulation platform. Simulation parameters are selected from reference [2], using the Mica motes [3] as underlying hardware. Table 1 shows main simulation parameters. Aditionally, the following options are set for all the simulations:

- A simulation finishes when all the nodes have sent 1000 data packets (70% unicast and 30% broadcast). Data packets are 100 bytes long.
- Network packet generation starts after a transient time (100 s) plus a random number of cycles uniformly distributed between 0 and 50. Packet generation is then deterministic: packets arrive after a selected IAt.

Maximum and Average Latency. Figures 5(a) and 5(b) show the maximum and the average latency, respectively. A bounded latency is expected for VTS as discussed in section 4.4. Experiments confirm that in all the cases latency never exceeds the superframe length (as obtained from eq. 3). VTS effectively adapts the frame length to the actual number of nodes present. In comparison, S-MAC maximum packet latency is clearly not bounded, even with adaptive listening.

Under high load conditions (low IAt), VTS keeps average latency equal to the superframe length (20 $T_C = 26$ s). For low and moderate loads (medium and high IAt), the average latency depends on the packet generation time, which is uniformly distributed in the timeslot, yielding a latency reduction of one half. In S-MAC, latency depends on the number of nodes contending for the medium. For moderate loads, only a few nodes contend and latency reduces below that of VTS, because VTS nodes must wait for their timeslots to transmit. Adaptive listening is an improvement of S-MAC to reduce latency. Consequently, it outperforms both VTS and S-MAC. Although this is a trade-off between average latency and energy consumption, as it will be shown later.

Power Consumption. Figure 6(a) shows the average network power consumption. S-MAC consumes a 18% more than VTS at high loads (due to the double

---
[2] http://www.omnetpp.org
[3] http://www.xbox.com

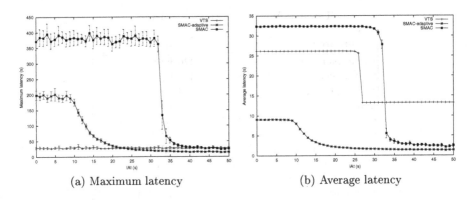

(a) Maximum latency   (b) Average latency

Fig. 5. Single-hop configuration (average ± 99% confidence interval)

contention interval per slot and the collisions). S-MAC with adaptive listening consumes two times more power than VTS. This is the cost of reducing latency. In this case, nodes wake up many more times and try to send packets during the scheduled sleep time, consuming the energy of an additional listen interval. As load decreases, the adaptive listening mechanism is not necessary and the behavior is similar to normal S-MAC. In this case, nodes sleep early in VTS, which increases power saving up to 75%. Reduction of VTS power consumption is higher than S-MAC one as load decreases. Under very low loads (high IAt), VTS will significantly increase the network lifetime compared to S-MAC (the peak at IAt=30 is due to a steeped decrease in latency 5(b), since time to deliver all the packets is reduced and power is measured as total energy consumed divided by total time). In conclusion, in VTS there is a trade-off between latency and energy consumption at low loads, while it guarantees latency at high loads.

Throughput. Figure 6(b) shows that at high loads VTS performs slightly better than S-MAC. VTS can handle traffic peaks as properly as a contention protocol. S-MAC with adaptive listening outperforms VTS but at the cost of a higher consumption.

Transient Time. An experiment was conducted to evaluate the time needed to reconfigure the timeslot arrangement when nodes appear in the network. In this experiment, a 16 nodes network is set and progressively 4 additional nodes join the cell, causing allocations loops (see Sect. 4.1). The results show that the average transient time until superframe is established again is 30.08 s (slighty higher than a single superframe time, $N_C T_C = 26$ s).

Multi-hop Scenario. Scenario of Fig. 4 is set for the multi-hop configuration experiments. That is, two clusters (A and B) with 3 and 2 nodes respectively, plus one common border node (A_1). IAt was set to 0 (always one packet to send), One node of cluster A sends packets to another node of cluster B through the border node. The rest of the nodes send packets to randomly selected intra-cluster nodes. As expected, from 0.15 to 1 s offset there is no overlap between schedules, thus all the experiments exhibit a maximum latency under the upper

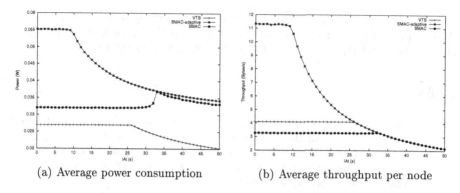

(a) Average power consumption   (b) Average throughput per node

Fig. 6. Power consumption and throughput for single hop (average $\pm$ 99% confidence interval)

bound obtained in eq. 3 ($7T_C$ in this case). Average latency depends on the offset between schedules. If there is overlapping, VTS still works and delivers all the packets but latency is not bounded.

6   Conclusions

In this paper we proposed VTS, a protocol for WSNs with bounded latency. VTS dynamically creates a superframe of timeslots and adapts its length to the number of actual nodes in a cell for optimum performance. VTS implements a very simple mechanism to adjust and assign timeslots to the nodes (Sect. 4.1 and 4.2). This protocol may be extended to a multi-hop network if the medium is shared by multiplexation of activity/sleep cycles of clusters (this access scheme is called ATDMA). Its behavior is examined in Sect. 4.5, concluding that, as long as nodes do not overlap, multi-hop operation has a bounded latency. Finally, expressions for the maximum latency of both intra and inter-cluster links have been obtained (Sect. 4.4 and 4.6). VTS further proposes to use a short single control packet to announce any node intentions during its timeslot. Thereby, VTS saves energy by reducing the amount of time a node needs to listen to the channel. Simulations reveal that VTS has an excellent power consumption profile, which is crucial in WSN. Under low loads VTS compromises latency and energy consumption, while it guarantees latency at high loads. Our future work includes the development of a generalized mechanism that ensures proper ATDMA operation (independently of the relative schedule delay among clusters) and an evaluation of scalability. We plan also to implement and test it with real devices.

Acknowledgments

This work has been cofunded by the Economy, Industry and Innovation Council, with the SOLIDMOVIL project (2I04SU044), supported by Fundacion Seneca, from the Region of Murcia with the ARENA Project (00546/PI/04), with the ARPaq project (TEC2004-05622-C04-02/TCM) by the Spanish Research Council and the CSI-RHET project (TEC2005-08068-C04-01/TCM).

References

1. Akyildiz,I. F., Kasimoglu, I. H.: Wireless sensor and actor networks: Research challenges. Elseveier Ad Hoc Networks, Vol. 2, issue 4 (1995) 351-367
2. Ye, W., Heidemann, J., Estrin, D.: Medium Access Control with Coordinated, Adaptive Sleeping for Wireless Sensor Networks. ACM/IEEE Transactions on Networking, Vol. 12 (2004) 493-506
3. Stemm, M., Katz, R. H.: Measuring and reducing energy consumption of network interfaces in hand-held devices. IEICE Transactions on Communications, Vol. E80-B (1997) 1125-31
4. Singh, S., Raghavendra, C.: Power efficient MAC protocol for multihop radio networks IEEE Interational Symposium on Personal, Indoor and Mobile Radio Communications, Vol. 1 (1998) 153-157
5. van Dam, T., Langendoen, K.: An adaptive energy–efficient MAC protocol for wireless sensor networks. SenSys 03-ACM Conference on Embedded Networked Sensor Systems (2003) 171-180
6. Zhu, C., Corson, M. S.: A five–phase reservation protocol (FPRP) for mobile ad hoc networks. Kluwer Wireless Networks, Vol. 7, no. 4 (2001) 371-384
7. van Hoesel, L., Nieberg, T., Kip, H., Havinga, P.: Advantages of a TDMA based, energy–efficient, self–organizing MAC protocol for WSNs. IEEE VTC (2004)
8. van Hoesel, L., Havinga, P.: A lightweight medium access protocol (LMAC) for wireless sensor networks. INNS 04-International Workshop on Networked Sensing Systems (2004)
9. Langendoen, K., Halkes, G. Energy–efficient medium access control. In: Zurawski, R. (ed.): Embedded Systems Handbook, CRC Press (2005)
10. Basagni. S.: Distributed clustering for ad hoc networks. Proc. 1999 Int. Symp. on Paralled Architectures, Algorithms and Networks (1999) 310-315

An Effective Video Streaming Method for Video on Demand Services in Vertical Handoff

Jae-Won Kim, Hye-Soo Kim, Jae-Woong Yun, and Sung-Jea Ko

Department of Electronics Engineering, Korea University,
Anam-Dong Sungbuk-Ku, Seoul, Korea
{jw9557, hyesoo, jyun, sjko}@dali.korea.ac.kr

Abstract. Vertical handoff (VH) is required to achieve anywhere and anytime internet access in the fourth generation (4G) network providing interoperability between universal mobile telecommunications system (UMTS) and wireless LAN (WLAN). However, video data can be lost due to latency caused by VH. To solve this problem, in this paper, we propose an effective video streaming method for video on demand (VOD) services that provides seamless playout at the client in VH. Experimental results show that our method can provide seamless playout at the client in VH while preserving image quality.

1 Introduction

Currently, the research community and industry in the field of telecommunications are considering the possibility of the choice for handoff which could be the solutions for the 4G of wireless communication [1]. The 4G wireless networks will integrate heterogeneous technologies such as WLAN and third generation (3G) network because no single wireless network technology simultaneously can provide a low latency, high bandwidth, and wide area data service to a large number of mobile users [2].

The movement of a user within or among different types of networks is called the vertical mobility. One of the major challenges for seamless service in the vertical mobility is VH, where handoff is the process of maintaining a mobile user's active connection by changing its point of attachment [3]. In the 4G wireless systems, seamless handoff with small latency and packet losses should be executed. Handoff latency is one of important factors that decides the quality of service (QoS) in the 4G wireless networks. In the deployment of multimedia services with real-time requirements, the handoff process can significantly degrade the QoS from the user's perspective [4]. Especially, since video data can be lost due to latency caused by VH, video quality degradation caused by VH is the critical problem in video streaming. In order to solve this problem, a successful video streaming solution is required to adapt appropriately to mobile handoff scenarios for maximum user-perceived quality.

There are several methods for video streaming in VH [5]-[7]. The multimedia transport protocol (MMTP) determines the encoding rate according to the

W. Grass et al. (Eds.): ARCS 2006, LNCS 3894, pp. 397–406, 2006.

measured available bandwidth for VH [5]. However, this protocol does not concern packet losses caused by VH. In [6], the required buffer size of the client is determined to achieve lossless VH. However, since this method does not perform QoS control for video streaming, the large buffer size is often required to adapt various network. The seamless VH scheme in [7] implements soft handoff based on the stream control transmission protocol (SCTP). However, this scheme requires the support of the system-level design such as the hardware configuration and the lower layer protocol design.

In this paper, we present an effective video streaming method for VOD services that provides seamless playout at the client in VH between the WLAN and the 3G network without the system-level design. For seamless video playout, the streaming server predicts the channel rate and the client buffer status by analyzing the RTCP receiver report (RR) and the application-defined packet (APP). And, we propose a frame selective pre-transmission (FSP-T) method using the predicted results to minimize visual quality degradation caused by VH. The FSP-T method selectively transmits frames with high activity for the VH preparation period. The motion vectors (MVs) of skipped frames are also transmitted to support error concealment (EC) of skipped frames in the client.

The rest of the paper is organized as follows. Section 2 presents the proposed video streaming method for VH. Experimental results are presented in Section 3. Finally, our conclusions are given in Section 4.

2   Proposed Video Streaming Method for Vertical Handoff

Before introducing the proposed video streaming method for VH, we first consider VH scenario as follows:

Fig. 1 shows the VH when the mobile station (MS) moves between the 3G network and the WLAN. In our scenario, the MS automatically transits to a

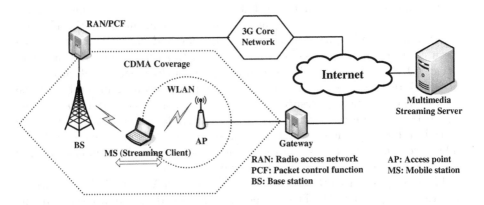

Fig. 1. Vertical handoff scenario

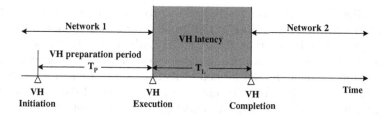

Fig. 2. Vertical Handoff procedure

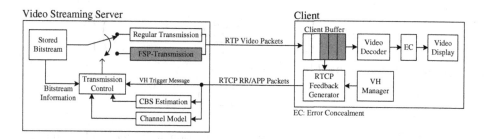

Fig. 3. Video streaming framework

new network attachment between the 3G network and the WLAN, based on WLAN availability. That is, considering the WLAN with high priority, it would be preferable to seamlessly and automatically switch to a higher data rate network connection whenever it is available.

Fig. 2 illustrates the VH procedure in the heterogeneous network where significant events have been pointed out. When the streaming client needs VH, it transmits the trigger message indicating the VH initiation to the streaming server. At this time, the streaming server performs the proposed FSP-T to minimize visual quality degradation caused by VH. The trigger message indicating the beginning of VH is transmitted to the streaming server before executing VH. Finally, the client informs the server of the VH completion. Note that T_P and T_L, respectively, are the period for VH preparation and the VH latency.

According to the VH scenario, after receiving the trigger message indicating the VH initiation, the client buffer status is predicted by analyzing RTCP feedback and the channel rate is estimated by using the channel model [8] at the streaming server. Using the predicted results, the video stream is transmitted by the proposed FSP-T method during T_P. After finishing VH, the streaming server transmits the video bitstream by using the regular transmission that is the basic transmission method of the streaming server. Fig. 3 shows the proposed video streaming framework that can overcome handoff problems.

Before VH, in order to achieve seamless playout in the client for T_L, the proposed FSP-T method attempts to transmit in advance all frames that can be lost due to T_L as well as frames that are transmitted for T_P. However, the picture quality may be degraded since all the frames can not be transmitted in advance because of the channel rate and client buffer constraints. Thus, the Lagrangian rate-distortion (R-D) method is employed to dynamically select frames to be transmitted during T_P according to the frame activity while minimizing visual quality degradation. In addition, the proposed method also transmits in advance only MVs for frames to be skipped in order to enhance the performance of EC in the streaming client. In the proposed method, since the frames with lower activity are skipped, the streaming client can easily conceal the effect of frame-skipping with received MVs while minimizing visual degradation.

Let S be all frames that are assigned for $T_P + T_L$ and S_T be frames to be transmitted during T_P. The optimal frame set, S_T, is determined from the set S by

$$S_T = \arg\min_{S_t \subset S} \left\{ D(S_t) + \lambda \cdot \left(\sum_{i \in S_t} B_i + \sum_{i \in S - S_t} B_i^{MV} \right) \right\}, \tag{1}$$

with the distortion caused by skipped frames

$$D(S_t) = \sum_{i \in S - S_t} A_i, \tag{2}$$

where A_i, B_i, and B_i^{MV}, respectively, are the motion activity of and the number of bits of, and the number of bits for MVs of the ith frame. In order to comply with rate and client buffer constraints, the optimal set, S_T, is obtained by minimizing (1) subject to the rate constraint:

$$\sum_{i \in S - S_t} B_i^{MV} + \sum_{i \in S_t} B_i \leq \widehat{B}, \tag{3}$$

the client buffer constraint:

$$B_C + \sum_{i \in S - S_t} B_i^{MV} + \sum_{i \in S_t} B_i - \sum_{i \in S_P} L_i \leq B_C^M, \tag{4}$$

where $\widehat{B}$ is the total number of bits allocated for $T_P + T_L$, B_C^M is the maximum level of the client buffer, and S_P represents frames to be played for T_P in the client buffer. In (4), the client buffer fill level, B_C, can be predicted by analyzing RTCP RR and APP at the streaming server [9]. Thus, B_C is given by

$$B_C = \sum_{i=\text{LPSN}}^{\text{HTSN}} L_i, \tag{5}$$

where L_i is the size of the packet with the ith sequence number, HTSN is the highest transmitted sequence number kept by the server, and LPSN is the last played sequence number which is calculated by using the playout time. The playout time is calculated by using the fields the oldest buffered sequence number (OBSN) and playout delay (PD) contained in the RTCP APP OBSN extension as proposed by 3GPP-SA4 [10]. OBSN is the sequence number of the first packet in the sequence of packets to be played out in the client buffer. PD is the difference between the scheduled playout time of the oldest packet and the time of sending the OBSN APP packet in milliseconds.

Note that since MPEG bitstreams typically consist of the group of pictures including B-frames, e.g., IBBPBBPBBP⋯, P-frames are kept preferentially in order to minimize re-coding errors caused by skipping frames. Thus, the proposed method first skips B-frames and then skips P-frames.

3   Experimental Results

We have simulated VH according to the VH scenario to show the effectiveness of the proposed video streaming method. The "Foreman" sequence with 300 frames of QCIF format (176×144) is used for our experiments. The test sequence is encoded to the MPEG-2 bitstream of 128kbps with 30fps. M and N, respectively, are 3 and 6. For buffering simulations, a 35KB client buffer is assumed and we specify an 1.25 sec pre-buffering time for playout.

Fig. 4 shows the variation of the channel rate for the VH simulations. In our VH simulations, there exist two times transitions where T_P and T_L, respectively, are 1 sec. Each transition is described as follows:

Transition 1) 3G → WLAN: (2.33 sec ∼ 4.33 sec)
    The handoff process including the handoff initiation is performed from the 70th frame to the 130th frame. In this transition, the dominant factor of constraints is the channel rate of the 3G network, 190kbps.
Transition 2) WLAN → 3G: (4.66 sec ∼ 6.66 sec)
    The handoff process is preformed from the 140th frame to the 200th frame. In this case, although the channel rate of the WLAN is high enough to transmit in advance all frames that can be lost due to handoff latency, the client buffer does not provide sufficient empty space to receive all frames from the 140th frame to the 200th frame.

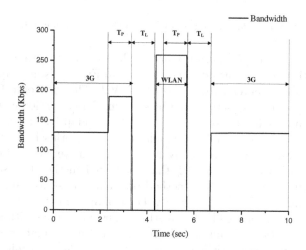

Fig. 4. Channel rate variation for the vertical handoff simulation

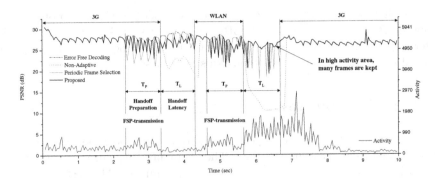

Fig. 5. PSNR performance of the proposed method without error concealment

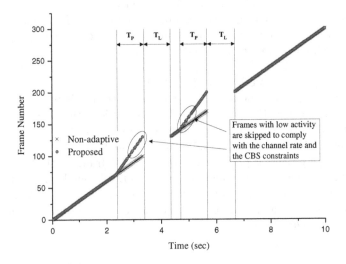

Fig. 6. Frames transmitted according to the vertical handoff scenario

Fig. 5 shows the PSNR performance of the proposed method in VH based on the transition scenario as described before. In Fig. 5, "Non-adaptive" means that the streaming server does not consider VH. The "Periodic Frame Selection" indicates that S_T is determined by selecting frames periodically to comply with the rate and buffer constraints. For the "Non-adaptive" case, every transition produces tremendous quality degradation. On the other hand, the proposed methods show that VH can be effectively overcome. In every transition, the FSP-T method shows better visual quality than the PFS-T method that selects frames just periodically since the FSP-T method preferentially skips frames with lower activity according to the frame activity. For example, in the second transition, we can see that the proposed FSP-T method transmits frames with high activity. Fig. 6 shows the frames transmitted according to the simulation scenario. We can see that the proposed method provides seamless video transmission although the non-adaptive method produces tremendous lost frames caused by VH.

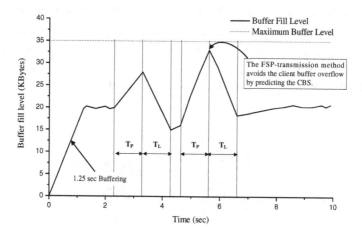

Fig. 7. Client buffer fill level for the proposed video streaming method in vertical handoff

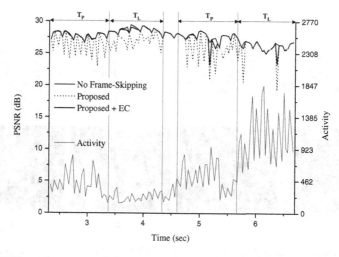

Fig. 8. PSNR performance of the proposed method with error concealment between 70th frame and 200th frame

Fig. 7 shows the client buffer fill level of the proposed method. For the proposed method, we chose B_C^M to be 95% of the client buffer size to give marginal spaces enough to prevent the client buffer overflow caused by abrupt transmission. Thus, the proposed method controls the transmission rate to prevent the client buffer overflow around 5.6 sec. As shown in Fig. 7, despite of two times VHs, the client buffer is maintained stably without the underflow caused by VH and the overflow by overtransmission.

Fig. 8 shows that the EC method using pre-transmitted MVs can be applied easily to the result of the proposed FSP-T method in order to conceal skipped

Table 1. Comparison of the PSNR performance of the FSP-transmission method

Transition	Average PSNR [dB]			
	Non-adaptive	FSP-T	FSP-T+EC	No Frame-Skipping
1 (3G → WLAN)	25.10	26.83	28.07	28.13
2 (WLAN → 3G)	20.53	26.17	26.99	27.15

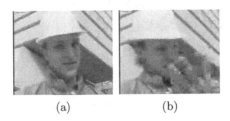

(a)   (b)

Fig. 9. Error-free decoded frames of the "Foreman" sequence: (a) 113th frame with low activity; (b) 155th frame with high activity

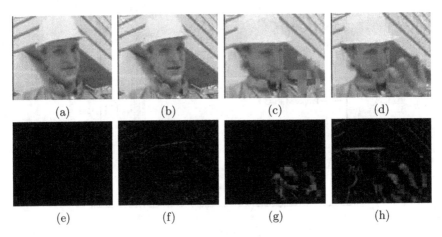

(a)   (b)   (c)   (d)

(e)   (f)   (g)   (h)

Fig. 10. Reconstructed and error images for 113th frame and 155th frame of the "Foreman" sequence: For 113th frame, (a), (b), (e), and (f), respectively, are the reconstructed image by EC, the previous frame, the error image of (a), and the error image of (b); For 155th frame, (c), (d), (g), and (h), respectively, are the reconstructed image by EC, the previous frame, the error image of (c), and the error image of (d)

frames since skipped frames have lower motion activity as compared with non-skipped frames. Table 1 shows PSNR comparison for two transition cases. In Fig. 8 and Table 1, it is seen that the PSNR result of the FSP-T method with EC is very close to that of the error-free transmission. In order to show the visual quality of EC, we show estimated frames for the "Foreman" sequence; for comparison, Fig. 9 reports 113th and 155th frames after decoding in the no frame-skipping case. In Fig. 10, we report the frames reconstructed by EC using pre-transmitted MVs for the "Foreman" sequence, in which 113th and 155th frames are lost (The 113th frame has low activity and the 155th frame has high activity.) As can be seen from these images, the EC using MVs provide a reconstruction of good visual quality. Especially, since the proposed FSP-T method skips frames with lower activity, many skipped frames are closely reconstructed as shown in Fig. 10. Especially, Fig. 8 shows that some frames are reconstructed perfectly because of very low activity of those frames. Thus, the simulation results show that the proposed method that transmits in advance the MVs of skipped frames improves the performance of EC effectively.

4   Conclusions

VH is required to achieve anywhere and anytime internet access in the 4G network providing interoperability between UMTS and WLAN. However, video data can be lost due to latency caused by VH. To solve this problem, in this paper, we have presented an effective video streaming method for VOD services that provides seamless playout at the client in VH. For seamless video playout, the streaming server predicts the channel rate and the client buffer status by analyzing the RTCP RR and APP. And, we propose a FSP-T method using the predicted results to minimize visual quality degradation caused by VH. The FSP-T method selectively transmits frames with high activity for the VH preparation period. The MVs of skipped frames are also transmitted to support EC of skipped frames in the client. Experimental results show that the proposed method provides seamless video streaming in VH with both utilizing the channel bandwidth highly and maintaining the client buffer stably. In addition, through EC using MVs transmitted of skipped frames, it is seen that the streaming client can reconstruct skipped frames successfully.

References

1. Savo, G. G.: Advanced wireless communications 4G technologies. WILEY (2004) 3-3
2. Stemm, M., Katz, R.-H.: Vertical handoffs in wireless overlay networks. ACM Trans. Networking and Applications **3** (1998) 335-350
3. McNair, J., Zhu, F.: Vertical handoffs in fourth-generation multinetwork environments. IEEE Wireless Communication **11** issue.3 (2004) 8-15
4. Varshney, U., Jain, R.: Issues in emerging 4G wireless networks. IEEE Computer **3** (2001) 94-96
5. Wu, H., Zhang, Q., Zhu, W.: Design study for multimedia transport protocol in heterogeneous networks. IEEE International Conference on Communications **1** (2003) 567-571
6. Salamah, M., Tansu, F., Khalil, N.: Buffering requirements for lossless vertical handoffs in wireless overlay networks. The 57th IEEE Semiannual Vehicular Technology Conference **3** (2003) 1984-1987
7. Ma, L., Yu, F., Leung, V. C. M., Randhawa, T.: A new method to support UMTS/WLAN vertical handover using SCTP. IEEE Wireless Communications **11** (2004) 44-51

8. Wang, H., Moayeri, N.: Finite state Markov channel: A useful model for radio communication channels. IEEE Trans. Veh. Technol. **44** (1995) 163–171
9. Baldo, N., Horn, U., Kampmann, M., Hartung, F.: RTCP feedback based transmission rate control for 3G wireless multimedia streaming. Personal, Indoor and Mobile Radio Communications, PIMRC 2004. 15th IEEE International Symposium **3** (2004) 1817–1821
10. Transparent end-to-end packet-switched streaming service (PSS): protocols and codecs, (2004) 3GPP TS 26.234 Rel. 6

A High-Throughput System Architecture for Deep Packet Filtering in Network Intrusion Prevention*

Dae Y. Kim[1], Sunil Kim[1], Lynn Choi[2], and Hyogon Kim[2]

[1] School of Information and Computer Engineering, Hongik University,
72-1 Sangsu-Dong, Mapo-Gu, Seoul, Korea
{hansol, sikim}@cs.hongik.ac.kr
[2] The Department of Electronics and Computer Engineering, Korea University,
Anam-Dong, Sungbuk-Ku, Seoul, Korea
{lchoi, hyogon}@korea.ac.kr

Abstract. Pattern matching is one of critical parts of Network Intrusion Prevention Systems (NIPS). Pattern matching hardware for NIPS should find a matching pattern at wire speed. However, that alone is not good enough. First, pattern matching hardware should be able to generate sufficient pattern match information including the pattern index number and the location of the match found at wire speed. Second, it should support pattern grouping to reduce unnecessary pattern matches. Third, it should show constant worst-case performance even if the number of patterns is increased. Finally it should be able to update patterns in a few minutes or seconds without stopping its operations. We modify Shift-OR hardware accelerator and propose a system architectures to meet the above requirement. Using Xilinx FPGA simulation, we show the new system scaled well to achieve a high speed over 10Gbps and satisfies all of the above requirements.

1 Introduction

The explosive growth of the Internet and the emergence of new applications, such as P2P file sharing, video-on-demand, and e-commerce, dramatically increases network traffic. Network speed and bandwidth is also rapidly increasing to satisfy demand for high-speed Internet access and high bandwidth. These trends have made malicious network attacks, such as Denial of Service (DoS), e-mail virus, and Internet worm, faster and more destructive and damaging. For example, Code Red worm [1] and SQL Slammer worm [2] spread over the world within a few hours and minutes, respectively to cause billions of dollars in damage.

Network Intrusion Prevention Systems (NIPS) have recently emerged as one of the most promising technologies against such network attacks. The NIPS combines both firewall and NIDS [3]. It inspects both packet headers and payloads as a NIDS does and blocks suspicious packets from entering the network as a firewall does. The NIPS lives in-band on the network and processes packets in

---

* This work was supported by 2005 Korea Sanhank Foundation Research Fund.

W. Grass et al. (Eds.): ARCS 2006, LNCS 3894, pp. 407–421, 2006.
© Springer-Verlag Berlin Heidelberg 2006

real-time at wire speed. The performance of NIPS is critical because a poorly performing NIPS would be detrimental to the whole network. At the heart of most NIPS is pattern matching to find attack string patterns in the payload. Pattern matching is computationally intensive. The pattern matching routines in Snort [4], a widely used open-source NIDS/NIPS, account for up to 70 % of total execution time and 80 % of instructions executed on real traces [5]. Therefore, a pattern matching method for NIPS should be highly efficient to keep up with ever increasing speed demand.

Pattern matching for NIPS has several domain-specific characteristics [6, 7, 8]. First, the number of patterns is very large and is keep rising. In Snort, a rule describes the pattern of attack signature and an action to take if a packet matches the signature. The number of the patterns is increasing and more than 2100 in the current Snort. Second, the size of patterns varies widely ranging from 1 to 122, although most pattern sizes are below 32. Third, a large number of string patterns are non-case sensitive. More than half of the string patterns used in Snort are non-case sensitive.

A great deal of research has concentrated on developing pattern matching hardware that satisfies all or some of the domain-specific characteristics. However, there are other important features that pattern matching hardware must support to be useful and effective for NIPS.

1. *Pattern match information at wire speed – at least the pattern index number and the location information should be provided:*
   When a pattern match occurs, rule-checking software further examines the packet to check if other rule options are satisfied. Snort uses pattern index information to find the related rule and the location information to decide whether the packet satisfies other content options, such as *depth* and *offset*, which specify how far into a packet should be searched and where to start searching in the packet, respectively. Such information for all matched patterns should be generated at wire speed. Otherwise, pattern matching hardware eventually stalls to process the information.

2. *Pattern grouping support – only patterns related to the rule group a packet belongs to are checked against:*
   In Snort, rules are divided into rule groups by the protocol type and source and destination port numbers specified in the rules. An incoming packet is classified by its protocol type and source and destination ports, and its payload is checked against only those patterns in the corresponding rule group. Without pattern grouping in hardware, there could be many matches against patterns that belong to other unrelated rule groups and this could results in unnecessary software executions.

3. *Worst-case performance:*
   This requirement is also discussed in [6, 9]. The worst-case performance of a NIPS has to match network speed. Otherwise, an attacker can devise a packet with content that results in the worst-case performance of NIPS and

continuously send the packets to render the NIPS unusable, which will eventually block all other legitimate traffic. In addition the worst-case performance should remain constant and predictable even when more patterns are added. If not, it would be hard to predict when the NIPS would fail to meet the speed requirement.

4. *Fast non-interrupting pattern update:*
This requirement is important to protect networks from a fast spreading Internet worm like SQL Slammer worm. Content-filtering, used in NIPS, should start to filter the new worm within a few minutes after the worm outbreaks in order to successfully quarantine the worm propagation [10]. This implies that pattern matching hardware should be able to update patterns in less than a few minutes or seconds for Internet worm quarantine. Considering the amount of damages caused by latest worm outbreaks, this feature becomes very important. Only the pattern matching architecture in [9] explicitly addressed this issue.

Most pattern matching hardware based on FPGA [11, 12, 13, 14, 15, 16, 17] likely fails to satisfy the worst-case performance requirement. When the number of patterns is increased, the operating frequency of FPGA pattern matching hardware tends to increase due to the increase in the amount of combinational circuits for state transitions. This makes NIPS performance unpredictable and eventually leads to the failure of NIPS performance at some point, not matching network speed. These approaches also most likely fail to meet the fourth requirement, fast non-interrupting pattern update, because they need to re-synthesize and reprogram FPGA for new patterns, which usually take a long time for a large number of patterns. Bit-split FSM approach [9] based on Aho-Corasick algorithm [18] uses SRAM for state transition tables. The approach shows excellent performance and hardware area utilization as well as satisfies two requirements, the worst-case performance and fast non-interrupting pattern update.

In this paper, we propose a pattern matching system architecture for the wire-speed pattern match information and pattern grouping requirements. To the authors' best knowledge, this is the first work that successfully addresses these two requirements. Two papers [16, 17] addressed issues related to the pattern match information requirement and proposed two similar architectures that generate signature indexes using pruned priority binary tree and highly pipelined binary-OR tree. However, these architectures cannot handle multiple matches that simultaneously occur and also do not provide any information on the location of a match in a payload. Our study on string patterns used in Snort shows that there are many suffix matches of patterns. The maximum number of patterns in the same suffix match group is 5. This implies that there could be up to 5 multiple matches for a given input character.

In this paper we also introduce some improvements to Shift-OR pattern matching accelerator [8] for fast non-interrupting pattern update. The Shift-OR pattern matching accelerator uses SRAM as Bit-split FSM does and does not need to change hardware when a pattern is added. This allows the accelerator to have constant worst-case performance. The proposed pattern matching system architecture with the updated Shift-OR pattern matching accelerator successfully satisfies all of the above four requirements.

We evaluate our proposed architecture using Xilinx FPGA tools. We design the proposed pattern matching system and obtain timing and area results through FPGA simulation. This paper begins by briefly describing Shift-OR algorithm [19] in Section 2. Section 3 presents the pattern matching system that consists of the updated Shift-OR pattern matching accelerator, pattern grouping hardware, and pattern match information system. We evaluate the proposed architecture by Xilinx FPGA tools in Section 4 and conclude in Section 5.

2   Shift-OR Pattern Matching Algorithm

In this section, we briefly describe Shift-OR pattern matching algorithm for a single pattern, which is the basis of the pattern matching architecture we present in this paper. The algorithm uses bitwise techniques. It keeps a bit array of size m (pattern length), a state vector R that shows if prefixes of the pattern match at the current place. For example, there are a pattern $P = p_0 \ldots p_{m-1}$ and input string $X = \ldots x_{i+j} \ldots$. After processing x_{i+j}, $R[j] = 0$ if $x_i \ldots x_{i+j}$ matches $p_0 \ldots p_j$, otherwise $R[j] = 1$. There is another bit array of size m, a character position vector S_c, denoting the position of character c in pattern P. For example, $S_c[i] = 0$ if $p_i = c$, otherwise $S_c[i] = 1$. If we know that the bit value of $R[j]$ after processing x_{i+j}, we can easily compute $R[j + 1]$ by knowing whether the next character x_{i+j+1} appear at pattern position p_{j+1}. $R[j + 1]$ can be defined as follows:

$$R[j + 1] = \begin{cases} 0 \text{ if } R[j] = 0 \text{ and } S_c[j + 1] = 0 \text{ where } c = x_{i+j+1} \\ 1 \text{ otherwise.} \end{cases} \tag{1}$$

$$R[0] = S_c[0] \text{ where } c = x_{i+j+1} \tag{2}$$

$R[m - 1] = 0$ means the pattern $x_i \ldots x_{i+m-1}$ matches $p_0 \ldots p_{m-1}$, that is, the matching pattern is found. The computation of new R for the next input character c reduces to Shift and OR operations ($SHIFT(R)$ OR S_c).

This algorithm easily handles any finite class of symbols, complement symbols and even don't care symbols. If position i of a pattern allows a class of symbols $\{x, y, z\}$, then letting $S_x[i] = S_y[i] = S_z[i] = 0$ handles the case. Complement symbols and don't care symbols can be handled in the same way. Therefore, noncase-sensitive matches can be easily processed without any additional overhead. The algorithm can be extended for multiple patterns. It first concatenates all state vector R for each pattern into one large state vector. It also concatenates all character position vector S_cs for each pattern into one large character position vector for a given character c. The only difference from single pattern match is that when the new bit value of the large R corresponding to the first position of a pattern, i, is computed, the value is only affected by the large $S_c[i]$, not by shifted value from $i - 1^{th}$ position. In the remaining of the paper, '*vector*' denotes a concatenated vector.

3   Pattern Matching System

The pattern matching system presented in this paper has multiple pattern matching units (PMU). PMU is the updated Shift-OR pattern matching accelerator that can do fast non-interrupting pattern update and have constant worst-case performance. The pattern matching system provides pattern grouping and can generate pattern matching information at wire speed.

3.1   Pattern Match Unit

The pattern match unit performs Shift-OR pattern match algorithm for multi-patterns. Figure 1 shows the components of the pattern matching unit (PMU). PMU has a multiport SRAM that stores 256 character position vectors, one per an 8-bit character. Multiple characters are read from the payload and used to address the multiport SRAM. The size of the SRAM is 256 x W bits, where W is the width of the SRAM. It is also the size of the character position vector that the PMU uses. The character position vector is a concatenated character position vector for a character for all the patterns assigned to the PMU. These vectors are precomputed from string patterns and loaded into the SRAM. The number of SRAM ports, N, determines the number of input characters processed together. PMU has four registers for bit vectors: pattern boundary vector (B),

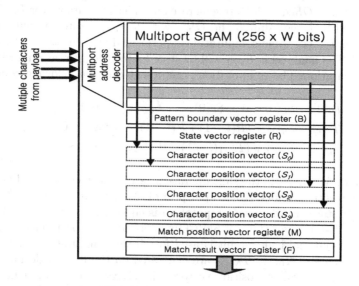

Fig. 1. Pattern Matching Unit

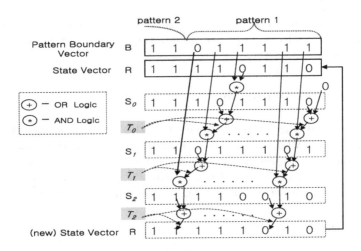

Fig. 2. Shift-OR Computation

state vector (R), match position (M), and match result vector (F). The size of all vector registers is the same, W bit wide.

Once N character position vectors $S_0, \ldots, S_{N-1}$ are read from the multiport SRAM, Shift-OR computation is performed using state vector R generated from the previous cycle and pattern boundary vector B to compute a new state vector R as shown in Figure 2. The pattern boundary vector B denotes boundaries of each pattern by bit value '0' and is used to prevent the Shift-OR computation result from propagating cross pattern boundaries. Initially R is ANDed with B, then shifted and ORed with S_0 to generate intermediate state vector T_0. Next, T_0 is ANDed with B, then shifted and ORed with S_1 to generate next intermediate state vector T_1. The same computation is performed at each stage until T_{N-1} is generated. The final result T_{N-1} will be stored into R register again for the next cycle computation. The computation is represented in the following equations.

$$T_k(0) = S_k(0) + 0 = S_k(0) \qquad \text{for all } k \qquad (3)$$
$$T_0(i) = S_0(i) + (R(i-1) * B(i-1)) \qquad \text{for } i > 0 \qquad (4)$$
$$T_k(i) = S_k(i) + (T_{k-1}(i-1) * B(i-1)) \quad \text{for } k > 0, \, i > 0 \qquad (5)$$

As shown in Figure 2, the shift operations are performed by simply connecting the ith position results to one input port of the OR gate of the $i+1^{th}$ position at the next stage. Each stage computation is equivalent to one Shift-OR operation in Shift-OR algorithm. N Shift-OR operations are performed in a single cycle. Combinatorial logic circuit is used for all the computation, and intermediate state vectors, $T_0, \ldots, T_{N-1}$, are generated on the fly and do not need to be stored. The character position vectors, $S_0, \ldots, S_{N-1}$ also do not need to be stored. They are the output of the multiport SRAM and directly used for the computations.

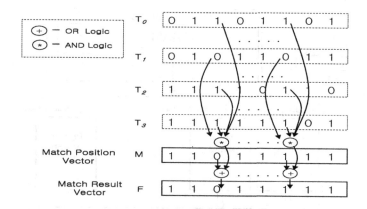

Fig. 3. Match Result Vector Generation

While N input characters are simultaneously processed, several matches can be found. Figure 3 shows the architecture that detects all the matches from all the intermediate state vectors. All the bits at the same position in the intermediate state vectors are *ANDed* and then *ORed* with the bit at the same position in match position vector M. Match position vector has 0 bit at a pattern's end position. The result is match result vector and stored in F register. If the match result vector has zero bits (*match bits*), it means there are matches. The output of F vector register becomes the output of PMU.

PMU can perform fast non-interrupting pattern update. A pattern can be easily ignored by resetting M vector bit at the pattern's end position to 1. The effect is the same as deleting the pattern. Adding a pattern requires reinitializing pattern boundary vector B and match position vector M registers and reloading the multiport SRAM. Updating and initializing B and M registers can be done by writing the vector values into SRAM, reading the vector data from the SRAM, and finally loading them into the corresponding registers. For this, we can use a separate SRAM or the same multiport SRAM by increasing its depth by 2 for the vectors. The time for reloading the multiport SRAM for new character position vectors takes the same number of cycles as the length of the new pattern. We need to write only the character position vectors for characters in the new pattern. Writing multiport SRAM can also be performed without blocking any read operations. Therefore, pattern updates can be done without stopping the system.

3.2 Pattern Group Unit

In hardware pattern matching where all patterns are searched together, the time taken for the pattern match process itself is not affected by grouping patterns. However, pattern grouping can reduce many unnecessary matches against patterns that belong to other unrelated rule groups. Rule groups are classified by the protocol type and source and destination ports specified in the rules. Patterns in the same rule group form a pattern group. The patterns are assigned to PMUs

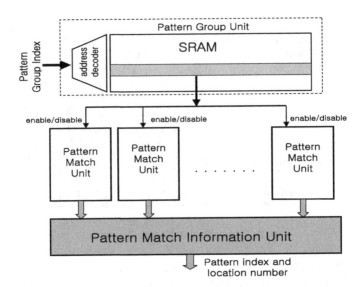

Fig. 4. Pattern Matching System

such that a PMU processes only patterns in the same pattern group. A pattern group index is obtained by inspecting an incoming packet's protocol type and source and destination ports and used to access Pattern Group Unit (PGU) as shown in Figure 4. The PGU enables only those PMUs that handle the corresponding pattern group. A PMU activation vector is read from the SRAM accessed by pattern group index, and each bit of the vector is used to enable or disable a PMU. When a PMU is disabled, the match result vector of the PMU generates all 1's, effectively having no effect on the match result.

3.3   Pattern Match Information Unit

Pattern matching hardware usually raises a signal line when a pattern matches. For Snort, pattern matching hardware may need almost 2000 signal lines and more. The software cannot read all of the signal lines at once. Therefore the signal line index (or *pattern index*) should be provided to rule checking software for further examination. Pattern Match Information Unit (PMIU) reads the match result vectors of all PMUs and generates pattern indexes and the location information of the matching patterns in the payload for all match bits. PMIU speed should match the processing speed of core pattern match hardware. Otherwise, the pattern match hardware would stall at some point to wait for all the match results to be processed.

Example architecture of PMIU is shown in Figure 5. It is a pipelined priority tree with special functionalities. The figure shows how PMIU receives a match result vector from F register and generates a position index of the match bit at the 35th bit position. The position index can be used as a pattern index. First, an Input Vector Encoder (IVE) receives each 4 bits in the match result vector

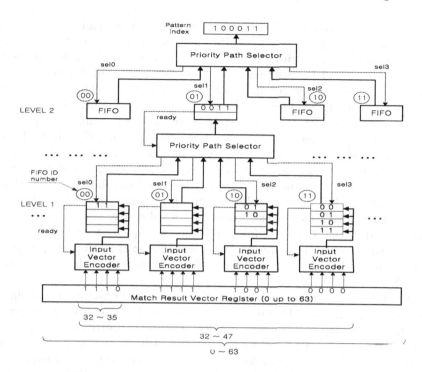

Fig. 5. Example of Pattern Match Information Unit

and encodes the relative position indexes of all match bits in those 4 bits. The encoded values are put into the first-level FIFO. The first-level FIFO with ID '00' has the relative position index of the match bit at the 35th bit position, and the index value is '11'. The next level Priority Path Selector (PPS) selects the first-level FIFO '00' out of the four first-level FIFOs. The four FIFOs have the relative position indexes of match bits in each 4 bits at the bit position 32nd to 35th, 36th to 39th, 40th to 43rd and 44th to 47th, respectively. The PPS uses the relative position index ('11') from the first FIFO and the FIFO ID ('00') to generate position index '0011'. The position index is stored in the second level FIFO '01'. Note that the value '0011' is the relative position index of the match bit at 35th bit position in 16 bits, from 32nd to 47th position. The final PPS selects the position index ('0011') from the second-level FIFOs and uses the FIFO ID number '01' to generate the final position index '100011'. In the next, we describe three main components of the PMIU.

FIFO. The FIFO stores the position index of matching bits. A FIFO entry consists of three control bits, tag (T), dummy (D), empty (E), and index bits (I). In Figure 5, only the index bits are shown for simplicity. The index bits store the relative position index of a match bit. At the first level, the size of the index bits is $\log_2 N$ where N is the number of bits processed by an IVE. As the level goes up, the size of the index bits is increased by $\log_2$ of the number of the lower level FIFOs connected to a PPS.

An empty control bit (E) shows whether the corresponding FIFO entry is empty or not. A tag bit (T) is used to represent the sequence of match results. A tag bit is associated with a match result vector register, and the value is toggled between 0 and 1 every time a new result vector is loaded into the register. All PMUs generate new result vectors at the same time. The tag bit value is moved along with the index bits for the match result vector. We can compute the location information of the pattern by counting the number of the tag bit changes when the final pattern index is generated. Using the tag bit, PPS selects input index bits such that the index bits for earlier match results vector are moved to the upper levels before the index bits for any subsequent match result vectors. The dummy bit tells whether the index bits have a real position index. An IVE fills one FIFO entry with dummy index bits when there is no match bit. This prevents index bits for different match result vectors, but with the same tag value from appearing as inputs of a PPS at the same time. Dummy index bits are eliminated by PPS so that there is one dummy index left at the final stage of PMIU for each match result vector with no matches.

The FIFOs at each level create a pipeline stage. The first-level FIFO connected to IVE is different from FIFOs at the other levels. The size of an IVE input bits determines the depth of the first-level FIFO. All the relative position indexes of match bits are generated and loaded into the FIFO in one cycle. The depth of FIFOs at the other level should be at least two. Two entries are required not to make a bubble in the pipeline stage. With two-entry FIFO, a new relative position index can be generated and stored into the FIFO by the lower-level PPS connected as soon as there is at least one empty entry. This prevents a bubble from being introduced in the pipeline.

Priority Path Selector. A Priority Path Selector (PPS) selects the highest priority index bits from all the connected input FIFOs and generates a new relative position index from the input index bits and the ID number of the FIFO selected. The selected FIFO entry is erased, and the new relative position index is stored in the output FIFO connected to the PPS. The priority selection should consider tag and dummy bit values as well as the priority of input FIFOs. The operation of a PPS is executed in one cycle.

The priority mode of a PPS changes between 1 and 0-mode. In a given priority mode, input FIFO entries with the same tag value as the mode are considered for selection and subsequent operations. The mode changes only when the first entries of all input FIFOs have the same tag value, and then the priority mode is changed to the tag value. This is to compute all the relative position indexes in the same order of the match result vector generation. When a PPS finds at least one non-dummy entry, then it selects one entry among them and erases all dummy entries by sending a select signal to all related input FIFOs. If all entries are dummy entry, only one dummy entry is move to the upper level, and all the other dummy entries are erased as well. By doing this, at most only one dummy entry is left when it reaches the top-level PPS. The dummy entry is for a match result vector with no matches.

Input Vector Encoder. An Input Vector Encoder (IVE) receives a part of a match result vector and generates all the relative position indexes of match bits in the partial match result vector. If there is no match bit, the IVE generates only one dummy index. The IVE stores all the relative position indexes into the first-level FIFO in one cycle and set its mode to the same as the tag value of the match result vector. As far as the mode of an IVE is the same as that of the match result vector, no further operation is performed. When the tag of the match result vector changes, that is, a new match result vector is generated for the new input payload byte and loaded into the vector, the IVE generates the relative position indexes again.

4   Evaluation

We design PMU using the latest Xilinx FPGA Virtex-4 [20]. Virtex-4 has the largest number of embedded RAMs, called block RAMs, which are used to construct multiport SRAM in our design. Unfortunately it has only dual port memory configuration. Therefore, we have to duplicate memory banks to simulate the multiport SRAM when the number of ports becomes larger than 2. In this experiment, we choose 256 bits for the size of the character position vector. Therefore a PMU can handle the total pattern length of 256 bytes. The average size of patterns in Snort is about 12 bytes and hence a PMU can process more than 20 patterns in average.

Figure 6 shows the processing speed of a PMU as the number of Shift-OR stage is increased. The number of Shift-OR stages is shown in logarithmic scale. We can process the same number of input characters together as the number of Shift-OR stages. There are two different versions of the designs. The one labeled as *'pipeline'* has a pipeline stage between the memory bank and Shift-OR computation circuits, and the other one labeled as *'non-pipeline'* does not have a pipeline stage. The graph shows that the processing speeds of both versions of a PMU can reach up to 14 and 14.5 Gbps, respectively, with 64 Shift-OR stages.

The pipelined design shows up to 58 % improvement over the non-pipelined design. The performance difference is more noticeable when the number of Shift-OR stage is small. This is because the effective memory access time is reduced by overlapping memory accesses and a few stages of Shift-OR computations. This shows that memory access time is critical when the number of Shift-OR stages is small. As the number of Shift-OR stages is increased, the total Shift-OR computation time for all stages becomes the dominant performance factor.

Figure 7 shows the resource count for different hardware resources, such as RAM banks, LUT, flip-flops for the non-pipelined design and flip-flop for the pipelined design. They are labeled as *RAM, LUT, FF(NP), FF(P)*, respectively in the figure. The resource count counts the number of resources needed per one pattern character. The increase in the number of RAM banks is due to the simulation of multiport memory. As the number of Shift-OR stages is increased, we need more memory read ports. Duplicated memory banks are used instead of memory ports, and this leads to the large number of memory banks for a

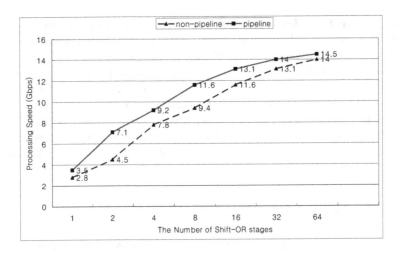

Fig. 6. PMU Processing Speed vs. The Number of Shift-OR Stages

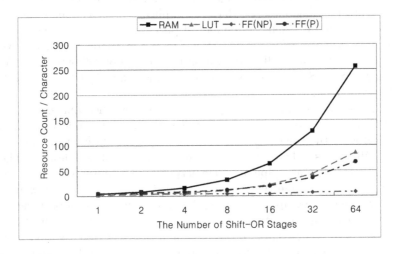

Fig. 7. Resource Count per Pattern Character vs. The Number of Shift-OR Stages

large number of Shift-OR stages. The number of LUT and flip-flops for the pipelined design is increased as well. This is because Shift-OR stages use LUTs for the logic, and the number of flip-flops for memory pipeline is increased due to memory port increase for more Shift-OR stages. Note that the number of flip-flops for the non-pipeline design is almost constant. This implies that non-pipeline is a good choice when memory is fast enough and many Shift-OR stages are needed.

Overall, there are trade-offs between the processing speed and the amount of hardware resources available for Shift-OR pattern matching architecture. As we add more Shift-OR stages, we need more read ports or memory banks and LUTs even for the resource-efficient non-pipeline design. However, note that

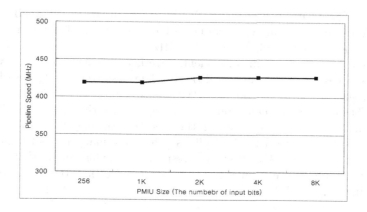

Fig. 8. PMIU Pipeline Speed vs. PMIU sizes

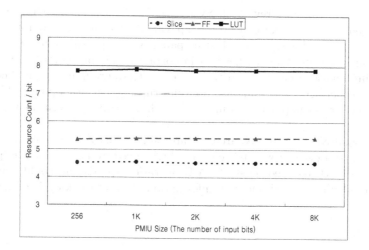

Fig. 9. Resource counter per one PMIU bit vs. PMIU sizes

when more hardware resource is available, it is relatively easy to improve the processing speed of a PMU by adding more Shift-OR stages. This is an important advantage of Shift-OR pattern matching architecture over other previous pattern matching hardware.

We implement PMIUs with 256 inputs through with 8K inputs. Figure 8 shows the pipeline speed of PMIU as its input size increases. The pipeline speed remains almost constant for all PMIU sizes we test and successfully matches the speed of all the non-pipelined PMUs and the speed of pipelined PMU except those with 1 or 2 Shift-OR stages. Figure 9 shows the resource count for different hardware resources, slices, LUTs, flip-flops for different sizes of PMIUs. The resource count counts the number of resources per one input bit of a PMIU. The hardware resource used to construct a PMIU increases linearly as the size increases. These data show that the PMIU architecture uses a reasonable amount of hardware resources and can produce a pattern index and the location information at least every clock cycle of 420 MHz.

Finally we put all system components together on one single Xilinx Virtex-4 chip and measure the resource utilization. The designed architecture has one PGU of size 512 x 32 bit wide, 32 PMUs with 4 Shift-OR stages, one 8K-bit PMIU. The architecture can support total pattern length of 8K bytes. The slice is the most constraint resource in the design, reaching 94 % utilization. A slice consists of two LUTs and flip-flops. There are many flip-flops and LUTs left unused (54 % and 88 % utilization, respectively). This implies that a custom design may improve the balance of the resource utilization. However, we do not further investigate the issue in this paper.

5   Conclusion

In Network Intrusion Prevention Systems (NIPS), pattern matching is extensively used to find attack signatures in a payload and is the most computationally intensive part of the execution. In this paper, we proposed a pattern matching system architecture that satisfies four important requirements for NIPS: pattern match information generation at wire speed, pattern grouping support, constant worst-case performance, and fast non-interrupting pattern update. These requirements are as important as finding matching attack patterns at wire speed for NIPS.

We evaluated the proposed architecture using Xilinx FPGA tools and showed that the system scaled well to achieve a high speed over 10Gbps. The pipeline speed of PMIU matched most of PMU operation speeds and could generate a pattern index and match location information at every clock cycle of 420 MHz.

References

1. Code Red worm exploiting buffer overflow in IIS indexing service DLL. CERT Advisory CA-2001-19 (2002)
2. MS-SQL Server Worm. CERT Advisory CA-2003-04 (2003)
3. Xinyou Zhang, Chengzhong Li, Wenbin Zheng: Intrusion Prevention System Design. In: The Fourth International Conference on Computer and Information Technology (CIT'04). (2004)
4. Snort. (http://www.snort.org)
5. S. Antonatos, K. G. Anagnostakis, E. P. Markatos: Generating Realistic Workloads for Network Intrusion Detection Systems. In: Proceedings of ACM Workshop on Software and Performance. (2004)
6. N. Tuck, T. Sherwood, B. Calder, G. Varghese: Deterministic Memory-Efficient String Matching Algorithms for Intrusion Detection. In: Proceedings of the 23rd Conference of the IEEE Communication Society (INFOCOM04). (2004)
7. R. Liu, N. Huang, C. Chen, C. Kao: A Fast String Matching Algorithm for Network Processor Based Intrusion Detection System. ACM Transaction on Embedded Computing Systems 3 (2004) 614–633

8. Sunil Kim: Pattern Matching Acceleration for Network Intrusion Detection Systems. In: Embedded Computer Systems: Architectures, Modeling, and Simulation (SAMOS V). (2005)
9. Lin Tan, Timothy Sherwood: A High Throughput String Matching Architecture for Intrusion Detection and Prevention. In: The 32nd Annual International Symposium on Computer Architecture. (2005)
10. David Moore, Colleen Shannon, Geoffrey M. Voelker, Stefan Savage: Internet Quarantine: Requirements for Containing Self-Propagating Code. In: IEEE INFOCOM. (2003)
11. Sarang Dharmapurikar, Praveen Krishnamurthy, Todd Sproull, John Lockwood: Deep Packet Inspection Using Parallel Bloom Filters. In: Proceedings of the Symposium on High Performance Interconnects (HotI). (2003) 44–51
12. B. L. Hutchings, R. Franklin, D. Carver: Assisting Network Intrusion Detection with Reconfigurable Hardware. In: Proceedings of the 10th Annual IEEE Symposium on Field-Programmable Custom Computing Machines. (2002)
13. J. Moscola, J. Lockwood, R. P. Loui, M. Pachos: Implementation of a Content-Scanning Module for an Internet Firewall. In: Proceedings of the IEEE Symposium on Field-Programmable Custom Computing Machines. (2003)
14. M. Gokhale, D. Dubois, A. Dubois, M. Boorman, S. Poole, V. Hogsett: Granidt: Towards Gigabit Rate Network Intrusion Detection Technology. In: Proceedings of International Conference on Field-Programmable Logic and Applications. (2002)
15. I. Sourdis, D. Pnevmatikatos: Pre-decoded CAMs for Efficient and High-Speed NIDS Pattern Matching. In: Proceeding of the 12th Annual IEEE Symposium on Field Programmable Custom Computing Machines. (2004)
16. Young H. Cho, W. H. Mangione-Smith: Programmable Hardware for Deep Packet Filtering on a Large Signature Set. In: Workshop on Architectural Support for Security and Anti-Virus. (2004)
17. Young H. Cho, W. H. Mangione-Smith: Deep Packet Filter with Dedicated Logic and Read Only Memories. In: Proceedings of the 12th IEEE Symposium of Field-Programmable Custom Computing Machines. (2004)
18. A. V. Aho, M. J. Corasick: Efficient String Matching: An Aid to Bibliographic Search. Communications of the ACM 18 (1975) 333–340
19. R. A. Baeza-Yates, G. H. Gonnet: A New Approach to Text Searching. In: Proceedings of ACM 12th International Conference on Research and Development in Information Retrieval. (1989)
20. Xilinx, Inc. (http://www.xilinx.com)

A Hierarchical Key Management Approach for Secure Multicast

Jian Wang[1], Miodrag J. Mihaljevic[2], Lein Harn[3], and Hideki Imai[4]

[1] College of Information Science and Technology,
Nanjing University of Aeronautics and Astronautics,
Nanjing 210016, China
wangjian@nuaa.edu.cn
[2] Mathematical Institute, Serbian Academy of Sciences and Arts,
Belgrade, Serbia and Montenegro
[3] Computer Networking Department, University of Missouri, Kansas City, USA
[4] Institute of Industrial Science, The University of Tokyo, Tokyo, Japan

Abstract. The problem of secure multicasting in a large and highly dynamical group of users is addressed, and a novel hierarchical key management framework is proposed, based on an appropriate combination of the updatable and static logical key hierarchies. It fits to the underlying architecture of an IP-based network, and reduces the synchronization problem which is a main issue regarding the necessary key update upon membership changes. The proposed solution employs a hybrid two-layer approach with the updatable key hierarchy in the upper layer and the static one in the bottom layer. It provides scalability, flexibility, efficiency and security. Although any static and updatable logical hierarchies can be employed, certain architectural issues of the proposed framework are considered. The security and performance of the proposed approaches are discussed and compared with the previously reported schemes, and advantages of the proposed approach are pointed out.

1 Introduction

Multicast is commonly employed in the context of group communication over an IP-based network in order to save network bandwidth and server capacity by sending some message only once to several recipients, and therefore securing the multicasting sessions appears as a very important issue.

When cryptography is used for secure multicast communications, a session-encrypting key (SEK) is used to encrypt the data. Ensuring that only the valid members have SEK at any given time instance is the key management problem in the secure multicasting. Whenever the SEK is invalidated, there needs to be another set of keys called the key-encrypting keys (KEKs) to encrypt and transmit the updated SEK to the valid members of the group. Hence, the key management problem reduces to the problem of distributing the KEKs to the members such that at any given time all the valid members can be securely reached and updated with the novel SEK. The difficulty of managing cryptographic keys used arises from the dynamic characteristics of membership.

W. Grass et al. (Eds.): ARCS 2006, LNCS 3894, pp. 422–434, 2006.

Accordingly, from a security point of view, an efficient key management for a very large, highly dynamic multicast group is a challenging issue. Among the results addressing this problem the approaches based on the logical key hierarchy have appeared as very important ones. Roughly speaking, there are two main logical key hierarchy concepts: one is based on the updatable KEKs (see [1,2], for example) and the other is based on the static KEKs (see [3,4], for example). A number of proposals on scalable key management for establishing the secure multicast or broadcast sessions have been reported including the ones discussed in [1-15].

This paper mainly intends to propose an alternative approach which yields some advantages over the previously reported results, i.e. the novel proposal will accommodate higher frequency of membership change with moderate communication overload but not reducing the security. Particularly, our approach is motivated by a very recently reported concept of the sectioned tree logical key hierarchy [13] which has been also employed for developing particular reconfigurable key management schemes reported in [14,15].

This paper is organized as follows. In the next two parts of this section, the related works on key management and our contributions are summarized. Some preliminaries, including formal definitions, are given in Section 2. The novel framework for key management and certain implementation issues are discussed in Section 3. The security and performance of the proposal are addressed as well as some comparisons with the previous results in Section 4. A concluding discussion is given in section 5.

1.1   Background

The subsection overviews some results on the hierarchical approaches for developing scalable key management schemes which provides the main origins for our approach. These schemes are based on the underlying tree structures, and these tree nodes play different roles in different schemes. According to the nature of the elements forming a hierarchy, there are the following two main classes: (i) hierarchy of the domains, and (ii) hierarchy of the keys (KEKs). The second further includes, as the subclasses, the hierarchies with updatable nodes and the static ones.

Hierarchy of Domains. The hierarchy of domains is proposed in [6]: The proposed tree hierarchy consists of receivers at the leaves with multiple intermediate levels of group security agents (agents, in short) above. Each agent tree node and its children (clients or lower level agents) form a subgroup and share a subgroup key. Thus, there is no globally shared group key. Thus a join in or a leave from a subgroup does not affect other subgroups; only the local subgroup key needs to be changed. Therefore, in the tree scheme [6], only the members in the same subgroup are influenced upon membership change.

On the other hand, the scheme [6] requires synchronization of the state upon a user addition or removal, but within the subgroup only. Thus, suitable division strategy makes it scalable for a very large, dynamic membership. But, due to its computational overheads for decrypting and re-encrypting data (not only key update message)in each agent, it consumes a pretty large amount of computation resources and produces extra delays. Thus, it is not suitable for real-time applications (e.g. video multicasting).

Hierarchy of Keys

Updatable Tree Nodes. The logical key hierarchy (LKH) scheme [1,2] uses a hierarchy of keys to solve the scalability problem, and LKH was the first secure multicast protocol that incurs sub-linear re-keying cost for single membership change.

The approach is based on a different hierarchy in comparison with [6]. The tree hierarchy consists of keys, with individual keys at leaves, the group key at the root, and subgroup keys in intermediate node. There is a single key server for all the users (clients). Without any agents, each user is assigned multiple keys (its individual key, the group key, and some subgroup keys).

A number of results to improve LKH have been reported in the literature including [11] and [12], for example. The approach reported in [12] is particularly efficient in some revocation situations: It yields a small communications overhead in the multiple revocations at the expense of a pretty large, computation overhead that limits its scalability.

A drawback of LKH is that it requires dealing with the synchronization for the keys updating. This operation, if implemented in the acknowledgement manner, makes LKH unsuitable for a very large, highly dynamic membership. Certainly, other reliable multicast approaches, e.g. FEC, can also be used for the required state synchronization, but, they can not guarantee complete synchronization of the state. Hence, up to now, acknowledgement manner is still a popular one. Accordingly, the state synchronization (StateSyn) problem appears to be a limiting issue regarding the updatable logical key hierarchies (U-LKH). An additional problem with LKH is related to the users who were off-line during the resynchronization. These users should be provided with all updates while they were off-line.

Static Tree Nodes. When the members of a session are stateless receivers, broadcast encryption techniques, based on a static logical key hierarchy (S-LKH) appear to be the suitable one for key management.

The basic idea in the most efficient broadcasting encryption schemes is to represent any privileged set of users as the union of s subsets of a particular form. A different key is associated with each one of these sets, and a user knows a key if and only if he belongs to the corresponding set. The broadcaster encrypts SEK s times under all the keys associated with the set in the covering message. Consequently, each privileged user can easily access the SEK but even a coalition of the non-privileged users cannot recover SEK. The simplest implementation of this idea is to cover the privileged set with singleton sets. A better solution is to associate the users with the leaves of a binary tree, and to cover the privileged set of leaves with a collection of sub-trees.

Let N be the number of receivers, R the number of revocations, and let all the logarithms be the base 2.

In [3], a generic framework based on the tree graph approach is given by encapsulating several previously proposed revocation methods called Subset-Cover algorithms. These algorithms are based on the principle of covering all non-revoked users by disjoint subsets from a predefined collection, together with a method for assigning KEKs to subsets in the collection. The first proposed scheme, called the Complete Sub-Tree scheme (CST), requires a message length of at most $R \log(N/R)$ and storage of $\log N$ keys at the receiver and constitutes a moderate improvement over previous schemes. The second scheme proposed in [3] is based on the Subset Difference algorithm (SD), and further improvement of this technique called Layered Subset Difference (LSD) is reported in [4].

Recently, a divide-and-conquer strategy and the sectioned key tree were reported in [13] for developing improved key management schemes based on the trees with static nodes which yield a possibility for appropriate trade-offs between the main overheads related to the key management.

1.2   Motivation for Our Work and Summary of the Results

The previous discussion has pointed out the main characteristics of certain reported techniques for developing the secure multicasting. The techniques based on the updatable LKH (U-LKH) have a number of favorable characteristics but their main disadvantage is related to StateSyn problem which is an essential and restrictive factor regarding U-LKH based techniques. The simplification of StateSyn problem opens a door for higher frequency of the membership changes to be accommodated. On the other hand, a main advantage of the static LKH (S-LKH) techniques is that they do not require the synchronization. But, S-LKH will produce more communication overload that tightly relevant with the scale of whole network not only the number of legitimate receivers. Also, fitting of the key management architecture to the underlying network architecture appears as an interesting issue, as well as employment of a dedicated divide and conquer concept. Accordingly, in this paper we consider a hybrid approach for developing the key management scheme for secure multicasting.

This paper proposes a novel LKH based key management framework suitable for a variety of secure multicasting scenarios, which combines U-LKH and S-LKH techniques in a suitable manner to yield more powerful hybrid LKH (H-LKH) approach.

The integration of S-LKH into U-LKH simplifies StateSyn, so that U-LKH can support very high frequency of membership changes. U-LKH assumes that a receiver keeps a number of updatable keys whereas the keys at a receiver related to S-LKH scheme are fixed (not changeable). The proposed hybrid approach increase the fixed part of key materials and reduce the changeable part of it through employing a suitable two-layer structure where the upper layer of the tree has updatable nodes and the bottom layer has static nodes.

The employed two-layer structure partitions all receivers/users into a number of different logical domains and fits to the network underlying structure. This paper gives only a hierarchical infrastructure of key management with hierarchical key centers, and they can be run by some network service providers (NSP) cooperatively, e.g. Master Key Center is run by a NSP, and Master Key Agents are run by other NSPs.

2   Preliminaries

A key management scheme can be denoted as a triple (U, K, R) as follows:

- U is a finite and nonempty set of users, $U = \{u_1, u_2, \ldots, u_n\}$
- K is a finite and nonempty set of KEKs
- R is a corresponding relationship of key assignment. $R(u_i) = K_i$, $u_i \in U$ and $K_i \subset K$ and $\bigcup_1^n K_i = K$

The security of key distribution requires that the session key is only distributed to all authorized receivers excluding all revoked receivers and that any coalition T of revoked receivers cannot get this key even with all secret information $\bigcup_{u_i \in T} K_i$ they hold. Therefore, key assignment method R must meet: $K_j|_{u_j \notin T} \not\subset \bigcup_{u_i \in T} K_i$ for any coalition of receivers T. Certainly, $K_i \neq K_j$, when $i \neq j$.

Definition 1: StateLess Protocol (SLP) Key Management. SLP key management is one where K is not changed when membership change event (e.g. a user addition or removal) happens, which implys that $K'|_{event} = K$, where K' is the set of keys to be used after a change event.

Definition 2: StateFul Protocol (SFP) Key Management. SFP key management is one where K must be updated when membership change event happens, which implys that $K'|_{event} \neq K$, where K' is the set of keys to be used after a change event.

SLPs include subset cover revocation scheme [3] and its variants. They assign the secret information to all receivers: at certain time instance some of these receivers will be the legitimate ones, and some of them will be revoked. Thus, the set of users can be considered as $U = U_L \bigcup U_R$, where $U_L = \{u_i : u_i$ is a legitimate receiver$\}$ and $U_R = \{u_i : u_i$ is a revoked receiver$\}$. Thus, K is fixed for fixed U.

The most prominent SFPs are LKH [1]-[2] and their variants ([10] and [16], for example). Let $U = \{u_i : u_i$ is legitimate receiver of session$\}$, and $K = K_{ind} \bigcup K_{KEK}$, where $K_{ind} = \{k_i : k_i$ is individual key of user$u_i\}$ and $K_{KEK} = K - K_{ind}$, is set of all changeable KEKs. The state of SFP is determined by K_{KEK}. StateSyn intends to assure $\bigcup_1^n K_i|_{receiver-end} = K|_{center}$ by acknowledgement mechanism. Sender is not permitted to transmit the encrypted data with renewal session key and the next update cannot be handled until StateSyn is set up. The more legitimate receivers, the more packets of acknowledgement are required, and the higher possibility this will bring packet dropout during a session, thus the higher probability of retransmitting key update message. Thus, the complexity of StateSyn is completely determined by the parameter $|U|$ of SFP.

3 Novel Approach

3.1 Underlying Ideas and the Framework Proposal

According to Section 2, $K = K_{ind} \bigcup K_{KEK}$ can be generalized as $K = K_{fixed} \bigcup K_{changeable}$ where $K_{changeable}$ specify the state of SFP, and therefore generally speaking, decreasing $K_{changeable}$ implies a possibility to accommodate a higher membership dynamic in comparison with the ordinary SFP.

This paper indicates a possibility for integration of SLP into SFP and development of a hybrid key management protocol. Generally speaking, this approach employs two cryptographic components F_K and E_L, related to SFP and SLP, respectively. The security requirements of these two components are different, since F_K uses short-lived keys whereas E_L uses long-lived keys. E_L is required to be semantically secure against chosen ciphertext attacks, and F_K to be chosen-plaintext, one-message semantically secure. Key-indistinguishability property, identified and utilized in [3], may be utilized in our approach, as well. Any scheme in which all the keys are chosen independently satisfies this property.

Accordingly, the novel framework is based on the following:

1. Two-layer heterogeneous hierarchy with SFP over the upper layer and a number of SLPs over the bottom layer is employed where the internal tree nodes correspond to the keys and the members are at the tree leaves
2. The upper layer contains a number of the key management agents (KMA), and members in a subgroup are connected to the center via an intermediate tree node corresponding to a KMA;
3. The members are at bottom of the bottom layer, and all the members are partitioned into several subgroups;

Regarding the above proposed framework please note the following:

- The employed two-layers hierarchy is used for secure transmitting of the session key only, but not for data itself. Here, we should emphasize that after the SEK distribution, all members share the same session key for decrypting the payload data, just like that used by previously reported systems.
- Employment of the two-level hierarchy in a general setting implies existence of the following four possibilities related to the upper and bottom layers: (i) SFP+SFP, (ii) SFP+SLP, (iii) SLP+SFP, (iv) SLP+SLP. StateSyn requires that all members correctly obtain the renewed session key. Therefore, SFP+SFP implies the same complexity as a simple SFP over the entire structure (yielding the same performance, as well). SLP+SLP mode will require too much communication overhead. On the other hand, the upper layer corresponds to a bigger zone than the bottom one: Therefore, if SLP is employed in the bottom layer, its inherent disadvantages will have not too significant impact particularly in comparison with the synchronization advantages. Accordingly the combination SFP+SLP appears as the most favorite one.

– In a scenario with trustable KMAs, after a KMA receives a session key encrypted by the center, it will decrypt it with some key it has been assigned to recover the new session key and then re-encrypt it with relevant keys assigned to this subgroup, and finally transmit the encrypted session key to the subgroup members.

3.2   Architectural Issues

Upper Layer Issues. For a concrete secure multicast session, there certainly exists the smallest domain that contains all potential members, and the corresponding (the hierarchically highest) key center is assigned to be the master key center (MKC) for this multicast session, e.g. c_2 (fig.1) is the MKC of a multicast session whose members all lie in this domain. The MKC (e.g. c_2 in Fig. 1) and the key management agents, KMAs, of the session lying in the BLDs which contain the legitimate members of the current session (e.g. c_4 and c_5 in Fig. 1), constitute a backbone for the key management (see Fig. 1). All KMAs to the session are placed at the leaf nodes of the upper layer key tree that is built and maintained by the MKC. The keys are assigned according to the path from associated leaf node to the root, following the ordinary LKH [1]-[2] approach.

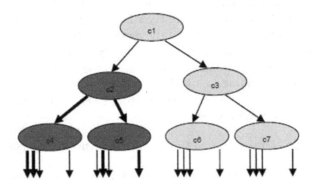

Fig. 1. Key centers for a multicast session, here $c_1, \ldots, c_7$ are prospective key centers

When a KMA enters into or leaves from the session due to a membership change, associated keys should be updated as follows: MKC will generate the renewal session key and transmit it securely to KMAs of BLDs that contain legitimate members of the current session in the same way as in the ordinary LKH. The employed MKC is an entity that is temporarily in charge of the key management functions for a multicast session.

LKH is employed between the MKC and KMAs so that only those KMAs of BLDs that contain legitimate users of the current session can securely obtain the new session key. If a membership change implies that a KMA joins or leaves a session, the key tree needs to be updated in the same way as in the ordinary LKH scenario. Otherwise, only the session key needs to be updated and relevant

KMA needs to re-compute subset cover so that forward/backward secrecy can be assured, but the state of the upper layer does not change.

Bottom Layer Issues. Within every bottom-layer domain (BLD), a SLP key management, e.g. subset cover revocation approaches [3,4] or a similar suitable one (such as [13]), is employed. This scheme assumes that all the users within BLD are arranged at the leaf nodes of the underlying binary tree, and that the key center in this domain, for each multicast session, can generate a subset cover based on this tree to include all legitimate receivers and to exclude all revoked receivers within the domain.

Suppose that a subset cover $S_1, S_2, \ldots, S_n$ is generated within a BLD. Then the message, $(E_{k_1}(k_s), E_{k_2}(k_s), \ldots, E_{k_n}(k_s)), E_{k_s}(M)$, can be constructed where $E_k(L)$ stands for encrypting L with key k, k_i is the key corresponding to subset S_i, k_s is the session key and M the message securely transmitted. Accordingly, each legitimate receiver of the session within this domain can derive the key of subset it belongs to from pre-assigned key material so that it can get the session key to decrypt the message. So, each BLD can be considered as a subgroup within the two-layers underlying structure corresponding to the members partitioning according to their physical locations in the network.

4   Security and Performance

4.1   Security

The consideration is related to the following two variants of the proposed approach. The first variant is related to the scenarios with trustable KMAs, and the second one is related to the scenarios with untrustable KMAs. In the both cases the security of the proposed schemes is discussed assuming LKH+CST combination over the upper and the bottom layers as an illustrative example. The session key must be updated upon membership change and that the upper layer state should be updated only if the event of a KMA addition/removal takes place.

After receiving key update message, KMAs are in charge of two kinds of operations depending on their trust assumptions. If KMAs are trusted ones, they are authorized to decrypt the key update message and recover the new session key - otherwise, they are not authorized to do this. In the two scenarios, KMA should encrypt the session key (or key update message itself) using the relevant KEKs of the employed broadcast encryption scheme (CST) within the BLD in order to securely transmit it to legitimate end-nodes. The main difference between the scenarios with trustable and un-trustable KMAs is that the un-trustable scenario requires extra keys and more computations at the end-node.

Key materials of different BLDs are absolutely independent mutually. Therefore, collusion of users from different domains does not provide them any additional power owing to re-encryption of the update messages with independent keys within different BLDs. On the other hand, as pointed out in [3] and [4], any collusion of users from the same domain cannot recover the current session key unless at least one of them is a legitimate member of the session.

Different trust relations requires different key pre-assignment. Here, if KMA doesn't leak out the session key he gained, KMA is trustable.

Trustable KMAs. In this scenario, the users keep those keys assigned by SLP within the corresponding subgroup (BLD). After a user is joining in or removed from a multicast session, corresponding KMA will re-generate a subset cover which including all legitimate receiver and excluding all revoked receivers, and a new session key will be generated by MKC and then distributed to all the session members. Both of the employed key management schemes (LKH and CST) provide the required secure updating of the session key. Accordingly, the proposed scheme is forward/backward secure.

Un-trustable KMAs. The scenario with un-trustable KMAs requires the following deployment of the keys: (i) Each receiver keeps the keys related to the both layers, i.e. to the both components SFP and SLP; (ii) Each KMA keeps all the SLP related keys in its BLD only. SFP related keys should be updatable and SLP related ones are fixed. Untrustable KMAs is not authorized to decrypt and just re-encrypt the key update message from the key center. MKC works as usual to encrypt the key update message with SFP-related key. Each legitimate receiver needs double decryptions to get the SEK and possibly update the SFP-related keys.

We assume that the "un-trust" implies that KMA works improperly , and accordingly, in general case, removal of a untrustable KMA includes the following. An alternative KMA will be established and the main center will update related SFP keys at each receiver, and finally distribute the new encrypted SEK. As the previous discussion, in the same manner as in the case of a user revocation, the security under the KMAs change can be shown.

Finally, note that in the scenario when KMAs are un-trustable, the updating of SFP keys at a receiver is required only when some KMA should be removed, and it is likely that this event appears with a much lower probability than appearance of a user revocation request.

4.2   Performance

The proposed approach mainly intends to simplify StateSyn problem related to the SFPs in order to boost the frequency of the allowed membership change with integrating SLPs (e.g. subset cover revocation scheme) into the entire structure. As well, the proposed approach intends to minimize the overall overheads of the system.

System Overheads. The main overheads of any key management are related to the following: (i) required storage at a receiver, (ii) required processing at a receiver, and (iii) the communications overhead. Additionally the synchronization requirements should be taken into account.

In a scenario with un-trustable sub-centers (KMAs), each receiver should keep as well the KEKs involved in the upper layer besides the keys used in the SLPs within the subgroups. These keys can be divided into two types, fixed and changeable. The fixed part corresponds to the employed SLP while the changeable part corresponds to SFP. The proposed approach can also be regarded as integrating SLPs into SFPs so that increasing the fixed part that makes the changeable part smaller implies simplification of the StateSyn problem because only the changeable keys require the synchronization.

On the other hand, if some subgroups/domains are merged to become a bigger one, the changeable portion of the keys will be further reduced while the fixed part will be increased because some previous changeable keys can be as the fix ones. In general case, it also slightly increases the number of keys each receiver should keep. Therefore, complexity of StateSyn becomes lower while overhead regarding the subgroup related storage and communication become slightly larger. If this process continues until only one subgroup contains all members (only one BLD contains all users within a network), the approach becomes a SLP one involving only unchangeable keys. As another extreme, the approach becomes SFP one (like LKH) when each subgroup contains only one user. In this case all the keys are changeable implying that complexity of StateSyn becomes the largest and this makes membership change harder.

The proposed framework yields a variety of possibilities for combining particular SFP and SLP in order to achieve different tradeoffs and to fit the performance within the given limits. Therefore, the proposed architecture can accommodate different characteristics and performance requirements, and as a result, the scheme is highly scalable and highly flexible.

Suppose that a particular framework employs SFP with basic LKH [1,2] and the subgroup oriented SLP with CST [3].

Let the total number of members of a session is N, and that the proposed hybrid approach allows that they can be partitioned into P subgroups where each subgroup contains Q members. Let R revocations in total should be performed assuming that R/P revocations should be performed within each of the subgroups.

Assuming the above notation, it can be directly shown that the following two propositions hold.

Proposition 1. When the sub-group centers (KMAs) are trustable, the proposed hybrid key management requires the following overheads.

1. Storage overhead at a receiver: unchangeable storage $\log Q$
2. Processing overhead at a receiver: 1
3. Communications overhead within a BLD sub-group for R/P revocations: $(R/P) \log(N/R)$.
4. Synchronization requirements at a receiver: None.

Proposition 2. When the sub-group centers (KMAs) are not trustable, the proposed hybrid key management requires, in a general case, the following overheads.

1. Storage overhead at a receiver: unchangeable storage $\log Q$ and changeable storage $\log P$
2. Processing overhead at a receiver: $2 + \log P$ (when KMAs structure is changed) or 2 otherwise
3. Communications overhead within a BLD sub-group for R/P revocations: $(R/P)(\log P + \log(N/R))$ (when KMA structure is changed) or $R/P \log (N/R)$ otherwise
4. When a change appears in the structure of KMAs, synchronization requirements at a receiver is $\log P$ or none otherwise.

Summary comparisons between the proposed scheme and the ordinary LKH [1,2] and its recent improvement [12] are given in Tables 1 and 2.

Table 1. Comparison among our proposed scheme, ordinary LKH [1]-[2] and its recent improvement [12] on receiver's side overhead assuming N users partitioned into P subgroups and each one of dimension Q, $N = PQ$, and assuming that there are no changes within KMAs

Evaluation Scheme	changeable storage	unchangeable storage	computation overhead	required synchronization
LKH basic scheme [1,2]	$\log N$	0	$\log N$	$\log N$
LKH version [12]: restricted revocation scenario	$\log N$	0	$\log N$	$\log N$
proposed scheme (LKH + CST) with trustable KMAs	0	$\log Q$	1	0
proposed scheme (LKH + CST) with untrustable KMAs	$\log P$	$\log Q$	$2 + \log P$ or 2	0

Table 2. Comparison of the proposed scheme, ordinary LKH [1]-[2] and its recent improvement [12] regarding the communications' issues, assuming N users partitioned into P subgroups and each one of dimension Q, $N = PQ$, and R user's revocations in total with R/P random revocations per a subgroup (domain)

Evaluation Scheme	# domains	comm. overhead per domain	# users domain that require syn.
LKH basic scheme [1,2]	1	$R \log N$	$N - R$
LKH version [12]: restricted revocation scenario	1	$2 \log N$	$N - R$
proposal1 (LKH + CST) with trustable KMAs	P	$(R/P) \log(N/R)$	0
proposal2 (LKH + CST) with untrustable KMAs and no changes within KMAs	P	$(R/P) \log(N/R)$	0
proposal3 (LKH + CST) with untrustable KMAs and a changes within KMAs	P	$\log P + (R/P) \log(N/R)$	$\log P$

State Synchronization. Due to non-reliability of Internet, some packets may be dropped out. And in certain LKH based scenarios, if some of the acknowledgements have not been received upon expiration of timeout, key center is required to retransmit key update message and keep on waiting for the acknowledgement, until it is sure that the focused receivers have updated the keys. During this procedure, the key center cannot handle any membership change. Hence, StateSyn determines the upper bound on frequency of membership changes that SFPs can support and the problem become more serious with larger membership. If a session has larger membership, this will not only imply possibly longer duration of StateSyn and as a consequence a lower frequency of the supportable membership change, but also significant implications to other applications within the same network due to increased overhead of communications. Therefore, there is a trade-off between the number of members and frequency of the changes in an ordinary LKH.

Contrarily, the proposed approach with trustable KMAs requires synchronization only among the KMAs. On the other hand, it is obvious that both the number of KMAs and the frequency of theirs change are much smaller in comparison with the the same issues related to the members. Thus, the proposed scheme can remarkably simplify the StateSyn problem to yield a shorter duration of StateSyn and be able to handle a higher frequency of the membership change.

5   Concluding Discussion

This paper points out a hierarchical infrastructure for key management regarding the secure multicast. The hierarchical and autonomous structure of Internet allows allocation of key centers in each of the domains supporting the hierarchical infrastructure for key management. Also, for each particular multicast session, a dynamic hierarchical structure for key management is feasible.

A novel key management approach for secure multicasting is proposed. It is based on a hybrid underlying structure which contains updatable and fixed nodes and where the synchronization problem, as well as the overall overheads are reduced.

The underlying hybrid structure is two-layer, i.e. the upper layer employs an updatable logical key hierarchy, e.g. LKH scheme [1,2], and the bottom layer employs CST scheme [3] (alternatively SD [3] or LSD [4] schemes can be employed as well).

The proposed key management appears as a very suitable approach for a different Internet oriented applications. Main advantages of the proposed hybrid framework include the following: (i) reduction of the synchronization problem in comparison with employment of an updatable (U-LKH) scheme; (ii) reduction of the permanent keys to be kept at each end users (receivers at leaves in the bottom layer) in comparison with employment of a static (S-LKH) scheme; (iii) reduction of the overall system overheads; (iv) fitting the system architecture to the underlying environment (Internet).

References

1. D. M. Wallner, E. J. Harder and R. C. Agee: Key management for multicast: Issues and architectures. IETF draft, July 1997. ftp://ftp.ietf.org/internet-drafts/draft-wallner-key-arch-01.txt.
2. C. K. Wong, M. Gouda and S. Lam: Secure Group Communications Using Key Graphs IEEE/ACM Transactions on Networking, vol. 8, no. 1, pp.16-30, Jan 2000.
3. D. Naor, M. Naor and J. Lotspiech: Revocation and Tracing Schemes for Stateless Receivers CRYPTO 2001, Lecture Notes in Computer Science, vol. 2139, pp. 41-62., 2001.
4. D. Halevi and A. Shamir: The LSD broadcast encryption scheme CRYPTO 2002, Lecture Notes in Computer Science, vol. 2442, pp. 47-60, 2002.
5. R. Canetti, T. Malkin, K. Nissim: Efficient communication-storage tradeoffs for multicast encryption. EUROCRYPT'99, Lecture Notes in Computer Science, vol. 1592, pp. 459-474, 1999.
6. S. Mittra Iolus: A framework for scalable secure multicasting Proc. ACM SIG-COMM'97, pp. 277-288, Sept 1997.
7. R. Molva and A. Pannetrat: Scalable multicast security with dynamic recipient groups. ACM Transactions on Information and System Security, vol. 3, no. 3, pp. 136-160, Aug. 2000.
8. S. Setia, S. Koussih, and S. Jajodia: Kronos: A scalable group re-keying approach for secure multicast. Proc. IEEE Symposium on Security and Privacy, pp. 215-228, 2000.
9. M. Waldvogel, G. Caronni, D. Sun, N. Weiler, and B. Plattner: The VersaKey framework: Versatile group key management. IEEE Journal on Selected Areas in Communications, vol. 17, no. 9, pp.1614-1631, Aug. 1999.
10. S. Zhu and S. Jajodia: Scalable group rekeying for secure multicast: A survey. IWDC 2003, Lecture Notes in Computer Science, vol. 2918, pp. 1-10, 2003.
11. G. Di Crescenzo and O. Kornievskaia: Efficient re-keying protocols for multicast encryption. SCN2002, Lecture Notes in Computer Science, vol. 2576, pp. 119-132, 2003.
12. J. H. Ki, H. J. Jim, D. H. Lee and C. S. Park: Efficient multicast key management for stateless receivers. ICISC2002, Lecture Notes in Computer Science, vol. 2587, pp. 497-509, 2003.
13. M. J. Mihaljević: Broadcast encryption schemes based on sectioned key tree. ICICS 2003, Lecture Notes in Computer Science, vol. 2836, pp. 158-169, 2003.
14. M. J. Mihaljević: Key management schemes for stateless receivers based on time varying heterogeneous logical key hierarchy. ASIACRYPT 2003, Lecture Notes in Computer Science, vol. 2894, pp. 137-154, 2003.
15. M. J. Mihaljević: Reconfigurable key management for broadcast encryption. IEEE Communications Letters, vol. 8, 2004 (accepted for publication).

A Cache Design for a Security Architecture
for Microprocessors (SAM)

Jörg Platte, Edwin Naroska, and Kai Grundmann

Robotics Research Institute: Section Information Technology,
University Dortmund
{joerg.platte, edwin.naroska, kai.grundmann}@udo.edu

Abstract. Protecting software and data becomes more and more important, especially, when sensitive or expensive software is executed on remote hosts. This protection includes copy protection, prevention of disassembling, prevention of altering the program flow and protection of processed data. For personal computers protection is more focused on copy protection. However, providing extended security to prevent data and algorithm disclosure is very important to increase the acceptance for GRID computing.

In this paper we present a cache design for a secure combined hardware and software architecture called *SAM*. For *SAM*, the cache provides transparent encryption/decryption and content verification using hash values. Additionally, the cache has to consider different memory views and protection levels as well as support for protected shared memory, a key feature of *SAM*.

1 Introduction

SAM was introduced in [1]. The architecture provides a secure execution environment for programs by providing register protection, encryption/decryption of program code and prevention of memory manipulations by using hash trees. Since all encryption and protection is done inside the CPU, even direct hardware access (for instance by sniffing on busses) or software based attacks (for instance by administrators) cannot be used to alter or disclose protected data. All protection schemes are implemented transparently and therefore typically invisible to the executed program. Protected and unprotected programs can be executed in a multitasking environment without interfering each other.

SAM was designed to achieve the following two goals:

1. Protection of program code and data: It should be impossible for an attacker to get information about the executed program code and the computed data.
2. Preventing any external modifications during program execution: The program must be executed in the intended way or aborted immediately.

The major parts of the operating system can be unchanged. *SAM* requires only changes in the lower level parts like TRAP handling and context switching. These parts must be trustworthy and each protected program has to provide hash values for them. Fortunately, these parts occupy only 64 kByte of memory.

W. Grass et al. (Eds.): ARCS 2006, LNCS 3894, pp. 435–449, 2006.
© Springer-Verlag Berlin Heidelberg 2006

Since the operating system (OS) typically has full control over all executed programs and their memory contents a partly trustworthy OS requires changes in the memory management to prevent successful attacks by a modified OS.

This paper is focused on *SAM's* cache design. Compared to normal caches additional verification and cryptography units have to be added. They are implemented using dedicated queues to parallelize most of the required work. The cache provides different memory views required to keep the protected part of the OS as small as possible. Furthermore, the cache keeps track of which cache lines have already been verified. This is required because the protected parts of the operating system are shared between all executed programs and each program must trust them individually. Therefore, *SAM* adds support for protected shared memory.

Section 2 gives an overview the architectural changes introduced by *SAM*. Then the cache design is described in detail in Sec. 3. Section 4 gives an overview over other approaches to provide a secure execution environment. The next two sections describe the simulation environment (5) and simulation results (6). Section 7 concludes this paper.

2   Architecture Overview

SAM is currently implemented using a modified SPARC processor design (LEON [2]) and a modified Linux kernel. Encryption and verification is implemented transparently in the L2-cache. A more detailed description of the cache design is given in section 3.

The operating system (OS) must be adapted to support *SAM*. But only a small part of the OS (approx. 64 kByte) dealing with context switching and TRAP management must be trustworthy. The main part with drivers, networking and filesystems can remain untrusted and mostly unchanged.

Tamper detection has to be done on different levels. Hardware manipulations on the processor core must be detected just like software based attacks and external data manipulations. Hardware manipulations of the processor core are not covered by this work. In the final implementation they are reported like all other detected tampering attempts to the tamper detection unit. This unit deletes all process related sensitive data stored in the processor. This includes keys and cache contents.

2.1   Data and Program Verification

Overview. *SAM* provides transparent verification of memory contents by checking corresponding hash values for each fetched cache line. Additionally, these hash values are updated transparently during write back.

AES [3] is used as the hashing algorithm H^1, because the program encryption (see section 2.2) is based on AES, too. In the current design of *SAM* a L2 cache line consists of 64 byte which is equal to four AES blocks. As can be seen in

---

[1] Unlike the proposed size of 256 bits, we are using only a key and block size of 128 bits resulting in a 128 bit hash value.

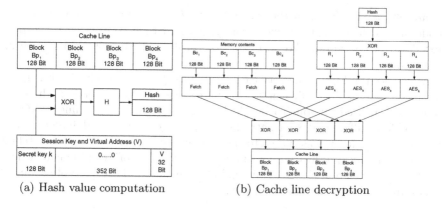

(a) Hash value computation   (b) Cache line decryption

Fig. 1. Hashing and decryption

Fig. 1(a) the hash value is computed over the unencrypted cache line. To prevent data disclosure and to bind the cache line to its address in main memory, the virtual base address V and the program specific secret AES-key k^2 are included in hash value computation. This results in an unique hash value. To prevent replay attacks, a set of four hash values is protected by another hash value. This results in a hash tree [4]. The root hash is permanently stored in the cache to prevent manipulations of the tree during runtime.

The hash values are stored in the cache like any other cache line[3]. This can speed up data verification, because already stored and checked hash values in the cache are trustworthy and need not to be re-verified.

Each protected program contains pre-computed hash values for all protected parts including all trustworthy parts of the OS. Each time the cache detects modified memory parts, the particular program is terminated immediately and all program related parts in the cache including the secret key k are deleted and the operating system is informed by generating a TRAP.

Fast Verification. The whole hash tree is only required for non static data, because replay attacks on static data are not possible. Even parts of other programs in the same memory region cannot be used as a replacement due to different secret keys. Furthermore, the unique secret key k prevents calculation of valid hash values by an attacker. As a result, for static program code only the corresponding hash value in the parent node is checked, but not the whole tree. This helps to speed up program verification, especially for the often used protected OS parts.

2.2   Data and Program Encryption

To prevent program and data disclosure transparent memory content encryption and decryption is supported. Like all other protected parts encrypted parts are protected by hash values. Each cache line can be encrypted and decrypted

---

[2] This key is chosen randomly when building a *SAM* executable.

[3] In the following, cache lines containing hash values are denoted as hash lines.

separately using AES with the secret key k (E_k) in counter mode. In counter mode, a so called counter value is encrypted and then XORed with the plain text data for encryption. We are using the hash value described in section 2.1 as a counter.

As can be seen in Fig. 1(b), every cache line consists of four cache blocks. Hence, one hash value is not sufficient as a counter, because this would result in the same pattern used for four cache blocks. Therefore, the hash value is XORed with the four different 128 bit patterns $R_{1...4}$[4] to generate four different counter values. Counter mode was chosen to speed up cache line fetches, because fetching memory contents and the time consuming encryption E_k of a counter can be done in parallel as shown in Fig. 1(b). When both the data and the encrypted counter values are available, they must only be XORed to get the decrypted data.

2.3 Memory

SAM provides execution of encrypted and normal programs at the same time using multitasking. Therefore, depending on the application, shared memory parts of the main memory must not be encrypted, to allow access by other programs running at the same time. Further, parts of the main memory used for DMA are modified from external devices like network cards. Hence, the corresponding memory regions cannot be protected by hash values. This results in different context specific memory regions where each region can either be unprotected, protected or protected and encrypted.

Memory Layout. Figure 2 shows this relatively fixed layout. It was chosen with hardware implementation in mind. For each protected context only four addresses are stored. Their base addresses are marked in this figure with the following labels:

- *HASH_BASE* denotes the position of the root hash and therefore the beginning of the hash tree.
- Between *ENC_BASE* and *PROT_BASE* the cache transparently decrypts and encrypts all code and data and verifies the contents using the hash tree.
- All code and data between *PROT_BASE* and *UNSEC_BASE* is unencrypted, but protected by hash values. This memory region is typically dedicated to trustworthy parts of the OS.
- All memory above *UNSEC_BASE* and all memory below *HASH_BASE* is unprotected. These parts are dedicated for the OS, DMA areas and parameter passing between the operating system and the protected program.

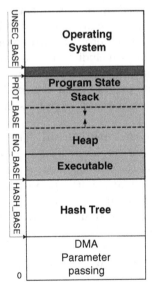

Fig. 2. Memory Layout

---

[4] These four patterns are constant and the same values are used by all *SAM* enabled processors. Their values were chosen randomly.

Memory Views. The L2-cache transparently decrypts encrypted parts of main memory and computes new hash values for modified memory regions. But access to decrypted parts cannot always be granted and hash values must not always be computed or checked: For example, memory contents are decrypted and hash values are computed during write back only if the line was written by an instruction protected by hash values of the same context. This results in the internal classification of protected or unprotected instructions, depending on the existence of hash values for these instructions. Hence, SAM provides two different *views* of the main memory:

- Protected instructions can access all memory regions and encrypted main memory contents are decrypted in SAM's L2 cache. On write back hash values are computed and the hash tree is updated.
- Untrusted instructions can access the whole memory area, too, but encrypted parts remain encrypted and hash values are not generated during write back of dirty parts.

Sparse Hash Trees. The hash tree protects the whole memory area containing the executable, stack and heap and parts of the OS (see Fig: 2). It consumes 33% additional memory compared to the original memory region. Hash values need to be provided for all memory areas containing data to protect. On the other hand, parts like heap or stack that are unused at time of program start do not need pre-computed hash values. These values can be calculated the first time a corresponding region is used.

To distinguish used and unused memory areas, unused areas are marked with a hash value of zero. Fortunately, all pages containing only zeros need not to be stored within the executable to reduce its size. During runtime, the OS maps pages containing only zeros to this areas. Each time zero is read, the protected content is assumed to be valid, regardless of the actual contents. However, the cache still verifies this zero value using the corresponding parent in the tree. To cope with the unlikely case of a computed hash value of zero, this value is stored as "1" in memory. The following pseudo-code describes the checking procedure:

```
valid=0
if (computedHash==0) computedHash=1
if (HashBlock==0 || computedHash==HashBlock) valid=1
if (valid==0) informTamperDetectionUnit()
else checkHashBlockwithParentHash()
```

2.4   Operating System

In a multitasking environment the OS manages execution of different processes. Hence, it must be adjusted to support SAM's security architecture. Additionally, approx. 64 kBytes of the OS mostly used for the TRAP handling must be stored in protected memory. The other parts can remain unprotected. SAM provides special instructions described in [1] to prevent attacks on the protected program when leaving the protected part of the OS during a TRAP.

3   Cache Design

In this section implementation details of the L1 and L2 cache will be discussed. As encryption and verification takes place in L2 cache most architectural changes are located there. Data encryption and verification leads to additional latencies. *SAM* was designed to keep read latencies as small as possible. On the other hand, the time until protected data is written back to memory is increased. *SAM* tries to hide these additional latencies where possible.

3.1   Comparison with Other Caches

Both the L1 data and instruction caches are operating on virtual addresses. The L2 cache operates on physical addresses but additionally stores the virtual address of each cache line. This is required because the virtual address is used for encryption, decryption and to compute the address of the hash value.

Because of the memory verification of the L2 cache parts of its contents are hash values. They are stored in cache lines (here called hash lines) like other data requested by the processing unit and treated equally regarding to the line exchange algorithm. The cache automatically computes the memory address of the corresponding hash value to the requested data and fetches it.

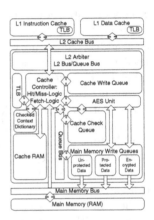

Due to the different memory views the cache hit logic is more complex than in other caches. For example, a requested cache line already stored in the cache could be treated as miss, if it has been fetched for a different memory view. In cases of a permission related miss the cache line is written back to main memory and fetched again with the correct permissions.

Fig. 3. L1/L2 cache design

3.2   L1 Cache

The L1 cache has to keep track of the memory views of all stored cache lines. *SAM* uses one additional bit, the *unprotected* bit, to reflect the memory state. It is set for each unprotected cache line and each time a cache line was fetched due to an unprotected instruction access. This information is passed to the L2 cache during write back to prevent hash updates. Each time a protected instruction tries to access an unprotected line this access is treated as a miss and the line is written back to the L2 cache and re-fetched.

3.3   L2 Overview

The L2 cache has been newly designed, because most security related functions are located here and therefore, its design requires most changes compared to standard caches. Figure 3 contains an overview about the caches internal units. The most noticeable change are five queues. They are used to process all functions related to protected memory and hash values in parallel to the normal cache logic. They are described in Sec. 3.8.

The cache supports only a limited amount of encrypted processes. This helps to reduce the overhead caused by storing process related data. Our implementation is able to execute up to 16 protected processes at the same time. The next subsections describe all parts shown in Fig. 3 in detail.

3.4   TAG RAM

Protection. The L2 cache uses two bits to reflect the protection level of each cache line: The *unprotected* bit serves the same purpose as in the L1 cache. The cache refuses to update the hash tree during write back if this bit is set. Additionally, for encrypted memory regions the *decrypted* bit indicates an decrypted cache line. This bit is used to prevent read or write access from other contexts to decrypted memory parts.

The L2 cache operates on physical addresses, but additionally stores the corresponding virtual TAG part of this address. This is required because it is impossible to compute the virtual address only from a given physical address. The virtual address is required at three times:

1. The virtual address is part of the hash value computation.
2. It is required to determine the parent node in the hash tree.
3. The stored virtual address of a cache line and the requested virtual address must match in case of protected memory. If not, the cache initiates a recheck of the stored hash line regardless of the checked context bits described in the next section.

On write back, the cache has to select the matching secret key k for hash value computation and encryption. Thus, the context number of the fetching context (here called owner context) is stored, too.

Multitasking. *SAM* provides multitasking support and shared protected read only memory. This memory area is mainly used for the protected part of the OS (see Fig. 2).

The L2 cache checks each cache line accessed by a protected instruction. Already checked cache lines need not to be rechecked, as long as they remain inside the cache. Obviously, a cache line already stored in the cache and checked for a protected context A may be not trustworthy for a protected context B. Since frequently used parts of the OS

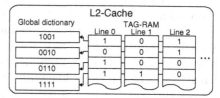

Fig. 4. Context Dictionary

remain in this kind of shared memory the cache has to keep track of the contexts the current cache line has been checked for.

Special care must be taken to reduce the overhead caused by storing this information, because it has to be stored for each cache line in the cache, Therefore, *SAM* uses a dictionary based approach shown in Fig. 4 to minimize the amount of RAM to store this information. The last four context numbers a check was processed for are stored in a global dic-

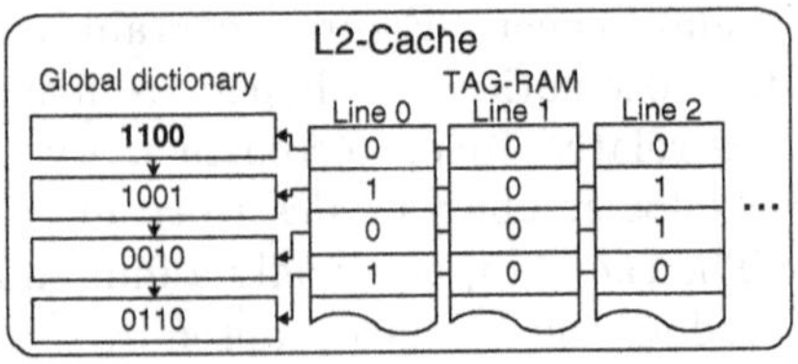

Fig. 5. Adding context "1100"

tionary. Each cache line (Fig. 4 shows three sample lines) now has to keep track for which of the global contexts it has been checked for which requires only four additional dictionary bits for each cache line.

Each time a new entry is added to the dictionary the oldest entry has to be removed first and the dictionary bits in each cache line must be updated. This is shown in Fig. 5 for the new protected context "1100". To speed up this task, the global dictionary and the dictionary bits for each cache line are stored in shift registers. Hence, they can easily be updated in one clock cycle. On write access, the context bits of others than the writing context are deleted.

3.5   Hit Logic

The L2 cache contains a complex hit logic. The cache sets the following internal status bits if the requested cache line is already stored in cache RAM:

- Write: This bit is set on write access.
- Protected Memory: Set, if the requested data is located in protected memory.
- Encrypted Memory: Same for encrypted memory.
- Protected Instruction: Set, if data is requested by a protected instruction.
- CTX: Set, if the owner context and the requesting context are different.
- Dirty: The accessed cache line is dirty.
- Unprotected: The accessed cache line is unprotected.
- Decrypted: The accessed cache line is decrypted.

Table 1 illustrates the action to be taken based on these internal status bits[5]. Each column represents another protection combination of the requesting instruction. For example, the first column represents an unprotected instruction accessing unprotected memory whereas the last column represents a protected instruction accessing encrypted memory. Each row in this table shows the different states of the cache line already stored in cache RAM. For example, the actions for shared protected memory are shown in column 5, rows 1, 3, 7 and 9. Possible actions are:

---

[5] The following invalid status bit combinations are omitted, because they are prevented by the cache logic: "Unprotected Memory, Encrypted Memory" and "Unprotected, Decrypted".

- "WB": Write back current line and fetch the same line again with a different protection level.
- "F": Fetch line and overwrite selected line in cache.
- "R": Process read requests, equals "WB" on write access.
- "RW": Cache hit, process read or write access based on Write bit.

After a line fetch or on write access the status bits of the corresponding cache line are updated according to the following Boolean functions:

$$dirty = \text{Write}$$
$$unprotected = \sim \text{Protected Memory} \ \lor \ \sim \text{Protected Instruction}$$
$$decrypted = \text{Protected Instruction} \ \land \ \text{Encrypted Memory}$$

Table 1. L2 hit logic

| | | | | 0 | 1 | 1 | 0 | 1 | 1 | Prot. Memory |
| | | | | 0 | 0 | 1 | 0 | 0 | 1 | Encr. Memory |
CTX	Decr.	Unprot.	Dirty	0	0	0	1	1	1	Prot. Instruction
0	0	0	0	RW	RW	F	RW	RW	F	
0	0	0	1	R	R	R	WB	RW	WB	
0	0	1	0	RW	RW	RW	RW	RW	F	
0	0	1	1	RW	RW	RW	WB	WB	WB	
0	1	0	0	F	F	F	F	F	RW	
0	1	0	1	WB	WB	WB	WB	WB	RW	
1	0	0	0	RW	RW	RW	RW	RW	F	
1	0	0	1	R	R	R	R	WB	WB	
1	0	1	0	RW	RW	RW	RW	RW	F	
1	0	1	1	RW	RW	RW	RW	WB	WB	
1	1	0	0	F	F	F	F	F	F	
1	1	0	1	WB	WB	WB	WB	WB	WB	

3.6   TLB

The L2 cache must be able to compute physical addresses of parent hash lines determined by their virtual address. Hence, as can be seen in Fig. 3, the L2 cache contains its own TLB[6]. This design was chosen because the VHDL implementation is based on the LEON design. LEON contains one TLB's for the L1 instruction cache and another one for the data cache and these TLB's cannot be accessed by the L2 cache. Therefore, the cache has its own TLB.

3.7   AES Unit

The AES unit is a central part in this design and used by many other units (see Fig. 3). It is used to compute hash values and encrypted counter values. Due to the counter mode design and the hash value computation algorithm no

---
[6] Translation Lookaside Buffer.

decryption part is required. In our implementation the AES unit is controlled by a simple scheduler. This scheduler can pass a new cache line to be encrypted to the AES unit within each clock cycle. In our VHDL design a pipelined version of the AES unit was replaced with four sequential AES units to reduce the required chip space. In this case the scheduler waits until one AES unit is free.

3.8   Queues

The cache contains three different data queues to hide cache latencies:

1. **Cache Write Queue:** On write miss this queue stores the value to be written to cache RAM until the missing cache line is fetched. After each fetch all queue contents are processed to find entries which can now be stored in the newly fetched line. This queue is primary used to store computed hash values from the Main Memory Queue until the corresponding line is fetched.
2. **Main Memory Write Queue:** This queue contains cache lines to be written to main memory. Internally this queue is split into the following three queues:
   – Unprotected Data Queue: This queue is used for unprotected data to be written back to memory.
   – Protected Data Queue: This queue is used to compute hash values for protected data to be written back. The computed hash value is passed to the cache which may write it in the Cache Write Queue on write miss.
   – Encrypted Data Queue: This queue serves the same purpose as the Protected Data Queue but additionally encrypts the given line before writing it back to memory.
3. **Hash Check Queue:** The purpose of this queue is to verify cache or hash lines. A cache line is passed to this queue if it is protected and unchecked for the accessing context. This queue then computes the hash value and compares this hash value with the parent hash values. The parent hash value is fetched from the cache. On a miss the queue waits until the requested data is fetched.

Each queue has a predefined size and only the first element can initiate a cache or memory access. Note that all queue elements can access the AES unit as needed.

3.9   Cache Arbiter

The arbiter controls internal and external access to the cache controller. External access is initiated by the L1 I/D cache and internal access is requested by the queues. The arbiter considers the following information when granting access to the cache:

– If a requested cache line is in one of the Main Memory Queues cache access is deferred until the line is written back to memory.
– A cache line can not be accessed until all data for this cache line is written from the Cache Write Queue to cache RAM.

- The size of all queues is monitored. If one of the queues has less than 2 free elements all L1 requests are stalled until one element left the queue. This prevents deadlocks on full queues caused by L1 requests.
- Queues with more active entries have higher priority to access the cache than queues with less active entries.

4   Related Work

Using cryptography to protect algorithms and data in a tamper resistant environment is not a new approach. Secure co-processors have been proposed which provide a tamper-sensing and tamper responding secure environment. These processors can be implemented on smart cards (for example, [5]) or as a co-processor shown by [6] in a PC (for example, the IBM PCIXCC [7]). These co-processors provide a secure environment. But they are limited in terms of processor speed and memory and often, programs must be significantly modified to be suitable to this kind of co-processors. Therefore, they do not provide an easy to use and expandable secure environment.

A more related approach to ensure a secure execution of programs is the AEGIS [8] architecture. The architecture provides transparent program and memory encryption using an enhanced standard processor. Protected parts begin with a special instruction and all further instructions are encrypted. Unfortunately, only small parts of a program can be encrypted, because it does not allow system calls while in encrypted mode.

The AEGIS architecture provides status changes during an interrupt and guarantees correct restoration. But an AEGIS program contains unprotected parts used for system calls. During execution of this parts, a malicious OS can alter the program counter or modify register values and therefore, the unmodified execution of a whole program with encrypted and unencrypted parts cannot be guaranteed. As a result, only sensitive algorithms can be protected, but not the whole program.

In AEGIS, memory protection is done by encrypting the memory contents with AES [9] and protecting them by hash values. Like our approach, both encrypted and normal programs can be executed in a multitasking environment. But encryption is done by encrypting the data directly. This increases the decryption latency, because all data must first be read and can then be decrypted instead of doing both in parallel as SAM does. On the other hand, writing encrypted data is slower in our case, since the hash value must be computed first. But fortunately, this additional latency caused by SAM can mostly be hidden by the Main Memory Write Queues. For most programs the read latency is more important, since a program can only be continued after providing the requested data.

Another advantage of SAM is is the amount of memory required to encrypt and validate cache lines. We must only store the counter value, which can be used as a hash value to validate the integrity of the cache line and as a counter value to decrypt the cache line. Therefore, only one additional read access is required to encrypt and check the contents of a cache block. In the AEGIS architecture the hash and an initialization vector must be stored. Additionally, *SAM's* design does not require a full hash tree walk for instructions.

Other approaches to provide a trusted environment, like the TCG [10] can provide only a trusted software platform. Hardware attacks, like sniffing on busses, are still possible. Additionally, compared to our design larger parts of the OS must be trusted which increases the possibility of exploitable errors in these parts. Therefore, mostly software based systems do not provide the same protection level as our architecture.

5   Simulation Environment

SAM's development efforts are focused on a hardware based FPGA implementation and a software simulator. The hardware is used to proof the design on the hardware side. Unfortunately the VHDL model is too slow when it is used for software based simulations. Simulations using the FPGA are much faster, but much harder to debug, especially when developing the OS changes. Hence, a fast software based simulator is required. The freely available system emulator qemu[11] has been chosen as platform, because it provides a good performance by using dynamic translation and a reasonable detailed hardware simulation. To fulfill all requirements for *SAM* qemu has been modified in many ways:

 - Due to its main purpose to provide a fast environment qemu does not count the number of simulated clock cycles and the program counter is only updated on branches. Since we need detailed clock information for benchmark purposes and memory protection qemu was modified to provide this information. The current implementation executes one instruction in *each* simulated clock cycle. A pipeline or stalls due to branch misprediction are not simulated.
 - The whole memory access is logged into a trace file.
 - Qemu supports *SAM's* changed instruction set.
 - The memory protection levels are honored and checked for each instruction.

The trace file that is generated during simulation logs following data: The virtual and physical address of the accessed memory, the program counter, the type of access (instruction, data, I/O or raw), the number of bytes read or written and information about TRAP or context switch occurrences.

The trace file is then used as input for a L1/L2 cache simulator to estimate the overhead of the security mechanisms of *SAM*. The discrete event simulator simulates the whole cache system described in section 3. Special care has been taken to build the simulator as close as possible to the hardware design. But due to the trace file, it is impossible to feed back timing impacts caused by the cache simulation back to qemu. Therefore, the next step is the integration of the secure cache directly into qemu.

6   Simulation Results

The following results are generated using a standard Linux kernel because the *SAM* enabled kernel is still under development. As most of the protected and encrypted part of a protected context are located in userspace, we expect the results with a *SAM* enabled Linux Kernel to be similar.

The SPEC suite was used as a base for the following simulations. In this paper, not the whole runtime of all benchmarks was simulated. Due to the long simulation times for a full benchmark (up to two weeks on a Pentium 4, 3 GHz) and due to the size of the resulting trace file (approx. 2-3 bytes per clock cycle) the benchmarks were terminated after 2^{32} simulated clock cycles.

A cache line of the different simulated L1 and L2 caches equals 64 bytes in each simulation. The L1 caches are always direct mapped and the L2 caches 4-way set associative organized. The benchmarks were executed on the following cache configurations using five non-pipelined AES units:

- BC: 16 KB data instruction cache, 1 MB L2 cache
- SC: 8 KB data instruction cache, 128 KB L2 cache
- TL1: 4 KB data instruction cache, 1 MB L2 cache
- TL12: 4 KB data instruction cache, 64 KB L2 cache
- BCA: Like BC, but using only a single pipelined AES unit[7]

Each benchmark was executed without *SAM* enhancements used as a reference, fully encrypted (E), fully encrypted with full hash walk even for instructions (EH) and only protected without encryption (P). All programs have been statically linked with a base address of 0x70000000. The region between 0x70000000 (*ENC_BASE*) and 0xf0000000 (*UNSEC_BASE*) was protected by hash values for the E, EH and P runs.

Fig. 6(a) shows the results for most of these configurations. As expected, the performance penalty is lower for a bigger L2 cache. For most benchmarks the speedup is between 0.99 and 0.80 for the BC and TL1 configuration. But increasing the L1 cache does not always increase the speedup as can be seen by comparing both configuration. The SC and TL12 configurations could not hide the additional latencies as good as the BC and TL1 configurations resulting in a speedup down to 0.61 for one benchmark and the smallest cache. The abdication of a full hash walk for instructions can increase cache performance slightly especially for small caches. On larger L2 caches this optimization has no effect.

When using mostly protected, but unencrypted programs, the performance penalty is near zero in most cases as can be seen in Fig. 6(b). Therefore, in cases, where the program code must be encrypted, but the stack and heap contents can remain unencrypted, the performance penalty can further be reduced. Using a pipelined AES unit does not increase performance significantly. Hence, five non-pipelined AES units are sufficient which reduces the required chip space.

---

[7] A pipelined AES unit consumes approx. 11 times more chip space than a non-pipelined unit.

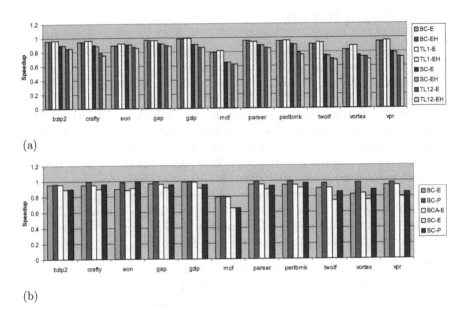

(a)

(b)

Fig. 6. (a)Various cache configurations (b)AES and no encryption

7   Conclusion

In this work we presented a cache design suitable for the *SAM* architecture. The architecture was designed to provide a secure execution environment even for hostile environments where an attacker might have direct hardware or software access.

SAM mainly consists of security enhanced L1 and L2 caches. The L1 cache provides basic security support by using additional TAG bits to represent the additional protection. The L2 cache additionally provides transparent data and code encryption, decryption and verification. As a result, *SAM's* hit logic has to consider the protection of each cache line on each access. Most additional encryption and verification steps are done by dedicated queues. This enables concurrent access to the cache either by the L1 cache as well as internal accesses by the queues and helps to hide most additional latencies caused by these steps.

SAM was designed to support concurrent execution of unprotected and protected programs. The cache design supports multitasking in many ways: Data from different contexts can be held in the cache because *SAM* stores for each cache line the owner context. Additionally, shared protected memory is supported by providing a dedicated context dictionary to prevent unneeded cache line verifications.

The size of the required hash tree stored with each executable can be limited by using sparse hash trees. By using a full hash walk only for data and not for instructions, the resulting performance penalty can further be reduced. Simulations show, that the overall performance penalty is acceptable and in some cases only detectable by benchmarks.

References

1. Platte, J., Naroska, E.: A combined hardware and software architecture for secure computing. In: CF '05: Proceedings of the 2nd conference on Computing frontiers, New York, NY, USA, ACM Press (2005) 280–288
2. Gaisler, J.: LEON2 Processor User's Manual - XST Edition (Version 1.0.24). Gaisler Research, http://www.gaisler.com/doc/leon2-1.0.24-xst.pdf. (2003)
3. Cohen, B.: AES-hash. http://csrc.nist.gov/CryptoToolkit/modes/proposed-modes/aes-hash/aeshash.pdf (2001)
4. Gassend, B., Clarke, D., Suh, G.E., van Dijk, M., Devadas, S.: Caches and Hash Trees for Efficient Memory Integrity Verification. In: Proceedings of the Ninth International Symposium on High Performance Computer Architecture (HPCA-9). (2003)
5. Microsystems, S.: Java card security white paper. http://java.sun.com/products/javacard/JavaCardSecurityWhitePaper. pdf (2001)
6. Yee, B.: Using secure coprocessors. PhD thesis, Carnegie Mellon University (1994)
7. Arnold, T.W., Van Doorn, L.P.: The IBM PCIXCC: A new cryptographic co-processor for the IBM eServer. IBM Journal of Research and Development **48** (2004) 475–487
8. Suh, G.E., Clarke, D., Gassend, B., van Dijk, M., Devadas, S.: AEGIS: architecture for tamper-evident and tamper-resistant processing. In: Proceedings of the 17th annual international conference on Supercomputing, ACM Press (2003) 160–171
9. NIST: Specification for the Advanced Encryption Standard (AES) - Federal Information Processing Standards Publication 197. National Institute of Standards and Technology, http://csrc.nist.gov/publications/fips/fips197/fips-197.pdf. (2001)
10. TCG: Trusted computing group. http://www.trustedcomputing.org (2005)
11. Bellard, F.: QEMU. http://fabrice.bellard.free.fr/qemu (2005)

Constraint-Based Deployment of Distributed Components in a Dynamic Network

Didier Hoareau and Yves Mahéo

Valoria Lab – University of South Brittany
{Didier.Hoareau, Yves.Maheo}@univ-ubs.fr

Abstract. Hierarchical software components offer interesting characteristics for the development of complex applications. However, supporting the deployment of such applications is difficult, especially on challenging distributed platforms. This paper addresses the distribution and the deployment of hierarchical components on heterogeneous dynamic networks. Such networks may include fixed and mobile resource-constrained devices and are characterized by the volatility of their hosts and connections, which may lead to their fragmentation. The distribution scheme and the associated mechanisms we propose allow a component to provide its services in an ubiquitous way and to operate in a degraded mode. The deployment of hierarchical components is described: we present an ADL extension for specifying a context-aware deployment and we detail a hierarchically-controlled deployment designed for dynamic networks. This deployment is performed in a propagative way and is driven by constraints put on the resources of the target hosts.

1 Introduction

Distributed platforms are no longer restricted to stable networks of workstations. One of the archetype of a distributed platform is now a network that may comprise stable and powerful workstations but also a number of mobile and resource-constrained devices. Although this kind of distributed platform is increasingly common, it remains a challenging target for building, deploying an maintaining distributed applications. Specific techniques must be applied to cope with the heterogeneity of the hosts and links as well as with the dynamism of the network. What we call dynamic networks are especially a difficult target, as hosts may become unaccessible because of their mobility or their volatility. As a consequence, one cannot rely on models and algorithms designed for fully connected networks. A dynamic network is rather described as a partitioned network, viewed as a collection of independent islands. An island is equivalent to a connected graph of hosts that can communicate together, while no communication is possible between two islands. In addition, the configuration of the islands may change dynamically.

Figure 1 shows an example of such a dynamic network. It is composed of a number of hosts a user has access to and on which a distributed application is meant to be accessible. This set of hosts includes fixed and mobile machines. Connectivity is not ensured between all the hosts. Indeed, at home, the user's connection to Internet is sporadic and some of the devices are mobile (as such, they may become out of reach) and/or volatile (a PDA may for example be switched off frequently).

W. Grass et al. (Eds.): ARCS 2006, LNCS 3894, pp. 450–464, 2006.

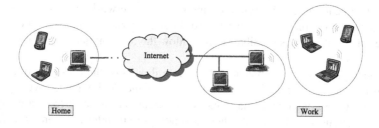

Fig. 1. Example of a dynamic network, possibly partitioned in three islands

The applications that are to be executed on dynamic networks can be inherently complex. This complexity is even increased by the need to produce code that can adapt to the changes of the execution environment. Since a few years, the use of software components proved to be useful for developing complex distributed applications and many component models and their associated technologies are now available. In the component-based approach, the application is designed as an assembly of reusable components that can be bound in a versatile manner, possibly dynamically. Some of the proposed models are known as hierarchical models. They offer the possibility of creating high level components by composing components of lower abstraction level, which represents a software construction principle that is natural and expressive. In such models, a component –that is then called a composite component– can be itself an assembly of components, recursive inclusion ending with primitive components that encapsulate computing code.

Using a hierarchical component-based approach for building an application that targets a dynamic network seems an attractive solution. Yet, several problems remain that are not dealt with available component models and component execution supports. In particular, the two following aspects have to be dealt with: (1) how to deploy a hierarchical component in a dynamic network while ensuring that this deployment respects the architecture of the application and adapts itself to the resource constraints imposed by the target platform? (2) how to allow a distributed execution of the components, i.e. to allow interactions between components in a not-always-connected environment? This paper describes a distribution scheme of hierarchical components and its associated deployment process that target dynamic networks. Because of the very constrained environment in which the application is to be deployed, we can hardly envisage a permanent access to the services offered by the application or an optimal utilization of the resources. The emphasis is put on finding a distribution scheme and some deployment mechanisms that achieve a minimal availability while taking account of the environment.

Outline of our approach. The distribution scheme we propose is related to the hierarchical structure of the application. This scheme is based on the replication of composite components. Indeed, we allow a composite to be accessible on a set of hosts, although each primitive component is localized on a single host. Besides, we also allow a component to operate in a degraded mode in order to account for network disconnections without making the entire application unusable. The notion of *active interface* is added to the component model. Our runtime support detects network disconnections and de-activates some components' interfaces accordingly. Introspection on the state (active or inactive) of an interface is possible so as to allow the development of adaptive components.

The deployment of a component covers several parts of the life-cycle of a component. In this paper we focus on the last phases of the deployment, covering the in-stantiation of the component (that creates an executable instance from a component code), its configuration (that establishes the bindings to its interfaces) and its activation (that allows the other components to invoke its interfaces). The presented techniques should be complemented with component delivery mechanisms such as those described in [1].

The deployment of the hierarchy of components is specified in a constraint-based declarative way. The architecture descriptors of the components are augmented with deployment descriptors in which constraints on the resources required by components and on their possible location can be specified.

When the deployment is triggered, all the constraints listed in the deployment de-scriptor may not be satisfied immediately. The dynamism of the network makes the sit-uation even more difficult as it may occur that the set of hosts that would satisfy globally the deployment constraints are never connected together at the same time, precluding any deployment. Instantiation of some components and their activation is however pos-sible as we allow the components to operate in a degraded mode through the dynamic management of interfaces' activation. The deployment process we implement is thus a propagative process : the instantiation and the activation of a component are performed as soon as some resources that meet its needs are discovered. We propose an algorithm that supports this propagative deployment. The scalability of the process is ensured by the distributed and hierarchical organisation of the control. Moreover, we implement a distributed consensus that guarantees that the location constraints are satisfied even in the context of a partitioned network.

The paper is organised as follows. First, the model of hierarchical component we work on is presented and we explain how a hierarchy of components is distributed over a network. The concept of activation at the interface level is briefly exposed. In section 3 we give some details on the form of the deployment descriptor that complements the architecture description. Section 4 presents the overall propagative deployment process and details the distributed instantiation algorithm that forms the basis of the distributed deployment. Section 5 briefly describes the status of the development of our prototype. Finally, we cite the related works before concluding.

2   Distributed Hierarchical Components

We describe in this section what we understand by distributed hierarchical components, through the description of the basic features of our component model and of the way we have chosen for distributing the components over a network of hosts. Further details can be found in [2].

2.1 Hierarchical Component Model

In this paper, we consider a widely applicable hierarchical component model in which a composite component represents a more or less complex structure of interconnected components that can be used as a simple component with well-defined required and provided interfaces. Recursion stops with primitive components that correspond to computing units. Components are interconnected through bindings that each represents a link between a required interface and a provided interface. For practical reasons, we have chosen to base our development on the Fractal component model [3] and more precisely on its reference Java implementation Julia. However, the concepts developed in this paper could easily be applied to other hierarchical component models such as Koala [4], Darwin [5] or Sofa [6].

The notion of composite component is often used at design time and is found in so-called architecture description languages (ADL) [7]. In the applicative framework we have chosen, it is however interesting to also be able to manipulate a composite at execution time in order to ease dynamic adaptation. Therefore the composite is reified at runtime namely by a membrane object that stores the interfaces of the component and its configuration (the list of its subcomponents and the bindings between these subcomponents).

2.2 Distribution Model

As mentioned in the introduction, we wish to deploy a hierarchy of components on a distributed platform that is characterized namely by its heterogeneity and the volatility of its hosts. The application components are distributed on a set of hosts. The way this placement is performed is detailed in section 4. We focus here on the description of the mechanisms allowing a distributed execution of hierarchical components.

In our approach, the architecture of a component is coupled to its placement and this relationship is dealt with differently for composite components than for primitive components. As far as distribution is concerned, a primitive component executes on one host whereas a composite can be physically replicated on a set of different hosts. The main goal of composite replication is that the component's interfaces become directly accessible on several hosts. A composite component can then be seen as providing a ubiquitous service.

A single host is associated with a primitive component whereas a set of hosts is associated with a composite component. This set must be a subset of the set of hosts associated with the including component. By default, the placement set of a composite component is inherited from the including component.

At execution time, each instance of a composite component maintains locally information about the configuration of its subcomponents. Hence, a distributed composite component c distributed over a set of hosts $\mathbb{H}$ respects the following properties:

- The provided and required interfaces of c are accessible on all the hosts h_i of $\mathbb{H}$.
- Let c be a composite component that contains a *primitive* subcomponent p. There exists a single host h_i on which p executes. For every host $h_j \in \mathbb{H}$ ($j \neq i$), there exits c_j, an instance of c on h_j. Each c_j holds a remote reference to p (in a proxy).

2.3 Example

We give in this section an example of an application made of hierarchical components and we detail how it can be distributed on a given set of hosts.

Figure 2 depicts the architecture of a photo application that allows the user to search for a number of photos in a repository and to build a diaporama with the selected photos. The top-level composite component (*PhotoApp*) includes a generic component devoted to document searching (*DocumentSearch*). This component is also a composite component (taken off the shelf); it is composed of a *DocumentFinder* and a *DocumentBuffer*. The primitive *DocumentFinder* component provides an interface for issuing more or less complex requests based on the names of documents, on their subjects or some other meta-information, and for selecting the corresponding documents from a given set of documents (a repository). The selected documents are passed to a *DocumentBuffer*. Apart from an interface for adding new documents, the primitive *DocumentBuffer* component provides an interface for sorting and extracting documents. This provided interface and the one of *DocumentFinder* are accessible as provided interfaces of the *DocumentSearch* component. Finally, the *DocumentSearch* component is bound to a *PhotoRepository* component that constitutes the specialized document repository and a *DiapoMaker* component which allows the selected photos to be assembled in a parameterizable diaporama.

Consider that the photo application is meant to be usable from any of the five machines owned by the user (hosts h_1 to h_5), in a dynamic network similar to the one depicted in figure 1. Hence, the target set of hosts associated with the *PhotoApp* component is $\{h_1, h_2, h_3, h_4, h_5\}$. A subset of these hosts is dedicated to the distributed execution of the composite component *DocumentSearch*, say $\{h_1, h_2, h_3\}$, h_4 and h_5 being excluded for licence reasons for example. Moreover, some constraints on the required resources result in the following placement of the primitive components (see section 4 for details): *DocumentFinder* on h_1, *DocumentBuffer* on h_2, *PhotoRepository* on h_4 and *DiapoMaker* on h_5.

At runtime the membranes of the composite components are maintained on each of their target hosts. A membrane contains the interfaces of the component as well as the description of its architecture (subcomponents and bindings). The instances of components (primitive or composite) that are not present are represented by proxies. Note that for a primitive component, the proxy is linked to the distant (single) instance of this primitive whereas for a composite component, the proxy is linked to one distant instance of the (partially replicated) membrane.

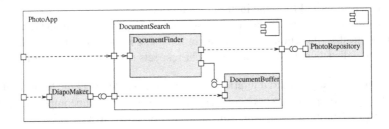

Fig. 2. Architecture of the photo application (in UML 2.0)

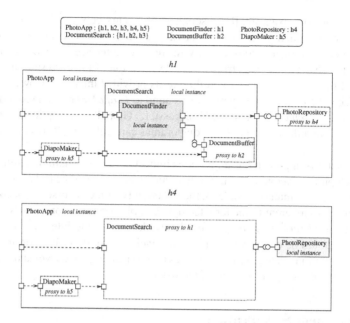

Fig. 3. Placement of components and entities maintained on host h_1 and h_4

Figure 3 summarizes the placement of the components and shows the runtime entities (architectural information and instances) maintained on h_1 and h_4 for our PhotoApp example.

2.4   Support for Disconnections

The replication of a composite component eases the access to the services it implements as it makes possible to use its provided interfaces on each host. However, because of network disconnections, from a given site, access to a remote component can be interrupted. Consequently, a method invocation in this case may raise some kind of a network exception. This problem is not specific to our approach but appears as soon as remote references are used, that may point to unaccessible components at any time. In a context of hierarchical components, the technique that consists in deactivating a component as soon as one of its required interface is unbound is very penalizing as a single disconnection will end up by ricochet with the deactivation of the top-level component, that is the deactivation of the entire application. In the dynamic environments we target, where disconnections are frequent, the application is likely to be rarely usable.

We address this problem in the following two ways:

– We introduce the notions of active and non active interfaces. We maintain the state (active or not) of an interface according to the accessibility of the component's instance it is bound to. Moreover, we add a control interface to components to allow introspection on the state of its provided and required interfaces.
– We allow the execution of a component even if some of its interfaces are not active.

On the PhotoApp example, if a disconnection occurs between h_1 and h_4, the *PhotoRepository* component is no longer accessible from h_1. The disconnection is detected by a dedicated monitor, and consequently, the required interface of the *DocumentSearch* component is deactivated. This triggers the deactivation of the corresponding required interface of the *DocumentFinder* and then of its provided interface. However, the second interface of *DocumentSearch* (the one bound to *DiapoMaker*) can remain active as the *DocumentSearch* component is still accessible. Globally the application is still usable, although in a degraded mode, as diaporamas can still be built from the document buffer.

Notice that this approach has an obvious impact on the programming style required when developing components, as the state of an interface should be tested before invoking methods on this interface. Indeed, the uncertainty of the accesses to needed (or required) services –inherent to the targeted dynamic platforms– enforces adaptable code. The provision for tools to introspect on the availability of the interfaces is a minimal answer that should be complemented by other facilities for describing or applying, for example, adaptation strategies. This involves research at language level and middleware level that is out the scope of the presented work.

3 Deployment Specification

When considering the deployment of distributed components, the key issue is to build a mapping between the component instances and the hosts of the target platform. This task implies to have some knowledge not only about the identity of the hosts involved in the deployment phase, but about the characteristics of each of them as well. Moreover, for a hierarchical component-based application, every component instance at each level of the hierarchy has to be handled.

At design-time, the designer is unlikely to know where to deploy each component regarding resource availability. This motivates the need to differ this task at runtime. We propose to add a deployment aspect to an existing architecture description language (such as [8, 9]).This will allow the description of the resource properties that must be satisfied by a machine for hosting a specific component.

We propose an extension to ADLs that makes possible the description of the target platform in a declarative way. The language we propose is purely declarative and descriptive and has a similar objective to the language described in [10]. It is not mandatory to give an explicit name or address of a target machine: the placement of components are mainly driven by constraints on the resources the target host(s) should satisfy. The choice of the machine that will host a component will be made automatically at runtime (during the deployment).

The description of the resources that the target platform must satisfy is defined in a deployment descriptor in which references to component instances (defined in the architecture descriptor) can be made. For each component, a *deployment context* is defined. Such a context lists all the constraints that a hosting machine has to satisfy. If these constraints are associated with a primitive component, one host will be authorized to instantiate this component whereas several hosts may be selected for hosting the membrane of a composite component, in accordance with our distribution model.

There are two types of constraints that can be defined in a deployment context: resource constraints (*ResCst*) and location constraints (*LocCst*). *ResCst*s allow hardware and software needs to be represented. Each of these constraints defines a domain value for a resource type that the target host(s) should satisfy. *LocCst*s are useful to drive the placement choice of a component if it occurs that more than one host is applicant.

```
                                                  <component name="PhotoApp">
                                                    <component name="DiapoMaker">
                                                      <deployment-context>
40                                                      <cpu freq="1.5" unit="GHz"
                                                          operator="min" />
      <component name="DocumentSearch">                 <memory
        <component name="DocumentFinder">        free="50"
          <deployment-context>
            <resource-constraint>                           directory="/home/"
5           <cpu freq="1.2"                                 unit="MB"
              unit="GHz"                         45           operator="min"/>
              operator="min" />                         </resource-constraint>
            </resource-constraint>                    </deployment-context>
                                                    </component>
10          <location-constraint>
              <target varname="x"/>             50   <component name="PhotoRepository">
            </location-constraint>                    <deployment-context>
          </deployment-context>                         <resource-constraint>
        </component>                                       <memory free="1" unit="GB"
15                                                55            directory="/home/"
      <component name="DocumentBuffer">                       operator="min" />
        <deployment-context>                            </resource-constraint>
          <resource-constraint>                       </deployment-context>
            <memory free="200"                      </component>
20            unit="MB"                        60
              operator="min" />                   <component name="DocumentSearch">
          </resource-constraint>                   <locationconstraint>
          <location-constraint>                      <operator name="exclude">
            <target varname="y"/>                       <arg value="egilsay" />
25        </location-constraint>             65          <arg value="parvati" />
          </deployment-context>                        </operator>
        </component>                               </locationconstraint>
                                                  </component>
        <deployment-context>
30        <location-constraint>                   <deployment-context>
            <operator name="alldiff">        70     <locationconstraint>
              <arg varname="this.DocumentFinder.x" />   <target hostname="ambika"/>
              <arg varname="this.DocumentBuffer.y" />   <target hostname="dakini"/>
            </operator>                                 <target hostname="mafate"/>
35        </location-constraint>                        <target hostname="egilsay"/>
        <deployment-context>                 75         <target hostname="parvati"/>
      </component>                                 <deployment-context>
                                                </component>
```

(a)   (b)

Fig. 4. Deployment descriptor

An example of use of *ResCst* and *LocCst* is illustrated in Figure 4 which shows the deployment descriptor, in an XML notation, of the photo application introduced in the previous section. The descriptor (**a**) contains the constraints associated with the *DocumentSearch* composite component and descriptor (**b**) contains those of the *PhotoApp* component. Resource constraints are defined within the *resource-constraint* element. For every component, adding an XML tag corresponding to a resource type (e.g. cpu, memory) specifies a constraint on this resource the target host has to verify.

Location constraints are declared within the *location-constraint* element. The *target* element defines the set of hosts among which our runtime support will have to choose. Hosts can be represented in two ways: (1) by their hostname if their identity are known before the deployment or (2) by a variable. Such a variable can be used at the composite level to control the placement of components. This feature is achieved by the use of the *operator* element. This element allows relations between variables to be expressed. For example, in descriptor (**a**), the *DocumentFinder* component is said to be deployed on host *x* and *DocumentBuffer* on host *y*. Constraining *DocumentFinder* and *DocumentBuffer* to be on two distinct hosts is achieved by using the *alldiff* operator that declares *x* to be different from *y*. For a primitive component, at most one variable can be declared (because a primitive component will be placed on an unique host). Several variables can be used for a composite component, which is physically distributed over several hosts.

When composing the application, it is possible to use only variables. Then, the definition of the target platform is made at the first level of the hierarchy (for the component *PhotoApp* on the example) by adding the list of the machines that will be involved in the deployment (lines 71–75 on Figure 4). During the deployment, as it is detailed in next section, this set of machines, together with the location constraints will be inherited by the sub-components.

4   Deployment Process

4.1   Overview of the Propagative Deployment

Because of the dynamism of the network on which we deploy our applications, it is not possible to base a deployment on a full connection of the different hosts. We are interested in a deployment that will allow an application to be activated progressively, that is, part of its provided services can be put at disposal even if some machines that are required for the "not yet" installed components, are not available. As soon as these machines become connected, the deployment will go along. Moreover, resource changes on any host may yield the deployment of components although is was not possible before. The deployment we present in this paper is thus asynchronous as it may not be possible to deploy every component immediately.

Once the architecture descriptor and the deployment descriptor have been defined, the deployment phase we consider in this article consists in choosing a target host for every component of the architecture. This selection has to be made according to the deployment context associated with every component. Indeed, the selected machine has to satisfy all the resource constraints and this machine must not contradict the location constraints. In the case of a primitive component, a single host has to be selected among several applying machines. For a composite component, the number of applicants can be greater than the set of machines over which this composite component has to be distributed. Controlling the selection of the target hosts is essential to guarantee the consistency of the application. Indeed, in a dynamic network where islands of machines may appear, we must avoid inconsistent decisions in two different islands. For example, we have to ensure that two distinct machines from two islands will not be selected for the hosting of the same primitive component.

In the following we present the general propagative deployment algorithm in two steps. First, we consider a fully connected environment. This will help us to focus on the resolution of the constraints expressed in the deployment descriptor and to describe a possible distribution of the instantiation tasks (thus the selection of target hosts) within a hierarchical architecture. Then we present the complete propagative deployment in a dynamic network where the main difficult aspect is to ensure a unique decision regarding component instantiation.

4.2 Deployment in a Connected Network

We consider in this section a fully connected network composed of a finite set of machines. Each machine is identified and no disconnection may occur. The propagative deployment in such a network consists in diffusing the architecture descriptor and the deployment descriptor to all the machines that are listed at the top level of the application (with the XML *target* element).

Then, once a machine has received these descriptors, a recursive process is launched in order to select the components that can be hosted on this machine. The main steps of this process for a machine m_i, for a component C are the following:

1. machine m_i checks if it satisfies the location constraints associated with C. This corresponds to verifying if m_i belongs to the set of the target hosts (see XML `target` element). If the m_i is not concerned by the deployment (instantiation) of component C, the process returns for this component, else,
2. machine m_i has to launch probes corresponding to the resource constraints of C (e.g. `CPUProbe`, `MemoryProbe`). If at least one probe returns a value violating a resource constraint (e.g. not enough free memory available), the process returns, else,
3. machine m_i declares itself as an applicant host for component C and a collective decision has to be made. Indeed, more than one host may apply and if C is a composite component, it may have subcomponents with location constraint such as $x \neq y$
4. once a choice has been made, all the applicants are informed of the value of the free variables and of the fact that they are authorized (or not) to instantiate component C. The process stops for hosts that are not authorized. For the others,
5. if C is a composite component, the process is performed recursively for all the subcomponents of C

In a connected network, there is no difficulty to make the collective decision described in point 3. We could for example choose before the deployment a machine S whose role is to decide a host among applicants. In this case, when a host h satisfies all the constraints attached to a component and thus becomes applicant, h announces itself to S and waits for a decision. However we prefer the approach of [11] where a deployment controller, which is in charge of well-defined tasks of the deployment, is defined for each composite component of the hierarchy. The main reason for such a distribution of the deployment controllers is scalability. Indeed, with this approach, parts of the application can be deployed independently according to its topology. Thus, we define a machine S_i per composite component of the hierarchy. This machine is responsible for the decision-making of its direct sub-architecture, *i.e.* it must choose among applicants those who don't contradict the location constraints. Applicants must be informed of the results. Thus, after a decision, each representative S_i sends to the applying hosts a new deployment descriptor which is updated with the new location information, *i.e.* the actual name of the machine hosting a specific component is added to the location constraints. Indeed, before the deployment, no explicit machine name is given and variables can be used to indicate applicant machines. For example, if the machines *ambika* and *dakini* are respectively attributed to components *DocumentFinder* and *DocumentBuffer*, the following lines are added to descriptor (**a**):

```
// replace line 11 by:
<target varname="x" value="ambika"/>
```
```
// replace line 23 by:
<target varname="y" value="dakini"/>
```

As a consequence of the decision, some components can be instantiated. In the case of composite components, the deployment process (local evaluation, applicant announcement, decision-making) goes along recursively.

However, it may be possible that a representative machine could not find any placement solution (because no combination of applicants fullfills all the location constraints). In order to propose to the representative a new possible placement, a machine that newly satisfies some resource constraints (for uninstalled components) declares itself as applicant.

4.3 Deployment in a Dynamic Network

The previous section, with the assumption of a fully connected network, has highlighted two main ideas of the propagative deployment: (1) each host does the evaluation of the constraints attached to the components and (2) the decision making is distributed over several machines, each of them representing a composite component of the application.

In a dynamic network all the machines may not be connected at the same time. In this kind of network, islands may exist and communication paths between machines may disappear. In such an environment, a deployment based on a full connection of the different machines at the same time is not conceivable. We may want to start the deployment (*i.e.* the instantiation of parts of the components and thus to put parts of the services offered by the application at disposal) while some machines may be disconnected or inaccessible. The component model presented previously (see section 2) allows an application to run in a degraded mode but the main difficulty here is to deal with the unicity of the instantiation of the–possibly statefull–components, which is difficult to ensure in a dynamic network. Indeed, we must avoid conflicting decision to be made in the different islands that may exist in such an environment. On one hand, a machine that represents a composite component, cannot be selected before the deployment, as in a fully connected network, since this machine may not be connected. On the other hand, if we let each of the machines that host the same replicated composite component make a decision, we cannot guarantee that in two different islands contradictory instantiations may not be performed. We tackle this difficulty by considering the consensus problem: a set of machine has to decide on a same value regarding the representative of composite components.

We use the results of [12], in which the requirements of the consensus problem are relaxed. The authors have identified *conditions* for which there exists an asynchronous protocol that solves the consensus problem despite the occurrence of t process crashes. We define the consensus to select, for each composite that is replicated on several machines, a representative host that will make future decisions on where the direct subcomponents have to be instantiated.

Algorithm. The main steps of the algorithm described in the previous section are not modified. The only change concerns the designation of a representative host for each node of the hierarchy. We use the algorithm of [12] to elect such a representative and to build a common view of the placement of the components.

The consensus algorithm requires that a majority of machines can be reached among the target hosts of the composite component. This majority is not the same depending on the composite component. For example, the photo application is distributed over $\{h_1, h_2, h_3, h_4, h_5\}$, as a consequence, the majority is reached when at least three of these machines are in the same island. Whereas for the composite DocumentSearch component, which is distributed over $\{h_1, h_2, h_3\}$, the consensus is possible when an island, composed of at least $\{h_1, h_2\}$, $\{h_1, h_3\}$ or $\{h_2, h_3\}$, is formed.

The consensus-based algorithm consists in:

1. ensuring that the selection of a host for a representative composite component is possible if an island is composed of a majority of machines,
2. selecting a machine S_i for the future instantiation decisions for each composite component of the hierarchy
3. updating the deployment descriptor with the identifier of the selected machine.

Points 1 and 3 guarantee that if a new island composed of a majority of machines is created, there is at least one machine that possesses the most recent version of the deployment descriptor. Thus no contradictory decision can be made in this island.

The consensus may not terminate (e.g. the number of hosts within an island may not be sufficient). In order to prevent this situation, we allow a newly connected machine to participate in this consensus. This is achieved by periodically broadcasting a message asking if a consensus is still in progress. In that case the newly connected machine collects the data that have already been exchanged between the other machines and proposes a value that can make the consensus evolve.

Once a representative composite component is chosen, due to the dynamism of the network, this composite may be in a non-majority island during a more or less amount of time. In this case, if an instantiation decision is made, it cannot decide any more whereas it may exists an other island in which a consensus can be reached. Thus, if such a decision has to be made and a majority of machines composes the islands, a new representative machine is selected and the deployment descriptor is updated. No conflict will arise later, *i.e.* when the older representative belongs to a new majority islands. Indeed in such an island, it exists at least one machine that possesses the most recent version of the deployment descriptor, thus during the consensus, the older representative will learn the existence of the new one.

5   Implementation Status

The propagative deployment presented in this paper is based on a constraint based-language for the description of the placement of components according to resource requirements. Our current prototype has been implemented using Julia, a Java implementation of the Fractal component model [3]. The features of the ADLs described in section 3 have been implemented as new modules into the Fractal Architecture Description Language. Deployment descriptors can be specified graphically through an extension of FractalGUI.

In order to evaluate the constraints defined in the deployment descriptor, we have to collect information about resources on every host. We use D-Raje [13] –a framework developed in our team, dedicated to the observation of distributed system resources in

Java– to define specific probes related to resource constraints. D-Raje is also used to model and to monitor the state of physical links between hosts. A disconnection can then be captured with the result that bindings between components are withdrawn and the corresponding interfaces are deactivated. Further details can be found in [2].

We are currently implementing a distributed test platform in order to tune our consensus algorithm considering parameters such as the numbers of hosts and the frequency of disconnections.

6 Related Work

The main aspects developed in this paper are related to a distribution scheme for hierarchical components on dynamic networks and to a resource-aware and propagative deployment.

Many works have taken into account a context-aware deployment, that is, the placement of components onto hosts according to some resource requirements. A formal statement of the deployment is given in [14] and a set of algorithms that improve mobile system's availability is presented. In [15] the authors propose a deployment configuration language (DCL) in which properties on the target hosts can be expressed. The deployment considered in this work extends the Corba Component Model, which is a flat component model. In [10], the authors present the Deladas language that also allows constraints to be defined on hosts and components. A constraint solver is used to generate a valid configuration of the placements of components and reconfiguration of the placement is possible when a constraint becomes inconsistent. But this centralized resolution is not suited to the kind of dynamic network we target. Moreover, the current version of Deladas does not consider resource requirements. These abovementioned works aim at finding an optimum for the placement problem of components. This aspect is not one of our objectives. Indeed, due to the dynamism of the environment, it is hardly feasible to define a quiescent state that will allow our consensus algorithm to decide on an optimal placement. Moreover, the solutions proposed are centralized.

In [16] a decentralized redeployment is presented. The configuration to be deployed is available on every host involved in the deployment. A local decision can then be made according to the local subsystem configuration state. However the choice of the components' location is made before the deployment process. The works presented in [11] on the deployment of hierarchical component-based applications is probably the closest to ours'. The authors describe an asynchronous deployment and use the hierarchical structure of the application in order to distribute deployment tasks. In the solution developed by the authors, a deployment controller is statically chosen and defined in the deployment descriptor. In our approach we could not decide at design-time which machine will host such a controller. The approach proposed by the authors focuses on functional constraints and thus resource requirements have not been taken into account.

7 Conclusion

This paper has presented a support for deploying and executing an application built with hierarchical components on an heterogeneous and dynamic network. The main contribution of this work is that it attempts to take into account a challenging distributed target platform characterized by the heterogeneity and the volatility of the hosts, volatility that may result in the fragmentation of the network.

A distribution method has been proposed for hierarchical components. Composite components are made accessible on a set of hosts whereas each primitive component is localized on a single host. Besides, via the notion of active interface, we allow a component to operate in a degraded mode in order to account for network disconnections without making the entire application unusable.

We have presented a purely descriptive language for specifying deployment descriptors that allow for a context-aware deployment. This language is meant to extend some existing ADL. A deployment descriptor allows the description of the resource needs of a component and some placement constraints.

The deployment process we have defined is a propagative one. The instantiation and the activation of a component is performed as soon as some resources that meet its needs are discovered. This early activation is possible as some of its interfaces can remain inactive (the component then executes in a degraded mode).We have designed an algorithm that supports this propagative deployment in a dynamic network. The scalability of the process is ensured by the distributed and hierarchical organisation of the control. Moreover, we have presented a distributed consensus that guarantees that the location constraints are satisfied even in the context of a partitioned network.

The main direction of our future work consists in taking into account the possible modifications on the resources' availability after some component instantiations have been made. Indeed, even if we can respect for example a memory constraint on the instantiation of a given primitive component, the memory conditions may change that invalidates the choice afterwards. The mechanisms we have implemented in our deployment algorithm could be adapted for solving this problem, provided the component can be safely stopped. An autonomic deployment could thus be defined.

References

1. Roussain, H., Guidec, F.: Cooperative Component-Based Software Deployment in Wireless Ad Hoc Networks. In: 3rd International Working Conference on Component Deployment (CD 2005). LNCS, Grenoble, France (2005)

2. Hoareau, D., Mahéo, Y.: Distribution of a Hierarchical Component in a Non-Connected Environment. In: 31th Euromicro Conference - Component-Based Software Engineering Track, Porto, Portugal, IEEE CS (2005)

3. Bruneton, E., Coupaye, T., Leclercq, M., Quéma, V., Stefani, J.B.: An Open Component Model and its Support in Java. In: Proceedings of the International Symposium on Component-based Software Engineering (CBSE7). Number 3054 in LNCS, Edinburgh, Scotland (2004)

4. van Ommering, R.C.: Koala, a Component Model for Consumer Electronics Product Software. In: ESPRIT ARES Workshop, Las Palmas de Gran Canaria, Spain (1998) 76–86

5. Magee, J., Dulay, N., Eisenbach, S., Kramer, J.: Specifying Distributed Software Architectures. In: Proceedings of the 5th European Software Engineering Conference (ESEC), Sitges, Spain (1995) 137–153

6. Plasil, F., Balek, D., Janecek, R.: SOFA/DCUP: Architecture for Component Trading and Dynamic Updating. In: Proceedings of the 4th International Conference on Configurable Distributed Systems (ICCDS '98), Annapolis, Maryland, US (1998)

7. Medvidovic, N., N. Taylor, R.: A classification and comparison framework for software architecture description languages. IEEE Trans. Software Eng **26**(1) (2000) 70–93

8. : xacme: Acme extensions to xarch. School of Computer Science Web Site: http://www-2.cs.cmu.edu/ acme/pub/xAcme/ (2001)

9. Dashofy, E.M., van der Hoek, A., Taylor, R.N.: An infrastructure for the rapid development of xml-based architecture description languages. In: In proceedings of the International Conference on Software Engineering (ICSE'02), Orlando, Florida, USA (2002) 266–276

10. Dearle, A., N. C. Kirby, G., J. McCarthy, A.: A framework for constraint-based deployment and autonomic management of distributed applications. In: ICAC. (2004) 300–301

11. Quéma, V., Balter, R., Bellissard, L., Féliot, D., Freyssinet, A., Lacourte, S.: Asynchronous, hierarchical and scalable deployment of component-based applications. In: Proceedings of the 2nd International Working Conference on Component Deployment (CD'2004), Edinburgh, Scotland (2004)

12. Mostéfaoui, A., Rajsbaum, S., Raynal, M., Roy, M.: Condition-based consensus solvability: a hierarchy of conditions and efficient protocols. Distributed Computing **17**(1) (2004) 1–20

13. Mahéo, Y., Guidec, F., Courtrai, L.: A Java Middleware Platform for Resource-Aware Distributed Applications. In: 2nd Int. Symposium on Parallel and Distributed Computing (IS-PDC'2003), Ljubljana, Slovenia, IEEE CS (2003) 96–103

14. Mikic-Rakic, M., Medvidovic, N.: Software architectural support for disconnected operation in highly distributed environments. In: CBSE. (2004) 23–39

15. Li, T., Hoffmann, A., Born, M., Schieferdecker, I.: A platform architecture to support the deployment of distributed applications. In: ICC, IEEE International Conference on Communications. Volume 4. (2002) 2592–2596

16. Mikic-Rakic, M., Medvidovic, N.: Architecture-level support for software component deployment in resource constrained environments. In: Component Deployment. (2002) 31–50

Comparative Analysis of Ad-Hoc Networks Oriented to Collaborative Activities*

Sebastián Echeverría, Raúl Santelices, and Miguel Nussbaum

Departamento de Ciencia de la Computación,
Escuela de Ingeniería, Pontificia Universidad Católica de Chile,
Vicuña Mackenna 4860, Santiago, Chile
secheverria@ing.puc.cl, rasantel@ing.puc.cl, mn@ing.puc.cl

Abstract. Mobile ad-hoc networks are suitable for collaborative applications, whose objective is to reach a common goal through the cooperation of the members involved. These networks have to be trustworthy in message delivery and fault-tolerant. We developed two different frameworks to satisfy these needs, and evaluated the performance of each network. This paper describes both frameworks and the results obtained from the experiments. We observed important differences between the networks in the results. This is explained by the two different development environments used, C++ and .NET, and the specificity versus generality of the frameworks. Combining the advantages of both frameworks could present a platform that satisfies all the needs for mobile collaborative activities.

1 Introduction

In recent years, mobile devices such as cell phones and Personal Digital Assistants (PDAs) have become part of our daily lives. With their increasing improvements on both hardware and software, the scope of their possible applications has extended. At the same time, new wireless technologies such as Bluetooth and Wi-Fi have taken these devices out of their isolation, allowing the advantages of mobility to be used in combination with inter-device interaction.

In particular, mobile ad-hoc networks present a particularly attractive environment for collaborative applications [1]. Since in ad-hoc mode the wireless connection does not need a central server, execution of these activities can be achieved anywhere and with any number of people. This potential, enhanced by the handheld size of the PDAs, presents a proper ground for the development of collaborative applications, whose objective is to reach a common goal through the communication and cooperation of the various members involved [2]. This type of collaborative work can be seen in collaborative learning, in simulations which involve several people working together, etc.

Among the problems that standard ad-hoc networks deal with are the frequent peer transit and the indirect peer routing [3]. Peer transit refers to the

* This work was partially funded by FONDECYT/CONICYT grant 1040605.

W. Grass et al. (Eds.): ARCS 2006, LNCS 3894, pp. 465–479, 2006.

successive entrance and exit of peers to the network, while indirect peer routing refers to the generation of the adequate routes, through other peers, to carry messages between peers which are not directly connected (i.e. out of reach) [4][5]. Nevertheless, these concerns do not apply to collaborative activities. In these, it can be considered that the users do not transit, because the purpose of these activities is for a pre-defined group of people to collaborate for a period of time to reach a common goal. Thus, the transit requirement is reduced to the need of a discovery method at the beginning of the activity. Moreover, because collaboration is intended to take place in a face-to-face interaction, indirect peer routing does not apply.

On the other hand, collaborative activity networks must outperform standard ad-hoc networks in two main subjects: trustworthiness of message delivery and fault-tolerance. Trustworthiness of messages delivery is a high priority in the development of a collaborative activity. The correct progress of such an activity relies on the effective arrival of all the shared information. Due to the fact that these activities tend to have a considerable duration, and a progress that depends on the communication inside the group, the successful exchange of information between peers must be ensured in order to be able to reach the goals of the activity [6]. This is not an easy task in a wireless mobile network, especially if there is much traffic and a high number of users involved.

A high level of fault-tolerance is another important factor. Wireless networks are prone to disconnections and other similar problems [7]. If one of the peers accidentally leaves the network, the whole activity could be compromised. In the best case, the remaining users could be able to go on without that peer, but that user looses the possibility to complete the activity. Therefore, the recovery of both the network and the application is essential to repair the possible problems that may show up.

Networks in collaborative activities share specific characteristics that need custom made solutions. We developed two different networks which satisfy these needs as a part of two different collaborative activity frameworks. Although they share the same common objectives, their aim and design was different.

Though the services provided by both networks are similar, they hold important differences. Both are designed to be used with PDAs. The protocols used in each network are different, as is the way they solve problems such as fault-tolerance. The first framework, named Edunova, was implemented in embedded C++. This is a lower-level language compared to other possible platforms, but it provides better control of the network and other operating system functions with less overhead. The second framework, called Activity Framework (AF), was developed using the .NET Compact Framework and the C# language [8]. .NET provides better functionality and is easier to use, but it adds a new middle layer to the applications, which may slow down the execution of the software.

This paper describes the architecture and protocol of each framework. It also shows the results of a set of performance experiments we designed, which give a measure of the limitations and advantages of each framework's functionality and physical behavior. These results help to understand each design, protocol and the advantages/disadvantages of the corresponding implementation environment.

The document is structured as follows: Sect. 2 details the objective and architecture of each framework. It also shows the features and structure of the network developed for each framework. Section 3 explains the experiments designed to test both networks. Section 4 presents the results of the experiments performed, and Sect. 5 finishes with the conclusions and future work.

2 Frameworks Developed

2.1 Objectives and Main Features

The purpose of both frameworks is to provide the services required to build a collaborative activity (see Table 1). By using a framework, the developer of an activity can focus on its objectives, without considering the lower-level functionality.

Table 1. Objectives and features of each framework

	Edunova	AF
Main objective	Specific collaborative activities for the classroom (MCSCL [2] [9])	Generic collaborative activities
Applications developed	MCSCL implementation for the use in school's classrooms [2] [9]	Learning to Collaborate Collaborating (LCC) [10]
Implementation language	Embedded C++	.NET Compact Framework C#

The first framework, Edunova, was developed to implement face to face collaborative learning [2][9]. Mainly, activities consist of questions stored in a database, where students have to agree on an alternative, with the teacher acting as a mediator. Even though there is the potential to add new functionality, the main underlying frame of the activities will persist.

The second framework, Activity Framework (AF), was designed to unify the lower level functions into a generic, complete and coherent framework. Two of the main objectives of AF were the modularity and ease of extension. One application developed over the AF framework is called Learning to Collaborate Collaborating (LCC) [10], where collaboration and coordination between the members is essential to successfully solve the problems presented.

Being more specific, Edunova has the possibility of functioning more finely-tuned to the kind of collaborative activity that uses its services. However, it can't be used as a framework for other types of applications, at least not without extensive changes. On the other hand, AF provides services that may not be specifically made for a given application, but provides a higher level of flexibility for multiple applications of different kinds.

Another difference arises from the implementation language used in each case. The Edunova framework was developed in Embedded C++, because of the speed and efficiency it provides. It also allows a considerable level of control over the lower operating system calls, and the way the communication is done. Nevertheless, developing the platform in this language implies a very high level of complexity in producing and maintaining the code.

The AF platform was developed in C# over .NET Compact Framework. One of the reasons we chose this environment is the high level of functionality it provides, which simplifies considerably software development. .NET also is platform-independent, so AF can be used over multiple operating systems. However, the .NET layer may diminish the efficiency of the platform, especially when many resource-limited devices, such as PDAs, are interacting. Also, it may reduce the level of control the developer has over the inner workings of the operating system and network calls.

2.2   Framework Architectures

The architectures of both platforms are similar, based on a series of hierarchical components. They both have a certain degree of modularization, to allow the easy expansion of new functionalities and activities.

The architecture of the Edunova framework is organized in several hierarchical layers, as shown in Fig. 1. The upper layers handle the functionality for different high-level purposes, such as group management, image processing, and visual interface. The lower layers consist of the network and the basic functional blocks. The communication between the modules is either direct, calling functions of the lower layers, or through "handlers", objects that register their functions to be called when an event is generated.

Edunova's components are modular. The functionality of each one of them is clearly defined and separated. However, due to the platform's objective and its development, there are some strong relations between the components, which make the process of isolating or replacing them complex.

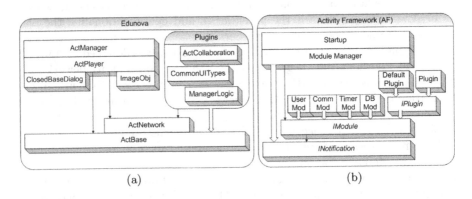

(a)   (b)

Fig. 1. (a) Architecture of the Edunova framework, (b) Architecture of the AF framework

AF's architecture is completely modular, as shown in Fig. 1. It has a main manager, called ModuleManager, which coordinates the rest of the modules. The manager acts as a mediator, so that each module only knows one interface, the manager's, and they are independent among themselves. Besides, the manager only sees one interface, IModule, which is implemented by each module. Therefore, there is no need to modify the inner workings of either the manager or the other modules when adding new ones.

Each module adds a specific functionality, such as network functions or peer management. The services of each one of them are used by sending specific messages through the IModule interface. Each module sends messages intended for other destinies to ModuleManager, who in turn re-sends them to the corresponding module.

Both platforms allow the user to select one of the available activities in the device. Activities have a different definition in each framework, as shown in Table 2. In Edunova an activity is a specific instance of the MCSCL type of collaborative activities. In AF, an activity is the complete definition of a generic collaborative group work which meets certain conditions to function with the framework. In both cases the concept of "plugin" is used for an object that extends the functions of the platform, though with different scopes in each case.

Table 2. Comparison of activities in each framework

	Edunova	AF
Definition of an Activity	XML object that contains graphic design, logic and information; other resource files used by the activity	Plugin contained in a DLL file with graphic interface, logic, functionality and resources
Extra Functionality for an Activity	Can't have specific new functionality	Included in definition
Extra Functionality for the Framework	Plugin contained in a DLL file with the functionality	Modules implementing the IModule interface
Purpose of a Plugin	Component that adds new services and functionality to the framework	Complete activity, including custom-made functionality
Activity Execution	Controlled by the framework	Controlled by the plugin

The development of new activities in Edunova is relatively simple, due to the fact that the definition is isolated in an XML file. The person creating them doesn't need to have knowledge of C++, as he/she can easily adapt an activity XML template to his needs. However, he will not be able to add new functionality inside the XML, and the complexity of implementing new plugins with some added features to the framework, or of modifying the framework itself, is extremely high. This is due to Edunova's architecture, and the little facilities for reusability that embedded C++ offers when compared to other alternatives, such as .NET or Java [11]. Though it is true that C++ is object oriented, the settings needed to operate in a Windows environment, and to connect to libraries in the operating system, hinder the ease of development.

On the other hand, the development of activities in AF requires a high level of knowledge in the C# language, as they are implemented directly on the code. However, this gives a high flexibility for the possible applications to be designed, without loosing the advantages of the services provided by the framework. .NET provides much more functionality and it is easier to use than the libraries and methods of C++. However, this usually implies sacrificing some of the efficiency and control that C++ provides.

Figure 2 shows the architecture of the network level of both frameworks.

Edunova's network is organized as a library. It has a hierarchical structure divided in layers. Higher modules in the framework can access its services calling the corresponding functions.

The network components are organized so that each has clear and differentiated functions. The access to each component is direct, so that high level modules call specifically the component they require. This allows the network to

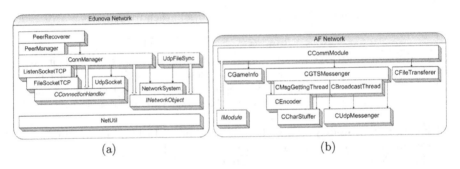

(a)   (b)

Fig. 2. (a) Architecture of Edunova's network, (b) Architecture of AF's network

Table 3. Main components of the Edunova network

Component	Functions
ConnManager	- Starts and stops the WinSocks [12] library for TCP/IP communication. - Sends and receives messages inside the logic network of the system, offering both TCP and UDP protocols for sending them.
PeerManager	- Connects and manages the peers in the logic network.
PeerRecoverer	- Broadcasts by UDP the state of the application and network. - Helps the recovery in case of network failures. - Negotiates the reentry into the network, the change of a device for a user and the late entries into the network.
UdpFileSync	- Implements a UDP trusted file transfer protocol, to help broadcast files through the network. It works directly over WinSocks.

Table 4. Main components of AF's network

Component	Functions
CCommModule	- Interacts with ModuleManager and gets the messages requesting network services from other modules. - Centralizes and unifies the functions of the lower components in the network.
CGTSMessenger	- Codifies and sends the messages on the network. - Handles the threads that send and receive messages.
CGameInfo	- Handles the network status, and the information about connected peers.
CFileTransferer	- Provides file transference between peers.
CUdpMessenger	- Implements a UDP trusted communication protocol between peers.

be efficient, but it makes the relation between the components stronger, being harder to isolate the network module to be reused in a simple way.

On the other hand, AF's network architecture has a more modularized design, also using several layers. The upper interface is used to hide the complexity of the lower layers, so when there are changes inside the module, they are not seen by the outside components (either ModuleManager or any module requesting the network services).

Inside the module, the components possess a low level of coupling and a high level of cohesion. This makes the components highly reusable. As an example, the component in charge of the file transference was easily reused in another application for the quick updating of the AF files between different devices.

2.3   Network Model and Services

Both network modules allow the setup of an ad-hoc network among several mobile devices. The way the network works after it has been setup is ad-hoc. In both networks, there are two kinds of peers: Master and Slaves, which are shown in Table 5.

The peer we call Master provides certain specific services, but in general it acts as a simple peer. However, there are some differences regarding the Master in each network. In Edunova, the Master centralizes the activity around it, as the activities developed for this framework need a main peer. Some functions in Edunova are limited to the Master. On the other hand, the AF network sees the Master as another peer during the progress of the application. The only special functionality is the initial network setup, and the recovery and re-entry into the network by other peers. After the setup, the Master is only different in that it can communicate with all the groups. It depends on the application if it uses the Master as the center of the activity, as a monitor, or as another peer.

The setup is similar in both networks. The Master chooses the activity to be loaded from the list of available activities. Then, it broadcasts a message about the new activity, and registers every peer that answers. Once they are all connected, it starts the activities. The only differences in this setup between the

Table 5. Comparison of Master and Slave functions

	Edunova	AF
Master	- Creates the network. - Registers peers into the network. - Acts as a peer. - It is the center of the activities. - Broadcasts and file multicast limited to Master-Slave model. - Coordinates the recovery after network problems.	- Creates the network. - Registers peers into the network. - Acts as a peer; it knows and handles several peer groups. - Tends to be the center of the activity, but it depends on the application. - All communications peer-to-peer. - Coordinates the recovery after network problems.
Slave	- Can communicate with Master directly. - May communicate with other peers, depending on the configuration. - Doesn't have access to all functions.	- Can communicate with Master directly. - Can communicate will all peers in the group directly. - Has access to all functions.

frameworks are in the coordinating protocol and the methods for peer registry, but the outcome is the same.

Lastly, the AF network handles the groups directly at its level. The Edunova framework allows the creation of groups, but at a higher level, above the network layer.

Table 6 shows the services provided by each network. The basic services are similar, and cover the main functions a network must provide for a collaborative activity. Both networks function mainly at the Session (layer 5) and Transport (layer 4) levels of the OSI model [13]. However, there are some differences.

Regarding the transport protocols, the Edunova network allows sending messages both through TCP and UDP, while the AF network implements its own trusted protocol over UDP. UDP has less overhead than TCP, but it's not trustworthy. AF's protocol is similar to TCP, but lighter. Each time a message is received, an acknowledgement is sent back. In case this acknowledgement does not arrive after a certain amount of time, the message is assumed lost, and the higher application is notified.

Both networks have a recovery mechanism, in case a peer drops out of the network. The Master is constantly sending a broadcast containing the basic network configuration. In Edunova, it also includes the activity state. When a peer resets its network interface, it is able to detect the recovery message, and uses it to re-enter the network. In both frameworks it communicates with the Master to be re-accepted. In Edunova, it also returns to the place it was in the activity before it dropped out. In the case of AF, there is an activity recovery mechanism, where the Master and the Slave coordinate to return to the previous state. Due to the fact that AF activities are more generic, the implementation

Table 6. Description of the services provided by the networks in Edunova and AF

Services	Edunova	AF
Send Text Messages	Sends messages between Master and Slaves. There has to be some additional setup to send messages between Slaves. Allows trusted (TCP) and not trusted (UDP) communications.	Sends messages, usually smaller, between all members of a group, or to or from the Master. Uses a trusted protocol over UDP.
Send Binary Messages	Sends binary data in the same way as a text message.	(No corresponding service)
Send Broadcasts	Sends broadcasts to the entire logic network from the Master.	Sends broadcasts to the entire logic network, or to a group, from any peer.
Send Files	Sends files through TCP between two peers, or multicast through UDP (from Master to all the Slaves).	Sends files through TCP between any pair of peers.
Recovery	Can return to the network and the activity state if disconnected.	Can return to the network if disconnected. May return automatically to the activity state if the application detailed the structure of a state.
Saving and Loading ofStates	(No corresponding service)	Can save the network state to the device, and load it later. May save the activity state and load it later if the application detailed the structure of a state.

of the state structure for the activities is left to be defined by the application, though the recovery of such state is handled by the framework automatically.

3   Empiric Framework Comparison

3.1   Test Environment

The PDAs used were Compaq iPAQ Pocket PC h3760. Each one has an Intel StrongARM 1110 processor at 206 MHz, with 64 MB of SDRAM memory, running over Microsoft Pocket PC 2002. The network interface is the Compaq WL110 Wireless PC Card, Wi-Fi certified, working at 11 Mbps (802.11b [14] specification). These cards were setup in ad-hoc mode, so there was no need for an access point.

Due to the short battery life of the PDAs, the tests were run having all the devices plugged in to their power sources. In this way we avoided the possible negative effect of differently charged batteries, or low power of a device.

3.2   Experiments

These experiments are intended to get a measure of the behavior of both networks under typical conditions. The service evaluated was the sending of text messages through a trusted protocol. The values measured were the latency (time between the moment when the message was sent by a peer, and the moment when it was received by the destiny peer, measured in milliseconds) and the percentage of lost messages (proportion between the total amount of messages that were received, and the total amount of messages sent). Both give an idea of the behavior and limits of each platform and network.

The parameters that were controlled for the measurements were three: the amount of network peers, the size of the message, and the time between sending one message and the next. This last parameter allows controlling indirectly the frequency of the messages. Each one of the tests was repeated at least five times in each peer, to get stability in the values measured. The averages were calculated among all the peers to get the final values.

Table 7. Controlled parameters

Parameter	Values Used
Amount of peers	2, 4, 8
Message size	From 1 B to 1024 B
Time between messages	From 1 ms to 4096 ms

For each framework, we developed small test applications. The logic of the program is the same in both frameworks; only the use of the corresponding services varies. In Edunova, we designed an activity to handle the experiments, and an extra plugin with the new functionality required. In AF, we created a specific new plugin, which implements the required experiments. Both applications simulated the environment conditions of traffic in a network, to evaluate its performance with minimal interference from the higher layers.

Experiment 1. An evaluation of the performance in mutual communication. Peer-to-peer communication was simulated, with each peer sending messages to each of the rest of the peers in the network. This simulates the traffic occurring when the peers are working collaboratively in a group. In this experiment, the Master is considered just another peer.

Experiment 2. An evaluation of the capacity of the Master (peer) to receive messages from the peers. It measures how much traffic the Master can handle in the different scenarios. All the peers send messages continuously to the Master. This simulates the messages that the Master receives when supervising the work on the network.

Experiment 3. Combination of experiment 2 and traffic from the Master. The Master receives messages from all the peers, and is also continuously sending messages back at them. This experiment is the closest one to the functioning of a Master/Slave network.

4   Results

Here we present the results obtained with the experiments on both networks.

From the results of the first experiment in Fig. 3, we can see that the distributions bear a certain similarity between both networks, but differ in some considerable aspects. The latencies of both networks are very different, with the ones in AF being much higher than the ones in Edunova. While Edunova has a tendency to stabilize along 50 ms, and it peaks no more than 200 ms, AF is more stable around 1300 ms for large messages, and peaks up to 2300 ms. These differences show that, in peer-to-peer high traffic mode, Edunova is around 10 times faster than AF.

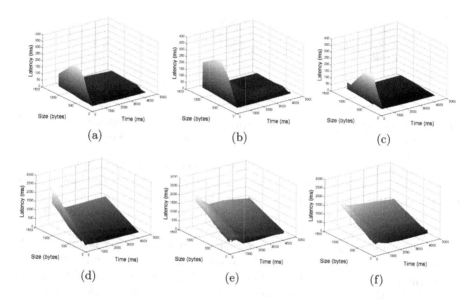

Fig. 3. Peer average behavior in experiment 1. First row: Edunova, with (a) 2, (b) 4 and (c) 8 peers. Second row: AF, with (d) 2, (e) 4 and (f) 8 peers.

The tendency in Edunova is to have high latencies when there is little time between messages, and to remain more stable for any values after that. AF is more strongly affected by the size of the messages, and shows a higher latency with larger messages. Also, in AF, the highest latency is at the point of higher message size and lower time between messages, as it should be expected. In Edunova, however, there seems to be a peak around 500 - 1000 bytes, and then the latency goes down. This is probably due to the fragmentation of packages around that message size, which speeds up the data transfer.

In Fig. 4, we can see the results of the second experiment. In Edunova, the graphics are stable and unaffected by the time between messages, except for some brief peaks at the lowest times. The rest of the time, the latency peaks up to 500 ms, and goes steadily down along with the package size. In AF, the same tendency observed in the previous experiment is maintained, having the

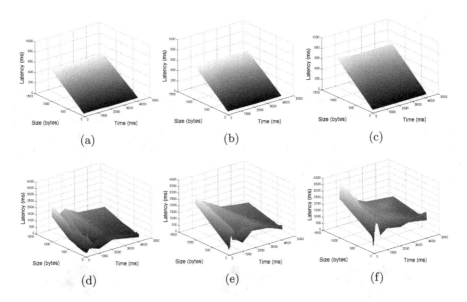

Fig. 4. Behavior of the Slave peers in experiment 2. First row: Edunova, with (a) 2, (b) 4 and (c) 8 peers. Second row: AF, with (d) 2, (e) 4 and (f) 8 peers.

highest latency when the message size is highest and the time is lowest. The lowest latency values are observed when the message sizes are smallest and the in-between times are highest. The latency in AF peaks up to 3000 ms, but it tends to stabilize around 1000 - 1500 ms for large messages. In this case, Edunova is around twice as fast as AF, and more stable in its results.

The behavior of the peers in Edunova shows that the Master is able to with-stand the traffic from the peers, and it is only barely affected by the frequency of the messages. This is probably due to the Master/Slave design of Edunova's network. In AF, the peaks are more notorious than in the previous case, and the rest of the time the latency is stable. This shows that AF is strongly af-fected when there is high traffic, but it is stable in other cases, even with large messages, due to its particular protocol.

Figure 5 shows the results of the Master peer in experiment number 3. The shapes of the graphics are similar for both networks. In Edunova the peaks are around 90 - 110 ms, and the latency stabilizes around 50 ms for large messages. In AF, the peaks are near 2300 ms, and it stabilizes around 1000 ms for large messages. It can also be seen that in Edunova with 8 peers, there is an increase of the latencies with small packages and small in-between times, probably due to the high amount of traffic that this situation generates. AF has a similar shape, but it is not affected by the number of peers; the graphics show only a peak for lower in-between times and larger messages.

Edunova seems to be unstable in this experiment with many peers, because the Master is not designed for constant bi-directional communication. Its protocols are optimized for receiving messages, or sending them to peers, but the Master is unstable if it has to do both things at a time. AF is very stable, even with

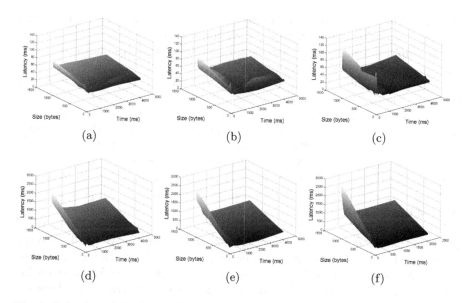

Fig. 5. Behavior of the Master peer in experiment 3. First row: Edunova, with (a) 2, (b) 4 and (c) 8 peers. Second row: AF, with (d) 2, (e) 4 and (f) 8 peers.

Table 8. Percentages of messages lost

Number of peers	Edunova (%)			AF (%)		
	2	4	8	2	4	8
Experiment 1	0	1.068	1.739	0	0.398	0.444
Experiment 2	0	0	0	1.111	3.504	10.51
Experiment 3, Master	0	0	0.0360	0	0	0
Experiment 3, Slaves	0	0	1.514	2.393	8.119	21.32

many peers, though the same tendency to be strongly affected by high traffic is maintained. The time AF protocols need to process the messages is an important factor when there is little time between the messages.

Regarding the packages lost, it can be seen in Table 8 that Edunova is more trustworthy than AF on average. However, in the first experiment, AF looses fewer packages than Edunova. This may be because AF is a little more oriented to pure peer-to-peer than Edunova. In the second experiment, Edunova has a far higher performance than AF. This may be due to the fact that Edunova's Master is more suited for Master/Slave activities, and therefore can handle better the reception of many peers communicating with it at once.

5   Conclusions and Future Work

We have presented two frameworks developed for collaborative activities. Both frameworks have similar purposes and services, though one is more generic than the other. The networks of each framework offer the same kind of services, though the implementation and protocols in each one of them are different.

The empirical results show that the targeted framework (Edunova) is, in general, much faster in its message sending, especially with more users and larger message sizes. It also appears to be more trustworthy. Its better results are probably due to being custom-made, and to the use of embedded C++. Being custom-made for the activities it supports, it is more finely-tuned for the services required, and makes the components more efficient in their communications. Embedded C++ offers a degree of control, speed and efficiency that is much higher than the one .NET can provide. However, the generic framework (AF) still presents an environment in which the development of activities is faster and easier. It also provides platform-independence, and the support for many types of collaborative activities.

Selecting the best traits of each framework could be very useful in creating a platform that would have the advantages of both systems. If AF can be brought up to speed with Edunova, it would become a competitive generic framework, while still allowing for easier development and maintenance. Working on improved transport protocols, and tuning the network parameters and mechanisms, could yield a substantial improvement in AF's performance.

References

1. Edwards, W., Newman, M., Sedivy, J., Smith, T., Balfanz, D., Smetters, D., Wong, H., Izadi, S.: Using Speakeasy for Ad-Hoc Peer-to-Peer Collaboration. In: Proceedings of the CSCW'02, ACM (2002)
2. Zurita, G., Nussbaum, M.: Computer Supported Collaborative Learning Using Wirelessly Interconnected Handheld Computers. Computers & Education 42 (3) (2004) 289–314
3. Iwata, T., Miyazaki, S., Takemoto, M., Ueda, K., Sunaga, H.: P2P Platform Implementation on PDAs organizing Ad Hoc Wireless Network. In: Proceedings of the International Symposium on Applications and the Internet Workshops, IEEE Computer Society Press (2004)
4. Maibaum, N., Mundt, T.: JXTA: A Technology Facilitating Mobile Peer-To-Peer Networks. In: Proceedings of the International Mobility and Wireless Access Workshop, IEEE Computer Society Press (2002)
5. Sunaga, H., Takemoto, M., Iwata, T.: Advanced Peer-to-Peer Network Platform for Various Services - SIONet (Semantic Information Oriented Network). In: Proceedings of the Second International Conference on Peer-to-Peer Computing, IEEE Computer Society Press (2002)
6. Vedula, I., Han, R.: A Distributed Software System Architecture for Wireless Peer-to-peer Collaborative Learning. In: Proceedings of the Third IEEE International Conference on Advanced Learning Technologies, IEEE Computer Society Press (2003)
7. Thilliez, M., Delot, T., Lecomte, S., Bennani, N.: Hybrid Peer-To-Peer Model in Proximity Applications. In: Proceedings of the 17th International Conference on Advanced Information Networking and Applications, IEEE Computer Society Press (2003)

8. .NET Framework Homepage. (http://msdn.microsoft.com/netframework/)
9. Cortez, C., Nussbaum, M., Santelices, R., Rodriguez, P., Zurita, G.: Teaching Science with Mobile Computer Supported Collaborative Learning (MCSCL). In: Proceedings of the Second IEEE International Workshop on Wireless and Mobile Technologies In Education (WMTE 2004), IEEE Computer Society Press (2004) 67–74
10. Cortez, C., Nussbaum, M., Woywood, G.: LCC: Learning to Collaborate Collaborating, a Mobile Collaborative Activity for Learning Basics about Collaboration and Teamwork. (In: Working paper)
11. Java Technology, Sun Developer Network. (http://java.sun.com)
12. Winsock Reference. (http://msdn.microsoft.com/library/default.asp)
13. ISO/IEC JTC1, Information Technology - Open System Interconnection - OSI Reference Model: Part 1 - Basic Reference Model, ISO/IEC 7498-1: (1994)
14. IEEE 802.11: Protocol Standard for Wireless LANs. (http://standards.ieee.org/getieee802/802.11.html)

Fault Tolerant Time Synchronization for Wireless Sensor Networks

Soyoung Hwang and Yunju Baek

Department of Computer Science and Engineering,
Pusan National University, Busan 609-735, South Korea
{youngox, yunju}@pnu.edu

Abstract. Time synchronization is a prerequisite in sensor network applications such as object tracking, consistent state updates, duplicate detection, and temporal order delivery. In addition, reliability issues and fault tolerance in sophisticated sensor networks have become a critical area of research today. However, most research on time synchronization does not consider clock faults of nodes such as fluctuation, severe changes in drift rate, and so on. In this paper, we propose a fault tolerant time synchronization method for wireless sensor networks. In the proposed method, two cases of fault model: (1) clock faults and (2) network faults (topology changes) are assumed. In order to evaluate the performance of the proposed method, a simulation model is established in the NESLsim based on the PARSEC platform. In the simulation, the effect of clock faults is analyzed. Simulation results show that the proposed scheme has about 1.5x~2x better performance than TPSN (Timing-sync Protocol for Sensor Networks) in the presence of faults.

1 Introduction

A sensor network is composed of a large number of sensor nodes which have sensing, computation and wireless communication capabilities. Sensor network applications need synchronized time to the highest degree such as object tracking, consistent state updates, duplicate detection, and temporal order delivery. In addition to these domain-specific requirements, sensor network applications often rely on synchronization as typical distributed systems do: for secure cryptographic schemes, coordination of future action, ordering logged events during system debugging, and so forth [1]. Besides, reliability issues and fault tolerance in sophisticated sensor networks have become a critical area of research today. From a fault-tolerant computational perspective this encompasses issues like: (1) the integration of information in real-time when the clocks at the nodes are not so perfect, (2) the transmission and integration of information without incurring heavy losses (communication, information or otherwise), and (3) the fault tolerance of the network topology in the presence of not working or dead nodes [2]. These issues are closely connected with time synchronization in sensor networks to improve synchronization accuracy and reliability; but there is little research on these problems.

W. Grass et al. (Eds.): ARCS 2006, LNCS 3894, pp. 480–493, 2006.

This paper proposes a fault tolerant time synchronization for wireless sensor networks. In the proposed scheme, we assume two cases of fault model: (1) clock faults and (2) network faults. The clock faults mean timing faults such as fluctuation of clocks, changes in drift rate, and so on. The network faults mean communication or crash faults due to hardware failure, moving of nodes, or running out of energy which bring topology changes. Simulation results show that the proposed method has about 1.5x~2x better performance than TPSN [3] in the presence of faults.

The remainder of this paper is structured as follows. In section 2 related work and motivation are discussed. Section 3 describes proposed fault tolerant time synchronization method. Next, simulation and performance analysis are presented in section 4. Finally, we conclude in section 5.

2 Related Work

2.1 Traditional Time Synchronization Protocols

Most traditional time synchronization protocols share the same basic design: a connection-less messaging protocol, exchange of clock information between client and server(s), methods to reduce the effects of random non-deterministic communication delay, and a method to upgrade the client time based on the information from the server [4]. Several standard time synchronization protocols were defined in a series of RFC (Request for Comments) documents. The three major time synchronization protocols are the Time Protocol, the Daytime Protocol, and the Network Time Protocol (NTP). NTP is widely deployed in the internet, since it is scalable, robust and has good performance. It consists of various stratums of servers in a hierarchy providing synchronization to the clients which are leaves in a hierarchical tree [5].

Table 1. Internet time synchronization protocols

Name	Document	Format
Time Protocol	RFC-868	– Unformatted 32-bit binary number – UTC seconds since January 1, 1900
Daytime Protocol	RFC-867	– Exact format not specified in standard – Time code as standard ASCII characters
Network Time Protocol (NTP)	RFC-1305	– 64-bit timestamp – UTC seconds since January 1, 1900
Simple NTP (SNTP)	RFC-1769	– Same format with NTP version 3

2.2 Time Synchronization Protocols in Sensor Networks

Since the characteristic of sensor nodes with limited computation and energy, traditional time synchronization protocols in distributed systems can not be applied to the sensor networks directly. So existing synchronization methods are revised or new approaches are proposed to synchronize the sensor networks. In the following we survey time synchronization protocols for sensor networks and present a classification for the various approaches pursued.

In the first stage of research on time synchronization in sensor networks, most approaches are based on the synchronization model such as event ordering or relative clock. These methods do not synchronize the sensor node clocks but generate a right chronology of events or maintain relative clocks of nodes. From a viewpoint of network topology, synchronization coverage is limited in a single broadcast domain; however, typical wireless sensor networks operate in areas larger than the broadcast range of a single node, so network-wide time synchronization is needed essentially. Besides, adjusting the local clock has better efficiency than maintaining relative clocks since it requires more memory capacity and communication overheads. TPSN [3] and FTSP [6] are the representative ones which meet these requirements [7].

TPSN works in two phases: level discovery and synchronization. The aim of the first phase is to create a hierarchical topology in the network, where each node is assigned a level. Only one node is assigned level 0, the root node. In the second phase, a node of level i synchronizes to a node of level $i - 1$. At the end of the synchronization phase, all nodes are synchronized to the root node, and network-wide synchronization achieved [3]. The goal of the FTSP is to achieve a network wide synchronization of the local clocks of the participating nodes. The assumptions in FTSP are that each node has a local clock exhibiting the typical timing errors of crystals and can communicate over an unreliable but error corrected wireless link to its neighbors. The FTSP synchronizes the time of a sender to possibly multiple receivers utilizing a single radio message time-stamped at both the sender and the receiver sides. It compensates for the relevant error sources by utilizing the concepts of MAC layer time-stamping and skew compensation with linear regression [6].

FTSP achieves robustness against node and link failures by utilizing periodic flooding of synchronization message and implicit dynamic topology update. On the other hand, TPSN does not handle dynamic topology changes; however, FTSP can not be applied generally since the synchronization accuracy in FTSP is seriously affected by the analyzed source of delays and uncertainties which are varied according to changes of the systems. Our previous work, RTSP solves these problems by maintaining candidate parents list and performing pair-wise synchronization. It handles topology changes through candidate parent and improves synchronization accuracy through constructing a tree with lower depth and pair-wise synchronization [8].

Recently, reliability and fault tolerance in sensor networks have become critical issues; however, most research on time synchronization does not consider clock faults of nodes such as fluctuation, severe changes in drift rate, and so on. If these faults are not considered in a synchronization mechanism, the synchronization error is propagated hugely in the network. Therefore, new approaches are required to manage these problems.

3   Fault Tolerant Time Synchronization

In the following, we present a synchronization method called *Fault Tolerant Time Synchronization* (FTTS) for wireless sensor networks. As mentioned before, reliability and fault tolerance issues are increased in sensor networks. In this paper, we consider two cases of fault model.

3.1   Fault Model

A sensor node fails when its output deviates from the desired value. Communication faults occur due to hardware failure, moving of nodes, or energy depletion. These faults can be permanent, temporary or transient [2].

From a viewpoint of clock management, a clock H is correct if it measures the length $t' - t$ of any real time interval $[t, t']$ with an error of at most $\rho(t - t')$, where ρ is the maximum clock drift rate from external (or real) time specified by the clock manufacturer:

$$(1 - \rho)(t - t') \leq H(t) - H(t') \leq (1 + \rho)(t - t')$$

A clock fault occurs if the previous clock correctness condition is violated. Examples of clock fault types are: crash faults (e.g. the clock stops), timing faults (e.g. a change in the frequency of the quartz oscillator driving the clock counter causes the clock value to be incremented too fast or too slowly), and Byzantine faults [9].

In this paper, we assume two cases of fault model: (1) clock faults and (2) network faults. The clock faults mean timing faults such as fluctuation of clock, changes in drift rate, and so on. The network faults mean communication or crash faults due to hardware failure, moving of nodes, or running out of energy which bring topology changes.

3.2   Basic Concept

The proposed FTTS works in two phases. It is assumed that: (1) nodes in the network have a unique ID, (2) root clock has no clock fault, and (3) a synchronization group meets the following condition $n \geq 3m + 1$ where n is the number of nodes and m is the number of fault nodes. It does not need that each node is aware of the neighbor set. The management of neighbor nodes is included in the operation of the scheme.

In the first phase – hierarchical topology setup – a hierarchical topology is created in the network. Root node with level 0 initiates topology setup. A node receives topology setup messages and assigns its level by selecting a parent with lowest level to reduce the depth of tree in the network. This improves synchronization accuracy since the accuracy is a function of the construction and depth of the tree in network-wide multi-hop time synchronization. Other parent information is stored in the reference parent list for fault management. Eventually every node is assigned a level and a tree structure is constructed.

In the second phase – fault tolerant synchronization – a node belonging to level i exchanges time-stamp messages and calculates offset and delay with its parent node and two reference nodes from the reference parent list which are belonging to level $i-1$. It removes a false-ticker node and synchronizes to one of the true-chimer nodes using averaged offset. When a node can not communicate with its parent or reference nodes, it selects another parent in the reference list and performs synchronization. If the reference list is empty, it requests level setup to its neighbors and assigns a new level, a new parent and reference parents.

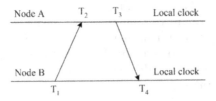

Fig. 1. Measuring delay and offset

As in the NTP, the roundtrip delay and clock offset between two nodes A and B are determined by a procedure in which timestamps are exchanged via wireless communication links between them. The procedure involves the four most recent timestamps numbered as shown in figure 1. The measured roundtrip delay δ and clock offset θ of B relative to A are given by [10]

$$\delta = (T_4 - T_1) - (T_3 - T_2), \ \theta = \frac{(T_2 - T_1) + (T_3 - T_4)}{2}.$$

Figure 2 shows how to define a false-ticker. First, a node exchanges time-stamp messages with its parent node and two reference nodes. Then, it calculates offsets and delays respectively. After that, it averages offsets and finds majority using averaged offset. A false-ticker is defined as what is not included in the majority. A node synchronizes to one of the true-chimer nodes.

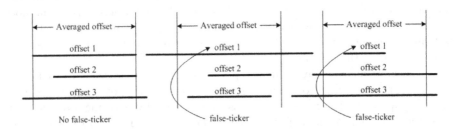

Fig. 2. Defining a false-ticker

3.3 Protocol Description

(1) The first phase: Hierarchical topology setup
In the first phase, a hierarchical topology is created in the network. This phase enforces to create a tree structure with lower depth and reference parent list is generated to manage fault of nodes in the network. Figure 3 shows the operations of the first phase.

Step 1: The root node initiates topology setup phase. Level 0 is assigned to the root node. It broadcasts topology setup message with its ID and its level.

Step 2: A node receives topology setup message during pre-defined time interval. Root node discards this message. It selects a parent with the lowest level number from received messages and stores other information to the reference parent list according to the level number. Then it broadcasts topology setup message with its ID and its level.

Step 3: Each node in the network performs step 2 and eventually every node is assigned a level.

Step 4: When a node does not receive topology setup message or a new node joins the network, it waits for some time to be assigned a level. If it is not assigned a level within that period, it broadcasts topology setup request message and then performs step 2 with reply of its neighbors.

(2) The second phase: Fault tolerant synchronization
In the second phase, a node belonging to level i synchronizes to a true-chimer node which is one of parent or reference nodes by exchanging time-stamp messages. When a node can not communicate with its parent or reference nodes, it selects another parent in the reference list and performs synchronization. Operations of the second phase are presented in figure 4.

Step 1: The root node initiates synchronization phase by broadcasting synchronization pulse.

Step 2: On receiving synchronization pulse, nodes belonging to level 1 exchange time-stamp message with the root node and adjust the local clock and then broadcast synchronization pulse.

Step 3: On receiving synchronization pulse, each node belonging to level i exchanges time-stamp message with its parent and two reference nodes. It removes a false-ticker node (if it presents) and synchronizes one of the true-chimer nodes using averaged offset. Eventually every node is synchronized. Once it receives a synchronization pulse, it discards additional pulses from other upper level nodes.

Step 4: When a node can not communicate with its parent or reference nodes, it selects another parent in the reference list, updates own level (if it is needed) and performs step 3. The level of its child nodes will be updated when they execute synchronization. If the reference list is empty, it performs step 4 of the topology setup phase ahead. The reference list can be updated periodically by listening to communications of neighbors.

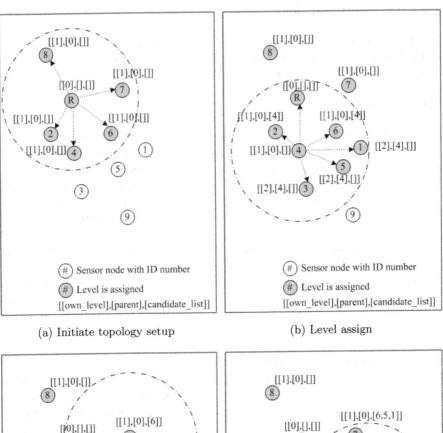

(a) Initiate topology setup

(b) Level assign

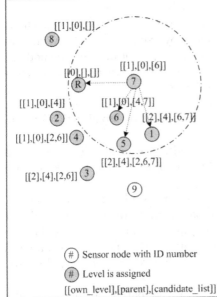

(c) Level and candidate assign

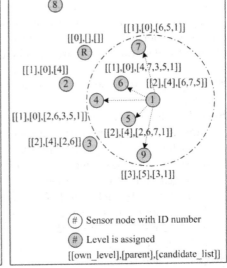

(d) Level and candidate assign

Fig. 3. Hierarchical topology setup

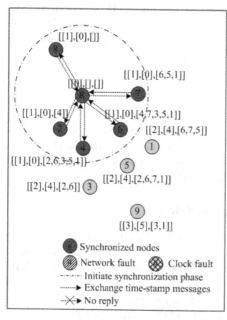

(a) Initiate synchronization

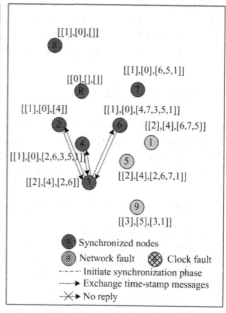

(b) Exchange time-stamp messages

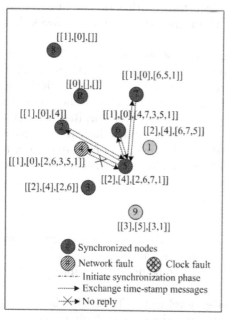

(c) Network fault handling

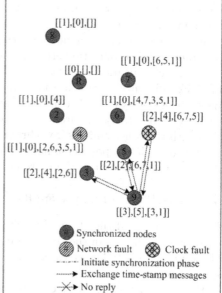

(d) Clock fault handling

Fig. 4. Fault tolerant synchronization

When the root node fails, a node which has the lowest ID in the next level takes it over. The synchronization accuracy may be improved by utilizing the concepts of MAC layer time-stamping and the random back-off mechanism can be adapted to avoid the collision of wireless links.

4   Experiments

In order to evaluate the performance of the proposed method, we established a simulation model in the NESLsim based on the PARSEC platform [11, 12]. In NESLsim, a sensor network is modeled as a collection of sensor nodes, a channel, and a supervising entity to create the nodes [11].

4.1   Environment and Performance Metrics

N nodes are deployed in a uniformly random fashion over a sensor terrain of size 100×100. Each node has a transmission range of 28. The number of nodes, N, is varied from 100 to 300 with step of 50. The setup includes a CSMA MAC. The radio speed is 19.2kb/s, similar to the UC Berkeley MICA Motes, and every packet has a fixed size of 128bits. The granularity of the node clocks, which is the minimum accuracy attainable, is 10μs. The clock model used in simulations has been derived from the characteristics of the oscillators used in sensor nodes. The frequency drift is varied randomly with time, within the specified range, to model the temporal variations in temperature. All sensor node clocks drift independently of each other [13].

Followings are performance metrics in the experiments: (1) synchronization accuracy or synchronization error, (2) number of messages and (3) synchronized ratio. Synchronization accuracy is defined as average and standard deviation of clock differences between a node and a root node. Number of messages is a measure of energy costs. It consists of send, receive and overhear. Receive means reception with its own address or broadcast address and overhear means reception with the other address. Synchronized ratio is a metric of fault tolerance. It is defined as the proportion of nodes that their synchronization error is bounded in defined accuracy when there are faults.

4.2   The Effect of Clock Faults

First, we analyzed the effect of clock faults since there are few researches considering clock faults. In the simulation environment, 200 nodes are deployed and clock faults are set. The clock of fault nodes set to be fluctuated rapidly or fault nodes have error in drift rate.

Figure 5 shows the effect of fault nodes' level in the TPSN. In the simulation, 1% nodes are set as clock fault nodes and the clock of fault nodes set to be fluctuated rapidly. The y-axis represents the proportion of nodes that their synchronization error is bounded in $m + 3\sigma$ where m is average and σ is standard deviation when there is no fault of nodes. The synchronization error is defined as the difference between the clocks of the sensor nodes and the root node. As

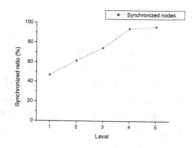

Fig. 5. The effect of fault nodes' level

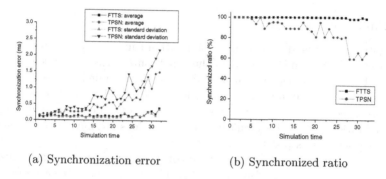

(a) Synchronization error   (b) Synchronized ratio

Fig. 6. The effect of clock fault

Table 2. Number of messages

	Total	Send	Receive	Overhear
FTTS	43459	1062	1073	41324
TPSN	16323	401	414	15508

can be seen in the result, the synchronization error is increased the more the fault nodes have the higher level.

In the following, we compare the effect of clock faults in the FTTS to that in the TPSN. In the simulation model, 200 nodes are deployed and 5 nodes are set as clock fault nodes. Clock fault nodes are set step by step during the simulation. First, 2 nodes are set as fault nodes, then each 1 node is set as a fault node additionally at each determined time up to 5 as simulation time goes by. The fault model is that fault nodes have error in drift rate. Figure 6 shows the synchronization accuracy and the synchronized ratio. The synchronized ratio represents the proportion of nodes that their synchronization error is bounded in defined error boundary of 1ms. Table 2 presents average number of messages each synchronization phase.

The proposed scheme, FTTS restricts the propagation of synchronization error when there are clock faults of nodes, but it needs improvement in the number of messages. Theoretically, FTTS has 3x amount in the number of messages than TPSN.

4.3   Simulation Model

In the proposed method, FTTS, two cases of fault model: (1) clock faults and (2) network faults are assumed. In the following simulation, we applied these fault model and analyzed synchronized ratio and number of messages during synchronization phase. A clock fault is set as error in drift rate of a node's clock; therefore, the clock is fluctuated. A network fault is set as communication failure between a node and its parent or reference node. These faults are set after first synchronization round. Simulations are performed when there are 10% clock fault of nodes, 10% clock fault and 10% network fault of nodes and 10% clock fault and 20% network fault of nodes. Fault nodes are selected randomly.

4.4   Simulation Results

All results are averaged over hundred simulation runs. The performance is compared to the TPSN and the RTSP. The synchronized ratio represents the proportion of nodes that their synchronization error is bounded in $m + 3\sigma$ where m is average and σ is standard deviation when there is no fault of nodes. The fault nodes are selected randomly and these nodes are excluded in calculating synchronized ratio. During the simulation, if a node does not have enough reference nodes, it synchronizes just to its parent node.

Table 3 and figure 7 show the number of messages and the synchronization accuracy when there is no fault of nodes. The FTTS has better performance than the TPSN in synchronization accuracy since it creates tree topology with lower depth according to the operation of the topology setup phase; however, the number of messages in the FTTS is more than that it the TPSN since it exchanges time-stamp messages with multiple reference nodes to discard a clock fault node.

Figure 8 depicts the synchronized ratio and the number of messages when there is 10% clock fault of nodes. The FTTS has 1.5x~2x better performance in synchronized ratio. The number of messages in the FTTS is 2.4x~2.8x more than that in the FTTS since it exchanges time-stamp messages with multiple reference nodes to discard a clock fault node; however, fault tolerant synchronization is a critical factor because clock error is propagated hop-by-hop.

Figure 9 shows the synchronized ratio and the number of messages when there is 10% clock fault and 10% network fault of nodes. The FTTS has 1.5x~2x

Table 3. Number of messages without fault

Nodes	Send			Receive			Overhear		
	FTTS	RTSP	TPSN	FTTS	RTSP	TPSN	FTTS	RTSP	TPSN
100	507	202	202	512	208	209	9354	3649	3650
150	795	303	305	803	312	320	22127	8251	8415
200	1092	404	406	1104	416	419	42006	15206	15318
250	1364	504	505	1380	519	529	65561	23815	24000
300	1665	604	605	1684	623	629	95986	34149	34519

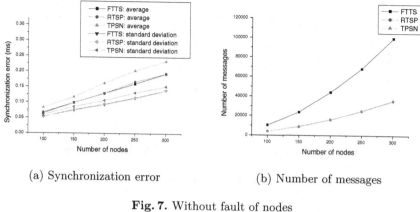

(a) Synchronization error   (b) Number of messages

Fig. 7. Without fault of nodes

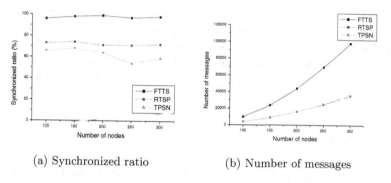

(a) Synchronized ratio   (b) Number of messages

Fig. 8. 10% clock fault of nodes

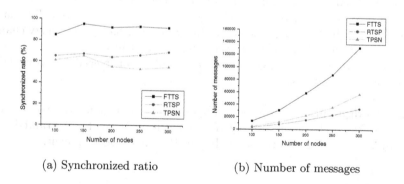

(a) Synchronized ratio   (b) Number of messages

Fig. 9. 10% clock fault and 10% network fault of nodes

better performance in synchronized ratio. The number of messages in the FTTS is 2.3x~2.8x more than that in the FTTS. Figure 10 shows the synchronized ratio and the number of messages when there is 10% clock fault and 20% network fault of nodes. The FTTS has 1.5x~2x better performance in synchronized ratio. The

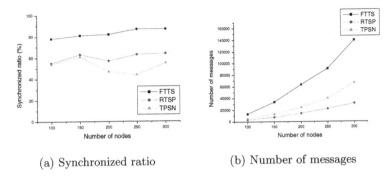

(a) Synchronized ratio   (b) Number of messages

Fig. 10. 10% clock fault and 20% network fault of nodes

number of messages in the FTTS is 2.1x~2.6x more than that in the FTTS. The number of messages in the FTTS is decreased the more the network fault ratio is increased since it handles dynamic topology changes with the candidate parent list as described in the operation of the fault tolerant synchronization phase.

As can be seen in the results, the proposed method has about 1.5x~2x better performance than TPSN in the presence of faults; however it needs improvement in the number of messages.

5   Conclusions

In this paper, we proposed a fault tolerant time synchronization method for wireless sensor networks considering two cases of fault model such as clock faults and network faults. The proposed scheme restricts the propagation of synchronization error when there are clock faults of nodes such as rapid fluctuation, severe changes in drift rate, and so on. In addition, it handles topology changes. Simulation results show that the proposed method has about 1.5x~2x better performance than TPSN in the presence of faults; but it needs improvement in the number of messages.

Acknowledgment. This work was supported by the Regional Research Centers Program (Research Center for Logistics Information Technology), granted by the Korean Ministry of Education and Human Resources Development.

References

1. Elson, J., Romer, K.: Wireless Sensor Networks: A new regime for time synchronization, ACM Computer Communication Review 33(1), pp.149–154, 2003.
2. Jacob, C. and Mathai, R.J.: Fault tolerance in sensor networks: A survey of fault tolerant sensor network algorithms and techniques, ECE753, Univ. of Wisconsin, Madison, 2004.

3. Ganeriwal, S. Kumar, R., Srivastava, M.B.: Timing-sync protocol for sensor networks, Proceedings of the ACM International Conference on Embedded Networked Sensor Systems, pp.138–149, 2003.
4. PalChaudhuri, S., Saha, R.K., Johnson, D.B.: Adaptive clock synchronization in sensor networks, Proceedings of the ACM International Conference on Embedded Networked Sensor Systems, pp.139–149, 2004.
5. Lombardi, M.: Computer time synchronization, Time and Frequency Division, NIST, http://tf.nist.gov
6. Maroti, M., Kusy, B., Simon, G., Ledeczi, A.: The flooding time synchronization protocol, Proceedings of the ACM International Conference on Embedded Networked Sensor Systems, pp.39–49, 2004.
7. Hwang, S., Baek, Y.: A survey on time synchronization for wireless sensor networks, ESLAB Technical Report, 2004.
8. Hwang, S., Baek, Y.: Reliable time synchronization protocol for wireless sensor networks, Proceedings of the IFIP International Conference on Embedded And Ubiquitous Computing, pp.663–672, 2005.
9. Cristian, F.: A probabilistic approach to distributed clock synchronization, Proceedings of the IEEE International Conference on Distributed Computing Systems, pp.288–296, 1989.
10. Mills, D.L: Network Time Protocol (Version 3) Specification, Implementation and Analysis, RFC1305, 1992.
11. Ganeriwal, S., Tsiatsis, V., Schurgers, C., Srivastava, M.B.: NESLsim: A parsec based simulation platform for sensor networks, NESL, 2002.
12. PARSEC User Manual, http://pcl.cs.ucla.edu/projects/parsec, 1999.
13. Ganeriwal, S., Kumar, R., Adlakha, S., Srivastava, M.B.: Network-wide time synchronization in sensor networks, NESL Technical Report, 2003.

Author Index

Aisopos, Konstantinos 114
Ali, Shoukat 17
Amft, Oliver 99
Anliker, Urs 217

Baek, Yunju 480
Bannach, David 99
Bell, Ian 252
Ben Atitallah, Rabie 298
Bharatula, Nagendra Bhargava 217
Biles, Stuart 283
Bohn, Jürgen 69
Bueno-Delgado, M. Victoria 382

Chen, Xiaoyong 191
Cher, Chen-Yong 232
Choi, Lynn 407
Chu, Yul 130

de la Hamette, Patrick 31
Dekeyser, Jean Luc 298
Dittrich, Steffen 202
Dutta, Hritam 176
Dybdahl, Haakon 145
Dynia, Miroslaw 341

Echeverría, Sebastián 465
Egea-López, Esteban 382
Eliassen, Frank 84

Fenne, Martin 56

Gade, Arul Sandeep 130
García-Haro, Joan 367, 382
Ghosh, Mrinmoy 283
Grannæs, Marius 145
Greiner, Alain 298
Grundmann, Kai 435

Han, Tack-Don 160
Hannig, Frank 176
Harn, Lein 422
Hasasneh, Nabil 252
Haubelt, Christian D. 202

Hoareau, Didier 450
Hwang, Soyoung 480

Imai, Hideki 422

Jesshope, Chris 252
Jóźwiak, Lech 1

Kaxiras, Stefanos 114
Keramidas, Georgios 114
Kim, Dae Y. 407
Kim, Hye-Soo 397
Kim, Hyogon 407
Kim, Il-San 160
Kim, Jae-Won 397
Kim, Kyung-Su 160
Kim, Sunil 407
Ko, Sung-Jea 397
Koch, Dirk 202
Korzeniowski, Miroslaw 341
Kunze, Kai 99

Lafond, Sébastien 311
Lee, Hsien-Hsin S. 283
Lee, Kil-Whan 160
Lee, Won-Jong 160
Lilius, Johan 311
Lukowicz, Paul 99, 217
Lundesgaard Amundsen, Sten 84

Maciejewski, Anthony A. 17
Mahéo, Yves 450
Malgosa-Sanahuja, Josemaria 367
Manzanares-Lopez, Pilar 367
Martínez-Sala, Alejandro S. 382
Maskell, Douglas L. 191
Meftali, Samy 298
Mihaljevic, Miodrag J. 422

Naroska, Edwin 435
Natvig, Lasse 145
Niar, Smail 298
Niemann, Jörg-Christian 268
Nussbaum, Miguel 42, 465

Özer, Emre   283

Park, Il   232
Park, Woo-Chan   160
Pavón-Mariño, Pablo   382
Platte, Jörg   435
Porrmann, Mario   268
Puttmann, Christoph   268

Rückert, Ulrich   268

Salomon, Ralf   352
Sanchez-Aarnoutse, Juan Carlos   367
Santelices, Raúl   465
Schindelhauer, Christian   341
Shestak, Vladimir   17
Shriraman, Arrvindh   326
Siegel, Howard Jay   17
Sill, Frank   352
Soundararajan, Niranjan   326

Stöcker, Benjamin   56
Streichert, Thilo   202
Strengert, Christian   202

Teich, Jürgen   176, 202
Tröster, Gerhard   31, 217

Vales-Alonso, Javier   382
Venkateswaran, Nagarajan   326
VijayKumar, T.N.   232

Wang, Jian   422
Wieland, Thomas   56

Yang, Sung-Bong   160
Yoon, Duk-Ki   160
Yun, Jae-Woong   397

Zurita, Gustavo   42

Lecture Notes in Computer Science

For information about Vols. 1–3792

please contact your bookseller or Springer

Vol. 3901: P.M. Hill (Ed.), Logic Based Program Synthesis and Transformation. X, 179 pages. 2006.

Vol. 3899: S. Frintrop, VOCUS: A Visual Attention System for Object Detection and Goal-Directed Search. XIV, 216 pages. 2006. (Sublibrary LNAI).

Vol. 3894: W. Grass, B. Sick, K. Waldschmidt (Eds.), Architecture of Computing Systems - ARCS 2006. XII, 496 pages. 2006.

Vol. 3889: J. Rosca, D. Erdogmus, J.C. Príncipe, S. Haykin (Eds.), Independent Component Analysis and Blind Signal Separation. XXI, 980 pages. 2006.

Vol. 3884: B. Durand, W. Thomas (Eds.), STACS 2006. XIV, 714 pages. 2006.

Vol. 3881: S. Gibet, N. Courty, J.-F. Kamp (Eds.), Gesture in Human-Computer Interaction and Simulation. XIII, 344 pages. 2006. (Sublibrary LNAI).

Vol. 3879: T. Erlebach, G. Persinao (Eds.), Approximation and Online Algorithms. X, 349 pages. 2006.

Vol. 3878: A. Gelbukh (Ed.), Computational Linguistics and Intelligent Text Processing. XVII, 589 pages. 2006.

Vol. 3877: M. Detyniecki, J.M. Jose, A. Nürnberger, C. J. '. van Rijsbergen (Eds.), Adaptive Multimedia Retrieval: User, Context, and Feedback. XI, 279 pages. 2006.

Vol. 3876: S. Halevi, T. Rabin (Eds.), Theory of Cryptography. XI, 617 pages. 2006.

Vol. 3875: S. Ur, E. Bin, Y. Wolfsthal (Eds.), Haifa Verification Conference. X, 265 pages. 2006.

Vol. 3874: R. Missaoui, J. Schmidt (Eds.), Formal Concept Analysis. X, 309 pages. 2006. (Sublibrary LNAI).

Vol. 3873: L. Maicher, J. Park (Eds.), Charting the Topic Maps Research and Applications Landscape. VIII, 281 pages. 2006. (Sublibrary LNAI).

Vol. 3872: H. Bunke, A. L. Spitz (Eds.), Document Analysis Systems VII. XIII, 630 pages. 2006.

Vol. 3870: S. Spaccapietra, P. Atzeni, W.W. Chu, T. Catarci, K.P. Sycara (Eds.), Journal on Data Semantics V. XIII, 237 pages. 2006.

Vol. 3869: S. Renals, S. Bengio (Eds.), Machine Learning for Multimodal Interaction. XIII, 490 pages. 2006.

Vol. 3868: K. Römer, H. Karl, F. Mattern (Eds.), Wireless Sensor Networks. XI, 342 pages. 2006.

Vol. 3863: M. Kohlhase (Ed.), Mathematical Knowledge Management. XI, 405 pages. 2006. (Sublibrary LNAI).

Vol. 3861: J. Dix, S.J. Hegner (Eds.), Foundations of Information and Knowledge Systems. X, 331 pages. 2006.

Vol. 3860: D. Pointcheval (Ed.), Topics in Cryptology – CT-RSA 2006. XI, 365 pages. 2006.

Vol. 3858: A. Valdes, D. Zamboni (Eds.), Recent Advances in Intrusion Detection. X, 351 pages. 2006.

Vol. 3857: M.P.C. Fossorier, H. Imai, S. Lin, A. Poli (Eds.), Applied Algebra, Algebraic Algorithms and Error-Correcting Codes. XI, 350 pages. 2006.

Vol. 3855: E. A. Emerson, K.S. Namjoshi (Eds.), Verification, Model Checking, and Abstract Interpretation. XI, 443 pages. 2005.

Vol. 3853: A.J. Ijspeert, T. Masuzawa, S. Kusumoto (Eds.), Biologically Inspired Approaches to Advanced Information Technology. XIV, 388 pages. 2006.

Vol. 3852: P.J. Narayanan, S.K. Nayar, H.-Y. Shum (Eds.), Computer Vision - ACCV 2006, Part II. XXXI, 977 pages. 2005.

Vol. 3851: P.J. Narayanan, S.K. Nayar, H.-Y. Shum (Eds.), Computer Vision - ACCV 2006, Part I. XXXI, 973 pages. 2006.

Vol. 3850: R. Freund, G. Păun, G. Rozenberg, A. Salomaa (Eds.), Membrane Computing. IX, 371 pages. 2006.

Vol. 3849: I. Bloch, A. Petrosino, A.G.B. Tettamanzi (Eds.), Fuzzy Logic and Applications. XIV, 438 pages. 2006. (Sublibrary LNAI).

Vol. 3848: J.-F. Boulicaut, L. De Raedt, H. Mannila (Eds.), Constraint-Based Mining and Inductive Databases. X, 401 pages. 2006. (Sublibrary LNAI).

Vol. 3847: K.P. Jantke, A. Lunzer, N. Spyratos, Y. Tanaka (Eds.), Federation over the Web. X, 215 pages. 2006. (Sublibrary LNAI).

Vol. 3846: H. J. van den Herik, Y. Björnsson, N.S. Netanyahu (Eds.), Computers and Games. XIV, 333 pages. 2006.

Vol. 3845: J. Farré, I. Litovsky, S. Schmitz (Eds.), Implementation and Application of Automata. XIII, 360 pages. 2006.

Vol. 3844: J.-M. Bruel (Ed.), Satellite Events at the MoDELS 2005 Conference. XIII, 360 pages. 2006.

Vol. 3843: P. Healy, N.S. Nikolov (Eds.), Graph Drawing. XVII, 536 pages. 2006.

Vol. 3842: H.T. Shen, J. Li, M. Li, J. Ni, W. Wang (Eds.), Advanced Web and Network Technologies, and Applications. XXVII, 1057 pages. 2006.

Vol. 3841: X. Zhou, J. Li, H.T. Shen, M. Kitsuregawa, Y. Zhang (Eds.), Frontiers of WWW Research and Development - APWeb 2006. XXIV, 1223 pages. 2006.

Vol. 3840: M. Li, B. Boehm, L.J. Osterweil (Eds.), Unifying the Software Process Spectrum. XVI, 522 pages. 2006.

Vol. 3839: J.-C. Filliâtre, C. Paulin-Mohring, B. Werner (Eds.), Types for Proofs and Programs. VIII, 275 pages. 2006.

Vol. 3838: A. Middeldorp, V. van Oostrom, F. van Raamsdonk, R. de Vrijer (Eds.), Processes, Terms and Cycles: Steps on the Road to Infinity. XVIII, 639 pages. 2005.

Vol. 3837: K. Cho, P. Jacquet (Eds.), Technologies for Advanced Heterogeneous Networks. IX, 307 pages. 2005.

Vol. 3836: J.-M. Pierson (Ed.), Data Management in Grids. X, 143 pages. 2006.

Vol. 3835: G. Sutcliffe, A. Voronkov (Eds.), Logic for Programming, Artificial Intelligence, and Reasoning. XIV, 744 pages. 2005. (Sublibrary LNAI).

Vol. 3834: D.G. Feitelson, E. Frachtenberg, L. Rudolph, U. Schwiegelshohn (Eds.), Job Scheduling Strategies for Parallel Processing. VIII, 283 pages. 2005.

Vol. 3833: K.-J. Li, C. Vangenot (Eds.), Web and Wireless Geographical Information Systems. XI, 309 pages. 2005.

Vol. 3832: D. Zhang, A.K. Jain (Eds.), Advances in Biometrics. XX, 796 pages. 2005.

Vol. 3831: J. Wiedermann, G. Tel, J. Pokorný, M. Bieliková, J. Štuller (Eds.), SOFSEM 2006: Theory and Practice of Computer Science. XV, 576 pages. 2006.

Vol. 3829: P. Pettersson, W. Yi (Eds.), Formal Modeling and Analysis of Timed Systems. IX, 305 pages. 2005.

Vol. 3828: X. Deng, Y. Ye (Eds.), Internet and Network Economics. XVII, 1106 pages. 2005.

Vol. 3827: X. Deng, D.-Z. Du (Eds.), Algorithms and Computation. XX, 1190 pages. 2005.

Vol. 3826: B. Benatallah, F. Casati, P. Traverso (Eds.), Service-Oriented Computing - ICSOC 2005. XVIII, 597 pages. 2005.

Vol. 3824: L.T. Yang, M. Amamiya, Z. Liu, M. Guo, F.J. Rammig (Eds.), Embedded and Ubiquitous Computing – EUC 2005. XXIII, 1204 pages. 2005.

Vol. 3823: T. Enokido, L. Yan, B. Xiao, D. Kim, Y. Dai, L.T. Yang (Eds.), Embedded and Ubiquitous Computing – EUC 2005 Workshops. XXXII, 1317 pages. 2005.

Vol. 3822: D. Feng, D. Lin, M. Yung (Eds.), Information Security and Cryptology. XII, 420 pages. 2005.

Vol. 3821: R. Ramanujam, S. Sen (Eds.), FSTTCS 2005: Foundations of Software Technology and Theoretical Computer Science. XIV, 566 pages. 2005.

Vol. 3820: L.T. Yang, X.-s. Zhou, W. Zhao, Z. Wu, Y. Zhu, M. Lin (Eds.), Embedded Software and Systems. XXVIII, 779 pages. 2005.

Vol. 3819: P. Van Hentenryck (Ed.), Practical Aspects of Declarative Languages. X, 231 pages. 2005.

Vol. 3818: S. Grumbach, L. Sui, V. Vianu (Eds.), Advances in Computer Science – ASIAN 2005. XIII, 294 pages. 2005.

Vol. 3817: M. Faundez-Zanuy, L. Janer, A. Esposito, A. Satue-Villar, J. Roure, V. Espinosa-Duro (Eds.), Nonlinear Analyses and Algorithms for Speech Processing. XII, 380 pages. 2006. (Sublibrary LNAI).

Vol. 3816: G. Chakraborty (Ed.), Distributed Computing and Internet Technology. XXI, 606 pages. 2005.

Vol. 3815: E.A. Fox, E.J. Neuhold, P. Premsmit, V. Wuwongse (Eds.), Digital Libraries: Implementing Strategies and Sharing Experiences. XVII, 529 pages. 2005.

Vol. 3814: M. Maybury, O. Stock, W. Wahlster (Eds.), Intelligent Technologies for Interactive Entertainment. XV, 342 pages. 2005. (Sublibrary LNAI).

Vol. 3813: R. Molva, G. Tsudik, D. Westhoff (Eds.), Security and Privacy in Ad-hoc and Sensor Networks. VIII, 219 pages. 2005.

Vol. 3812: C. Bussler, A. Haller (Eds.), Business Process Management Workshops. XIII, 520 pages. 2006.

Vol. 3811: C. Bussler, M.-C. Shan (Eds.), Technologies for E-Services. VIII, 127 pages. 2006.

Vol. 3810: Y.G. Desmedt, H. Wang, Y. Mu, Y. Li (Eds.), Cryptology and Network Security. XI, 349 pages. 2005.

Vol. 3809: S. Zhang, R. Jarvis (Eds.), AI 2005: Advances in Artificial Intelligence. XXVII, 1344 pages. 2005. (Sublibrary LNAI).

Vol. 3808: C. Bento, A. Cardoso, G. Dias (Eds.), Progress in Artificial Intelligence. XVIII, 704 pages. 2005. (Sublibrary LNAI).

Vol. 3807: M. Dean, Y. Guo, W. Jun, R. Kaschek, S. Krishnaswamy, Z. Pan, Q.Z. Sheng (Eds.), Web Information Systems Engineering – WISE 2005 Workshops. XV, 275 pages. 2005.

Vol. 3806: A.H. H. Ngu, M. Kitsuregawa, E.J. Neuhold, J.-Y. Chung, Q.Z. Sheng (Eds.), Web Information Systems Engineering – WISE 2005. XXI, 771 pages. 2005.

Vol. 3805: G. Subsol (Ed.), Virtual Storytelling. XII, 289 pages. 2005.

Vol. 3804: G. Bebis, R. Boyle, D. Koracin, B. Parvin (Eds.), Advances in Visual Computing. XX, 755 pages. 2005.

Vol. 3803: S. Jajodia, C. Mazumdar (Eds.), Information Systems Security. XI, 342 pages. 2005.

Vol. 3802: Y. Hao, J. Liu, Y.-P. Wang, Y.-m. Cheung, H. Yin, L. Jiao, J. Ma, Y.-C. Jiao (Eds.), Computational Intelligence and Security, Part II. XLII, 1166 pages. 2005. (Sublibrary LNAI).

Vol. 3801: Y. Hao, J. Liu, Y.-P. Wang, Y.-m. Cheung, H. Yin, L. Jiao, J. Ma, Y.-C. Jiao (Eds.), Computational Intelligence and Security, Part I. XLI, 1122 pages. 2005. (Sublibrary LNAI).

Vol. 3799: M. A. Rodríguez, I.F. Cruz, S. Levashkin, M.J. Egenhofer (Eds.), GeoSpatial Semantics. X, 259 pages. 2005.

Vol. 3798: A. Dearle, S. Eisenbach (Eds.), Component Deployment. X, 197 pages. 2005.

Vol. 3797: S. Maitra, C. E. V. Madhavan, R. Venkatesan (Eds.), Progress in Cryptology - INDOCRYPT 2005. XIV, 417 pages. 2005.

Vol. 3796: N.P. Smart (Ed.), Cryptography and Coding. XI, 461 pages. 2005.

Vol. 3795: H. Zhuge, G.C. Fox (Eds.), Grid and Cooperative Computing - GCC 2005. XXI, 1203 pages. 2005.

Vol. 3794: X. Jia, J. Wu, Y. He (Eds.), Mobile Ad-hoc and Sensor Networks. XX, 1136 pages. 2005.

Vol. 3793: T. Conte, N. Navarro, W.-m.W. Hwu, M. Valero, T. Ungerer (Eds.), High Performance Embedded Architectures and Compilers. XIII, 317 pages. 2005.